A HISTORY
OF THE
ANGLO-SAXONS

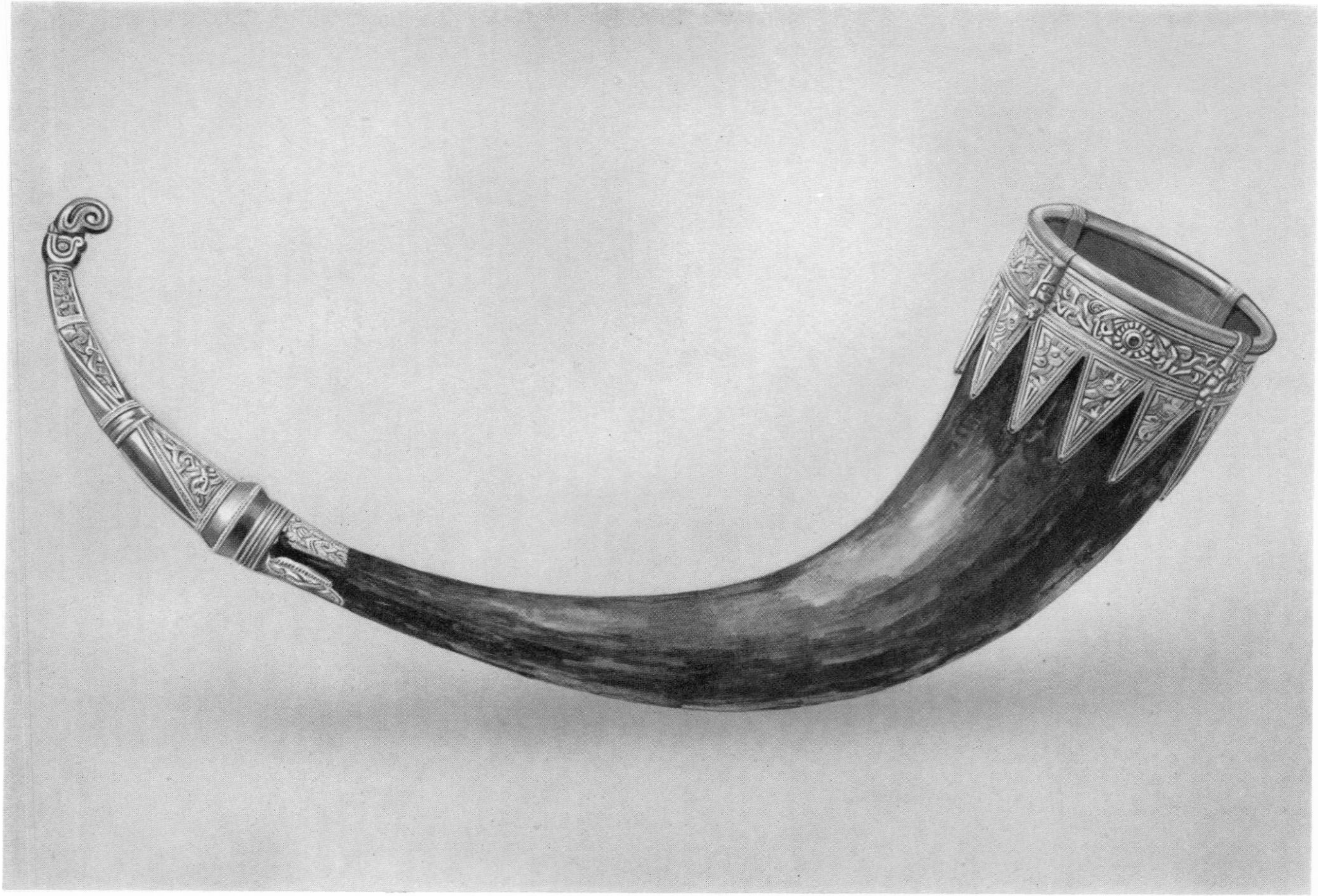

I. DRINKING-HORN FROM TAPLOW ON THE THAMES
About $\frac{1}{3}$

A HISTORY

OF THE

ANGLO-SAXONS

By

R. H. HODGKIN

FELLOW AND TUTOR OF QUEEN'S COLLEGE, OXFORD

VOL. I

OXFORD

AT THE CLARENDON PRESS

1935

OXFORD UNIVERSITY PRESS
AMEN HOUSE, E.C. 4
LONDON EDINBURGH GLASGOW NEW YORK
TORONTO MELBOURNE CAPETOWN BOMBAY
CALCUTTA MADRAS SHANGHAI
HUMPHREY MILFORD
PUBLISHER TO THE UNIVERSITY

PRINTED IN GREAT BRITAIN

PREFACE

DURING the last thirty years, while important advances have been made in the study of Anglo-Saxon history, there has, I think, been some loss of general interest in the subject. The Victorians turned with zest to the Saxon period because Stubbs, Freeman, and Green showed them there the dawn of English democracy. Now, however, the colour has faded; and democracy, both the primitive and the modern varieties of it, has lost its glamour. It is left to the Germans to idealize the virtues—but not the liberties—of our Nordic ancestors. In this island it too often happens that our history is made to start only at the conquest of England by the Norman-French, and that our Germanic ancestors, the Æthelberhts, the Ælfgifus, and the rest, are regarded as uncouth, like their names. But even if we have no wish to seek our ideals or our politics in the Dark Ages, the Anglo-Saxon dawn should never be a subject of indifference to us. That is a general excuse for this book; a special one is that the Anglo-Saxon period of English History more than any other needs to be retold. During the last decades old views—especially those about the Saxon conquest of Britain—have been challenged. Mr. E. T. Leeds and others, 'drawing their conclusions from the more perfected methods of archaeology', have argued that the early annals of the Saxon Chronicle are incredible. Important work has also been done in other directions. Professor Chadwick has offered us new interpretations of the constitutional data. Armies of philologists, both here and abroad, have joined battle over the problems of Old English literature. Other valuable work has been done on the place-names, the charters, and the art of the Anglo-Saxons. There has been a definite strengthening of knowledge all along the line. In the following pages I attempt to adjust the new views and the old.

I have kept in my mind the needs of students, including students of the Old English language, who wish to understand the background of its literature. At the same time I hope there may be other readers ready to endure the more arid tracts of pre-Norman history in order to learn what may now be believed about the beginnings of our Germanic forefathers, our monarchy, our Church, our literature, and our art.

I have focused on the great men and the big subjects—the Conquest, the Conversion, the results of the Conversion, the success of the Southerners in the struggle for supremacy, the Viking invasions, the life and beliefs of the people. My choice of the great men has necessarily been determined by the fullness of our information about them. It is fortunate that the layman whom it is possible to know most intimately was also, it seems, the greatest of all—King Alfred. He must be the centre in any picture of Saxon times. Accordingly the story of England before the Norman Conquest divides into two parts. The first leads up to Alfred, and this is contained in the present volumes: the second follows the influence of Alfred and that of the Danes who during his reign made their home in England, and this I hope to narrate in a sequel.

There are features of the book which need defence. My readers will, I trust, agree that the dearth of written authorities is reason enough for making the fullest use of illustrations. At the same time I must confess that my illustrations vary greatly in evidential value. The modern 'reconstructions' are sometimes open to criticism. There is still much difference of opinion about some of the objects illustrated; for instance, the Lindisfarne Gospels. Others, like the drawings of the Utrecht Psalter, which can now be analysed with some certainty, are composite productions, in which features derived from different centuries are blended. The maps also unavoidably contain more guess-work than I like. I have tried to give guidance on many of these points in my notes.

Something must also be said about the plan of the book. My experience in teaching this early history has shown me that beginners are often baffled by the strange names. I have therefore deliberately abstained from crowding my pages with the record of kings and others who can never be much more than names. This policy may have led me to do less than justice to certain parts of the subject, such as the history of Mercia, but some of the gaps thus left are filled in the genealogical and chronological tables at the end of Vol. II. I have written at some length because I believe that students thrive best when they are not brought up on too condensed a historical diet.

Throughout the book, alike in my figures, my maps, and my text, I have acted on the principle that an approximation to the truth is better than a complete blank. This principle is far-reaching; but I fear that it will not cover all my statements on the highly controversial subjects which thrust themselves forward in this period. Since a general historian, who has to assemble the parts made by specialists, is obliged to cut and shape those parts before they can be made to fit, it is, I fear, inevitable that he should make mistakes. And apart from the fallibility of the human worker, it has also to be admitted that Saxon archaeology has not yet attained to a high degree of scientific security. In so far as the following pages rest on its dicta, or what I have taken to be such, they must be regarded as nothing more than an interim report.

ACKNOWLEDGEMENTS

One great difficulty of a synthesis is that of acknowledging fully indebtedness to other works without over-weighting the text with an apparatus of notes. The references at the end of each volume will, I hope, sufficiently indicate the books which I have used; but I must here acknowledge more generally my debt to the works of the late Professor G. Baldwin Brown, of Edinburgh; to Professor H. M. Chadwick, of Cambridge; and to Professor F. M. Stenton, of Reading. There are others who have kindly helped me by their advice as well as by their writings; and among these I must specially mention Mr. E. T. Leeds, Keeper of the Ashmolean Museum; Mr. T. D. Kendrick, of the British

Museum; Dr. R. E. M. Wheeler, Keeper of the London Museum; Professor Roeder, of Göttingen; and Professor R. G. Collingwood, of Pembroke College, Oxford. In view of the uncertainties of the subject I need scarcely add that some at any rate of them will think that I have erred in what I have written about the Saxon Conquest.

The list of those who have been good enough to answer my questions on all kinds of points is a long one. It includes: Miss M. V. Taylor, Miss M. H. Longhurst, the Provost of University College, London (Dr. Allen Mawer), Dr. E. C. Curwen, Mr. T. C. Lethbridge, Mr. J. P. Bushe-Fox, Mr. R. G. de Beer, Dr. Gudmund Hatt, and Dr. Hans Kjær, of the National Museum, Copenhagen. Those whom I have pestered in an attempt to make my maps reproduce as far as possible the natural features of the Dark Ages are the following: Major Gordon Fowler, Dr. Gordon Ward, Mr. R. Rainbird Clarke, Mr. C. E. Stevens, Dr. H. Schütte of the Landesverein Oldenburg für Heimatkunde und Heimatschutz, and Dr. H. Hesmer of the Forstliche Hochschule, Eberswalde. My questions to the last two were about the coastline and the forest conditions of North Germany in the fifth century; and I much regret that I was unable to follow up the information which they gave me, so that my map of North Germany is still not all that I could wish. To this list I must add the name of Dr. G. B. Grundy, Fellow of Corpus Christi College, Oxford, who kindly copied for my map of the Athelney campaign his own map of trackways indicated by Saxon charters; and also the name of Mr. O. G. S. Crawford, of the Ordnance Survey. It has been unfortunate for me that the projected Ordnance Survey map of Anglo-Saxon England has not appeared before this book goes to press. When it does appear, it will, of course, be the standard map which should be used by all students of the Saxon period; and I can only hope that my own maps will be found roughly to agree with it.

I am under obligations of a different kind to the many authors and publishers and others who by their kind permission have enabled me to make this book well illustrated. My thanks, even when unexpressed, must be read into my List of Figures. In this preface it is right that I should thank Miss E. D. Brinton, Mr. E. W. Oldham, and the members of the Staff of the Clarendon Press who have made drawings for the book; Mr. C. D. Waterhouse, of the British Museum, on whose sketches most of my coloured plates are based; and others who have helped me to obtain photographs and the like, namely: Miss M. P. Ramsay, of the Fine Art Department of Edinburgh University; Dr. C. Rothmann, of the Schleswig-Holsteinisches Museum, Kiel; Mr. H. St. George Grey, Curator of the Somerset County Museum; Mr. Norman Cook, of the Maidstone Museum; Mr. C. W. Pugh, of the Devizes Museum; the Rev. E. C. Ratcliff, of Queen's College, Oxford; and Mr. J. E. Hodgkin, of Darlington.

In the next place I must thank the publishers who have allowed me to quote from their publications: Messrs. G. Bell & Sons, the Cambridge University Press, Messrs. Chatto & Windus, Messrs. J. M. Dent & Sons, Messrs. Longmans, Green & Co., and the Society for the Promotion of Christian Knowledge. My obligations to the authors I have acknowledged in my notes.

Finally, I am deeply indebted to Mr. C. L. Wrenn, who devoted part of his summer holiday in 1932 to reading and criticizing this book in manuscript; and of those who have given me the greatest help of all there is no need to say anything in public.

R. H. H.

April 1935

CONTENTS

VOLUME I

VOLUME II

LIST OF PLAT S

VOL. I

The passage is as follows:

> In illo tempore Saxones invalescebant in multitudine et crescebant in Brittannia. Mortuo autem Hengisto Octha filius eius transivit de sinistrali parte Brittanniae ad regnum Cantorum et de ipso orti sunt reges Cantorum. Tunc Arthur pugnabat contra illos in illis diebus cum regibus Brittonum, sed ipse dux erat bellorum. Primum bellum fuit in ostium fluminis quod dicitur Glein. Secundum et tertium et quartum et quintum super aliud flumen, quod dicitur Dubglas et est in regione Linnuis. Sextum bellum super flumen, quod vocatur Bassas. Septimum fuit bellum in silva Celidonis, id est Cat Coit Celidon. Octavum fuit bellum in castello Guinnion, in quo Arthur portavit imaginem sanctae Mariae perpetuae virginis super humeros suos et pagani versi sunt in fugam in illo die et cedes magna fuit super illos per virtutem domini nostri Iesu Christi et per virtutem sanctae Mariae virginis genitricis eius. Nonum bellum gestum est in urbe Legionis. Decimum gessit bellum in litore fluminis, quod vocatur Tribruit. Undecimum factum est bellum in monte, qui dicitur Agned. Duodecimum fuit bellum in Monte Badonis, in quo corruerunt in uno die nongenti sexaginta viri de uno impetu Arthur: [et nemo prostravit eos nisi ipse solus, et in omnibus bellis victor extitit].

VOL. II

COLOURED PLATES

VOL. I

VOL. II

LIST OF TEXT FIGURES

(† = Headpiece or Tailpiece)

VOL. I

VOL. II

LIST OF MAPS

VOL. I

VOL. II

I

THE ANGLES AND SAXONS IN GERMANY

DRIFT TOWARDS THE WEST

THE subject of this book is the history of the Angles and Saxons from the time when they are first mentioned among the German tribes. We shall be following the main stream in the rise of the English, that which gave them their name, their speech, and their fundamental institutions; but in doing so we shall obtain some ideas about the course of other tributaries to our nation, Celtic, Roman, Danish, and Norwegian.

If we seek out the original England of the continental Angles, we must go to the district of Angel,* in the Cimbric, that is the Danish, peninsula. Whatever its original extent, Angel is now only a small district, a part of Schleswig. It is no bigger

HEADPIECE.—Destruction of a German village by Roman soldiers. From the Column of Marcus Aurelius at Rome. Reconstructed.

* Spelt in German *Angeln*.

than an average English county, stretching for some forty miles along the Baltic coast between the Flensburg fiord and the Schlei. In this old 'England' there is still much to make those of us who belong to the new England of Britain feel at home. Not only do the faces of the men and women constantly remind us of types to be seen in the Anglian districts of our island, but by some chance the appearance of the land itself, with its irregular fields and hedgerows and undulating well-timbered country, is also what we should call typically English.

The emigrants to Britain preserved, at least from the time of Bede, a continuous tradition that their forefathers dwelt in these lands before they came to Britain. The passage in Bede's history in which this is stated as a fact must ever remain the starting-point for investigation into the continental homes of our race:[1]

> 'Those who came over were of the three most powerful nations in Germany—Saxons, Angles, and Jutes. From the Jutes are descended the people of Kent and of the Isle of Wight and those in the province of the West Saxons who are to this day called Jutes, seated opposite to the Isle of Wight. From the Saxons, that is, from that region which is now called Old Saxony, came the East Saxons, the South Saxons, and the West Saxons. From the Angles, that is, from that country which is called Angul* and which is said from that time to the present day to have remained deserted (between the province of the Jutes and the Saxons) are descended the East Angles, the Midland Angles, the Mercians, all the race of the Northumbrians . . . and the other nations of the Angles.'

No passage in Bede has evoked more controversy. One recent writer[2] has argued that Bede's statements are unreliable since they were 'in a great measure founded only on conclusions drawn from similarities of names'. We are told that Bede blundered both when he implied that the Jutes came from Jutland, and also when he asserted that the Angles came from the district of Angul.

* Latin *Angulus*.

In the present chapter our chief object will be to test and supplement Bede's statement about the Angles and Saxons, leaving on one side the problem who were the Jutes until we come to the Jutish settlement in Kent. We shall try to supplement Bede in two directions. In the first place we shall seek for information on questions such as what were the relations between the tribes along the Germanic seaboard; what was the determining cause that brought these Germans to Britain; and by what stages and by what routes they were drawn towards our island. Afterwards we shall try to find out what these 'barbarians' were like; how they were armed, how clothed, and what were their gods.

The chief contributions to these subjects in recent years have come from archaeologists, and it is on archaeology that we shall have to place our hopes of learning more about these matters than has usually been told us in text-books. But before we can understand the bearing of the archaeological evidence we must, as a preliminary, set out some of the fragmentary and confusing information which comes to us from Greek and Latin writers.

Let us then begin with Tacitus' well-known division of the 'Germans' (really the West Germans only) into three groups, and with the identification of the group called the Ingaevones as that which comprised the tribes spread out along the coast of the North Sea, the tribes which spoke the Germanic dialects commonly described as 'Anglo-Frisian'. About the position of some of these tribes at the end of the first century of our era when Tacitus wrote his *Germania* there is no serious doubt. The Frisians were the inhabitants of modern Friesland, and the Chauci, praised by Tacitus as 'the noblest of the German race', were on the coast between the Ems and the Elbe.

It is unfortunate that the position of the tribes among whom the Anglii are enumerated is not made clear beyond dispute. Tacitus mentions the Lombards as situated apparently on the lower Elbe. 'Next come the Reudigni, Aviones, Anglii, Varini, Eudoses [and others]. . . . They are fenced in by rivers and forests. None of these tribes have any noteworthy features except their common worship of Nerthus, who is the same as Mother Earth.' Tacitus describes the island of the ocean, where is the sacred grove of the cult, and ends with the remark that 'this branch of the Suevi stretches into the remoter regions of Germany'. But what was the principle on which Tacitus was

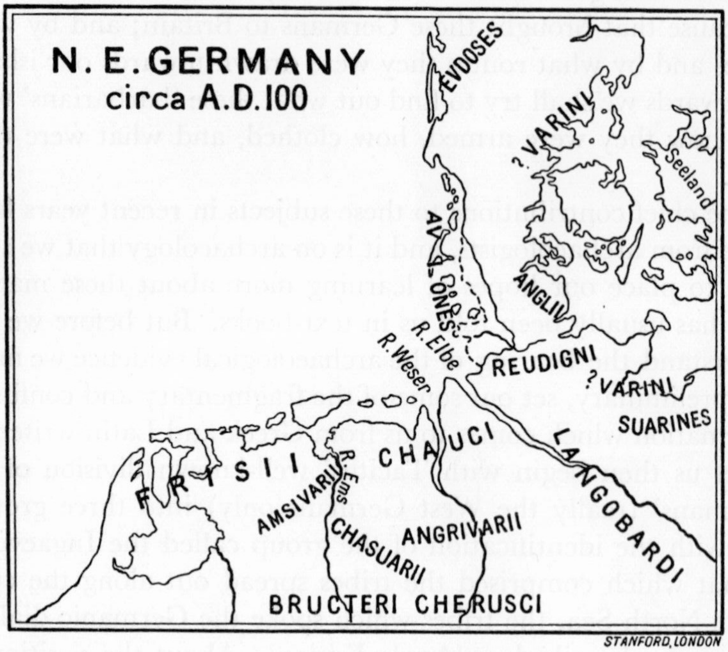

enumerating these tribes? Was he working from south to north? If we accept this, the most reasonable assumption,[3] we must look for the Reudigni beyond, that is to the north of, the Elbe, and then for the Aviones, the Anglii and the Eudoses (? Jutes) up the Cimbric peninsula.

But the Saxons? For the first mention of these we must go to Ptolemy, who, writing about the middle of the second century, places them 'on the neck of the Cimbric peninsula', that is presumably in Holstein. The great puzzle is to know how to explain the failure of Tacitus to mention the Saxons. Shall we by a simple equation say that they are the Reudigni and some of their neighbours? If so, the name 'Saxons' even from the first was a group-name for an alliance of tribes—a group-name like that of the Franks (the spearmen) and that of the Alemans (the men of all kinds), great Germanic confederacies which

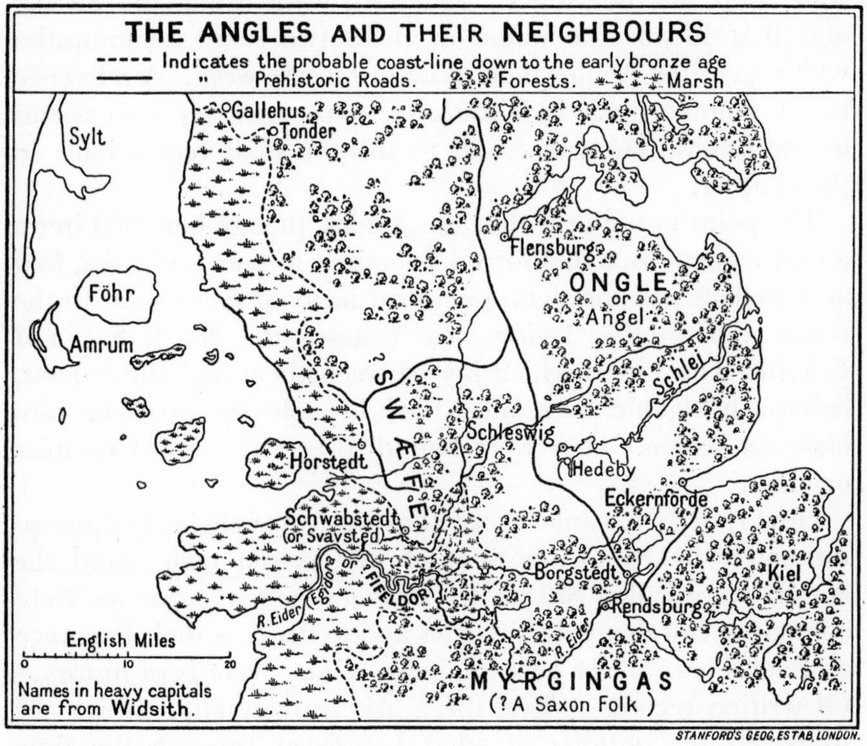

appear in the second century, the one on the lower, the other on the upper, Rhine. It is natural to suppose that this group-name like the others had a meaning; and scholars are fairly well agreed that the Saxons were so called because they were the users of the *seax* or *sahs*, a short one-handled sword.

The map above indicates what seems to have been the position of the Angles and their neighbours three centuries after Tacitus. It shows how in prehistoric times the settlements of the Angles, though mainly on the middle of the peninsula and round the inlet from the Baltic called the Schlei, were within easy reach of good harbours giving access to the North Sea, so long as the marshland of the lower Eider was navigable for light craft. On the strength of a place-name it is suggested[4] that the next-door neighbours of the Angles, that is the people who lived on the western seaboard, were called the Swæfe, and that it was the union of these two small communities which gave the Angles their 'window to the west'. A reference to this union is made in *Widsith*, one of the earliest extant poems in the English language; and to this we shall return later in the chapter.

The point to notice is that the Angles, though hemmed in on a narrow peninsula and forced by nature to take to the sea, had an excellent position, with one good harbour facing east to the Baltic and another facing west towards the North Sea and Britain. The Eider, which lay between them and the Saxons, being a navigable river, must have brought the two folks into close connexion. They were bound to be either great enemies or allies.

How exactly it came about that the two peoples became so intimately linked to one another that in our own island the Angles were called Saxons by strangers and the Saxons were content to call themselves Angles and to speak of their language as English can never be explained by any records of history.* Of written records indeed there are scarcely any. If we try to sketch the outlines of what happened between the time of Tacitus and the migration to Britain, we have to give our attention to the theories of the archaeologists, and to these we must now turn.

In the study of primitive peoples scientific archaeology has of course to depend mainly on the evidence provided by their burial customs. Now the peoples of northern Germany at the time of the migration to Britain, and for many centuries before that, had as a rule followed the custom of cremating their dead.

* See below, pp. 157–61.

They had placed the ashes and what was left of the brooches and buckles which had fastened the clothes of the dead body when it was placed on the fire, in an urn, either an elaborately ornamented urn made for the purpose, or else any cooking-pot

FIG. 1. Typical Saxon and Anglian urns of the first and second centuries (according to Plettke). *Above.* From Bornhöved, Holstein. $\frac{1}{4}$. *Below.* From Nottfeld, Schleswig. $\frac{1}{4}$.

which might be handy. Since the fashions in urns, and to a less extent in brooches also, varied from region to region and changed like any other fashion, it may be possible with their evidence to fix the distribution of a tribe and to follow its movements. The most interesting attempt as yet published to detect in this way the distribution and the expansion of our Anglo-Saxon ancestors is that made by A. Plettke, a young German who was killed in the Great War. Plettke claimed that the type of urn to be identified as that of the Anglo-Saxon section of the Ingaevones is one found during the first two centuries of our era in the cemeteries of west Holstein and southern Schleswig. Two cremation urns from this district assigned to this period are shown in Fig. 1. The type is differentiated both by its shape and by its ornamentation with 'hatched triangles'.

Now the fact that the Angles and Saxons in their original homes resembled one another in their funeral fashions is certainly significant, especially in view of the contrasts between their urns and those of their neighbours: the handled urns of the Lombards to the south, and the few and poorly ornamented urns of the Chauci across the Elbe.

A story can be extracted from the changes—or what Plettke takes to be the changes—occurring in the urn-fields during the next centuries. While those of the Angles in Schleswig and those of the Saxons in west Holstein seem for the most part to have been used continuously down to about A.D. 500, the great Lombardic cemeteries near the lower Elbe came to an end about A.D. 200. These folk who buried their dead in the handled urns disappear. What had happened? Presumably they had packed their families and scanty goods into their wagons and, driving their herds before them, had set off on their long wanderings seeking—who knows?—richer lands, the spoil of the south, a place in the sun. At any rate the Lombards passed away. Their old neighbours, the Saxons, remained on the neck of the Cimbric peninsula. For some hundreds of years after the Lombards had vanished from the scene these Saxons continued to plough the lands of north Germany.

The changes to be detected west of the Elbe in the lands of the Chauci concern us more closely. Here, says Plettke, none of the earlier cemeteries are continued into the period of the later Roman Empire, but all the cemeteries of that period seem to begin about A.D. 200. Moreover, the characteristic urns of these new cemeteries are similar to those of west Holstein.

Early fourth century—one type

Later fourth century—narrower in the mouth and more spherical

From about 400—many are stamped

During the fifth century bosses and moulded feet come into fashion

SOME SAXON URNS OF THE FOURTH AND FIFTH CENTURIES ($\frac{1}{4}$)

(*After* PLETTKE)

PLATE 2

A and *B*. Oldendorf-Weissenmoor, near Stade; window urn. $\frac{3}{8}$

C. Wester-Wanna; spout-handled urn.
About $\frac{1}{4}$

D. Wester-Wanna; holed urn.
About $\frac{1}{7}$

PECULIAR URNS FROM THE ELBE-WESER REGION

The conclusion which he draws is obvious. The Chauci—or most of them—had migrated, and the Saxons, having overrun the lands about Hamburg formerly possessed by the Lombards, had drifted still farther west to take the place of the Chauci, or absorb what was left of them. On the spits of higher

FIG. 2. Issendorf, near Stade; Saxon urn, *c.* 450.
The boar on the lid is the only excavated sculpture of the early Saxons.

ground which lie between the marshes of the Elbe and those of the Weser the Saxons seem to have found a promised land. The soil was light and easily worked. There were open spaces free from the endless trees which made so much of the interior of Germany hard to colonize. In this region between the Elbe and the Weser the Saxons increased and multiplied. We know of no less than sixty urn-fields, many of them very large—that at Wester-wanna, the only one which has been completely excavated, yielding no less than four thousand urns.

It is still impossible to say with any finality whether those

North Germans who were packed so closely on the cultivable land between the Elbe and the Weser were composed mainly of descendants of the Chauci, the tribe once belauded by Tacitus, or whether they were, as Plettke and others have argued, immigrant Saxons from beyond the Elbe.[5]

Whatever view we take about the origin of the so-called 'Saxons' who were so thickly strewn in the lands between the Elbe and the Weser, one fact indicated by their cemeteries need not be questioned. These lands clearly did not give enough elbow-room for so prolific a people. Crowded out from this district, their overflow can be traced farther to the west. The lands between the Weser and the Ems, though barren or swampy, have some traces of them.[6] But west of the Ems, that is in Frisia, their urns and brooches reappear in some numbers.

Such are some of the conclusions drawn by Plettke from the cemeteries of north Germany. Once more we must protest that these conclusions are quoted here not because they are to be received as a sure and ascertained truth, but because they illustrate the kind of story which may finally emerge from the testing fire of controversy.

In recent years some important contributions to the subject have been made by the German archaeologist F. Roeder. He has studied with exemplary thoroughness the development and distribution first of one type of urn or brooch then of another, bringing within his survey both the cemeteries of the continental Saxons and those of the migrants to Britain. The reader will find in the illustrations specimens of the peculiar vessels and of certain brooches which appear on the Continent and then reappear in Britain: the pots with perforated handles,* strange vessels called 'window urns', which have pieces of glass let into them; and even more mysterious 'holed urns', that is urns with holes deliberately made in them.[7] The map on page 33 shows

* This statement must be modified in so far as it is now proved (cf. Roeder, *Neue Funde*, 24 ff.) that the only English example—from Great Addington—has Scandinavian rather than Saxon affinities.

the distribution of other significant objects, and it provides one of the best arguments which help to fix definitely the home of the men who invaded the eastern Midlands of Britain.

FIG. 3. Nydam Moor, north of Flensburg fiord; archetype of the cruciform brooch. $\frac{1}{1}$.

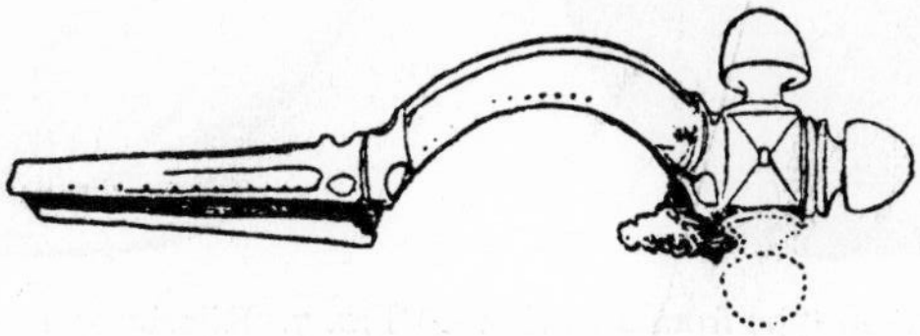

FIG. 4. Tolkwade, Schleswig. Cruciform brooch. The lower end has no trace of an animal's head as in examples found in England. $\frac{3}{4}$.

FIG. 5. Perlberg, near Stade. A 'round' brooch (of the 'saucer' variety) with spiral design. $\frac{1}{1}$.

In the past it has been very difficult to relate the brooches of the continental Saxons with those of the invaders of Britain, owing to the fact that well-preserved brooches were hardly ever found in their cremation urns.[8] Now, however, this gap in our knowledge is being filled by the fortunate discovery of one or two 'mixed' cemeteries,[9] that is cemeteries in which the Saxons can be seen passing, as in Britain, from the older custom of cremating their dead to the new custom of burying them unburnt with their ornaments and weapons of war. The types of brooch which appear on both sides of the North Sea, and are most useful in helping us to trace the migration of our Germanic ancestors, are the following: the 'cruciform' brooch, the 'round' brooch (in two

FIG. 6. Urn of Saxon type from a Frisian terp.

FIG. 7. Rijnsburg, near a mouth of the Rhine; urn (?) of Saxon type.

varieties), the 'Luton' type, and the 'equal-armed' brooch (see Figs. 3, 4, 5, 8, 9, 28).

All these grave-goods help us to pick up the tracks of our ancestors as they moved westwards towards Britain. As we have seen, the traces are most numerous and unequivocal along the north German coast. They appear sparsely west of the Weser. They become numerous again in Frisia, especially in the district between the mouth of the Ems and the Zuyder Zee. Here the Anglo-Saxons found a half-way house—or let us rather say a stepping-stone—of so strange a kind that we may well pause to observe it.

It seems that about the first century B.C. the sea began to break through the rampart of sand-dunes which had previously protected this low-lying coast. The inundations in course of time became so bad that the unhappy Frisians had to choose between deserting their homes or constructing mounds, or terps, from clay and sods and reedy manure on which, during the

FIG. 8. Dösemoor, north of Stade, equal-armed brooch. Roeder's date, *c.* 500.
(*Slightly enlarged.*)

FIG. 9. Nesse, near Geestemünder, equal-armed brooch. Roeder's date, *c.* 500.
(*Slightly enlarged.*)

high tides, they could find safety for themselves and their belongings. No existence could well have been more miserable than theirs in this corner of the Continent opposite our own shores. So at any rate it appeared to Pliny the Elder.[10]

'With immense tidal flow the Ocean floods over the land twice in every twenty-four hours, spreads its waters wide, and raises Nature's eternal question, whether these regions are to be regarded as belonging to the land or to the sea. Here the wretched inhabitants dwell upon high mounds, as it were platforms constructed by men's hands above the level of the highest tides. Thus when the waters cover everything around, they are like sailors on board a ship; but are more like shipwrecked men when the sea retires, and around their huts they pursue the fish receding with the tide. . . . They dig the peat up with their hands and dry it, more in the wind than in the sun, and then with it cook their food and warm their bodies benumbed by the north wind. Their only drink is rain water, which they collect in holes dug at the entrance of their huts. And yet these tribes, were they to be conquered by the Romans to-day, would call it slavery!'

The fact that the migrant Anglo-Saxons found lodging on the terp mounds, and perhaps for a time dominated all this sea-swept corner of the Continent, is attested by the discovery of many 'Saxon' cremation urns buried in the mounds beside the inhumed skeletons of the Frisians, and also of cruciform and 'round' brooches.

If, therefore, we try to construct a map* to show the routes by which the Teutonic invaders found their way to Britain, the route by Frisia is the first and most obvious one which we must mark.

In what direction they set their course when they rowed away from the terps of Frisia is more open to question. Many of them no doubt turned to the south, either down the coast or inland by the waterways which could conduct their boats through still waters to the Rhine. But others may have waited for calm summer weather and then pointed their bows due west and

* See map facing p. 9.

made out into the open sea with a view to striking the Wash and the rivers of the Wash which could bring them without fear of molestation into the heart of Britain. It was only a hundred and thirty miles of open sea—less than the distance which was regularly crossed by traders from Ireland or western Britain to Gaul.

We have said that many ships of the Saxons would turn from the Zuyder Zee by inland waterways to the Rhine mouths. This brings us to what we may consider the second route to Britain. Let us call it the Rhine ferry—the ferry running, needless to say, down the coast to the narrow straits so as to gain the shortest crossing of open sea. What is not obvious is whether the Saxon invaders had access to the Rhine also by an overland route through the heart of north Germany, and whether they remained settled about the lower Rhine for some time before they crossed to our island. These are points about which archaeology supplies a little evidence. There is no series of cemeteries in southern Hanover and Münster corresponding to that which can be traced along the north coast of Germany. Those lands were indeed mostly forest and moor. They did not attract colonists. Dutch archaeologists, however, claim[11] that urn-burials of the Saxon kind are found in some eastern districts of Holland—in Drenthe and the Veluwe—and again in one or two cemeteries near the mouths of the Rhine, notably at Rijnsburg (Fig. 7). But these urns are few, and this evidence is clearly not sufficient in itself to lay any solid foundation for the theory that the Teutonic invaders of Britain, or a section of them, had occupied lands about the lower Rhine before they crossed the sea.

But the theory has won adherents on grounds other than archaeological. Most notable among these is J. Hoops, who, in a learned work on the trees and plants of ancient Germany,[12] built up an argument that while certain Old English words, derived from Latin, such as *pipor* (pepper), *mynet* (money, from *moneta*), might have been imported through the ordinary intercourse of trade, and while others such as *cāsere* (Caesar), *pīl* (a pointed stick, from *pilum*), were no doubt carried home by Angles and Saxons who had served in imperial armies, there are yet others which cannot be so explained. For instance, the English resemble the Frisians and Dutch in calling the seventh day of the week Saturday,* the other Germanic peoples speak of *Samstag*. The only explanation, according to Hoops, is that Angles and Saxons must have picked up the expression before they conquered Britain, when bands of them were for a time settled somewhere near the lower Rhine. So also the Old English *cleofa* (a chamber) and *miltestre* (a loose woman, from Latin *meretrix*): these too, it is said, must have been learned by our migrant ancestors when they were in contact with Latin-speaking peoples in the Low Countries before they crossed the Channel and conquered Britain. This theory has not won general favour. A distinguished French historian has called attention to its 'extreme fragility'.[13] Is it not rash, he says, to assert that the words enumerated by Hoops must have been transferred into the English language before A.D. 600? Why should not the English and Dutch have borrowed them independently of one another?

The philological foundation of the theory being weak like the archaeological, an attempt has been made to obtain support from a famous sentence in Adam of Bremen's twelfth-century chronicle which says that the Saxons were at first settled about the Rhine before a part of them came into Britain and drove out the Romans.† But this corrupt passage in a work written some six centuries after the event is scarcely calculated to add much solidity to the theory. Such strength as it still possesses is derived from arguments about the origin of the Jutes and from occasional mentions of the doings of 'the Saxons' by writers who lived within the Roman Empire. To these passages we must now turn, postponing the Jutish problem till our Chapter III.[14]

How incomplete is the information about the Saxons to be

* OE. *Sæterdæg*.

† I. c. 3: 'Igitur Saxones primo circa Renum sedes habebant, (et vocati sunt Angli) quorum pars inde veniens in Brittanniam, Romanos ab illa insula depulit.'

obtained from the Roman world is at once brought home to us by the fact that after Ptolemy's statement that the Saxons were to be found 'on the neck of the Cimbric peninsula', we have to wait for more than a hundred years before we again hear of them. Then about A.D. 286 they are mentioned along with the Franks, first as pirates who infest the coasts of Gaul and later as allies of Carausius, the Roman admiral who revolted and established himself as emperor in Britain. In the course of this long interval covering the end of the first century and the greater part of the second, most of the changes which we have already traced from the archaeological evidence had taken place. The Chauci had been absorbed or displaced. The Frisians had been overcome. Men of Germanic stock who called themselves 'Saxons' (they may have been mere confederates of the Saxons of the Elbe lands) had become a power on the lower Rhine. In the fourth century these Saxons of the west trod on the heels of the Salian Franks as the latter moved step by step into Gaul. Zosimus, the Byzantine, could read into the story the idea that the Saxons were pushing the Franks forward from behind. When the government of Roman Gaul crumbled in the first decades of the fifth century and Rome finally gave up the attempt to control the waters of the Rhine mouths, this way to the sea was completely opened to the Saxons. Accordingly while the Franks, now confining their operations to the land, were occupied in building up a kingdom in the north-east of Gaul with a capital at Tournai, the Saxon marauders were left free to establish themselves at various points on the Gallic coast, settling now, if not earlier, in the villages round Boulogne (names of which still betray their Saxon origin by the ending *-thun* or *-tun*),[15] and establishing themselves also in the Bessin round Bayeux and near the mouth of the Loire.

Though no consecutive story can be built up from the occasional references to the Saxons in the writings of the later Empire, enough is said to justify us in showing on our map the Saxon confederation reaching almost up to the lower Rhine, and in shading the Boulonnais and the Bessin as nests of the Saxons on the northern shores of Gaul.

This completes our sketch of the westward drift of the Saxons, the drift which had been going on for some three centuries before it brought them to the settlement of Britain. We have already noted at least two possible bases from which their ships could sail to our island: one the most northerly in the terps of Frisia; the other somewhere about the lower Rhine. Now, from the written authorities and the place-names, we have found traces of a third possible base, namely these nests of Saxons on the coast of Gaul.

Of the three the situation on the Rhine is in every way the most obscure. We do not know for certain where exactly it was, nor how large, nor whether it should be thought of as a populous settlement or as a merely temporary post. We do not know who these hypothetical folk were—whether Saxons from the Elbe or men of neighbouring tribes such as Jutes, Angles, and Chauci, passing under the name of Saxons. Common sense suggests to us that the Rhine-Meuse-Scheldt mouths opposite the Thames must have been the taking-off place for many of the invaders of Britain. But so far we have had no good proof of its existence; it remains no more than *x*, the unknown quantity in the problem.

For the present it will be sufficient if in thinking of the three possible bases we understand how different the invaders might be who came from these different quarters. The Saxons who had been established in the advanced posts of Gaul may have learned something of the ways either of the Franks or of the provincials around them. They were probably federates like the Franks and the other barbarians who had established themselves on Gallic soil; and it is possible that they contributed the Saxon levies who fought on the imperial side in the army of Aëtius against Attila's Huns.[16]

The 'Saxons' of the Rhine, if they existed, may also have been changed by long contact with the Franks. They also may have grown unlike their kinsmen in the homelands, those who were

Details, doubtless mythological, from the upper sections of the horn

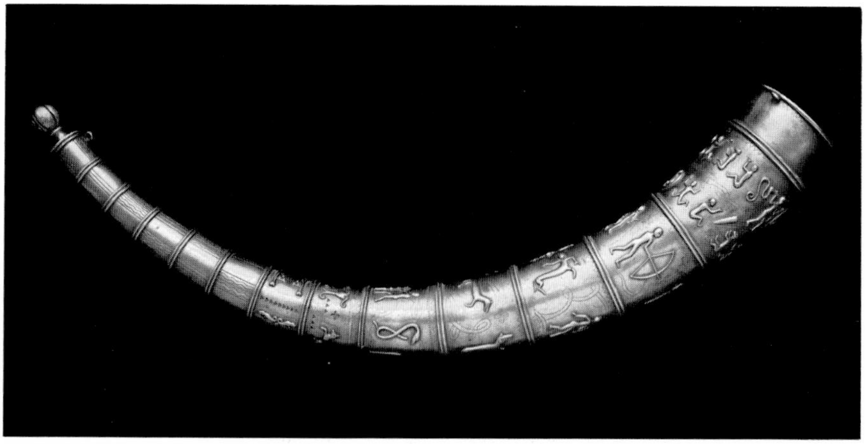

Replica of golden horn, found at Gallehus, near if not within the ancient Angel

It is not certainly of Anglian workmanship

PLATE 4

German chiefs in council, a moot of a free people
From the column of Marcus Aurelius

still living in old-fashioned ways by the North Sea or the Baltic. This is not an empty conjecture. We seem to trace some differences of this kind reflected in their burial customs. Re-examine the evidence: in the Elbe-Weser country, cremation urns crowded together by the thousand in numerous cemeteries; in the terps of Frisia, similar finds, but few of them; on the lower Rhine, finds still fewer and less characteristic; but in Gaul, though Saxons must have died there in their thousands, not a single Saxon burial-place has been discovered.

This question of the character of the Saxons cannot be dismissed in a paragraph. We must now take it up and devote to it a new section of the present chapter.

CHARACTER AND BELIEFS

The fullest description which has come down to us of the Saxon pirates was written by Sidonius, a Gallo-Roman noble who flourished in the latter half of the fifth century. He was writing to a friend who, he had heard, was at the moment combining the duties of a sailor and a soldier, 'looking out for the curved longboats of the Saxons'.[17]

'When you see the rowers of that nation,' he says, 'you may at once make up your mind that every one of them is an arch-pirate; with such wonderful unanimity do all at once command, obey, teach, and learn their one chosen business of brigandage. For this reason I ought to warn you to be more than ever on your guard in this warfare. Your enemy is the most ferocious of all enemies. Unexpectedly he attacks, when expected he escapes, he despises those who seek to block his path, he overthrows those who are off their guard, he always succeeds in cutting off the enemy whom he follows, while he never fails when he desires to effect his own escape. Moreover, to these men a shipwreck is capital practice rather than an object of terror. The dangers of the deep are to them, not casual acquaintances, but intimate friends, for since a tempest throws the invaded off their guard, and prevents the invaders from being descried from afar, they hail with joy the crash of waves on the rocks which gives them their best chance of escaping from other enemies than the elements.

'Then again, before they raise the deep-biting anchor from the hostile soil, and set sail from the continent for their own country, their custom is to collect the crowd of their prisoners together, by a mockery of equity to make them cast lots which of them shall undergo the iniquitous sentence of death, and then at the moment of departure to abandon every tenth captive to the slow agony of a watery end, a practice which is the more lamentable because it arises from a superstitious notion that they will thus ensure for themselves a safe return.'

Sidonius, repeating the hearsay about an enemy, gives us a vivid but evidently an exaggerated picture of the Saxons. To obtain truer notions about them, we must leave these, the advanced bands of the Saxon marauders, and, studying the Angles and Saxons in their continental homes, see if we can find any answers to the questions: What they were really like? How did they live? How was it they came to give up their old homes and to venture forth into strange lands across the North Sea?

In the first place, what did they look like? Roman sculptors carved representations of German barbarians on their monuments. On the column of Marcus Aurelius at Rome they are portrayed clothed in shirts to the knee, cloaks buckled on the right shoulder, and long trousers to the ankle. Look, for instance, at the scene on page 1 where Roman soldiers burn a German village. The German men (*Marcomanni*) with arms upraised beg for mercy as their huts are burned. The Roman soldiers slay the village folk with the sword and the spear, they burn their huts, and the German mother, with long hair falling over her shoulders, hurries away from the scene of the destruction of her home and the slaughter of her kinsmen, pulling her young son by the arm—a fitting introduction to the later invasion of the Roman Empire by the Germans. On another relief (Pl. 4) of the same column, German chiefs are represented sitting in an assembly; again it is a memorable scene, the moot of a free people.

The bust in Berlin (Pl. 5) was for long said to illustrate how a primitive German man wore his hair. Now, however, it is

PLATE 5

An idealized German. Bust of the eighteenth century
Königl. Museum, Berlin

Bust of a German woman
British Museum

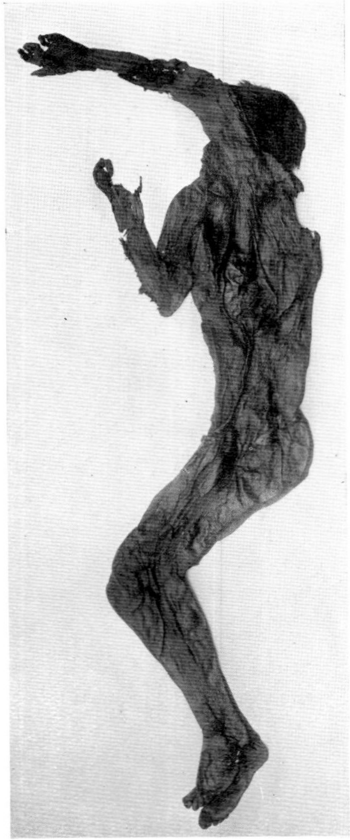

A. The Damendorfer man

B. Tunic or shirt found at Thorsberg

All in the Kiel Museum

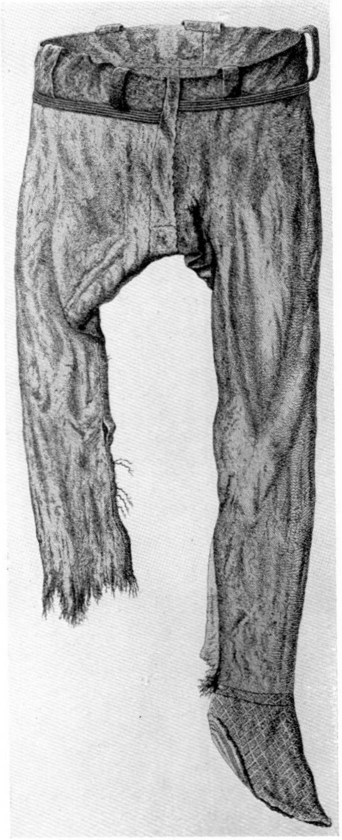

C. Trousers from Thorsberg

certain that it is only a 'fake' of the eighteenth century.[18] The bust in the British Museum (also on Pl. 5) has a pedigree and some claim to illustrate the Roman idea of a German woman; but there is no certainty about her race and the bust has been much mended. Such works of art cannot well be produced to support the statements of Tacitus about the nobility of the Germans. They are not evidence for the existence of a Teutonic type in general; still less for a Saxon type in particular.

And what we want to see is not a Nordic man or German in the abstract, but if possible an Angle or Saxon of the time of the invasion. Such a one may be found in the museum at Kiel (Pl. 6A), no idealized portrait in marble, but the veritable man himself, preserved for some fifteen centuries beneath the heather of Damendorf in Schleswig—preserved, or rather pickled, in the peat of the moor; his flesh, his skin, his long fair hair (dyed red by the peat), and his clothes—all are there; but by some strange chemical action of the peat, his bones have disappeared, and the weight of the earth above him has pressed his body till it is little more than a silhouette. There lying in the peat he was found in the year 1900, his left arm stretched out and his head resting on it as if in sleep. Whatever beauty he may once have had could no longer be discerned in his wrinkled skin, his gaping mouth, and his tangled hair. More interesting than the man himself are his clothes. Spread out over his naked body was found a large woollen cloak almost two yards square, and at his feet, wrapped up in his trousers, were his shoes, his puttees, and his belt. These and similar finds elsewhere (Pl. 6B and C) not only tell us how our Anglian forefathers were dressed, but they give a good idea of the daily work and the skill of their womenfolk. One could weave a diamond pattern into the cloth for a tunic. Another, to give her man protection against the storms and rains of a northern winter, sewed a covering of hides on to his cloak. Thus did the women of the Anglo-Saxon tribes spend their days: spinsters, weavers, sewers, producing clothes for their families while their menfolk were ploughing in the fields or were out on the war-path with spear and bow.

Now it so happens that the peat moors in the neighbourhood of Angel have yielded their richest harvest of finds from the period preceding that of the migration to Britain. Those which concern us most immediately are the finds at Nydam, north of

FIG. 10. The Nydam boat.

the Flensburg fiord. There parts of three ships—three 'keels' we may call them if we use the old Germanic word—were dug out; but only one of them, a ship made of oak, was sufficiently preserved to be repaired—the long ship which is now to be seen in Kiel Museum. Since the Anglo-Saxons presumably crossed over to Britain in somewhat similar vessels, the Nydam boat and the things found with it are worth our attention. The boat is very long (77 feet) and very narrow (less than 11 feet) and very low amidships (Fig. 10)—so long and so low and so narrow that it almost recalls a modern racing 'eight' or a Pacific canoe. It had provision for fourteen oars on either side. When propelled by its twenty-eight oars it must have been fast, fast enough to elude the clumsier Roman galleys. It is generally said that it possessed among other merits notable buoyancy and elasticity. The way in which its builders obtained these results is interesting.

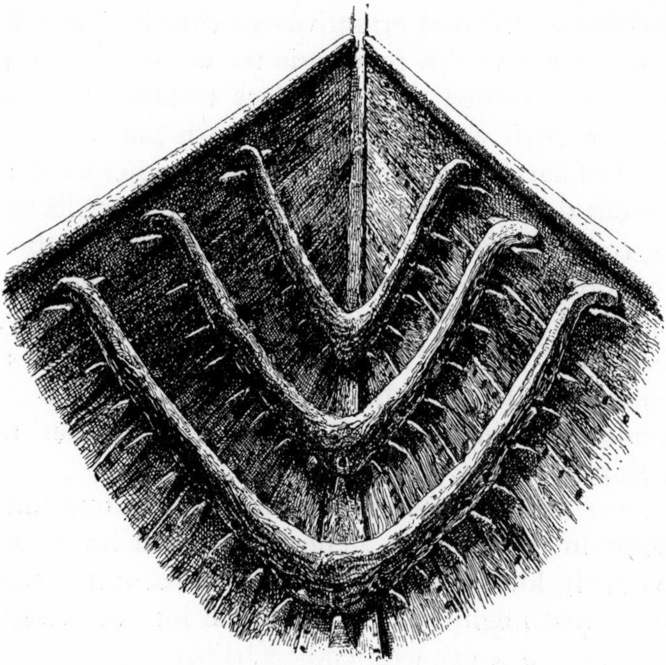

Fig. 11. Prow of Nydam boat, to show construction.

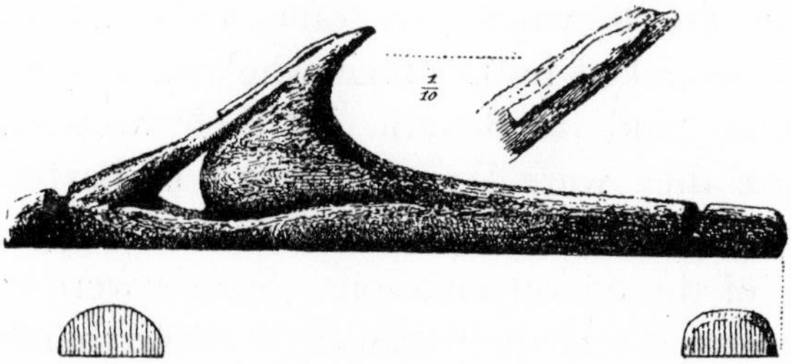

Fig. 12. Rowlock of Nydam boat.

The vessel was clinker built and the five oak planks on each side were held together by large iron rivets fastened on the inside with washers or nuts, but these side-planks were not nailed on to the main framework: they were tied to the ribs by ropes made of bast.

The arrangement of the rowlocks exhibits a somewhat similar mixture of ingenuity and primitive experiment. They also were tied on to the gunwale by ropes, and the oar was passed through another rope attached to the rowlock to keep it in its place. The rowlock itself with its sloping form is said to be stronger than our ordinary double rowlock. On the other hand the boat had obvious defects: owing to the form of the rowlock it could only be rowed in one direction; since it could not be backed with any force and could only be steered by a large paddle over the stern, its manœuvring capacity was slight. Moreover,[19] its keel was weak. It could not carry a mast or sail. Its stability was so poor that heavy ballast was necessary to keep it steady. This would accordingly make it harder to propel than the later Viking ships.

The experience of crossing the North Sea in it must have been unpleasant in the extreme. The waves must have constantly broken over its low sides; and the soaked passengers—some forty persons all told might have been packed into the vessel—must have been kept at work with endless baling.

At the bottom of the Nydam peat moor, mixed up with the fragments of boats, were exhumed quantities of weapons and miscellaneous articles which give some idea of what it must have meant to be attacked by the men who rowed these long ships from the Elbe lands to Britain. Of their swords we need say little because they were largely imports of barbarian-Roman make from the Rhine lands, such as could no longer be bought in the time of the Saxon invasions. Spears were evidently the commonest weapons of the marauders. More than five hundred spear-heads were found in the deposit. The shafts were mostly made of ash, and varied from eight to ten feet in length. Formidable weapons these, almost like the pikes of the seventeenth century. There were also spears of other kinds, some to be used as missiles and some for hunting purposes. Such spear-heads

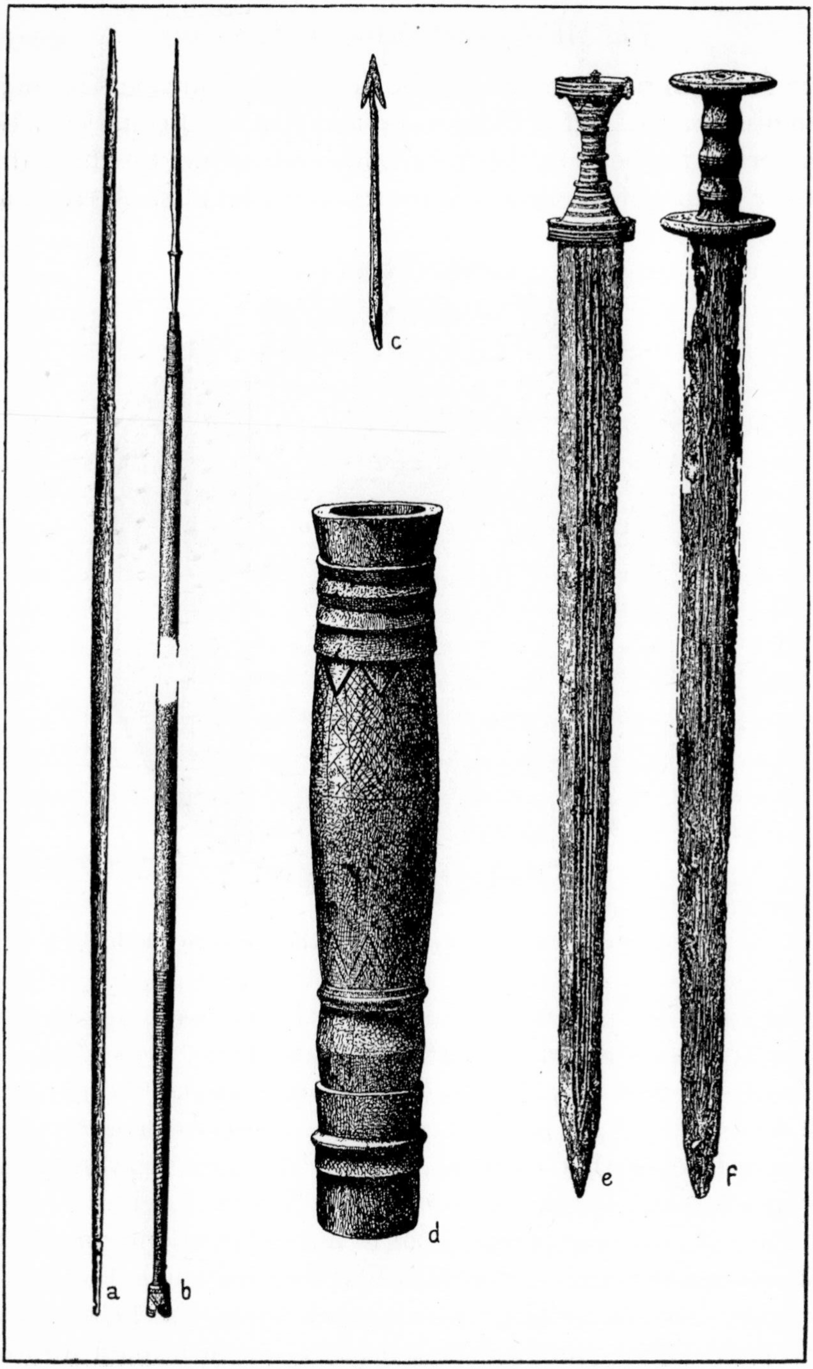

Fig. 13. Nydam Moor, weapons, &c.:
(*a*) bow, about 5 ft. long; (*b*) spear, 10 ft. long; (*c*) arrow;
(*d*) wooden quiver; (*e*), (*f*) imported swords.

are found in numbers among the bones of the invaders in their English graves. But at Nydam we also find what could only be preserved in the peat, the long bows and arrows to which the battle poetry of the Anglo-Saxons so often alludes. At Nydam

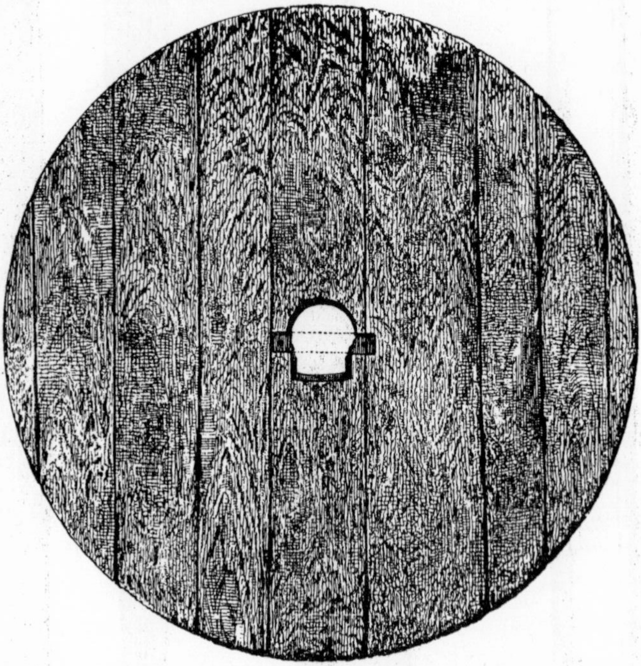

FIG. 14. Thorsberg Moor, north of the Schlei: wooden shield. $\frac{1}{12}$.

some forty bows, usually about five feet long, were discovered. The arrow-heads were made of iron and bone. The shafts of the arrows generally had notches or other marks, the purpose of which may have been to enable the owners to collect their own arrows so that each could prove his own prowess when their warriors 'held the place of slaughter' after a fight.

For defence these people seem to have trusted only to round shields of wood covered probably with hide, having in the centre a raised boss, or *umbo*, by which the weapon was held in the left hand. Their mail-coats and helmets, like their finest swords, seem to have been imported from the Rhine lands. The supply of such luxuries failed in the fifth century, and few even of the Anglian and Saxon chiefs, when they landed on the shores of Britain, can have been equipped with a shining helmet or byrnie.

So far we have been studying all that is external about our Germanic forefathers—their brooches, their clothes, their weapons, their ships. Is there any way by which we can discover something more important than these buried belongings of theirs? Can we penetrate beneath the surface and see how their minds worked?

Now without doubt even the material objects excavated from their graves should throw some light on the ideas of these men, if only we could read them aright. It is just here that difficulties become most acute.

For instance, if we try to understand why it was that the men were buried in the bogs, and why the ships and all the paraphernalia with the ships were sunk at Nydam, what are we told by the experts? At one time it was said[20] that when these things were deposited there was at Nydam a lake, evidently a sacred lake; and that into it the men of that age had cast their most precious belongings; that the motive at work had been the religious motive of sacrifice, for holes had been cut in the boats, the swords had been bent, the spear-shafts had been broken. And if this were true, the character of the gods who had been propitiated by such orgies of destruction might be guessed, and the character of the men who made their gods in their own image. And noting these things we might remember that the periodic rites of Nerthus—rites in which our Anglian ancestors participated—were concluded with the cleansing of the car of the goddess in a lake by slaves who were instantly swallowed up in its waters. This sacrificial view of the deposits in the peat has been succeeded by many others.[21] One theory explains them as dumps of worn-out things collected at the end of a campaign. Another holds that they were depots of war-booty, 'hidden treasure to which men meant to return'. Yet another interprets them by the primitive belief known as animism. The things themselves were thought to have souls, and to set their souls free for a dead owner they must be bent or broken, i.e. they must be 'killed'.

On the whole a quasi-religious motive seems to be the most adequate explanation. It is a useful reminder of the childlike ideas which from remote ages had been working in the minds of these Germanic tribes, and which were still so powerfully operative that they impelled men to destroy, to sacrifice, those things which they valued most.

Our clearest information about the religion of the Ingaevonic tribes, including the ancestors of the Angles and Saxons, is a famous description given by Tacitus of the worship of 'Nerthus, that is Mother Earth': of the sacred grove on the island where is the sanctuary of the goddess, and the sacred car which no one except the priest of the goddess may touch; of the procession of the car through the villages, the peace and festivity which reign wherever the goddess goes, and the cleansing in the secret lake, ending with a sacrifice of the slaves which the deposits in the Nydam Moor have just recalled to us. It is now usual[22] to recognize in the Nerthus cult of the Ingaevonic tribes some influence from oriental religion—'vegetation rites' which may have drifted in the Bronze Age along with the rites of the over-sexed Cybele down the trade route from the Black Sea to the Baltic. In historic times the cult passed from the Danish islands to the Swedes, where the place of Nerthus was taken by the god Frey, the son of Njorth, that is of Nerthus. The Scandinavian traditions tell of a war between the Njorth-Frey family ('the Vanir') and the family of Odin ('the Anses'). Here we have a true reminiscence of the rivalry between the competing cults which no doubt caused a great stir among the Angles and Saxons in the centuries preceding their migration. It was a struggle between the cult of Mother Earth on the one hand—bountiful Mother Earth, with her gods who gave peace and who blessed agriculture with plentiful increase—and on the other hand the heroic gods, the gods of war who gave victory.

Woden himself was the chief god of the warriors at the time of the migration because, in the early centuries of our era when the worship of Christ was advancing from Palestine to Britain, the worship of Woden, coming probably from the Rhine lands, was spreading both east and north. Woden, it seems, was driving out Thunor, the Thunderer, the weather-god beloved by the common people, much as Thunor coming at an earlier age from the west had driven out Tiw (the god of our English Tuesday), the oldest of the great gods, so old indeed that by the fifth century he had faded into the background of men's minds. It was the kingly families who looked to Woden. From him they traced their descent. His character varied. Originally, it is said, a wind-god, a god of the homeless dead, followed through the air by the Wild Hunt of disembodied spirits; lord of life and of death; lord of fighting and inspirer of battle fury—Woden appealed in a variety of ways to the kingly dynasties and the aristocrats. In all probability he was now becoming, as in Scandinavia, the master of potent spells. He could arm men with the mysteries of the Futhorc, the new runic alphabet. Thus it was easy for him to dethrone his rivals among the gods, Tiw and Thunor and the peaceful prolific Vanir gods.

Lastly, let us seek an approach to the minds of our Germanic ancestors by the way of literature. Probably the oldest poem in English, the oldest at any rate in parts, is *Widsith.* It takes its name from the far-travelling minstrel to whom the poem is attributed. Though Widsith, the nominal author, can be no more than the creation of some later poet's fancy, and though the poem itself, even the oldest parts of it, cannot well have been composed till about the beginning of the seventh century, it does still preserve for us some of the traditions carried by the Angles and Saxons from their continental home.[23]

We must not expect to get much from the poem, for it is little more than a 'Who's Who' for the Heroic Age, a catalogue of the kings and heroes whose deeds stirred the imaginations of the Germanic peoples in the age when there was an Empire to be sacked and kingdoms to be won. Even a catalogue like that, however, is something for which we may be thankful. This is how it begins:

'Widsith spake, unlocked his store of words, he who of all men had wandered through most tribes and peoples throughout the earth: oft in hall had he received the lovely treasure. . . .

'He began then to speak many words: "Of many men have I heard ruling over the nations. Every chieftain must live virtuously (one lord after another, ruling his land), he who desires his throne to flourish.

' "Of these was Hwala for a time the best, and Alexander most mighty of all the race of men, and flourished most of those of whom I have heard tell throughout the world. Attila* ruled the Huns. Ermanaric† the Goths . . . Caesar‡ ruled the Greeks, and Caelic the Finns" ' . . . and so on.

Widsith himself, the reputed author of the poem, is introduced to us as a travelling minstrel, from 'Angel in the East', that is the continental home of the Angles, and he is represented as the one who of all men had wandered through most tribes and peoples throughout the earth. He enumerates in all sixty-nine tribes and tribal heroes. Those which he knows best are the tribes and heroes of the northern seas. In the myths of northern tradition Baltic chiefs assume heroic proportions. Kings and tribes are mentioned who never appeared above the horizon of the southern Roman world.

Among the crowd of obscure northern heroes mentioned by Widsith there is one who concerns us directly. Recent writers[24] have given Offa of Angel his proper place at the head of English history as the first king of the English who is something more than a mere name. What Widsith tells us is that in those days when 'Offa ruled Angel; Alewih the Danes, he was the boldest of all these men, yet did he not in his deeds surpass Offa. But

* *Aetla.* † *Eormanric.* ‡ *Casere*—the Eastern Emperor.

Offa gained, first of men, by arms, the greatest of kingdoms whilst yet a boy; no one of his age [did] greater deeds of valour in battle with his single sword; he drew the boundary against the Myrgingas at Fifeldor.* Engle and Swæfe held it afterwards as Offa struck it out.'

Now the interesting thing about Offa of Angel is that traditions about him continued to flourish both among the English in Britain and among the Danes, who in appropriating the province of Angel took over some of its Anglian folk-lore. The Danish version which emerges in the twelfth century in the History of Saxo portrays Offa† as a prince of great stature who in early youth was considered to be dull and silent and useless in all affairs, and whose true worth was only revealed to the Angles. For it was then agreed that the fate of the kingdom should be decided by a duel between Offa and the son of the aggressor. These were the circumstances under which a duel was fought on an island of the river Eider—the duel in which Offa 'whilst yet a boy . . . with his single sword drew the boundary' for the Angles, when the kingdom of his father, an old man, was attacked by the king of the Myrgings from the south of the Eider.

Since there are eight steps in the Mercian genealogy (vol. ii, p. 719) between Penda (? 626–55) and his ancestor Offa, we may calculate that the incident which gave birth to these traditions probably occurred about the end of the fourth century; and we may accept as highly probable the conjecture that Offa of Angel was remembered because his reign had been in fact unusually successful. Thus at a time when the Roman power in the west was beginning to crumble, when the Saxon raiders were an increasing menace in Britain and Gaul, the Angles of Schleswig were enjoying the rule of a strong king.

This introductory chapter is already long enough; yet the picture of the Angles and Saxons on the Continent before their migration is lamentably incomplete. Some of the blanks which

* The river Eider (but cf. Siebs, 65). For the Swæfe see above, p. 6. † Spelt Uffo.

have been left are inevitable; some will be in part filled up when we learn about the emigrant peoples in their new colonies; others may be made good by the reader in his own mind from the evidence which has already been given.

The deficiency which is perhaps most likely to give a wrong impression is the omission so far of any description of the wild nature surrounding these Germanic tribes—the vast stretches of forest and marsh and heath which hemmed them in and did so much to form their characters. This is one of the subjects about which little is here said because the conditions will be much the same when the emigrants reappear in Britain. The forests and heaths of Britain will be less extensive, but the struggle of the farmer with forest and moorland will continue with little change or abatement.

For a like reason little has been said about the agriculture of the Angles and Saxons, though this rather than the chase or cattle-raising must have been the pursuit which filled the day of most men from morning till night. At this point it must suffice to say that in Britain the skill of Anglo-Saxons in ploughing the heavy clay lands of the river valleys will be an all-important factor in their successful advance.

Again, little has been said about many points made familiar by the sketch of Tacitus. In his own day the common characteristics which he ascribed to scores of different 'German' tribes can have been but half-truths. By the fifth century they were necessarily something less. The lazy life in which sleeping and feasting alternated with fighting and hunting may still have existed in some war-bands of chiefs or kings at the time of the migration as in the time of Tacitus; but it was clearly not the normal life of the farming folk who made the villages of England and laid out their open fields.

The evidence which has been already produced will, on consideration, supply answers to many of the questions which rise in the mind when we try to picture the society of our forefathers by the Elbe and the Eider.

What arts did they possess? We must remember their runes. We must remember their cremation urns with ornamental lines and stamps and bosses. Above all we must remember their brooches. The 'round' and the 'equal-armed' brooches (Figs. 5, 8, 9) are good examples of what is called 'chip-carving' or

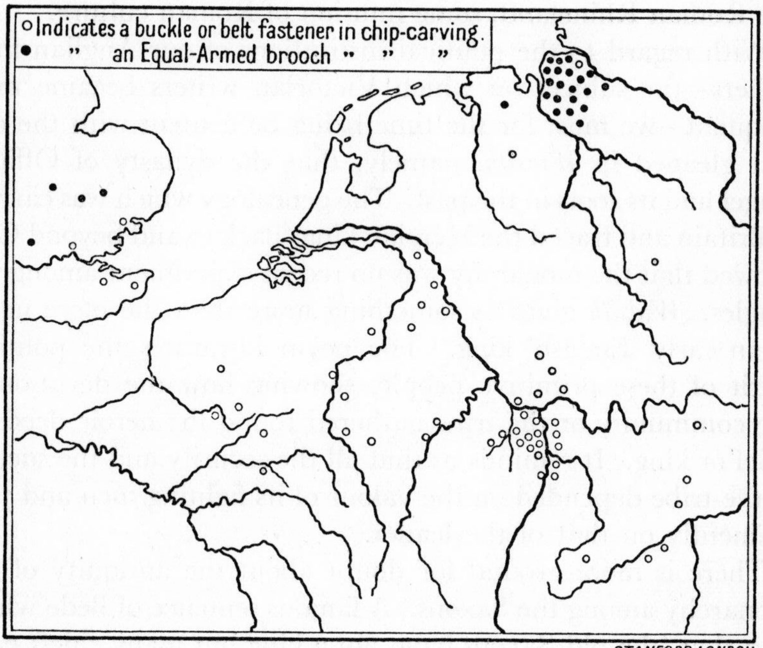

Kerbschnitt technique. This was the last fashion in metal-work to gain sway in the Western Empire before the Empire was inundated by barbarians in the fifth century. The map, showing the distribution of certain objects made in this style in western Europe, indicates that the chief home, perhaps the factory, of the chip-carving craftsmen was the region of the middle Rhine. That was a region where 'barbarian' influences were strong, and it may well be that the influence of German woodcraft is reflected in the designs of this chip-carving. It is true that in the art-motives and in the technique there is much borrowing from Roman-provincial work both of the Rhine lands and of north-east Gaul. This is the important point, for here we see the contrast between the Germans who invaded Britain and the Germans of Tacitus—the contrast between a people almost untouched by Roman influences and a people who for many generations had received, along with goods manufactured in the Roman Rhineland, some infusion of Roman culture.

With regard to the political institutions of our Anglian forefathers—the subject on which Victorian writers became most eloquent—we must for the time being be content with the one fact gleaned in *Widsith*, namely, that the dynasty of Offa of Angel had its roots in the past. The genealogy which was carried to Britain and traced the Mercian kings back to and beyond Offa showed that the monarchy was no recent experiment among the Angles. *Widsith* gives us something more than the mere name of an early 'English' king. The poem illustrates the political spirit of these primitive people, showing how the devotion of the community or the tribe gathered round the heroic deeds of chief or king. It reminds us that all the security and the success of the tribe depended on the valour of its fighting men and pre-eminently on that of the leader.

There is more ground for doubt about the antiquity of the monarchy among the Saxons. A famous sentence of Bede which says that 'the old Saxons have not a king but many chiefs each set over his own tribe' certainly suggests that the conglomerate of tribal communities calling themselves Saxons had been less unified in a common obedience than the Franks and other new confederate groups of the Germanic world.

We need not discuss here how the German tribal system worked, since the migration of the Angles and Saxons over sea could not be a migration by tribes. The crews who manned the longboats may have been animated by a strong sense of equality bred on the fields of northern Germany, but the success of their enterprise, whether on sea or on land, depended primarily on the skill of the leader and the discipline of the followers. The spirit which permeates *Widsith* was no later invention. It was an essential to success in the age of the migration.

One last question remains: What were the motives which impelled these peoples to leave their former homes and risk everything in a long voyage to Britain?

Remembering that the invaders may have come from regions as widely sundered as is the north coast of Gaul from the Jutish peninsula and that they probably continued to come for more than a century, we shall see that many different causes must have been at work. For example, some of the Saxons in Gaul may have been squeezed out by the advance of the Franks, but this would chiefly be towards the end of the fifth century. Then some fifty years later the northward expansion of Frankish power may have moved any Saxons still camped about the Rhine mouths and have closed that route to the emigrants. Some writers, observing that the first Saxon settlement in Britain coincided roughly with the climax of the Hunnish power in western Europe, have argued that 'panic-stricken tribesmen—English, Saxons, Jutes and others—took to their ships and fled overseas'[25] in order to escape from Attila. But this is a mere guess; and it seems to exaggerate the terror caused by Attila in north Germany and the suddenness of the migration. It may well be doubted whether the migration was ever such a mass movement as Bede[26] implied. When Bede spoke of the old home of the Angles being still a desert in his day, he may not have realized how much of it was then rendered uninhabitable by nature.[27]

There is, however, no need to seek further for motives. In the fifth century the Germanic nations were on the move. The unrest in the souls of men is reflected even in Widsith's jejune catalogue of the nations and their great men. The stories of Ermanaric the Goth, of Gundahari the Burgundian, and many of the other heroes, known and unknown, to which he alludes, had no doubt stirred the minds of Germans even when they lived in remote wastes near the shores of the Baltic. They had helped to bring home to them the truth that the Empire was crumbling, that the old defences were broken down, that the way was open to those who had followers ready to risk death in the hope of winning gold or land. And apart from the tales of the minstrels, the ordinary talk of the shipping folk along the north German coast must have kept rumours circulating about the events in Gaul and Britain: rumours of the outposts of Saxon adventurers thrust forward to the Rhine lands, to the Loire; rumours of world-shaking events such as the advance of the Germanic peoples into Gaul; then finally of the lodgements effected by Jutish or Saxon adventurers in Britain. When these rumours reached the villages crowded on the narrow spits of habitable land by the Weser and Elbe, the minds of men along the over-populated seaboard must have been seized with a new contagion. For long it may have been a fever which only attacked the young and the adventurous, like one of the gold manias which in modern times have driven descendants of the Anglo-Saxons to the Rand or Klondike. In the end the epidemic clearly became less virulent but more universal, a land-hunger which drove whole families, sometimes whole communities, to make the great resolve, to take the step which required much more faith than is needed for a colonist in our modern mechanical days, to pack their stores and weapons on one of their long narrow ships and to adventure into the unknown world. In this phase the motive force of the migration was a land-hunger like that which has carried men of Anglo-Saxon stock as migrants round the globe.

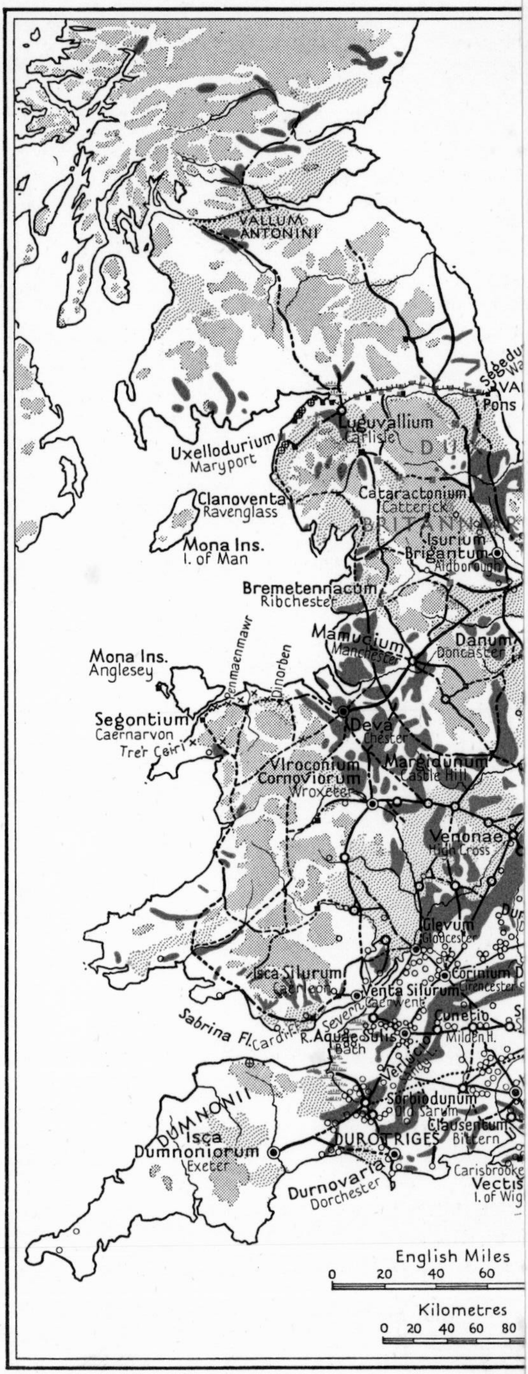

VALLUM ANTONINI
Luguvallium
Carlisle
Uxellodurium
Maryport
Clanoventa
Ravenglass
Cataractonium
Catterick
Isurium
Brigantum
Aldborough
Mona Ins.
I. of Man
Bremetennacum
Ribchester
Mamucium
Manchester
Danum
Doncaster
Mona Ins.
Anglesey
Penmaenmawr
Dinorben
Segontium
Caernarvon
Tre'r Ceiri
Deva
Chester
Viroconium
Cornoviorum
Wroxeter
Margidunum
Castle Hill
Venonae
High Cross
Glevum
Gloucester
Isca Silurum
Caerleon
Venta Silurum
Caerwent
Sabrina Fl.
Cardiff
Severn
R. Aquae Sulis
Bath
Cunetio
Mildenhall
Sorbiodunum
Old Sarum
Clausentum
Bittern
DUMNONII
Isca
Dumnoniorum
Exeter
DUROTRIGES
Durnovaria
Dorchester
Carisbrooke
English Miles
0
20
40
60
Kilometres
0
20
40
60
80

Redditor lucis aeternae.

II

THE END OF ROMAN BRITAIN[1]

THE UNDERWORLD OF ROMAN BRITAIN

THE chief aim of this chapter is to throw such light as there is upon the condition of Roman Britain in the middle of the fifth century. At the outset we have to admit that we are facing a dark tract of history which can never—not even with the help of archaeology—be made clear; all that can be done is to approach the unknown through the known, to get as near as we can and then to conjecture the state of Britain in the fifth century from what we have seen of it in the preceding period, when it was still an integral part of the Western Empire.

The civilization of Roman Britain—the 'known' which is to be our starting-point—need be represented in this book only by a 'reconstruction' of Roman London (Pl. 7 A) which may serve to remind those whose imaginations are not stirred by objects in museum cases, of the majesty and wealth of the Roman world—the majesty which for long awed the barbarians and the wealth which in the end attracted them. There is also no need

HEADPIECE.—Gold medallion celebrating the relief of London, A.D. 296, by Constantius Chlorus. $\frac{1}{1}$.

to describe the Romanized superstructure of society during the first centuries of the Roman occupation—the three strongholds of Roman culture: first, the military garrison and the lesser army of civil servants; secondly, the Romanized communities of the towns; and thirdly, the Romanized country gentlemen who inhabited the larger villas of the countryside. These need not detain us, since they had little connexion with the Saxons. In this history we shall be more concerned with the offspring of the underworld of Roman Britain, the descendants of the serfs living in the outhouses of the villas along with the animals, or of the natives whose primitive round huts were clustered in villages and homesteads on the outskirts of civilized society. They are the people who in the long run were to come into chief contact with the Saxons and who, whether as enemies or subjects, were to influence them through the succeeding centuries. The future of Celtic Britain was to be determined by these backward communities of the country districts rather than by the more civilized inhabitants of the towns and villas; and it is therefore these that we should study. Though our knowledge of the native settlements is still far from complete, we can see their varying gradations of Romanization in different regions. At the top of the scale we may place the villages excavated in Cranborne Chase, headed by Woodcuts. Here the usages of civilized society had made such way that the huts were roofed with tiles and sometimes heated with a rough type of hypocaust. The villagers bought such goods as they could afford in the Roman towns—their furniture, their glass, their spoons, their jewellery, their tools. They could write with iron *styli* in the Roman manner. In some ways they were worse than barbarians; for example, they buried their dead in ash-pits without order or decency.

Next in the scale of superficial civilization we may place other upland settlements on the open hills of southern Britain. The plans of their habitations and fields have been recently revealed to us by air photography (Pl. 8). Their culture and habits

A. Roman London—reconstructed
From a drawing by the late Mr. A. Forestier

B. Roman soldiers
From the column of Marcus Aurelius

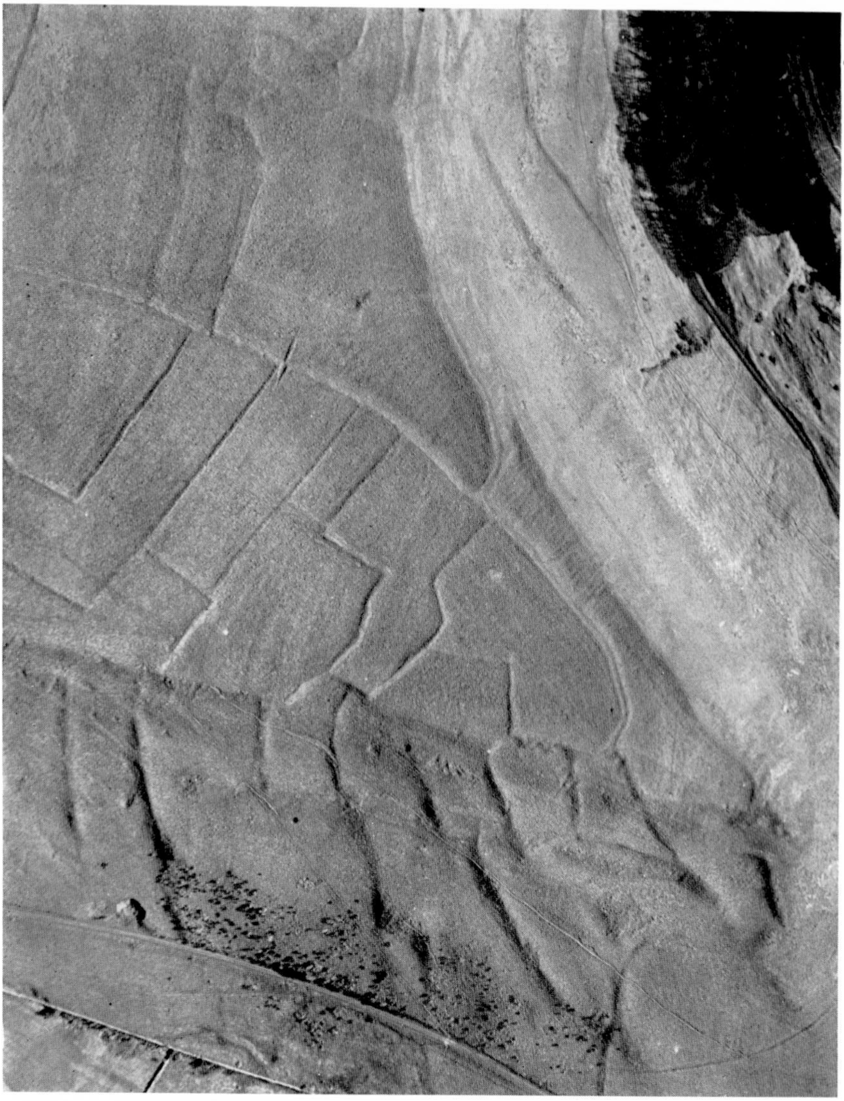

Air-photograph of Celtic Fields, near Kingston, Dorset

There are faint indications of habitations near the top. The double line (right centre) is a lane leading to the fields. The fields were here separated by stone walls and within them may be seen the ancient 'lands', two or three yards wide

are well illustrated by the excavations of a homestead at Lowbury Hill on the Berkshire Downs above Moulsford, where

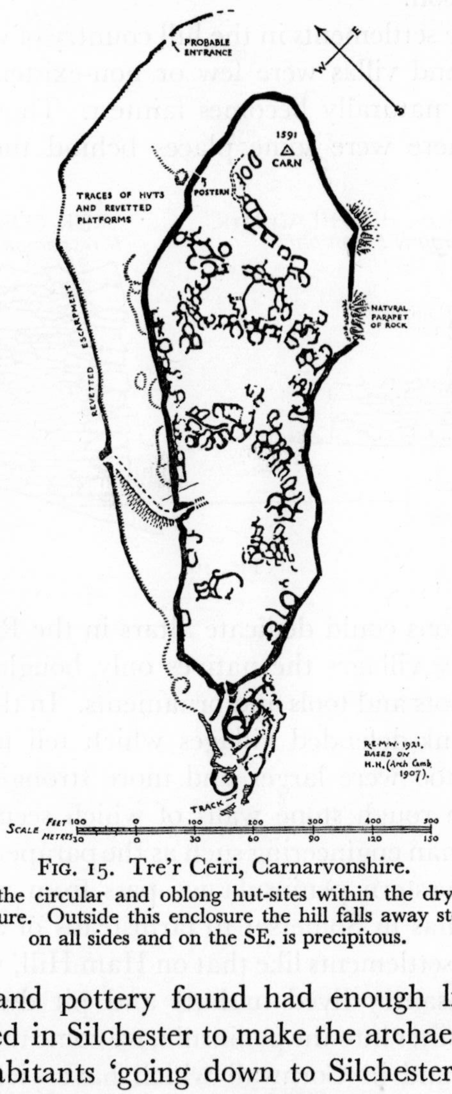

FIG. 15. Tre'r Ceiri, Carnarvonshire.
Note the circular and oblong hut-sites within the dry-wall enclosure. Outside this enclosure the hill falls away steeply on all sides and on the SE. is precipitous.

the jewellery and pottery found had enough likeness to the things excavated in Silchester to make the archaeologist picture the Celtic inhabitants 'going down to Silchester from time to time to do their marketing and see life'.[2]

The identification of other British settlements is now being pursued by archaeologists all over the country. They are found not only on the chalk hills but on gravel patches in the valleys and wherever in those days there was open ground with a dry, easily worked soil.

In the native settlements in the hill country of western Britain, where towns and villas were few or non-existent, the tinge of Romanization naturally becomes faintest. Thus in the north-west, while there were some places behind the frontier forts

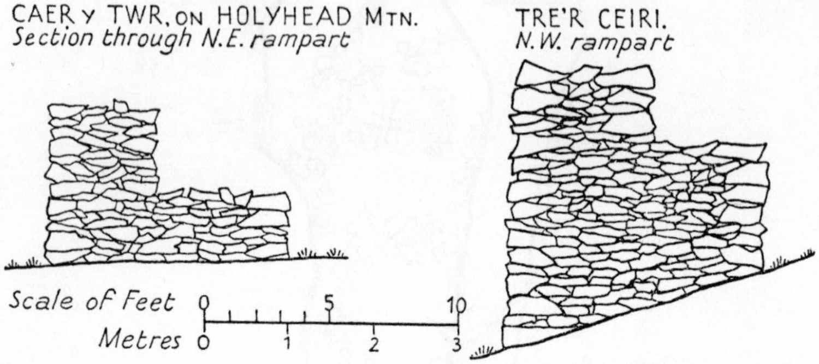

FIG. 16.

where the Britons could dedicate altars in the Roman manner, in the ordinary villages the natives only bought from Roman traders a few pots and tools and ornaments. In the hills of Wales there were bank-defended villages which tell much the same story. There too were larger and more strongly fortified hill-top towns, the rough stone walls of which seem to reproduce features of Roman engineering such as the parapet walk (Fig. 16). In the south-western peninsula we pass from a few luxurious Romanized villas in Somerset to farmsteads of a humble type, and to upland settlements like that on Ham Hill, where the semi-barbarous peasantry lived in huts and pit dwellings. Then, penetrating farther into the peninsula, we come to hill-top villages on Dartmoor and in Cornwall which have yielded few or no traces of Roman culture. Homes such as these were the strongholds of the Celtic race and the Celtic spirit. Here the more civilized fugitives from the east would find some kind of shelter.

Here too they could soon forget their Latin and lose the habits of Romanized life.

Thus excavation is constantly giving us new glimpses of the more primitive communities of Roman Britain—those which,

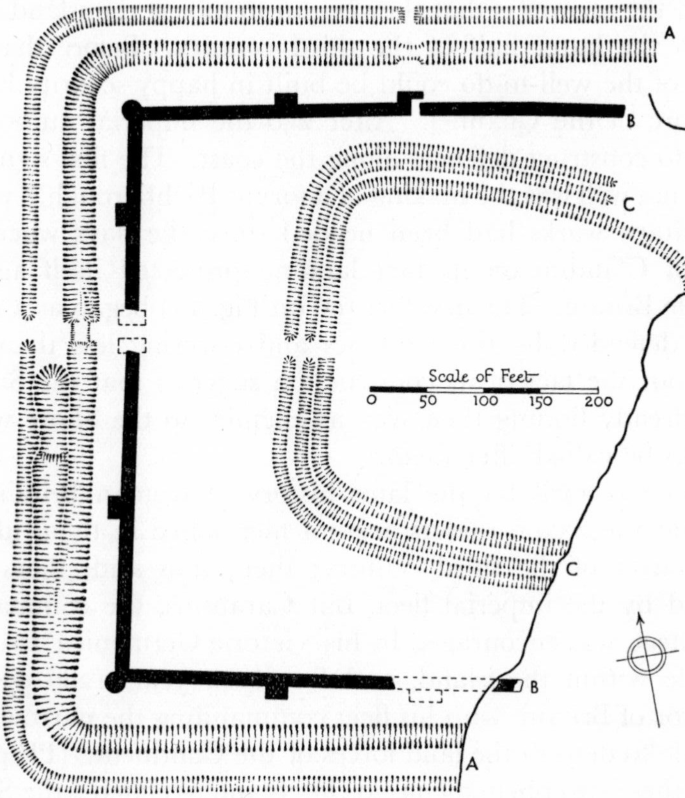

FIG. 17. Plan of Richborough, showing earlier (CC) and later (BB, AA) forts.

owing partly to their poverty and the small temptation they offered to the spoiler, and partly owing to their hills, were able to escape the first waves of invasion: islands in the deluge, where remnants fleeing from the cities and the lowlands could find a refuge in the evil days, and where Romano-Britons could grow into Welshmen.

THE LATER DEFENCES OF ROMAN BRITAIN

When exactly was it that the evil days did come? When did the Golden Age of Roman Britain end? About this there is room for difference of opinion. So far as it is a question of the Saxons' advent, the answer is that they began to molest the island some time in the latter half of the third century. Before that the houses of the well-to-do could be built in happy security beside the shore of the Channel. After 250 the imperial authorities began to construct defences along the coast. The first sign that all was not well was the making of a fort at Richborough,* where no military works had been needed since the days when the army of Claudius on its first landing protected itself against a hostile Britain. The new fort (CC on Fig. 17) began as a small affair, defended by three ditches and covering less than two acres, but the fact of its construction suggests that the Saxons were already finding their way as enemies to the Shore which came to be called after them.

Written records for the later history of Roman Britain are few; and the Saxon raiders are not mentioned in them till the last quarter of the third century; then, it is said, they were repelled by the imperial fleet, but Carausius, the commander of the fleet, was encouraged by his 'victoria Germanica' to usurp the rule within the island, and for seven years (286–93) the Emperor of Britain, with his fleet commanding the narrow seas, was able to defy all the land forces of the Continent. (Pl. 43, 1.)

It is these two phenomena, so closely inter-related—the Saxon raids and the revolt of the Roman fleet—which explain the developments of the following century, the last century of Roman rule in our island.

When Constantius Chlorus re-established the authority of the Empire in Britain in 296–7 and in 305–6, he organized as part of the permanent defences of Roman Britain the chain of massive forts along the coast between the Wash and Southampton

* Rutupiae.

Water, some of which had perhaps been begun in the disorders of the preceding period.[3]

For the scheme of defence of Roman Britain in its last phase we have to consult the government handbook called the *Notitia Dignitatum*. The edition of this book which has come down to us seems to date from about 428. Whether it in truth gives the dispositions of that age or those of the fourth century is a disputed point. With this caution, we may gather from the *Notitia* that the garrison which had to protect Britain in the period when the Saxons became a menace was disposed as follows.

(1) The command in the north was given to a 'Duke of the Britains'.* Under him were the Sixth Legion, 'Victrix', based as of old on York, and a number of auxiliary troops. (2) The commander-in-chief of the new south-eastern forts was the 'Count of the Saxon Shore'.† The centre of the defence was at Richborough, to which fortress the Second Legion, 'Augusta', had been wholly or partly removed from the borders of Wales. At the eight other forts were stationed auxiliary units, each with an establishment of five hundred or one thousand men. Then (3), at any rate in the last phase of Roman rule, there was in reserve somewhere—we do not know where—a field army, a mobile striking force under the 'Count of Britain'.‡

The disposition of the Roman army in Britain described in the *Notitia* and the ruins of the fortresses of the Saxon Shore rising from the meadows of our south-east coast, both speak to us with equal emphasis of the serious view of the Saxon menace taken by the imperial government during the last phase of Roman Britain. The walls of these forts of the Saxon Shore are more imposing at the present day than the ruined foundations of the Roman forts in northern Britain. No quarrying of post-Roman times has been able to destroy the concrete core of their

* *Vir spectabilis Dux Britanniarum* ('Britains' in the plural because there were now five provinces within the 'Diocese' of Britain).

† *Vir spectabilis Comes Litoris Saxonici per Britanniam.*

‡ *Vir spectabilis Comes Britanniae.*

walls. The modern excavations at Richborough and at Pevensey (Pls. 9, 10) are enabling the present generation to see these fortresses with a new understanding. Their walls, rising in places to a height of twenty-five feet, their ditches, their bastions—such things as these show how the Romans in this latest period were thrown upon the defensive. In name and in appearance the *castella* of the Saxon Shore were coming to resemble the castles of the Middle Ages. But while the medieval castles were well adapted to protect a local magnate from the attacks of his neighbours, the forts of the Saxon Shore were not so well devised to meet the raids of volatile sea-raiders. We seem to see in them a scheme stamped with the mentality of generals accustomed to the land warfare of the continental Empire and obsessed with a theory about a new artillery defence. It looks like the scheme of men who did not sufficiently understand that the main protection of an island must be with ships rather than walls, even the highest, the solidest, the most impregnable walls. None the less, it must be confessed that at present we do not know enough about the Channel fleet of the Romans in the fourth century to condemn their High Command for stupidity. The positions of the Saxon Shore forts, placed at what were in those days the harbours of that coast, and the fact that their walls were extended to the sea, suggest that they were planned for the protection of shipping; and that the communications between the forts were maintained by sea rather than by land.

It is possible to claim a high strategic value for the forts. Thus it is argued:[4] 'These forts which formed a strong coastal defence and were also probably supply bases for the fleet, must have done much to minimize the raids, as, although the Saxons might have penetrated inland between them, the fear must always have been present that their retreat would be cut off by the garrisons, and their ships destroyed by the patrolling Roman galleys.'

Enough has been said to show that we have here a good example of the perennial controversy about the relative value of

Richborough—an air-photograph
Royal Air Force Official. Crown copyright reserved

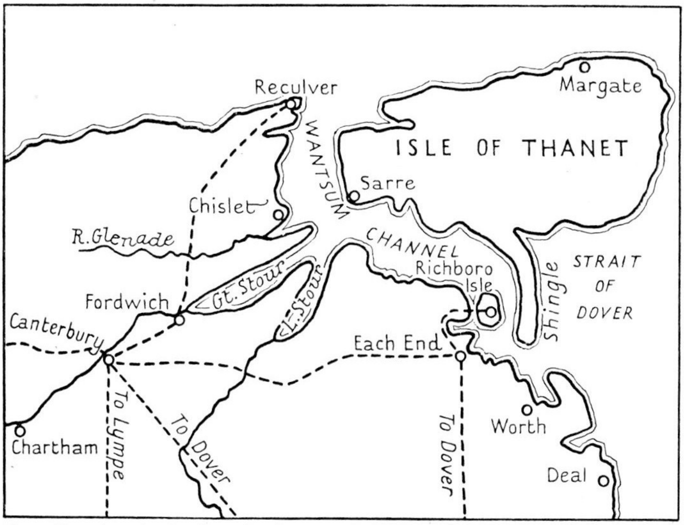

From Chartham to Deal is 16¾ miles

N.E. Kent—probable waterways of the Roman period
To show the importance of Richborough as a port

Richborough. North wall of the Saxon Shore Fort
By permission of the Controller of H.M. Stationery Office

mobile forces and fixed defences in warfare. But until the spade turns up more substantial evidence that a strong Roman fleet was based on the harbours of the Saxon Shore, we may continue to suspect that the Romans, with their massive concrete walls, were acting like children who attempt to keep out an incoming tide with a dam of stones; efforts may be made to fill in the gaps, but they are doomed to fail. Indications that the rulers of Roman Britain in the fourth century experienced something of this kind may be found in the existence of other fortifications along the Saxon Shore supplementary to those enumerated in the *Notitia*. There was, for instance, Walton Castle (now covered by the sea), near Felixstowe, and at the western end of the Shore there have been discovered traces of a fort at Carisbrooke, which in the Middle Ages was used as a foundation for the castle. A fort at Cardiff occupied down to 375, or later, shows that some attempt was made to extend the system even to the west coast. In Lincolnshire, walls of the new type at Caistor and at Horncastle illustrate a modification in which inland fortifications were used to supplement, or to take the place of, shore defences. Even a posting station like Margidunum on the Fosse Way was given its strong walls.

Significant additions were also made to the defences of London and of York. At London the river wall was probably built about the same time as the forts on the Saxon Shore, and was evidently intended to protect the city from Saxon attack by river. Bastions also were built on to the walls on the landward sides. At York the river wall was constructed about 300, and some fifty years later magnificent corner bastions were added, one of which, the Multangular Tower (Pl. 68), topped with medieval work, may be seen in the Museum Gardens. Then, when peace had been permanently dispelled by great barbarian inroads about 360, further attempts were made to strengthen the defences of northern Britain. Small stations were built at intervals of about ten miles along the coast of Yorkshire and elsewhere. Those of which the clearest traces remain extend from Huntcliff to Filey.

Being placed at the top of the cliffs, they were not intended like the forts of the Saxon Shore to protect shipping. All that their small garrisons could do was to watch for the approach of an enemy from the sea and then to signal a warning which could be brought back to the base fort at Malton and so to the head-quarters at York.

FIG. 18. Restored view of north corner of Roman fort at Malton.

What is most extraordinary about the disposition of the Roman army detailed in the *Notitia* is the fact that, apart from some garrisons posted in the extreme north-west to guard the flank of the great Tyne–Solway Wall, there is an almost complete absence of regular troops in the west of Britain. This official record of the imperial army assigned no units to any station in the west of the island between the Ribble and Southampton Water. Here the *Notitia* does not tally with the discovery of the Roman fort at Cardiff, or with the evidence that Segontium (Carnarvon) was repaired and re-garrisoned about 364. However, it is indubitable that towards the end of the Roman rule there was no adequate defence of western Britain by the imperial troops.

What is the explanation of this strange gap in the British defences? To answer this we are thrown back on mere conjecture. We may say that the scheme revealed in the *Notitia* was planned before the danger from the Irish had been brought home to the government, and that the later Emperors, being too much occupied with dangers nearer home to do more than tinker at the old plan, failed to recast it thoroughly and readjust it to the new situation. Or we may say[5] that the defence of the western uplands was informally handed over by the Romans to the friendly natives; in other words, that the tribes of Wales and of the south-western peninsula were left to their own devices because they were, as has been seen, too little Romanized and their hills too barren to justify the organization of an Irish Shore with a network of costly forts like those on the south-eastern coast. But the root of the matter no doubt was this: the Empire was suffering from a shortage of men, or rather of the money to pay for them. It was one thing to see that the west of the island needed systematic defence, and it was quite a different matter to find the wherewithal. What was of primary importance was that the communications between Britain and the Continent should be kept open and that the corn-land and sheep-walks of the eastern half of the island should be protected. Thus did the military policy of the later Empire accentuate the contrast between the two sides of Britain: that contrast between the more civilized lowlands and the wilder hill country which had its origin in remote geological ages.

However we explain the contrast between the Roman defences on the east and the west of the island, there can be no question that the incomplete, lop-sided disposition of the troops did as a matter of fact expose the country to its enemies. In one way or another, by peaceful infiltration or by violent conquest, a tribe like the Irish Desi from county Waterford was able to settle in

Pembrokeshire; and the extent of the Irish penetration of the west is marked by the finds of stones with Ogham inscriptions in the Irish manner—incised probably about the fifth century.

THE LAST PERIOD OF ROMAN RULE (360–(?)410)

The beginning of the end of Roman rule may be placed about 360. The preceding period had in general been one of peace and of some prosperity. British corn and cloth had been exported; Britain like the rest of the Empire had benefited from the reforms of Diocletian (284–305) and Constantine (306–37). Its civil government had been separated from the military, and had been reorganized into five provinces. Christianity had been introduced as the official religion. The first half of the fourth century has accordingly been described by Haverfield[6] as 'the zenith of ancient history in Britain'. Nowadays our attention is more drawn to the shadows in the picture; to the sense of insecurity in the hearts of men, revealed by the new forts on the coast and the new walls round inland towns. Recent excavation has also supplied evidence that even from the beginning of the fourth century—or earlier—there was a decline of prosperity in the towns. When buildings in Viroconium (Wroxeter) were burnt about 300 they were not rebuilt. The pavements of Verulamium (St. Albans) when injured were rudely patched up with clay. In the fourth century the arts were less cultivated than in earlier times. Fewer inscriptions were set up. The builders who added bastions to the walls of London used ruins of neighbouring houses, including their columns and sculptures, as material. These houses were presumably derelict, because London, like other towns, was on the decline. The kernel of inhabited houses had shrunk within the shell of its walls.[7] Our best experts are now agreed that the town had been overbuilt. The imperial government had, like Peter the Great, been in too great a hurry to civilize its barbarians. Accordingly in the fourth century, even before the troublous times, the towns were becoming depopulated and impoverished. Then about 360 the troubles began,

An Elk fight, an amusement in the Roman Empire. *c.* A.D. 400–450

A. Reconstruction of the temple-settlement, Lydney

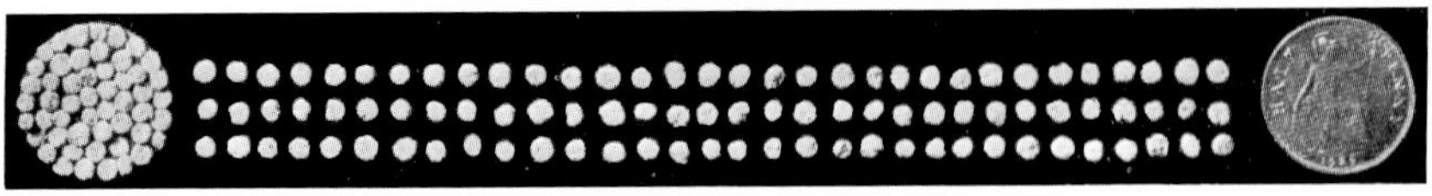

B. Minimissimi, minute sub-Roman coins. From Lydney. $\frac{1}{2}$

C. Bronze Dog from the Temple of Nodens at Lydney. $\frac{1}{1}$

and first one and then another part of the Roman superstructure crumbled: first the villas of the well-to-do landowners, next the civil service and the army, lastly the towns. The years from 360 to 367 were a crescendo of ravage. In 360 the Picts from north Britain and the Scots from Ireland broke into the province and harried the lands near the frontier. By 364 the Saxons and other barbarians had joined in and were taking their share of the spoil of the province. Then in 367 the Count of the Saxon Shore was slain by the enemy and the Duke of the northern army was surprised and overwhelmed. London and the other towns were cut off and threatened by the wandering bands of plunderers. Theodosius, the imperial general who was sent to restore order, had to wait for reinforcements before he could advance from Richborough to London. In the following year the situation was restored by him. The enemy were punished and their wandering bands expelled; the discipline and morale of the garrisons were re-established. Outwardly the military situation was restored, but the old social order was wrecked and the prestige of the Empire was dangerously shaken.

The importance of the devastation caused in these years has recently been emphasized by R. G. Collingwood. He has argued[8] that 'Roman Britain, by 367, had all her eggs in one basket'—the villa; and that the coin finds prove that the disaster was fatal to most of the villas, and therefore was irreparable. This view of the ruination caused by the raids of 360–7 is now generally credited, though it is admitted that there were many exceptions up and down the country, especially in Kent, Somerset, and the Cambridge region, and it is probable[9] that many villa owners saved themselves, though not their villas, by fleeing to the towns.

An illuminating sidelight has been cast on one spot in Roman Britain in this latest age after the beginning of the troubles, and it is a reminder that the shadows must not be made too black. Recent excavations at the Temple of Nodens at Lydney, a temple placed on a hill by the Severn, nine miles north of Chepstow,[10] have shown that soon after 364–7, elaborate Roman buildings were constructed within a prehistoric earthwork: large bathing establishments, a row of shops (or priests' rooms), and a large guest house for visitors to the shrine. The masonry is solid; floors are tessellated: there is no sign here that the civilization of the Severn valley had been destroyed. Nor is there any sign that Christianity had long been the official religion of the Empire. The priests of Nodens, evidently a Celtic divinity, found that the healing powers ascribed to the god were profitable. Of the 8,000 Roman coins which have been recovered from the neighbourhood most were of the fourth century. We see then that even towards the close of this century life could in places still be lived on much the same peaceful lines as of old, and that in the Severn valley men were still able to bring themselves and their families to enjoy the luxury of a 'cure' in the quiet of the Lydney woods. Soon, however, events occurred across the seas which turned the order of Britain, as of all the civilized world, into irretrievable confusion.

On the death of the Emperor Theodosius in 395 the Empire was cut into two; thenceforth the two halves of it went their different ways to ruin. Honorius, to whom was bequeathed the rule of the Western Provinces, was a child, and remained till his death in 423 childish in mind (Pl. 13 A), without wisdom or capacity, a breeder of pigeons. Yet the dangers now threatening the Western Empire were so great that only the highest qualities of foresight and leadership could have saved the State. Germans had gained the chief positions in the government; German troops had become the backbone of the Roman army; Germans hesitating between service and spoliation were both within and outside the Empire—within its borders Alaric the Goth was already beginning to see the truth that the Empire could not withstand those determined to seek kingdoms for themselves; outside, wild bands of Alans, Vandals, and Sueves were massed beyond the Rhine like the besiegers of a city, restlessly waiting an opportunity to assault Gaul and to sack it. In the north, Franks were pushing persistently from Toxandria into the valleys of the Scheldt and the Lys, ever planting their villages farther into the heart of Belgic Gaul, and thus threatening the line of communication between Britain and the Continent. And behind the Franks there came, as we have seen, the Saxons —Saxons pressing on their heels in the forest lands of western Germany; Saxons packed in long boats, exploring the waterways of the Low Countries and looking to the sea and to the sea-coasts of Britain and Gaul for their fortunes.

FIG. 19. A Pict.

FIG. 20. A Scot.

The generation which had the ill fate to be born in the latter half of the fourth century was to see the civilized world end in catastrophe. Everything was going wrong at the same moment, and for that reason the troubles were becoming unmanageable. The Empire was sick, not only in its head but in every one of its members; and the Saxons, though they were still a nuisance to those who lived near the sea (as they had been for well over a century) were one of the lesser evils of the age.

So far as the Roman provinces of Britain were concerned, the danger which threatened civilization came from nearer home. It was raiding bands of Picts from the north who brought fire and slaughter to the country round York and then penetrated to the heart of Britain. It was the men of Ireland (then called 'Scots') who destroyed the civilization of the west and carried off thousands of peaceful Britons to sell them as slaves.

This was the general situation. And in such a world three well-known incidents by ill luck combined to denude the island of its regular garrison and sever its effective connexion with the central government.

First, in 383, Maximus (Pl. 43, 2), who held a high command in Britain, revolted and led a considerable part of the British garrison across the narrow seas to Gaul to assert his claim to the imperial diadem. It was the selfish act of an adventurer, and its effect on Britain was to expose the north to the barbarians. Coins found in the forts of the Roman Wall go down to the year 383, but only one* has been found of a later date. For a few years Honorius allowed the military prestige of the Empire to be restored by Stilicho, a man of Vandal origin, who had climbed to the position of commander-in-chief. Thanks to Stilicho, wrote a court poet of the age,[11] Britannia need no longer fear the Scot and the Pict, nor keep watch along all her coasts dreading the coming of the Saxons with every change of wind. But he spoke too soon. For (this is the second incident of the three) in 401, when Alaric and his Visigoths advanced against Italy, Stilicho did not hesitate to withdraw another 'legion' (perhaps no more than a thousand men) from Britain.

Then, thirdly, in 407, the Roman troops in Britain, revolting against the incapacity of Honorius, set up successively three usurpers, of whom the last, Constantine, followed a course outwardly not unlike that of Maximus in 383. Constantine was no sooner hailed as Caesar in Britain than he transported his army to Gaul, and the troops withdrawn never returned.

The event of 407 which had stirred the troops of Britain to this feverish insubordination was the terrible irruption of Vandals, Sueves, and Alans into Gaul. In midwinter they had crossed the Rhine. Gaul had then become a stormy sea of barbarians, or rather one vast, smoking, funeral pyre.† Britain seemed to be cut off from the imperial government. In this

* A copper coin of Arcadius at Heddon-on-the-Wall.

† *Uno fumavit Gallia tota rogo.* S. Orientius, in Migne, *P. L.*, lxi, col. 995.

The Emperor Honorius and his wife, a daughter of Stilicho the Vandal (his commander-in-chief)

A plundered Roman flagon of silver. From the Traprain hoard. About $\frac{1}{3}$

PLATE 14

Air-photograph of Cissbury, Sussex, a disused fort reoccupied about the fourth century

By permission of the Controller of H.M. Stationery Office and the Director-General, Ordnance Survey. Crown Copyright reserved

crisis, Constantine and the troops who followed him to the Continent may have dreamed that in Gaul they would defeat the enemies of the State, or they may have been thinking less of the State and more of themselves, their own fortunes, and their own pay in a dissolving world.

In 407 the situation of the Roman army in Britain may well have seemed desperate. Britain was raked by barbarians attacking from three sides. Some signs of the barbarities which

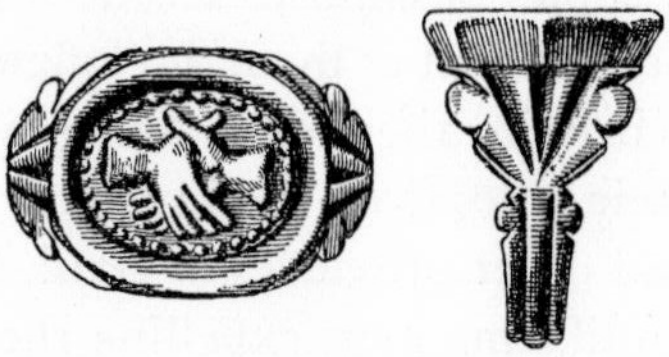

FIG. 21. Silver ring buried with a horde of coins near Wilton, about A.D. 400. The device is found on coins with the legend, *Concordia militum*.

made the Pictish or the Saxon invasions a terrible reality have been found. For instance, in the Yorkshire coastguard station at Huntcliff, when the fort was stormed about the year 400, the defenders were slain and their bodies, together with those of their women and children, were tossed into a well. At Caistor by Norwich a house has been excavated which was inhabited till about 400 and was then burnt with thirty-six persons, presumably refugees, inside it. It was probably about this same time—about the turn of the century—that Niall of the Nine Hostages, the first High King of Ireland known to history, overran the west of Britain, and in a merciless raid Patrick, the son of a British decurion, and 'many thousands' of other captives were carried off to slavery.

The end of the connected story of Roman Britain—such as it is—is contained in two passages referring to the year 410. One from a contemporary Gallic chronicle says briefly[12] that 'the multitude of the enemy so prevailed, that the strength of the Romans was extremely diminished. The provinces of Britain were laid waste by an incursion of the Saxons.' This disaster is placed in the chronicle side by side with the devastation of Gaul by Vandals and Alans and the sufferings of Rome, 'the head of the world'. The strength of the Romans in Britain passed away in the same year that Rome itself endured the three days' sack at the hands of Alaric and his Visigoths.

The other passage is contained in some ambiguous sentences of Zosimus:[13]

'... The barbarians from beyond the Rhine [i.e. the Saxons] ravaging everything at pleasure compelled both the inhabitants of the British Isle and some of the peoples of Gaul to secede from the Empire of the Romans and to live independent of them, no longer obeying the Roman laws. The people of Britain, therefore, taking up arms, and braving every danger, freed their cities from the invading barbarians. And the whole of Armorica, and other provinces of Gaul, imitating the Britons, liberated themselves in like manner, expelling the Roman officials and setting up a civil polity according to their own inclination.

'This secession of Britain and of Gallic peoples took place during the time of Constantine's usurpation, the barbarians rising up in consequence of his neglect of the government. . . .

'Honorius moreover having written letters to the cities in Britain urging them to look to their own safety . . . lived at ease.'

The value and real meaning of this passage is one of the puzzles of history, but if, as is probable, Zosimus, who lived in the latter half of the fifth century, drew his information from an earlier writer (Olympiodorus), we may give weight to the statements that the people of Britain now took up arms; that they fought well; and that the local rulers in 'the cities'*—some of them old centres of cantonal administration—sundered from the central government by the force of circumstances and the waves of barbarism which now flowed between Italy and Britain, found that in practice they were left to shift for themselves.

THE SUB-ROMAN PERIOD (*c.* 410–*c.* 450)

And so we pass to the age of the greatest darkness: it is so dark that neither the date of its beginning nor of its end can be fixed

* e.g. Exeter, Dorchester, Winchester, Chichester, Canterbury, Silchester, Caerwent, Colchester, Caistor by Norwich, Leicester, Wroxeter.

with certainty, and in calling it 'sub-Roman' we are simply confessing our ignorance of its positive characteristics.

We can say vaguely that while Roman Britain in the previous generation had lost most of its civilized villas, now in this sub-Roman period it had to struggle on without the main body of the Roman garrison and without the unifying authority of the bureaucracy appointed by the Emperor. In spite of the catastrophes which at this time destroyed so much of the old order, the change now as elsewhere in history came gradually.

Just how far the circumstances of Roman Britain were changed about 410 is still a subject of controversy. Bury, the historian of the later Roman Empire, whose opinions must carry great weight, has argued that the *Notitia Dignitatum* gives something like the real distribution of the Roman troops in the period 428–37, and that 'the true date of the Roman abandonment of Britain [is] A.D. 442'.[14] Now while Bury's view has received some important support, it is contrary to the evidence of the coins. This last is held to point decisively to the abandonment of the Wall by its garrison about 383, and to the abandonment of most of Britain even before 410. The coins which have come to light at Richborough in recent years number more than sixty thousand. The examination of the first finds has shown that the great bulk of them, where they could be identified, were minted in the last thirty-five years of the fourth century and a considerable number about A.D. 400. This coin evidence is believed by at least one expert to indicate that most of Britain was lost to Roman authority even before 400, and that the strip of eastern Britain which remained under the protection of the forts of the Saxon Shore was abandoned before 410.

The coin evidence, however, is not as conclusive as could be wished, owing to the fact that the continental bronze and silver mints which had supplied the pay for the troops in Britain were closed about the end of the fourth century, and that consequently the coins of Honorius and of Arcadius (his brother and colleague in the East) remained in circulation as no other imperial coins had done before them.

At present all that can be said is that while the argument from the coins is sufficient to discredit Bury's theory in the eyes of most experts, it is not sufficient to prove a complete negative. Regions on the Continent can be pointed out, such as Noricum

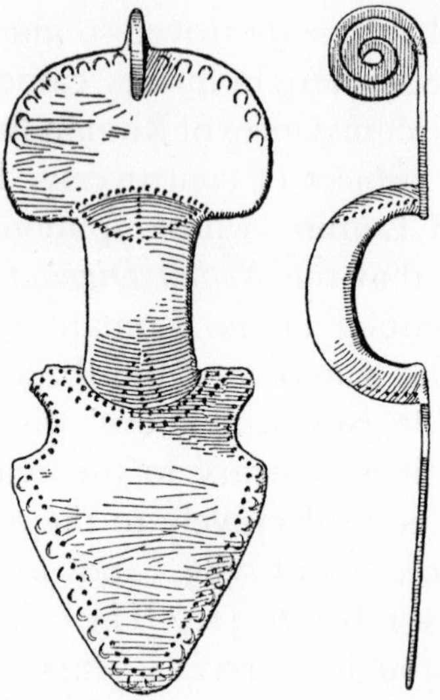

FIG. 22. Lydney; brooch excavated in 1928–9, assigned to the post-Roman period. $\frac{1}{1}$.

Ripense and parts of Normandy,[15] where the coin finds ceased as in Britain though the authority of the Emperors survived down to the middle of the fifth century. We may still hesitate before we assert that no Roman troops whatever, no cadre of the former garrison supplemented it may be with occasional new levies, lingered on in forts of the Saxon Shore for many years after 410.

In other directions also the results of the troubles of the early fifth century are often exaggerated. When Honorius sent his rescript to the cities of Britain urging them to look after their own safety, he was taking a sensible step which may have given

Britain a fairly satisfactory government for some decades. The presumed condition of affairs has been summed up by R. G. Collingwood in the following words:*

'What the cities lacked was a co-ordinating power; they must therefore have run on more or less parallel but unconnected lines, always in danger of getting to cross-purposes, and also in danger of becoming the tools of ambitious men bitten by a desire for local greatness. They continued also to raise and employ local militia: but these forces, adequate for a defence of town walls against casual barbarian raids, would be useless for a campaign and therefore unable to drive an enemy out of a countryside.'

Archaeology unfortunately can do little to fill in the gaps in our knowledge of the sub-Roman period. The Romano-British provincials, engrossed by the immediate necessities of their existence, seem to have used up their old belongings, or if they made new things they must have made them out of perishable materials like wood and leather. None the less, even for the fifth century the spade has supplied some data, few but significant. At Silchester and elsewhere a town gateway has been found half blocked up with masonry; an entrance built in the Golden Age could be dangerously wide in days when the *pax Romana* was ending. At Lydney, by the Severn, men thought it necessary to strengthen a prehistoric rampart. In the southern downlands disused earthworks like Cissbury (Pl. 14) and Yarnbury were reoccupied, doubtless by refugees, some time towards the end of the Roman period. In the north a rude fort like 'the Castles' near Hamsterley in County Durham may tell a similar tale, since it is built on a Roman plan, though with stones neither squared nor cemented.

Two other finds in this necessarily disconnected list are specially interesting. One is a memorial stone with an Ogham inscription, excavated at Silchester, which shows that the Irish, either as friends or foes, penetrated into the heart of southern Britain. The other is the hoard of spoil carried off about the

* Privately communicated.

beginning of the fifth century from a Roman province (probably Gaul) and buried on the top of Traprain Law, the hill which is a well-known landmark in the country south of the Forth. The beautiful silver flagons and dishes (Pls. 13 B and 15), now in the Museum at Edinburgh, were evidently loot from a church and from the mansion of some wealthy landowner. Since many of them had been hacked in two, it is conjectured that two bands had co-operated in the raid and had then divided the spoil equally. Thereafter one band, being surprised in their lair on the hill, buried their treasure in haste, and were overtaken by death before any of them could return and recover the hoard. In these battered silver vessels we see the process by which the beautiful things of the Roman world were carried off to be melted down and converted into jewellery for the barbarians.

External ravage was accompanied by internal decay. It is now possible to study the latter in the coins (some of them scarcely deserve that name) found at Richborough and Lydney. These show the makeshifts used by the people of Britain when, isolated from Roman mints, they had to produce a currency of their own. Sometimes they minted small barbarous copies of genuine Roman coins in base metal, sometimes they used minims or minimissimi, the smallest coins ever produced in this island. Since they are so small that fifty of them can be placed side by side on a halfpenny (Pl. 12 B), we need not wonder that they have rarely been noticed by previous excavators. Now, however, they are our best illustration of the poverty and degradation which overtook the deserted provincials. The sub-Romans could attempt to repeat on their barbarous imitations the inscriptions of happier times—'Victoria'; 'Gloria Romanorum'; 'Fel[ix] Temp[orum] Reparatio'.[15a] But these were mere parrot-cries. The figure of Mars was so badly copied that it became a woman: in another series a female figure with arms outstretched was copied till in time it became a Saxon cross.

Are these miserable substitutes for a coinage a fair measure of the degradation to which the Romano-Britons succumbed in

A view of Traprain Law

The treasure as found

the fifth century? This is a question of which we are likely to hear more in the coming years. The advocates for the survival of Romano-British art after the departure of the Roman army can produce some finger-rings found at Amesbury (Wilts.) and can recognize Celtic art in some of the treasures found in Anglo-Saxon graves, such as the enamelled plaques of numerous hanging bowls.[15b] But on the other hand the clumsy masonry of the sub-Roman period, the barbarous patchings of tessellated pavements, the mud floors, the resort to earthworks of the primitive type, the lettering and grammar of the tombstones and the minims—all these tell a convincing story of rapid demoralization.

Having obtained from the archaeologists some information, however fragmentary, about the sub-Roman period, we have next to fall back upon the few references to it in literature.

Nennius,* the Welsh antiquary of the early ninth century, who did his best to be the historian of the Britons, relates, in one of the more reliable sections of his book,[16] a tradition that Cunedda, son of Eternus and grandson of Paternus, came towards the end of the fourth century† with his eight sons from the north, that is, from the region called Manaw Gododin, near the Firth of Forth, and expelled the Irish from Gwynedd and other parts of Wales, defeating them so utterly that never again did they try to settle there. The Britons among the hills of Wales were thus reanimated; they obtained a vigorous dynasty, tinged with Roman civilization but essentially Celtic in thought and language. This story illustrates the complexity of the situation in Britain about the time of the great catastrophe. There was no simple straightforward conflict between provincials and barbarian invaders. A chieftain with a Roman pedigree could come

* I retain the name by which he has been known in the past, though R. Thurneysen (in *Zeitsch. f. Celtische Philologie*, xx (1933), 97–138) argues that the name should be read as Nemnius or Nemnivus.

† i.e. '146 years before Maelgwn reigned'. Maelgwn died in 547.

from beyond the pale of the Empire. When he settled in Wales, those whom he drove out were not Britons but Irish, who had for some indeterminable period been in possession of this region.

For the rest, British sources are too untrustworthy to be of much help in disentangling fact from fiction. Even Gildas (of whom as of Nennius we shall have more to say in the next chapter), though he ought to have possessed some traditions of value about the sub-Roman period since he lived in the middle of the sixth century, allows his main story to be discredited by a schoolboy howler about the Roman Wall. A few details remain which carry conviction. Gildas tells us of 'civil wars' which broke out among the Romano-Britons, and civil wars were surely inevitable where competing cities and individuals were left stranded without a central government. He refers to an appeal made to Aëtius in his third consulship; and Aëtius at any rate was an historical figure, a commander who for thirty years was the mainstay of Roman power in the West and whose third consulship is known to have occurred in the year 446.

If we discard the narrative of Gildas as improbable (and there is almost general agreement that it is necessary to do so for the first half of the fifth century, but not, be it noted, for the second half) we surrender the hope of obtaining any sort of connected history for the sub-Roman period. What remains? We have two contemporary writings which throw some light on the general condition of the country in the fifth century; and we have certain contradictory statements about the date of the first submergence of Britain—or of part of it—by the Saxons. The two books which help us to understand the former, the more important, subject are the *Life of St. Germanus* and the writings of St. Patrick.

The *Life of St. Germanus* is no better than the ordinary run of hagiography in its accumulation of miracles, but we do at any rate know that it must have been written before 490 (probably about 480), and that the author, Constantius, a priest of Lyons,

Portrait from diptych, now identified as Stilicho, at one time supposed to be Aetius

Reconstruction of the Gate through which St. Germanus probably entered Verulam
(? already falling into ruin by the fifth century)

had opportunities of learning about Britain at first or second hand, since he was a friend of Sidonius, who was in his turn a friend of Lupus, a companion of Germanus on the journey to Britain.[17] The *Life* tells us that Germanus, archbishop of Auxerre, paid two visits to Britain with the purpose of stamping out in the island the heretical views concerning free-will propagated throughout the Empire by Pelagius, a man of British* birth. On his visit in 429 Germanus showed the Britons that he was an old soldier as well as a saint. He held a council in which the damnable heresies of Pelagius were denounced. He accompanied the clergy attending the council to the tomb of St. Alban the Martyr, and he then taught the Britons how to defeat a combined army of Picts and Saxons by shouting 'Alleluiah' three times as they closed with the enemy. At first sight the alliance between Gaelic-speaking Highlanders and German-speaking Saxons seems so great an improbability that it is reasonable to see in it one of the author's imaginative touches intended to enhance the fame of the saint, a victory over two peoples being more miraculous than a victory over one. He would regard the change as a laudable improvement of the story, quite in keeping with the principles of hagiography. Another explanation, however, is possible. There is, it is asserted,† archaeological evidence for the view that Saxons were entering the eastern Midlands for some time before 429. These, being hard pressed, might conceivably call to their aid Pictish pirates—and we have the authority of Gildas for thinking that the Pictish raiders came by sea rather than by land. Such bands might well cause fear among the militia of London and of Verulam, unused to fighting in the open. The skirmish between the Christian and the heathen might occur in the hills of the Chiltern escarpment. The 'Alleluiah' shout may have been intended to beat the Germans at their own game, the battle shout—a custom as old as the time of Tacitus. These are possibilities rather than probabilities; and when we are told that the 'Alleluiah' was re-echoed by the rocks

* Or Irish. † See below, p. 116.

of the surrounding mountains we recognize the easy rhetoric of a hagiographer.

But whatever view we take of the Alleluiah victory of St. Germanus, we need not doubt that his *Life* contains a residuum which may reasonably be accepted. We have the significant points: that a Gallic archbishop could cross to Britain as a matter of course and co-operate with the clergy of Britain; and that south-eastern Britain was still a land where Romano-Britons lived their old life even though they were vexed by invaders as well as by Pelagian heresy.

About 447 or somewhat earlier Germanus returned to Britain, but he was then an old man and his second visit supplied fewer incidents to the biographer. The saint on landing was welcomed by a certain Elafius, the leading man of the district. Britain still does not appear to be submerged by barbarians. But what is most remarkable of all is that at the time when the *Life* of the saint was composed—say about 480—the author could still think of Britain as a wealthy island,* and boast that the pure doctrine taught by Germanus was still preserved in those parts. Even in the last quarter of the fifth century the encroachment of the Saxons had not become so flagrant that it was necessary for a Roman provincial to observe that the Britons, in spite of their orthodoxy, were no longer in possession of Britain. The *Life of St. Germanus* thus supplies some local colour which we cannot afford to disregard, even when we admit that it comes from an alien author writing about fifty years after the chief event which he describes.

More satisfactory and more vivid are the short writings of St. Patrick, the only Briton of the sub-Roman period whose words take us straight to the heart of the man and near to the spirit of the age. We have the *Confession* in which he pours out a wandering but a glowing defence of his career:[18]

'I, Patrick the sinner, am the most illiterate and the least of all the faithful, and contemptible in the eyes of very many. My father was

* *opulentissima insula* (c. 18).

Calpurnius, a deacon, one of the sons of Potitus, a presbyter, who belonged to the village of [?] Bannavem Taberniae. Now he had a small villa* hard by, where I was taken captive.

'I was then about sixteen years of age. I knew not the true God; and I went into captivity to Ireland with many thousands of persons, according to our deserts, because we departed away from God, and kept not His commandments, and were not obedient to our priests, who used to admonish us for our salvation.'

The raid which carried off Patricius, the well-born Romano-Briton, to Ireland, and which, as we have seen, probably occurred about 400, helps, like the Traprain hoard, to bring home to us what really happened in the interminable wars which distressed the wretched inhabitants of our island decade after decade from 360 onwards. A boy of sixteen driven off to slavery with 'many thousands' of others, sold and set to tend swine in a remote part of Ireland—that may stand for the fate of untold numbers of Romano-Britons. The matter-of-fact way in which St. Patrick speaks of his misfortune is also typical of the times. The raid is accepted as a matter of course: it is simply one of the punishments with which God is admonishing His people for their own good. Misfortune is fostering religion.

Let us quote once more from the *Confession*:

'Now after I came to Ireland, tending flocks was my daily occupation; and constantly I used to pray in the day-time. Love of God and the fear of Him increased more and more; and faith grew and the spirit was moved, so that in one day [I would say] as many as a hundred prayers, and at night nearly as many, so that I used to stay even in the woods and on the mountain [to this end]. And before daybreak I used to be roused to prayer, in snow, in frost, in rain; and I felt no hurt. . . . And there verily one night I heard in my sleep a voice saying to me, "Thou fastest to good purpose, thou who art soon to go to thy fatherland". And again after a very short time I heard the answer [of God] saying to me, "Lo, thy ship is ready". And it was not near at hand, but was distant, perhaps, two hundred miles.'

The story which follows, of his escape on the heathen trading-

* *villulam.*

ship (probably to Gaul), of his wanderings with the crew for twenty-eight days, through country devastated so that it was little better than a desert: all this need not detain us, though the story itself illustrates the curious juxtaposition of civilization and barbarism which marks this age—here merchants who trade in Irish sporting-dogs, there a countryside so wasted that travellers may almost die of hunger.

Other allusions in St. Patrick's writings also help us to conceive the conditions of the sub-Roman period. For instance, when he speaks of his return to Britain (probably in 414–15) there is no suggestion that he is returning to a country given over to abnormal anarchy. 'And again, after a few years, I was in Britain with my kindred, who received me as a son, and in good faith besought me that at all events now, after the great tribulations which I had undergone, I would not depart from them anywhither.' It was there in Britain, about 432, while living with his kinsmen that he heard the voice of the Irishmen crying to him, 'Holy youth, we beseech you to come and walk among us once more'—the call which gave a new purpose to his life. What concerns our present point is that his kinsmen evidently thought that residence with them in Britain would be sufficiently peaceful to compensate him 'after the great tribulations' of his earlier years. Patrick is at pains to defend himself from the charge of shirking his duties by departing from his kinsmen to 'live as an exile among barbarians'. In one place, he says, 'I am born of a father who was a decurion, but I sold my noble rank . . . for the profit of others'. This is a course which needs justification. It is heavily on his conscience. Accordingly at the date when Patrick wrote—probably well into the middle of the fifth century—the imperial system of local government was, it seems, intact in so far as the decurions or *curiales* (the members of the town council) were still the class who were mutually responsible for the load of taxes due to the government. Furthermore, in the eyes of Patrick, Britain is still a land where 'lordly rhetoricians' flourish. He is always expecting these elegant stay-at-homes to laugh at his 'rusticity'. He knows he cannot write Latin as if it were his own tongue. This distresses him; but 'I wish my brethren and kinsfolk to know what manner of man I am, that they may be able to understand the desire of my soul'. Britain might have its rhetoricians; but, as we may gather from the *Life of St. Germanus*, it was far behind Gaul as a school of Christianity. Patrick turned for his religious training to Gaul and not to Britain, to Lérins and Auxerre and not to London. Britain was backward, but there was no question of its not being the home of Romans—Romans regarded from an angle different from that of the fourth century—'holy Romans'. Patrick's ideas on the subject come out in his letter to Coroticus, the Briton who had somehow or other obtained rule over the Britons of Strathclyde. The soldiers of Coroticus had made a raid on the north of Ireland; they had 'cruelly butchered with the sword' newly baptized converts of Patrick, 'while the chrism was still fragrant on their foreheads'; they had carried off girls and distributed them; and when Patrick had sent clergy to ask the raiders to return some of the booty and all of the baptized captives, they had laughed at his messengers.

In the shaft of sunlight cast by this letter to Coroticus what is shown to us is once more a topsy-turvy world; not Irish raiding Britons but Britons raiding Irish. Patrick, the Briton, appeals to the soldiers of this chieftain living beyond the old Roman frontier as men who are discrediting the Roman name. 'I have written these words to be sent . . . to the soldiers of Coroticus; I do not say to my fellow-citizens* or to the fellow-citizens of the holy Romans, but to those who are fellow-citizens of demons because of their evil deeds.' He upbraids them for having dealings with 'the most vile and apostate Picts'. The world is still divided into men of civilization and barbarians, but the differentia is changing. To Patrick the name 'Romans' means those who are baptized into the society of Rome. Here, then, in the middle of the fifth century we see in the writings of Patrick a new state

* *civibus meis.*

of things. The Roman provinces are not simply beleaguered, as at the end of the fourth century, by barbarians. The Roman world is barbarized; but the barbarian world increasingly reflects sunset tints from the sinking Roman civilization. The Irish are ceasing to be the terror of the western seas because Patrick and his fellow workers are baptizing them by the thousand and are teaching them—not always it must be admitted with complete success—that it is a barbarous thing to live by plunder.

And even 'the vile Picts' had begun to change under the teaching of St. Ninian, a Briton, an elder contemporary of St. Patrick. For some years after 400, Ninian from his new church built of stone, the *Candida Casa*, which gave its name to Whitern, had sown Christianity among the Picts—those of Galloway and, it is sometimes claimed, those also who lived beyond the Forth.

In all the countries bordering on the western seas of Britain we see, not stagnation or mere decline, but activity and the beginnings of new life.

Before we can grope our way any further in this fifth century, we must try to come to an understanding about the date at which the permanent Saxon occupation of British territory began. Three dates have rival claims for acceptance.

(1) A date corresponding to A.D. 428 is one of the suggestions thrown out in the *Historia Brittonum*. But Nennius—or the other writers whose works were incorporated in the *Historia*—weakens the value of his words by offering his readers a confusing choice of dates for the advent of the Saxons.[19] The date 428 also fits in with the story of the Alleluiah battle and possibly with the evidence* of some early Saxon brooches found in the eastern Midlands. When two or three pieces in our jig-saw puzzle can be fitted together in this way, one is loath to say there is a mistake. But looking at the other pieces of the puzzle, we may

* See below, pp. 116–17.

with some confidence add that if there was infiltration of Saxons at this time, it was comparatively unimportant. They were probably raiders rather than settlers. They cannot have been the conquerors of south-eastern Britain who cut the communications between the island and the Continent.

(2) A.D. 441–2. In favour of this date there is a single short sentence in a Gallic chronicle[20] which says: 'The eighteenth year of Theodosius II [A.D. 441–2] the provinces of Britain which up to this time had been on all sides harassed* by various slaughters and disasters, are brought under the dominion of the Saxons.' Some historians[21] think that since the Gallic chronicler was a contemporary, the above statement is sufficient evidence that what the Welshmen later called the *adventus Saxonum* was an accomplished fact by 441–2. If it is objected that the words of the chronicler are vague and that they may describe a temporary submission during a raid like that of 367, a later Gallic chronicler[20] (he wrote about 511) can be produced who says with reference to 441–2: 'The provinces of Britain are lost to the Romans and yield to the rule of the Saxons.' This is indeed more definite; but it is at the best a gross exaggeration.

(3) A.D. 449.† The date which has for so long been current among English historians is derived from Bede. The objections to it are that Bede's statements in his various works are not quite consistent,[22] and, more serious, that Bede, writing some three hundred years after the event, seems to have arrived at his date only by an inference of his own from Gildas. Since Bede's tables showed him that the third consulship of Aëtius was in 446–7, he assumed that the invasion followed within a few years.

Thus when the rival claims of 442 and 449 are compared, we find that we have to balance the words of a chronicler from the south of Gaul, who could only know about events in distant Britain through a fog of rumour, against the words of Gildas, who, though removed by time as well as by place, had none the

* *Latae* emended to *late vexatae*.

† Or, owing to Bede's inconsistencies, A.D. 446–57.

less a chance of hearing genuine traditions. If Gildas was right in thinking that when in 446 the Britons appealed to Aëtius for help, their enemies were Picts and Scots, and that the Saxon troops were introduced into the island as friendly auxiliaries, the Gallic annal was misleading. But in truth the words of the chronicler and the words of Gildas cannot fairly be weighed against one another; both are imponderable.

If we are agreed that 'the coming of Hengist and Horsa' occurred within about ten years of 450, that is enough for all practical purposes, and we shall feel that we are not far from the truth if we continue to speak, as in the past, of 'the middle of the fifth century' as the turning-point at which decades, even centuries, of Saxon raiding gave place to decades of Saxon conquest and settlement.

We shall see more fully in the next chapter how the coming of Hengist's band differed from that of previous Saxons who had landed in Britain. They came as federates; they seemed to the British king who employed them unlike the primitive Saxons from the north. And they were unlike. They were trained fighting men, supplied with instruments of warfare such as battering-rams. They could take and sack the towns of sub-Roman Britain. They could penetrate to the western sea. They could conquer and retain a favourite region of the provincials.

At the beginning of this chapter we set out with the purpose of discovering what there was to be learnt about the condition of Britain at the period when the Saxons began their conquest of the country. The time has now arrived to collect the impressions suggested by the few glimpses permitted us as we look back through the almost impenetrable screen of fifteen centuries.

Britain appears before us as a land which for eighty or ninety years, that is ever since 360, had been periodically swept by barbarians and wasted. The villas of the well-to-do had never recovered from the destruction of the years following 360. The imperial officials and the garrison had been the next supports of Romanism to vanish. The towns for a time remained; but if, as is now known, many of them were declining as early as the third and fourth centuries, what chance had they when the peace of Roman rule came to an end? We shall see in later chapters how various were the fates which befell them. No one can say for certain whether their strong walls and their militia were able to preserve them in the sub-Roman period. But if the towns were not sacked many of them were strangled or half-strangled. With pirates on the sea and barbarians molesting the old trade routes on the land, prosperity must have crumbled. In 410 it was the cities which were told to look to their own safety. By the middle of the fifth century it was a 'tyrant', not self-governing towns, who according to Gildas invited the Saxons into the island.

In these ways the three strongholds of Romanism had been largely destroyed by 450. With the well-to-do villas wiped out in the country districts, the Roman garrison dissipated, and the towns in rapid decay, the barely Romanized country folk in the villages were left the chief element in the population. But how far were they indeed left? If the Irish raid which carried off Patrick, and along with him some thousands of other captives, was typical of the anarchy of the fifth century, large tracts of Britain must have been emptied of inhabitants. Patrick's account of his wanderings in a hungry land for twenty-eight days after his escape from Ireland suggests that barbarian devastation in this age could leave a country little better than a desert.

Here, then, we reach a crucial point. If the native villages had been destroyed as the villas before them, the Saxons and Angles might indeed have found Britain, as some archaeologists have believed, a land of great unoccupied spaces which were only waiting for settlers from overseas to come and cultivate them. But does such a picture of Britain fit in with the fragments of our written information?

It is obvious that the available evidence is too defective to permit of any positive assertions; but so far as it goes it tells against the idea that Britain was in any sense derelict. Gildas speaks of the period which followed the appeal to Aëtius—that is, the middle of the fifth century—as a period which saw abundant plenty and the growth of *luxuria.* And putting Gildas aside, we have in the *Life of Germanus*, positively, a statement about the 'great wealth' of the island, and, negatively, an absence of reference to any abnormal dearth of population in sub-Roman Britain. But the evidence of any kind is so meagre that it is needless to labour the question.

If we try to obtain a general view of the Britain which in the middle of the fifth century confronted the incoming Saxons, it is much easier to conceive what things were like in the west than in the east. In the west the folk in the hill-top villages and the rude hill forts were living much the same strenuous life, only slightly tinged with Roman civilization, as had existed in the days of the Empire. We can form our opinions about these Celtic-speaking Britons. We know them from their descendants, the Welsh of later times. We know, too (from our written authorities), how in the west military leaders of different kinds during the fifth century established their power as political rulers—men like Coroticus in Strathclyde, commander of the lawless soldiery who raided St. Patrick's catechumens; or like Cunedda, who with war-bands from beyond the Wall 'drove out the Irish from Wales'. But in the east of the island there is nothing to fill the blank between the imperial rescript of 410 and Vortigern, the Celtic king of about 450.

The period which we have been specially studying in this chapter closes with what Gildas calls 'the groans of the Britons' to Aëtius. *Repellunt barbari ad mare, repellit mare ad barbaros.* It is not so easy, as some critics suggest, to dismiss these words as mere rhetoric. Gildas writes as if he had here some document before him. Rightly or wrongly this cry of the Britons will remain in the ears of posterity like a cry coming through the night from men in a sinking ship.

The ninety years between 360 and 450 seem in retrospect to be filled with little else but raids and destruction and every kind of violence. If we knew more about it we should, of course, see the light as well as the shade. That can be done in the history of the end of Roman Gaul, the nearest, though not a close, analogy to the end of Roman Britain. The letters of Sidonius show how a Gallic aristocrat of the fifth century could enjoy the sociabilities of life and leave the barbarians on one side with little more than a shrug of his shoulders and a contemptuous reference to their greased hair, their gluttony, their harsh and ugly language. None the less the shadow was deep enough in Roman Gaul. To some it seemed that they had reached the end of all things—'*ultima pertulimus*'; '*ultima quaeque vides*'[23]—and in Britain it must have been much the same. There, according to Gildas, pestilence and famine were added in the middle of the fifth century to barbarian invasion and to civil war.

As in all times of great calamity, the troubles affected men in opposite ways. Some were turned to debauchery—'We will eat and drink, for to-morrow we shall die,' quotes Gildas; others turned to religion.

It was in these decades that the British provincials became Christian in more than name. Before this age Christianity had been an official religion; the churches few and small; the Christian emblem, the ☧, used as a charm and stamped like a trade-mark on jewellery or pewter. After this age, i.e. towards the end of the fifth century, we shall come to the development of monastic Christianity. Britons returning from the monasteries of Gaul will teach their countrymen to despise and renounce the world. But in this sub-Roman twilight, the Christianity of Britain was in an intermediate stage. The Britons, deserted by the Empire, divided, beset by barbarians, turned to Christianity as the City of God. The religious temperament, once evident in their cult of Druidism, began in the period 360–450 to reappear in their Christianity. The new-found zeal of the Briton Pelagius and his denial that all men were born evil owing to the sin of Adam disturbed the whole Roman world. It is true that the other Britons who became notable in this period were, like Pelagius, men who made their name outside Roman Britain; some of them missionaries like Palladius, Patrick, and Ninian; others learned men who attained fame in Gaul, such as Fastidius and Faustus. But the *Life of St. Germanus* indicates that there was Christian agitation also within Britain itself. It was the recrudescence of Pelagianism or semi-Pelagianism in Britain which necessitated the visits of the saint to our island. The fire of heresy had to be extinguished in Britain lest it spread to the Continent. The interest in religious matters or personages was not confined to a select few only. When St. Germanus moved about in Britain the people pressed upon him in their enthusiasm.

The writings[24] of Fastidius, 'bishop of the Britons', composed about 420–30, and the help sent later to St. Patrick from Britain, show that Christianity was now penetrating as a living force. It was the great discovery of the age, and probably occupied the minds of thinking men more than did fear of the Saxons.

In fact, looking at this period, 360–450, it is as fair to fix our eyes on the new life which was stirring among the peoples of Britain as on the decay of the State and the destruction of wealth. If the growth of the spiritual life of man counts for more than changes in political systems or the distribution of material wealth, then it may be held that this period, which witnessed a transition in Britain from the Roman culture of the later Empire through sub-Romanism to a Celtic and a Christian renaissance, was a period of creation rather than of destruction. The Roman Britain which was now to be the prey of the Saxons had passed in ninety years from the age of Julian to the age of Germanus, from an age of toleration to an age when belief was so intense that it was an offence to have mistaken notions about the sin of Adam; from an age when the imperial officials and drafts of imperial troops were guided across the Channel by the lighthouses on the cliffs of Boulogne and of Dover to an age when

St. Germanus, an emissary of Gallic bishops, in crossing the Channel was obstructed by demons.

The world had changed. The Romano-Britons who were about to be submerged by a new flood of barbarians had, by the middle of the fifth century, obtained a source of spiritual consolation for the loss of the lands and goods of this transitory world.

Remains of Roman lighthouse at Dover. In Roman times it was probably eight stories and about 80 feet high.

III

THE CONQUEST OF KENT

THE STORY IN THE WRITTEN AUTHORITIES

WE have now to change our point of view and look back at the fifth century with the eyes of later generations. Through the obscurity of the middle years of that century when the Huns were daring to advance towards the heart of Gaul; when the Franks were consolidating a kingdom round Tournai, in regions not far distant from Britain; when the Empire still lingered as a shadow of its former self in other parts of the West—in this storm-darkened period we have to try to discern what really happened when our Germanic forefathers first effected a permanent lodgement on the shores of Britain.

The event which the Britons in later times remembered as the *adventus Saxonum* is one of the most dramatic stories in the history of our island, and it was in that way that the descendants of the Britons told it. When genuine traditions failed, others were supplied to meet the demand of a later age, and thus came into existence, as we shall see below, the romantic tragedy centring round Vortigern, Hengist, and Rowena.

The critical methods of the nineteenth century shattered most of this picturesque narrative. In the present century experts have been trying to produce from the study of antiquities and of place-names the material out of which a new story may perhaps some day be built up. How far these new materials can be fitted together so as to form a safe groundwork for a revised history is the chief theme of this and the following chapters. One thing is certain—that for the time being the Germanic conquest of Britain cannot be told as a narrative. How then are we to treat it? There is no choice. It is a great enigma and we must treat it as such. The problems which it presents may interest us in much the same way as a detective story. Using the jargon of that form of fiction we may call it 'a mystery', the first and greatest in the history of England. There is no doubt about the crime itself. But the questions to which we have to seek an answer are the following. Was the general appropriation of the land of the Britons aggravated by wholesale murder? Who exactly were the invaders? What were their numbers? Where exactly did they come from? How did they make their way into the country?

Thanks to the progress made by modern archaeology we are now able to set out on our inquiry with a hope of arriving not at the whole truth—not at as much of it as will be known in, say, ten or twenty years time—but at more than appeared in the history books of the last generation. It is unfortunate that the subject of this chapter, the problem of what happened in the invasion of Kent—it may be called the problem of the Jutes—is the most difficult and confusing bit of the whole question.

We must begin by making clear what are the different kinds of evidence which lie before us, and much in these preliminary remarks will be an introduction to the subject as a whole.

First we shall follow a well-worn path and trace the growth of the legend of the Conquest. Later we shall see how far the old scraps of tradition can be fitted into the new fragments of a different kind, the inferences which experts in archaeology and other subjects have been trying to patch into some sort of history. For the legend we have the following sequence—Gildas, Bede, Nennius, the Saxon Chronicle, and a few odd sentences from other authorities. These are the witnesses. They are all unsatisfactory in various ways; but the first, the familiar statement of what happened, must come from them, and we must now hear the beginnings of their several stories and form a general impression of the credibility of each.

Gildas[1] comes before us, a middle-aged Romano-Briton—really a Briton, it seems, by blood; but enough of a Roman by culture to have a fairly wide knowledge of Latin literature and to write Latin with fluency, though in an over-elaborate style, the fashion for which was spreading from Gaul to Celtic Britain. It is clear that he considers himself and his countrymen as still belonging to the Roman world. They are the *cives*, the citizens, in contrast to the barbarians. He speaks of Latin as 'our language'. Except for the facts that Gildas was born somewhere about 500, that he wrote his book shortly before 547,[1a] that he visited Ireland about 566 and died in 570, there is little else that can be said about his career, since the lives written of him date from the eleventh century or later and are not to be trusted.

His book *De Excidio et Conquestu Britanniae* was written in the form of an Epistle, but was pitched on the high note of a Hebrew prophet. Its purport was to denounce the wickednesses of five British kings and to point out to the Britons in general and especially to the clergy the error of their ways. The History with which he introduces his subject is not a history in the ordinary sense. The author is not trying to inform his readers about events. Hardly any names or dates are mentioned. He is simply a prophet preaching at large against the sins of the Britons; an impressionist seeking to obtain bold effects by massing subjects in the blackest shadows; a patriot, of that melancholy kind which finds most satisfaction in uncovering the faults of his own countrymen.

We see then that while Gildas is our best source of information, since he wrote within about a century of the reputed 'Coming of the Saxons', he is as vague as a man can be. As far as dates are concerned, he may have talked to old men who could remember the first employment of 'Saxons' as mercenaries by a British king—the event which Gildas describes as 'the germ of iniquity and root of bitterness'. But on the other hand, living, as it seems he did, far away in the west of the island (at any rate the five kings whom he denounced lived in those parts), he may give us only hearsay which distorts the truth when he speaks of events in the east.

What he says is this: that all the counsellors, together with a certain 'proud king'* whom he does not name, 'introduced the fierce Saxons, hateful alike to God and man, into the island to repel the northern nations'. He laments this as the most pernicious of all steps ever taken, and he laments the king's hopeless stupidity. He tells how the invaders arrived in what they called three *cyulae*, 'what we call warships'.† He tells how their motherland, finding that the first contingent had prospered, sent a larger body of warriors‡ who joined forces with the others; how they demanded that *annonae* (the allowances or payments in kind which for centuries had been rendered to the 'federates' who fought for the Empire) should be paid to them as if they were troops who were about to undergo great hardships on behalf of their kind host; how for a considerable time the grants which were given them stopped their mouths, but how they then complained that their monthly supplies were not enough and did their best to pick a quarrel, saying that they would break the agreement and plunder the whole island if they were not treated more liberally; finally, how they quickly followed up their threats with actions, 'for the fire of righteous vengeance . . . blazed from sea to sea' until 'having burned nearly the whole island it licked the western ocean with its red and savage tongue'.

Though there are no names or dates attached to this story by Gildas and the number of the ships has a legendary sound, the story in itself is by no means improbable. The Romans had increasingly used barbarians to fight their battles, and nothing could be more natural than that a hard-pressed British king

* *superbus tyrannus.*

† *lingua . . . nostra longis navibus.* *Cyula* is the English word 'keel' latinized.

‡ *satellitum.*

should follow that example. This story of Gildas does not go far, but it may be accepted as part of the truth.

Some two hundred years later the Northumbrian monk Bede (672–735), in reproducing the story of Gildas, filled in a few details. Somehow Bede knew the name of the 'proud tyrant', Vortigernus, and those of the two brothers who were the first leaders of the immigrants, Hengist and Horsa. He knew that they were Jutes and not Saxons, and that the monument of Horsa, killed in battle, was still to be seen in the east of Kent.

Some historians, strong in criticism, think that Bede's additions make the story less credible. They assert that the names Hengist and Horsa, meaning Stallion and Mare, have a legendary origin. They see in Bede's reference to Horsa's monument an etymological fiction. They think that the location of the incident in Kent scarcely tallies with the story that Hengist's war-band was introduced, as Gildas said, to repel 'the northern peoples', that is presumably the Picts—Kent is a curious base for operations against Caledonian invaders. But too much is often made of these difficulties.[2] Hengist was a well-known name. It was borne by a real war-leader mentioned in *Beowulf*, one who has some resemblance to the conqueror of Britain and was perhaps a Jute. It is also more consistent with the usual custom of the Germanic invaders to suppose that the Horstead near Aylesford in Kent took its name from a real man rather than a legendary hero.[3] It is worth noting that Horstead in Kent has its counterpart, Horsted in Angel (north-east of Husum). Lastly, though it is a far cry from Kent to the land of the Picts, the Picts seem to have been sea-raiders much like the Saxons themselves (they are described as a 'transmarine' enemy by Gildas), and we may suppose that Hengist was introduced to operate against the Picts by sea as well as by land.

Bede is careful to say that the Hengist story is only tradition; it is 'what men say'. But we may suppose that it was the legend believed by intelligent Kentishmen in Bede's own day, since he was the friend and correspondent of such men.

The next additions to the legend of Hengist reflect the new antiquarian and historical interests stimulated by the revival of learning in the Carolingian period. In the early decades of the ninth century Nennius, a Welshman, and in the later decades an anonymous Saxon chronicler each collected what information he could about the first coming of the Saxons. Both works are composite productions. The fragments of information about the past which were tacked together by their compilers were in either case many and various. In either case the date of the compilation and the value of the component parts are still subjects of controversy. In other respects the contrast between the two works is as great as can be.

The doubts about Nennius spring primarily from the fact that his *Historia Brittonum* survives in very different forms, some short, others long, some with a preface, others without. Owing to this, Mommsen, the editor of the book, in the *Monumenta Germaniae Historica*, and other historians before and after him[4] have concluded that the nucleus of the *Historia* was written by some anonymous writer about the end of the seventh century, and that Nennius in the ninth century only added a preface and some trifles of his own to the History which has passed under his name. A different and in some ways a more satisfactory explanation has been suggested by Liebermann. This view regards Nennius as the real compiler (one can hardly call him the author) of the History. All that is known about Nennius himself is that he was a 'disciple' of Elfodd, the chief bishop of Gwynedd and a man of importance, since though he did not die till 809 he had as early as 768 brought the Church of North Wales into closer harmony with the Roman Church. Following Liebermann we may picture Nennius as a learned man according to his lights, one who did his best to write the History which other Britons hitherto had failed to accomplish. He pieced together extracts from Jerome and Isidore; from a *Life of St. Germanus*; from 'annals of the Irish and of the Saxons'; and from what he calls the 'tradition of our elders'. If industry could give his country a History which might rival that of Bede, his industry would do it; so he worked on, patching together his authorities and his 'traditions'. He found himself confused by different stories and by different baffling systems of chronology. But he refused to be daunted. The different versions and the discordant dates were all placed side by side, Saxon and British genealogies, the wonders of Wales, the Lives of saints and heroes, were all brought in, and the centre of all he made the romance of Vortigern, which, with details unimagined by Gildas or Bede, might point the moral of the calamity which had befallen his countrymen.

Now if we are to understand the *Historia Brittonum* what matters is less the editorial functions performed either by Nennius or the hypothetical earlier editor than the nature of the several parts which were somehow incorporated in the History. Each section of the book should be judged by itself; such a judgement, however, is complicated by the interaction of popular tradition and pseudo-historical speculation among the Welsh. Of the sections which bear most directly on the subject of the present chapter, one which enumerates the battles of Arthur has on it some stamp of popular tradition. The chapters about Vortigern, on the other hand, are more suspect. The romantic tales woven round him, his love for the daughter of Hengist, his fatal cession of Kent in return for her hand, the details of victories won over Hengist by Vortimer, the son of Vortigern, the final conference in which the invaders, with the basest treachery, pulling knives from their boots killed three hundred of the British nobles—all this was good entertainment for Welshmen and helped to reconcile them to their defeat and provide a national scapegoat. According to Nennius, the Britons fought magnificently; it was by Saxon treachery that their nobles had been slaughtered. One need not suppose that Nennius himself invented his highly coloured stories, and it is certainly carrying criticism to an extreme to assert, as some have done, that the whole Vortigern romance was a fabrication based on a few words of Bede and without roots in Welsh tradition. None the less, Welsh imagination, whether of antiquaries or bards, ran so wild that the occasional touches in the story which are not in themselves improbable (such as the assertion that Hengist and his band came as exiles to Vortigern to seek his protection) are rightly discredited by the transparent fiction in which they are embedded.

Very different, once more, are the additions made to the story in the Saxon Chronicle. The Chronicle is short and matter-of-fact. Its author resembled Nennius in one respect; he made a show of knowing too much. Nennius supplied five or six different dates for the same event. The chronicler does not hesitate to supply one date for every event. His story for the first twenty-eight years after the landing of Hengist at Ypwines-fleot (Ebbsfleet in Thanet) is little more than the enumeration of four battles: the first being at Ægelsthrep (probably near Aylesford), and the second at Crecganford where they 'slew four thousand men; and the Britons then forsook Kent and fled to London in great terror'. Finally, in 473, 'Hengist and Aesc fought against the Britons and captured innumerable spoils, and the Britons fled from the English like fire'.

It is still permissible to give some credence to these entries, since they have a look of being derived from an old saga or poem. 'A look', however, is not a good argument with which to confute a sceptic; and it is most improbable that the dates are anything more than the guesses of a later age.

THE PROBLEM OF THE JUTES

Let us now turn from the stories of Hengist and of Vortigern to the more general problem of the Jutes: who they were and whence they came. Here the foundation from which every argument must start is the statement of Bede that *Angulus*, the home of the Angles, lay 'between the provinces of the Jutes and the Saxons'. This familiar view has for long been questioned on archaeological and philological grounds, but the critics of Bede's statement have generally tried to fortify their argument with one or more *obiter dicta* drawn from continental writings.

The more noteworthy of these *dicta* cannot be ignored. They are:

First, a passage of Procopius, a contemporary of Gildas but a Byzantine. Britain, he states, contains three nations, the Angles, the Frisians, and the Britons. By taking his Angles to mean both Angles and Saxons, and by a simple subtraction sum, it is found that the Frisians of Procopius may be equated with the Jutes.[5] In defence of this statement it is urged that Procopius met certain Angles who accompanied a Frankish embassy to the East and that he may therefore have known what he was talking about. Some hardihood, however, is required by those who maintain that Procopius was well informed about the circumstances of Britain, inasmuch as this author elsewhere says that human life could not be lived in the country beyond the Roman Wall and that Britain itself was a ghostly region to which the souls of the dead were ferried in phantom ships by night.

A second passage is one in which Theudebert, a Frankish king, writing to Justinian about 540, asserts that among the tribes who had voluntarily submitted to him are the 'Saxones Eucii'.* The name *Eucii* can fairly be corrected to *Eutii* and regarded as the equivalent of the *Jutae* of Bede; but it is uncertain whether a hyphen or a comma should be inserted between the two words—that is, whether the Eutii were in American language 'hyphenated' Saxons or whether they were a distinct folk, presumably neighbours of the Saxons and, since they thought it wise to submit to the Franks, not far distant from the Frankish kingdom; possibly therefore within the region loosely described as 'Frisia'.[6]

A third passage from the poet Venantius Fortunatus,[7] who died in 609, mentions a people, the Euthiones, between the Saxons

* *Cum Saxonibus Euciis qui se nobis voluntate propria tradiderunt*; the phrase occurs in a corrupt sentence in which the king claims that in addition to the Visigoths and to northern Italy his *dominatio* extends from the Danube and the borders of Pannonia to the Ocean. *M.G.H.*, Ep. iii, 133.

and the Danes, and for those who are prepared to accept the name as another equivalent for the Jutes, it is a reminder that enough of the tribe must have remained in the Jutish peninsula to pass on the name of Jutland to that region when, probably about the fifth century, it was overrun by the Danes.[8]

The mere enumeration of these passages, slender bases for argument but at times used for the building up of a top-heavy superstructure, is enough to show that the problem of the Jutes can never be settled by reference to our written authorities. If there is an answer it must be obtained from other investigations. Before we diverge on to these other lines which may perhaps be tedious, we may strengthen our resolve with a conviction that the subject is worth pursuit. Since Kentishmen have so often taken the lead in English affairs, we cannot shirk the attempt to discover who they were and whence they came.

The discussions of the philologists about the form of the name which appears in Bede's *History* as Iutae have been prolonged. Their conclusions (anticipated in what has been said above) mostly support the view that the correct equivalent of the Latin Iutae is Iote, which becomes in West Saxon Yte. This rules out the theory which once obtained that the Jutes were to be identified with the 'Geatas', the Götar of south Sweden. It does not in itself decide whence they came; but it assists the argument of those who hold that the Jutes of Kent were related to the Eutii mentioned in Theudebert's letter, that is, to a Saxon tribe thought to be settled in or near Frisia.[9]

In the next stage of our investigation we must ask the archaeologists what light they can throw on the problem. We find that there are difficulties, and these must be faced at the outset.

One might suppose that it would be an easy thing to compare the graves of the Jutish and Saxon settlers in Britain with the graves of their kinsmen on the Continent. But the first difficulty arises from the fact that men in the early centuries of our era, and especially in the Migration Age, were liable to change from one mode of burying their dead to another. Their minds were in a state of flux. They were unsettled in their views about what happened after death; and this unsettlement expressed itself in changes in their burial customs. The idea that it was better not to burn but to bury a dead kinsman and to give him ample supplies of everything he might require in the next world was just beginning to affect the tribes of north Germany about the time

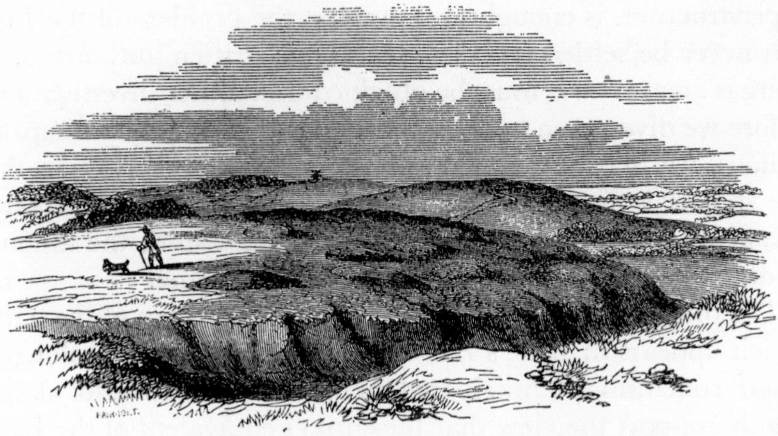

FIG. 23. Barfriston Down, Kent; Jutish Burial Mounds.

that they migrated, as is now shown in the newly discovered cemeteries at Nesse and Galgenberg. Otherwise the almost universal custom of the Anglian and Saxon tribes in Germany had been to cremate their dead. In their cemeteries in Britain the modes of burial adopted by the German immigrants were various. Cremation appears to have been still the prevailing custom among those who came direct from Germany to this island. But cremation is rarely found in the burial-places south of the Thames valley, and it is clear that in the south almost from the first the burning of a corpse was regarded as something primitive, contrary to the new fashions which were spreading in from other Germanic peoples, especially from the Franks.

Thus, while cremation urns are no reliable indication of date, their appearance in any cemetery may justify the opinion that

Anglo-Saxon cemetery at Saffron Walden, Essex

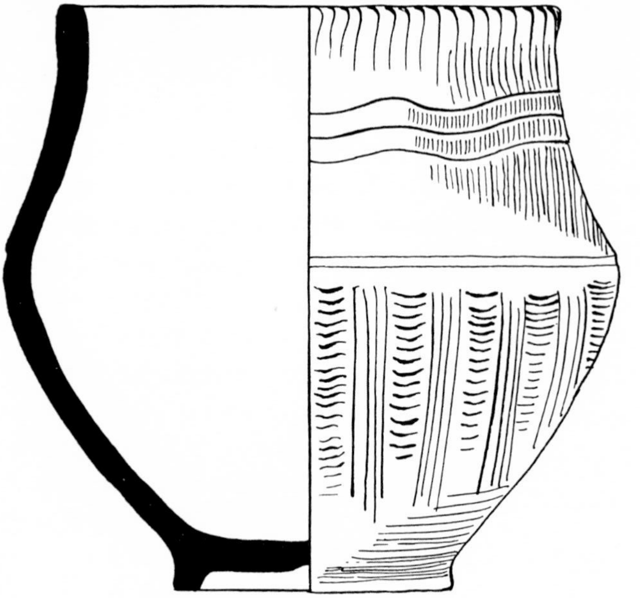

A

B

Kentish vases of Saxon type

A. From Hersden, near Sturry. $\frac{2}{3}$

B. From Sarre, Isle of Thanet. $\frac{2}{3}$

here are traces of some of the original settlers or their children. There were, no doubt, certain groups, especially among the Anglian settlers, who were more conservative than others in their ways. Sometimes in out-of-the-way places the good old custom might be maintained to the end of heathen times.[10] Cremation is thus a positive test of early invaders, but not a negative one. Though we may be sure when we find it that we have to do with invaders who were either newly arrived from Germany or else conservative in their customs, we cannot, on the other hand, assume that cemeteries where it is not found are not early.

So far the change from cremation to burying the dead, while it has made it difficult to trace the migrants with the exactness which might otherwise have been possible, has only presented minor difficulties. At this point, however, we must introduce a further complication; the men of this age had not to choose simply between cremation and burying in the heathen fashion, i.e. with many grave-goods. There was a third choice. They could give up the custom of burning the dead without adopting the new costly custom of burying them with all war-trappings and finery. They could copy the Romano-provincials rather than the Franks; they could bury their dead without anything at all. We shall find that the failure of the archaeologists to reckon with this radical change has falsified not a few of their conclusions.

It must, however, be admitted that an unfurnished grave does not necessarily mean that the Saxons or Angles who made it had been influenced either directly or indirectly by later Roman customs. It may only mean that the kinsmen were too poor to afford the cost of furnishing a grave. It may also mean that the graves are late and reflect the influence of Christianity. In most cases the records of past excavations do not enable us to decide between these possibilities except by conjecture.

The other great difficulty which besets any attempt to reconstruct the early history of the Germanic invaders by archaeological evidence is fundamental; it is the doubt whether the date of a brooch or buckle, still more whether the date of a grave containing such an object, can be determined with sufficient accuracy to be of use for the historian. Now there are one or two burials which have been identified as those of historical persons. There are others, more numerous, which contain a datable coin, often a coin worked up into a brooch or a bracteate. These at any rate give a *terminus post quem*, and by com-

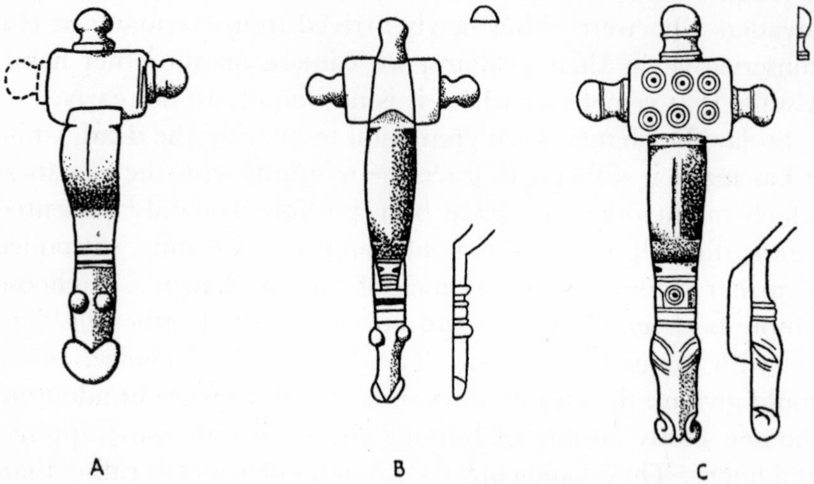

FIG. 24. Typological development of the cruciform brooch. A (Bifrons, Kent) and B (Faversham, Kent) show the second stage—that assigned to the latter half of the 5th century. C (Lyminge, Kent) shows the third stage assigned to the early 6th century. All $\frac{2}{3}$.

paring the objects in one grave with those found in another (i.e. reasoning from what the archaeologists call 'the correlation of associated finds') it has been possible to link up the chronology of one kind of grave furniture with that of another. But the line of argument on which archaeologists have chiefly relied in fixing their dates has been that of 'typological development'. Since the validity of their results depends mainly on this method, it will be well at this point to illustrate it from what they have to tell us about the early evolution of the cruciform brooch.

(1) There is no doubt that this kind of brooch, like many others, was ultimately derived from the simple safety-pin type. It has an uncertain relationship with the crossbow brooches common

among the Roman provincials in the fourth century.[11] But the starting-point of the Germanic development is represented by the specimen (Fig. 3) found in the peat at Nydam with the famous boat, and another found in a mysterious grave at Dorchester on the Thames (Pl. 21E). These are generally assigned to about the end of the fourth century.

(2) The second stage was probably evolved in the latter half of the fifth century. At this time the brooches in use in north Germany and Frisia, as well as among the invaders of Britain, were characterized by a full round knob at the top and a narrow head-plate. To this head-plate side-knobs were attached to hold the cross-bar round which the pin was coiled. As these side-knobs were fitted and not welded to the head-plate, they are often missing in the specimens which have been excavated. Examples of this type have been found chiefly in certain Kentish cemeteries, in East Anglia, and in the Cambridge region.

(3) In the next stage the knob at the top became only half round instead of full round and the lower end of the brooch developed horse-like nostrils which became a special characteristic of the English design. This class is assigned to the first half of the sixth century, and of its fifty-seven examples in England, three or four come from Kent, thirteen from East Anglia, twenty from Cambridgeshire, and eight from Lincolnshire.[12]

We need not here concern ourselves with the later stages, in which the side-knobs were cast all in one piece with the rest of the brooch, and the ornamentation elaborated with a great variety of ever-changing fashions. Our present concern is only with the early forms which help us to trace the course of the first invaders.

Now it is obvious that the room for mistakes in such schemes of typological development is large. The change in one country may be different from that in another. A type which goes out of fashion in one place may remain in fashion elsewhere. At times the genius of an individual craftsman may falsify all ordinary calculations. Inevitably there are disagreements among experts about the dating of any stage and about the normal margin of error on either side. One expert puts this margin at twenty-five years. Others admit that it may be much wider. For the time being, however, our only practicable policy is, while recognizing the element of uncertainty, to accept the chronology worked out by archaeologists in the last decades, and the maps in this volume are based on their results.

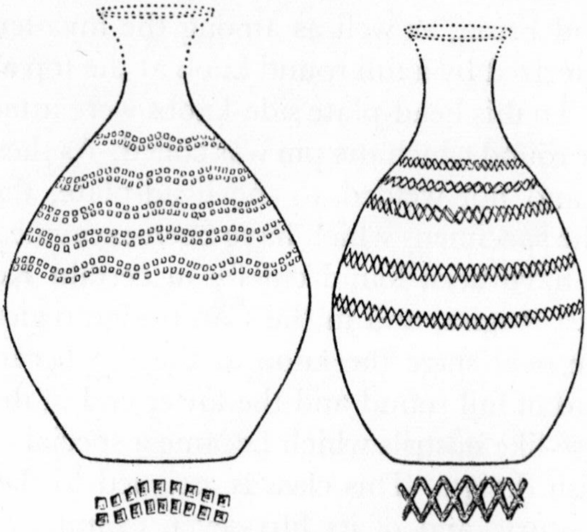

FIG. 25. Kentish bottle vases. $\frac{1}{5}$.

These, then, are the chief difficulties. They are not so discouraging that we need turn from archaeology in complete scepticism; but they are enough to explain why the study is not an exact science, and why we must be cautious in accepting its pronouncements.

The limitations of archaeology are more than usually apparent as soon as we ask about the first conquerors of Kent in the middle of the fifth century, and about their continental home. Any visitor to the Anglo-Saxon room of the British Museum cannot fail to be struck by the beautiful grave furniture found in typical Jutish cemeteries in contrast with the ordinary objects produced by Anglian and Saxon craftsmen. For example, the characteristic pottery which he will see from Kentish graves is not hand-made and wide-mouthed urns like those of north Germany, but bottle-necked vases made on a wheel (Fig. 25). He will also see a profusion of fine goldsmiths' work, decorated with garnets and other jewels, some beautiful glass vessels, and curious things like perforated silver spoons and mounted crystal balls, the use of which has never been fully explained.

The first systematic attempt to extract the early story of the Jutish kingdom from its graves was made by E. T. Leeds in his *Archaeology of the Anglo-Saxon Settlements*, a book which must be

FIG. 26. Sarre, Kent; gold bracteate. $\frac{1}{1}$.

the starting-point of all subsequent discussions of the subject.[13] The point which specially impressed Leeds was the resemblance between these finds from Kent and the finds from Frankish cemeteries, especially those of the Rhineland between Coblenz and Düsseldorf. Leeds inferred that these Frankish fashions must imply that the Jutes were of Frankish origin, or at least that they had long resided among the Franks before their migration. But in the cemeteries of east Kent he noted a second distinct culture 'which can only be ascribed to admixture of race'. The lesser culture, which appeared in cemeteries 'all close to the Thames or the scene of the earliest landing', was represented by cruciform brooches such as we have seen both north and west of the lower Elbe, and by gold bracteates (Fig. 26). Such finds were only intrusive material among the typical Kentish relics. To Leeds, therefore, the evidence from archaeology seemed clear. It proved that the bulk of the Kentish settlers did not come from Jutland or from Friesland, but from the middle Rhine. They were presumably Ripuarian Franks.

Among subsequent discussions of the subject two constructive theories call for attention. N. Åberg, a Swedish archaeologist, has argued that the grave-goods which seemed to Leeds to be 'intrusive' among the Jutish objects should instead be regarded as those of the earlier settlers. The eight or ten cruciform brooches found in Kent, thanks to the better-established chronology of the type, show 'a development extending over the second half of the fifth century and a little into the sixth century. Then development ceases in Kent, but proceeds with undiminished vigour north of the Thames.' On this kind of evidence Åberg concluded that the peculiarities of Kentish culture did not go so far back as to the time of the invasion. They 'did not exist from the beginning, but developed during the course of the sixth century'.[14]

Thus while Leeds saw in eastern Kent two cultures representing two streams of immigrants, the main one drawn from the Frankish Rhineland, the other from the north, Åberg saw a later and an earlier culture. The earlier was the culture of the original Jutish settlers, the later represented the new fashions which developed in Kent as the Jutes, exploiting their nearness to the Continent, traded with Franks and Frisians, copied their luxuries, and so, growing rich, generated an art and culture of their own superior in many ways to the art and culture of the Franks themselves.

The other contribution comes from T. D. Kendrick.[15] He admits that the evidence is at present insufficient for a trustworthy theory, but he makes a guess which well illustrates the uncertainties now surrounding the whole subject. The way for Kendrick's theory was prepared by Lindqvist, another Swedish archaeologist, who maintained that the Vendel style (which is the Swedish counterpart of the Jutish style in England) was much earlier than had hitherto been thought. Kendrick, following

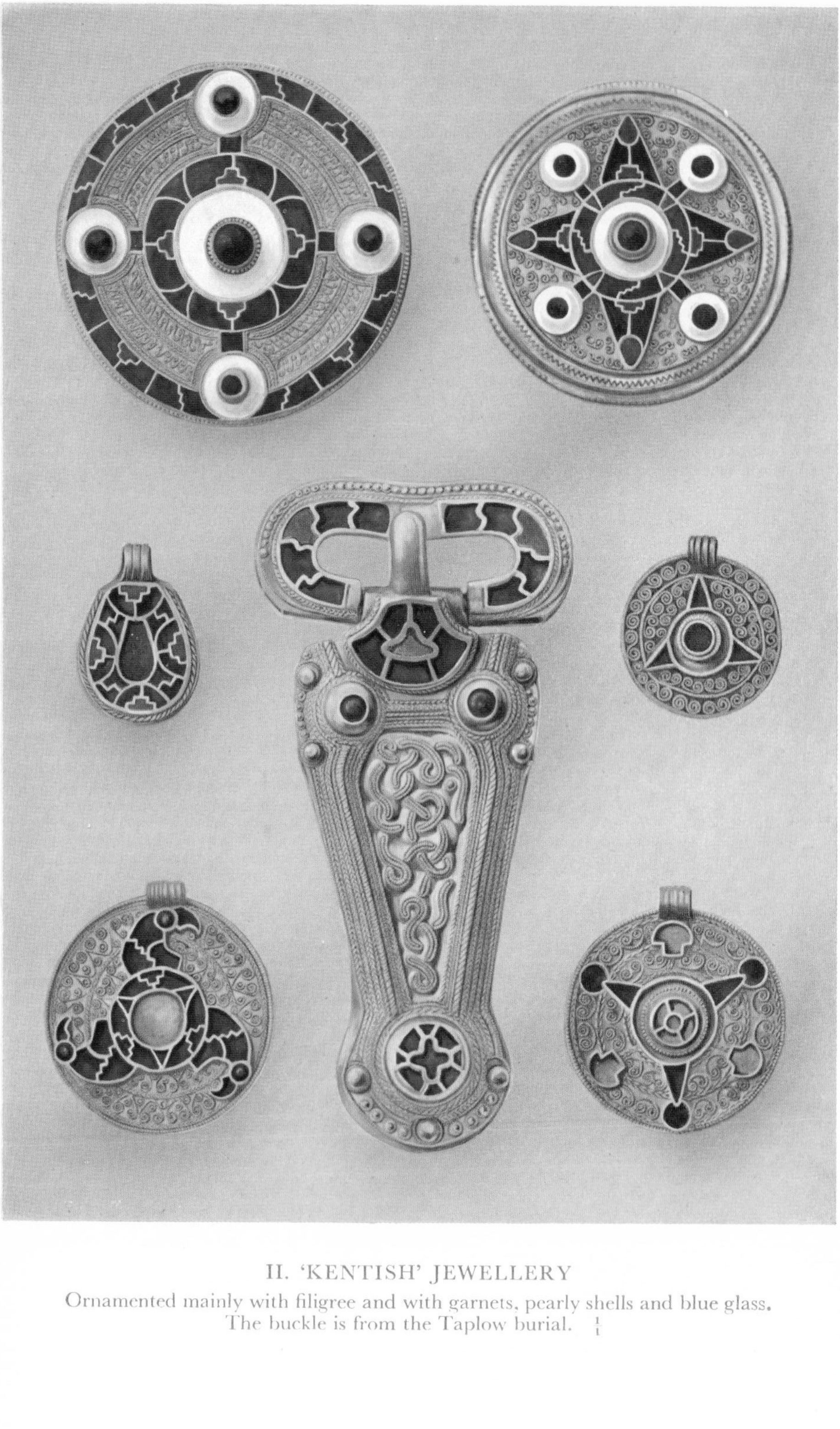

II. 'KENTISH' JEWELLERY

Ornamented mainly with filigree and with garnets, pearly shells and blue glass. The buckle is from the Taplow burial. $\frac{1}{1}$

up this clue, examined the gorgeous barbaric jewellery of Kent, and divided it into two main varieties. Style A chiefly used garnets and blue glass, with *cloisonné* (that is, cell-work) setting and with filigree decoration, as in the coloured plate. Style B inlaid its jewels in cast settings, and used chip-carving ornament and niello (a black inlay on metal), but not *cloisonné* or filigree, producing disk brooches and long brooches, both square-headed and radiated, like those in the next plate. Kendrick rejects Åberg's view that the first of these styles was the work of Ethelbert's golden age (the end of the sixth and beginning of the seventh centuries), and thinks that both styles are contemporary and go back to the period of the Jutish invasion and settlement, in other words, that most of the gorgeous jewels of Kent were being worn 'about A.D. 500'. The guess with which Kendrick ends is admittedly daring. He claims that the *cloisonné* jewellery was a British craft, and was taught by Britons to 'federate Teutons (probably Angles, Saxons and Frisians)'; and that the cast jewellery was Jutish and was chiefly used by Hengist's Jutes who occupied Thanet and its neighbourhood.

These rival theories may some day be decided on archaeological grounds either by further excavation or by more intensive study of those antiquities already in our museums. The amateur, pending the decision of the experts, can only call attention to some aspects of the problem.

With regard to the original home of the Kentish immigrants, the fact that the graves in Kent only resemble those of the middle Rhine in some respects[16] seems to agree with the view that the similarities were the result of trade between the Rhine and Kent, rather than of a Frankish migration. For instance, if the resemblances between long-necked vases of the two districts did not arise simply from like conditions (in other words, from the survival of a Roman-provincial craft of pottery in either district), they may conceivably be the wine vessels in which Rhenish wine was imported—imported to the only communities in Britain that could afford to pay for such a luxury. One clue which has recently come to light, points us away from the middle Rhine to the settlements of north Germany; urns of a Saxon type have been unearthed at Hersden, between Thanet and Canterbury—a reminder that in the past generations, when archaeology was a hunt for treasure rather than for knowledge, such pots may have been often found but disregarded.*

In the next place it must be admitted that archaeology has failed to support Bede's statement that the Jutes came from Jutland; indeed, it has not yielded any positive support for the view that migrants from Jutland were one among the component elements of the Kentish population. The cemeteries of Kent are certainly unlike those of east Jutland, where, in the Migration Age, the dead were inhumed with an exceedingly generous spread of food and drink, supplied to them in as many as fourteen to sixteen vessels.[17] In west Jutland, on the other hand, the cremation cemeteries seem to come to an end in the second century. A conjecture of Plettke and others that the Jutes migrated from Jutland at that time and reappeared in Kent under Hengist centuries later, can only be accepted if their half-way house is allowed to be some region where they might have remained in touch with folks of Anglo-Frisian speech.

In the end the chief impression which the archaeological controversies leave on the mind is that the Jutish problem is much more complicated than was at one time supposed. It is not enough to ask whether the settlers of Kent came from Jutland or the Rhineland or from both, or from any one or two districts. The different fashions found in Kentish graves are many. They must be explained not only by heterogeneity among the invaders (important as that is), but also by the variety of experiences enjoyed by the different communities during the two or three centuries in which Kentishmen furnished the graves of their

* To illustrate this point I add in Pl. 19 another vase of Saxon type from Sarre, now in Maidstone museum. I may also mention that a vase, formerly preserved at Queen's College, now in the Ashmolean, Oxford, *may* have come from Faversham. See Rolleston in *Arch.* xlii. 432.

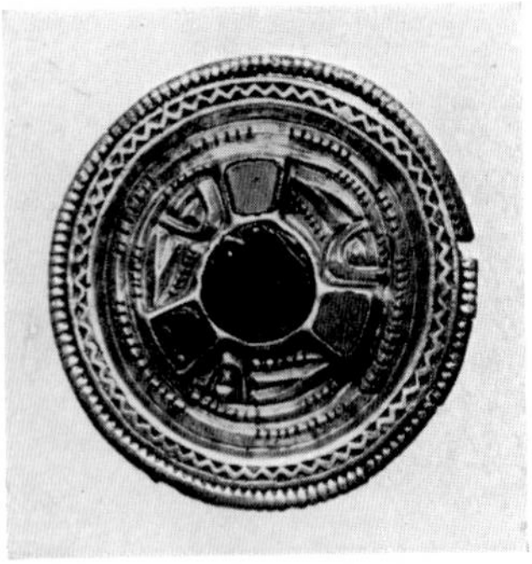

1

2

3

4

Kentish chip-carving jewellery. (Kendrick's 'Style B'. See *Antiquity*, vii, p. 432 and Plate II.) Above, disk brooches. Below, a radiated and a square-headed brooch. About $\frac{2}{5}$

dead. For example, the fact that the chip-carving jewellery (Style B) is found mainly in the Thanet region, and the *cloisonné* jewellery (Style A) mainly on the Dover–Canterbury line may be a result of some change that occurred in the trade route—perhaps owing to the tendency of the Wantsum Channel to silt up. We are all tempted to interpret any peculiarity in terms of race: we must be careful therefore not to overdo that explanation.

Archaeology having up to the present failed, it becomes necessary to point to the other lines of investigation which may supply clues. These are (1) the field system of Kent; (2) the social institutions revealed in Kentish laws; and (3) the evidence of the place-names.

The field system of a people is its signature written on the earth's surface. Once formed, it can scarcely be defaced. Even when incoming races destroy an old system, field survey and air photography are often able to read the old writing on the palimpsest. Being almost unchangeable and indelible, a field system supplies evidence of the highest value.

Now the system of medieval Kent was unlike the two- or three-field system which prevailed through mid-England from the Channel to the Humber and beyond (see map, p. 174). The holding of a typical Kentish cultivator was not a number of strips scattered in large, open, common fields. It was consolidated. Instead of scattered strips, members of a Kentish family as a rule had fields grouped together much like a modern farm.

Other points of contrast between Kent and the rest of England in the Middle Ages are well known. Gavelkind, that is the ancient custom of dividing a holding among coheirs; the division of the kingdom into *lathes*; the measurement of land by the unit called the *sulung* (or plough-land) and its quarter-share the *jugum* (or yoke)—these are only three out of many peculiarities. Their antiquity is ably demonstrated by Jolliffe.[18] His explanation of their ultimate source is less convincing. He assumes that the field system must be Teutonic and not, as some previous historians[19] have supposed, partly a survival from Romano-

British times. If Teutonic, he maintains that it is necessary to ascend the Rhine to Düsseldorf and beyond to find a district where land was reckoned by jugera and plough-lands, much as in Kent. From this and from other similarities in their institutions he concludes that the Jutes were nothing else than Franks from the middle Rhine.

Here is a theory which, like the middle-Rhine theory of Leeds's *Archaeology*, seems to be contradicted both by the language and by the traditions* of the Jutes of Kent. It asks us to believe that a branch of the Franks ceased to be proud of their descent from that all-conquering race, and forgot their Frankish language so completely that there are not even traces of it in the Kentish dialect.[20]

These aspects of our problem, while they are too involved to be examined in our present survey of the ground, are clearly of great significance.

For the same reason we shall do no more than mention the evidence which may be extracted from the early Kentish laws.† These show that the freemen, the *ceorls*, of Kent were more substantial persons than the ceorls of the neighbouring kingdoms; that their dependent and servile classes were more elaborately classified, and that one of these classes, that of the *læt*, is clearly identical with the *litus*, or *lazzus*, of the Frisian, Frankish, and Old Saxon laws. This evidence seems to strengthen the argument for the connexion of Kent with the neighbouring continental lands rather than with Jutland.

A last line of investigation is that of the place-names of Kent. Here again we can only say that the subject is still waiting for its specialist.[21] In the meantime valuable attempts have been made to differentiate the place-names which contain the element *-ing*, representing the Old English plural *-ingas*.[22] These have the strongest claim to antiquity. They seem to represent a stage

* Bede's statements may perhaps have the force of traditions since they were accepted by the Kentish clergy and later by Alfred, a king of Kent.

† See below, p. 205.

in the settlement, perhaps the first stage, when men identified districts by the groups of settlers which were to be found in them rather than by the name of any one farm or village. There are a few of these group-names in the east of the county, especially round Richborough, but the district where they are found most thickly is the Medway valley with its Barming, Binling, Halling, Malling, Yalding, and others.[23]

Our excursion into the Jutish problem has now been long enough to give the reader an idea of the possible lines along which the question must be approached. Much of the evidence is at present incomplete and ill-digested. The problem is not ripe, perhaps it never will be, for solution. It has only been possible to indicate some of the considerations which must in the future be more carefully sifted and weighed. Looking at the problem as a whole, we see that Bede's statement that the home of the Jutes was beyond that of the Angles receives but little support and is in some directions contradicted. In itself, however, it carries weight; Bede's correspondents, the educated clergy in Kent, were presumably in contact with traditions about the early history of their people. Bede's statement needs to be qualified, but it should not be wholly set aside unless the arguments against it become overwhelming.

How is it to be qualified? If we are aiming at safety, we may say that what is needed, the well-constructed theory in which each piece of evidence finds its proper place, cannot be built up until the materials to which we have pointed are better squared by the experts. Let us, however, change the analogy, and revert to that of the detective story. Every reader knows that a stage comes when a working hypothesis is required, one which may help to clear the mind even if it cannot claim to be well ascertained truth. With this justification, let us put together a working hypothesis, basing it frankly on conjecture as well as on evidence.

We begin, as of old, with Hengist and Horsa, since there is no sufficient reason for abandoning these characters of the story. In order to explain Bede's statement, we think of these adventurers and their immediate followers as natives of Jutland who, like other adventurers of the age, as of the Viking age, had been long absent from their original home. When they appear on the scene, since Vortigern thought it worth his while to take them into his pay, they were presumably commanders of a company of some repute. It is possible that they may already have served for a short time as federates or as less formal auxiliaries in Gaul; Aëtius, we know, had 'Saxons' on his side when he defeated the Huns in 451. It is tempting to speculate whether there was any kind of connexion between the appeal to Aëtius and the employment of Hengist's force. There is just a bare possibility that Aëtius, unable to send regular Roman troops, may have recommended the Britons to hire the services of Hengist's war band. But though it is tempting in this period, where we possess only a few fragments of information, to put those few together as cause and effect, it is historically unsound and the temptation should be avoided. All that we can really say is that, if there is truth buried in the story of Gildas, it is probable that the *superbus tyrannus* (that is Vortigern) took Hengist into his pay because more trustworthy reinforcements from Gaul were not to be had. Remembering that the Roman emperors had been for centuries accustomed to employ German barbarians as mercenaries, we must discount the violent abuse which Gildas heaps on the king who admitted the Saxons. It was easy to be wise after the event. When Vortigern handed over Thanet to them, he no doubt imagined that that island with its definite bounds would save the farmers of Kent and their families from molestation. In fact, however, he was giving them the perfect base, that which the Vikings selected four centuries later.

A point which one would like specially to clear up is how long the mercenaries were in the pay of Vortigern before they got out of hand. Gildas says it was 'a long time',* but that might mean, say, ten months or ten years. The Saxon Chronicle implies that it was five or six years; but little reliance can be placed on

* *multo tempore.*

its early dates. In any case, the period was long enough to enable Hengist to bring over large reinforcements. No doubt the barbarian chief had during this interval a good opportunity to form ideas about the military features of the country. Both at this time and possibly during earlier employment on the Continent he and his men had been in close touch with sub-Roman civilization; and the kind of civilization to be assimilated by German mercenaries was the use of engines of war such as battering-rams. Then, when it came to a quarrel and the Germans turned against Vortigern, it was easy for Hengist to obtain his reinforcements. Gildas says that these came from the 'motherland' of the Saxons; but it is more likely that in reality Hengist recruited other roving bands like his own, and drew also from the 'Saxons' who had established themselves in the corner of Gaul immediately opposite the Kentish coast. The supposition that Hengist's forces were composed of adventurers of diverse origin drawn from different folks of the Germanic seaboard—Frisians, Saxons, Angles, even Franks, in addition to the 'Jutes' themselves—may help to explain some of the striking variations in Kentish graves. It may also explain why there are now conflicting theories about the Jutes: why this expert finds in Kent affinities with the Frisian language and another with the Frankish laws. No one theory indeed can yet pass unchallenged. The philologists are not agreed; the jurists without full early codes from the peoples of Jutland and the Saxon-Frisian coast cannot well assess the value of the few resemblances between Frankish and Kentish laws. It may indeed be held that the competing arguments simply cancel one another, and therefore betray no mixing of the races. If so, we may still guess, as a mere probability, that the followers of Hengist, like the Great Army of the Vikings in the ninth century, were a coalition of many bands of different origin.

In any case, it is at least possible that some of Hengist's contingents had been long enough in contact with the Franks to adopt many of their ideas. The early dominance of Hengist and his own *comitatus* of Jutes among the heterogeneous bands of new settlers, and the outstanding qualities of personality and leadership of this Jutish hero himself, may well have set going a tradition which survives in Bede's words.

Lastly and more confidently, we may attribute the sustained development of Kentish culture to the fact that Kentishmen, living on the old trade route and being pre-eminently the trading people of the island, were exposed in a unique way to all kinds of continental influences. Kentish culture was a cross between Frankish and northern cultures, with perhaps some mingling of a British strain in its remoter ancestry; but it was a new type, a native growth.

Three or four other features of this conquest may perhaps be distinguished in the black night of the time. First, some sense of strategy may be detected not only in Hengist's choice of Thanet, but also in the establishment of the group communities —shall we call them in this case detachments from the army of invasion?—in and about the Medway valley. To begin with, Thanet was, as we have said, an ideal base. Later, when the invaders mastered east Kent, it may be inferred from the place-names that they planted their group communities thickly along the Medway valley. By so doing, thanks to the great tract of the desolate Weald to the south, they succeeded in accomplishing what the clever Viking leaders attempted but failed to do in the last war against Alfred; that is, they nipped off a territory which was well defined and easily defensible—a territory almost like an island, one which tended to separate Britain from the Continent.

What happened after the conquest of east Kent is another obscure point. Here we come up against the question whether the invasion of Kent was really the first permanent occupation of British territory by the Germanic peoples. We shall hear in the following pages more about the theory, based on the grave-finds, that the settlement of the eastern Midlands—the country opened by the rivers of the Wash—was begun about the middle of the fifth century. The evidence of the heathen graves, however, is as yet not strong enough to justify us in abandoning the old story that Hengist's seizure of Kent was the turning-point, the event which came to be remembered in Welsh tradition as the *adventus Saxonum*.*

Gildas draws a picture of the first invaders after they had broken faith with the British king, harrying 'the whole island'. It may well be true; and these first bands may indeed have poured down the Roman roads in all directions, plundering and destroying. These raiders, however, have given the archaeologists no clear trace of themselves or of their violence.

The story must end with the establishment of the invaders in east Kent, perhaps a sequel to the return of the bands from raiding up to the western sea. Narratives which introduce other details, such as battles of Vortimer, successor to Vortigern, must be suspect, since they are derived from Nennius.

One point, however, should be noticed before we leave the Jutes, namely, that at some time they made a second settlement in the Isle of Wight and yet another in the country opposite, round Southampton Water.[24] In the Isle of Wight some of the characteristics which we call Jutish can be recognized. For instance, in its graves, as in those of Kent, we see the garnet and square-headed brooches, the crystal balls, and the perforated silver spoons.† This evidence, agreeing with the statement of Bede that the people of the Isle of Wight and of the opposite mainland were sprung, like the people of Kent, from 'the nation of the Jutes', seems at first to drive us back to the idea that the distinction between the Jutes and the other immigrants was a matter of race and of little else but that. The conjectures to which we have been led in the present chapter point to a somewhat different conclusion. We do not reject Bede's statement as a mere blunder, but for us who, unlike Bede, are seeking for an explanation of the peculiarities of the Kentishmen and their culture, any talk about 'the Jutish nation' is quite inadequate. Our conclusion, our 'working hypothesis', is different: namely,

* Cf. above, p. 67. † Cf. above, p. 89.

that the peculiarities of Kent were less the result of blood than of time, circumstance, and place.

As for the blood of the Kentishmen, we believe that to have been more than usually mixed, but the ingredients and their proportions to be not yet ascertained.[25] The circumstances of the conquest of Kent were, we have seen, unique and formative: first, the previous experience of Hengist and his men, their discipline as federates, and their consequent knowledge of Frankish and sub-Roman civilization; then, the survival of numbers of the British natives whom the conquerors were sufficiently civilized to employ as their potters and craftsmen and as their serfs on the land—circumstances which combined to produce some parallelism between the conquest of Kent and the regulated occupation of certain parts of Gaul by Goths, Franks, and Burgundians.

Then in point of time, we must remember that the dynasty of Hengist had a start of something like a generation over the other small local monarchies—a generation in which they and their followers were sufficiently cultured to make a good use of their advantages. The decades in the middle of the fifth century when the Teutonic kingdom of Kent was an organized state surrounded, not by the primitive tribesmen of western Britain, but by the more Romanized Britons of the south-east, may have done much in fixing the contrast between the 'Jutes' and the Angles and Saxons.

But, above all, it was the geographical position of the Jutes at the bridge-head between Britain and the Continent which enabled them to generate a culture far above that of the other invaders of the island. The trade of the Jutes was the determining factor in their rise.

This explanation would, it is true, be falsified if it could be shown that the Jutes occupied the Isle of Wight and the opposite coast at the same time as Kent, and that from the first they displayed all the characteristics of Jutish civilization. But there is no evidence that this was what happened. These secondary

Jutish settlements seem to be in the main offshoots, overflowings from Kent. The graves indicate that for a time in the sixth century the Isle of Wight had contact with Kent, presumably political as well as cultural, and that it shared in the Kentish monopoly of trade. These western Jutes were, however, exposed to the influence and enmity of their Saxon neighbours, and this may be the reason why their graves fail to yield objects made in the most magnificent style of the golden age of Kent.

The Jutish problem, therefore, is not decided one way or another by the appearance of Jutish culture in the Isle of Wight and its neighbourhood. 'The Jutish nation' with its peculiar culture was made like the 'English', and so many other hybrid nations, out of different elements, and was made after the conquest. It was to all intents made in Kent.

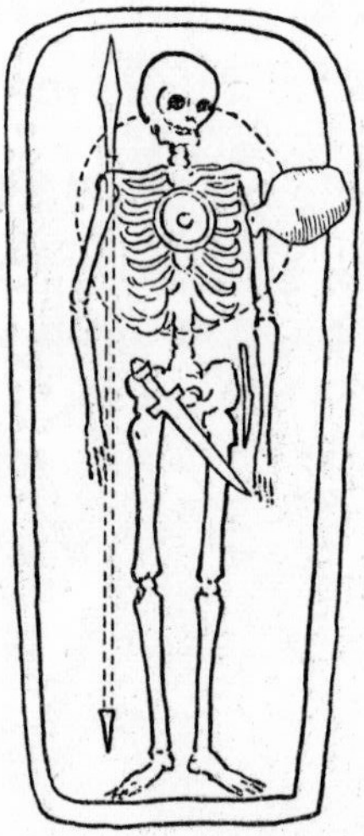

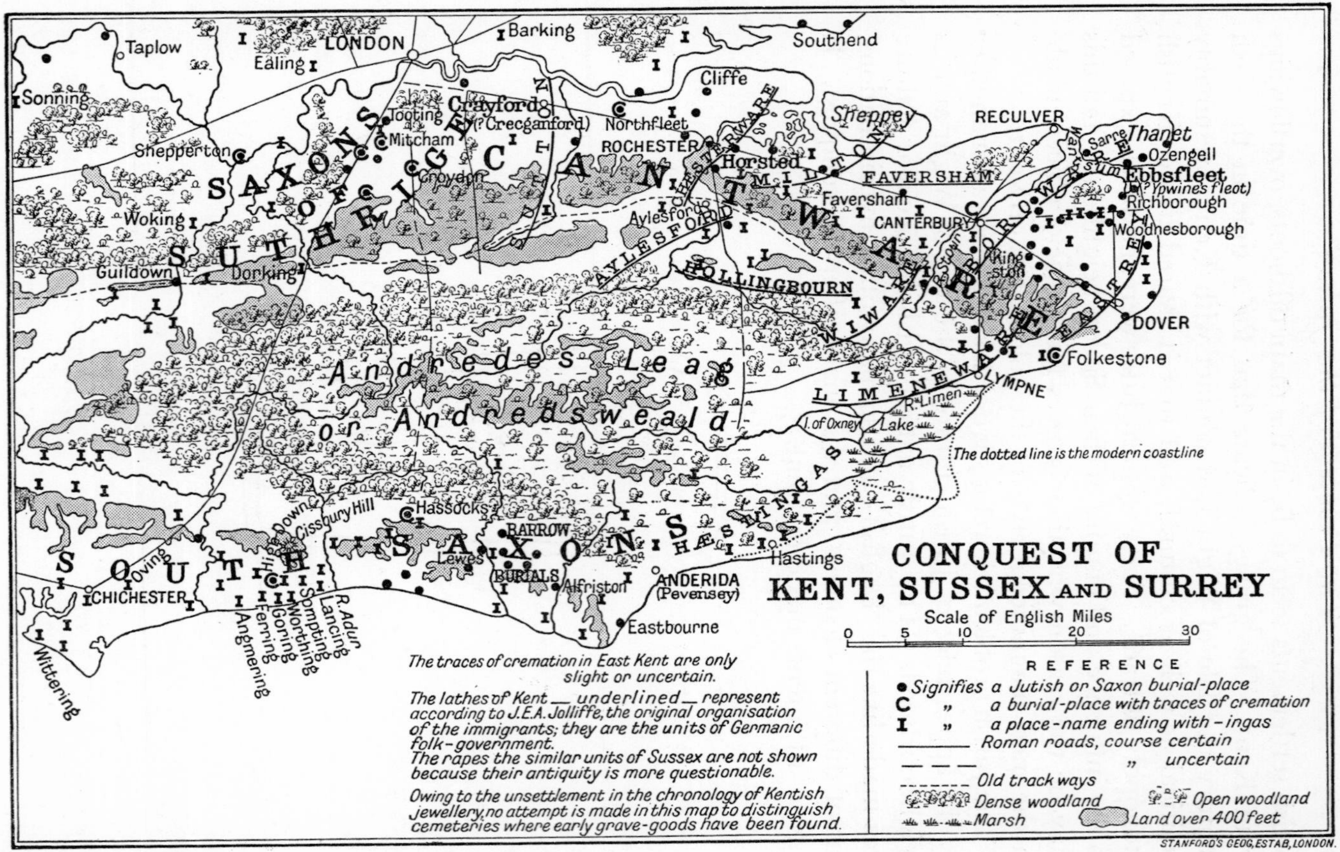
CONQUEST OF
KENT, SUSSEX AND SURREY
Scale of English Miles
0 5 10 20 30
REFERENCE
● Signifies a Jutish or Saxon burial-place
C " a burial-place with traces of cremation
I " a place-name ending with -ingas
Roman roads, course certain
" uncertain
Old track ways
Dense woodland
Open woodland
Marsh
Land over 400 feet
The traces of cremation in East Kent are only slight or uncertain.
The lathes of Kent — underlined — represent according to J.E.A. Jolliffe, the original organisation of the immigrants; they are the units of Germanic folk-government.
The rapes the similar units of Sussex are not shown because their antiquity is more questionable.
Owing to the unsettlement in the chronology of Kentish jewellery, no attempt is made in this map to distinguish cemeteries where early grave-goods have been found.
The dotted line is the modern coastline
SAXONS OF SUTHRIGE
CANTWARE
SOUTH SAXONS
Andredes Leag or Andredsweald
HÆSTINGAS
Taplow
Sonning
LONDON
Ealing
Barking
Southend
Cliffe
Sheppey
RECULVER
Thanet
Sarre
Wantsum
Ozengell
Ebbsfleet
(? Ypwines fleot)
Richborough
Woodnesborough
Shepperton
Tooting
Mitcham
Croydon
Crayford
(? Crecganford)
Northfleet
ROCHESTER
Horsted
CESTERWARE
MIDDLETON
FAVERSHAM
Faversham
CANTERBURY
BOROWARE
EASTRY
Aylesford
AYLESFORD
HOLLINGBOURN
WIWARWE
Sturry
Kingston
DOVER
Folkestone
LYMPNE
LIMENEWARE
R. Limen
I. of Oxney
Lake
Woking
Guildown
Dorking
Hassocks
Cissbury Hill
High Down
BARROW
BURIALS
Lewes
Alfriston
ANDERIDA
(Pevensey)
Eastbourne
Hastings
Oving
CHICHESTER
R. Adur
Lancing
Sompting
Worthing
Goring
Ferring
Angmering
Wittering
STANFORD'S GEOG. ESTAB. LONDON.

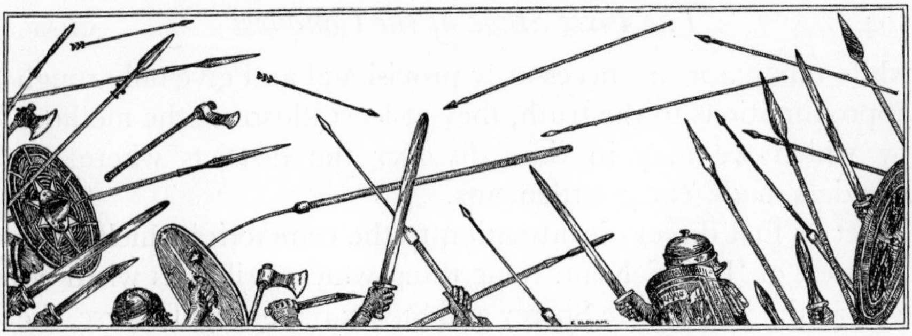

IV

THE FIRST STAGE OF THE SAXON AND ANGLIAN CONQUESTS

THE SAXONS

FOR the conquest of Kent it was reasonable to hear first what legend had to tell us and then to inquire whether the legends were confirmed by evidence from the graves. But for the rest of England the legends are so late or so meagre that we have often to reverse the procedure and to look at the archaeological evidence first, before we pay attention to any written statements made in the Saxon Chronicle. The maps which follow in this chapter attempt to summarize some results of the archaeological evidence. They show two ways by which we may try to trace the presence of early invaders, the distribution first of Saxon cemeteries where the dead were cremated, and secondly of burials containing grave-goods assigned to about the fifth century.

The reasons for caution to which we have drawn attention in previous chapters of course hold good whenever we use the evidence of Anglo-Saxon archaeology as a basis for history. In this even more than in most subjects we must expect to have the conclusions of one generation questioned by another.* But

* Indeed, the datings on which these maps are based, those of Baldwin Brown, Reginald Smith (in the volumes of the *Victoria County History*), and of Åberg, are already challenged; and owing to the great unsettlement in the chronology of Kentish jewellery I have given up the attempt to show the distribution of early grave goods in my map of southern Britain.

while our maps are necessarily provisional and give only rough approximations to the truth, they at least illustrate the methods by which we may in time discover the districts where the invaders made early settlements.

Let us first direct our attention to the cemeteries which lie to the west of 'Jutish' Kent. One thing which strikes us when we look at the map of the Surrey and Sussex region is, of course, the great extent of the uninhabited Weald country, and the smallness of the few districts to the north and south of it where there are archaeological traces of pagan settlement. In Sussex there are no cemeteries whatever at the eastern end of the county, in the Hastings district. Towards the west also they almost disappear, and in this direction we have only some barrows on the downs near Arundel to tell us of the presence of heathen Saxons, barrows which, in the phraseology of the archaeologists, were scantily 'furnished', and yielded little more than knives buried with the dead. There is a fairly thick cluster of cemeteries in the chalk country behind and around Brighton. Here in two cases only there were traces, and these slight, of cremation.

To form plausible theories about the conquest of Sussex it is essential at the outset to give special weight to what the place-name experts have to tell us. In no county have their studies been more illuminating.[1] If we accept the axiom that the suffix *-ing* (representing the Old English plural *-ingas*) betokens a colony made by a group in the early days of the settlement, perhaps by a group of the original invaders, we shall be forced to modify the ideas which we had formed from the cemeteries. The name Hastings itself, and a number of *-ing* names round the present town, suggest that the Hæstingas established themselves in these borderlands in an early phase of the migration.* Turning westwards along the coast, we find but few *-ing* names in the downlands around Eastbourne, Lewes, and Brighton,

* Certain Kentish features in the ancient field-system of the district have been taken to mean that these settlers were Jutes, and point at any rate to some connexion with Kent before their absorption into the kingdom of Sussex. Cf. Jolliffe, 73–97.

where the signs of heathen burials are most plentiful. But west of the Adur they reappear in a long sequence up to and beyond Chichester: Lancing, Steyning, Sompting, Worthing, Goring, Angmering, Oving, Wittering, and many others. Thus the burials and the place-names of Sussex both show marked changes in local custom as we go from east to west. We therefore infer that the later kingdom of the South Saxons was a union of at least three earlier folks, and the inference receives some confirmation from a record of the eleventh century in which one of these small units, the Hæstingas, is mentioned as distinct from the South Saxons. Here, then, we have an example of the process by which the Heptarchic kingdoms were forged from smaller units.

After these preliminaries we are ready to hear what the written authorities have to tell us. In the Alfredian Chronicle,* immediately after the entries about the conquest of Kent, there come two laconic annals about Sussex.

> '477. Ælle landed in Britain and his three sons—Cymen and Wlencing and Cissa—with three ships, at the place which is called Cymenes ora; and there they slew many of the Welsh and some in flight they drove into the wood that is called Andredesleage.'

Then, after another battle:

> '491. Ælle and Cissa besieged the stronghold† of Anderida [Pevensey] and slew all that were therein, nor was one Briton left there afterwards.'

The dates of the Chronicle, here as elsewhere in this early period, are not to be relied on. But it is noteworthy that in the opinion of Baldwin Brown[2] 'none of the finds of Teutonic character that have been made in the district suggest a date earlier than the last quarter of the fifth century, which tradition assigns for the first entry of the invaders'. Whether 'tradition' is a word than can rightly be applied to these annals of the Chronicle, is a question which can be better discussed when we come to the

* The Anglo-Saxon Chronicle is called Alfredian in order to remind the reader of the period when it was compiled. The term does not necessarily imply that King Alfred himself was the author. See vol. ii, pp. 624–8.

† *ceaster*.

early history of Wessex. On the face of things, however, it seems reasonable to infer from all the evidence (such as it is) that the Saxons who followed Ælle to Sussex had been campaigning so long either in France or Britain that for the most part they had given up their old custom of cremation burial; that the nucleus of the main settlement on the coast was somewhere about the middle of the modern county; and that the story of the massacre of Britons who had taken shelter at Anderida behind the walls of the old fort of the Saxon Shore, must be genuine enough—it reads much like a passage from an encomium of a Viking hero.

The massacre at Anderida may perhaps be explained by the old Germanic idea that a wasted land was the safest kind of frontier. Something similar, yet different, may well have happened also at the western end of Sussex. At any rate the name of the Roman *Regnum* vanished and the place which succeeded it was thenceforth known as the 'fort' (*ceaster*) of Ælle's son Cissa, that is, Chichester.[3]

The only other information about Ælle comes to us from Bede, and all that he tells us is this: that Ælle was the first king to have an *imperium* over all the invaders south of the Humber. Now *imperium* is an ambiguous word. Later in this passage Bede uses it as meaning something like our 'empire'; he enumerates kings who held imperial sway over wide tracts of country south of the Humber. Since, however, Ælle lived in a very early phase of the Conquest, it is fair to argue that his *imperium* was military rather than territorial—a command. No one need doubt that this mysterious Ælle, founder of the kingdom of the South Saxons, played a decisive part as a leader of the Germanic invaders of the second generation. But it must be an open question whether he was a mere war-leader—a commander-in-chief who at the end of his life settled down in Sussex—or a petty king, recognized as the most capable among a number of confederate chiefs who co-operated in wars against the Britons.

Remembering this uncertainty we will once more refer to the archaeologists and hear what they have to tell us about the

Pevensey Castle (Anderida), West Gate

A About $\frac{1}{8}$

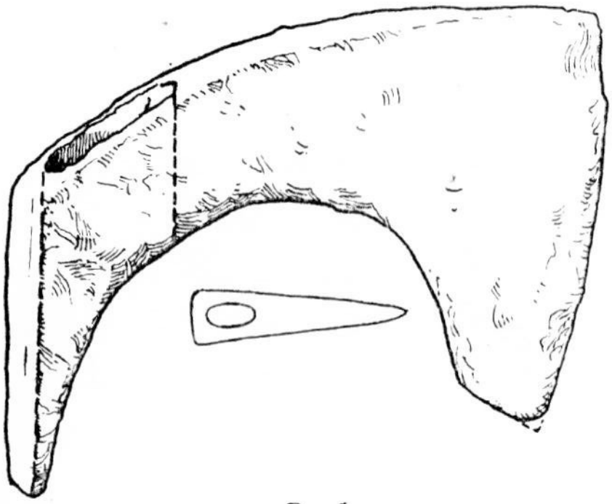

B $\frac{1}{2}$

C $\frac{1}{1}$

D $\frac{1}{1}$

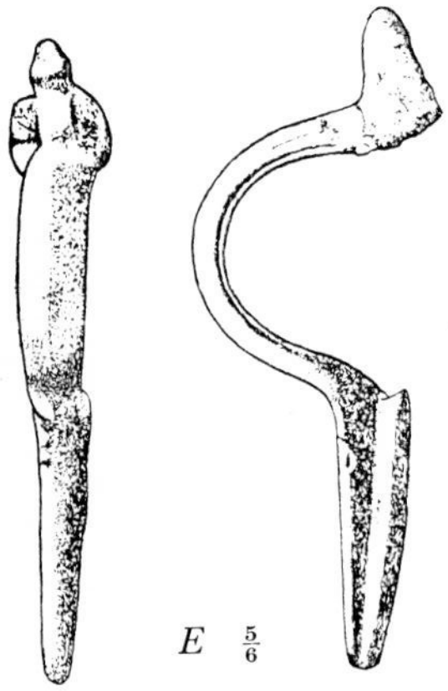

E $\frac{5}{6}$

F $\frac{3}{4}$

A, *B*, *C*, *D*—Grave finds from Sussex and Surrey

A, An angon, and *B*, a throwing axe or Francisca, illustrate Frankish influence; *C*, a ring brooch, and *D*, a button brooch, illustrate Kentish influence

E and *F* are from the Upper Thames Valley

E, Long brooch of primitive type from Dorchester; *F*, Equal-armed brooch from Sutton Courtenay

conquests of Saxons to the north of Sussex, and especially about the conquest of the Thames valley.

After the first Saxon settlements in west Kent, we next find a large group on good dry soil in the Croydon area, sheltered from London by marshes and woodland. One cemetery of the group, that at Mitcham, with over 300 graves, indicates a place of some importance.

Now the first thing suggested by the cemeteries of Surrey, so widely sundered from those of Sussex, is this: that if the Saxons of the two regions were confederates, if both recognized, as Bede implies, the authority of Ælle, they did not maintain touch with one another by land. There is not a sign of any heathen settlement, late or early, along the Weald section of the Stane Street, the old Roman road which connected Chichester with the Thames valley. The Saxons who ploughed the coastlands and the river valleys of Sussex were effectually cut off from their kinsmen in Surrey by the greatest forest of southern Britain. If Ælle's *imperium* was a reality, it must have rested on communications by sea rather than by land. He must have been the leader of a fleet which could operate both along the Sussex coast and in the Thames valley.

Next we find that there are marked resemblances between the cemeteries of Surrey and Sussex. In both areas the practice of burning the dead yielded quickly to the new fashion of burying the dead uncremated. But none the less there are differences: in Surrey cremation seems to have been practised for a generation or two; in Sussex the old custom seems to have been much more exceptional and evanescent. Another characteristic common both to the Saxons of Sussex and those of the lower Thames valley is that when they buried bodies unburnt they laid the bodies east and west. This orientation is no evidence of Christianity, but it is perhaps a sign that these invaders had been in contact with the more advanced Germanic peoples, like the Franks, and had learnt something of Frankish customs. Then, too, much of the gear which was placed with the dead was similar. For example, around Croydon in Surrey and at High Down in Sussex were found, in addition to Kentish fashions such as 'button' and 'ring' brooches and looted glass vases, round brooches with geometric patterns, like those of the Elbe lands, and Frankish imports such as 'angons', long barbed spear-heads which could transfix an enemy's shield and could not be cut by his sword.[4] (Pls. 21 and 22.)

It is possible to claim that the similarities of the graves indicate that somewhere in the past the history of the Saxons of the lower Thames touched that of the South Saxons. Thus it has been said that 'a study of the Saxon relics of the period seems to offer proof that the tradition of Ælle's hegemony contains at least a kernel of truth'. But other explanations are also legitimate. The resemblances between the two may have resulted not from co-operation in war under the command of Ælle, but from a similarity in their circumstances—their nearness to Kent and the fact that they bought their goods from the same or similar traders.

SETTLEMENTS ON THE UPPER THAMES

Having learnt something about early settlements of the Saxons on the Surrey side of the lower Thames, our obvious course is to track the invaders up the river. But at once we are checked. The following map shows us that there is a great gap between the Saxon cemeteries in the Croydon area and those ranging from Reading to Fairford in the valley of the upper Thames, a country which may for the sake of convenience be called after its modern centre, the Oxford region.

We shall discuss in a later section the question of what happened to Roman London. Here we need only remark in passing two things: first, that there is scarcely a trace of a pagan Germanic cemetery within some thirty miles of London on the northern bank of the Thames; and, secondly, that the Alfredian chronicler believed, whether rightly or wrongly, that as late as 571 there were British forces north of the Thames large enough to fight an important battle with Saxons who had, it seems, advanced from the Salisbury region. It is certainly curious that the settlements in the Oxford country, though they are so far from the sea, and though one of them, Fairford, is within eight miles of Cirencester, which, according to the Chronicle, was only conquered in 577, none the less seem from their graves to go back to an early date, that is to a period somewhere about 500. Two graves at Dorchester on the Thames have indeed produced the earliest Germanic objects yet excavated in this country—a brooch anticipating the cruciform type, buckles, and various oddments which were made about 400 or perhaps earlier[5] (Pl. 21 E). The significance of an isolated find such as this may clearly be questioned. The warrior who was buried here may have been a mercenary in the service of the Romano-Britons, or he may have been unusually old-fashioned in his equipment. On other grounds, however, Leeds[6] inferred that 'there must have been not inconsiderable settlements of Saxons in the upper Thames valley by the beginning of the sixth century at latest'; and[7] that 'it is archaeologically certain that the Saxons held the district immediately south and west of Oxford at least three-quarters of a century before . . . A.D. 571'. This point is of such importance that it is incumbent upon us to have some knowledge of the arguments upon which this view is based, even though it is only possible to give here a few samples of the evidence.

To begin with we must notice that in many of these cemeteries of the upper Thames valley there are unmistakable traces of cremation. It is found at Reading, at Long Wittenham near Dorchester, and at four or five other burial-grounds as far west as Fairford. It is true that the cremation urns are not numerous, but they are enough to suggest that the original settlers in this region had come direct from Germany, and were not offshoots from those who had been long established in the east of the island. A stronger argument is constructed from the brooches of these Saxons. One is an 'equal-armed' brooch, a type found in England in a few other places (in settlements on the Ouse and its tributaries), and elsewhere, as we have seen above,* only in the Elbe-Weser region. Now the ornamentation on these unique curiously shaped brooches is of the fifth-century kind, made with 'chip-carving'. The specimen to which we are referring in the Oxford area was found not in a grave, but buried in earth which had once been the floor of a Saxon hut, near Sutton Courtenay.† True, it is, like the Dorchester burial, an isolated find. But it is a strong reason for thinking that the village here was inhabited by Saxons in very early days of the invasion.‡

The other kind of Saxon brooch, common both in the Elbe-Weser region of Germany and in the upper Thames valley in Britain, is the 'round' brooch made in two varieties, called respectively 'saucer' (or 'cast') and 'applied'. Some of the patterns of the English examples—especially those with spirals (Pl. 22)—resemble so closely the round brooches of north Germany that we are compelled to think that the immigrants brought their first models with them, and that they must have brought them at an early date.[8]

Another, though a fragile, argument can also be constructed from the evidences of continuity between the Romano-British and the Saxon settlements which have been found in quite a number of these upper Thames burial-places: at Long Wittenham, at Frilford, at East Shefford (up in the Downs), and elsewhere. Turn up the records of one of these, for example that of Frilford.[9] Here, as elsewhere, the excavators found that the Saxons had buried their dead in a cemetery of the conquered people. They were side by side with Romano-Britons who had sometimes been placed in leaden or wooden coffins, sometimes had been committed to the earth with a coin in their mouth—an obol for Charon—sometimes had been orientated like Christians,

* See map, p. 33.

† See below, p. 223, and Pl. 21 F.

‡ The date assigned to this brooch by Roeder is *c.* 475.

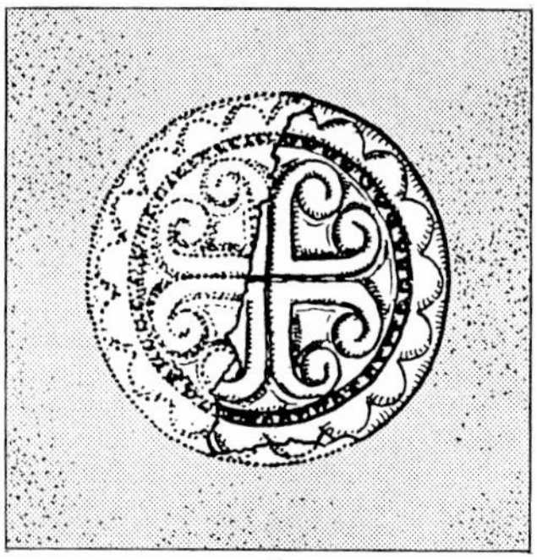

A

B

C

D

E

F

ROUND BROOCHES FROM GERMANY, SUSSEX, AND SURREY

A, *B*, *C*, and *D*—with floreated cross design (*A*, mounted on a square plate, from Wester-Wanna, N. Germany; *B* and *C* from High Down, Sussex; *D* from Mitcham, Surrey). *E* and *F*—with running spiral design (*E* from Wester-Wanna; *F* from Mitcham). $\frac{1}{1}$

with their heads to the west. Again, every stage of transition from provincial-Roman to Saxon seemed to be represented in this Frilford cemetery. There were a few urns of the first intruders, those who for a time kept up their old Germanic customs (Fig. 27), ornamented vessels, or unadorned pots, such as the new-comers used for their everyday cooking. Then, when the immigrants began to bury instead of to cremate their dead, their graves

FIG. 27. Frilford, Berks.; urn. Less than ½.

showed evident signs of persistent Romano-British influence. Sherds of Roman pottery were found thrown into the Saxon graves just as into those of the natives. Moreover, in addition to the round brooches of which we have already spoken, there were Saxon buckles and other goods which showed resemblance either in shape or in the style of ornamentation to the things which had been used by the natives before the invasions. Now it may be said that these signs of continuity do not prove that the settlement of the Saxons at Frilford was early. This on the whole must be granted; but it may still be claimed that the British community which had sufficient influence to pass on its customs and designs to the new-comers was not removed by many generations from the times when Romano-British civilization had been vigorous.

The reasons for thinking that the Saxons found their way to the open spaces of the upper Thames at an early stage of the invasion are none of them perfectly strong; but taken together they have a certain cumulative strength—enough to justify us in provisionally marking the upper Thames valley as occupied by Saxon immigrants by the beginning of the sixth century.

And still we have not done with these Saxon graves and the lessons to be learnt from them. We must give due attention to the surprising fact, on which the experts have rightly laid much stress, that 'it is well-nigh impossible to single out any one cemetery as earlier archaeologically speaking than the rest'.[10] Now even if we allow the archaeologists an extra large margin of error, since the dating of these round brooches is admittedly insecure; even if we argue that the burial-grounds of the upper Thames basin, like Fairford, only go back to, say, 525, we still have this result, that for nearly fifty years before the reported capture of Cirencester (according to the annal of the Chronicle for 571) the Saxons at Fairford were settled within eight miles of the Britons who still clung to the old Roman town. And if it is true that the boundary between the two peoples did here remain almost unchanged for a generation or two, this fact is full of significance and must be remembered when we form our opinion about the general character of the Conquest.

In the next place we must direct our attention to two important cemeteries which have been excavated in recent years. One of these is at Bidford on the Avon, where the finds indicate that the colony was a large one, that it was Saxon—apparently an offshoot from the Thames valley people—and that in the opinion of the excavators it was 'established quite early in the sixth century'.[11] The cremation burials were numerous, and plain square-headed brooches were recovered of a type assigned to about 500. Here, then, we seem to have evidence that a strong outpost of Saxons was placed at Bidford not long after the upper Thames valley was occupied. The position of Bidford was one of some strategic importance, since it marks the point at which Ryknield Street, a branch of the Fosse Way, crosses the Avon. When the Bidford post was established, Saxons had penetrated the line of the Fosse Way. The Britons had ceased to control this road, all-important for the defence of the west.

The other significant cemetery excavated was at Luton, near the Icknield Way, the track which follows the escarpment of the Chilterns and which from remote ages had been the chief line

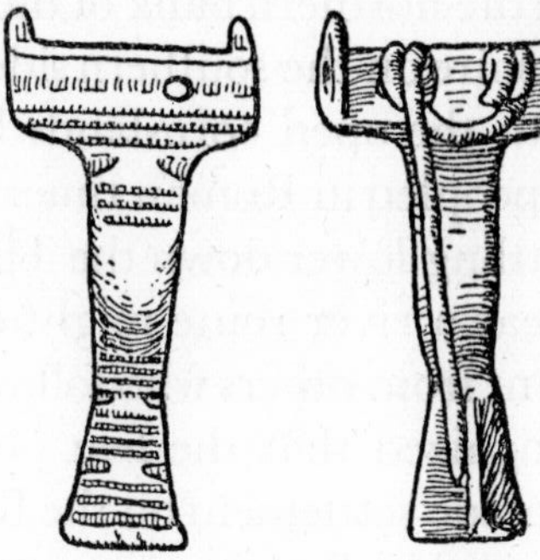

FIG. 28. Luton, Beds.; brooch with primitive headplate. $\frac{1}{1}$. (Roeder's date, *c.* 400.)

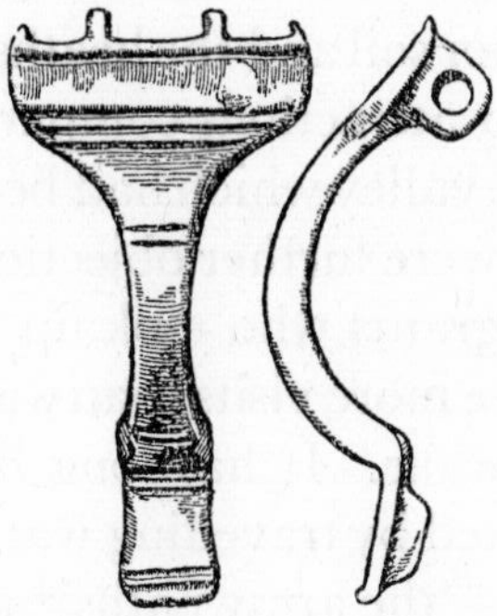

Fig. 29. Kempston, Beds.; brooch of the 'Luton' type. $\frac{1}{1}$. (Roeder's date, *c.* 450.)

of communication between the country south of the Fens and the region of the upper Thames. The interest of the settlement is enhanced by the fact that it was placed about three miles from the Watling Street. Luton, therefore, near the junction of the two highways, had even more strategic importance than Bidford. It is said[12] that some of its grave-goods, like the above brooch, are early—indeed among the earliest of all such finds in Britain. But the chief importance of the finds here was that they added strength to a notable theory propounded by Leeds,[13] that the Saxons reached the upper Thames country, not by the natural route up the river, but by 'a land route from the Wash along some such line as the Icknield Way'. Leeds, however, admits that when once the settlement had been made there would be nothing extraordinary in further bands of immigrants making their way up the Thames to join the first comers. If we accept the fact that Saxons entered the Midlands by both routes, the question whether the first Saxons round Oxford came overland rather than by the river loses much of its importance. The dearth of Saxon graves on the middle reaches of the Thames—a dearth somewhat magnified by Leeds—does not mean that the river was not used for traffic. It is easy to see why the early settlers were unwilling to fix their homes on the middle reaches. The Chiltern woods which fringed the northern bank of the river, the poor soil and the heaths of Berkshire on the southern side, held out no attractions comparable with the open corn-lands higher up the valley which had been well-peopled in Roman times. And there were further objections to settling lower down the Thames. Immigrants who took up lands near a river route might expect to have more visits than was pleasant from others who followed in their wake. It has long been recognized that the fear of being molested by travelling war-bands made settlement on the Roman roads—'the army paths'* as the English called them—unpopular in the early days of the Conquest. And a similar fear must have acted as a deterrent to settlement near waterways like the Thames. Disorderly Saxons were more to be dreaded than hostile Britons; and so for safety's sake immigrants stuck together and made for the upper waters of the river. There was nothing abnormal in the neglect of the middle Thames country by the colonists.

Oxford may therefore repudiate the suggestion that the first settlers in its neighbourhood came from Cambridge (what fuel the suggestion would have given the controversialists of the seventeenth century!); but the evidence that Saxons entered the Midlands in some numbers by way of the Cam and of other Fen rivers is so strong that we must now turn our attention in that direction.

SETTLEMENTS IN THE CAMBRIDGE REGION[14]

A glance at the last map shows not only the density of the settlement in this region, but also the reason for it. When the

* *herepaðas.*

Romano-British inhabitants had been somehow or other disposed of, there was no safer channel into the heart of the Midlands than the Ouse and its tributaries. For thirty miles or more the

FIG. 30. Kempston, Beds.; equal-armed brooch. $\frac{1}{1}$. (Roeder's date, *c.* 450.)

FIG. 31. Haslingfield, Camb.; equal-armed brooch. $\frac{1}{1}$. (Roeder's date, *c.* 500.)

shallow boats of the invaders could paddle up through the marshes of the fenlands unobserved and unmolested. Those who turned south-west and west found at last in the valleys of the Cam, the Ouse, the Nene, and the Welland the dry lands which were suitable for habitation. This region in later times was known as the territory of the Middle Angles. The archaeologists mark it as a distinct 'cultural area'. It contains an unusually large number of grave-goods which can be assigned to the fifth century or thereabouts; and Saxon and Anglian things are curiously mixed. Roeder, the German archaeologist to whose careful studies of Saxon grave-goods we have already referred,*[15] dates a brooch of the 'Luton' type, from Kempston, back to about 425. Two equal-armed brooches from the Cambridge area he assigns to about the end of the fifth century (Figs. 30, 31). Equally significant are the unusual urns found both in the Elbe-Weser country and in our eastern Midlands: 'window urns', with pieces of glass fixed into the vessel, sometimes at the side, sometimes at the bottom; 'holed urns', that is, urns in which holes have deliberately been made.† These urns are strange vessels. Their peculiarities need not be explained in terms of religion. The glass was probably fitted into the clay because glass was a rarity, and even a fragment of it was worth framing in a pot.

There can be little doubt that many of these things were treasured belongings brought over by very early immigrants; and if others, like some of the equal-armed brooches, were made in England, then though we may not feel confident about the dates assigned to brooches on the strength of typological development, we may at least accept Roeder's argument that the invaders must have been settled in the Cambridge region for a long time before a craftsman could find an opportunity to produce these elaborate ornaments.

Now the interest of these 'freak' urns and of the 'Luton' and equal-armed brooches is, we repeat, twofold. Besides proving that the Germans were dribbling into the country through the Fens at some very early phase of the invasion they have something else to tell us. They come from definitely Saxon districts of Germany rather than Anglian. Their home is not Schleswig but the district to the west of the Elbe. Moreover, these peculiar grave-goods are not the only things which link up the so-called

* Above, p. 10.

† As mentioned above, p. 10, note, the Great Addington urn with a handle perforated so as to form a spout (Pl. 27D) may now be regarded as evidence for an early Scandinavian contingent in the Midlands.

A and *B*. Heslingfield, Cambridge; window urn. $\frac{5}{8}$

C. Great Addington, Northants; spout-handled urn. About $\frac{1}{6}$

D. Kempston, Beds.; holed urn. $\frac{1}{2}$

PECULIAR URNS FROM THE EAST MIDLANDS

'Middle Angles' with the Saxons of Germany. The urns in which they were buried can more nearly be matched with those recovered from the Elbe-Weser cemeteries than from the cemeteries of Schleswig. On the other hand, the Cambridge region has produced unusually large numbers of early cruciform brooches —those with full-round and with half-round detachable knobs. On the strength of these and of other supposed Anglian *differentiae*, and above all, of course, on the strength of their name, the Middle Angles are often included within the boundary-line of the Anglian culture. The confusion of Anglian and Saxon things in the graves of the eastern Midlands points to there having been a mixture of Anglian and Saxon settlers rather than to mere trading intercourse. One may suppose that the Saxons who entered Britain by the back door of the Wash instead of by the front door of the Thames were, perhaps, even from the first intermingled with Anglian migrants, and that they were only transformed into 'Middle Angles' in the seventh century owing to the political conquest of all the Midlands by the Angles of Mercia.

These speculations for the time being can be put aside. What is essential is that we should treat with respect the view that the settlements round Cambridge go back to the fifth century —possibly to the middle of that century—and that others also in the eastern Midlands, such as that at Kempston on the Ouse, may be almost as early.

At this point we finish for the moment with the evidence of the archaeologists. They have said their say, and if their version of what happened is accepted, the new story of the Conquest is something very different from the old story. For their evidence amounts to this: that at an early period of the invasion, probably before the end of the fifth century, there were clusters of Germanic invaders both in the Cambridge region and also, less certainly, on the upper Thames. Between the two in the sixth century, intermediate Germanic settlements were multiplied until they stretched like the string of a bow across the eastern Midlands. The existence of these, and the unearthing of early brooches at Luton, while they show that the Wash rivers and the Icknield Way were early used as an important means of entry into the island, scarcely prove that this was the main, much less the only, route used by the invaders of southern Britain.

THE STORY OF GILDAS

It is time to return to the story of Gildas, the only British writer who was in any sense contemporary with the Conquest. When last we referred to him he was speaking about the 'fire of the invaders' licking 'the western ocean with its red and savage tongue'—rhetorical words which may be interpreted to mean that a mobile force of the first permanent invaders, Hengist's or another's, made destructive marches right across the island before returning to the east to appropriate the best lands available. Now Gildas, in spite of his extravagances, his querulous tone, and his vagueness, is of the greatest value in certain ways. He does give us one side of the story—the British side. Moreover, he brings home to us the truth that the Conquest which we have unavoidably to treat as a tangle of inter-related problems was in fact a series of human tragedies involving as much destruction of life and of civilization as has ever occurred in the history of our island. Gildas was not able to detect, like some modern historians, 'peaceful yeomen farmers' behind the brutal Saxon marauders. He tells, apparently at first-hand, of what was to be seen in the cities of Roman Britain, after the fury of the invaders had done its worst—of the ruined towns; the tops of towers and stones from high walls tumbled to the ground; the fragments of unburied human bodies lying, covered with clotted blood; the widespread devastation in the countryside, where there was hardly an ear of corn to be seen. He tells how the Britons, sheltering in the hills, were caught and murdered; how some were compelled by hunger to come and give themselves up as slaves to the enemy, so running the risk of being slaughtered at sight; and how others fled, lamenting, over the sea.

This is rhetoric rather than history; it is intended to rouse his countrymen, and not to inform posterity. Gildas is no more attempting to describe all the aspects of the invasion than to weigh his words. But, so far as it goes, we need not question the general truth of the picture. On the contrary, if we admit that it is not the whole truth of what happened, we may accept its lurid details as a part of the truth; and apply it not only to the west of Britain, which was the chief concern of Gildas, but also to the east. Massacres, a flight to the hills, enslavement, migration over sea—these are incidents of the Conquest which undoubtedly occurred. And if Gildas could only have told his story in simple language instead of in the tortured style which he adopted and helped to make fashionable among his countrymen, the miseries and horrors which this generation of Britons endured would have been remembered ever since, as one of the most moving catastrophes in history. As it is, we must not be deterred by his verbiage about the clotted blood and the wolfish, dog-like barbarians, for he tells us just enough of his ideas about the course of the Conquest for it to be possible to extract from it at least a bare sequence of events. What we obtain is the following story.

(1) After the petition of the Britons to Aëtius in 446, there ensued the age of the 'proud king' (Vortigern), who called in the accursed 'Saxons' (Hengist and company) to repel the Picts. It was at this stage, when the Saxon mercenaries turned against the king who was their paymaster, that 'the fire of their rage licked the western ocean with its red tongue'. Thus, apparently during the third quarter of the fifth century—if we accept the chronology of Bede—there occurred the episode of the hopeless collapse when the Britons, too demoralized to put up an effective resistance, endured the horrors of the pitiless raids, which, according to Gildas, left behind them tracks of unburied corpses and ruined towers. In this period we may place the evacuation of Kent. The double burial at Dorchester may be a solitary witness to the bands of marauders who at this time,

when there was little organized opposition, rode across the island. But we have seen in the graves little or no proof of settlement at this stage.

Then (2) 'after a certain interval of time' there followed, according to Gildas, the age of Ambrosius Aurelianus, a man of a distinguished Roman family whose kinsmen, before they were killed in the storm of war, had 'worn the purple' (having presumably been proclaimed emperors by the Britons or by some section of them). Gildas tells us that Ambrosius Aurelianus himself was 'a discreet man';* that he might be considered the only survivor of the Roman nation; and that he became the leader of the remnants of the wretched *cives* (the Romano-Britons) who flocked to him from all sides like bees.

Then (3) from that time there ensued a period of alternate victory and defeat. Sometimes the Romano-Britons, sometimes the Saxon enemy, had the upper hand. When the chronology is as vague and elastic as it is both in the words of Gildas and in the dating of the grave-gear, there can be no exact adjustment between the two. One can therefore only speculate whether the rally of the Britons under Ambrosius came before or after the Saxons established themselves in the eastern Midlands and in the upper Thames valley. If Ambrosius lived during the time when these regions were inundated by Saxons, then one may guess that the great work of this 'last of the Romans' was to organize resistance along the Fosse Way, in that central part of the line where the Saxon advance had broken most dangerously into the centre of Britain. And if so, the road which had been made to enable the generals of Claudius to consolidate the first Roman attack on the Midlands was now used to prolong the last Romano-British defence. One suspects that the short generalization of Gildas about the alternate victory and defeat of the Britons from the time of Ambrosius conveniently covers up much ignorance and confusion in his mind. For the period of alternating success was prolonged apparently for one or two generations.

* *vir modestus.*

It lasted, says Gildas, 'until the siege of the Badon hill, almost the last and not the least slaughter of the rascals'. And when was that siege or battle? Here we encounter another well-known puzzle. It is one that cannot be avoided; and a glance at it will at any rate serve to show how insecure is our footing throughout this tract. Gildas intended for once in a way to fix the date of this slaughter of the Saxons. The event had a special interest for him as being the year of his own birth. In his original manuscript he said it occurred in the forty-fourth year from something or other; from what he reckoned soon became doubtful owing to mistakes in copying the manuscript. Bede, in reproducing the passage, understood him to mean that it was the forty-fourth year 'after the first coming of the Saxons', i.e. after about 449, so it is evident that Bede assigned the victory to about 493. Was Bede reproducing the original reading? Some think it unlikely that a Briton would wish to set up a national defeat as the beginning of a new era of chronology. Moreover, to Gildas writing about 546, the victory of Mount Badon was 'almost the last slaughter' of the enemy; it was 'in our times' and therefore can scarcely have occurred more than fifty years earlier, in the previous century. Or did Gildas mean to say that the battle was in the forty-fourth year after the time of Ambrosius Aurelianus—the last subject about which he had been writing? That is possible, but since he failed to mention the date of Ambrosius, it is not helpful. Or was he measuring backwards and trying to say that the fight occurred in the forty-fourth year from that in which he wrote? This view has behind it the support of Mommsen, and a conjectural emendation in his edition of Gildas.*

In these uncertainties we can only say that the battle was fought some time between 493 and 516 (or 518), the date found in the *Annales Cambriae*.[16]

* C. 26. 'Ex eo tempore nunc cives, nunc hostes, vincebant . . .; usque ad annum obsessionis Badonici montis, novissimaeque ferme de furciferis non minimae stragis, quique quadragesimus quartus ut novi [or, according to Mommsen's emendation, est ab eo qui] orditur annus, mense jam uno emenso, qui et meae nativitatis est.'

One reason for approaching the fringe of this tangled controversy is, as we have said, that it illustrates the chronological uncertainties of the age in which we are groping and of Gildas, our sole contemporary guide. But there is also what we may call a sentimental reason. The British 'traditions' preserved in *Nennius* tell us that the battle of Mount Badon was the twelfth and last battle in which Arthur, the *dux bellorum*, together with the kings of Britain, fought against the Saxons, and that 960 men fell in that one day from the onslaught of Arthur alone. This is one small ray of light which comes from the Dark Ages to show the historian how already, in the ninth century, and doubtless much earlier, the Romano-British commander had caught the glowing colours of heroic tradition.[17]

But it is worse than useless to try to weave Arthur into the story of the invasions. A few vague things can be said: that in point of time Arthur probably lived about a generation after Ambrosius; that the Cornish traditions of him must be erroneous, since Cornwall was quite outside the fighting area; that the attempt[18] to locate Arthur's battles in Sussex is unacceptable, because it places them too far to the east, and the names do not fit.

An Arthur connected with north Britain has advocates. They find significance in the fact that as early as the sixth century Aedan, king of Dal Riata, named his heir Arthur. Certain Arthurian battles also are identified best in the north. Thus 'the wood of Celidon', where the seventh battle was fought, points to Caledonia. These arguments are far from conclusive. King Aedan was a Scot, not a Briton. South Wales as well as north Britain can produce an early namesake, an Arthur of Dyfed, who lived about 600. Again, Mount Badon, which Nennius calls the twelfth battle of Arthur, should be placed in the south, since that was the region which interested Gildas, the only good authority for the battle. Gildas was probably referring to a struggle of the Cirencester and other Britons against the invaders of the upper Thames. Likely spots for the

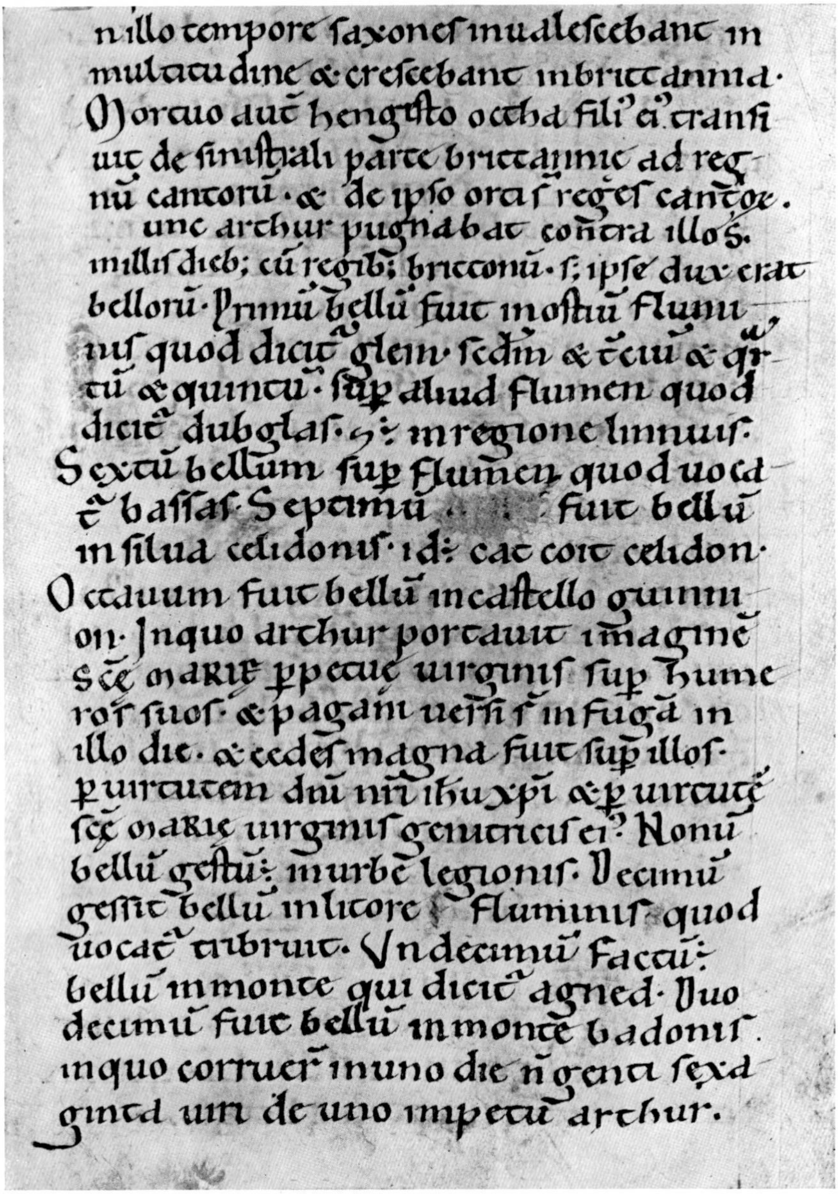
n illo tempore saxones inualescebant in
multitudine & crescebant in brittannia.
Mortuo autẽ hengisto octha fili' ei' transi
uit de sinistrali parte brittannie ad reg
nũ cantorũ. & de ipso orti s' reges cantor.
unc arthur pugnabat contra illos.
in illis dieb; cũ regib; brittonũ. s; ipse dux erat
bellorũ. Primũ bellũ fuit in ostiũ flumi
nis quod dicit' glein. secũdm & tciũ & qr
tũ & quintũ. sup aliud flumen quod
dicit' dubglas. & ẽ in regione linnuis.
Sextũ bellum sup flumen quod uocat'
ẽ bassas. Septimũ . . . fuit bellũ
in silua celidonis. id ẽ cat coit celidon.
Octauum fuit bellũ in castello guinni
on. In quo arthur portauit imaginẽ
scẽ mariẽ ppetuẽ uirginis sup humeros suos. & pagani uersi s' in fugã in
illo die. & cedes magna fuit sup illos.
p uirtutem dnĩ nr̃i ihu xpi & p uirtutẽ
scẽ mariẽ uirginis genitricis ei'. Nonũ
bellũ gestũ ẽ in urbe legionis. Decimũ
gessit bellũ in litore fluminis quod
uocat' tribruit. Undecimũ factũ ẽ
bellũ in monte qui dicit' agned. Duo
decimũ fuit bellũ in monte badonis.
in quo corruer' in uno die nongenti sexa
ginta uiri de uno impetu arthur.

The earliest mention of Arthur. From Nennius, *Historia Brittonum*, ch. lvi, Harleian MS. 3859. British Museum. About A.D. 1100

(For transcription of this passage see p. xvi. See also p. 122)

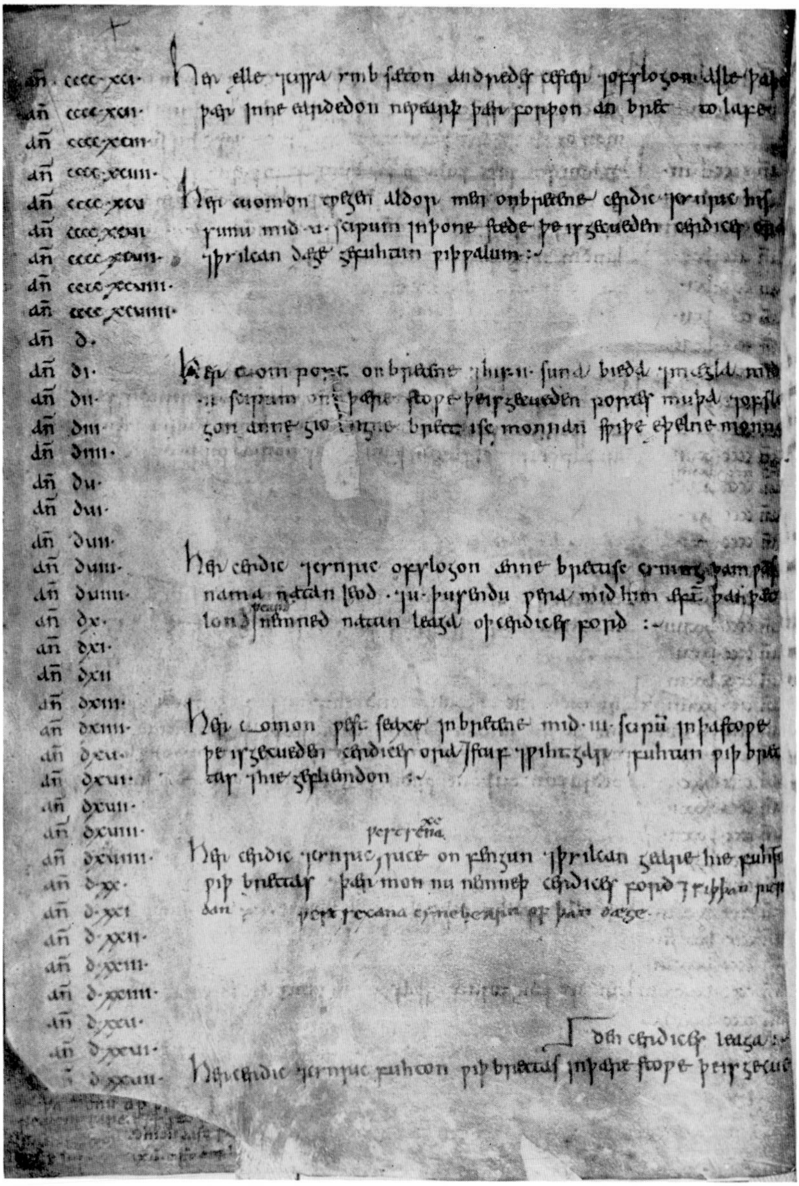

The Alfredian Chronicle (Parker MS.). Facsimile of entries about Ælle, Cerdic and Cynric, and Port. $\frac{1}{2}$

fight can be found either at Badbury Hill, near Faringdon, or at the hill above another Badbury, near Swindon.[19] If this reasoning is accepted, it leads further. The grave-finds of the upper Thames region suit a date nearer to 516 than 493 for such a fight. And Arthur's participation in it? Is this not a fable which has grown from the two facts, that Badon was the one contest mentioned in Gildas, and that Arthur was tradition's favourite leader?

(4) After the siege of Mount Badon we come, in the story of Gildas, to what we distinguish as a fourth period. It was the beginning of a time in which, though the cities still lay desolate and though civil wars continued, the foreign wars ceased. This period of victory, of rest from Saxon aggression, was still continuing when Gildas wrote.

On the whole, the story of Gildas harmonizes well with what may be inferred from the cemeteries. We see that the invaders had, early in the sixth century at latest, thrust themselves far up the valleys on the east side of Britain. It is likely enough that the years following Mount Badon were a period when the Saxons were mainly occupied in making good the footing they had already obtained.

This peaceful period lasted long enough for the generation which had been eyewitnesses of the earlier desolation to die out. Looking back at the previous age it seemed to Gildas that, in the bygone generation, owing to the remembrance of those troubles, the kings, the public officials, the private men, the priests and ecclesiastics, had all done their duty.

(5) But in the middle of the sixth century when he wrote, a new generation had grown up, which knew nothing of the past storm and had only experienced the existing peace. Accordingly, in the age in which Gildas flourished, truth and justice were subverted—or so it seemed to him—by his countrymen, and there were very few of them who were not gaily rushing down to hell.

The above five periods of Gildas make up what we may call

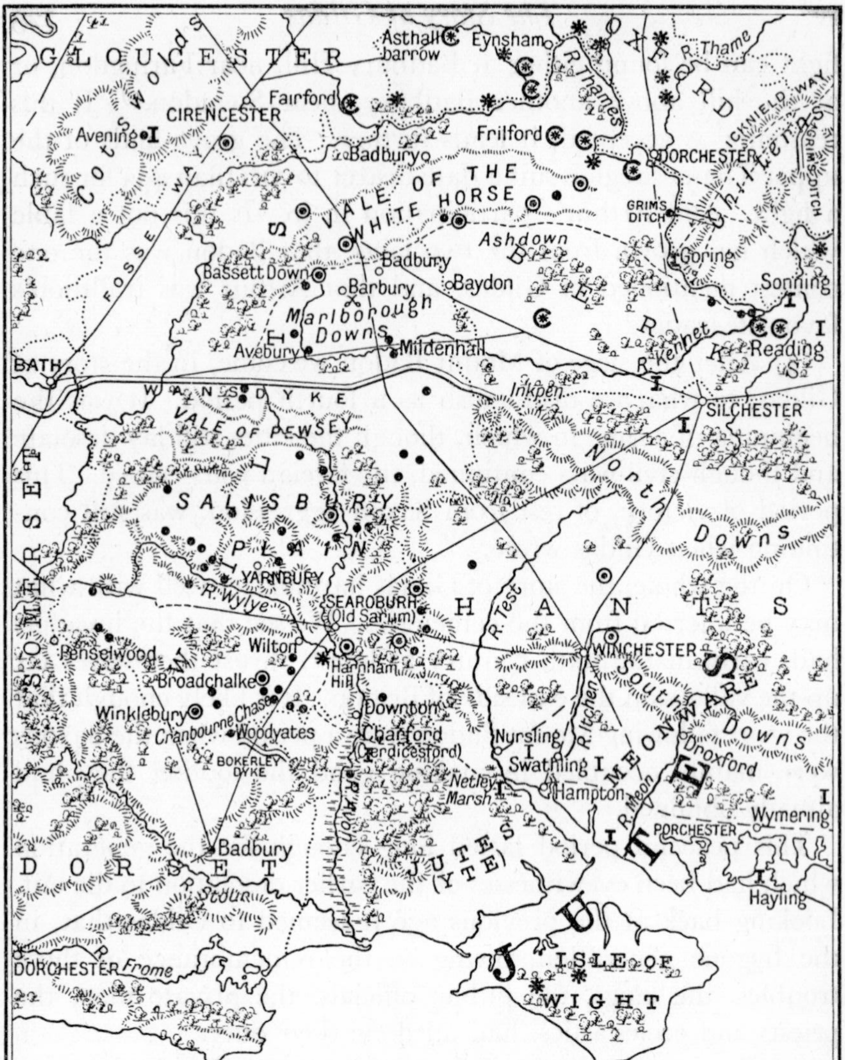

BEGINNINGS OF WESSEX

Scale of English Miles

0 5 10 20 30

REFERENCE

- ● *indicates a Saxon burial (often in a barrow)*
- ◎ „ *an ill-furnished cemetery of the Saxon type.*
- ✱ „ *a well-furnished cemetery either of the Thames-valley or of the Jutish type.*
- C „ *a burial-place with traces of cremation.*
- I *indicates a place-name ending in -ingas*
- ——— *Roman roads, course certain.*
- — — — „ „ „ *uncertain.*
- - - - - - *Old track ways.*
- .... *Modern County boundaries.*
- *Woodland*

STANFORD'S GEOG. ESTAB., LONDON

'the first stage' of the Saxon Conquest. The beginning is fixed by the appeal to Aëtius, whose third Consulship we know to have fallen in the year 446. The final date is approximately fixed by the fact that Gildas was writing shortly before the death of Mælgwn (Maglocunus), king of Gwynedd—an event which (according to the *Annales Cambriae*) occurred in 547, or 549, when Britain was swept by one of the periodic plagues which visited the island. From 446 to 547 is a century of shifting, dangerous chronology—a great slough to discourage the student of English history at the beginning of his pilgrimage. A slough, however, is not the best simile; though it is better than that of Professor Lot,[20] who calls the age 'a blank page'. Let us rather resume our earlier idea and remember that in the complex of problems before us many are soluble.

THE BEGINNINGS OF THE WEST SAXON MONARCHY

Any one looking at a map in which the heathen cemeteries of the Anglo-Saxons are marked, will at once observe that there are three large areas where the invaders might have been expected to settle, but where in fact there is little or no evidence of their settlement. The first of these areas almost bare of recorded Germanic cemeteries which we propose to investigate is the territory lying between the upper Thames valley and the Channel, that is, roughly speaking, our counties of Hampshire and Wiltshire. The subject is of peculiar interest because we have numerous entries in the Alfredian Chronicle which profess to give something like a story of those settlements, and this story is often said to be at variance with the archaeological evidence.

Our approach to the subject must be through the Chronicle. Let us first read a sentence or two from the genealogy of Alfred's ancestors which was inserted as a preface by Alfred or his helpers.

'In the year when 494 winters had passed from the birth of Christ, Cerdic and Cynric his son landed at Cerdices-ora with five ships. Cerdic was Elesing [the son of Elesa].'

The descent from Woden is then given, the most noteworthy name being that of the great-grandfather of Cerdic, Gewis, the eponymous hero of the Gewisse, the West Saxons.

'And about six years after they landed, they took the kingdom of the West Saxons, and they were the first kings who took the land of the West Saxons from the Britons. And he [Cerdic] had the kingdom for sixteen years, and when he died his son Cynric succeeded and held the kingdom for seventeen winters. . . .'

Turning to the annals we find (cf. Plate 25) these entries:

'495. Two ealdormen [war-leaders] came to Britain, Cerdic and Cynric his son, with five ships, at the place which is called Cerdices-ora, and the same day they fought against the Britons.

'501. Port came to Britain and his two sons, Bieda and Mægla, with two ships, at the place which is called Portsmouth, and they slew a young British man, a man of very noble birth.

'508. Cerdic and Cynric slew a British king, named Natanleod, and five thousand men with him. And afterwards the land was called Natan-leaga up to Cerdicesford.

'514. The West Saxons, Stuf and Wihtgar, came to Britain with three ships, in the place which is called Cerdices-ora; and they fought against the Britons, and put them to flight. . . .

'519. Cerdic and Cynric succeeded to the kingdom, and the same year they fought against the Britons where it is now called Cerdicesford.

'527. Cerdic and Cynric fought against the Britons in the place which is called Cerdices-leaga.

'530. Cerdic and Cynric took the Isle of Wight, and slew a few men in Wihtgaræsburh.

'534. Cerdic died, and his son Cynric continued to reign for twenty-six winters: and they gave the Isle of Wight to their two grandsons [or nephews] Stuf and Wihtgar. . . .

'544. Wihtgar died and was buried at Wihtgaraburh.'

Two subsequent entries about fights of Cynric will come in more appropriately at a later point in the story.

There may well be differences of opinion on the question how far the Alfredian editor had earlier material before him when he wrote the above annals. The forms of some of the names appear to be antique: Wihtgaraburh, for instance, almost certainly contains an archaic genitive singular; and *leag* is said to be used in the primitive sense of a 'wood' instead of the later sense of a 'field' or 'clearing in a wood'.[21] Again, the fact that the editor conflates two discrepant versions of the story—a landing in 495 and a landing in 514—shows that he is incorporating with honesty, though with little skill, narratives which were already put on record. There is a stronger case for considering the preface to be early, since there are philological reasons for thinking that the names of its genealogy had been written down 'as early as the eighth century, probably before A.D. 750'.[22] This line of argument would carry back the tradition to at least the early eighth century. But even that leaves too long an interval for the handing down of accurate details.

The transparent blunders made by the chronicler have long been notorious. Port, perhaps a genuine Saxon hero, was connected with Portsmouth by some ingenious antiquary who did not realize that the prefix of that place-name was derived from the Latin word *portus*, a harbour. Though Wihtgar may also be a genuine Germanic name, there is a suspicious resemblance between the initial syllable of his name and that of Vectis, the Roman name for the Isle of Wight.[23] Natanleod may be another fictitious personage.

Are we then to give any credence to Cerdic when he is found in this shady company? In recent years historians have regarded the existence of Cerdic with suspicion owing to his Celtic name. This scepticism is a natural rebound from the extreme credulity of the Victorians, and notably of J. R. Green. On the strength of the annals which we have quoted and of the natural features of the country, Green described in a long and vivid narrative exactly what happened in this advance; 'as if he had been present at the landing of the Saxons, and had watched every step of their subsequent progress'.[24] The picturesque imaginings of J. R. Green have been long discredited. At the present day it is more needful to correct the bias to scepticism than that to credulity.

Let us then inquire whether anything of this early story can be saved from the critics.

Professor Lot[25] wishes to sweep aside all the entries of the Chronicle, and insists that tradition cannot survive for so many centuries and that the people remember nothing, even of the greatest events. This cannot, however, be accepted as an axiom; a people's memory may be either short or long. Gildas and the Britons clearly forgot within a century and a half what had happened on the extinction of Roman rule. The Scandinavians, on the other hand, can be proved to have carried certain facts in their memories not for a mere four, but for fourteen centuries.[26]

The Chronicle itself tells us so little about the Saxon Conquest, so little is narrated about the heroes of the invasion, that the English cannot be said to have preserved traditions of their ancestors as carefully as did the Scandinavians. But one thing, it seems, they did try to remember in each of the Heptarchic kingdoms; that was, the succession of their rulers. The lists of kings, and sometimes even the number of the years which they reigned, seem to have been carried in the mind like a kind of chant. They were naturally among the first things to be written down on parchment as soon as the art of writing was introduced.[27] In the West Saxon genealogy, though there are discrepancies in places, there is no confusion about the head of the dynasty. All were agreed that Cerdic was the founder of the fortunes of the family. The Chronicle is most careful to trace the pedigree of one king after another back to Cerdic. Clearly a king was not considered to be in the right line of succession unless it could be said of him that 'his kin goeth back to Cerdic'.

This surprising fact should really be another argument for the view that we are here encountering a genuine tradition. What Germanic invader would go out of his way to invent a despised British name as that of the ancestor of all his kings? One thing, and one thing only, could pass such an idea into general currency—the existence of such a founder in actual fact. The modern sceptic says that Cerdic must have been born at a time (about 450) when 'intimacy with the Britons and the borrowing of a name from them seems almost incredible'. Such things are incredible only when this dark period is approached with preconceived opinions. How exactly it came to pass that Cerdic was so named we shall never know, but it is easy enough to imagine a number of ways in which it might have occurred. For instance, the ancestors of Cerdic—Gewis and his brood—may have been Saxon chiefs who cruised in the Channel for generations. Cerdic's father may well have been called in to help some local British leader against his enemies, Irish from the west, Jutes from the east;* it may be, even against rival Britons. Germans in the fifth century were in one country after another introduced in this way. Military service in the Empire had long since been considered a reputable life for a German chief and his followers—it was a natural and normal proceeding; nor is there anything unnatural in intermarriage under such conditions, nor anything improbable in a British mother giving a Celtic name to the son of a Saxon chieftain.

Now if Cerdic is accepted as the genuine leader of this invasion, it is reasonable to believe that Cerdices-ora, Cerdicesford and Cerdices-leaga, being well-known places in the ninth century, had obtained their names on account of some real connexion with the first king of the West Saxon dynasty.[28] Cerdices-ora may indeed have been the place where by a genuine tradition it was believed that Cerdic had landed. An interesting attempt has recently been made to fix this place. O. G. S. Crawford[29] revives the old identification of Natan-leaga with the district Netley, of which a trace is left in the modern name Netley Marsh; and since Cerdicesford has always† been identified with Charford on the Avon, it is likely enough that Cerdices-ora was in the neighbourhood of Netley Marsh, at the top of Southampton Water. It is claimed that even the road by which

* But cf. note on p. 382 *b*. † Ever since Ethelweard. Cf. *M.H.B.* 503.

Cerdic advanced can be identified by an air photograph which shows an ancient track leading from Southampton Water to Charford.

Now the fact that the chronicler did find two other place-names formed with the name of the reputed founder of the West Saxon dynasty apparently not far from Charford has definite significance. The bad guesses which he made about Port and Natanleod do not in themselves put this other guess about Cerdic out of court. The author of the Chronicle was in a better position than we are to speculate about the history of Cerdic, since he knew of three place-names embodying Cerdic's name. It does not follow that because we suspect half, or more, of these entries we must needs reject the remainder. The dates, the number of the ships, and many other details are clearly dubious. They may be mere speculations. The entries about the Isle of Wight may be echoes of some rivalry of the seventh century between West Saxons and Jutes. About these things scepticism is justified. But we turn our backs on the truth if we deny the existence of Cerdic and do not see that the place-names go some way to justify the Alfredian theory that Cerdic's invasion occurred in this southern borderland of Hampshire and Wiltshire.

Other objections which have been raised to the story contained in the Chronicle must be considered. One[30] is the assertion that southern Hampshire was, like the Isle of Wight, a Jutish district. There is no doubt that it was so in the time of Bede; but it does not follow that the Jutes were already in possession when Cerdic landed. The Jutes on the mainland may well have been an overflow from the Isle of Wight, coming in at a later period. Even if the assumption is right that the Jutes had occupied southern Hampshire before the war-bands of Cerdic appeared on the scene, even if Southampton Water and the country to the north of it was closed to his Saxons, it is not necessary to regard his invasion as a fiction imagined by a later age. For the Hampshire Avon was a navigable waterway; it led to the region of Charford, and to the good open lands of Salisbury Plain.

But then comes the archaeological argument which is generally said to be fatal to the Chronicle's story—the remarkable dearth of heathen Saxon graves in Hampshire and their rarity in Wiltshire. According to Leeds,[31] 'the absence of pagan cemeteries south of the [Berkshire] Downs suggests that the Saxon occupation of that area did not materialize before the time when pagan burial was gradually going out of practice'. Now it has been suggested above (p. 85) that the principle, 'No heathen settlement where no heathen grave', is unsound. It reduces the whole history of Wessex to an absurdity.[32]

Our contention is that the Saxons of Wiltshire and Hampshire must have conformed to some of the Christian fashions of their neighbours before they actually adopted Christianity. The vital point is, when did they conform? Was it before their arrival in the island when they were unsettled in their religious practices by a long course of piracy, perhaps by living in one of the Saxon colonies in Gaul? Was it in the early days after their arrival, in times when they were perhaps employed by some hard-pressed British chief against his enemies? Or was it on the eve of the Conversion?

Now the fact that the Saxons of Sussex almost ignored the old rite of cremation and began from the earliest times the new custom of disposing of their dead by inhumation is not without significance. If the South Saxons could surrender the burial tradition of centuries so easily, is there anything improbable in the supposition that another group of invaders, giving up cremation, adopted burial customs such as those which they saw practised by the Britons with whom they came into contact, whether in war or friendship? One need only suppose that Cerdic and his chiefs were clever and adaptable men who saw that the depositing of weapons and jewellery with the corpses was an unnecessary extravagance.

If it is true that Cerdic's people were disinclined to bury with the dead their most precious belongings, we are deprived of the means of estimating their numbers and of following their course.

Most of their graves containing mere bones could no more be identified as Saxon than can those of the provincials be recognized as British. Such Saxons imitating Romano-British customs would disappear from the world and leave no sufficient evidence of their existence. As a matter of fact, Wiltshire can produce one fair-sized Saxon cemetery—at Harnham Hill near Salisbury—a few smaller ones, and many isolated Saxon burials scattered about the district. These last are being steadily revealed by excavation, especially in the uplands to the south-west of Salisbury—often secondary burials in and around old tumuli, sometimes primary mound burials;[33] but no solid argument can at present be built on the evidence either from Harnham Hill or from the other burials of this region. The graves were for the most part poorly furnished. They were only recognized as Saxon owing to the occasional presence of a sword, a spear-head, a knife, a shield boss, a bead, or suchlike.

A clue of a different kind which should be noticed is that an earthen rampart, Bokerly Dyke, was at some time in the fifth century[34] enlarged so as to protect the east of Dorset from raids coming from the direction of Salisbury. There is some excuse for jumping to the conclusion that this dyke, which still in part forms the boundary between Wiltshire and Dorset, was a British defence, and that the enemy in view were Cerdic's war-bands established in the uplands near Salisbury.

It is now time to put together the different lines of our argument. We have first the general probability that a waterway as easily navigable for the light-draught Saxon ships as the Hampshire Avon would not escape the attention of the invaders. Next we have the positive statements of the Chronicle, which in spite of its late date and in spite of some obvious errors cannot be altogether brushed aside; they show that Cerdic and his war-band were located by place-names, probably also by genuine tradition, in the country near Charford on the Avon, that is in the Wiltshire-Hampshire borderland. Lastly, we have found reasons for questioning the common view that the scarcity of

Saxon cemeteries is fatal to the story of the Chronicle; and we observe on the map that this scarcity is in some measure compensated by Saxon burials of a different kind.

We may strengthen the archaeological argument by approaching it from another direction. If we reject the theory of an early occupation of Wiltshire and Hampshire by some Germanic people who quickly ceased to bury their dead according to the ordinary modes of the Germans, the only alternative is to suppose that the Saxons descended at some later date from the north, that is from the Thames valley, as overland migrants. But this migration from the north, if it had ever occurred, should have been marked by a series of cemeteries such as those which we have seen in the Thames valley at Frilford, at Wittenham, and elsewhere. The track of these Saxons across the Marlborough Downs and Salisbury Plain should have been blazed with well-furnished heathen cemeteries. Since we must think that much of Hampshire and Wiltshire was occupied before the coming of Christianity, and since these early Saxon inhabitants left little or no trace of themselves, may we not infer that in their burial customs they resembled the migrants who entered Wessex from the Channel rather than those who came by way of the Thames?

Thus from many angles, but chiefly from the Chronicle, arguments converge to a conclusion very much like the story with which we have been long familiar in the Victorian histories. It is like; but it is not the same. While we accept the main tradition of the Chronicle, we reject many of its details. We no longer believe, as did J. R. Green, that the county boundaries of Hampshire mark the line which the invaders had reached when their advance was arrested for thirty years by the victory of the Britons at Mount Badon. That battle is rightly, as we have already seen, out of the picture. If it was an attempt of the Britons to stem the main advance of the Saxons up the Thames valley, it naturally found no place in the traditions of the small community which had established itself round Salisbury.

Leaving the beginnings of Saxon Hampshire[35] as one of the

pages which are almost blank in our island's history, let us continue to piece together the existing fragments of information about the Saxon community in the valley of the Avon. The two short annals of the Chronicle which profess to give facts from the last years of Cynric's long—indeed, incredibly long[36]—career are the following:

> 'A.D. 552. Cynric fought against the Britons at the place which is called Searoburh [Old Sarum] and put the Britons to flight.
>
> 'A.D. 556. Cynric and Ceawlin fought against the Britons at Beranburh.'

Since Old Sarum is within, or at any rate quite close to, the district which we have taken to be the core of Cerdic's kingdom, it is reasonable to suppose that in the battle of 552 the Saxons were on the defensive. But if the fight of 556 is rightly located at Barbury camp[37] near the highest part of the Marlborough Downs, overlooking the valley of Swindon, we must infer that Cynric in his last years launched out into an ambitious campaign far from his base. Such an advance suggests that the victory at Sarum had been a smashing one; it also suggests that the Saxons had already overrun Salisbury Plain up to its northern edge. The expansion had now begun which was in time to give the dynasty of Cerdic predominance in the Thames valley, and ultimately the rule over all the English.

Before we leave the obscure beginnings of these men who first among Englishmen marched and fought on the soil of England under the command of the founders of our present monarchy, we must take note of evidence which is perhaps the most interesting of any which has been produced in recent years: that is, of the results obtained for the historian by the miracle of modern air photography. Our thanks are due to O. G. S. Crawford, who has put the miracle to good use.[38] The air photographs which he has published reveal to us the roads, villages, and fields of the Celtic inhabitants of southern Britain in the days before the coming of the Saxons (cf. Pl. 8). These photographs demonstrate that the settlements of the Britons round Salisbury were placed almost invariably on the crests or higher slopes of the hills. Their upland villages, set among more or less rectangular fields, are in every way differentiated from the Saxon villages which in time took their place—these villages of ours which are still to be found in the valleys close to the rivers. Crawford claims that in not a single instance did any British village remain inhabited after the Saxon Conquest.

> 'Their sites were abandoned and may often be seen to-day exactly as they were left, though now of course a maze of grass-covered mounds. We do not know of course what happened during that century and a half of darkness and confusion; but when the dawn broke through once more, we find a totally new system, Teutonic in character and differing in every way from its predecessor. New villages with new Saxon names have sprung up along the valleys; the once populous uplands are deserted; the Celtic fields, now grass-grown, have reverted to grass, thick scrub, or forest. The boundaries of the new "manors" disregard the old field system entirely.'

The change from the hill-villages of Romano-British times to the compact valley settlements of the Saxon period is one of the fundamental facts in our period. But how is it to be explained? Does it necessarily mean that the Saxon intruders into these 'hills of sheep and howes of the silent races', these beautiful chalk uplands of Salisbury Plain, were superlatively ruthless and destructive? That is a possibility; but not the only possibility. When we know little about a period we are always inclined to exaggerate its catastrophic features. The destruction of the Celtic villages need not have been sudden and remorseless. The plantation of Saxon villages in the valleys was certainly a slow process, of which a mere beginning can have been made in the heathen period. Indeed the Saxon practice of burying their dead in or near old tumuli on the hills may mean that there was a phase when they themselves were hill-dwellers before they cleared the land near the rivers and settled down to plough the heavy soils of the valleys. It is conceivable that when a well-watered site for a village came to be preferred to the high and dry uplands, the Celtic inhabitants of the hill-tops may have been induced by fair means as well as foul to come down from their old settlements. The inhabitants who clung to the hills would be a prey for violent men. Even if the Saxon thegn did not reduce the Celts of his neighbourhood to serfdom, the latter might think it desirable to seek his lordship and put themselves under his protection. For whatever reason, the change of fashion became complete.* Since the peasantry of Wiltshire are said to have a high ratio of brunettes (see map, p. 171), it does not seem likely that the Britons of this district were massacred or driven out with any special ruthlessness by the invaders.

One subject remains about which historians who are not prepared to surrender the early Chronicle *in toto* must be ready to meet the arguments of archaeologists. Was the Wansdyke—the massive earthwork which extended from Inkpen near Newbury almost to the Severn—thrown up by the Britons to repel Saxon aggression? (Pl. 26 B.) The existence of a ditch on the northern face of the dyke proves that it was intended as a defence against an enemy from the north. Excavations of the dyke have indicated that the men who made it were using Roman pottery and wearing Roman boots which left a hobnail behind them. It is therefore thought to be either a late provincial-Roman or an early post-Roman work, perhaps the last great effort of the Britons to save the south-west of the island from Saxon barbarism.[39]

Until the early Chronicle is proved to be mere fiction, historians may well continue to place some, though not complete, reliance on its general story. And they must therefore believe that the Wansdyke was either made at different times or that it was constructed, as Sir Charles Oman has argued, to mark the boundary of one British kingdom against another.

Unless some view like this which we have outlined in the present section is accepted, it is impossible to reconcile the

* There seems to have been a Celtic drift from the hills to the valleys apart from Saxon compulsion since there are some signs of it even in Wales.

A. An ancient downland trackway

B. Course of the Wansdyke over the Marlborough Downs (St. Anne's Hill)

PLATE 27

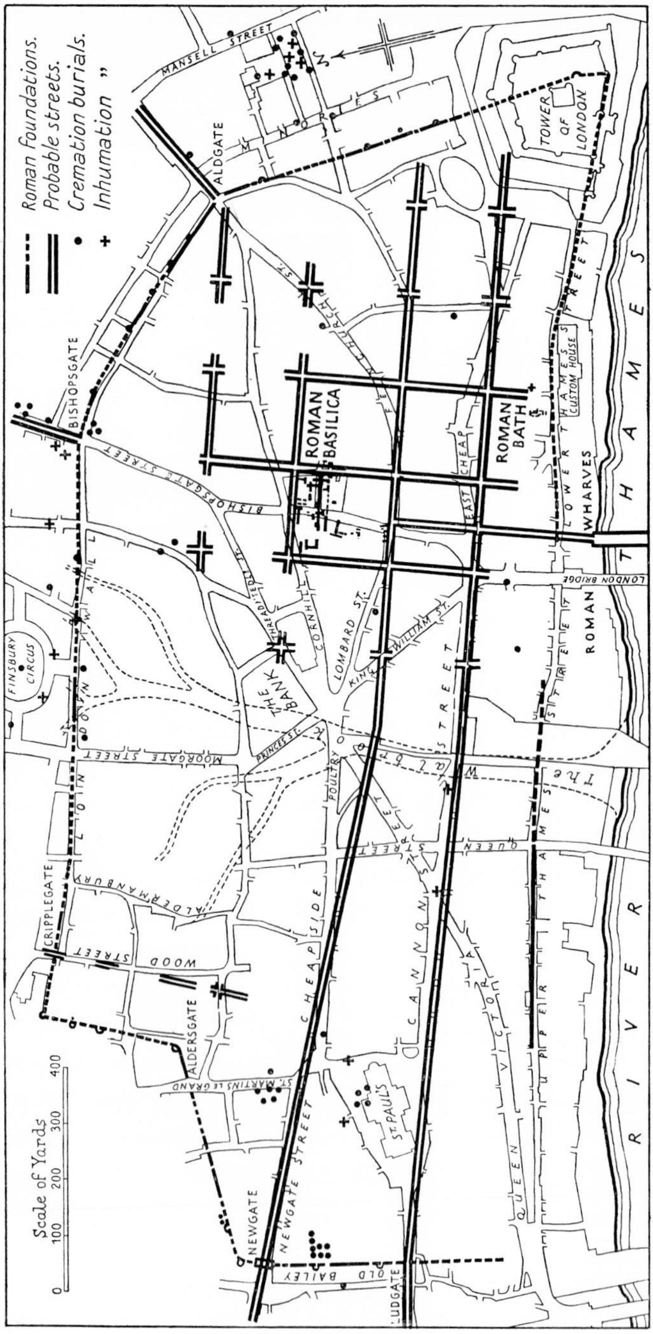

Plan of London, showing lines of Roman streets and walls

evidence of the Chronicle and that of the graves. It is indeed possible to hold that in the period which we have been studying the entries of the Chronicle are mere fiction. But the balance of probabilities is against that view. These early entries cannot be jettisoned without impairing the story of Ceawlin which follows. The misty legends about the origin of the West Saxon dynasty and its first petty conflicts in the borderlands of Hampshire and Wiltshire still deserve a place in our history. The war-bands of Cerdic's family were being trained for the great forward movement which, in the second half of the sixth century, was to change the whole situation.

THE FATE OF LONDON AND ITS HINTERLAND

We have now to investigate the dearth of archaeological evidence for early Saxon settlement in the country round London. Here we have not isolated burials instead of cemeteries. The absence of heathen graves is almost complete.

To appreciate this fact let us examine in some detail the few finds which have come to light. In London itself the chief early Saxon relics (39 A) cast up have been a buckle outside the Roman walls and a brooch from Thames Street, dropped possibly by a trader or a migrant breaking his journey up the river. Down the Thames on the northern bank no burials have been recorded except some discovered in 1923 near Southend.[40] These show that Jutish influence could be exerted across the Thames towards the end of the heathen period, but they have no bearing on the early history of Essex. Besides this nothing Saxon has been unearthed except some spear-heads found at Witham and some possibly Saxon graves found near Shoeburyness. These were arranged in a circle—an unusual plan for Saxons, but not unique. However, an isolated burial of this kind is without clear significance.

To the north-east of London there are only one or two burials of the late sixth or of the seventh century, until round Colchester we come to cemeteries which seem to mark one of the first settlements of the East Saxons. To the north of London there have been no pagan Saxon finds either late or early. To the north-west there has been little or nothing until the country of the Icknield Way is reached, and though this is within about thirty miles of London it is really outside the London region; the cemeteries of the Icknield Way have their own story to tell—a story which has no relation to London. Circling round to the west we still find no trace of these early invaders; a barrow at Taplow displayed the remains of a magnificent chieftain—but a chieftain who lived long after the Conquest.

Only at Shepperton do we meet the exception which proves the rule; for from Shepperton have come cremation urns which show that here indeed the invaders did occupy a position on the northern bank. It must be noted, however, that at this point the Thames makes its farthest bend to the south. The Shepperton cemetery may therefore not unfairly be assigned to the branch of the invaders who elsewhere, as in the Croydon area, thought well to keep the Thames between themselves and London.

We see then that with this one exception and the doubtful burials at Shoeburyness the country round London to the north of the Thames within a radius varying from thirty miles up to fifty miles was, according to the archaeological evidence at present available, free from early Saxon settlements.

This is the London 'gap'—no small one—in the Germanic occupation of Britain. How are we to explain it?

Shall we say with F. M. Stenton[41] that the discovery of Saxon cemeteries depends on chance; and that it is therefore not strange that in Essex few burial-places have been discovered? Chance of course there is; but the contrast between the grave-finds in Essex and those in the Cambridge region or in the valley of the upper Thames is too marked to justify us in putting everything down to that factor. We must seek for other explanations.

One partial solution may certainly be found in the physical character of much of this country round London. To E. T. Leeds the fact that one-third of the surface of modern Essex consists of London clay and that 'areas of clay-land were carefully avoided by the earliest settlers' is the chief explanation for the 'extraordinarily disappointing' results of archaeology in Essex.[42] Moreover, the marshes which to the east stretched down the Thames and up the Lea impeded an enemy advancing from that direction, while dense forest was almost continuous from the Essex marshes to Buckinghamshire and southern Hertfordshire, and only became a patchy and open woodland on the eastern slopes of the Chilterns. The London area was thus screened from the invaders who penetrated Britain from the Ouse and the Cam; and the Essex clay and the woodlands, effective as physical barriers to armies, were even more effective as a discouragement to colonists. But we must not spread our forests and swamps too generously. Even Essex and the north bank of the Thames above London have their patches of gravel; and the forests round London were never such an extensive tract as the famous Andredsweald round Sussex. The great Roman cities of Colchester, London, and Verulam must have had in their neighbourhood some agricultural land to supply their wants. In Roman times the villas and farms in this area, few and poor though they mostly were, might have been expected to tempt barbarians who entered the island by way of the Thames; yet except near Colchester there is no outward sign that the invaders squatted on these agricultural lands as, south of the Thames, they settled in the Romanized district round Croydon.

We are driven, therefore, to contemplate the possibility that there was another reason, apart from the clay and woodland, for the distaste felt by the invaders for this region. It looks as if there was something repellent to them in the proximity of London. And what else can this something have been except the survival of a Romano-British population in and around London itself, and if in London, why not also in Verulam or Camulodunum?

This is a question to which Haverfield, writing in 1911 from the point of view of Roman archaeology, returned an emphatic negative. 'Nothing has been found', he said,[43] 'to suggest that Roman Britons dwelt in London long after A.D. 400. . . . London doubtless fell in the early fifth century. Then it lay waste a hundred years and more.' Latterly, however, the views of archaeologists have been modified.[44] Since the question is of great importance, it will be well to illustrate here some of the lines on which it may be argued.

Now, if we examine the grounds for the old view, that London was destroyed soon after the year 400, we find that it rested in part on a literal interpretation of the extravagant statements of Gildas; in part on the fact that the streets of medieval London did not coincide with the rectangular streets of the Roman city; but mainly on the fact that when men dig deep into the soil of London to construct cellars and foundations for city offices, they find innumerable Romano-British coins, pots, and implements, but none which are assigned to the fifth or sixth century.

Let us gauge the force of these arguments. Against the theory that 'London was destroyed soon after the year 400' we may recall the picture of Britain given in the *Life of St. Germanus*.*

The only other piece of written evidence, apart from Gildas, is the annal in the Anglo-Saxon Chronicle under the year 457, which says that 'the Britons forsook Kent and with great fear fled to London'. It is one of those entries which seem to echo faintly some old poem.[45] If the annal is accepted, Haverfield's view becomes ridiculous. It asks us to believe that the Britons fled to a town which had been 'destroyed soon after 400'.

And the evidence of Gildas? Is this decisive against the survival of a Romano-British London? It is said[46] that the existence of British principalities in the south-east Midlands in the time of Gildas is incredible, because this author 'gives us a picture of Celtic Britain which does not extend anywhere towards the east coast'. But the preoccupation of Gildas with the politics and morals of the small British princes of the west is by no means

* Above, pp. 60–62.

inconsistent with a possible survival of British communities in the eastern half of the island, communities screened from the man living in or near Wales by the arch of Germanic invaders which archaeology detects in the Midlands. The Britons, it must be remembered, had not been fused into one solid nation, even though they had been subject for three or four centuries to one external government. There was no all-British nationalism. The patriots of the west had their work cut out in preaching unity and self-control to the Britons of the west. The horizon of Gildas no more included a *Britannia irredenta* in the east than it included the Britons of Strathclyde or those of Elmet.

It is true that certain statements of Gildas, if interpreted literally, contradict the idea of any continuity of society in London from Roman to Saxon times. '*All* the *coloniae* are levelled to the ground by the frequent strokes of the battering-ram.' Yes, and with them the *coloni*, the husbandmen—indiscriminately; and the cities—indiscriminately—are wasted and destroyed. These lamentations of Gildas were written in the spirit of a prophet. In his zeal he clearly does not weigh his words. If we are to take his statements literally, we must argue, not only that London and Verulam and all the cities of the east were levelled to the ground, but no less Gloucester and all the cities of the west. But this is to misinterpret the prophet. His intention was, as we have said, to arouse his countrymen by painting highly-coloured pictures of universal disaster. He does not contrast the east with the west. He speaks of the trade of the Thames in the past tense, but so also does he speak of the trade of the Severn.

On the whole, then, the words of Gildas cannot be pressed to exclude the possibility of a survival of a Romano-British London in this first stage of the Saxon Conquest, and we shall find later on, in the annal for 571 of the Chronicle, a record of a defeat of the Britons at Bedcanford, which points to the survival, even at that late period, of Britons capable of giving fight to a Saxon prince in the eastern Midlands.

The doubtful statements of Gildas have delayed us too long;

for, after all, the views of those who assert that London perished early in the fifth century and lay empty for a hundred years and more, are based mainly on the fact that no remains have been dug up which can be assigned to the fifth and sixth centuries. The words of Haverfield about Bath[47] can fairly be quoted to represent his general line of argument. 'If the Britons held it . . . after their severance from Rome some trace of this period ought to survive. Even savages use pots and pans and live in houses and bury their dead. The Romano-British pottery of the early fifth century would have given way to some newer, perhaps ruder, but certainly distinguishable style.' Here is the crucial point. The archaeologists see no traces of Romano-British life in London from the fifth century onwards, but where do they see traces of Romano-British life? A few grave-stones, especially in Wales;[48] three or four hoards of the debased and minute coins known as minims; possibly some 'Jutish' vases,* brooches, and hanging bowls found in the graves of the invaders. Those are all (or more than all) of the goods which can be credited to Britons in this age. Craftsmanship in durable materials had almost ceased throughout the island, and archaeology once more fails us. Since the provincials who undoubtedly survived in the west of Britain left behind them so little evidence of their existence, the absence of evidence from London, where excavation has been conducted for commercial rather than for archaeological purposes, cannot well be taken to prove the annihilation of London.

With regard to Haverfield's argument that London must have long lain waste because its medieval streets did not coincide with those of the Romans (Pl. 27), such a change does indeed prove that the flourishing city fell on evil days, that many of its buildings collapsed through age and neglect, that the old streets were blocked, and that in time new streets were made over or

* To these must now be added a two-armed, wheel-made pot (Fig. 32), supposed to be of the sub-Roman period (at latest of the sixth century) found at the Bran Ditch (*Proc. Cambridge A.S.* xxxii (1932), 54–6).

round the old ruins to suit the convenience of the inhabitants of a later and more prosperous age. We know that this was what happened in Rome, which certainly was not deserted for more than forty days. Why then should we assume that London lay waste and empty for a century and more?[49]

In recent years there has been more readiness to consider the possibility of some survival in post-Roman London. R. E. M.

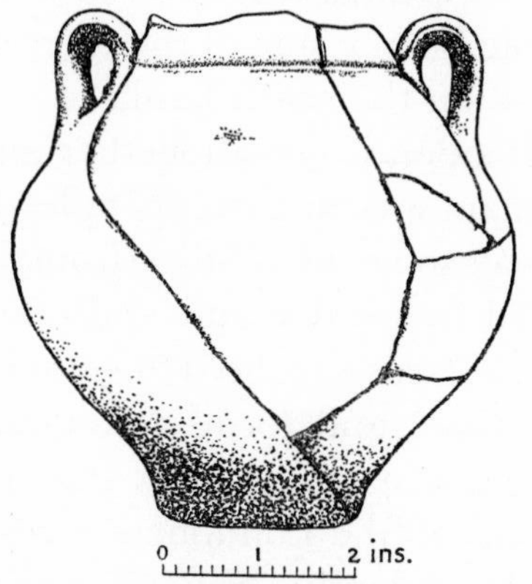

FIG. 32. Bran Ditch, nr. Cambridge. Two-armed post-Roman pot.

Wheeler[50] says: 'It is permissible to imagine their [the Saxons'] small fleets passing up-river beneath the closed gates of a London which may have regarded them with the same wary indifference wherewith, four centuries later, Saxon London often enough regarded the roving long-ships of the Vikings.' Here he is speaking of the decades which immediately followed 410. The London which may have lingered on later was, in his opinion, probably no more than a 'reservation' for the British which 'can have mattered little to any one save to the few decivilized sub-Roman Londoners'.

This view perhaps understates the part played by the remnant of the Londoners. For London was the natural, the traditional port for the Thames valley. It was the natural market for a large though thinly peopled district. Traders from London may have trafficked in such pots and weapons and jewellery as were not home-made. At any rate, among the 320 acres of ruined Londinium some houses may still have remained inhabited, not as the nests of brigands presumed by some, but as the homes of impoverished citizens who, with trade nearly suffocated, struggled on until the city rose in the sixth century from its desolation to be the metropolis of a Teutonic kingdom. If this was in truth what happened, it follows that one reason why the Saxons preferred the Surrey side of the river may have been the existence of London on the north bank.

But the fate of London is not altogether an isolated problem. Its neighbour Verulam was only twenty miles distant; Colchester, a smaller town, was some fifty miles from London; the three had been connected by good roads, and one may suppose that they would have the sense to hold together in the evil days, at any rate for a time, and form a Romano-British triangle. Later they were no doubt sundered by the incoming sea of barbarians. Bede speaks of 'the Londoners'[51] rejecting Christianity as if they acted independently. Saxon grave-goods found in the Roman burial-grounds round Colchester, though they are too late to throw much light on the beginnings of Essex, differentiate the Colchester region from the rest of the province, and suggest that here was a distinct component element which later went to the making of the Heptarchic kingdom. The fortunes of London were presumably linked most closely with those of Verulam, and the systematic excavation of that site should be continued in order to throw the light we need on this dark place of history.

We have taken note of three reasons which can be put forward to explain the dearth of Saxon graves in the London region: first, chance; secondly, forests and marshes; thirdly, the survival of a Romano-British population in London itself, perhaps also in Verulam and Colchester, and in the forest country which formed the hinterland of these ruined cities.

To these possible reasons we must add a fourth: that the East Saxons, or at any rate the greater number of them, resembled the followers of Cerdic in Wiltshire in so far as they discontinued from the first the heathen methods of burial, both the practice of cremation and that of inhuming a dead body with weapons and other gear. There are certain considerations which point to this. One is the fact that Essex possesses quite a large number of those villages with names ending in *-ing* which are supposed to be a mark of early settlement (see map at page 109)—Barking, Epping, Fobbing, Roothing, and a score of others. On the strength of these place-names it is asserted[52] that Essex, like Kent and Sussex, was among the counties first colonized. We might be sceptical if this were the only ground for considering the kingdom of Essex to be one of the early Teutonic settlements. The chronology extracted from place-names must be even more elastic than that which we derive from grave-gear. But we find a stronger and more compelling reason when we turn to Bede. For Bede's story gives the impression that the kingdom of the East Saxons (a kingdom which included Middlesex and parts of Hertfordshire) was a well-established state and that London with its Germanic priests was an important city at the time of the Conversion, soon after 600. It seems inconceivable that the East Saxons could have grown sufficiently strong to dominate London—a city described as 'the emporium of many peoples who came to it by sea and land',[53] unless they had been well established in Essex from an early decade of the sixth century; and it is no less inconceivable that if they were thus established in the kingdom of Essex and practised burial customs like those of the Saxons of the upper Thames or like those of the Middle or East Angles, more traces of their graves should not have been unearthed by excavators. The conclusion then is almost inevitable that there were East Saxons, as there were West Saxons of Wiltshire, who from the first did not use the ordinary Teutonic modes of burial. Whether this was due to the fact that these East Saxons and West Saxons had in any way a common history before they landed in Britain, or simply to similar influences after their arrival in the island, it is vain to speculate.

Historians, both in the Middle Ages and in modern times, have thought that the East Saxon monarchy had its beginning in or about 527.[54] Though the suggestion is not unreasonable in itself, it does not appear to rest on any adequate authority. An interesting point in the genealogy of the kings of Essex is that, unlike the other dynasties, they do not claim descent from Woden, but trace their line back to Seaxneat, a native Saxon god.

Enough has now been said to show how many pieces of the East-Saxon jig-saw puzzle have been lost, and how impossible it therefore is to obtain any picture of the story of Essex as a whole. Negations are indeed possible. We can deny the necessity for Haverfield's assertion that Roman London 'lay waste a hundred years and more'. We may be equally sceptical about Chadwick's guess[55] that Wessex was an offshoot from Essex and that 'Essex was in early times no doubt the most populous of these kingdoms'. Archaeology makes it clear that there was little in common between the East Saxons and the Saxons of the upper Thames.

Our positive conclusions about the end of Londinium and the beginnings of the East Saxons must be few and insecure. On the strength of the annal for 571 we can believe that the forest lands to the north and west of London remained the refuge of more or less independent Britons until that date. On grounds of probability we can assert almost with confidence that East Saxons, perhaps with little political unity, had been settled on patches of drier soil, especially near the coast and the rivers, from the early decades of the sixth century (perhaps earlier), and that most of them were sufficiently influenced by the modes of Christian civilization to have ceased to bury their dead according to the old Germanic rites. And if we seek for the sites of these early settlements our best guide must be a map showing the villages with names which end in *-ing*. Some, though not necessarily all, of these were no doubt the centres from which the population of Essex subsequently radiated.

And then between the Britons in the Chiltern country and

the Saxon migrants near the coast lay London and Verulam: but whether these cities remained before 571 in touch with the Britons of the woods or with the Saxons of the coastal valleys; whether they suffered an assault or quickly dwindled into insignificance; how long, if at all, they survived—these are questions on which excavation may possibly throw some light.

ANGLIAN SETTLEMENTS—ETHELFRITH

The darkness surrounding the Anglo-Saxon Conquest deepens as we move northwards from Saxon areas into Anglian. Something has already been said (above, pp. 114–18) about the 'Middle Angles' (the inhabitants of the patches of open land between the Welland and the Icknield Way), who in spite of the appellation Angle are proved by their grave-gear to have been partly drawn from the Saxon districts of Germany. It would be wearisome to discuss in any detail the evidence of the cemeteries for the other Anglian communities. Those who are interested in the early history of these Anglian districts will find the evidence, such as it is, set out in detail in the volumes of the *Victoria County History*.

In the following pages only a few suggestions will be noticed; and it must be stated at the outset that we are entering ground which is even more dangerous than that which we have already trodden. The only consolation to be obtained is that, since any theories can be little more than guesses, every man is almost free to construct his own.

If the reader looks at the map at page 9, he may feel disposed to begin his guesswork by conjecturing that the 'keels' which found their way to the Wash and the north-east coast crossed the 130 miles of open sea from Frisia instead of choosing the circuitous route by way of the Rhine mouths and Kent.

In East Anglia (see map at p. 109), while there are some cremation cemeteries near the coast which may mark early settlements, the most notable clusters of fifth-century finds are near the Little Ouse and the Lark. This may be taken to mean that most of the immigrants made their way up those tributaries of the Great Ouse, following the same course as many of the 'Middle Angles', until they turned east instead of west from the swamps of the Fens. The valleys of the Little Ouse and the Lark, and the flats extending as far as Cambridge, seem to have been the chief germinating centre of East Anglia, the next in importance being the district of the extreme north where the map shows many place-names ending in *-ingas* and cremation cemeteries.

Other expeditions of the invaders crossing the Wash made their way for twenty-seven miles up the marshes of the Witham and its tributary, the Slea, to Sleaford. Here the finding of some six hundred graves has indicated that Sleaford was the port where the migrants landed before they set off for the interior. Farther north, the district of Lindsey (taking its name from the Roman Lindum) may have been occupied by Angles advancing down the Roman road from the Humber. In the genealogy of their kings there is one (Cædbæd) whose name, like that of Cerdic of Wessex, indicates some blending with the Britons.[56]

In the valley of the Trent the boats of the invaders were paddled up-stream through long miles of unattractive swamps. Then from Newark up into Derbyshire a series of cremation cemeteries near the river mark out the core of the Mercian* settlement. Farther afield 'the distribution of the cemeteries', it is said,[57] 'points to a gradual occupation of Leicestershire, Warwickshire, and Rutland, probably along the old Roman roads leading from various points of access on the river'.

Beyond the Humber the heathen cemeteries indicate two main routes by which the invaders found their way into the country of the British Deras†: one a river route up the Ouse to York; the other northwards from the Humber by the wolds. Since the cemeteries round York differ considerably from the burials on the wolds, the two groups of migrants may have been independent of one another—independent also of some minor settlements on the coast—until they were united into a kingdom

* Mercians, OE. *Mierce* or *Merce* = Marchmen, i.e. borderers. † Or *Dere*.

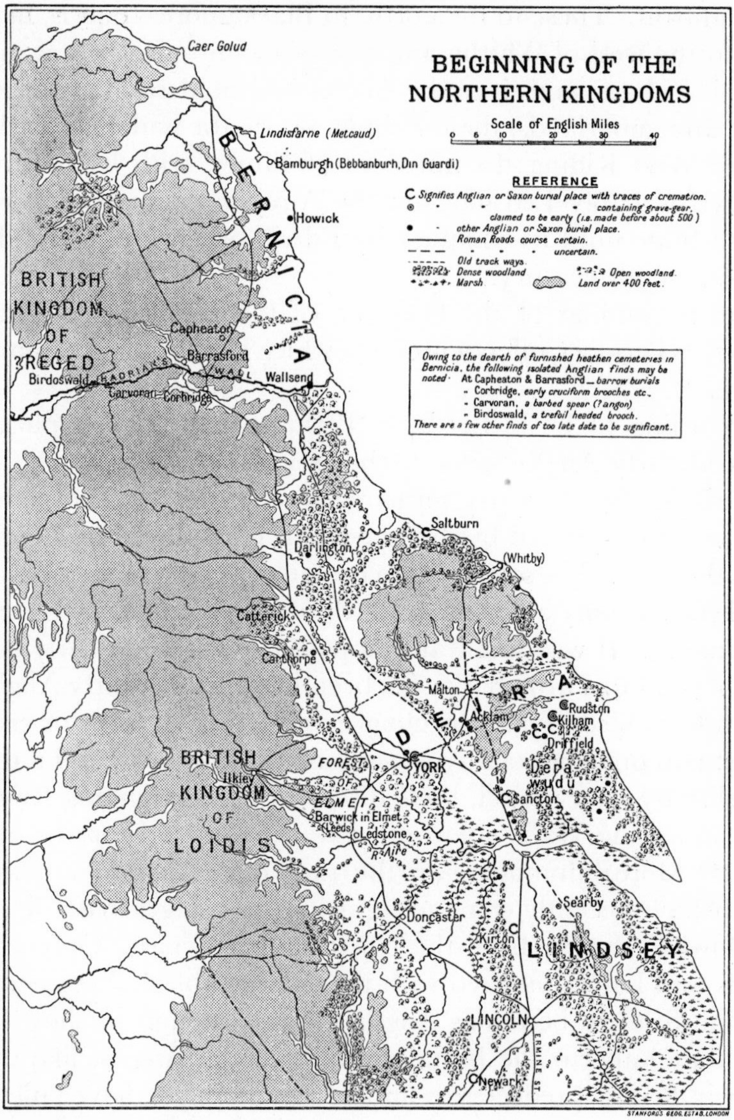

which took its name, Deira, from that of the conquered Britons. Thus a vigorous seed plot was planted in the East Riding. It was surrounded on three sides by Celtic populations. Those in the marshy flats of Holderness were probably few in number and insignificant. Those to the north, in Blackamore—that is, in the hills to the west of Whitby and Scarborough—also only wanted to be left alone; and since the Angles had no desire for unfertile dales and moorlands, these Britons no doubt had their wish.[58] In the West Riding the kingdom of Elmet, with its centre at Loidis (probably Ledstone on the Aire), remained a vigorous British State until its conquest by Edwin of York in the middle of the seventh century.

The beginnings of the kingdom of the Bernices,* generally known as Bernicia, offers a problem which calls for a less summary notice.

According to E. T. Leeds,[58a] 'Perhaps the most inexplicable point in early Anglo-Saxon archaeology is the astounding lack of evidence for the early settlements north of the Tees, which seem to be demanded by the important part played by Bernicia from the first'. The sole Anglian cemetery yet discovered beyond the Tees was only a few miles north of that boundary river near Darlington. It was small and apparently not of an early date; and beyond this little has so far been identified as early Anglian save a few objects found by chance and not in barrows or cemeteries: two brooches of a type assigned to about 500, and a third of a slightly later period, these discovered in excavating Roman sites along the Wall; elsewhere only a sword or *umbo* or other trifle.[59] More illuminating are the traces of an Anglian settlement which have recently come to light in quarrying a basaltic crag at Howick, not far from the Northumbrian coast. Only a few beads and knives interred with the dead enable modern experts to identify these bodies as Anglian,[60] just enough to show how it is that hitherto the burial-grounds of the Angles, like those of their British predecessors and contemporaries, have failed to be identified.

Thus Bernicia presents an even greater gap in the Anglo-Saxon grave-finds than does the country round London or that

* It is noteworthy that these settlers, like the Deras, seem to have taken over the name of a British tribe, the Brigantes of Roman authors. Cf. *Rev. Celt.*, li. 10–11.

of Wiltshire and Hampshire. Once more, therefore, we have to decide a question similar to that which has confronted us when dealing with the other two large districts bare of Teutonic burials. What are we to infer from the almost complete absence of urns or brooches buried by the English who first occupied this tract between the Tees and the Forth? About one thing we may feel certain. These invaders did not come direct from those parts of north Germany which had been the homes of the other Angles. If they had done so, it is inconceivable that they should not have cremated or buried their dead like the conquerors of the Midlands and York. If not from Germany, then whence did they come? Leeds[61] evidently thinks of them as emigrating northwards from Deira about the middle of the sixth century: it is probable 'that the Darlington cemetery represents the first successful attempt to plant a permanent settlement'. From then onwards 'the Angles seem to have been in constant conflict with the Britons'. Since the Bernicians were not only next neighbours to the Deirans, but later became united with them in one kingdom, there is undoubtedly on the face of things a presumption that Bernicia was an offshoot from Deira. But as usual there are difficulties. The union of the kingdoms here produced no union of hearts. Friction between Deirans and Bernicians was to be the bane of Northumbria. It may be said that nearest kinsmen can be the bitterest enemies, or that the strife between the two Northumbrian kingdoms was chiefly a feud between two rival dynasties; but this is scarcely sufficient to explain the unhappy relations which existed between Bernicia and Deira. The contrast is great between their hostility and the solidarity which we find elsewhere when a colony was pushed out from a parent kingdom; the Dorsæte, the Sumorsæte, and the Devonsæte, offshoots from the original Wessex, became the most loyal upholders of the West Saxon State.

The only piece of information about Bernicia which can claim much respect is a well-known passage[62] which asserts that in A.D. 547 'Ida began to reign from whom the regal stock of the

Northumbrians draws its origin'. A seventh-century genealogy carries Ida's ancestors back for nine generations to Woden, but as usual with these genealogies it does not indicate whether the persons named were of kingly rank or where they came from.

Nennius, whose passages about Bernician history have more value than his tales about Vortigern, adds[63] the words that 'Ida . . . joined the fortress of Gua[y]rdi to Berneich [Bernicia]'. It was only about the eleventh century that an interpolation into one version of the Saxon Chronicle[64] amplified the story further with the words, 'Ida reigned twelve years and he built Bebbanburh which was first enclosed with a fence and afterwards with a wall'. We have to go back to Nennius to learn that Bebba, the queen who received the rock fortress of Din Guardi as a gift and after whom it was renamed Bebbanburh or Bamburgh, was the wife of Ida's grandson.*

The year 547 is at any rate a landmark in the rise of the Bernician kingdom, even though there is doubt about what exactly occurred. One recent historian[65] thinks that the real settlement of Bernicia did not take place till a late period, 'when the influence of Christianity had led to a discontinuance of burial in pagan cemeteries'. This view, however, demands miracles—miracles of rapid settlement and propagation—to people the hills and valleys of Bernicia with those Angles who before the middle of the seventh century flocked to be baptized by Paulinus and by the Scottish missionaries.

Other historians go to the other extreme and ask us to believe that a settlement in Bernicia was begun near the beginning of the invasion by Octa, son (or grandson) of Hengist, after an expedition against the Orkneys. There could have been no better way than this of doing what Hengist had been called in to do; but the story, since it comes from Nennius, must be considered dubious, though not wholly incredible.

On *a priori* grounds we may suppose that these districts, being farthest from Germany and occupied by Celtic tribes with mili-

* Ethelfrith. According to Nennius, he was Ida's *great*-grandson.

tary traditions, would be among the last to be settled by Anglian war-bands and that the invasion therefore took place not long before Ida's kingship. If we attempt to decide what happened in these northern parts our views must be determined by probabilities, and by little else than probabilities. We may picture the pirate bands living for a time, as in the Salisbury Plain region, on plunder and tribute, then reinforced by colonies of fighting farmers, strung out along the coast and up the river valleys. The strips of land occupied by these adventurers were narrow and the Celtic natives up in the hills were not far off. From the first the Anglians of Bernicia were essentially borderers. Whether they were fighting the Celtic tribes or joining as hired troops in the feuds of the Celts, or ruling them as tributaries, the two peoples were in close contact. The Angles, who for safety's sake had established themselves on basaltic crags as at Bamburgh and Howick, must have lived a hard, tempestuous life. But they were being tempered by that life to be the northern spear-point of the invaders, and their proximity to the native hill tribes was preparing them and their race for the part they were to play in Christian times as the leaders in a remarkably vigorous Anglo-Celtic culture.

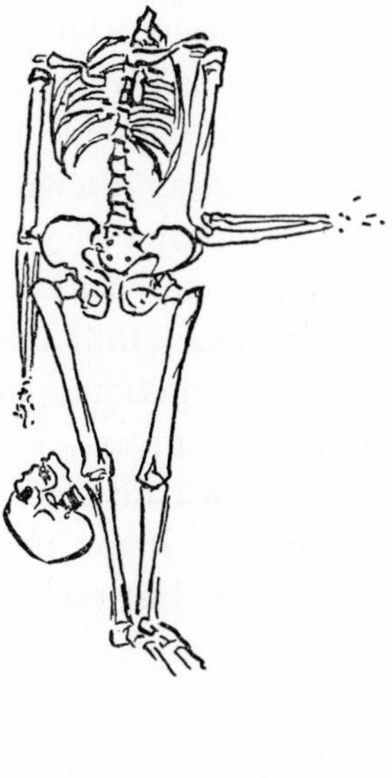

V

GENERAL CHARACTER OF THE SAXON CONQUEST

WE have now seen some of the evidence, chiefly the archaeological evidence, which bears on the opening phases of the Conquest down to the time of Gildas. We have covered what we may call its first stage, the hundred years from about the middle of the fifth century to the middle of the sixth century. On the strength of the grave-finds we may guess that the distribution of the immigrants about 550 was probably similar to that indicated on the following map. If the so-called 'Conquest' of Britain had really been a conquest, conducted on principles of regular warfare, the positions there shown might be pronounced incredible. But the truth is that the event which we are studying was more a colonization than a conquest. We might as well criticize the positions held, let us say, by early American farmers filtering out into the west of their continent, as apply principles of scientific warfare to the Anglo-Saxon migration to Britain. In saying this, we need not subscribe completely to the theory that the Saxons were 'peace-loving farmers'. The violence which accompanied the first over-running of the country may be grossly exaggerated by Gildas, but it had existed. We see it, for instance, in the cemeteries at Mitcham near Croydon and at Girton near Cambridge, where some of the warriors had been buried with extra heads—presumably the heads of enemies they had slain.[1] Regular fighting no doubt occurred locally in all stages of the Conquest. But the Britons were divided politically and socially. If the sense ot common interests was anything like as imperfect among them at the end of the fifth century as it was when Gildas wrote some fifty years later, they must have been incapable of joining in a united campaign.

On the Anglo-Saxon side also there seems to be no firm evidence to support the conjecture[2] that the invaders operated together for any length of time as one conquering host, like the later Great Army of the Vikings. In spite of Bede's reference to an *imperium* of 'Ælle of Sussex', it is inconceivable that the settlements south of the Humber can have been formed by sections of a once-united army. The contrasts between their cultures, the local peculiarities in their burial customs and in the fashions of their ornaments, are too great. Stubbs and Green were surely right in their assumption that the invaders normally operated in small groups. But where they and so many others who have written on this subject have erred, is in speaking ot the immigrants coming as 'tribes'. An oversea migration of that kind is most improbable owing to the difficulties of transport. The invaders must have trickled into the island in groups of adventurers rather than have flowed in with a tribal flood-tide. The cemeteries suggest that throughout the fifth century such bands as had obtained a foothold on our shores were small, and that except in Kent it was not until the sixth century that they increased and multiplied and coalesced until they formed some of the petty kingdoms which emerge into history in the chapters of Bede. This word 'coalesced' better than any other gives us the clue to the story of the invasion. The separate bands of the invaders were much scattered and rarely kept in touch with one another. They scored by the number of their aggressions, by their ubiquity, rather than by the shock of massed attack.

But these are generalizations, and generalizations are things of which above all others we must beware. We see now that the story of the Conquest was more complicated than was ever imagined by the historians who wrote before the evidence of the graves had been well sifted. It is folly to hunt for one master-key to all the settlements. In sampling the evidence from the different regions we have found hints of great diversity: in Kent a band of mercenary soldiers, who turn against their British employers; in Sussex an assault on a fort and a massacre; in the Salisbury district, it seems, a chief whose father had perhaps married a British woman and had given his son a British name; near the upper Thames, whole village communities which intermingle if they do not intermarry with the natives; and so on in endless variety from the war-bands of Bernicia to the colonists who only want land and a quiet life—the furtive immigrants who seek out empty spaces and derelict fields, especially those who creep stealthily into the Midlands through fen-protected waterways. When there was such diversity, is it possible to say that there was any normal pattern?

We may perhaps maintain that the frequency with which spear-heads appear in the graves testifies to the fact that these Germans were still for the most part, as in the days of Tacitus, armed cultivators, farmers who on occasions were prepared to fight, and soldiers who, when they found fighting unremunerative, were able to get a living from the land. The two activities could be combined in the same man, but they could also be separated, and it is possible that even from the first there may generally have been a division of labour; that the chiefs and their fighting retainers were the 'storm' troops who opened the way, and who continued to be the active warriors, protecting the ordinary folk, the ploughmen and the herdsmen. But it is much more doubtful whether, as is sometimes said,[3] the two classes came over in two distinct waves, first the adventurers, the fighting men, and then the farming folk with their wives. Such a plan might well be dictated by common sense, and it seems to accord with Bede's statement that the district of *Angul* lay waste and deserted after the migration. But it is the difficulties of the voyage which justify our doubt whether any mass movement across the North Sea was practicable. And once more we must refuse to tie ourselves to a generalization which claims to apply to all these diverse settlements.

ANGLES AND SAXONS

At this point, since we have referred to the question whether the migration can rightly be described as tribal, it will be well to return to a subject about which something has already been said*—the relation of the Saxons to the Angles. In the text-books the two are generally contrasted as if from first to last they had been distinct and well-defined tribes. In recent years there has been a tendency among the experts to insist on the closeness of their affinities. H. M. Chadwick—on this, as on so many subjects, a leader of heresy—has expressed his belief[4] 'that the invaders of Britain belonged not to three but to two distinct nationalities, which we may call Jutish and Anglo-Saxon. . . . The Anglo-Saxons may not originally have been a homogeneous people. . . . But there is no proof that any fundamental difference survived at the time when they invaded Britain.' Chadwick's view of the history of the Angles and Saxons before their migration is different from that suggested in our first chapter. On the strength of a tradition preserved among the Danes he has constructed a theory that the Angles early in the fifth century conquered the Saxons to the west of them, and that the apparent identity of the two peoples in Britain was produced by a union in which the Angles supplied the ruling dynasties (except that of Essex) and the dominant military aristocracy. Now while we need not follow Chadwick in this last speculation, the evidence which supports the idea that there was little or no distinction between Angle and Saxon is impressive. For example, the terms 'Angle' and 'Saxon' were confused both by themselves and by their enemies—they could be interchanged. The word *Angel-cynn*, which was regularly used in Old English literature as the

* Above, pp. 5–6 and 116–17.

equivalent to our 'English people', included equally Saxons and Angles; *Englisc*—English—was the word used to denote the language of the Saxons; both usages seem to be old-established, even if only found in writings of the ninth century. Similarly, the Angles as well as the Saxons were always called 'Saxons' by the Welsh, and *Saxonia* was the Latin word used by Anglian clerks when they described the country which was known in the speech of the natives as *Angelcyn*. Then, too, in Bede's history the recurrence of the phrase *gens Saxonum sive Anglorum* and the application of the name *Angli* to the Saxons of southern Britain contradict the idea of a radical distinction between the peoples; and modify what might otherwise have been inferred from Bede's well-known passage about the names of the three nations.

Chadwick's views about 'the absence of any fundamental difference' between Angles and Saxons have not passed unchallenged. It has been pointed out that the names of the 'Heptarchic' peoples, the East Angles (*East-Engle*), East Saxons (*East-Seaxe*), &c., and the names of places such as Englefield, the field of the Angles, alike show that the difference between the peoples was recognized by themselves, and that the custom of including Angles under the general term Saxon was a Roman practice easily intelligible in the circumstances of the early raids, and parallel to the later usage which included Norwegians under the term Danes. From the purely linguistic standpoint it must be admitted that the Anglian dialects in England do seem to have some affinities with the old Scandinavian language not shared by West Saxon or Kentish: yet these are mainly in vocabulary and generally confined to the specifically poetical language. Apart from this still incompletely explored matter of vocabulary, the outstanding differential characteristics of the Old English dialects are mainly to be seen in pronunciation.[5]

The archaeologists on their part are usually clear that, although the differences are slight, there are fairly well-marked boundary-lines between the Anglian culture in England and the Saxon. It is true that they have found it hard to determine

A. Wrist-clasps, from Malton, Cambridgeshire. $\frac{1}{1}$

B. Florid cruciform brooch, from Icklingham. $\frac{2}{3}$

C. Girdle-hangers, from Malton. $\frac{2}{3}$

ANGLIAN FASHIONS

Wester-Wanna. $\frac{1}{4}$ *A* Shropham, Norfolk. $\frac{1}{5}$

Wester-Wanna. $\frac{1}{4}$ *B* Heworth, near York. $\frac{1}{5}$

Quelkorn. $\frac{1}{4}$ *C* Heworth, near York. $\frac{1}{5}$

'SAXON' URNS FROM NORTH GERMANY AND 'ANGLIAN' URNS FROM ENGLAND

The resemblances though clear are not complete. In *A* the shapes correspond but not the markings (English urn has swastikas), in *B* the bosses but not the shapes. In *C* the foot, rim, and ornamentation of the German urn are better developed

what exactly were the *differentiae* between the two.[6] At one time it was thought that the Angle burned his dead while the Saxon buried his; but this we have already seen to have been a matter of time and circumstance rather than of people. Baldwin Brown tells us that the three main objects found in Anglian graves which 'do furnish us with very distinct *differentiae* between the two regions and races' (Pl. 28), are first, cruciform brooches, both the early types and the late florid; secondly, certain small clasps which were worn at the wrist, for holding together the sleeves of the women; and thirdly, certain iron implements called girdle-hangers. These last were hung from the waists of the women and were either used like a chatelaine, for the suspension of small articles, or were made in imitation of the keys habitually carried by Roman matrons.

These *differentiae* are certainly valuable; but the lines with which Baldwin Brown and Leeds mark on their maps the Anglian and Saxon districts really only show this, that in the sixth century the fashions on one side were different from those on the other. It is another matter to determine whether these differences in fashion went back to the age of the migration, and if so, whether they mean that all the colonists in the 'Anglian' districts of England had come from the Anglian districts of the Continent and belonged to a people different from the Saxons of the lower Elbe valley and of Hanover. Still less do these varieties of ornaments prove that there was any racial distinction between Angles and Saxons. We have here in fact another illustration of the insufficiency of archaeology to answer all our questions.

Such brooches as have been found in the continental cemeteries do, on the whole, confirm the old view that our Saxons came from the Elbe-Weser lands and that our Angles came from Schleswig or its neighbourhood; the round brooch ornamented with running spirals of the former district is lacking in almost all the Anglian kingdoms of England, while these Anglian kingdoms abound in the cruciform brooch which is characteristic of

Schleswig—that is, they abound in the later varieties of that type of brooch.

When, however, we compare the cremation urns which are so abundant in the cemeteries of the Elbe-Weser Saxons with the urns which have come to light in England, striking resemblances are to be observed between products of 'Saxons' on the Continent and of 'Angles' in our own island[7] (Pl. 29). The subject is one which calls for fuller investigation by experts; but in the meantime it is hard to resist the inference that many of our 'Angles' came in fact from the Saxon districts of Germany. Whether their German homes had been north of the Elbe or south of it, the Saxons were ready to think of themselves as Angles—that is, as English.

If it be asked how this came about, we are not likely to err if we guess that the confusion between Saxon and Angle goes a long way back, that it is older than the Conquest of Britain. In our first chapter we saw Saxons and Angles classed together as *Ingaevones*, and joint members of the religious confederation which worshipped the goddess Nerthus. But was this all? One may observe that there had been ample opportunity for Angles to be mixed with Saxons when, after the time of Tacitus, they turned westwards along the shores of the North Sea. There was a tradition[8] that the Saxons had come by sea to the Elbe-Weser region from the north. Nothing could be more likely than that the region in question should be peopled by oversea migrants voyaging from the Eider mouth, and we have seen that the Eider mouth was 'the window to the west' of the Angles, a window to which Saxons of Holstein as well as Angles of Schleswig could have access. It was thus easy for Angles to be intermingled with Saxons in all the sea-roving and colonizing of the fifth and sixth centuries—not only in the Elbe-Weser country but in Frisia, and again intermingled when they crossed the North Sea and disembarked in Britain, their plans disarranged by all the chances of wind and tide, of uncharted seas, and unmapped land.

If these guesses are near the truth, it follows that the diversities between Angles and Saxons in Britain were largely adventitious. They grew from differences in geographical situation and from different experiences. The 'Saxons' in Britain were among the earlier migrants; their leaders had probably been long in touch with the Empire, sometimes as mercenaries, more often as pirates and raiders. The Saxons were therefore readier than the Angles to give up the old ways of Germany and adopt the habits of the Roman Provincials. The so-called 'Angles' of Britain were more primitive folk, who came to the east coast direct from Germany. Among them were Saxons from west of the Elbe who became submerged by stronger Anglian neighbours. In short, the confusion between Angle and Saxon had many causes: they were originally akin; Saxons could regard themselves as men of Anglian stock, Angles could belong to the Saxon confederation; and lastly, in the course of the migration both folks were often mixed. Hence it was that the differences between the two peoples were only the minute points of apparel, ornament, or dialect, which were doubtless largely developed on British soil.

SURVIVAL OF THE BRITONS

In the next place we must give some attention to the well-worn controversy: how far did the Germanic stock of the invaders come to be mixed with Celtic blood? It is not a subject which need be treated at great length in these pages, since the contributions made to it in recent years have not materially changed the views expressed by the historians of the last generation. There is room for a large measure of agreement as well as for great differences of opinion.

The best way to find the points of agreement is to keep as distinct as may be the three questions: first, was there continuity between the Romano-British and the Anglo-Saxon towns? Secondly, was there continuity in the villages? And lastly, more generally, what proportion of the older population survived?

If we take the first point, we find that here again the problem must be analysed. 'Continuity' may be interpreted in different ways. We may mean continuity (1) of the site of the town, (2) of its name, (3) of habitation by the former occupants, and (4) of culture and institutions. But of these aspects of continuity the only one which as a rule is in serious doubt is that of habitation. Of the others, the discovery of Roman institutions in Saxon Britain is an employment which may be left to those who find amusement in making bricks without straw; the continuity of site is easily proved or disproved by the spade. The question of continuous habitation can in part be decided by excavation, but must be largely determined by inference.

Roughly speaking, three different fates befell these towns. A few, a very few, may have been overwhelmed suddenly. Many more declined—both before and after 410—until they disappeared altogether. But most, and especially the more important cities, seem to have shared the probable fortune of London, that is, they decayed and then revived. Like London, they suffered because the German immigrants, being country-folk, wanted to live in rural huts such as they had had in Germany. They wanted to have their cattle round them, and their fields near-by. The last thing they desired was to shut themselves up in half-ruined houses, constructed largely of stone in an unfamiliar way, ill-adapted for a farmer.

If a town survived, its survival must, as with London, have been due to the fact that its position fitted it to be the centre of what little marketing and trade lingered on. Such places in the eastern half of Britain were Colchester, Winchester, and York; these, being situated on waterways which gave good access into the interior, probably retained some of the characteristics which distinguished them from the surrounding villages, and thanks to an increase in prosperity, they were probably reviving for economic reasons when the Roman Church after the Conversion selected them as the sees for its bishops and restored them to a priority more like that which they had enjoyed under the Roman Empire.

Of the Roman places which degenerated into villages or became mere grass-grown ruins some, like Wroxeter (Viroconium), had failed to make good in the Roman age; many, like the forts of the Saxon Shore, had depended on their garrisons for their existence; or, like Corbridge (Corstopitum) and Caerwent (Venta Silurum), on proximity to a military camp. Some, like Richborough (Rutupiae), suffered owing to natural causes, such as the silting up of a harbour; some, like Silchester (Calleva Atrebatum), lost their *raison d'être* when they ceased to be centres of local government. Others suffered from their position on a Roman road, when the road became the army highway of the invaders, as may be seen from the disappearance of every Roman place-name on the Watling Street, from Verulam to the central water-shed.

With regard to the names of the towns, it is generally easy to understand how most of these came to be changed. We see that, as a rule, the German immigrants could not get their tongues round the whole of the Roman name, but they could catch the first syllable, and then add on to it one of their suffixes in common use. Thus, when referring to Camulodunum, the Britons of the neighbourhood spoke of the *colonia*, the Saxons took the first syllable and added *chester*,* Colchester. Similarly, *Venta* became *Win*chester. In the case of York the change was less obvious; the first two syllables of *Ebur*acum became *Eofer*, the suffix *wic* was added; and the whole, after the coming of the Danes, was contracted to its present form.† In the case of Lincoln the English did better, and managed to connect the *Lin* from Lindum with the *coln* from *colonia*. Altogether there are said to be more than two dozen Roman towns and stations which passed on their names to the German settlers.[9] There is room for controversy about the names of some other Roman towns—those which appeared in what seemed to be new forms in the Saxon period; but now even such a complete change as that of Ratae into Leicester cannot be brought forward as a

* OE. *ceaster* from Latin *castra*.

† Through the Old Norse form Jórvik.

conclusive proof that there was a breach in the existence of the town. For it has been argued that the first element in Leicester (Ligeraceaster in the Anglo-Saxon Chronicle) may represent an alternative British name current at the time of the Saxon invasion of England, in the same way that Legaceaster, 'the camp of the legion', later abbreviated to Chester, took the place of the official name Deva. So too the transformation of the Roman Durovernum Cantiacorum into Cantwaraburh (Canterbury) is not conclusive that the town was deserted; St. Petersburg could be renamed Petrograd and Leningrad without being emptied of its population. The Saxon name for the city supports the theory that the conquerors of Kent were far from being a well-defined homogeneous tribe. They used no tribal name for themselves. They were simply the inhabitants (*ware*) of Cantium, and having seized the old fortress they came to regard it as their own *burh*. The fact that their name for it ousted the old name implies that they were the dominant race, but not that they in any sense exterminated the Britons.

In the end, when the continuity of the towns has been discussed from every aspect, many may be tempted to agree with Collingwood's view that 'a handful of de-Romanized Britons, squatting among the ruins of a Roman town . . . from the point of view of the social, economic and political historian are discontinuity incarnate'.[10] But the British communities in losing their language and their institutions did not for ever lose their souls; in so far as British blood continued to flow in inhabitants of Britain, the spirit of the older race, though recessive, was not extinguished for ever.

We turn from the towns to the villages of earliest England and we put the same questions.

Was there continuity in the sites of the villages?

To this, at any rate as far as Salisbury Plain is concerned, we have already had a convincing answer. The fields and hut-circles of the British settlements revealed by modern air photography were found, it will be remembered, on the top or on the upper slopes of the chalk hills.* Quite distinct from these were the settlements which took their place after the Germanic con-

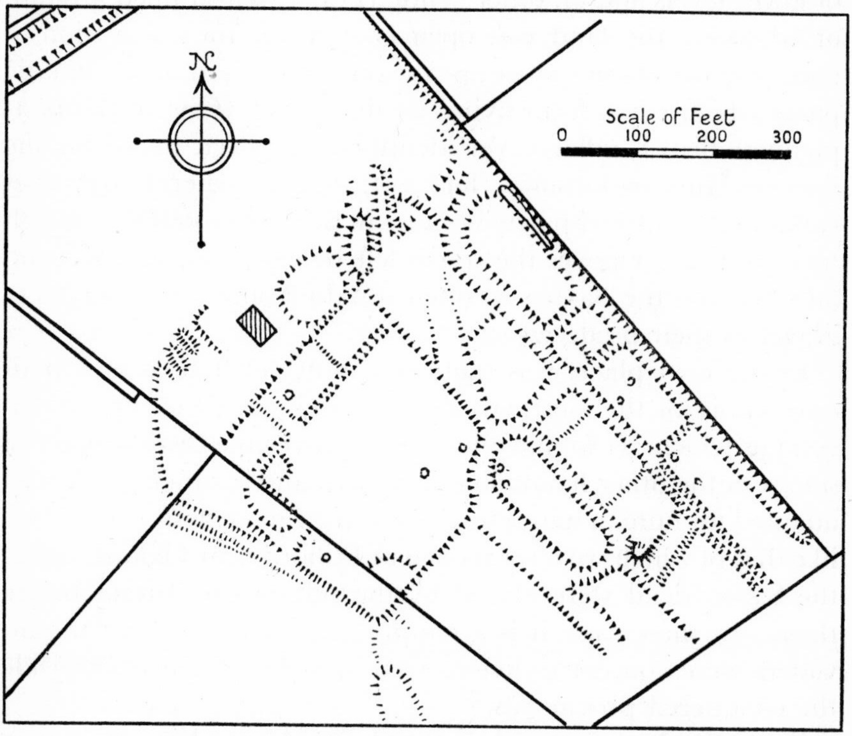

FIG. 33. Plan of Romano-British village at Colne, Hunts., probably inhabited by fishermen and hunters living as near as possible to the fens.

quest, the villages of the Saxons, placed in the valleys near the streams and rivers.

Similar changes have been observed in other parts of England, at any rate in those regions where the surface of the island has been allowed to retain the imprint of its earlier cultivation. Celtic lynchetts, or terraced fields of the Celtic type, have been recognized on the downs of Sussex, on the hills of Wharfedale in Yorkshire, on the Cheviots, and elsewhere.[11]

* Above, pp. 134–6.

It is not of course to be supposed that the Romano-British villages were only to be found where there were hills. Like those of the prehistoric peoples they were placed on the gravel beds of lower levels and on other gentle rises of well-drained ground, or wherever the land was open enough for the cultivation of corn, and dry enough to escape the discomfort and the rheumatic pains which came from living on damp soil. One of the best-planned British villages yet identified has been found on the flats of Huntingdonshire (Fig. 33); but in general such sites cannot be identified partly because in the valley-soils the plough more quickly removes the traces left by earlier cultivators; and also because the Saxons so often squatted on the same patch of gravel as their predecessors.

In the next place, was there continuity of habitation? This question is for the most part disposed of by evidence now forthcoming which, as we have just seen, proves the discontinuity of site. On the other hand, on gravel beds and at other places well adapted for human habitation, there are a good many cemeteries, like that of which we have spoken at Frilford near Oxford, where the Saxon dead were placed by the side of the Britons before them. In these cases it is a tempting presumption that the invaders were content to live as well as to lie in death alongside the conquered provincials.[12]

From the measurement of the skulls obtained in one Saxon cemetery, near East Shefford, it has been inferred that a generation of invading warriors intermarried with the conquered natives and that their offspring revealed intermediate characteristics.[13] This village, however, is at present the exception which proves the rule. Some day careful study of the skulls found in Anglo-Saxon cemeteries may possibly show that what is thought to have happened at East Shefford is not wholly exceptional as it now seems; but in the present state of knowledge nothing can seriously shake the conviction that the Saxon conquerors were not long in the island before they brought over their womenfolk from Germany. Their women are found in almost all the cemeteries, tall and 'long-headed', decked with their Teutonic brooches which only occasionally, as in the round brooches, reveal a liking for some provincial-Roman pattern—German matrons who were as loath to live in the huts of the Britons as in the stone-built towns of the Romanized provincials.

Lastly comes the question, what degree of continuity was there between the names of the British and of the Saxon villages?

The place-names of our English countryside which have been such poor guides when we wished to discover the course and date of the invasions, seem to be our best evidence when we ask how far the Romano-British population in the villages survived. They give us statistics, and statistics which at first sight appear to be almost decisive against the survival of any considerable proportion of the old population except in Cornwall, Wales, and their borders. The general result will be seen with sufficient clearness on the following map. It is based on the results of those who worked at the subject in the nineteenth century. The careful revision of the evidence which is now being carried out by the English Place-Name Society will in time enable new and more accurate statistics to be compiled, but enough has now been done to show that this new research will in the main confirm the old results. Among the counties which have now been investigated by the Society, no place-names clearly Celtic have been discovered in Bedfordshire, Huntingdonshire, and Sussex.[14] In Buckinghamshire only Brill and Chetwode and two or three others; in the North Riding of Yorkshire only about eight, and some six which possibly contain the old element *wealh* (Briton). In Worcestershire, a county which must have been mainly settled in Christian times, the number is inconsiderable. 'Three Celtic hill-names—*Bredon*, *Carton*, and *Malvern*; five names containing British *cruc*, hill, barrow; *Pensax*, containing Welsh *pen*, headland'; Worcester itself, and a few others. In Devonshire 'the total number of Celtic names in the county, excluding river-names, is less than 1 %'. The conclusion of an editor of the

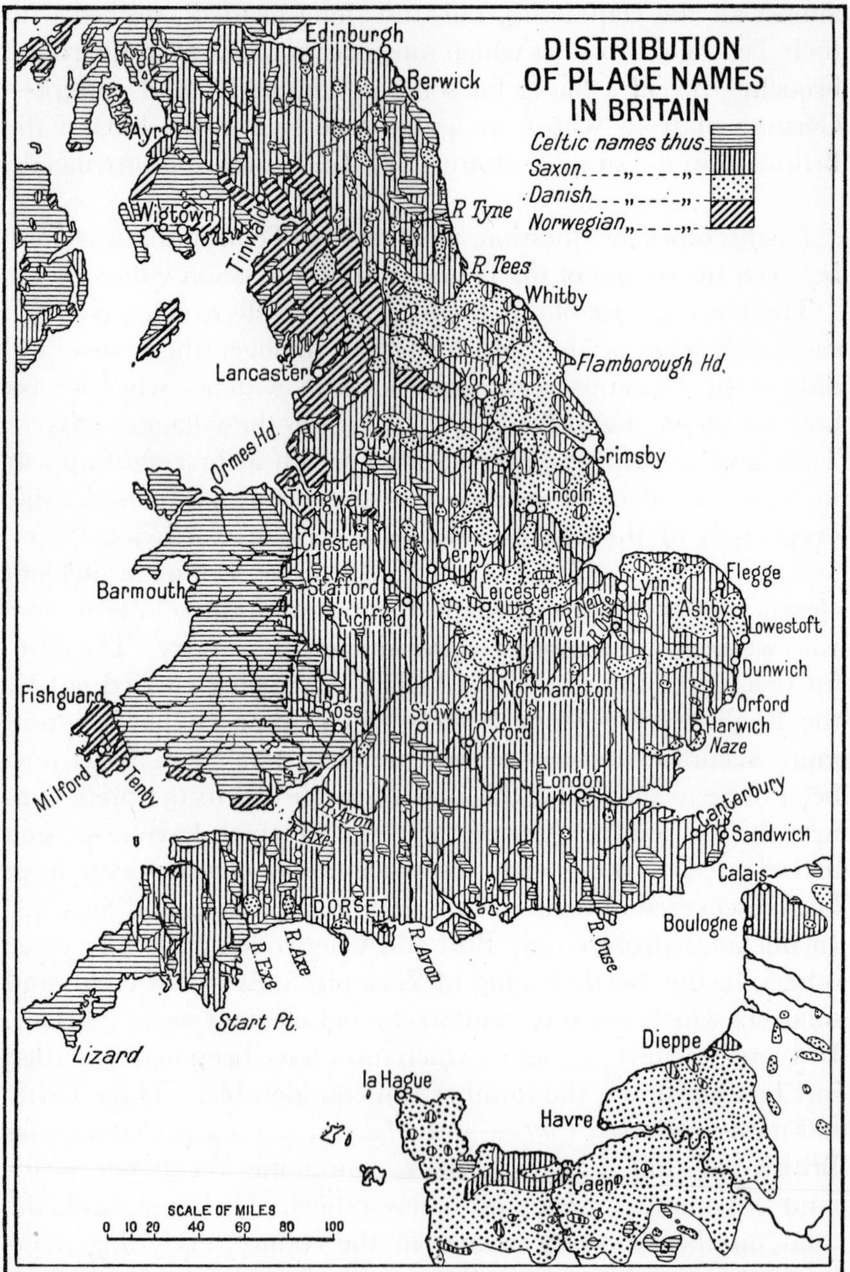

STANFORD'S GEOG. ESTAB., LONDON

Inaccurate in detail misleading in general effect. Arch. Jones.

Place-Name Society in what may be regarded as an interim report on the work of the Society is unequivocal:[15] 'Taking the place-name evidence as a whole, it is clear that in these counties at least, we can build little or nothing upon it in support of the idea of an extensive survival of a British population after the Saxon and Anglian conquests. That view may be correct, but it must be supported, if at all, on other grounds.' Similar results have been obtained from a study of the river-names of England.[16] Even in the east there are of course well-known Celtic river-names like the Thames, the Trent, the Cam, the Derwent, and some of the British names which meant simply 'water, river, stream'—Avon, Dover, Esk, Don, Ouse, &c. None the less, in counties like Essex, Suffolk, and Norfolk, 'the old theory of a wholesale extermination or displacement of the British population . . . may come near the truth'.

Is then the decision of the philologists so overwhelmingly against those who champion the theory of Romano-British survival that they have no chance but to yield? No, the Romanist, though caught in the net of the place-names, can still make a thrust or two. He may say: Your argument proves too much. You admit that counties verging on Wales, like Worcestershire, and counties in the south-west like Devon, conquered only in the latter half of the sixth or in the seventh century, are very largely Celtic in blood in spite of the fact that their place-names are predominantly Germanic.

And one cannot deny that in these counties the change in the names of the villages and hamlets is much greater than the change in the blood of the people, when we judge of the latter by a test such as that of the physical type. Take for instance the case of Devon. Not only have the river valleys their overwhelming preponderance of Saxon place-names, but even in the uplands and the outlying parts, even for example on Dartmoor, where, if anywhere, the Britons must have taken shelter, the newcomers discarded the old names. The editors of the Place-Name Society suggest that this may be explained by the fact that 'In the middle of the seventh century Devon was a sparsely settled Celtic kingdom, and that when once the resistance of its kings had been broken down, no considerable native population remained to complicate the life of the new settlers'.[17] But this view does not tally with the evidence of 'nigrescence', since we see from the map opposite that the statistics for Devon show about as many dark people in that county as in north Wales itself. It is clear that the place-names here are not an exact gauge of the percentage of British blood, and if they mislead us in the west why should we trust their evidence about the east of the island?

The place-name argument is, in fact, two-edged. For consider how it is that Worcestershire and Devon come to be so largely filled with English-named farms and villages. Was it not due to a combination of Anglo-Saxon energy in colonization with Anglo-Saxon intolerance? When a Saxon thegn or farmer pushed his way into British land by force or by peaceful enterprise acquired a new farm, he had little wish to live in the old buildings of his predecessor and he 'had no use for' the unintelligible names used by the natives. He had no use for their names, but he had plenty of use for their bodies. He wanted them as boors to help him in ploughing and as herdsmen for his cattle and swine. To sum up: it is certain that in many of these western districts where English place-names have ousted Welsh, there was no extermination but there was much absorption of the older population; and what is true of the west may in a lesser degree be true of the east.

The philologists are ready to supply arguments from the language as well as from the place-names of the English. The subject is, however, beset by difficulties,[18] and language is admittedly an imperfect test of race. In every direction examples may be found of subject races who have learnt to speak the language of their conquerors. Here it is enough to notice that the one *certain* 'carry-over' in vocabulary from Roman to Anglo-Saxon Britain is the Latin word *castra* which remained in Old

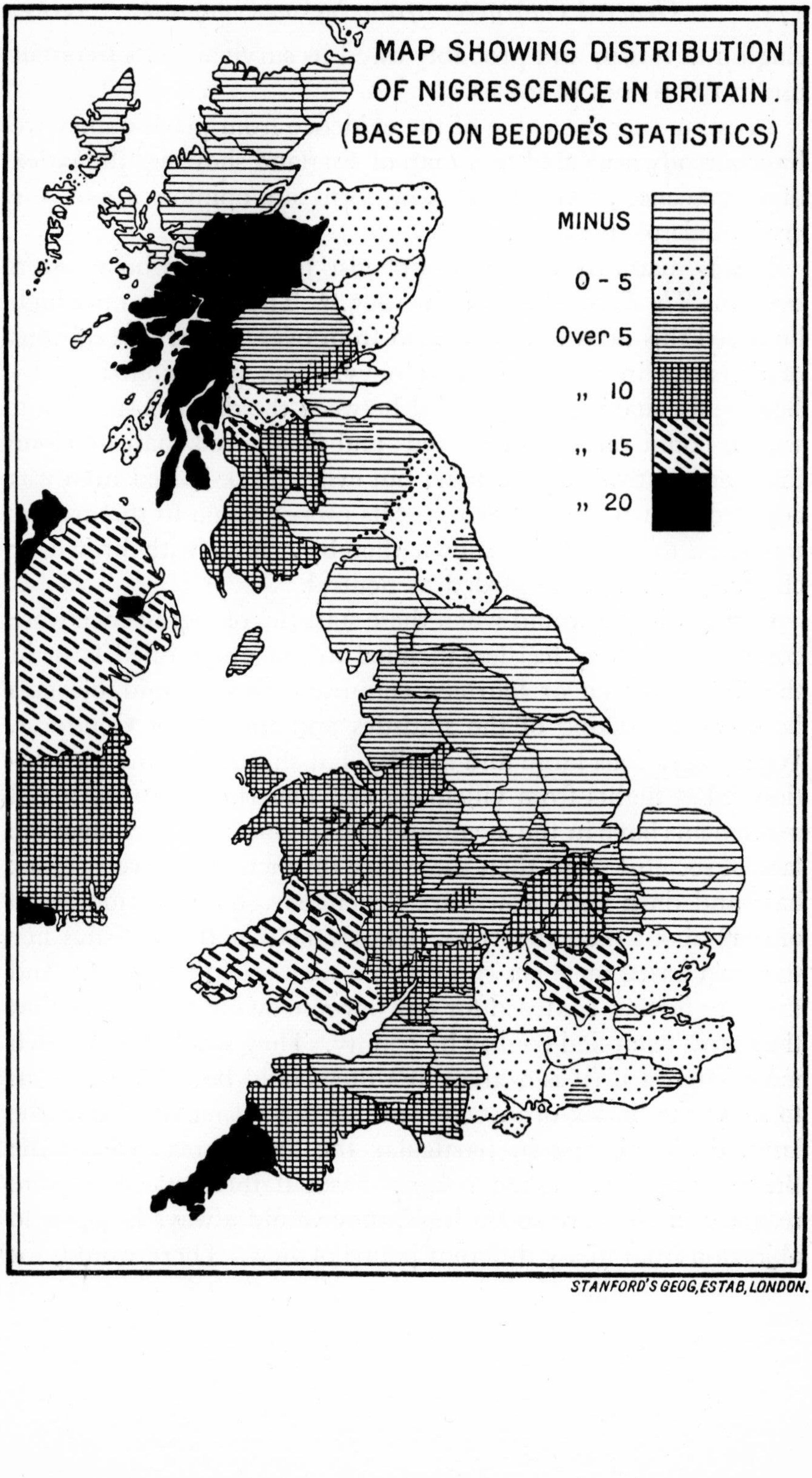

STANFORD'S GEOG, ESTAB, LONDON.

English as *ceaster*, and probably owed its survival to its frequent use in the names of towns.

In estimating the value of the evidence from place-names we have already appealed to a map of England showing 'the index of nigrescence'. We must now form an opinion about the credentials of this map.

It was made by the anthropologist J. Beddoe, who wrote a book on *The Races of Britain* in 1885.[19] The statistics on which he based this map were obtained from over 13,000 descriptions of deserters in the army and navy. The plan contrived by Beddoe for making the contrast between the districts stand out, was to count one for every red- and fair-haired man and one for every man with dark hair; but every black-haired man was counted as two 'in order to give its proper value to the greater tendency to melanosity shown thereby'. Men with brown or chestnut hair were regarded as neutral.

Considering how and when these statistics of nigrescence were compiled, we may feel less inclined to put unqualified faith in them.[20] Thirteen or fourteen centuries are a formidable gap between the taking of the statistics and the Saxon Conquest. What migrations large and small, what shiftings of the population, what flights from villeinage and poverty, what industrial movements have in the meantime worked together to change the face of society! And then these nice distinctions between black hair and dark and brown are dependent on the memories of officers about their deserters. Clearly neither the statistics nor the map based on them can claim a high scientific value. And they are further confused for our purpose owing to the fact that they were compiled county by county. They would be of much more interest if (it is a great 'if') they could be compiled so as to show the 'index of nigrescence' for the *natural* regions of the land, distinguishing in particular the forest areas where the Britons may have taken refuge. Even if these statistics were rearranged on more useful lines, they would always be open to objection from many different points of view. There would, for instance, be the well-known fact that the Celts proper belonged to much the same fair Nordic type as the Anglo-Saxons, and the darkness of the British population therefore must have varied in different districts according to the proportion of the pre-Celtic races with which it had been fused.

It would be possible to supplement the statistics of nigrescence with similar figures about such things as the stature and head-form ('the cephalic index') of men in different parts of the country. Statistics, discussions, and references bearing on these subjects will be found in the works mentioned above. But for our present purpose it must suffice to note the conclusion of a recent craniologist[21] that 'Angles, Saxons, and Jutes all belonged to one homogeneous racial type—clearly distinguished from that of the conquered people by its greater skull-height and absence of a retreating forehead', and 'that the male skulls are of precisely the same type as the female, suggesting that the two peoples lived side by side without mixing'.

Unsatisfactory as it is, Beddoe's map is in many ways the best evidence which now lies before us, and we cannot afford to disregard it. What is most significant in it for the first stage of the Conquest is the large pocket of dark men lying between the Thames and the Fen country. In so far as this dark patch corresponds with the wooded districts north-west of London it in the main supports what we have already learnt from the finds of Anglo-Saxon grave-goods, and what we are told in the Chronicle about the next stage of the Conquest. It is a notable piece of evidence that the counties of Buckinghamshire and Hertfordshire are shown to be as dark as the darkest parts of Wales.*

The reader must now compare with the two maps to which he has just been referred, a third map (p. 174), one compiled by H. L. Gray, to show the distribution of the 'two- and three-field system' of cultivation in England. Meitzen, the leading authority on this line of study at the end of the nineteenth

* But see on p. 382 *d* a criticism of 'the evidence of nigrescence' by a modern expert.

century, believed that large villages co-operating in cultivation on the three-field and similar systems were characteristic of the Germans, in contrast to the isolated homesteads—*Einzelhöfe*—of the Celtic or Romano-Celtic system. Gray's map follows up

Meitzen's theory and shows the limits of the supposed Germanic system both in the west and in the east of Britain. To the west of his line he naturally finds a Celtic system of cultivation. But what of the south-east? Gray is inclined to class East Anglia —more doubtfully Essex—with Kent* as an 'area within which Roman influence persisted', and to mark Middlesex, Hertfordshire, and the Chilterns as a borderland in which Midland Germanic influences were mixed with Kentish-Roman. If Gray's results could be accepted, they would be decisive in favour of the

* See above, p. 93.

view that a large proportion of the Romano-Britons survived in the district which had once been protected by the forts of the Saxon Shore. The map, however, may be challenged on grounds similar to those which make the previous map (that showing nigrescence) questionable. And though the evidence for the Kentish peculiarities can be carried back to Domesday Book and to pre-Norman charters, as has been done by Jolliffe,* his argument that the system was imported by the conquering Jutes direct from the middle Rhine illustrates the difficulty of interpreting the evidence. As a further illustration, reference may be made to another recent theory, which asserts[22] that the village systems are less a product of race than of geographical conditions; e.g. that in regions where there are hills and the water-supply is abundant men can live on their separate homesteads, but that when the water-supply is concentrated in large streams and rivers, men must collect in village-groups by the side of a stream. This is carrying the reaction against racialism to an extreme. For the present, it is only possible to 'put in' (using the phraseology of the Courts) Gray's map as evidence, and to note its disputed meaning.

We see now how imperfect and provisional is most of the information at the disposal of those who wish to draw conclusions about the survival of the Romano-British population. Once more the only inference which is safe is a negative one: that it is not and never will be possible to propound any simple solution of a problem which is itself complex.

If we are to generalize about England as a whole, we cannot hope to get beyond truisms. We can say that three fates befell the Romano-Britons. Some were slaughtered; some withdrew; some were absorbed. Extermination, withdrawal, absorption—these were not successive phases of the Conquest. They were almost equally possible from the beginning to the end of the story.

Extermination, the ruthless slaughter of a whole community,

* Above, pp. 93–4.

had long been accepted by the Germans as a practical policy. Before the time of Tacitus[23] the Bructeri had been 'utterly wiped out by neighbouring tribes'. As late as the year 686 a king of Wessex (Cædwalla) 'endeavoured by merciless slaughter to destroy' all the Jutes of the Isle of Wight.[24] Ruthlessness of this kind was specially characteristic of the Germans, but it was not confined to them. It was a British prince (another Cædwalla) who in 632 resolved 'to cut off all the race of the English within the borders of Britain'.[25] Even in Ireland it was possible for an enemy to contemplate making the destruction of a tribe so complete that there should not be a single survivor. Clearly there is no need to rule out extermination, if we mean by this only a local extermination, as one of the ways which helped to change Britain into England. Heathen Saxons, who had the reputation of being the fiercest of the barbarians, were doubtless ready enough to massacre the Britons. None the less, we shall probably be nearer the truth if we guess that the second of the three fates was commoner than the first; in other words, that many more Britons were driven out or had the foresight to flee to the west or to Brittany than were killed. It seems to be in this sense that the Britons are said by Bede to have been *exterminati* by Ethelfrith, king of the Northumbrians.*

A recent writer[26] has pointed out that the colonization of south Pembroke in the eleventh and twelfth centuries by Norman and English adventurers produced results just like those of the sixth-century Conquest. 'Here was a settlement where the colonists drove out the old inhabitants, where they divided the land among themselves and gave places new names from their new owners.'

Absorption, the last of the three fates, is that on which other recent writers have dwelt with special emphasis. Thus, a Swedish philologist has declared:[27] 'The only theory that reconciles all the clashing evidence is that the Britons were not exterminated but absorbed by their Saxon conquerors. Their civilization

* Below, p. 197.

vanished, but the race remained.' This process was in a sense even more prolonged than the others. It has been claimed that there were Welsh-speaking Britons in the heart of Wessex, for instance in Wiltshire, as late as the ninth century.[28] We all know that the Anglicization of the western districts of England was far from complete at the time of the Norman Conquest, and that the Celtic speech, Cornish, was spoken in 'the Duchy' down to the nineteenth century.

We see then that the problem how far the Britons survived in the first stage of the Anglo-Saxon Conquest involves us in the much wider question, how they were absorbed through the subsequent centuries. These are questions which must not be further anticipated. The truth that remains is that if we are to get beyond unsatisfying generalizations, the survival of the Romano-British population must be treated as a separate problem in each area. In this as in other matters each part of the island has its own secret.

Take Kent for example. We have the tradition embodied in the Saxon Chronicle (anno 473) that the Britons 'fled from the invaders like fire'. The index of nigrescence shows that the countries bordering on the Weald had a low ratio of the dark races. We may therefore infer that the Britons did not flee in very great numbers to the Weald. On the other hand, we have noticed above many small though disputed indications that a number of the older inhabitants survived in Kent: the fact that its potters continued to use a potter's wheel, and perhaps the peculiarities of the Kentish field-system and of the detailed classification of the servile population in the Kentish laws.

Or take Wiltshire; the index of nigrescence shows that many more of the British survived than the place-names of this region would lead us to suspect. The air-photographs of the British villages suggest that the British population in this neighbourhood had been considerable. Here then the inference is that while a large fraction of the population was absorbed, the rest were either massacred or scared into flight.

Take the upper Thames region: here again we carry away a picture constructed on different lines. We see the invaders in touch with the Britons in many directions, living on the same gravel-beds as those on which the Britons had dwelt, and using ornaments which somehow or other reproduce Roman or British motifs. British influence was here inevitable, since within a few miles there existed to the west a British kingdom at Cirencester, and to the east a large pocket of Britons sheltering in the woods of the Chiltern hills; and modern measurements of the heads of village folk round Oxford are thought to prove that the general type has scarcely changed since Romano-British times.[29]

Let us agree without more ado that this question about the proportion of British blood in the population of England demands not one but at least a dozen answers.

THE FAILURE OF THE BRITONS

Our last question is this: why did the Britons fail? How came it that they yielded to an enemy lacking in cohesion and long inferior in point of numbers? To this question Gildas supplies the best answer. He supplies it both in the accusations which he scatters broadcast against his fellow countrymen, and also in his own character. He makes specific charges against the Britons as a people and against the princes of the Britons. Let us begin with the latter. Gildas gives the details, or what he believes to be the details, of the scandalous careers of five of the princes who were his contemporaries. The foremost of them was Maelgwn (Maglocunus), 'the Dragon of the Island',* who seems to have ruled north Wales from Anglesey. He was, says Gildas, foremost in evil as well as in power and in military strength. His misdeeds, it is asserted, were known to all men: the violence by which in his early youth he had usurped the crown from an uncle; his short-lived remorse, which led him for a time to atone for his sins by taking monastic vows; his detestable relapse,

* *Insularis draco.*

'like the return of a dog to his vomit'; above all, the double crime of his later years, the murder of his first wife and of his nephew in order that he might take to himself that nephew's wife.

The other British princes denounced by Gildas resembled Maelgwn in wickedness. One, Constantine of Dumnonia, had murdered two 'royal youths' in church before the altar. Another, Aurelius Caninus, whose kingdom was probably in the west Midlands, was a murderer and a maker of civil wars. Both these are also denounced for their adulteries. Yet another, Vortipore, prince of Dyfed, the region round Pembroke, was even more abandoned; and the last of them is accused of putting away his wife to marry her sister, a professed nun.

Gildas is as unsparing in his general as in his particular accusations. According to him it was the feuds as much as the lusts of the British princes which diverted them from the task of expelling the barbarians.[30] He says, 'It has always been a custom with our nation to be impotent in repelling foreign foes but bold and invincible in raising civil war'. Again:[31] 'It has become a proverb that the Britons are neither brave in war nor faithful in time of peace.' What are we to think of these denunciations? How was it that this patriot came to foul his own nest? Are we to give any weight to his unmeasured abuse?

Plainly we may be generous in discounting the words of a moralist who has modelled himself on the Hebrew prophets. Vortipore, for instance, who in the pages of Gildas appears as a deceitful and foolish king, a murderer and adulterer, is described on a memorial stone as 'the protector' (Pl. 30). But there is enough in the specific charges of Gildas to prove that the ruling families of the Britons were in his day profoundly demoralized. He throws on the screen scenes of wild passion and lust which were being enacted in the west of Britain. That is not all. In the *De Excidio* we see clearly the Celtic separatism of which we have already detected signs in the fifth century. We infer that from the first the Romano-Britons had faced the Saxons as a divided and broken race. It is true that, thanks to the tradition left by the centuries in which the Celtic tribes had been under the common rule of Rome, Gildas can think of Britain as a whole. He can speak of his 'country'. To him all Britons are nominally 'citizens': they ought to behave like Romans, but they do not do so. Part of the twist in his outlook is caused by the fact that he, as a Romano-Briton, is hopelessly out of sympathy with the rough country-folk who remained mere Celts in their thoughts and ways, and with those British princes who in his own day were combining the vices of an educated civilization with a barbarism like that of the backward natives, and thus among the hills of the west were now reverting to type. When Gildas for once in a way wishes to praise and not to blame, his praise takes the form of saying that Ambrosius Aurelianus was 'the last of the Romans'.

To understand the failure of the Britons, we must get rid of the idea that the conflict was one between civilization and barbarism. The educated Britons were indeed the *cives*, the heirs of the civilization of Imperial Rome, and the Saxons were, in the old meaning of the word, 'barbarians', that is, peoples outside the pale of Rome. But the verbal distinction rapidly ceased to correspond to the facts. The tendencies which had arisen in the sub-Roman period became fully developed. The remnants of Roman civilization and of Roman tradition died away.

The stages in the destruction of Roman culture among the Britons cannot now be traced. It is evident from Gildas that in the middle of the sixth century the well-to-do classes still retained some knowledge of Latin; it was of course the literary language of the clergy, and Gildas himself knew his Virgil and other classics as well as his Vulgate and the Fathers. Latin names were still in use in the leading families, alternating often with Celtic names, but by the middle of the sixth century we are nearing the boundary-line where the Britons ceased to be, even in their own estimate, Roman provincials, and disappear as Welshmen into the Celtic twilight. The transition of which we are speaking can be seen in the tombstones reproduced on

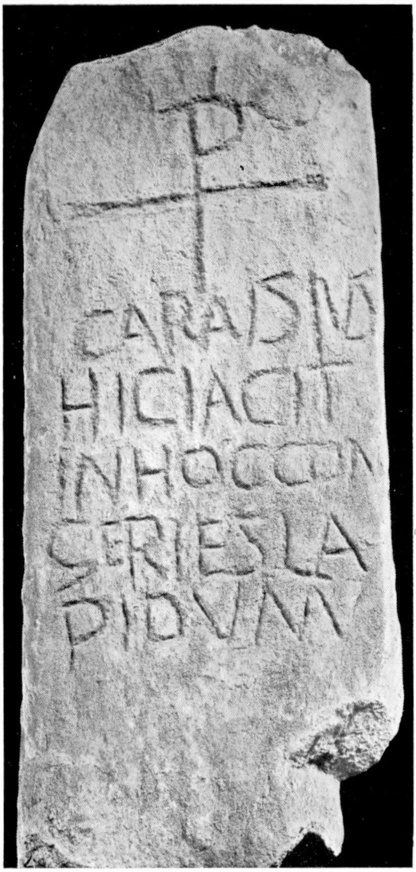

A

B

TOMBSTONES OF BRITONS

A. Of Carausius. Penmachno, N. Wales. Assigned to end of fifth century

CARAUSIUS HIC JACIT IN HOC CONGERIES LAPIDUM

B. Of Vortipore. Now in Carmarthen Museum. About A.D. 550

MEMORIA VOTEPORIGIS PROTICTORIS

The stone also bears in the Ogam script the name in its Goidelic form—Votecorigas

pp. 248, 183, and Pl. 30. Roman thoughts and ways yielded to Celtic. They were choked by new growths, especially by the rise of a monasticism so extreme in its ascetic repudiation of the world that its professors were often reduced in their poverty to the level of primitive men, and in their labour, yoked to the plough, to that of animals.

There is of course no denying that at times, especially in the later stages of the Conquest, the Britons did under good leaders put up a dogged resistance. If the drift of our argument in the previous chapters is correct, the faults on account of which they lost their predominance in the island were many and various: culpable blindness; failure to realize that Kent was the key to the whole island; lack of foresight also in allowing bands of Germans to establish themselves in the basins of the Ouse and the Nene and thus to drive a vast wedge into the heart of Britain; but the root cause of all their troubles was disunion.

It was this which made them prone to take the line of least resistance. When they found by experience that the Saxons were unusually fierce, they too readily consoled themselves with the thought that there was still room in the west of the island, and others—the more adventurous—taking a lesson from the invaders, sailed across the Channel to better themselves in the devastated or vacant tracts of the Armorican peninsula.[32] It seems that this migration began about the same time as the Saxon Conquest; we hear of a British prince in Gaul in 470, and by the beginning of the next century there had been a sufficient transfer of population for western Armorica to be renamed Brittany. Gildas tells us that the Britons as they fled, packed in their boats, 'beneath the sinuous sails raised their voices in loud lamentations, "Thou hast given us as sheep to be slaughtered and among the Gentiles hast Thou dispersed us" '. This may be another touch which Gildas supplied from his own imagination, but even so it is once more symptomatic of the fatalism of the Britons which led to their undoing. The lessons of confidence, unity, and efficiency, which they might have learnt from their Roman masters, were just those which they most ignored.

There was, however, one characteristic in which the Britons, released from the restraint of Rome, did now begin to excel; their powers of imagination were given free play. By the songs of their bards, the 'Histories' of their antiquaries, and the tales of their common folk, they succeeded in weaving a gorgeous web of fiction round the sordid realities of the long struggle and their ultimate defeat, and thus it came about that Artorius, the harassed leader of a rough war-band, living in a low state of civilization, without a currency (unless it were that of the contemptible minims) and without the comforts of life, was by the ninth century exalted into a wonder-working national champion who 'in all his battles was the victor',[33] who felled 960 men by his own onslaught at Mount Badon, and whose dog, Cavall, left a magical footprint on a stone in Buelt. Then, in the twelfth century, Geoffrey of Monmouth and the romancers transformed him further into a king whose court was the scene of all magnificence and chivalry.

Fancy can be more efficacious than fact. The Britons were left to themselves in the west of the island, celebrating in their poems their moral victories, creating a national hero whose fame was to obscure that of the unremembered Germans, the conquerors of the richest lands of Britain.

Thus in their virtues as in their vices the Britons were strongly contrasted with their enemies; they alternated between extremes of wild asceticism and self-indulgence, of patriotic endeavour like that of Ambrosius, 'the last of the Romans', and unpatriotic discord born of unrestrained passion. The Saxons aimed lower; they were perfunctory in their religion; they never dreamed of storming the heights of Heaven, but pushed forward their advancement in this world methodically, untiringly, showing at times ferocity to their enemies, but exhibiting also in their dealings with their own race no small sense of the importance of compromise and co-operation. If the Saxons of heathen times are truthfully reflected in the poem *Beowulf*, they set before themselves a high standard of character, of loyalty to the dead no less than to the living, of discretion, of calmness in adversity, and above all, of constant valour.

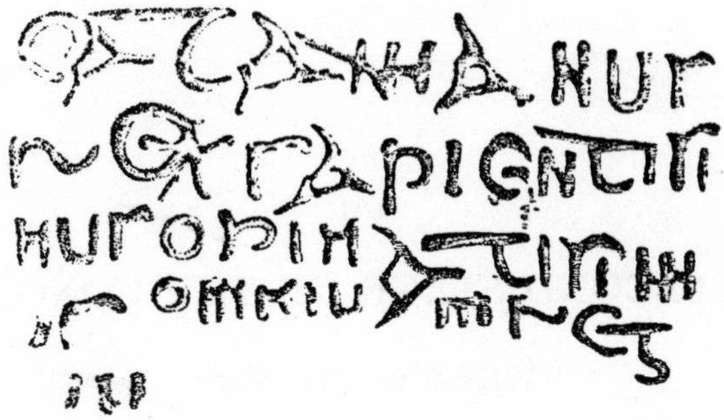

TAILPIECE.—Llangadwaladr, Anglesey; tombstone of Cadfan, King of North Wales in the early 7th century. The inscription runs—*Catamanus rex sapientisimus opinatisimus omnium regum.*

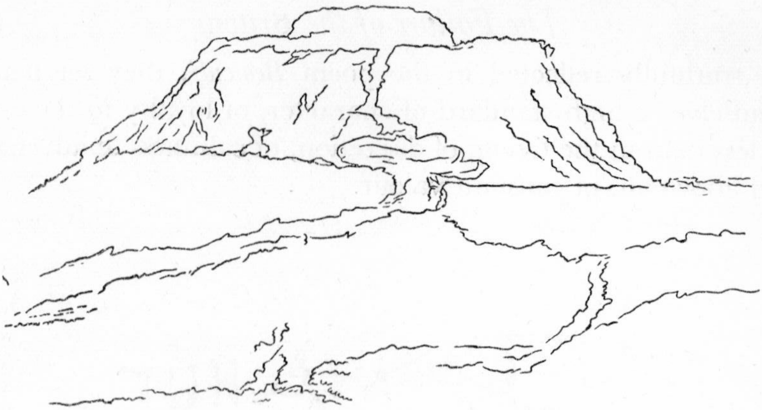

VI

THE SECOND STAGE OF THE CONQUEST

WESSEX—CEAWLIN

IN the middle of the sixth century, on the eve of the second stage of the Anglo-Saxon Conquest, it was by no means a foregone conclusion that the ultimate domination of the island was to fall to the Teutons rather than to the Celts. The position of the invaders was far from secure. They had fastened their hold, it is true, on many of the richest districts, the corn-producing plains of the east and south, the sheep-walks of the downs, and the navigable river valleys which faced towards the Continent. But the invaders were still, no doubt, a small minority. They had still, it seems, to reckon with numbers of Britons undigested, or only half digested, in their midst. The greater part of the island, all the west and the north, was still in the hands of the natives. Ambrosius Aurelianus and Arthur—and others whose names have not survived—had shown that the Celt, when well led, could still successfully resist the German. If the Romano-Britons could only have organized a united front, the future might have lain with them, and Britain might never have given place to England. But the unity of the Romano-

HEADPIECE.—Old Sarum, from Camden's *Britannia*.

Britons had vanished for ever. The five kings whose morals were denounced by Gildas were only one batch of the petty monarchs who now exercised rule in the west of the island. Two other principalities can be identified in the north in addition to the kingdom of Elmet in west Yorkshire: we can dimly discern a kingdom of Reged centred probably near the Solway, and a kingdom of Strathclyde, peopled by Britons of whom many may have forced their way northwards in order to escape from the pressure of the Angles.

In the Germanic half of the island the welter of small kingdoms and independent groups of settlers was, about 550, even more chaotic than among the Britons in the west. The Germanic kingdoms on the coast were the best defined. The natural features—the forests and the swamps—which did so much to mark their boundaries, prevented them from keeping touch with the invaders who were pushing forward in the centre of Britain, and thus caused them to lose the lead in the conquest of the island. The conquerors of Kent, for instance, were hemmed in by the Andredsweald to the south-west; and when they had absorbed a few Saxon settlers to the north-west beyond the Medway, they found their further expansion westward checked by the heaths and forests of Surrey. The *imperium* of Ælle of Sussex, whatever its real character, was certainly not maintained by his successors. The South Saxons, cut off on land by the Weald and at sea by the more enterprising Jutes to the east and west of them, inevitably lost touch with their fellow Germans, and fell to the rear. The condition of the East Saxons is certain in at least one respect—that landwards they were confined by the forest belt north of London and by what was described in the seventh century as the *deserta Ciltine*, the wastes of the Chilterns.[1] The East Angles were similarly shut in by the great fens and forests on their west; the people of Lindsey by the swamps of the Witham and of the Trent, and by the forests and wastes of Sherwood and Hatfield.

In the interior the groups of settlers were, it seems, small and embryonic. There was as yet nothing to indicate that in the south the followers of the House of Cerdic, or in the Midlands the petty Mercian kingdom of the Trent, ruled by princes sprung from Offa of Angel, were to become the great powers of the future. It is true that the advanced position held by either of these principalities on the western front of the German invasion kept their fighting men well exercised in war; but this advantage, if such it can be called, was enjoyed equally by the settlers on the upper Thames and by the Middle Angles in the country of the Cam, the Ouse, and the Nene. We can only say that the West Saxons who followed the House of Cerdic, and the Mercians who followed the House of Offa were, like the Bernicians to the north, well situated to lead the further attacks on the Britons. By itself, however, no one of these small principalities could hope to make any spectacular advance. The Germanic communities needed to be banded into larger federations before they could dislodge the Britons in the west of the island.

How these three small kingdoms succeeded in building up the greater kingdoms of Wessex, Mercia, and Northumbria, making these new states so powerful that they could out-distance the older and perhaps richer kingdoms of the south-east, is the chief subject of the present chapter.

We begin with the rise of Wessex. It centres round the career of Ceawlin, the son of Cynric and grandson* of Cerdic, founder of the dynasty. The hypotheses suggested above,† as those best calculated to reconcile the story of the Chronicle with the evidence of the graves—that Cerdic owed his Celtic name to a British mother and that Cerdic's band of invaders either plundered or ploughed the uplands of southern Wiltshire, expanding from a centre somewhere near the Avon—these guesses must be our starting-point. The early story of this group of settlers is irrecoverable, but it is natural to suppose that their pioneers spread both eastwards in modern Hampshire and northwards towards the Thames valley. These would presumably be the lines of

* Or more probably great-grandson. See note 36 on p. 373. † p. 129.

least resistance. What the Chronicle records is, as we have seen: first, in the year 552, the victory of Cynric over the Britons at Searoburh, Old Sarum, and then four years later the victory of Cynric and of his son Ceawlin at Beranburh (probably Barbury Camp, on the chalk hills between Swindon and Marlborough). With this emergence of Ceawlin we come to a section of the Alfredian Chronicle which seems more definitely than anything in the earlier annals to have a substantial basis, perhaps in some lost saga or poem. Though all is still obscure, with the career of Ceawlin we get near enough to the light to justify some conjectures—some may-have-beens which are preferable both to the must-have-beens of J. R. Green and to the 'blank page' of the strictest school of scientific historians.

Since guesses may help to clear ideas, let us speculate for a while about the outlook of Ceawlin at the beginning of his career.

If the usual identification of Beranburh is correct, we see the war-band which had advanced from the south across Salisbury Plain and the Vale of Pewsey, now established on the Marlborough Downs overlooking the upper reaches of the Thames valley. After holding out for two generations in the most exposed southern salient of the German line, the followers of Ceawlin are at last making permanent contact with their Saxon kinsmen who had penetrated into the heart of Britain by the Thames. Let us guess that Ceawlin, looking northwards from those heights, saw a land of promise and conceived ideas of conquest more grandiose than any which had hitherto contented his people—not schemes of petty ravage or of local thrust and parry with British neighbours; but schemes almost Roman in the scope of their ambition. There is of course another and perhaps a more likely possibility. His career may have been shaped throughout by less exalted motives, and by the circumstances of the moment. Even so, however, it is reasonable to credit him with sufficient intelligence to understand that consolidation in the east and confederation with the Saxons of the

Thames valley were good ways in which to prepare for the winning of more spoil and more land from the Britons.

We may ask ourselves this question and spin out our guesses, but all that remain in the end are the short, enigmatic annals of the Chronicle, sounding from those distant centuries like minute guns, at intervals which are almost regular.

Let us listen to those which tell of the new forward movements under Ceawlin and his kinsmen, and let us try to interpret them:

'560. In this year Ceawlin succeeded to the kingdom of the West Saxons.

'568. In this year Ceawlin and Cutha fought against Ethelbert [presumably king of Kent], and drove him into Kent and slew two ealdormen at Wibbandun. . . .'

Nowadays we are told that Wibbandun cannot be identified with Wimbledon, and that the Ethelbert who was driven into Kent cannot be the same king who some thirty years later introduced Christianity among the Germanic invaders.[2] These views, if correct, deprive the entry of 568 of such picturesqueness as could formerly be found in it; but its significance remains. It is the first warfare recorded, though surely not the first waged, between the invaders. It shows us the grandson of Cerdic asserting his superiority over the wealthiest of all the eastern kingdoms. He is clearing the country to the south of the Thames, preventing the Kentishmen from spreading westwards, and securing his own flank before sending Saxon armies into the Chiltern country.

Then we come to three notable annals.

'571. In this year Cuthwulf fought against the Britons [*Bretwalas*] at Bedcanford and took four towns: Lygeanburh [now identified as Limbury, near Luton in Bedfordshire],[3] Aylesbury, Bensington [now spelt Benson], and Eynsham, and the same year he died.'

If our former version of the events which happened to the north of the Thames in the first stage of the conquest is accepted, the difficulties found by Sir Charles Oman and others in this entry disappear. The writer does not, by a blunder, substitute

Britons for Angles; the Britons defeated by Cuthwulf were presumably the remnants of those who had long sheltered in the forest lands of the eastern Midlands, allied perhaps with other British forces from the London-Verulam enclave. The four towns which were taken by the West Saxon leader are rightly given with Germanic and not with Celtic names, because they were Germanic settlements. A glance at the map facing p. 109 suggests that they were the centres of four chief groups of immigrants who had penetrated into the country of the Chilterns and into the upper Thames valley, no doubt the people later known as Cilternsæte, whose territory was reckoned to contain 4,000 hides. They form sections of the Germanic arch which spanned the Midlands from Cambridge to Oxford.

We may think that Bedcanford (spelt Bedanford in Ethelweard's version of the Chronicle) was probably our Bedford, though the identification is denied by the experts of the Place-name Society.[4] If this is granted and the relationship of Cuthwulf to Ceawlin* is also accepted, the operation may be regarded as part of the general Saxon advance—a move intended to establish dominion over the still British woodlands of the eastern Midlands, with a view to encircling the Germanic Cilternsæte, and thus sweeping them into a West Saxon confederation.

What is important is to understand the historical significance of the annal of 571. The sequence of its statements suggests that the transfer of the four towns was the result of the victory at Bedcanford. The prestige gained by that victory seems to have prepared the way for the absorption of the Cilternsæte by Ceawlin's Saxons, and the fact that the new league of West Saxons was able to advance a few years later against the Britons of the Severn valley points to the adhesion of the Cilternsæte being voluntary rather than enforced after severe fighting. So far as we can see, there were no signs of ill-feeling between these new subjects of the West Saxon monarchy and the original followers of Ceawlin. When Ceawlin was defeated some twenty years

* See genealogy, vol. ii, p. 721.

later, the Cilternsæte did not break away from their connexion with the folk south of the Thames. The name by which the people of the greater Wessex were called was Gewisse. The theory which interprets the name as 'the confederates' is tempting, but not well-proven. The amalgamation of the four towns in 571 under the dynasty of Ceawlin seems to repeat a characteristic first noticed in the Saxon expansion in Germany before the migration. It recalls the advance of the 'Saxons' in which the remnants of the Chauci and other tribes of north Germany were absorbed into some kind of loose confederation. If this is right, it has significance for the future. It is prophetic of greater political combinations in subsequent ages, unions of Wessex with Kent, of Wessex with Mercia, of England with Scotland, of a Commonwealth of nations under a monarchy which still 'has its descent from Cerdic'. These Saxons of the sixth century, barbarous as they may be in many respects, by their political absorption of the four towns are exhibiting a gift for preserving themselves in the rough and tumble of this world by a readiness to unite and to make friends. Such speculations may be reading more than is warranted into the annal of 571, but this we take to be certain: that here more than in any other entry of the Chronicle we have the key to the history of the formation of Wessex into a great power.

'577. In this year Cuthwine and Ceawlin fought against the Britons and they slew three kings, Coinmael, Condidan, and Farinmael, at the place which is called Deorham [Dyrham, a village a few miles north of Bath], and they took three strongholds, Gloucester and Cirencester and Bathanceaster [Bath].' (Pl. 31.)

This battle at Dyrham is the decisive battle of the second stage of the Conquest. The slaughter of the Britons was evidently great. The territory of the three 'chesters', including the southern Cotswold country and the lower valley of the Severn, was considerable and fertile. We have seen archaeological reasons for supposing that the Britons at Cirencester had been for probably a generation or two near neighbours of the Saxons of the upper

Dyrham Camp, probable site of the battle of Deorham

End of the Western Towns; the South Gate of Caerwent, built-up for defence. The walls of Roman Gloucester and Bath were also of squared stones; the nature of those at Cirencester is disputed

Thames. Now in 577 the line which had there been held so long by the Britons was completely broken. The three kings, sons it may be of the degenerate princes whose crimes and adulteries had drawn the rhetoric of Gildas, brought on themselves and their subjects the punishment of heaven which he had threatened. The 'ruddy tongue' of the Saxons' fire again 'licked the western sea', and this time it betokened something more than a passing raid. Never again were the Saxons to be ejected from the west of the island. The importance of the battle has always been recognized and all modern historians have emphasized the fact that the victory of Dyrham drove a wedge between the Britons of Wales and the Britons of Dumnonia. It would be easier to gauge the element of truth in this assertion if we knew how far the newly conquered country was actually colonized by Saxons in subsequent years, and how far it was merely tributary. But at any rate, some thirty years later, when Augustine held a conference with the British bishops, the Severn was, it seems, the recognized boundary between the two peoples.

In another way also the battle of Dyrham placed the old inhabitants in an unfavourable position, for it brought the invading army on to the flank both of the Dumnonians (i.e. the inhabitants of our Somerset, Devon, and Cornwall) and of the Britons in the Severn valley.

Whatever the reason may have been, Ceawlin apparently turned his armies to the north rather than to the south. The development of the campaign is uncertain, because the next annal—the last of the series claiming West Saxon victories—introduces us to another battle-field which cannot be located with certainty.[5]

'584. In this year Ceawlin and Cutha fought against Britons at the place which men call Fethanleag and Cutha was slain, and Ceawlin took many places and countless war spoils, and in wrath he turned back thence to his own home.'

The generally accepted view is that Ceawlin continued his

victorious advance up the Severn. The settlers who percolated into this region, until they were checked in the north of Worcestershire by the forests of Wyre, of Morfe, and of Kinver, came in time to be known as the Hwicce. The later diocese of Worcester is thought to indicate the extent of their kingdom, and Wychwood (i.e. the wood of the Hwicce) in Oxfordshire is said to have been their eastern boundary. The new colony which is found later with its own line of local kings became another outpost of Germanism in the west—an outpost of Germanism, but not for long an outpost of the Saxons; for while the names of its early kings are thought to point to a connexion with the Bernician dynasty,[6] its later land charters, its traditions, and many of its place-names, bear witness to its association from the seventh century onwards with Mercia.

The last years of Ceawlin are left by the fragmentary notes of the Chronicle as a hopeless mystery. Who can say why it was that 'in wrath he turned back to his own home' after capturing 'the many places and countless war spoil' which fell to him as a result of the battle of Fethanleag. The words about returning in wrath sound like a snatch from some oral tradition. They suggest how it came to pass that our information about the first empire-builder of the West Saxons was preserved.

The next annal which tells of his surprising downfall is equally puzzling.

> '592. In this year was a great slaughter at Woddesbeorh and Ceawlin was driven out.'

Since Woddesbeorh seems to have been in the Marlborough region, seven miles east of Devizes,[7] we see that Ceawlin's career of conquest ended near the place where it had begun. Had he been expelled from some of his new conquests by Britons? Or had he been driven back to the support of his own folk when other Germanic peoples, newly subjected to his rule, revolted? Or were his victories in the north interrupted by troubles among his own kinsmen? Or had he to meet an attack from Ethelbert of Kent, the king whose power was thenceforth to be in the ascendant? The guesses have been endless, but there can be no sure answer. All that is told us is that Ceawlin survived his defeat for only one year; then, if our reconstruction of the genealogy of his family is correct,[8] the crown passed to his eldest surviving son.

The tradition of his conquests survived among the West Saxons for centuries. While Cerdic, the founder of the dynasty, became little more than a name, men looked back to Ceawlin, his grandson, as the second 'Bretwalda', the second Germanic war-leader who enjoyed south of the Humber an *imperium*—whatever *imperium* may connote. It was Ceawlin who had swept all before him from the Marlborough Downs to Kent, from the lower Thames in the east to the lower Severn in the west. It was Ceawlin who, profiting from the victory of Cuthwulf, had united the scattered Saxon settlements from the Chilterns to the Channel. It was Ceawlin who by the boldness of his schemes of conquest and by his generalship in the field had foreshadowed the ultimate supremacy of the Gewisse.

More than two centuries, however, were to elapse before the glory of the *imperium* was to be claimed once more by a descendant of the House of Cerdic.

MERCIA

The expansion of Wessex under Ceawlin may be supposed to represent roughly what happened also to Mercia and Northumbria, the two kingdoms which showed a corresponding capacity for growth. The Mercians failed to preserve a tradition, even a false one, of their early history; all that has come to us is a list of their kings and a document called the *Tribal Hidage*,* which gives what appears to be a summary of the districts liable for contributions to the armies and to the revenues of the Mercian monarchy in the seventh century. This document can be used to throw light on the political expansion of Mercia in that age,

* See genealogy, vol. ii, p. 719, and vol. ii, p. 389.

that is, in the time of Penda and his sons; but it scarcely helps to elucidate the story of the settlement. For instance, one people enumerated in it which can be clearly identified is the Pecsæte (Peak-dwellers); their territory is reckoned to contain 1,200 hides or households. Who were these Peak-dwellers and whence did they come? The natural inference would be that they sprang from small bands of Anglian settlers who pushed northwards from the older Mercia of the Trent valley and colonized new lands around the Peak. On the other hand, Bede tells us that Northumbrians early in the seventh century carried their conquests up to Chester, and a place-name expert[9] has claimed to find support for the view that south Lancashire was colonized by Northumbrians before it was re-colonized in the time of Penda by Mercians. This is only one example of many obscurities. It is enough to show why, in this second stage of the Conquest as in the first, the early history of Mercia is so dark that it is better to pass it by and admit the impossibility of putting together any trustworthy story.

NORTHUMBRIA—ETHELFRITH

We have seen* that the beginnings of the two Northumbrian States are purely conjectural until about the middle of the sixth century, when a leader called Ælle became king of Deira and one Ida, king of Bernicia. Practically nothing is known of Ælle. But some murmur of wars waged by the House of Ida comes down to us. Four of Ida's sons succeeded him on the throne. Nennius in the ninth century had earlier genealogies and fragments of apparently genuine information about some events of their time. He tells[10] that an alliance of four kings, Urbgen (known in later times as Urien), ruler of Reged,† Riderch, king of Strathclyde, Morcant (or Morgan), and another, fought against the successors of Ida. Then of Theodric, the son of Ida, who reigned about 572–9, he says: 'Theodric with his sons fought bravely against that Urbgen. At that time sometimes

* Above, pp. 148–53. † Or Rheged.

the enemy, sometimes our countrymen [*cives*] were defeated, and he beleaguered them for three days and nights in the island of Metcaud [Lindisfarne], and while he was on the campaign he was murdered at the instigation of Morcant from jealousy, because he was the most valorous and warlike of all kings.'[11]

Riderch appears also as an historical ruler in the *Life of St. Columba* and in the *Life of St. Kentigern* (based on earlier material, though written about 1175). He is Riderch Hael (the Generous), king of the Strathclyde Britons, and he has at his court a madman endowed with prophetic power. This madman is interesting because Chadwick has produced good reasons for thinking him to be the original (or rather one original) of Merlin of Arthurian romance, and it is interesting to find that Laloecen (as he was then called) was said to have become unbalanced owing to a conviction of blood-guiltiness which came to him in the middle of a battle. Later the same madman, after taking to the woods, 'used to come and sit on a rock over the stream Mellodonor—now called Molendinar—in the north of Glasgow, and interrupt the service of St. Kentigern's clergy by shouting prophecies; but his prophecies were never consistent with one another'.[12] The *Life of St. Kentigern* also relates that Urien, the most warlike king, was the patron of the Saint, and that Morgan the murderer of Urien was a persecutor.

The Welsh poems of Aneurin and Taliessin and of other poets who flourished about the end of the sixth century have something to contribute about the 'Men of the North'—'disintegrated' as these poems are, overlaid with later Bardic additions, and often unintelligible. The outstanding fact about the one fight which can almost be dated (to about 575) and located (at 'Arderydd', either Arthuret, near Longtown, or Airdrie in Lanark) is this, that it was fought by Riderch against other Britons and not against the Angles. One famous poem, the *Gododdin*, attributed to Aneurin and generally thought to contain some genuine tradition, seems to refer to a raid carried out by a small band of retainers of a prince living near the Forth against the Saxons at Catraeth (? Catterick), a hopeless venture by men 'fed with mead, and drunk'.

> The men went to Catraeth; merry was the host,
> The grey mead was their drink and their poison too.[13]

These side-lights, however flickering, help to illustrate the fatal elements of rivalry, of religious disunity, and of fecklessness, which prevented the Celtic tribes of the north-west from checking the Germans in Bernicia and Deira while these were still a small minority.

But on the whole it seems to be a fact that in this northern region the fighting was fiercer and more prolonged than in the Severn valley, and that the Britons of the north in the course of the struggle applied to themselves a new name, shared also with the Britons of Wales, but never given to those of Devon or Cornwall; they called themselves *Combrogies* or *Cymry*, meaning 'fellow countrymen', a word still recognizable in the first two syllables of our own Cumberland, the land of the Cymry. The name was evidence, if not of a new patriotism, at least of a new consciousness of Celtic racialism born during these struggles and, however imperfectly, superimposed over the old tribal and regional antagonisms.

It is not till we come to Bede's account of Ida's grandson Ethelfrith (593–617) that at last we have firm ground in the history of the rise of Northumbria. As with the rise of Wessex under Ceawlin, we find two distinct aspects of the process. There is the union of smaller kingdoms or districts, and there is conquest by the armies of the united kingdoms pushed forward till it reaches the western sea. The union of the northern kingdoms was a simpler affair than the union of those in the south and midlands, because in the north there were by the end of the sixth century only two, Deira and Bernicia; and when Ethelfrith of Bernicia married a daughter of Ælle, the old king of Deira, and succeeded in disinheriting Ælle's son Edwin (? 605), all that was required to merge the Northumbrian kingdoms into

View through the entrance of Dunadd, the rock fortress of the Scots

Alclyde (i.e. the rock of Clyde), also called Dumbarton (i.e. the fortress of the Britons)

one seemed for the moment to have been accomplished. But even before this union Ethelfrith had apparently carried all before him.[14] 'Throughout his reign,' says Bede, 'Ethelfrith more than all the chiefs of the English, harried the Britons. . . . Like another Saul he conquered more territories from the Britons than any other ealdorman or king of the English, either subduing the inhabitants and making them tributary, or driving them out (*exterminatis*) and planting the English in their places.'

The conflict culminated in 603. In that year Aedan, the Scotto-Irish king of Dal Riata (roughly equivalent to the modern Argyle), marched against Ethelfrith. The battle which ensued is the first recorded between Scots and English. Hitherto the colony of Scots, since they had crossed the seas from Ulster a hundred years earlier, had had enough to do in maintaining their footing against Picts and Britons. Now in 603 King Aedan, an old man of seventy, well known as the patron of St. Columba of Iona, seems to have been inspired by the idea of being a second Arthur (it is significant that his mother was British and that he christened his eldest son Arthur). He made a league with the Britons of Strathclyde and advanced 'with an immense and mighty army'. It is usual to identify Degsastan, the scene of the ensuing battle, with Dawston Rig in Liddesdale, and if we wonder how 'immense armies' could maintain themselves in that desolate spot among the bare hills of the borderland, we may remember that estimates of numbers are usually exaggerated, that the total area of Aedan's rock fortress at Dunadd (Pl. 32) in the Moss of Crinan could not maintain a population of more than some 700 people, and that the head-quarters of his ally, the king of Strathclyde, at Alclyde (Dumbarton) and of his enemy Ethelfrith at Bamburgh (Fig. 34) were similar rock fortresses. The smallness of their 'capitals'—if they may be so described—are a reminder of the diminutive scale on which these early kings of post-Roman Britain conducted their affairs.

But the battle of Degsastan, whatever its true site, and whatever the size of the armies engaged, was at any rate decisive.

FIG. 34. Bamburgh, the rock fortress of King Ethelfrith.

There was no glint of Arthurian romance in the sequel. Almost all the army of the Scots was slain, and the king fled with a few followers. 'From that day', says Bede,[15] 'no king of the Scots in Britain has to this day dared to meet the English nation in battle.' The predominance of the Angles south of the Forth was established in the west as well as in the east.[16]

The crowning mercy came about 616. Ethelfrith raised a great army and advanced boldly for almost a hundred miles from his own borders. In the neighbourhood of Chester, where once had been stationed the Twentieth Legion, he found himself opposed not only by a coalition of British princes but by 1,250 monks who had come from their monastery at Bangor to importune the God of battles. For three days the monks fasted, and then the wild group of holy men took up a position near the battle-field. Bede's well-known story of the massacre of the unarmed crowd illustrates the ruthlessness of this descendant of Ida, and the spirit of the age. The monks were fighting with their prayers; they must be the first to be cut down. The order was carried out, twelve hundred of the holy men were slaughtered. To Bede their fate appeared a punishment not unjustly inflicted on the Britons for their refusal to co-operate in the conversion of the heathen English. To us it helps to explain the loathing with which the Britons shrank back from contact with the Anglo-Saxon invaders.

The career of Ethelfrith like that of Ceawlin—and of so many another early king—ended in defeat and failure. The story of the defeat brings us to the rise of Edwin, the exiled son of Ælle of York, and it will find its place when we come to the history of the Conversion.

The meagreness of the present chapter shows how few are the facts that can be ascertained about the second stage of the Conquest.

We know something about Ceawlin of Wessex and something about Ethelfrith of Northumbria; but the rest is almost a blank. The gap in our written information might in places be filled with conjectures based on the grave-finds, but the reader has no doubt had his fill of the archaeological kind of history in previous chapters, and he may be spared any more of it in these later times when it is less essential. We have learnt enough from the written authorities to perceive that the advance made by the invaders in the latter half of the sixth century and the opening years of the seventh was all-important. It definitely turned the scale against the Britons and drove those who clung to their independence into the hill-country of the west. It also produced some sort of order out of chaos and brought to the front those states whose struggle for existence or for mastery make up so much of the history of the next few centuries.

Among the Germanic kingdoms in the east of the island events had occurred which were to determine the course of history in the seventh century. But in this period as ever, the all-important process in the making of England was more economic than political; it was the unrecorded expansion of Germanic cultivation. In every kingdom, small or great, the enterprising members of the community were farming new lands, and penetrating farther into the woodlands. The south-eastern kingdoms, such as Kent, Sussex, Essex, and East Anglia, were in this way being rounded off and delimited; and the others were stretching out longer tentacles among the Britons of the west.

This second stage has no well-marked termination. The story of the advance fades away. But when in coming chapters we focus our attention on the stories of saints and kings, it must not be forgotten that the process of gradual colonization, of gradual eating by Saxon and Angle into the lands hitherto British, continued unceasingly generation after generation.

VII

HEATHEN SOCIETY

KING AND PEOPLE

WE wish to know how our Germanic forefathers lived and governed themselves in Britain during those first generations which we must necessarily confuse under the phrase 'the heathen period' of Anglo-Saxon society. What stands in our way as we approach the subject is once more the uncertainty about the migration itself. How did the Jutes, the Saxons, and the Angles, cross the sea? Did they come in masses much as the Goths had crossed the Danube, and as the Franks had crossed the Rhine? Is it likely that peoples, the majority of whom must have lived some way from the coast, could have mustered a sufficient number of their elaborately made long keels to ferry more than small parties in any one year? Is it conceivable that, even in the later stages of the movement, tribes or even large groups of kindred could have been shipped from the Elbe to the upper reaches of the Thames, the Ouse, or the Trent? These questions are fundamental, and must determine our ideas about the kind of society which was formed by the Germanic immigrants into Britain.

If we turn to our best guides, we find a certain measure of agreement. Few could object to the main thesis with which Stubbs[1] prefaces his account of *The Anglo-Saxon System*. He

HEADPIECE.—Lid of Franks Casket; Ægil defending his home. ½.

points out that the process was not necessarily uniform in the several states.

'In some cases it [the transference of German institutions to Britain] may have been accomplished by unconnected bands of squatters, who took possession of an uninhabited tract, and, reproducing there the local system of their native land, continued practically independent, until the whole surrounding districts were organised by a central state-power. In other cases, the successful leader of a large colony or a victorious host, having conquered and exterminated [here, of course, Stubbs gives an opening to criticism] the natives, must have proceeded to divide their land according to a fixed scheme. The principle of this allotment he would find in the organisation of his host.'

What is objectionable in Stubbs's history is the social system which he builds on this foundation. The victorious host becomes the 'people in arms . . . united by the principle of kindred'; the allotment of the land is 'according to the divisions of the kindred'; the typical village is the community of equal freemen. In Kent, Sussex, and perhaps in Essex and East Anglia, the supreme authority in the State is probably a folk-moot of the freemen, meeting 'in primitive simplicity'. Elsewhere, this primitive simplicity is represented by the shire-moots. Between the shire-moots and the meetings of freemen in their townships or villages are the assemblies of the districts called 'Hundreds', probably introduced by the invaders, arranged in groups of a hundred warriors for the conquest of Britain. Stubbs is cautious in details, but he is clear that what is set up in Britain is a reproduction of the old tribal system of Germany, with little modification—a tribal system in which the old principle of kinship is still the chief force.

Among modern critics of Stubbs the most thorough-going is H. M. Chadwick.[2] He asserts that the Victorian's 'representation of Anglo-Saxon society rests upon a string of hypotheses not one of which is capable of proof', and that there is no evidence for self-government, either central or local, nor for the kindred as a definitely organized body. In his opinion 'it is not of national assemblies or responsible local bodies that we hear, but of kings and their officials'. The State is based on allegiance to the king and to the great men who surround the king; on lordship rather than on kinship. 'Indeed, it appears that with the exception of the king himself, every individual in the nation owed obedience to a lord.'

Now, there is no doubt about the main reason for the difference between these two views of the earliest Anglo-Saxon institutions. They are for the most part derived from different sources. While Stubbs drew his conclusions from the *Germania* of Tacitus, from analogy with what were supposed to be the Germanic institutions of the Continent, from place-names, and, above all, from the Saxon laws, Chadwick held that the best picture of early English society was to be found in the literature of the Anglo-Saxons, in their heroic poetry (especially in *Beowulf*), and in Bede's *Ecclesiastical History*. We must therefore begin by clearing our own ideas about the relative value of these several sources of information; and in doing so we find at once that the main defences of the old position must be almost surrendered. The *Germania* of Tacitus, eked out with analogies drawn from other Germanic States on the Continent, may supply us with ideas about the general principles on which Germanic society was organized; but it can do no more. The *Germania* must be out of our picture of Anglo-Saxon society, because it is too remote; and the institutions found among Franks and Lombards cannot be trustworthy parallels to those produced by an oversea migration. The main arguments of those who would emphasize the element of Germanic self-government or of a tribal system based on kinship, if they are to be valid, rest on the remaining sources of information—the Saxon laws, the place-names, and the village systems. Let us glance at the arguments constructed along these several lines.

First, with regard to the Saxon laws—it is sufficiently obvious that the only laws which can be quoted with confidence as evidence of the heathen stage of society are the laws of Ethelbert of Kent, compiled about five years after the Conversion. These can be interpreted, as by Stubbs, so that they tally with the Germanic systems of the Continent. They mention three classes in Kentish society. The *eorls* (a word which through the influence of the cognate Norse *jarl* acquired in time the more exalted force of our 'earl') may be taken as a hereditary nobility of birth. The *ceorls* (a word akin to our 'churl') are freemen—and freemen of substance, since the ceorl's *tun* or farm is protected against a breach of the peace in the same way as the king's or the eorl's, though with a lower fine. In the third class we have the half-free, the *læts*, corresponding to a similar class in the Frisian and Frankish laws. On the whole, it may be said that the social system in Kent is not far removed from those of their nearest neighbours on the opposite mainland. Thus in the law of Ethelbert (c. 2) which inflicts a special penalty 'if the king calls his *leode* to him and evil is done to them there', though the word *leode* may mean only personal dependants it may also mean, as Stubbs believed, the general freemen of the nation, and Jolliffe has recently given a new force and direction to the older views by equating the lathes of Kent with the *gaus*, the old local divisions, of Germany and by claiming that these districts were 'embodied folks'.[3]

Though these Kentish laws may be used as by Stubbs to support the theory which would transfer the tribal system of Germany almost ready-made to all the Germanic settlements in Britain, there are difficulties in the way. In addition to the uncertainty about the real meaning of the terms, there is the question why these laws differ so much from the later laws. Are they peculiar because they are generations earlier—because they describe primitive conditions of English society which later ceased to exist—or are they peculiar because they are Kentish? Now recent studies of Kentish institutions have all tended to stress the fact that the social arrangements of Kent were different from those of the rest of England. Nowhere else in Anglo-Saxon laws do we read of a ceorl's *tun* as if it were a separate estate—what the Germans call an '*Einzelhof*'. Nowhere else does the ceorl occupy such an independent position. In Kent his oath is about as good as that of a cleric, and he has under him dependants (*hlafætan*, 'bread-eaters').[4]

If we go on to the later law-books, those of the kings of Kent in the last quarter of the seventh century,* and that (dated about 690) of Ine of Wessex, we find that the Kentish ceorl is valued at least two and a half times as highly as the West-Saxon ceorl.[5] He seems to be a different kind of man from the normal peasant whom we encounter in the other kingdoms, and to have more independence as well as a more compact property. There is, then, much to be said for the view that since the Kentish men were a peculiar people, their laws cannot be taken to describe a stage of society through which the other kingdoms also passed. Some of the weighty arguments of Stubbs are thus put out of action, and it becomes less necessary to dwell further on the theory of Chadwick, that the *leode* whom Ethelbert specially protected when summoned to his presence were his fighting retainers rather than the members of a tribal folk-moot.

But even if the laws of Kent cannot teach us what had happened in the other kingdoms, there are yet other laws, notably those of Ine of Wessex, which, like outcrops from ancient buried strata, illustrate the nature of Anglo-Saxon society in its early epochs and show certain evidences of a primitive freedom. Thus one of Ine's decrees[6] regulates the fine (*fyrdwite*) which is to be paid by a man of the ceorl class who neglects his service in the *fyrd*, or national army. Another[7] deals with the obligations of ceorls who have 'a common meadow or other—partible—land (*gedalland*) to fence'. It is a mere glimpse of the corporate life of the village community. But it is enough to make it evident that in Wessex something like the later open-field system of cultivation goes back to the earliest centuries of the English occupation. No subject in early English history has received more attention since Seebohm first pointed out the historical significance of the

* Hlothere, reigned 673–85; Eadric, *c.* 685–86; Wihtred, 690–725.

typical arrangements of an old English village—its three great arable fields cut up into small strips which were distributed in such a way as to give each villager of substance his hide of land, his virgate (one quarter of a hide), or whatever smaller holding might be his portion, constituting a farm held not in one piece, but in a score or more of scattered strips mixed with those of his neighbours. It is now some decades since the works of Maitland and of Vinogradoff proved that these features of the English village system were Germanic rather than Roman; that they arose naturally as one piece of waste-land after another was taken into tillage; that they were not maintained to suit the convenience of a lord, whether Roman or Saxon, but sprang from a Germanic sense that men should share and share alike.*

So far in this chapter we have been examining what Chadwick meant when he asserted that the older view of Anglo-Saxon society 'rests upon a string of hypotheses not one of which is capable of proof'. We have seen that the early Kentish laws, the village system, the place-names, the meaning of a term such as *leode*—all are ambiguous. The interpretation put upon them by Stubbs and the nineteenth-century historians is open to criticism. The way is accordingly clear for us to go further, and see if the literary sources used by Chadwick—the *History* of Bede, the *Beowulf* and other poems—make it possible to reconstruct the conditions of early English society on other lines with better probability.

At the outset there is no denying that these sources have obscurities of their own, which render their evidence even harder to assimilate than the epigrams of Tacitus. Bede's aim was to

* The most interesting contributions to this subject in recent years have been the two books to which we have already referred (above pp. 173, 93). The books are: H. L. Gray's *English Field System*, whose map, p. 281, illustrates the absurdity of speaking about '*The* English Village Community', as if there were only one type of English village, and J. E. A. Jolliffe's *Pre-Feudal England, The Jutes*. Since it is only from the close of the pre-Norman period that satisfactory evidence about the different types of village communities in the different parts of England is forthcoming, it is better to postpone the attempt to understand the conditions under which the Anglo-Saxon peasantry lived and worked on the soil of Britain.

narrate the doings of kings and saints in the age of the Conversion, and his references to institutions are casual and never explicit. The epic of *Beowulf* and the other early poems which seem to refer to English society in the heathen period are as little concerned as Bede with the institutions of the English, and they plunge us into baffling cross-currents of modern theories and counter-theories. The *Beowulf* in particular is beset with difficulties. Modern critics now reject the idea that it is a composite work.[8] There is some measure of agreement that, while old myths, old legends, and old lays are of course woven into the epic, it is the work of a real poet, and not of a compiler; not a minstrel's casual outpouring, but the studied composition of a writer who could polish three thousand lines with care; one conversant both with Christianity and with heathen ideas. The author knows and loves the tales about the heroes who sailed the Baltic and the North Sea, who built their halls and fought out their feuds in that northern world during the fifth and sixth centuries; but he introduces his heathen heroes to instruct as well as to beguile the men-at-arms as they ate their bread and drank their beer in the halls of the great. The epic cannot have been composed long before the end of the seventh century, since we must allow for the lapse of some generations before Beowulf, the nephew of a Scandinavian king (one who appears in history fighting against the Franks about 525) could be mixed up in men's minds in adventures with dragons and monsters. On the other hand, it cannot well be later than the beginning of the ninth century, since there is no hint in the poem that the Danes, to save whom Beowulf fought the monsters, have yet become Vikings, hateful to the English.

But if in point of time the *Beowulf* poem is about as far removed from heathen England as is Bede's *History*, the pagan spirit animating the poem, and the setting, seem to take us back to the ideas and conditions which were to be found in England before the coming of Christianity. Though coloured, and at times distorted, by the ideas of the later century in which it was actually composed, the poem can yet be used as a guide to the ways and thoughts of the earliest Englishmen.

From this heroic poetry and from Bede, as well as from the laws and charters, Chadwick has extracted ideas which place the early institutions of the Anglo-Saxons in a new perspective. This is not the place in which to follow in detail his arguments or even his results, but his main contention, to which we have already alluded, is fundamental: namely, that the all-important element in the Anglo-Saxon State was the king himself and those officials and followers bound to the king by a personal tie. We shall, therefore, do well to glance at some of Chadwick's applications of his general theory. There is the idea that the kings themselves could dispose of their kingdoms—for instance on the death of the king who was Beowulf's uncle, his widow is said to have offered Beowulf the throne, because she considered her own son too young to defend the kingdom. There is a theory which cannot well be questioned, that the councillors (*witan*) were little more than the nominees of the Crown—the king's officials and his retainers. The central government, it is argued, was in the hands of the king and his court. 'It is clear from Bede's writings that the court consisted roughly of two classes, which we may describe as the "seniors" and "juniors" (*dugoð* and *geogoð*). The latter were young warriors (*milites*, *ministri*) in constant attendance on the king, while the former included persons of official position (*eorls*, &c.) as well as *milites emeriti* who had already been rewarded for their services with grants of land.'[9] The local government was administered by 'reeves'—a word which covers both the stewards of the king and those of the landowners under the king. 'There seems not to have been any difference in kind between the two classes. There is no evidence that either was controlled by or responsible to any authority, except their masters.' In this view the units of local government appear, not as natural growths from below, but as arrangements imposed by the monarchy from above: the shires of Wessex represent[10] 'divisions of the kingdom between members of the royal family'; and the smaller units which preceded the hundreds were administrative divisions grouped round the royal vills. Lastly, the army is not an assemblage of all the freemen of the nation. It is small and highly select, and there is no certain indication that normally any warriors came to the field except the king and his *gesiths*,* and those freemen who were bound by special personal ties to follow them.

We have now glanced at some of the older views of Stubbs, and also at some of the more recent theories put forward by Chadwick. When we make our choice between the two, we shall be wise to agree with Chadwick that in Bede's *History* and in Old English literature generally the kings and their personal followers fill the picture, and that little or nothing is to be seen of the tribalism, the self-government, and the democratic moots which fascinated Stubbs and his contemporaries. But as usual the two theories are not wholly irreconcilable. The question then arises, in what way they are to be combined. One historian[11] has suggested 'that when some adventurous king and his *comitatus* had made the first lodgement, free tribesmen were invited in to strengthen the new community', and that 'they would stipulate for the perpetuation of their old privileges, in their new homes, so that the state, when formed, would be much less autocratic in constitution than might have been expected'.

But this picture of the Conquest will not do—even as an hypothesis. Whatever happened, there can have been no bargain of this kind about rights. If we are to guess, we must think of the Germanic settlers introducing old privileges, laws, and customs, simply because these were all that they knew. The same thing happens whether Anglo-Saxon migrants are planting colonies in Britain in the fifth and sixth centuries, or in America and Australia in modern times. Most of the laws of the old country reappear in the new. None the less, profound changes were a natural consequence of the migration across the North Sea. To the old aristocracy of birth there was added a new aristocracy of

* See below, p. 210, for the general likeness of gesiths to thegns.

service and of wealth. Because the new land was won at the spear's point, the war-leaders, both the kings themselves and the warriors who were round them, stood to gain. But to talk about bargains being struck is as misleading as to assume that there was an importation of a constitution ready-made on the lines of the *Germania* of Tacitus.

All that we can say is that the Anglo-Saxons brought with them three Germanic ways of doing things, three principles on which society was built, principles which were not peculiar to the Germans, since they were found among other primitive peoples, but which stand out in all allusions to the Germanic tribes and are described in classic passages in the *Germania* of Tacitus.

First is the principle of the *comitatus*, which secured for a war-leader, great or small, a troop of devoted followers. We have already noticed the emphasis placed by recent writers on the part played by such war-bands in the conquest of Britain. Here we need do no more than recognize the various forms in which the principle could be embodied. The followers might be, as they were originally, the hearth-companions of their leader, receiving in return for their services board and lodging, supplemented by occasional special rewards, such as bracelets of gold and silver. Later, when fighting had ended in permanent conquest, the rewards of the followers naturally often took the form of land. This, of course, had the result of breaking up the closeness of the connexion between the lord and the follower, and gave rise to new quasi-feudal relationships, from which in time there sprang the tangled feudalistic growths of the later Saxon age.

The word chiefly used to describe the follower of a king in the early Saxon period is *gesith*, and it seems to contain the idea of companionship. It is gradually superseded, though not till the ninth century or thereabouts, by the word *thegn*, which places emphasis on the idea of service, rather than on that of companionship.[12]

The principle of the *comitatus* produces also retinues of humbler fighting-men for the gesiths and thegns themselves. All men, from the greatest landowners to the humblest peasants, can be bound to a lord by a devotion which is almost a religion. Since the groups of lords and of followers branching off from the principle of the *comitatus* were so diversified, it is natural that the numbers in the bands should be equally variable. In one of the oldest poems* we hear of a hero being accompanied by sixty champions. Beowulf sets out with fourteen, but later he offers to bring a thousand thegns and heroes to help his ally. We need not speculate here about the question how far a difference in degree produced a difference in kind. It is enough to see that, in the consolidation of the settlements, the small war-bands and the yet smaller informal followings of the local magnates could by simple addition be aggregated until the army collected by a wide ruler like the king of Greater Mercia might, according to one recent guess,[13] amount to 15,000 men.

Secondly, there was the principle of the free nation. The king could be no autocrat. Of necessity he must always gain the willing co-operation of his warriors. In so far as there was in these early times anything which could be called a constitutional theory, it might conceivably be held that the general assent of the freemen was desirable. In practice the barbarian nations worried little about theories. All that was really necessary was that a king should carry with him the leading men of his people. Having obtained this support, whether formally or informally, he could have things his own way.

In the nineteenth century much—certainly too much—used to be written about the functions of the 'Witenagemots', or of the local courts or 'folk-moots'. Now having acknowledged that the principle of popular assent existed, we need only recognize what is sufficiently obvious, that its application varied with time and circumstances, that is, with the size of the kingdom and with the character of the king and of his great men.

* The *Finnsburh Fragment.*

Kinship must be reckoned a third basic principle in Anglo-Saxon society. But kinship is a word which may cover much or little; and we must try to make its meaning more precise. Some things may be confidently asserted: that within historic times the unit of Anglo-Saxon society was never a well-defined cohesive kin-group; that it was no clan or sept of the Celtic type; that it was not exclusively patriarchic or agnatic like the Roman *gens*; that Anglo-Saxon armies were not, so far as we know, drawn up by families and clans, as Tacitus believed the German armies to be in his time. On the other hand, kinship brought with it duties greater and more definite than those which fall to the members of a modern family. If a man had the misfortune to kill another of a different kin, his family might sooner or later be called upon to pay a greater part of the money-compensation, the *wergeld*, which would be due to the family of the slain. The same principle would apply if a less serious injury had been inflicted. A man's kinsmen were expected to help him in every way they could—from swearing on his behalf in the local moot to enduring or pursuing a blood-feud if justice broke down. There is no question that this was in a general way the first principle of early English, as of Germanic and of most primitive justice. Moreover, the legal liability of the kindred, often of remote cousins, persisted among many of the north German and Scandinavian peoples throughout the Middle Ages. It was notably so in the regions whence had come the Anglo-Saxon conquerors of Britain. In Schleswig, the fourth cousin of a slain man might claim a few shillings, which were the recognized portion of his *wergeld*, and in the Hamburg district the kinsmen of slayer and slain were making treaties for composition in cases of manslaughter as late as the seventeenth century. There is earlier evidence also which shows that the continental Saxons, like their sometime neighbours, the Lombards, reckoned kinship for the purpose of primitive justice down to the seventh degree.

To what extent were such customs introduced by the conquering Saxons into Britain? Were families directly liable for the crimes of their members? Did the responsibility extend to remote cousins? Here we have a good example of the trend of historical thought in recent times. Scepticism about the 'Germanic' views of the nineteenth-century historians culminated in 1913 in a book entitled *Kindred and Clan*, by Miss B. S. Phillpotts;[14] and this will be our chief guide in glancing at the subject. The code of Ethelbert makes it clear that the primary responsibility for compensation fell, in Kent, on the individual, and only a secondary liability on the kinsmen—they are only called upon to pay if the real culprit has fled. But this was in Kent; and we have learnt that it is not safe to argue from the ways of Kentishmen to those of Englishmen in general.

The laws of the West Saxons (our only other laws) are unfortunately less explicit on this point. A man's *magas* (his kinsmen) have undoubtedly many responsibilities. They may be called in if he defaults and flees the land. They may have to act as guardians and to keep up the home of a dead man. Even the blood-feud is recognized, though the kings attempt to restrict it. A day may come in the life of any Anglo-Saxon when he has to call on the members of his family to take up their spears and defend him in feud or assist him to exact vengeance on another.

But what is this family? Did it include, as on the Continent, distant cousins? No answer to this question comes down to us from the Anglo-Saxon laws; and it is this fact, the complete dearth of regulations in England detailing the rights and liabilities of distant kinsmen, which justifies us in thinking that the Anglo-Saxon *mægth*, or kindred, meant little more than our 'family' in the modern loose sense of the word.

How then shall we explain the comparative insignificance of the kindred on the soil of Britain? Two reasons present themselves. One is the fact that an oversea migration is more upsetting to the old system than a land migration. The ship's crew must be a band of adventurers. It cannot well be a family party. The second cause was not peculiar to England. It was the difficulty of working a cognatic system, like that of the Anglo-Saxon laws, where the mother's relations were recognized as well as the father's. They were, it is true, less important; the relative responsibility was, as amongst many other peoples, two to one—i.e. when owing to the flight of a criminal the kindred had to pay for a murder, the relations on the father's side had to pay two-thirds of the fine, those on the mother's side one-third.* But the fact that there was no fixed kin-group like the agnatic *gens* of the Romans meant that the kin-group of a son was always different from that of his father. The complications arising from such a system were baffling. There was no end to them. Common sense pointed to substituting the family in its narrower sense for the wide and dispersed kindred.

The marvel is that the responsibility of the extended group could be retained for centuries in countries like Schleswig, and not that it disappeared in England.

Now it must not be supposed that there is any fatal antagonism between the older theories of Germanic freedom and the more recent theories which lay stress on the parts played by the kings and the dependants of the kings. The principles of freedom and lordship could exist side by side. For the king could be head of a free nation as well as lord of a war-band. The eorl—and even more eminently, the etheling, the member of a royal family—could be a noble, respected by the ordinary freeman on account of his good birth, and at the same time he could be raised above the common herd by the nobility of his services as a king's gesith. The ceorl might still be liable to perform the old duties once incumbent on all freemen, even when in actual practice those duties were only exacted from those who had bound themselves to follow some particular lord. Similarly in local government, a court might be held by the king's official—his ealdorman or his reeve—and it might assemble in a royal vill and yet be regarded as a popular court. The fighting freemen of the Conquest—such men as we see laid out in the cemeteries,

* See, however, Alfred's Law, c. 27, in Stubbs' *Charters*, p. 70.

sometimes in rows, each with his arms beside him—did not cease to be free because they followed a leader. They did not cease to be free even if the leader and his heirs after him came to be recognized as the lords of a settled community. They did not necessarily cease to be free when, frontier fighting having receded with the frontier, they were no longer practised in war. In fact, however, as these changes came about and the boundaries of the kingdom became enlarged, the ordinary freemen were left behind tending their cattle and ploughing their strips of land, content to leave the burdens of ruling and fighting to the king and to the king's men.

The principles of lordship and freedom could be intertwined in as many different ways as the knotted patterns of an Anglian or Celtic cross. For while on the one hand a free community was a good soil for the growth of lordship, on the other hand the *tun* of a single settler could, in the course of a few generations, so increase its population that to all appearances it became a community much like the settlement of a kindred.

It is sometimes said that 'the Conquest made the king'. This is untrue in so far as, among the Angles at any rate, the monarchy had been strong and the deeds of Offa of Angel by the banks of the Eider were praised, as we have seen,* by Anglian minstrels in Christian England. In other respects the saying is much less than the truth, for the Conquest also made the new aristocracy, and for a time—that is, as long as the war-bands were actually engaged in winning or holding the land of Britain —the Conquest may also have 'made' the freemen; that is, it may have increased the importance of the ordinary spear-wielding ceorls.

To understand the condition of the generality of the English when we first meet them in our literature and laws, it is of primary importance to remember that the freeman had been largely *unmade*, as we have just pointed out, by the extension of the kingdoms. As a state became bigger and the king and his

* Above, pp. 30–1.

men became further removed from contact with the village folk, the gulf between the men who ploughed and the men who fought became greater; and one reason why the ordinary freemen play no part in *Beowulf* and scarcely appear in the pages of Bede is that both these sources represent the conditions at or after the end of the heathen period rather than the conditions of the age of the migration.

One of the very few ways in which we can track the English village communities back to their beginnings is through the place-names of the villages. These were obviously given not long after the birth of the settlement. If they can be rightly interpreted they may tell us much. We have already tried to use them as material for the history of the Conquest. Now let us see whether they can help us to form any conclusions about the nature of the settlements. Historians of the nineteenth century were almost unanimous in accepting the view that the element *-ing* in our English place-names was patronymic; and that names like Tooting, Nottingham, Kennington all designated settlements made by groups of kinsmen. Nowadays the workers in this field of knowledge are comparing all the early examples of each name and are trying thus to decide whether the *-ing* represents an original plural form (*-ingas*) or a single *-ing* which is a mere possessive. But even in those cases when it becomes possible to assert that the original name was a plural name, we are still a long way from proving that the band of men who had established themselves in that locality were a group of kinsmen. It is said[15] that the plural forms *-ingas* or *-ingaham* often 'have nothing more than some rather indefinite linking force'. They may denote the descendant kin-group of a first settler; but they may also denote his squad of followers, or they 'need mean nothing more than "the people that have to do with" ' the man (or woman) whose name is preserved. All that we can say is that they are 'group names'. The fact is that we are still in the dark, and that if we assert that, say, the Tootings were either the descendants or the retainers of Tota we are dressing up a speculation in the guise of a dogma. Moreover, in almost all of our numerous names ending in *-ington* and in a few of those ending in *-ingham*, the *-ing* seems to be simply a singular possessive. These names witness it seems to the farms or settlements of individuals. The names containing an *-ing* which represent a plural *-ingas* are few and exceptional. The character of the settlement as a whole cannot be decided by them.

THEIR HOMES

In what follows we shall turn our backs on the controversies about the early institutions of the Anglo-Saxons, and shall collect what little information there is about their modes of life and thought; anything which can help us to conceive them, both the warriors and the workers, as living men. We shall begin by studying their homes.

In doing this, the first thing to strike our attention is that we find ourselves in an age of wood. The stone houses built in the great days of Roman rule are disused and falling into ruin. There is no new building in stone. The well-to-do, whether Saxon or British, are lucky if they now inhabit log houses. The humbler folk we shall find thankful for walls of wattle and daub, or mud and straw; but with them there is little change from Roman times. The character of the first habitation in any particular spot is often revealed by its place-name. Thus, a name ending in *-wick* (OE. *wic*) should tell us that the place probably came into existence as a building on the mead, or hayland, of an earlier settlement. Places ending in *stead* or *fold* originated in a similar way as outlying buildings; those ending in *worth* and *cot* had once been the cottages of men who, after the first colonization of England, were brave enough to live in lonely surroundings apart from some main community.[16] Since we are studying the heathen period we are not concerned with these secondary settlements but with the primary, the original, centres.

Leaving on one side those *-ing* place-names which denote a group of settlers rather than a place, the commonest term for an original settlement is our ending *-ton*.* The word could be applied indiscriminately to a large village containing a group of freemen, to the vill of a king or some other great man (this might equally well be described as a *burh*, a fort), or to the farm of a humble ceorl. It connoted an enclosed agricultural settlement, nothing more definite than that.

It is the existence of the enclosure, giving a fort-like appearance to a tun or burh, which would have seemed strangest to a modern man approaching one of the early settlements. He would see a rampart or stockade, pierced only by a narrow gate which could be held against marauders. But defence was only a secondary consideration; and the peaceful routine of the inhabitants would be clear enough inside the enclosure. There a man would see all the dirt and litter of a farmyard and the miscellaneous buildings of a farm—sheds and byres and barns. The number of these, of course, varied with the prosperity of the settlement. If the village had a lord of some importance, the wooden outhouses would be many, including a small building† for the women and children, a kitchen, and a larder. But the main building, the centre of the settlement where there was a lord, would always be the hall. Some idea about the way these were built can be had from the medieval halls or barns which have survived to our day (Pl. 33).

'Heorot', the hall of the king of the Danes, described in *Beowulf*, is magnificent beyond any ordinary building. It was the poet's ideal, the kind of hall to make men stare and envy. From afar could be seen its gleaming roof, with its stag-horns placed on top of the gables. Outside the hall was a bench on which visitors could wait, and there was a place where they could leave their spears before they entered. Inside the hall the first thing to strike a new-comer would be the smell of wood-smoke, and then through the dim light he would see the open hearth

* OE. *tūn*.

† OE. *būr*, 'bower'.

Fig. 35. A Saxon tun.

running down the centre of the building between the pillars which bore the roof—a hearth with piled-up logs and crackling flames, from which the smoke rose eddying round the draughty room before it could find its way out through holes in the roof. Then the walls would be seen to be hung with arms, and, if it were a royal hall like Heorot, there would be also woven hangings, gold-embroidered.

Round the walls were the benches where the retainers sat through the long evenings, when they feasted and drank and listened to the minstrel, or themselves took their turns at the harp. On these benches they pledged one another, they compared the rings and the arms which had been given them by their lords in return for their services. The veterans,* like petty officers, were separated on the benches from the young soldiers;† but none the less an old warrior could egg on one of the young men to revive an ancient feud and slay a foreign prince, the guest of their lord. The retainers talked of the wonders of their lord's sword, of its magical powers, of the runic lettering on the blade, the gold of its handle, and its ringed pommel. Half-way down one side of the hall was the high-seat of the king or lord. In front of the king sat his spokesman.‡ Along the opposite wall was the place next in honour to the high-seat. The queen or 'lady'§ sat by the side of her husband. The women, who had spent the day in housework or spinning, would come from their bower to attend in the hall during the earlier part of the evening's feast, and the 'lady' and her daughters would bear round the ale.

These feastings in the hall stood out in men's minds among the best things in life: the chink of a byrny when a well-armed warrior strode down the hall, the glint of the spears and swords hanging on the walls, cheered the spirits of the men as they drank at the tables. Their weapons were within easy reach; for who could feel sure that enemies, creeping up outside, might not

* OE. *dugoð*.
† OE. *geogoð*.
‡ OE. *thyle*.
§ OE. *hlæfdige*, 'bread-kneeder'.

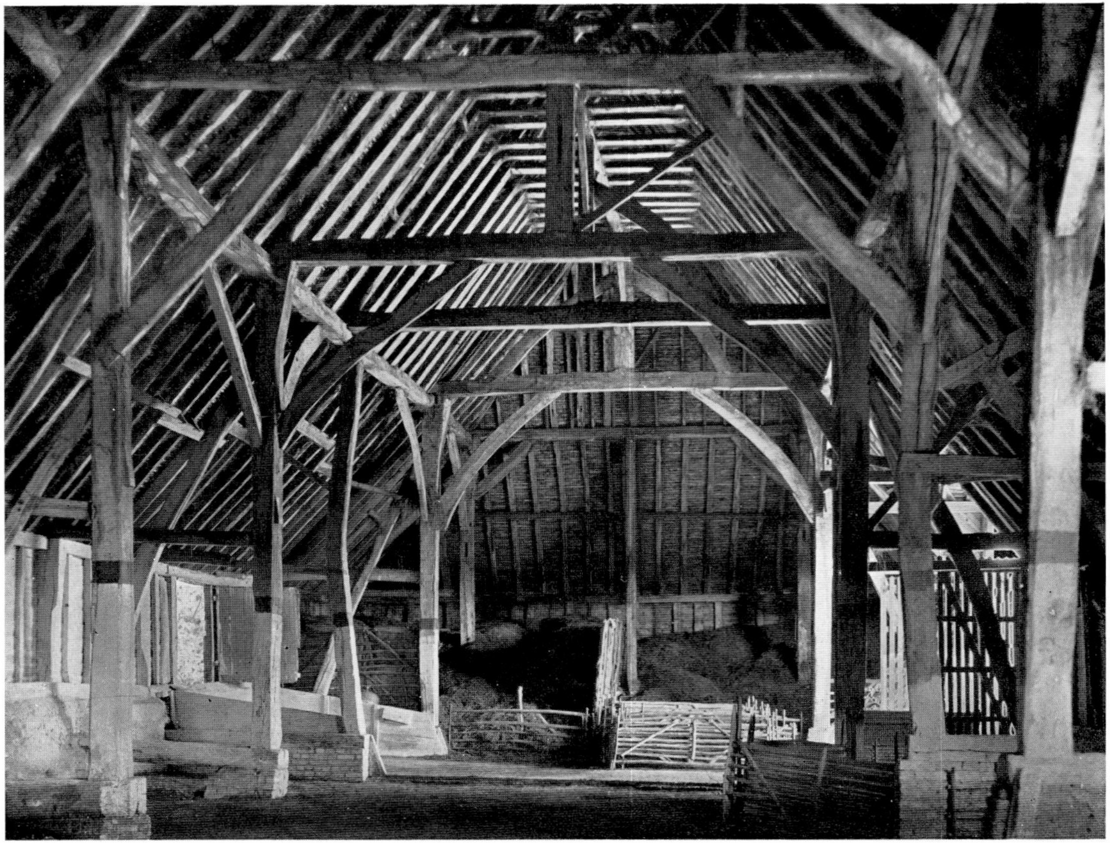

Godmersham, Kent. Old barn showing a type of construction used for halls, churches, and barns in the Middle Ages

Saxon weaver's hut at Bourton. A reconstruction in the British Museum

attempt a surprise attack? Who could tell whether the heavy drinking inside might not end in blows?

So far we have been chiefly concerned with the hall of a great king, as it appears in *Beowulf*. It is the most splendid of its kind; but it may stand for the type, since there was no small similarity in the homes and in the customs of all men of the fighting class. Even a lesser thegn or a substantial ceorl might build himself a log house which reproduced the main features of the larger hall of the great man. As we descend in the social scale, we find the hall becoming smaller, the surrounding outhouses in the *tun* becoming fewer, and the defences dwindling down to the mere hedge which protected the ceorl. Below these, however, in the lowest grades, we find small huts, miserable buildings crowded together in squalid conditions.

Only in the last few years have archaeologists, thanks to the more careful methods of modern excavation, been able to identify any house-sites of the Anglo-Saxons. E. T. Leeds has described[17] vestiges of an early village found in a gravel-bed near the Thames at Sutton Courtenay, south of Oxford. The huts seem to have been arranged in irregular lines (Fig. 36) The men who made them had first dug down for about two feet into the gravel. The construction of the huts above ground was partly revealed by the holes in the gravel, where once had stood the posts which supported the framework of the building. It was inferred that the roof-tree had been stretched from one post to another, perhaps about seven feet above the level of the floor, and that the walls had been formed of mud and straw in alternate layers. Assuredly they were rough-and-ready habitations. The irregularity of their construction can be seen in the inset, which shows the ground-plan of the largest house, one of three rooms. The rooms were separate buildings, but the potsherds found in them indicated that they had belonged to one household. Room no. 3 seemed to have been built as the kitchen for no. 2, and then, when the family increased in size or importance, no. 1 was added as an extra living-room. The floor of the

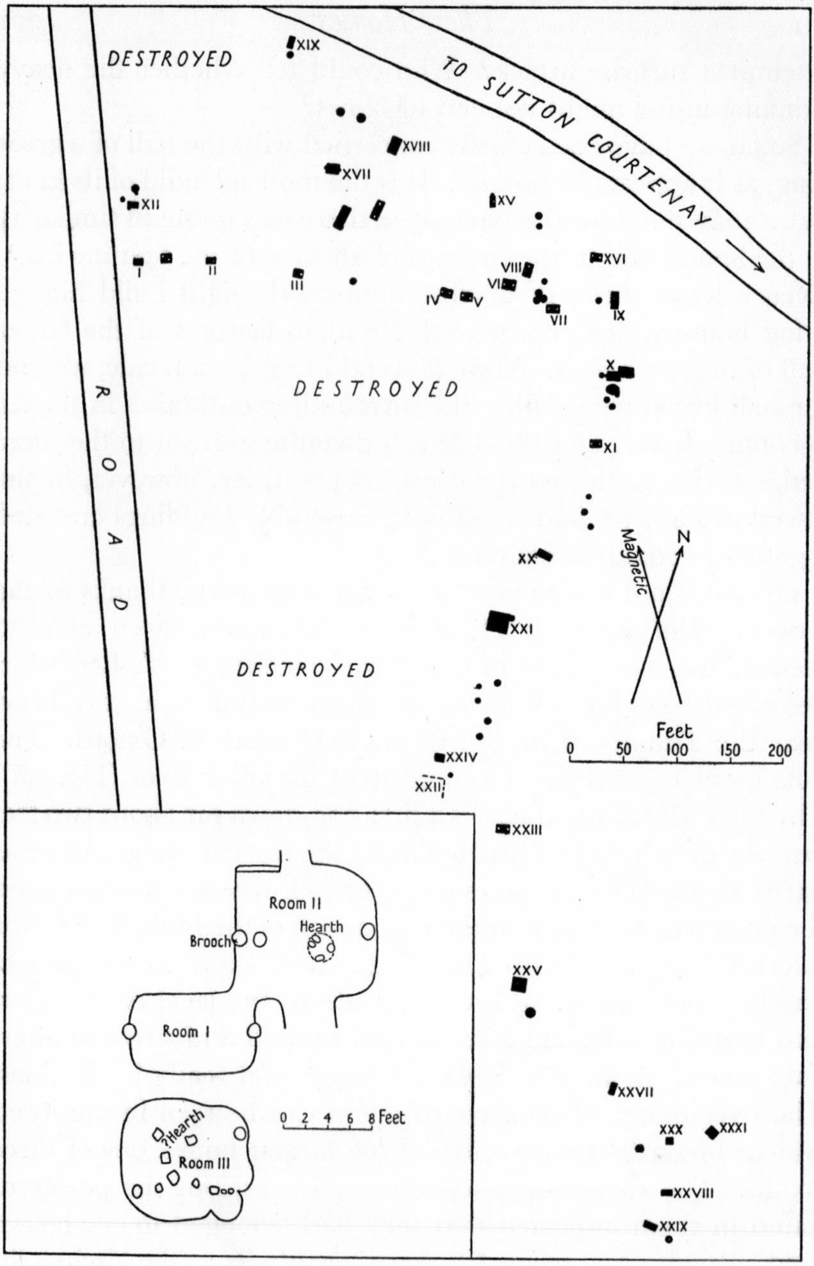

FIG. 36. Plan of Saxon village, near Sutton Courtenay. (The Roman numerals indicate the huts. The rounds in the inset (plan of hut x) indicate the post-holes.)

supposed 'kitchen' during the long period in which it had been used had risen six inches, owing to accumulations of broken pottery and rubbish. Among the things found inside these rooms were: in room no. 1, a bone stiletto, a comb, the pin of a large brooch, and (strange discovery) the skeleton of a middle-aged man, who had been 'buried' on the floor, covered by nothing but a thin blanket of clay, and with him were laid a knife and an ivory comb; in room no. 2, a circular hearth, $2\frac{1}{2}$ feet in diameter, some fragments of grey Roman pottery and Roman glass, and an equal-armed brooch of a fifth-century pattern, a close counterpart of those discovered in the lands between the Elbe and the Weser.*

A somewhat different type of house—perhaps the 'Anglian' type—has been identified on the Car Dyke, in Cambridgeshire.[18] Here there were no hearths, but the floor had been dug out as at Sutton Courtenay, and the shape was irregular. The short lengths of wood found on the site suggest that the walls may have been made of wattle and daub. The thatched roof may have rested on a ridge-pole supported on two posts. In some other respects, also, the hut near Cambridge resembled the Berkshire huts. The inhabitants seem to have been as unpleasant in many of their ways. The floor was a midden of broken bones and potsherds. In one part of the room a dog had been buried. The fragments of the cooking pots were often indistinguishable from the pots in the neighbouring cemeteries in which the ashes of their dead had been placed. These Anglian settlers by the Cam had been so primitive that they threw heated pebbles into their pots to make them boil. And yet they, like the cottagers by the Thames, left behind them traces of some wealth—an ivory armlet and a silver dirk—possessions to be compared with the equal-armed brooch of the Berkshire cottage.

These discoveries take us back better than any glass cases in museums to the actual homes and lives of the German peasants who crossed the North Sea to Britain. Here then we see our

* See Pl. 21 F, and above, Figs. 8 and 9.

Germanic forefathers in Britain at the bottom of the long ascent to civilization. They are beginning in 'filthy little dens'.[19] A weaver's hut at Bourton-on-the-Water suggests that things were better in the cottages of a later date (Pl. 34). And it is

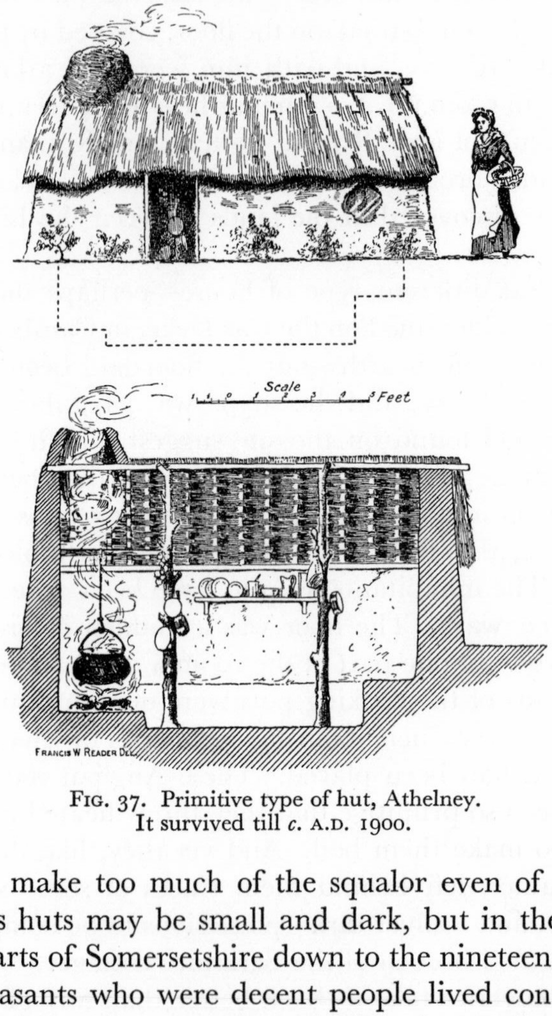

FIG. 37. Primitive type of hut, Athelney.
It survived till *c.* A.D. 1900.

possible to make too much of the squalor even of the Sutton village. Its huts may be small and dark, but in the Fens and in many parts of Somersetshire down to the nineteenth century, English peasants who were decent people lived contentedly in windowless huts of a somewhat similar size and construction (Fig. 37). The six inches of broken sherds and refuse trodden into the gravel of the floor are certainly no good testimonial to the cleanliness of the immigrants. On the other hand, such things, when meals have to be cooked for generations in one dark narrow chamber, do not necessarily prove an extreme of barbarism. But what are we to think about bodies buried in the living-rooms? What were the ideas which led the Berkshire widow to keep the corpse of her man covered with clay by her side, and why did the Anglian cottager leave his dead dog in the hut? Was it an utter devotion to the physical body, or an incredible slovenliness, curiously out of keeping with the ordered interments of the regular Anglo-Saxon cemeteries? Or are we here in contact with notions about the spirits of the dead? These are questions to be remembered, even though they cannot be answered.

THEIR DRESS AND ORNAMENTS

We have been able to say something about the best and the worst dwellings of heathen England, about the halls of the great at the end of the heathen period and the huts of the poor made at the beginning of the settlement. The men and women who lived in these surroundings still escape us. Is it possible to raise the ghosts of these heathen forefathers of ours, the men who spent their days in hunting, fighting, and ploughing, and the women who spun and wove at home and directed their house-slaves? Can we picture even the clothes they wore? This must be the first question to which we now direct our attention. Since there are not English peat-bogs like those of Schleswig, the only pieces of cloth preserved in the heathen graves in England are mere fragments. They are said[20] to be 'of various qualities, varying from about the texture of a modern flannel shirt to that of Harris tweed'. The best that we can do is to study the costume portrayed in the carving of the Franks casket in the British Museum. It must be remembered, however, that this whalebone box is, in all probability, a Northumbrian product, and that while it is the nearest that we can get to a representation of the men of heathen times, it is none the less assigned to a period as late as about 650–750.

On the casket we see that the fighting-men have tunics which hang down to above the knee, much like kilts; garments like sleeved jackets; and cloaks or mantles fastened on the shoulder. Some of the men have clumsy puttees wound round their legs; others have their legs either bare or covered with hose. Altogether it is a costume not unlike that of the Highlander. Close-fitting breeches reaching down to the ankle, like those at Kiel (Pl. 5), and cross-gartered, were also no doubt quite a normal mode of covering the legs throughout the Saxon period. The women shown on the casket, and the men when they are sedentary or men of dignity, wear long tunics reaching to the ankle or nearly to it, and longer mantles also—fine large sweeping garments, with hoods which can be drawn over the head.

With some exercise of imagination we may perhaps obtain a better idea of the appearance of these heathen men and women from their graves.* We can picture the Anglian women with their sleeves caught together at the wrist with the small clasps which are so characteristic a feature of their graves, and their girdle-hangers, like a chatelaine, depending from their tunic-belt and jangling as they move; their men-folk also, long-haired, proud of their cruciform brooches, which become long and flat and increasingly vulgar as the heathen age draws to its close.

The fashions of course changed with the changing decades or generations, if not like ours with the changing years. Even more than ours, in those days of isolation they changed from district to district. Thus, to take a single example, at Sleaford in Lincolnshire there was a large settlement of early immigrants in which the women commonly wore their beads slung in festoons from shoulder to shoulder, both ends of the festoon being fastened to the tunic with a pin.

Before we turn from the heathen graves of the Saxons, let us pick out one or two of those which are the most richly furnished

* e.g. Fig. on p. 101 (the man's shield is indicated by the round dotted line) and Fig. 38.

A

B

C

A. The Franks casket, Anglian work, about A.D. 650–750
B. The Visit of the Magi, on the front of the casket
C. A scene from the Capture of Jerusalem by Titus, on the back of the casket

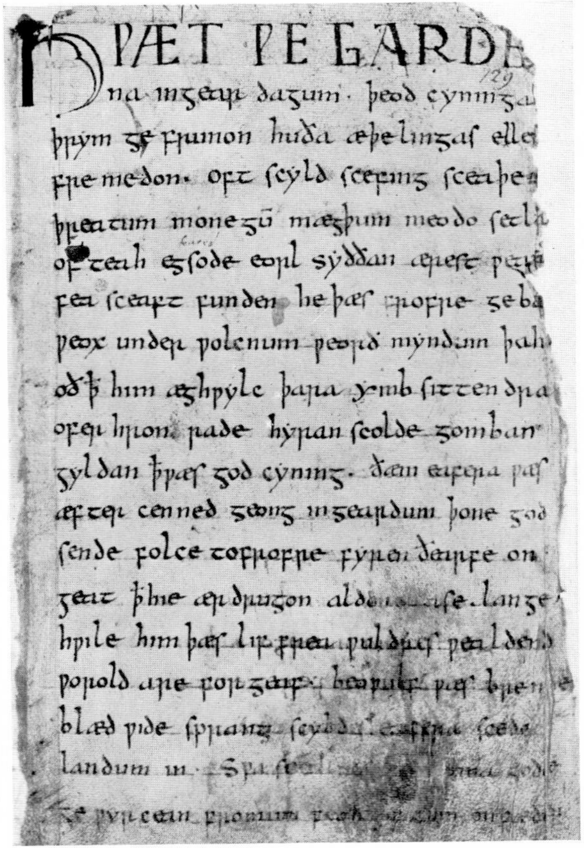

HWÆT, WE GĀRDEna   in ʒeardaʒum
þeodcyninʒa   þrym ʒefrunon,
hu ða æþelinʒas   elle[n] fremedon.
Oft Scyld Scefinʒ   sceaþen[a] þreatum,
moneʒum mæʒþum   meodosetl[a] ofteah,
eʒsode eorl,   syððan ærest wear[ð]
feasceaft funden;   he þæs frofre ʒeba[d,]
weox under wolcnum,   weorðmyndum þah,
oð þæt him æʒhwylc   þara ymbsittendra
ofer hron rade   hyran scolde,
ʒomban ʒyldan;   þæt wæs ʒod cyninʒ.
Ðæm eafera wæs   æfter cenned
ʒeonʒ in ʒeardum,   þone ʒod sende
folce to frofre;   fyrenðearfe onʒeat,
þæt hie ær druʒon   aldor[le]ase
lanʒe hwile.   Him þæs lif frea,
wuldres wealdend,   woroldare forʒeaf;
Beowulf wæs breme   —blæd wide spranʒ—
Scyldes eafera   Scedelandum in.
Swa sceal [ʒeonʒ ʒ]uma   ʒode ʒewyrcean,
fromum feohʒiftum,   on fæder

The beginning of the Beowulf MS. (Cotton Vitellius A. xv, reduced)

and which show best of all the degree of magnificence to which heathen Anglo-Saxons attained.

For our chief example we cannot do better than choose the great mound which was piled up probably about the end of the heathen period over the body of a dead chieftain at Taplow. There can be no question that this is the '*hlaw*', the burial-mound, of Tæppa, the unknown warrior from whom the place has borrowed its name.[21]

The site chosen was on a high hill above the Thames with a commanding view over the surrounding country. The mound is a big one, 240 feet round the base, 80 feet in diameter, rising to a height of 15 feet. Tæppa was supplied liberally with precious belongings ornamented for the most part in the Kentish style; and some of them are reproduced in colour in this book (Coloured Plates I, II).

So far no other mound has been opened which quite corresponds to the Taplow tomb. An interesting comparison may be found in the Asthall barrow which was excavated in 1924.[22] The barrow itself was not so big as that of Taplow, but its position on a spur of the Cotswolds, 440 feet above the sea, made it an even more conspicuous landmark from all the hills round the upper Thames and the Vale of the White Horse. Now while there was probably no great difference of time separating the burials of the two chieftains, there was a fundamental difference in their religions. The thegns of Tæppa laid his best belongings by his side. They thought of his body continuing in the next world as he had lived in this. The thegns of the nameless hero at Asthall, on the other hand, burnt their lord. They remembered that men had a dual character, and they therefore sent their lord to the other world in the mood of the thegns who buried Beowulf and no doubt with much the same rites. These tumuli, then, reveal to us not a little about the warrior class in the times of heathendom. They show us their magnificence in outward appearance, their gold-embroidered clothing, their gilt buckles and their drinking vessels mounted in silver-gilt. They show us too the devotion of their thegns and the uncertainty of their heathen beliefs. A great man on the lower Thames, having advanced perhaps from Kent, the kingdom of merchant princes who dressed in cloth of gold, might be buried much like a later Viking. On the other hand, a great man in the upper Thames valley, having perhaps pressed south from Mercia, may have notions about cremation which are deliberately old-fashioned.

These barbaric warrior chiefs, so much alike in spite of variations between cremation and inhumation, are a whole world away from our modern society; it is different if we turn to the homelier articles of the women's graves or consider the craftsmen who made the brooches of the heroes. Here there are points where this oldest England is in touch with modern times. Note for instance the bronze work-box found in an Anglian grave at Burwell, Cambridgeshire (Figs. 38 and 39). Similar though less ornamented work-boxes are not uncommon in women's graves. No doubt they were sold by pedlars. They were of bronze, sometimes gilt. They were neatly made and could be carried, as in this case, in a lady's bag or suspended from her belt. They could contain such sewing things as bronze needles, minute tweezers or knives, and threads of silk or wool. Here then we have a reminder that the gay dresses of the Saxon women about which the clergy will later have much to say were not enjoyed without much labour on the women's part. As formerly in Angel, so again in England, for the women there is an endless round of spinning, weaving, sewing, and dyeing. Of all these activities the work-boxes remain for us the best symbol.

Lastly, the Saxon graves have much to tell us about the skill and the assiduity of the craftsmen, especially of the Kentish craftsmen, who could make beautiful ornaments like the Kingston brooch[22a] and those illustrated in colour in this volume. Experts agree that some of these Kentish jewellers had few, if any, equals in western Europe in their own day and that their work can bear comparison with that of modern craftsmen 'armed with all the appliances of science and machinery'.[23]

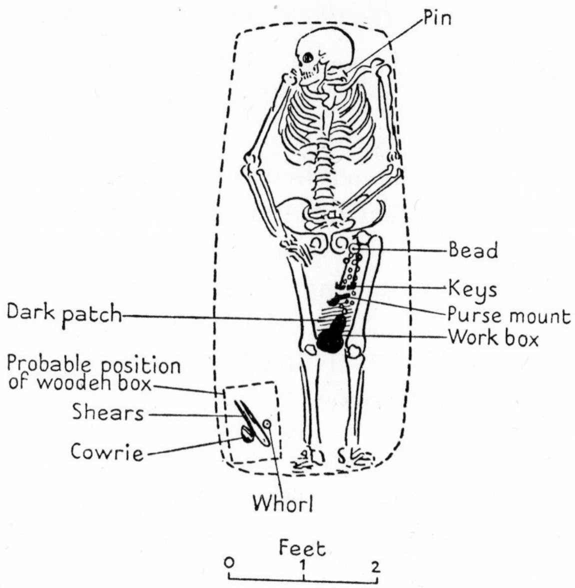

FIG. 38. Burwell, Cambridgeshire. Interment of Anglian woman, perhaps a Christian though buried in the pagan manner (*c.* A.D. 650 or later). The 'dark patch' had probably been a purse.

FIG. 39. Bronze work-box, from above, with repoussé ornamentation. The ends of the box (not here figured) show a man fighting a dragon, in panels.

So far we have picked up a few facts about the well-to-do, who lived in their timbered halls, and about the 'filthy dens' of the poor. What we have learnt is not much, but it is enough to remind us that life in the heathen period had its great contrasts, and that we must suspect historians who dismiss Anglo-Saxon society as if it were all of a piece, picking out a supposed fact about one generation, a surmise about another, and so producing a composite picture which is not true to any one time or place; and labelling it savage or civilized or liberty-loving, according to their varying predilections.

THEIR THOUGHTS

Is there any approach to the minds of the ordinary Englishmen, the ceorls, those whom King Alfred described as the *weorcmen*, 'the workmen'?[24] The nearest that we can get to them is in certain so-called 'Riddles' and gnomic poetry. Both writings come from the Christian period, but both, like *Beowulf*, seem to carry with them ideas from heathen times, mingled with material drawn from Latin literature and the Bible. The Riddle about the Plough, for instance, gives us a picture which, though true for any primitive agricultural society, has about it a characteristic Anglo-Saxon touch.[25] 'My nose is downward; I go deep and dig into the ground; I move as the grey foe of the wood [? man, the wood-cutter] guides me, and my lord who goes stooping as guardian at my tail; he pushes me in the plain, bears and urges me, sows in my track. . . . On one side of me as I go there is green, and on the other side there is black.' These few lines remind us once more of the unceasing labour of the Anglo-Saxon countrymen, which may rightly be mentioned in chapter after chapter since, year in and year out, from early morning to sunset, it was ever bringing wider tracts of forest and waste land under cultivation. Behind the turmoil of the war-bands—slaying and being slain for the honour of their lords, heroically winning (or losing) kingdoms—the ceorls and serfs with bent shoulders were driving their heavy German ploughs, turning the green sods into black furrows, and, as they slowly moved forward, shouting to their team.

The gnomic verses may be called the Book of Proverbs of the Anglo-Saxons, and as is the way with this type of popular literature, they abound with platitudes.[26] But however commonplace, a few quotations may help to bring certain aspects of the Anglo-Saxon world before us. We see, for instance, that these primitive men cling together for support, and pity or suspect those who are not anchored in a village community. 'Hapless is he who must needs live alone.' 'Well should one keep a friend in all ways; often a man passes by the village afar off where he knows he has no certain friend. Unfriended, unblessed, a man takes wolves for companions, a dangerous beast; full often that companion rends him. There should be terror of the grey wolf. . . .' This and other warnings about fierce beasts like the boar or the bear remind us of the constant apprehension in the minds of the country folk, isolated in clearings reclaimed from the wild nature around them—the fear of creatures of all kinds which lurked in the woods and the wastes. By the side of these passages let us place the early law found in the codes of both Kent and Wessex.[27] 'If a man from far or a stranger quits the road, and neither shouts nor blows a horn, he shall be assumed to be a thief [and as such] may be either slain or put to ransom.'

The thoughts of the seafaring folk are also illustrated in the gnomic poetry. 'Weary shall he be who rows against the wind. Full often one blames the coward with reproaches so that he loses courage, and draws his oar on board.' At the time when these verses were composed, the typical seaman had become a Frisian. But what is true of the Frisian in the eighth or ninth century must have been equally true of the Anglo-Saxon in earlier days.

'Dear is the welcome one to the Frisian wife when the ship comes to rest. His vessel has come, and her husband is at home, her own provider; and she bids him come in, washes his sea-stained garment, and gives him fresh clothes. She gives him on land what love requires. A wife should keep faith with her husband; often she defames a man with her vices; many a one is steadfast in mind, many a one is prying; she loves strange men when the other travels afar.'

Now let us again change our standpoint, and look, not at the 'workmen', but at the chiefs and their war-bands, the inhabitants of the great halls. For these we can turn to *Beowulf*, the only lengthy heroic poem of the Anglo-Saxons which has survived, and we shall be able to see therein much of the workings of the primitive English mind.

Since our last quotation from the gnomic poetry ended with a passage which took the low view of women so often affected by the writers of proverbs, let us make amends by saying at once that, as a rule, women appear in a more favourable light in Old English verse. They mix with the men on terms of equality. They minister to their wants. We recognize the important ladies of the heathen graves whose keys had jangled from their girdles, and whose work-boxes had been neatly supplied with needles and sewing materials. In *Beowulf* they are 'the people's pledge of peace', they 'weave peace' for their men-folk as well as their clothes. They help them with their advice and influence. They are respected, as Germanic women were said to be respected in the times of Tacitus.

In the men who appear in the heroic poetry, it is not mere fancy which inclines us to recognize features of family likeness to modern Englishmen—features both good and bad. Even the monster-fighting of Beowulf foreshadows the restless energy which has characterized men of Anglo-Saxon descent. Beowulf was not happy sitting still. He was said to be 'the strongest of mankind'; but the strongest in body and not in mind. His hunger to win fame, to do something that demanded endurance and heroism, made him seek out his monsters, as the moderns have sought out their conquests over nature in Central Africa, the Polar regions, or the Himalayas.

For those unacquainted with the plot of the *Beowulf* poem, it must suffice to say that the main story turns on three encounters. In the first of them Beowulf, the hero of the Geats (these almost certainly are the Götar, the southern neighbours of the Swedes), hearing that the country of the Danes is vexed by a monster called Grendel, goes with his followers to the court of Hrothgar the Danish king, at Leire in Zealand, and after some talk and feasting in Heorot, the splendid wooden hall recently built by that king, remains to fight the monster single-handed. In the second episode another monster, Grendel's mother, in revenge for Grendel's death, plays havoc in Heorot, and Beowulf seeks her out in her home beneath the waters of a mere in an eerie spot on a lonely heath. The third episode is later. After feats of war in the land of the Frisians and elsewhere, and after ruling well for fifty years as king of his own people, the hero engages in his last encounter. He kills a fire-breathing dragon who is guarding a hoard of gold; but in doing so receives a poisonous and fatal wound.

If we are to interpret the Anglo-Saxons by *Beowulf* we should know what was the intention of the poem. Did it aim rather at amusement or at edification, or was it simply a blend of old stories, a form of history?

The best way to understand what was supplied by the author is to understand what was demanded by his audience. What was it that the retainers in the hall wanted? First and foremost, to be taken out of themselves, and the commonplaceness of everyday life. Tales of monsters could do this, and the creatures of *Beowulf* were prize monsters: Grendel, the dark death-shadow from the misty moors, who entrapped warriors old and young, the creature from whose eyes came a weird light, who could open the door of the hall by touching it, who thirsted for human blood and swallowed men bite by bite, not leaving even their feet and hands. Grendel was frightful and Grendel's mother was equally uncanny—a mere-wife who clutched at men with horrid claws from the depths of a lonely lake. The world was full of monsters —animals of the deep, with tusks; and animals of the moors, like the spotted fire-breathing dragon who gave Beowulf his death-wound, biting his neck with its sharp teeth.

The warriors, returned from chase or war-path, and safe in their hall, when cheered by their ale-cups, liked to hug the thought of the fearful things outside the hall. And so the author of *Beowulf* enlarges on the horrors. For the first time the melancholy note of northern scenery is sounded. We move in a land of haunted moors, of 'wolf-slopes, wind-swept headlands, and dangerous marsh-paths, where the mountain-stream falls down under the darkness of the rocks'. There was the home of the monsters, a blood-stained and turbid lake overhung by gray rocks and mountain trees. The hunted stag would die rather than enter its water. Again those who seek out the lair of the 'twilight foe', that is, the dragon which flies flaming through the night skies, must go to the loneliest barrow of a desolate moor, where in subterranean chambers the enemy of mankind guards a hoard of heathen gold.

The warriors in addition to tales of dragon-killing expected to hear from their minstrels endless variations on the theme of fighting and bloodshed among men. No one could tire of such a subject (was it not at once the business and the sport of eorls?), but these stories also must be rendered in a minor key. Inside the hall revelry, and outside by contrast to it the evil things that beset men—a sobering thought. Even when the Danes are celebrating the double victory of Beowulf over Grendel and his dam, one of the braves 'told a true and *sad* tale'. Beowulf himself, before his last battle with the dragon, is made to dwell, in the characteristic Anglo-Saxon strain, upon the mournful lot of a father who loses a son. 'Unceasingly at every morn he is reminded of the passing of his son. . . . Sorrowful he gazes at his son's room . . . the deserted wine-hall, abandoned, a lodgement for the winds, its merriment all gone. The horsemen sleep, the heroes are in their grave, there is no music of the harp, no merrymaking in the courts as once there was.'

When the warriors were not exalted by battle-fury they

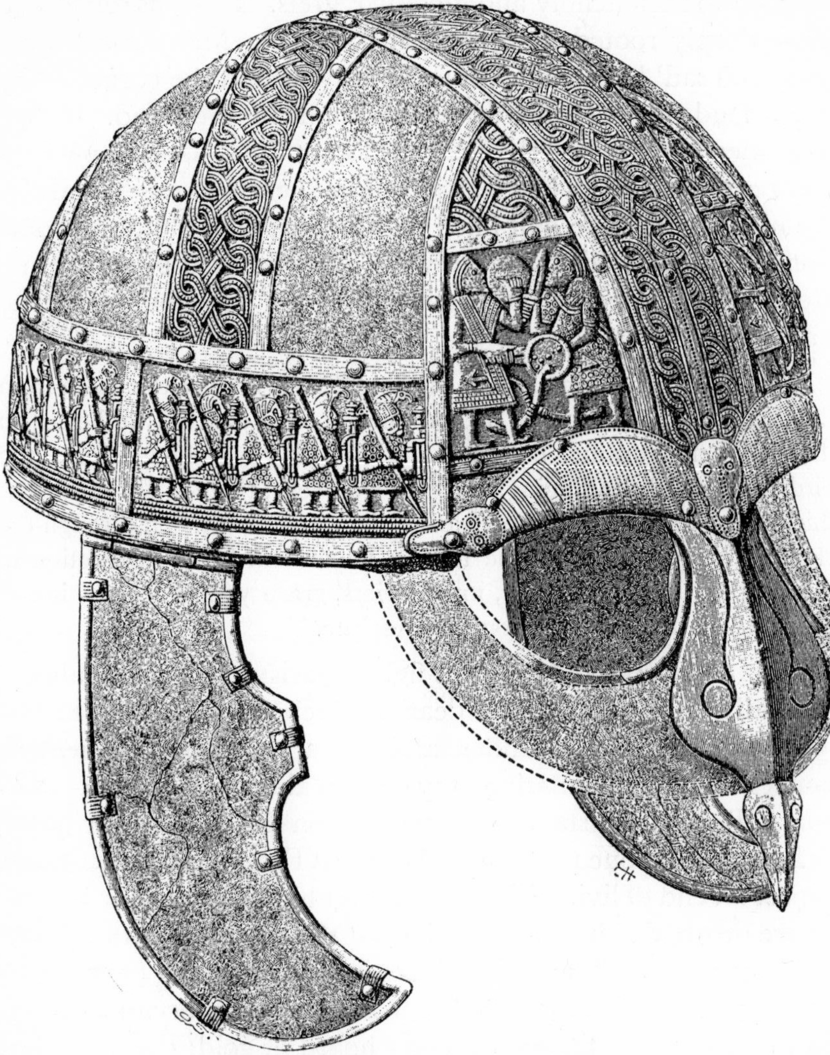

Fig. 40. Vendel, Sweden; helmet of iron with bronze mountings, partly gilded, showing warriors like those of *Beowulf*.

(Recent excavations show that the face guards were worn further forward than in the above reconstruction and were large enough to meet over the wearer's chin. A prototype of this helmet was used in the Roman armies in the fourth century. Cf. Lindqvist in *Acta Archaeologica*, iii (1932), 21–38).

inclined to melancholy and gloomy regrets. This was something more deeply rooted than a passing fashion. Men's songs were 'true and sad' because death was always round the corner. Any day a feud might spring up which might be their end. If they were merry in the hall they did not forget the stories of how men had been surprised when feasting. The spearmen might wake in the night to find the hall filled with smoke, which did not come from the hearth. The wooden walls could be fired by an enemy. Here, for instance, is the beginning of the fragmentary *Lay of Finnsburh.*[28]

> 'Then the king, young in war, spoke: "This is neither the dawn from the east, nor does a dragon fly here, nor are the gables [the horns] of this hall here burning, but they are launching a sudden attack; the birds (of battle) are singing; the grey wolf yells; there is din of spears; shield answers to shaft. Now gleams the wandering moon through the clouds; now evil deeds come to pass which will bring destruction to this people. But awake now, my warriors, grasp your shields, think of brave deeds, fight in the front, be resolute." '

Can it be wondered that this fighting aristocracy dwelt almost morbidly on the thought of death? They came back to it, but scarcely pretended to understand it, varying from moment to moment in the explanation they offered about the object of existence. Read, for instance, the speeches on this subject attributed to Beowulf. At one time the end of life is Fame: 'Each of us must expect an end of living in this world; let him who may, win glory before death, for that is best at last for the departed man of war.' Sometimes fame almost crystallizes into the winning of gold. In his dying speech Beowulf is reconciled to death because he has given his own life for the dragon's hoard of gold; the 'countless store of twisted gold' is an end in itself. None the less, the chief does not fight simply for his own gain. He fights for his people. He is the guardian, 'the shepherd of his people', and the warriors in their turn, and especially the hearth-companions of the chief, could find the effective religion of life in the service of their lord. The true thegn would rather die with his lord than desert him in the fight and carry back his weapons to his home. 'Death', says the one faithful follower of Beowulf, 'is better for all warriors than a shameful life.'

And when death comes, the warriors have to send their lord richly provided and with honour befitting his station to the realms of the dead. The poem of *Beowulf* opens with lines which tell how the companions of Scyld Scefing gave to the sea the eponymous ancestor of the Spear-Danes, equipping the ship with swords and coats of mail, laying out Scyld upon it with treasures on his breast and launching this kingly bier into the sea, to let the ocean carry him where it would. The same note is struck at the end of the epic, in the lines which describe the funeral of Beowulf.

'Then the people [*leode*] of the Geats made ready for him on the ground a splendid pyre, hung round with helmets, battle-targes, bright corselets, as he had craved; then the sorrowing men laid in the midst the famous prince, their loved lord. The warriors began to kindle on the barrow the greatest of funeral-fires; the wood-reek mounted up dark above the smoking glow, the crackling flame, mingled with the cry of weeping—the tumult of the winds ceased—until it had consumed the body, hot to the heart. Sad in spirit, they lamented the sorrow of their souls, the slaying of their lord; likewise the aged woman [? his widow] with bound tresses sang a dirge... [words missing in the manuscript]... the sky swallowed up the smoke.

'Then the people of the Weders [i.e. the Geats] wrought a mound, which was lofty and broad, at the edge of the headland, visible far and wide to seafarers; and in ten days they finished the beacon of the man mighty in battle; the remnant of the pyre they compassed round with a wall, as exceeding wise men might most worthily devise it. They laid in the barrow rings and ornaments, all such adornments as men, eager for combat, had erstwhile taken from the hoard; they let the earth keep the treasure of warriors, the gold in the ground. . . . Then men bold in battle, sons of chieftains, twelve in all, rode about the mound; they were minded to utter their grief, to lament the king, to make a chant and to speak of the man; they exalted his heroic life and praised his valorous deed with all their strength.'

Here, at the end of the poem, the intention of the author is put most plainly. He had aimed with all his skill at exalting the heroic life.

When we put *Beowulf* aside and glance at the other evidences of Anglo-Saxon heathendom, we realize at once how specially scanty these are.[29] The scantiness may be explained in two ways. We may, if we like, say that we have here a testimony to the efficiency of the censorship set up by the Christian Church in England. But other explanations cannot be disregarded: that Germanic heathenism had not stood well the crossing of the North Sea; or that it had never recovered its vigour in Britain. In northern Germany, in the first century of our era, the religion of Nerthus as described by Tacitus had been a well-organized cult, with its sacred island and its image of the goddess whose mysteries had drawn the neighbouring tribes together in a bond of common worship. But among the Germanic settlements in Britain we find no trace of religious centralization. There is no one holy place which is a centre for the different kingdoms. Even within the independent states there is little to suggest that religion is highly organized. A king has his own wooden temple within its sacred enclosure, and the wooden effigies of his favourite gods, each image placed on its small altar. But there is no great outcry when his temple is desecrated. There is not in heathen England, as among the continental tribes, an outstanding holy tree or holy pillar which attracts to itself the general devotion of the people. True, we hear of a chief-priest* in Northumbria, but if we may judge from his actions he was not the head of an organized hierarchy. In Norway and later in Iceland the great landowner who erected his temple and placed therein his images took it upon himself to set up, each in his own neighbourhood, as the priest† of the district, with a right of levying contributions for his trouble. If this custom was followed in England, it was not the only arrangement. There are

* *primus pontificum*, also called *pontifex sacrorum*. † *Goði*.

passages in Bede and elsewhere which indicate a more professional priesthood. Thus the Londoners, when they rejected their bishop Mellitus (617–18), preferred to be under their priests. The Northumbrian chief priest was not allowed either to carry arms or to ride on anything but a mare. The chief priest* of the South Saxons, who cursed Wilfrid when driven by a storm onto their coast, and sought to bind him with magic, has the look of an expert.

Since it is in London and in Sussex that we read of heathen priests taking a strong line in opposition to Christianity, it is interesting to note (though this may of course be only a coincidence) that it is also in the south-east of the island that we have the clearest traces of heathenism in place-names—for example, in names containing *harrow* (OE. *hearg*, a sacred place), and in those with an element derived from the Old English word *wig*, or *weoh* (meaning an idol, or something sacred), such as Weedon in Buckinghamshire.

As for the gods of the Germanic pantheon, it has been calculated that, out of the thousands of Saxon place-names, only six were compounded with the name of Woden, and only nine with Thunor.[30] The other Germanic gods were almost completely ignored. The settlers were matter-of-fact people in their nomenclature. They described their farms or villages by the names of their owners, or by physical characteristics. Is it probable that the gods who appear so little in their place-names came much into their thoughts?

The few glimpses which we catch of Woden in England reveal him in a variety of characters, but omit many features which in the past have been fastened on him by borrowing from the Odin of Scandinavian mythology. He is not the All-Father: he is no heathen counterpart of the Christian Deity; he has no well-appointed residence like Valhalla. He is not a one-eyed god who wanders about the world. He appears to be first and foremost the god of War. He can give the victory. He can be appealed

* *princeps sacerdotum.*

to in stress of battle; he can be appeased by a massacre. He can make an imposing earthwork like Woden's Dyke—'the Wansdyke'.

For the rest, we chiefly hear of Woden in England as a name which in later times could be employed in spells, or to head the genealogy of a royal family, and there, linked with other gods or demi-gods, give the dynasty the stamp of respectability. We have seen that in Germany Woden was a new-fashioned god, introduced late to the northern tribes as the special protector of the kings and the military class. In England the mass of the immigrants had for a time become fighting-men; and it was thus that Woden nearly rivalled Thunor in the number of his place-names, and obtained a lead in other directions.

The English Thunor, so far as our positive information goes, has even less in common with the Norse Thor than has Woden with the Norse Odin, for the fact is that we know Thunor only as the Thunderer.

He and the other gods and goddesses are mere names. The Tiw of our Tuesday, though equated with Mars, had clearly been given a back place among war-gods after the rise of Woden. The Frig of Friday was equated with Venus, and in late chronicles was said to be Woden's wife.

So little is known about these gods and the mythology of English heathenism that there can be no satisfactory comparison between the English and the Scandinavian systems. The similarities in the names and terminology are indeed notable. Thus the Saxon word for earth, *middangeard*, seems to carry with it an inference that the earth was the middle-dwelling, the habitation of men, because above or beyond it was the realm of the gods, and below it was hell, the place of spirits. If the gods were no happy family-party and their abode no Valhalla, it had at least a name, the unlovely name *neorxna-wang*.

Of lesser beings we hear of *wælcyrian*, corpse-choosing witches rather than reputable war-maidens like their counterparts the Valkyries of the north; also of *eotenas*, giants, not of the stuff to dream of waging war against the great gods, but mere unpleasant monsters, perhaps man-eaters.

Some knowledge of the ways of our heathen ancestors is derived from a work of Bede called *De Temporum Ratione.*[31] In it he explains the English names of the months and the reasons for them. February was called '*Sol-monath,* because of the cakes which were then offered to the gods'. 'To the gods'—surely to the oldest of all nature deities, the Sun. March was called '*Rhed-monath,* because of sacrifices to the goddess Rheda'. April was *Eostur-monath,* and its sacrifices were made to Eostra, apparently akin to the Greek Ἐώς, the goddess of the dawn. Then after the summer months—the months in which men were fully occupied with their milkings, their harvest, and their weeding—came September, the holy month (*Haleg-monath*),* the month of sacred rites; November (*Blot-monath*), the month of sacrifices, when the cattle which could not be fed through the winter were slaughtered and devoted to the gods; a season when heathenism more than ever spelt bloodshed—bloodshed no doubt accompanied by drinking and revelry. ('Gratia tibi, bone Iesu,' sighs Bede, 'Thou hast converted us from these deceits and hast allowed us to offer Thee sacrifices of praise.') Last (or more strictly first, since the Germanic year began with the winter) came the sixty days of Yule,† covering both December and January. It was only by Roman-Christian influence that this winter season Yule came to be restricted to Christmas. In the mid-winter feast of heathen times sacrifices were probably made for good luck and peace in the coming year, and men dressed themselves up in the skins and masks of animals. Bede calls the octave corresponding to our Christmas and New Year holiday, *Modranect,* Mother-night. In Roman days the pagan soldiers along the Wall erected their altars to the *Matres.* 'The Mothers' —but what Mothers?—were still remembered by their successors.

From glimpses of this oldest England given in passages like the above chapter of Bede, and from the survival of heathen

* Better *halig-monath.*

† *Geol* or *Guil.*

customs in Christian times, we see how mixed were the ideas and how diversified were the practices of Anglo-Saxon heathenism; and that the cults of Thunor and Woden were but novelties superimposed on far older and better-rooted beliefs. The king or rich landowner might build his timbered temple. The teaching of the priests might endow it with a tradition of sanctity. The slaughtering of the cattle might take place within the holy enclosure of the temple, surrounded by a holy wood. Men might troop to these sacred spots, and there see the blood flow, be themselves sprinkled or daubed with blood, gorge themselves on an unaccustomed superfluity of meat; they might drink and make merry. But the religious usages which were nearest their hearts were older, incalculably older, rites which they believed would appease the spirits of the sun and the corn, bringing fertility to themselves and their crops and their herds: the offerings of cakes to the Sun (if that is indeed the meaning of *Solmonath*); the charming of the plough on Plough Monday (the first Monday after Twelfth Night), and the May festival. In this the whole village joined in order to persuade the fertility spirit to return to their homes and fields, the villagers covering themselves in the greenery and flowers of the new spring life, dancing round a tree, washing in the dew, or ducking folk in water in order to mix with the water spirit, lighting 'need-fires' to attract the spirit of warmth and sunshine, passing their cattle through the fire, and processing solemnly through the fields, if not with the image then with the symbol of divinity. The vegetation rites which accompanied the coming of the spring, and the harvest rites were everywhere of first importance. But their details varied in different parts of the country. At any of the village festivals there might be sacrifices, since it was good to eat the spirit of the god. At any of them there might be sprinkling with blood, immersions, bonfires, since by such means there could be contact with the spirits of life, of moisture, of heat. Men danced and sang, but there was more than merry-making. The rites were necessary to bring good increase in agriculture.

Though the myths of the heathen English were almost entirely obliterated by the subsequent centuries of Christianity, a trace of them remains in the story of Scyld Scefing. The story as told by William of Malmesbury runs as follows:[32] 'Sceaf, as they say, was brought as a child in a ship without oars to Scandza, a certain island in Germany. . . . He was asleep, and a sheaf of corn lay beside his head. He was on this account called Sceaf (in modern spelling Sheaf) and was received as a prodigy by the people of that country and carefully fostered.'

This is not the place to enter into such controversial questions as the original version of the story or the relation of Sceaf to Scyld, to the Nerthus of Tacitus, or to the Vanir gods of the Scandinavians. What is undeniable and significant is that, though the organized Nerthus cult is not reproduced in England, some ideas and usages resembling those of the cult were clearly transferred from the Continent to our island; and that this primitive 'Fertility religion' was so well established that whatever the name of the great god who for the moment was favoured by the rulers of the State, whether Thunor or Woden—or Christ—the old practices could be maintained by the cultivators of the soil, practices essential for prosperity in farming and for good luck in life.

We see then that Woden and Thunor and the great gods introduced into Britain by Saxon conquerors were in some ways less important than the lesser powers like Sceaf and Weland the Smith (who was a living tradition in the times of Alfred) and Wyrd, the irresistible Fate who ruled even the gods; and all the rout of miscellaneous beings and spirits who accompanied the immigrants—elves of all kinds (of the downs, of the woods, of the fields, of the water), giants, nightmares, dragons, sea-monsters (*nicors*), altogether a mixed lot. The number and variety of these supernatural beings is another testimony to the confusion which reigned in the minds of the Anglo-Saxon immigrants. Remembering the diversity of their burial customs, we understand how the small communities of the heathen period were too isolated for their religious notions to be pooled or worked into a coherent system like that of the Icelanders in a later age. The unseen powers which surrounded the Anglo-Saxons filled them with all kinds of confused apprehensions. They had to resort in self-defence to charms and magic and sacrifices. So far as we know, human beings were not sacrificed as among the Scandinavians and the Frisians; but the pits of black greasy earth interspersed with bones of oxen, horses, pigs, and goats, sometimes found in the neighbourhood of Anglo-Saxon cemeteries remind us that their heathen customs were often ugly enough and reeked of blood. The feasts and the less horrid of their rites at the spring and autumn festivals had their hold on the people, but belief in the greater gods was weak. Heathen society was ripe for conversion. The world of Woden was ready to become a world created and ruled by an Almighty Father, dominated by his wonder-working saints, and tended by his bishops and clergy The heavenly powers might change, but the underworld of monsters and evil spirits would remain to be marshalled by Satan into a host of demons (*unholdan*), the enemies of Christian men.

From Franks Casket: Sigurd in his burial mound; his wife and horse standing near.

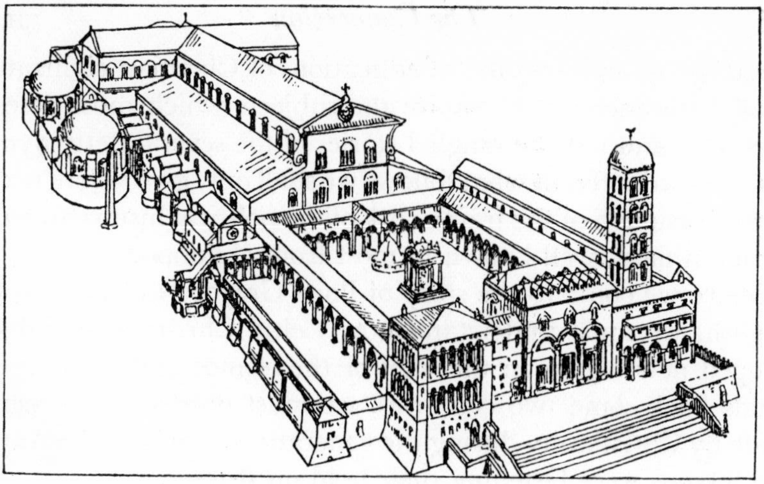

VIII—Part I

THE CONVERSION, TO 633

IT is inevitable that the history of the Conversion of the English should be told on different lines from that of their conquest of Britain. About the conquest so little is known that we have laboriously to fit together the few existing facts or clues. For the Conversion we have the lengthy *Ecclesiastical History* of Bede in addition to many *Lives* of saints. The difficulty is no longer one of accumulating material, but of eliminating it. Though the Conversion is from almost every point of view the most decisive event in the history of the English before the Norman Conquest, it does not call for minute treatment here. The modern reader who is interested in the subject should turn to the pages of Bede, or to classics based on Bede, like *The Early English Church History* of William Bright. All that need be done in this and the following chapter is to tell enough of the story to explain the change which transformed the Anglo-Saxon kingdoms in the seventh century—that century into which were crowded the establishment of the Church in England, the first stirrings of a sense of English unity, the beginnings of English

Headpiece.—Exterior of old St. Peter's, Rome.

literature, of architecture, of education, of Christian civilization in all its branches. These are the subjects which most deserve attention, and not the tangled stories of the several petty dynasties. Accordingly, in what follows we shall only give where necessary just enough of the framework of the political history to recall the main facts, well known to most from childhood.

Before we come to the story of Pope Gregory's mission to the English, we must understand how Celtic Christianity had developed new vigour in the west of the island; and, casting our minds back some two centuries, we must observe the progress made by Christianity during the generations in which the Angles and Saxons were fastening their hold on Britain.

THE BRITISH CHURCH

It will be remembered that as the world of Imperial Rome fell into ruins in the fifth century, as the civilized men within the Empire saw their homes destroyed by barbarians, their wives and families carried into slavery, and their best lands appropriated by the invaders, they turned from the disappointments of this world to hopes of redress in a future existence. Incidents which emerged through the obscurity of that age—the mission of St. Patrick to Ireland, and of St. Ninian to the Picts of Galloway; the controversy about the views of Pelagius the Briton; the visits of the Gallo-Roman, St. Germanus, to our island; other visits of Britons to Gaul—all these were illustrations of the new life now infused into British Christianity.

In the sixth century the force of the revival was directed into the monastic movement. This movement had taken its rise in the fourth century in Egypt, where hermits in the desert, refugees from the wickedness of the great cities, joined themselves into communities for common worship and discipline. When monasticism came to the west, it swept, with a current as irresistible as the gulf-stream, up to the remotest islands and headlands of Gaul, of west Britain, of Ireland. To understand how this came about, we must fix our eyes on Lérins, an island of the French Riviera. For in that spot were gathered Gallo-Romans who wished to emulate the holy men of the Egyptian desert, and others who had escaped from the shipwreck of the world. Thither Britons also had found their way; among them it seems Patrick, the runaway slave from Ireland, and Illtud, the reputed teacher of the Welsh saints, Samson, Paul Aurelian, and perhaps Gildas and David. It seemed, as well it might, a blessed and happy island, and there, in its sunshine and among its pine-trees and flowers, seeds of oriental asceticism and oriental lore were transplanted to the congenial soil of the Celtic spirit.

We may speak of such a spirit and of a Celtic Christianity, but we must remember that there was no one Celtic Church. Its two branches which for our present purpose must be distinguished are the Church of the Britons and that of the Irish. Among their common characteristics was the influence received from Lérins, which brought the monastic enthusiasm in both peoples to a white heat. The influence was transmitted to Ireland by St. Patrick, to the Britons by St. Illtud and his pupils.[1] Illtud himself, described in the eighth century as the *magister Britannorum*,[2] the founder of the first recorded British monastery and the first monastic school, that at Llanwyt,* is but a shadowy figure, for the legends which tell of him in youth as a keen hunter and a soldier of Arthur are not trustworthy. Of his reputed pupils David (*c.* 520–88) calls for notice, not only as the patron Saint of Wales, but as an extreme type of the new monastic Christianity of the Britons. We have no first-hand evidence for him as for St. Patrick, but the eleventh-century account of the austerities of his community at Menevia (now St. Davids) probably gives a fair idea of the way in which he encouraged his disciples to abandon themselves to unmitigated asceticism. To avoid idleness, the mother of vices, his monks yoked themselves instead of oxen to their ploughs. To avoid gluttony, they were

* i.e. Llan-Illtud, *Llan* meaning an enclosure, or more definitely a church or monastery.

allowed but one meal a day—a meal of bread and herbs, seasoned with salt. To enforce the monks' vow of poverty, not even one penny was received for the use of the monastery. To exclude the lukewarm in faith, any one who wished to join the community had to remain as a suppliant for ten days, as in Egypt, at the doors of the monastery, and then, whether rich or poor, he was 'received naked, as one escaping from shipwreck'.[3]

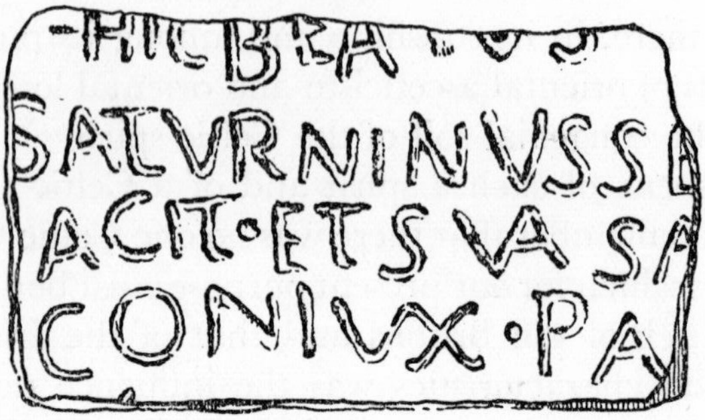

FIG. 41. Tombstone of Beatus Saturninus; from the churchyard of Llansadurn (a name which means the church of Saturn[in]us); inscribed 'Hic Bea[tus] Saturninus se[pultus j]acit et sua sa[ncta] coniux pa[ce]'. (? 6th century.)

The devotions required of the brethren after being admitted to the monastery were, it is said, no less exacting. Whole days and nights were spent without food and without sleep, in watchings and prayers and genuflexions. Thus, in an age of violence and crime, St. David and his disciples attempted to take the Kingdom of Heaven by storm, and in this way to assuage the memory of mundane defeats at the hands of the Saxons. Theirs was the extreme limit of austerity, and though there were among the Britons more moderate men, like Gildas, who criticized the ways of the extremists, David illustrates well enough the revolution which transformed the British Church during the fifth and sixth centuries.

The great number of saints who have left their names in the place-names of Wales and of Cornwall is in itself sufficient to justify the presumption that the tests of sanctity among the Britons were not usually so severe as those exacted at St. Davids. Many of these Celtic saints were, in fact, but well-born clerks in holy orders: men of sufficient wealth to be able to found and endow the small churches and monasteries which have perpetuated their names. Such a one was, for example, Saturninus, whose tombstone (Fig. 41) tells the world that by the side of 'The Blessed Saturninus' there was laid 'his holy consort'.

It has often been a reproach against the British Church that its saints were so fully occupied in saving their own souls that they had neither time nor energy left for the salvation of their neighbours. But this is an over-statement. To give the Britons their due, it must be remembered that in addition to Pelagius, the learned heretic, St. Patrick, and St. Ninian, they produced St. Kentigern (527–612), to whose preachings on the banks of the Clyde, those which were interrupted by a mad prophet, reference has already been made.* Moreover, there are abundant legends which record visits of Gildas, David, and other Britons to encourage the struggling post-Patrician Church in Ireland. Thanks to the enthusiasm with which the Celtic peoples adopted monastic Christianity at this time, there was during the period of the Saxon invasions a coming and going on the western seas of Britain in notable contrast with that on the eastern seas—holy men setting out from Ireland as well as from Britain, seeking both to learn from and to teach their fellow men on the opposite shore of the Channel. If, however, it be objected that the missionaries of British birth worked among their fellow Celts but never among their German enemies, the statement cannot be denied. Though the British clergy wavered for a moment when St. Augustine on his arrival in England asked for their co-operation, their aloofness was a deliberate policy. It was not the result of torpor, for the vitality of the Church is demonstrated by Bede's reference to the monastery of Bangor, near Chester. This community, founded at the end of the sixth century, was soon

* Above, p. 195.

reputed to number more than two thousand monks. It was organized into groups of three hundred and, according to Bede, it produced 'many most learned men'.[4] The Britons gloried in their policy of aloofness. It was a consolation to them to think that the invaders who had stolen their lands and slain their clergy were heading straight for hell-fire and an eternity of punishment.

Whatever the explanation, there is no doubt of the fact that while the British Church was not lifeless, it refused to propagate Christianity among the Anglo-Saxons. Thus the story of St. David, and of the Welsh Church, brings us to a dead end. Between the British Church and the English there was from first to last a complete, or almost complete, barrier. We must therefore turn to the other branch of the Celtic Church, to Ireland and to the followers of St. Patrick; and here it will at once become apparent that exclusiveness was not especially a Celtic characteristic.

ST. COLUMBA

The development of the Irish or 'Scottish'* Church after the death of St. Patrick (461) is obscure. When it reappears into clearer light at the end of the sixth century, the mission stations of St. Patrick and his disciples have blossomed into large monasteries. The period when these monasteries needed to learn from Britons like David and Gildas was passed, and the Irish were already excelling their masters. The monasteries were small towns or forts with inmates numbered by the hundred, and even by the thousand. The site of one of them—the monastery at Nendrum on Strangford Lough—has been recently excavated.[5] The spade revealed three concentric cashels, or dry-built stone walls, nearly circular in form. The church or oratory was the most important building inside the enclosure, and scattered round the

* It may be as well again to remind any readers not versed in the history of these times that the name 'Scots' designates until the tenth century, firstly the inhabitants of Ireland, and secondly, small colonies of Irish who had migrated to the west coast of north Britain, i.e. to Argyllshire.

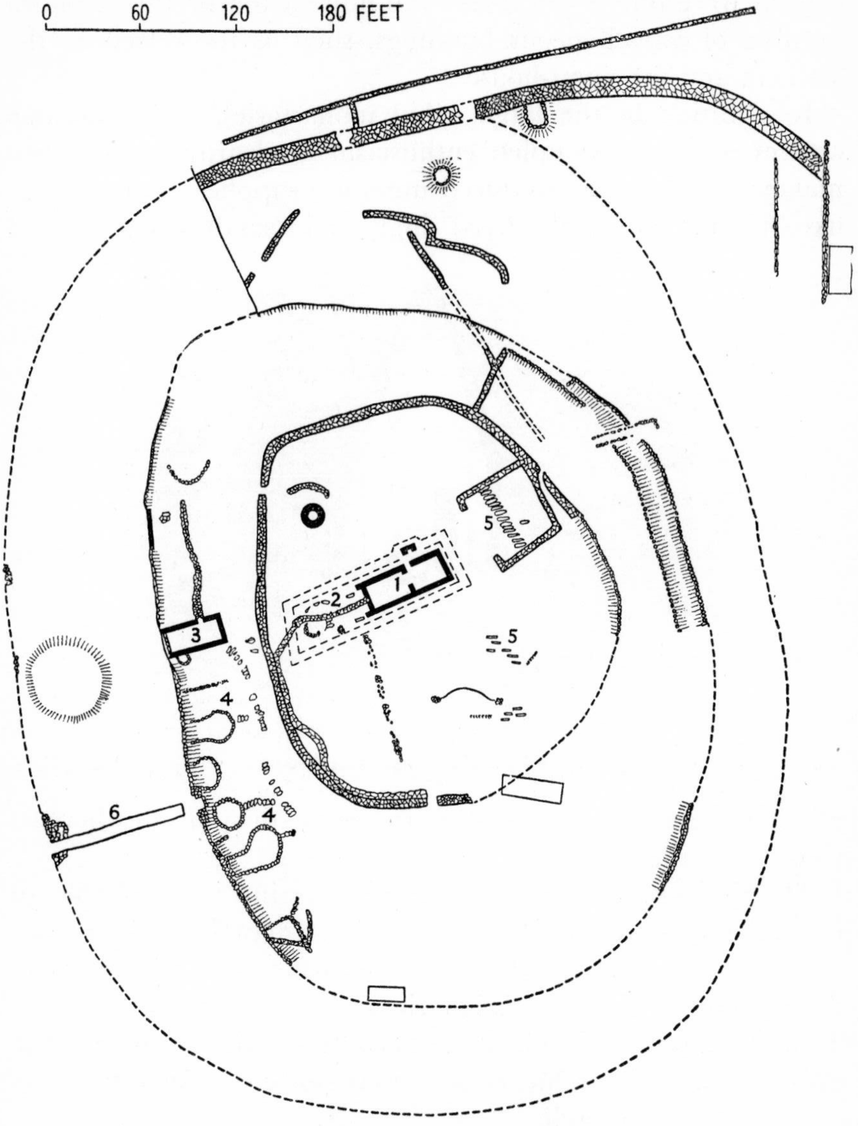

FIG. 42. Plan of Irish Monastery at Nendrum, Co. Down.
1. The Church. 2. Path round inner cashel wall. 3. The school. 4. Cells.
5. Graves. 6. Raised path to the quay.

church were others, no doubt the huts of the brethren, and a number of miscellaneous buildings, such as the refectory, the kitchen, and the guest-house.

In addition to the large tribal monasteries, which became centres of an unexampled enthusiasm for learning and book-making, Ireland also produced unfailing supplies of anchorites, like St. Mac Dara, who lived singly or in small groups, and of

FIG. 43. St. Mac Dara's primitive church on St. Mac Dara's Island off the coast of Galway.

religious wanderers who took to the sea to drift or sail wherever God might direct them.

The best authenticated of all the Irish saints is Columcille, or Columba (521–97),[6] the founder of Iona, a man of heroic temper, whose furious energy gave the impulse which was to carry Scottish or Scottish-trained missionaries from the Moray Firth to the Thames; and there can be no better introduction to the Scottish Church and to its influence on the Anglo-Saxons than the story of St. Columba himself.

The great-great-grandfather of Columba has already appeared in these pages. He was Niall of the Nine Hostages, High King of Ireland, whose raid on the west of Britain (*c.* 400) had helped to shake down the tottering Roman Empire in this island, and

Early monastic settlement on the rock of Skellig Michael, Kerry, Ireland

PLATE 38

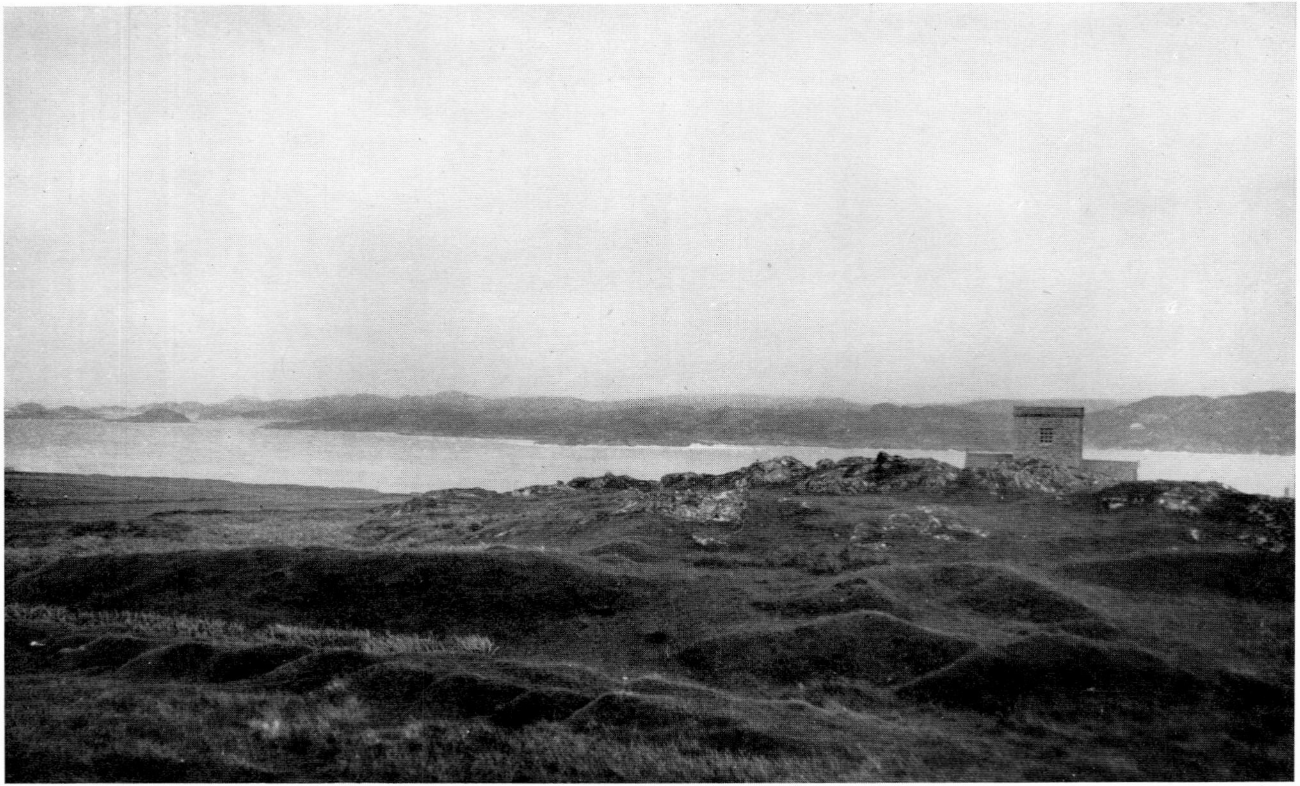

Iona, showing in the foreground the Vallum of the monastery

had probably swept off the boy Patrick into Irish captivity. Columba then, with the hot blood of Irish kings in his veins, was by nature impetuous, masterful, and adventurous. The story goes that when about forty years old he involved his clan in war for the possession of a book. He had surreptitiously copied the codex belonging to his former master, and the High King of Ireland had given judgement against Columba on the principle that 'To every cow belongs her calf and to every book its son book'.[7] Soon after the war, perhaps in expiation, Columba abandoned his native Ulster. 'He sailed forth resolving to go on pilgrimage for Christ from Ireland into Britain.'[8] He chose the island of Iona as the site of his new monastery because it was close to a colony of his countrymen (called after their Irish motherland Dal Riata). This was placed on the west coast of modern Scotland, near the point where the northern Picts marched with the Britons of Strathclyde. Columba succeeded in giving the Scottish colony a new political importance as well as in reviving their Christianity and in converting also their old enemies the Picts. Columba thus won for Iona an extraordinary supremacy. The Dalriatic Scots, if not also the Picts, regarded it as their mother-church. Columban communities arose even in Skye and the Islands. Many important monasteries in Ireland still obeyed him as their founder. All looked to Iona for direction and rule; and when Columba himself returned to Ireland in later life, he was received at Clonmacnois 'as if he were an angel'. Crowds bowed with their faces to the ground, and 'tying together a canopy [or barrier] of poles, they had it borne by four men around the Saint as he walked', lest he should be thronged by the crowd.[9]

What was it that raised Columba to such pre-eminence? From Adamnan's biography of the Saint (written about 100 years after his death) it is clear that it was his character rather than his royal birth which gave him his dominating influence. It would be hard to find a man more virile and untiring. 'He never could spend the space of even one hour without study, or prayer, or writing, or even some manual labour.' He was a typical Irishman, vehement, irresistible: hear him curse a niggardly rich man or bless the heifers of a poor peasant; see him follow a robber who had plundered a friend, cursing the wretch to his destruction, following him 'to the water's edge, wading up to the knees in the clear green sea-water, with both his hands raised to heaven . . .'[10] In the well-known story of

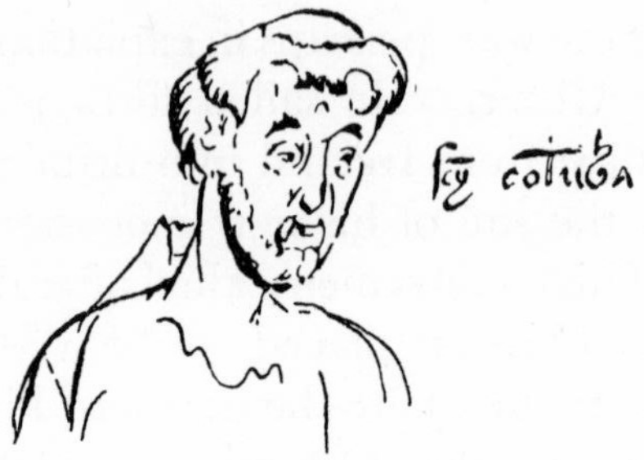

FIG. 44. St. Columba. From a ninth-century Codex at St. Gall.

his last day, what emerges is the love shown by and to the Saint as he wanders round the farmstead of the community: he gives thanks when he sees the two heaps of winnowed corn; he blesses the old white horse, which comes and puts its head into his bosom; he climbs the hill and blesses the whole monastery.

Here we have a good example of the spirit which will be transfused in the following epoch from the Scots to the Anglo-Saxons and will reappear in the lives and characters of men like Chad and Cuthbert and a host of other Englishmen who came under Celtic influences.

Columba is, in his life and character, an epitome of the Scottish Church. But since for a century or more the history of the English will centre round the interaction between Roman and Scottish Christianity, it will be well at this point to enumerate more systematically the chief features of the latter.

The foremost differences in the eyes of contemporaries were

disputes about the date at which the Easter festival should be celebrated, and about the shape of the tonsure. Of these we shall hear more—indeed, too much—when we come to the Synod of Whitby. Here it is more worth while to recall the fact that Christianity in Ireland, and probably also in Wales, had not adapted itself to the provincial and diocesan system of the Roman Empire. Each Irish king or chieftain had established his own monastery. It was ruled by an abbot who was commonly a member of the founder's family. Its population could grow to the hundreds or thousands sometimes recorded, because the monastery was both a sanctuary in an age of much tribal violence, and also a centre of education at a time when enthusiasm for the new learning was unbounded.

The abbot's power was supreme; it reflected that of the tribal king. The bishop, unless he happened also to be an abbot, was a mere official, whose function was to ordain. The Scottish Church was thus an aggregate of monasteries or of groups of monasteries. In so far as it enjoyed any unity, it was a unity of purpose and enthusiasm. A community like that of Iona might have rights over its off-shoots, but there was no other centralized government.

The monasteries were not only sanctuaries and schools of learning. They were bases for missionary work. The active and the contemplative ideals could be interchanged. Monks might wander abroad either to preach or to become anchorites. They could plant themselves in cells on lonely islands, on headlands, anywhere where they were far removed from their fellow men.

The Irish Church was less marked than the Welsh by extreme asceticism. But the oriental strain was there, and would in time find its way to the English. Mingling with it were other unusual strains of thought; sometimes derived darkly from ideas of magic, from worship of the elements, from Druidism buried deep in the inmost recesses of the Celtic mind; sometimes manifesting themselves in sympathies with the animal world or in ecstatic adoration of the forces of nature.

The best insight into these mysteries of the Celtic soul is to be had from the hymns of the Irish Church. The following are characteristic lines from a translation of the Irish *Lorica* (Coat of Mail) ascribed, perhaps rightly, to St. Patrick.[11]

I arise to-day:
in the might of Heaven
brightness of Sun
whiteness of Snow
splendour of Fire

. . . .

I arise to-day:
in the Might of God for my piloting
Wisdom of God for my guidance
Eye of God for my foresight
Ear of God for my hearing

. . . .

I invoke therefore all these forces:
against every fierce merciless force that may come upon my body and my soul;
against incantations of false prophets;
against black laws of paganism;
against false laws of heresy;
against deceit of idolatry;
against spells of women and smiths and druids;
against all knowledge that is forbidden the human soul.

Christ for my guardianship to-day:
against poison, against burning,
against drowning, against wounding,
that there may come to me a multitude of rewards;
Christ with me, Christ before me,
Christ behind me, Christ in me,
Christ under me, Christ over me.

. . . .

Other hymns the recital of which gave defence against the enemies of mankind are ascribed rightly or wrongly to well-known saints of the Celtic Churches. That of Columba, called from its first words the *Altus Prosator*, is probably genuine. It is in Latin, and approaches more nearly to the ordinary thought of the Latin world. None the less it is still far removed. Each stanza begins with a different letter of the alphabet. The fear of the *Dies Irae* sounds through it, but the devil who lies behind all the fear is 'The Dragon, great, most foul, terrible and old'—a monster ready to take the place of the Teutonic dragons which had brought Beowulf and the heathen heroes into action.

The important thing in the history of the English is to understand that while the sons and grandson of Ida were extending Anglian conquests north and west, a detachment of the Irish Church was established at Iona by a man of royal birth who could infect his followers with his own heroic temper, so that they in their turn could win their Teutonic neighbours to a new cult of dragon-slaying. At Iona there existed the enthusiasm which led men into great undertakings. Iona inherited the spirit of self-renunciation which we have seen inculcated by St. David, but it inherited also the devotion to learning somehow transmitted to the Irish Church, perhaps from Lérins through the medium of Illtud, Gildas, and other British saints. And above all it inherited the tradition of propaganda. The community at Iona could supply the evangelistic zeal which had led Columba to convert the Picts as Patrick had converted the Irish.

THE ROMAN MISSION TO THE ENGLISH

A generation elapsed before the Christianity of Iona was passed on to the English in Northumbria. Our attention must therefore now be diverted to Pope Gregory (540–604), a younger contemporary of Columba, one who during the last years of Columba's life was planning a missionary campaign for the conversion of the English with a clearness of purpose and a persistence worthy of his Roman ancestors. In the two centuries which had passed since the Roman armies had been withdrawn from Britain, Rome had seen Visigoths and Ostrogoths lording it in the land. She had seen the western Emperors come to an end and the eastern Emperors first establish and then relax their hold on central Italy. There were still in the peninsula imperial officials and generals—*duces, magistri militum, praefecti*—officials by courtesy still Most Illustrious, Glorious, Magnificent, as in the days of Constantine; but even at Rome the old world, like its temples, its aqueducts, and its theatres, was in ruins; the Romans found themselves face to face with the Lombards (those old neighbours of the English in the Elbe lands, who since the year 568 had been pouring a new flood of barbarism over Italy); and the Bishop of the Romans was left the only man with authority and vigour sufficient to save a remnant of the ancient order and uphold in a new ecclesiastical form the ancient traditions of the Imperial City. Gregory in his own life represents the bridge from the old Rome to the new. History has always recognized him as the last great official of secular Rome, the first great Pope of the medieval type. After rising as a Roman noble to be *Praefectus Urbis*, the highest official of the City, he had surrendered his enormous wealth; he had converted the palace of his father, on the Coelian Hill, into a monastery dedicated to St. Andrew, and he himself had entered it as a poor monk.

Thus he comes before us as a man with a conscience. It was conscience which had driven him to sacrifice his worldly position and wealth; it was this which made him miserable when he heard that a man had died of hunger in the City; it was this which made him oppose the traffic in Christian slaves; and once more it was his conscience, working like that of a nineteenth-century philanthropist, which moved him to form new schemes when he saw the Anglian boys with their fair hair, looking like angels in the Roman slave market. Whether or no his punnings are authentic, there must have been some such incident—some encounter with Anglian slaves—to start the oft-repeated story. We may believe that he then asked himself why these boys were vessels of the devil. Could he himself do nothing to rescue their nation from the devil?

The episode marks something more than the birth of an idea in the mind of one of the world's great men. It is a turning-point in the history of Latin Christianity. From that time the Roman Church becomes, as it had not previously been, propagandist, missionary, imperialist. It becomes the Church of the northern barbarians as well as of the Roman world. The sudden conviction of the man with a conscience who was also a man of

FIG. 45. St. Gregory. A modern reconstruction of his portrait based partly on a description of his contemporary portrait and partly on a copy of its copy.

action was equivalent to one of the grand discoveries of history, or one of the great inventions.

Before the idea bore fruit, years later, in the sending of Augustine to Britain, Gregory had made one attempt after another to have Christianity preached to the English. On one occasion he had begged permission from the Pope to go himself to Britain. He had persuaded the Pope by putting before him the thought which had been troubling his own mind. 'It is lamentable for such fair vessels to be full of the devil.'* [12] He had set out for Britain. He had travelled three days' journey to the north when the people of Rome made a tumultuous demonstration, and

* *Miserum tam pulchris vasis infernus* [*infernum*] *debuisse repleri.*

insisted that he should be brought back to the City. Later, in 595, after his accession to the papal throne, he had instructed his agents in Gaul to devote part of his revenues from Gallic estates to buying up Anglian slave-boys, evidently intending to have them taught Christianity, and sent back to Britain as missionaries.

But Gregory's life was full of more immediate cares—Lombards encircling Rome; quarrels, till 596, with the Franks; pestilence in the City; books to be written for the edification of the Church; immense papal lands to be administered in every province; a world-wide correspondence ever demanding his attention. The wonder is that Gregory, distracted by the pressure of such immediate necessities, and suffering, as he did, from gout and a bad digestion (the result of his monastic fasts), was ever able to drive the English mission through to completion.

There were many advantages in the plan of sending Augustine to Britain, the plan finally adopted in 596 when friendly relations with the Franks opened the road through Gaul. It held out a hope of earlier results than could be expected from the scheme of training heathen slave-boys as missionaries. Gregory could order Augustine and the monks of St. Andrew's to fulfil his wishes because that was his own monastery: he was their founder as well as their Pope. Augustine, the Prior, was well known to him, because at some time or other they had shared a cell. He could be trusted to do his duty. Some of the inmates of St. Andrew's had been trying to escape. The mission to Britain would give to all a new interest, to some a good employment.

In this way, it seems, the plan which was to change the destinies of the Anglo-Saxons grew to maturity.

Before we embark on the main story of the Conversion, it is needful to make clear our course by explaining the situation in Britain in 597, and the outlines of its subsequent political history. Some features of the situation have emerged in what has been already said. We have seen that, by 597, the Anglo-Saxons were almost encircled by Christians, but that while their nearest neighbours—the Franks across the Channel and the Britons in the west—were indifferent to the heathenism of the Anglo-Saxons, the more virile Christianity of the Scots of north Britain was confronted by Ethelfrith (593–617), king of Northumbria, who was only now beginning his career of ruthless war against Britons and Scots. There was little likelihood that he, 'the

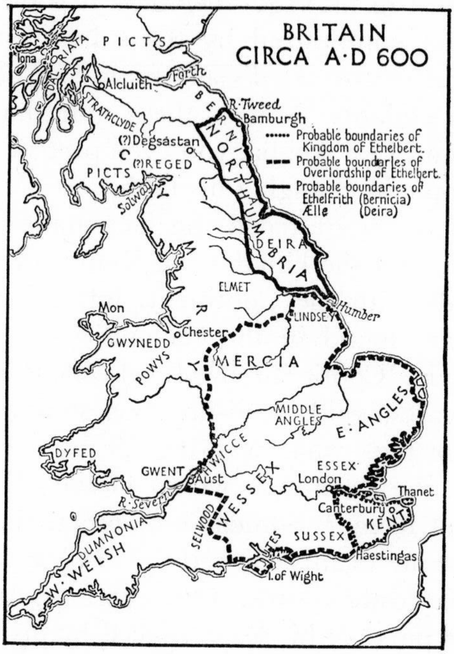

destroyer', the slayer of the monks of Bangor, would encourage any Christian propaganda. Of the other English kingdoms which were afterwards to play a chief part, the kingdom of Mercia on the upper Trent had not yet emerged into history; the kingdom of Wessex since the expulsion of Ceawlin in 591 had lost its effective unity and power. The small kingdoms south of the Humber had in general accepted the *imperium* of Ethelbert,* king of Kent (? 560–616).[13]

We know little about this *imperium* except that it was later

* OE. Æthelberht.

regarded as in some way a succession to that of Ceawlin, that it extended to the Humber and (apparently) to the Severn, and that it was fairly effective over Ethelbert's nephew, Saebert, king of the East Saxons, and in a less degree over Raedwald, king of the East Angles.[14]

To understand how loose was the tie which bound the under-kings to Ethelbert in his vague *imperium*, it is only necessary to remember a fact emphasized by the subsequent story of the Conversion, that the overlord's acceptance of Christianity will not bind his dependants. None of these under-kings, apart from those of Essex and East Anglia, will even pretend to follow their superior's example in changing his faith.

For the rest, we must recall the fact made evident by the Kentish graves, that the kingdom of Kent had long enjoyed a flourishing trade with the Continent: importing the beautiful things which are found in the cemeteries—golden bracteates from Scandinavia, 'Coptic' bronze bowls, shells from the Indian Ocean, glass vases, gold, semi-precious stones, and Frankish brooches; exporting—what was it?—perhaps rich cargoes of human beings, the slave-boys whom Gallic Jews resold in the slave-markets of Rome? Somehow or other, the Jutes became wealthy. These merchants enjoyed the display of having buried with them their costly swords. On occasions, too, one of them would have his purse or his scales placed by his side. This, like the sword, might be useful in the next world. Kent might seem barbarous to the Romans but to the peoples of Britain it was a centre of civilization. These prosperous, almost cosmopolitan Jutes were prepared to receive other things besides jewels and glass bowls from the Christian world.

We can now resume the history of Gregory's mission to England, and at the outset we are confronted by the fact that while Augustine and his companions had (apparently) left Rome in the spring of 596, they did not land in Thanet till shortly before Easter 597.

Why had they been so long upon the road? In part no doubt it was due to the difficulties of travel in those days; others in the Dark Ages besides Augustine consumed a year over the journey from Rome. But in part also the delay was due to the character of the men themselves. Augustine himself was as unlike the Celtic missionaries—St. Patrick, St. Columba, and the rest—as he could be. Here we are dealing not with a man who acted from passionate convictions and sudden impulses, but with a Roman, well-disciplined, discreet, learned in Holy Scripture, a man who was moved by a strong sense of duty. And the Romans who accompanied their prior were like him. They had been accustomed to the quiet routine of their monastery on the Coelian Hill. They had set out at the bidding of the Pope, little realizing what lay ahead of them. After sailing from Ostia to Gaul, they had spent some time in the island of Lérins, and there no doubt they had heard stories about the savagery of the Saxons, stories which may have originated with those holy men from Britain, such as Patrick, who, coming to Lérins in the fifth century, had doubtless scattered rumours which grew with the lapse of time. At any rate, when the party reached southern Gaul their fears became too much for them. They halted, 'and began to think of returning home rather than proceed to a barbarous, fierce, and unbelieving nation, to whose very language they were strangers'.[15]

Augustine went back to Rome to report their apprehensions, but he returned with papal letters of exhortation and, spurred on by Gregory, they again turned their faces to Britain. When at last they reached its shores, they landed where men said that Hengist and Horsa had landed before them, 'in the Isle of Thanet', within sight of the ruins of Richborough, the port of Roman Britain which, by 597, was suffering as much from the withdrawal of the sea as from that of the Romans. What then happened is a familiar story: how at close quarters the barbarians of Kent proved less terrible to the Italians than they had seemed at a distance; how when King Ethelbert was informed that the forty men who had appeared in his territory 'were come from

Rome and had brought a joyful message, which could undoubtedly assure to those that hearkened to it everlasting joys in heaven, and a kingdom that would never end',[16] he came to Thanet and ordered the men from Rome to be brought to him as he sat in the open air. 'For he had taken precaution that they should not come to him in any house lest . . . if they practised any magical arts they might impose upon him and so get the better of him. . . . But they came with Divine not with magic powers, bearing a silver cross for their banner, and the image of Our Lord and Saviour painted on a board, and chanting litanies.'

The point in the story which most calls for explanation is the facility with which Augustine secured his victory. For Ethelbert at once invited the new-comers to Canterbury, and promised to support them while they preached to his people. He there gave them the old Roman church of St. Martin, and though he refused to allow compulsion to be put upon his people, he himself accepted baptism, and presumably submitted to the rites for those of riper years—the priest blowing in his face to drive away the devil, placing salt in his mouth, and immersing him three times as he stood bare in the cold water. The King's lead was followed with little delay, first by the chiefs and then by the commons of his kingdom. By the end of the year, ten thousand men of Kent had been baptized (so Gregory asserted, no doubt with natural exaggeration), and Augustine had been consecrated in Gaul as 'Archbishop of the English'.

Now there is no difficulty in seeing why the kingdom of Ethelbert offered a good field for the mission from the Roman world. The Jutes, who had derived, or as traders had copied, so much of their material civilization from the Franks, were certainly well prepared to follow Frankish fashions in religion. They had a Christian Frankish queen, and she, with her chaplain Liudhard (Pl. 43, 3) and other Christian attendants, had accustomed the minds of the courtiers at Canterbury to Christianity. The church of St. Martin's had been repaired for her use. Whether Bertha and her retinue had done anything more positive to aid Christianity we cannot say; but Gregory, in one of his letters, written in 601, encourages Bertha by telling her that she should now act so as to make good what had formerly been neglected.[17] Ethelbert, in fact, was so friendly, tolerant, and hospitable to Augustine's party, that there is something to be said for the guess that he or Bertha had beforehand sent some kind of encouragement to the Pope. But what Gregory himself tells us is simply this: that 'the news had reached him that the Anglian people wished to become Christians'.[18] Ethelbert showed statesmanship as well as friendliness by moving with slow deliberation, and by consulting his great men he succeeded in carrying the bulk of his people with him. Though his chiefs might not be greatly moved by the preaching of Augustine, who could only address them through an interpreter, the old Germanic devotion of the *comites* to their lord would weigh heavily in favour of the decision of Ethelbert. If the chiefs could be persuaded the battle was won, for in those times we never hear of the humbler classes in society opposing a lead given them by their superiors. And if it is true* that the great landowners in England as in Scandinavia officiated as priests of the heathen gods, there would be few left to champion the cause of Thunor and Woden when their most powerful priests turned against them. As a further explanation of the rapid victory, we must remember what was said in the last chapter about the failure of Germanic heathenism to appeal either to the reason or to the better instincts of men. There had been no attempt to rationalize the heathenism of the north in the way that the paganism of Greece and Rome had once been doctored for the consumption of the educated. The methods recommended later to English missionaries in Germany show how easily the Christian could use the weapons of reason against the absurdities of the Teutonic gods. Daniel, bishop of Winchester, writing about 723,[19] suggested that Boniface, the English missionary to the Germans, should ask the heathen 'whether they think this

* Cf. above, p. 238.

universe had a beginning or was always in existence. If it had a beginning, who created it? . . . If they maintain that the universe always existed without a beginning, seek to refute and convince them by many arguments and proofs; if they go on contending, ask them: Who ruled it? How did they reduce beneath their sway and bring under their jurisdiction a universe that existed before them? Whence and by whom and when was the first god or goddess constituted or begotten?' The heathen were to be made to blush for their absurd opinions. They were to be shown that 'the Christians possess the fertile lands . . . and have left the heathen with their gods only the frozen lands in which their gods are wrongly thought to hold sway'.

These considerations help in some measure to explain the sweeping success of the mission. But first and last the credit must be given to Pope Gregory. Augustine and his companions did indeed, when established at Canterbury, show themselves to be both capable and obedient. But the hero of the story continued to be Gregory himself. Till his death he helped and guided the mission which had won such astonishing success in Kent. He sent Augustine reinforcements from Rome—Justus, Mellitus, Paulinus, and others. He sent him relics of the holy Apostles, and he sent him ornaments, vestments, and books. When Augustine propounded problems about liturgical discrepancies, or about the proper division of the offerings of the faithful, when he asked whether a man might marry his stepmother, and asked advice about sundry other questions which were troubling him and his converts, Gregory answered with admirable wisdom.

He told him to choose from the Roman or the Gallican or any other Church whatever custom 'may be more acceptable to Almighty God . . . for things are not to be loved for the sake of places'.[20] He told him that for those who like Augustine himself had taken the monastic vows, there could be no question about the division of church offerings, since they, like their fathers in the primitive Church, should have all things in common.

Marble throne in St. Gregory's Church, Rome, said to have been the chair of St. Gregory

Marble table 'of St. Gregory', also in St. Gregory's Church

PLATE 40

Part of the ivory back of the Drogo Sacramentary, written *c.* 830 and used in Metz Cathedral. The panels give views of the Mass in different stages of the ceremony

On the other hand, those in Augustine's mission who were clerics in minor orders were only 'to be kept under ecclesiastical rule that they may live orderly and attend to singing of psalms'. Accordingly, strict monastic rule need not be enforced on all.[21] On the other points, Gregory answered that it was a crime for a man to marry his stepmother. He told him to ordain plenty of bishops—twelve under a metropolitan at London, and twelve more under another metropolitan at York. He sent a special letter to tell Augustine his second thoughts about the treatment of heathen temples and rites. Let the idols be destroyed, but let the temples be converted into churches, sprinkled with holy water, and supplied with altars and relics; 'and because they are used to slaughter many oxen and sacrifice to devils [we have interesting light here on some of the rites of Germanic heathendom] some solemnity must be given them in exchange for this'. Therefore on feast days they should build themselves huts of the boughs of trees about those buildings which have been turned from temples into churches and they should 'kill cattle and glorify God in their feasts . . . for there is no doubt that it is impossible to cut off everything at once from their rude natures: because he who endeavours to ascend to the highest place rises by degrees or steps and not by leaps'.[22]

In one point only did the Pope lead Augustine to an unwise policy. Augustine had asked for instruction how he was to deal with the bishops of the Britons. Gregory in reply somewhat rashly committed all the bishops in the island to the care of Augustine, and his scheme for the organization of the Church in Britain was based on the same idea. Partly owing to these instructions, and partly owing to Augustine's failure to win the sympathy of the Britons in the conferences which he had with them (the first being at St. Augustine's Oak 'on the borders of the Hwicce and West Saxons'),* the Britons refused to co-operate. According to Bede's story, they thought Augustine proud because at the second conference he remained seated instead of

* Usually—but, as the map (p. 261) shows, wrongly—identified as Aust.

rising to greet them on their approach. The chance of a united Church in Britain was lost for centuries. 'It is to this day', said Bede in 731, 'the fashion among the Britons to reckon the faith and religion of Englishmen as naught, and to hold no more conversation with them than with the heathen.'[23]

The quarrel could hardly have been avoided. To have acknowledged the superiority of the metropolitan at Canterbury or London would have been worse for the Britons than a military defeat. It would have undermined their independence. The fault of the Britons was that for a century or more before the coming of St. Augustine they had despised their conquerors as barbarians and heathens. They had lost their opportunity before 597.

Was the Augustinian mission strong enough without the co-operation of the Britons to win over the other English kingdoms? Could it even hold its place in Kent when the personal influence of Augustine and of Ethelbert was withdrawn? The first twenty years of the seventh century brought an answer to these questions.

Ethelbert's *imperium*, at one time recognized up to the Humber, gave an opening for extending the work of the mission beyond Kent, and the last recorded act of Augustine was the consecration of Mellitus as bishop of London for the East Saxons. The deaths of Augustine and Gregory about 604[24] at first produced no obvious retrogression, and Raedwald, the king of East Anglia, when visiting his Kentish overlord, was admitted to the Sacrament. But the years which followed proved, in one kingdom after another, how slight was the hold of the new religion which rested on the patronage of a few great men, and how persistent was the old heathenism, in spite of its nominal defeats.

Thus, in East Anglia, Raedwald, having returned from his Christian overlord to his own heathen family, solved his religious difficulties by setting up in his 'temple' an altar dedicated to Christ by the side of another where victims were offered to 'devils'.

In Essex a Christian king was succeeded by pagan sons; and

when Mellitus, the bishop of London, refused in St. Paul's to give them 'that white bread'[25] which they had seen him give their father, he and his followers were ejected (617). Mellitus, with Justus who had been made bishop of Rochester, then retired to Gaul.

The death of Ethelbert (616) and the accession of his son Eadbald, a heathen, almost put an end to the mission in Kent itself. Laurentius, the successor of Augustine, is said to have agreed with the fugitive bishops 'that it was better for them all to return to their own country, where they might serve God in freedom of mind, than to continue to no purpose among barbarians, who had revolted from the faith'. According to Bede's well-known story, it was only a vision of St. Peter, appearing to Laurentius the night before his departure, which saved the situation. In the morning Laurentius showed King Eadbald his back scarred by stripes inflicted, he said, by St. Peter; and he so frightened the young king that from that time onward he became a supporter of the Church. Kent remained a Christian kingdom; but it was not till 640 that a king arose who eliminated outward heathenism, making Christianity compulsory on all his subjects and destroying the idols throughout the kingdom.

When Mellitus returned after one year's withdrawal, the Londoners, under the influence of their 'idolatrous high priest', refused to receive him. As the preaching of Christianity was not begun again in Essex till 654, the people to the north of the lower Thames continued for almost forty years to worship Woden and Thunor, while those on the southern bank were, at any rate nominally, Christians. During the ten years 617–27, Kent was the only Christian kingdom of all the English States.

Let us avail ourselves of this lull in the Conversion to note such traces of the handiwork of Ethelbert and of Augustine as have come down to us. They are of two kinds, the laws of Ethelbert, and fragments of the churches of Augustine—laws and churches which were to be models for after generations.

The primary motive of Augustine in guiding Ethelbert to formulate written laws is obvious in the first clause of the code. 'These are the decrees which king Ethelbert established in the lifetime of Augustine. (i) Theft of God's property and the Church's shall be compensated twelve-fold; a bishop's property eleven-fold; a priest's property nine-fold; a deacon's property six-fold; a clerk's property three-fold. Breach of the peace shall be compensated doubly when it affects the Church or a meeting-place.' The Roman mission must be protected. Since there were no traditional laws defending clergy, these new rules had to be formulated; and the introduction of parchment and ink made it possible for the barbarian king to imitate Roman methods of legislation.

Most of the ninety articles of the code detail the punishments for injuries to a man's person or property, including his wife and servants. Thus, 'If one man slays another, the ordinary wergeld to be paid as compensation shall be 100 shillings'; 'If a freeman breaks the fence round [another man's] enclosure, he shall pay 6 shillings compensation'; 'If a thumb is struck off, 20 shillings. If a thumbnail is knocked off, 3 shillings. If a man strikes off a forefinger, he shall pay 9 shillings. . . . If a man strikes off a ring-finger he shall pay 6 shillings compensation.'[26] This tariff may be all that the Kentish witan could recall when they were asked to sum up the traditional law of their folk. But something more than memorizing, recording, and adjustment, went to the making of Ethelbert's code. It stands for the Christian ideal which had just been introduced into the land. Order is to be enforced, morality upheld, the agents of the new religion are to be protected.

Of the churches built and repaired in and around Canterbury in this first generation of English Christianity, there exist only a few fragments. But these are now of special interest, because in the last few years they have been re-examined and their character is known to us as it was never known to our fathers.[27]

Two churches at Canterbury, used in the days of Ethelbert,

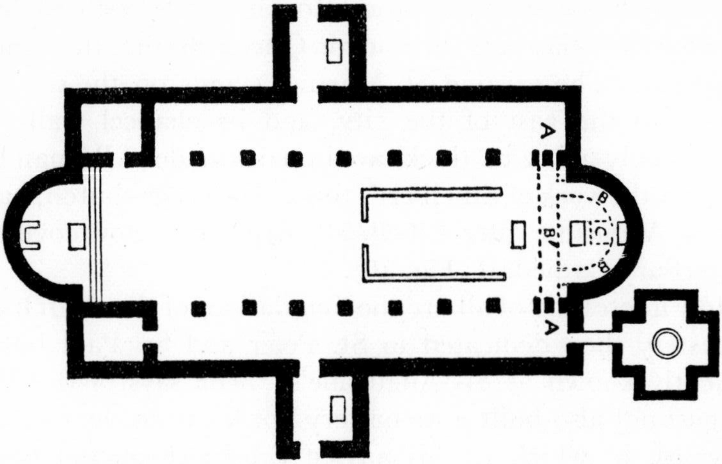

FIG. 46. Canterbury, plan of Saxon Cathedral. The Baptistery on the right was added *c.* 750. The dotted lines and the letters A, B, C, indicate the crypt.

The basilica which in Roman times pointed to the west, was reorientated by Augustine, who added an eastern apse and altar and placed the bishop's throne against the western wall.

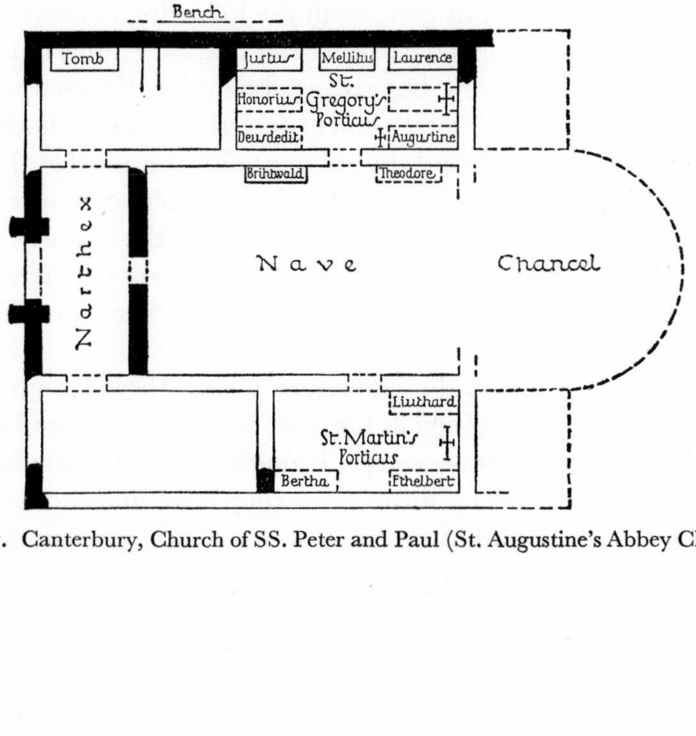

FIG. 47. Canterbury, Church of SS. Peter and Paul (St. Augustine's Abbey Church).

were said to be survivals from Roman times restored by the Jutes for Christian use, the one for Queen Bertha, the other for Augustine. The existing St. Martin's stands on the site of the former, to the east of the city, and its chancel walls (very narrow, only 2 ft. 2 in. thick) are in parts made of Roman brick, probably the work of Ethelbert's time. The other church, handed over to Augustine after Ethelbert's baptism, is now covered by Canterbury Cathedral (Fig. 46).

Most interesting of all are the foundations of the church of the monastery then dedicated to St. Peter and St. Paul but subsequently known as St. Augustine's. Bede says of this:[28] 'He [Augustine] also built a monastery not far from the city to the eastward, in which by his advice Ethelbert erected from its foundations the church of the blessed Apostles Peter and Paul, and enriched it with divers gifts; wherein the bodies of the same Augustine and of all the bishops of Canterbury and of the kings of Kent might be buried.'

In the ground-plans of this and of some other Kentish churches attributed to the period* we seem to see the Augustinian mission working out a type of its own, with the following characteristics: small proportions (the nave of St. Peter and St. Paul is only 39 ft. by 27 ft.); walls narrow but strong, being largely composed of Roman bricks and of good cement like the Roman; floors well constructed, coloured pink by mixing with the mortar the dust of pounded bricks; and lastly, the most distinctive feature of all, side chambers (*porticus*) opening either from the chancel or the nave. The characteristics are thought[29] to point generally 'to an Italian origin, with a strong eastern rather than Roman influence'.

Altogether, what little we know about these Augustinian churches, small and ruined as they are, leaves on the mind an impression of their great ancestry. Though they lack the columned beauty of the regular basilican type, they have inherited a tradition of strength, and they show a sense of proportion. The

* See Fig. 47 and those on p. 281.

evidence of the churches tallies with Bede's information, indicating that the influence of the mission was mostly concentrated at Canterbury. We see, moreover, that even at Canterbury Augustine's efforts were specially directed to the work of building a mausoleum where the souls of the king and queen, with their bodies in proximity to those of the holy men, might be defended alike from heathen spirits and from Christian demons. The foundations of this church, built to hold the tombs of kings and bishops, now that they have been excavated, are a visible reminder that, whatever the intention of Gregory might have been, the mission of Augustine in this first generation was, in fact, a mission to a court rather than to a people.

THE ROMAN MISSION IN NORTHUMBRIA

In 625 the interest of the story shifts from the south to the north. In that year Paulinus, one of the later reinforcements sent by Gregory to Augustine, journeyed from Canterbury to the court of Edwin, king of Northumbria. A Roman is once more seen at York, formerly the station of the Romans' Sixth Legion. His arrival in the wild north is almost as great an event as the coming of Augustine himself.

To understand its significance we must glance at the political developments which followed the year 616. Bede tells us that even before the death of Ethelbert, Raedwald, king of the East Angles, had been acquiring the leadership of the English provinces south of the Humber. The climax of Raedwald's power was reached in 617, when he defeated Ethelfrith, the king who had founded the greatness of Northumbria by overthrowing Celtic rivals at Degsastan (603) and at Chester (? 616). Raedwald's supremacy was, however, a mere flicker. He probably died some ten years after his great victory. The chief power then passed, not to his son, nor to any southern kinglet, but to Edwin, son of Ælle of Deira, who, after twenty-four years of exile, had been set up by the arms of Raedwald as king of Bernicia as well as of Deira. From that time till 633 Edwin gradually won his way to the foremost position in the island.*

These years also witnessed a change of wider significance than the transference of the supremacy from East Anglia to Northumbria. They saw the leadership among the Anglo-Saxons pass for ever from the small south-eastern kingdoms. These were pushed aside by the three states which were still able to expand by absorbing the Celtic inhabitants of the island. For a time East Anglia, Essex, Kent, and Sussex, might keep their own dynasties. But it was the beginning of the end for them when they all, save Kent, recognized the *imperium* of Edwin. Thenceforth the question which emerges is simply this—to which of the greater Powers are the small kingdoms of the south-east to be permanently attracted? If we employ the terms current in the nineteenth century, we may say that the rise of Edwin marks the end of the Heptarchy and the beginning of the Triarchy. However incorrect these terms may be, they have their uses, and the important thing is to remember that about this time the Anglo-Saxon world settled down from a confused strife between a large number of small kingdoms to a more clearly defined rivalry between Northumbria, Mercia, and Wessex.

Edwin's reign (617–33) brought Northumbria at one bound to the height of its power. Deira and Bernicia were strengthened as well as united. A British kingdom† (in what is now the West Riding), hitherto protected from the Angles by Elmet forest, was absorbed. Northwards, though the derivation of Edinburgh as 'Edwin's Burgh' should now be given up,[30] it is likely enough that his power was established up to the Forth. Edwin put to good use the knowledge of the affairs of Wales and of the south-Humbrian states acquired during his exile. His war-bands intimidated or

* See map, p. 275, and note, p. 378.

† The centre of this kingdom seems to have been Ledstone (in Bede, Loidis), where the Roman road crossed the Aire.

forcibly subdued all the British and English kingdoms except Kent, and his fleet reduced Anglesey and the Isle of Man. Then the greatness of his success brought about his fall. Cadwallon, king of North Wales,* a son of the King Cadfan who is said to have given shelter to Edwin as an exile, formed an alliance in

633 with Penda, king of the Mercians, that is the Angles of the upper Trent. Britons and English fighting side by side in their revolt overthrew and killed Edwin in the battle of Heathfield.† It was the beginning of a long feud between Northumbria and Mercia.

With this slight introduction we can now pass to the ecclesiastical history of Edwin's reign.

The conversion of Edwin of Northumbria was in its main outlines similar to that of Ethelbert of Kent. Once more a favour-

* Called by Bede, Caedwalla.

† OE. Hæðfelð (probably Hatfield Chase, east of Doncaster).

able opportunity came from the marriage of a heathen king with a Christian princess (Edwin's queen being Ethelburg, daughter of Ethelbert); once more a king acted with statesmanlike deliberation and referred the question of Christianity to his council of chief men. But there are novel features in the story. Edwin had himself enjoyed some contact with the new religion before his accession. When Deira had been annexed by Ethelfrith, Edwin, according to Welsh authorities, found refuge with Cadfan, a British (and therefore a Christian) king in North Wales. Later he had made his way to the court of Raedwald, and had no doubt seen the East Anglian temple with its altar to Christ alongside of the heathen altar. The other novelty in Edwin's conversion was a mysterious apparition which, like Macbeth's witches, promised him future greatness. But what chiefly distinguishes the story of Edwin is that it is narrated by Bede at such length that it is possible to see something of the workings of the barbarian mind as it turned gradually to the new religion. We see Paulinus, the chaplain who had been sent to the Northumbrian court with the Kentish princess, gaining influence over Edwin by claiming that the king's escape from the poisoned dagger of an assassin, and, on the same night (the night of Easter Sunday, 626), the easy childbirth of his queen, were both due to his prayers to the Christian God. We see Edwin then sitting much alone, brooding over the problem whether he should change his religion. Letters arrive 'from the Pope'; with them are a gold ornament for himself, and for the queen a silver mirror and a gilt ivory comb; then Edwin is victorious in a campaign against the West Saxons—his own mind is consequently made up. The question must, however, be referred to his counsellors, his *witan*. We have their arguments: the worldly wisdom of Coifi, chief of the priests (*he* had not got much good out of his service to the old gods); the more spiritual questionings of the counsellor who spoke of the shortness of man's life ('like the flight of a sparrow through a hall in winter') and of the uncertainty of what was to follow. This debate, and its sequel—the destruction of the heathen temple at Goodmanham with its idols, the chief priest himself leading the attack and casting a first spear at it—Bede's familiar story lays bare much of the heart of the barbarian; it reveals some of the mental processes which induced the fighting-men of the north to exchange Woden for Christ. But in all probability the proceedings were less spontaneous than is indicated by Bede. The part taken by Coifi at least must have been prearranged—a clever ruse for carrying the waverers over to the Christian camp. The leaders of the kingdom were infected by the enthusiasm of the moment, and quickly found that they had committed themselves, both by acclamation in the assembly, and also by the dramatic attack on the temple. Edwin's methods, like those of Ethelbert, were more skilful and happier than the arguments of force which in Norway gave Odin his sacrifice of blood before his adherents yielded to the sword of St. Olaf.

One reason for the calm with which the new religion was accepted was no doubt the fact that, after it had been officially adopted by the assembly, each individual was left free to choose whether or no he would come and ask for baptism. And as a matter of fact, the mission of Paulinus was evidently so short-handed—his only helper mentioned by name is James, the deacon—that the change had to come slowly. We hear of baptisms or other missionary work, but only at old Roman places such as York, Catterick, Campodonum,* and Lincoln. And it is perhaps significant that the place in Bernicia where Paulinus had remarkable success, being fully occupied in baptizing for thirty-six days, was Yeavering,† the centre of a district where place-names and hill-terraces point to a survival of the Celts. No doubt the people from the neighbouring villages who flocked to him to be baptized in the river Glen, as well as those who were baptized in the places which had once been Roman, were largely of British descent.

Bede[31] makes it clear how it was that information about these

* Perhaps Doncaster. † Adgefrin.

beginnings of Christianity in the north came to be conveyed to him.

'A certain priest and abbot of the monastery of Partney,* a man of singular veracity, whose name was Deda, told me concerning the faith of this province that an old man had informed him that he himself had been baptized at noon-day, by Bishop Paulinus, in the presence of King Edwin, and with him a great multitude of the people, in the river Trent, near the city, which in the English tongue is called *Tiouulfingacaestir*;† and he was also wont to describe the person of the same Paulinus, saying that he was tall of stature, stooping somewhat, his hair black, his visage thin, his nose slender and aquiline, his aspect both venerable and awe-inspiring. He had also with him in the ministry James, the deacon, a man of zeal and great fame in Christ and in the Church, who lived even to our days.'

Paulinus and James, the deacon, could catechize and baptize in a few places. They could do little more, and it was only a beginning. But the conversion of the Anglo-Saxons came without bloodshed because it came slowly, and with the minimum of compulsion. The Christian Edwin, his queen, and their Christian courtiers, brought some of the merits of the new religion to the notice of the Northumbrian people, as they made their progresses up and down the land. No ruler before Edwin had been so remarkably successful: before 616 a fugitive, and then after little more than ten years reputed overlord 'of all the parts of Britain that were provinces either of the English or of the Britons'—such an *imperium* as no English king had ever before possessed. When Bede wrote his history a hundred years later, the fame of Edwin and of his magnificence had become proverbial. However well-worn, the passage deserves to be quoted in full since it gives us the first picture of an English king.[32]

'It is told that there was then such perfect peace in Britain, wheresoever the dominion of King Edwin extended, that, as is still proverbially said, a woman with her new-born babe might walk throughout the island, from sea to sea, without receiving any harm. That king took

* In Lincolnshire. † Not identified.

such care for the good of his nation, that in several places where he had seen clear springs near the highways, he caused stakes to be fixed, with copper drinking-vessels hanging on them, for the refreshment of travellers; nor durst any man touch them for any other purpose than that for which they were designed, either through the great dread they had of the king, or for the affection which they bore him. His dignity was so great throughout his dominions, that not only were his banners borne before him in battle, but even in time of peace, when he rode about his cities, townships, or provinces, with his thegns,* the standard-bearer was always wont to go before him. Also, when he walked anywhere along the streets, that sort of banner which the Romans call *Tufa* and the English *Thuuf*, was in like manner borne before him.'

There are three points in this passage which should be noted: the emphasis put on the maintenance of order (the good king is the king who enforces order); the Germanic custom which made the king ride round his territory from one royal vill to another; and lastly, the Roman influence, coming probably through the court of North Wales, which induced the barbarian to imitate some of the pomp of a Roman ruler. Edwin's ambitions are heightened by some traditions of the bygone Empire, and the dignity of his migrant court is enhanced with some Romano-British trappings.

For six years (627–33) Edwin ruled as a Christian king. Then, in October 633, the blow fell. Cadwallon, 'King of the Britons', with the help of Penda and his Mercians wiped out the Northumbrian army at Heathfield. Edwin's head was carried to York. For a year, 'the hateful year', Cadwallon 'occupied the provinces of the Northumbrians, not ruling them like a victorious king, but ravaging them like a furious tyrant'.[33] Roman Christianity for a time died down in Northumbria as it had died in East Anglia and in Essex. But when Paulinus took ship back to Kent, his follower James, the deacon, bravely remained at his post near Catterick, baptizing and teaching. In 634 the tyranny of the British king was ended by his defeat near Heavenfield,†

* *Ministris.*

† OE. Hefenfelð.

and in 635 the whole religious situation was changed by the coming of two new missions to England, that of the Scots to Northumbria, and that of Birinus to Wessex.

Before we pass to this new phase in the Conversion, let us consider what had actually been accomplished by Augustine's followers since 597. Though Kent was still the only kingdom where the Roman Church had securely established itself, real progress had been made elsewhere by breaking the ground in Essex, East Anglia, Lindsey, and Northumbria. In East Anglia, Christianity made two false starts. The first of them, when Raedwald set up an altar to Christ by the side of a heathen altar, has been already mentioned. The second was about 628, when Eorpwald, Raedwald's son, was won over by Edwin's zeal to the new religion, but was soon murdered by a heathen. 'From that time the province was in error for three years.' Then a step-son of Raedwald, by name Sigbert,* gained the throne. Sigbert, 'a good and religious man', had been for some time an exile in Gaul, and had been 'there initiated into the mysteries of the faith, whereof he made it his business to cause all his province to partake as soon as he came to the throne. His exertions were nobly promoted by Bishop Felix, who, coming to Honorius, the archbishop, from the parts of Burgundy where he had been born, . . . was sent by him to preach the word of life to the aforesaid nation of the Angles.' Though the chief fellow-worker of Felix was for a time an Irishman, St. Fursey, the converts in this province looked towards Canterbury. Therefore Bishop Lightfoot's dictum that Augustine was but the 'Apostle of Kent'[34] is not the whole truth though it is near the truth.

There is no denying that the Augustinian missionaries showed eminent discretion in returning to their base when an advanced position became dangerous. There were, however, extenuating circumstances. They were city-bred; their earlier years had been spent within the four walls of a Roman monastery; they were men of southern ways and southern temperaments; and the

* OE. Sigeberht.

rough manners and hardly understood speech of the northern aborigines to whom they had been sent must, when combined with the sunless skies and cold and rain of our climate, have made missionary work in England as great an ordeal as the austerities imposed by St. David on the monks of Menevia.

The clergy of Augustine did their duty according to their lights, but, like English missionaries in India, they did not easily mingle with their converts; and it appears that some sixty years after the coming of Augustine, his Italian successors were still not able to speak the English language with any fluency.[35]

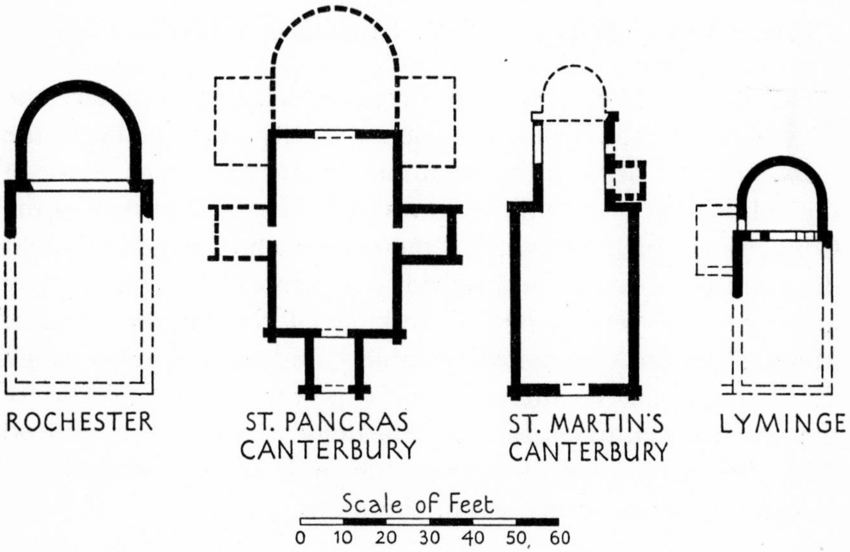

VIII. Part II

THE CONVERSION: THE SECOND GENERATION

THE outline of political events which has to preface the story of the Scottish Mission is chiefly concerned with the rivalry between Northumbrians and Mercians. Some of the political facts will find a natural place in the narrative of the Conversion which follows, but the reader who is not sure about the main story should now refresh his memory of its outlines by looking at the genealogies of the kings of Northumbria and of Mercia,* at the chronological table,† and at the maps which show the frequent alternations of power in the middle of the seventh century. In the genealogy it should be noticed that, though cousins of Edwin rule in Deira at intervals till eighteen years after his death, the murder of the last of these, Oswin (slain in cold blood by order of Oswy of Bernicia), brings the House of Ælle to an end. For the rest of the century, both Northumbrian kingdoms are ruled by the sons and grandsons of Ethelfrith. Three of these, Oswald (634–42), Oswy ‡ (642–71), Oswy's son Ecgfrith (671–85), are mentioned by Bede as kings who enjoyed the *imperium* (or *ducatus*).

Headpiece.—Celtic clergy, from Scottish sculptured stones. Note their book-satchels.

* Vol. ii, pp. 722, 719. † Vol. ii, p. 729.

‡ OE. *Oswio*.

But it is only necessary to glance at the maps to see that their supremacy was not as complete as that of Edwin, and that at certain periods the power of the House of Penda was more considerable than that of the House of Ida. On the whole, the Northumbrians were losing ground in this age, and the Mercians

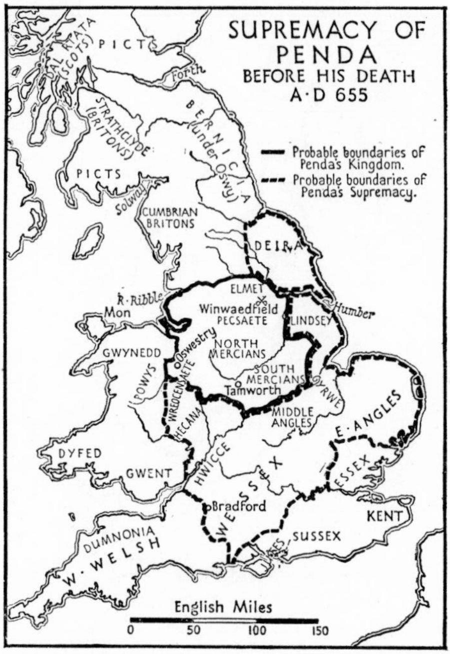

were gaining it. If we summarize the alternations of power, we have some such story as this.

Oswald, the representative of the Bernician dynasty, had defeated Cadwallon and his Britons near Heavenfield; since he came as a deliverer, he had no difficulty in establishing himself in Deira as well as in Bernicia. He also restored Northumbrian influence over some of the southern States, his position being illustrated by the part he took in the baptism of the king of Wessex (*c.* 635). But he did not recover any lasting authority over Mercia proper (that is, the original kingdom round the Trent) or over some of the neighbouring provinces. These remained in the hands of Penda (626–55), who made good use of his position on the flank of Northumbria's road to the south. By 642 Penda was strong enough to defeat and slay Oswald at the battle of Maserfield,* just as nine years earlier he had destroyed Edwin. Then followed a period of Northumbrian eclipse. The two

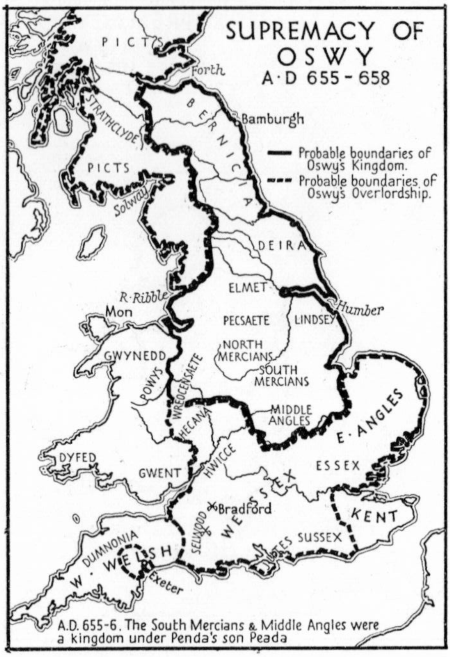

Northumbrian kingdoms were separated and Penda extended his power, first over Wessex (645), and then over East Anglia (650). By 654 he clearly had won to the south of the Humber an *imperium* approximating to that shown on the map. Penda had, in fact, built up for the first time a Greater Mercia. The king of Mercia had become king of the Midlands. When in 655 Penda vowed to blot out all the nation of the Northumbrians,

* OE. Maserfelð; Plummer (*Bede*, ii. 152) sums up the argument for locating this at Oswestry (Oswald's Tree) in Shropshire. The identification must be considered uncertain. A. Hunt, in *Journal of Arch. Ass.* (N.S.), xxx. 109–17, suggests a site in the Isle of Axholme, but this is improbable.

and Oswy, king of Bernicia, with a small army dared to oppose him, Penda was able to summon thirty 'legions'.[1] 'The engagement began; the pagans were put to flight or killed; the thirty royal commanders . . . who had come to Penda's assistance were almost all of them slain; . . . the battle was fought near the river

Winwaed.* Owing to the great rains the river was then in flood and had overflowed its banks, so that many more were drowned in the flight than were destroyed in battle by the sword.' Penda's legions did not avail to save him from defeat and death at the battle of the Winwaed. Thus, in the middle of Oswy's reign, that is during the years 655–8, Northumbrian authority once more reached the Severn and the Thames. For these three years Oswy was direct ruler of Mercia and appointed his own ealdormen. A revolt followed; and Wulfhere, the successful rebel,

* Apparently located by Bede *in regione Loidis*.

taking up the work of his father Penda, built anew on his foundations the kingdom of the Midlands which we have called Greater Mercia. Accordingly, when the Synod of Whitby was held in 664, the Humber[2] was again the dividing line between Northumbria and Mercia. Wulfhere before his death in 675 had spread Mercian rule over 'all the southern peoples',[3] including Kent and Wessex. His successor, Ethelred, another son of Penda, began his reign with a pitiless devastation of Kent, presumably to punish a revolt. In 679 he fought a great battle with Ecgfrith of Northumbria on the Trent, and was threatening 'a more bloody war',[4] when Archbishop Theodore intervened. A long peace between Northumbria and Mercia ensued. About the same time Mercia also suspended its schemes of aggression south of the Thames.

Thus, looking back on this stormy period, the age wherein the second generation of English converts played their parts, we see that its chief political phenomena were the following: first, the decline of the south-eastern kingdoms into second-class powers; then in the middle of the century the confederation of the Midland States into a Greater Mercia; and thirdly, towards the end of the century, a temporary condition of unstable equilibrium among the three chief kingdoms, Northumbria, Mercia, and Wessex.

THE SCOTTISH MISSION TO THE ENGLISH

We have now to return to the year 633 and to trace the coming of Scottish Christianity to the north of England and to the Midlands, a story which gives us the main theme of the middle period of the seventh century, and to which the wars and the political ambitions of the kings are but a rumbling accompaniment.

If we search back for the very beginning of the new movement, we may find it in the flight of Oswald and Oswy, the sons of Ethelfrith, from Edwin of Deira (617), a flight which brought them to Iona. This chance incident leading in the second generation of the Conversion to the Scottish mission may be regarded as a counterpart to the meeting of Gregory with the Anglian boys in the Roman slave-market, the incident which had led to the Roman mission of the first generation. A closer parallel offers itself if we compare the exile of Oswald at Iona with that earlier exile of Edwin, when fleeing from the father of Oswald. In either case, the feud between the dynasties of Ælle and Ida was the determining factor. The banishment of the princes caused them to mingle with the Christians in the west of the island. Oswald and Oswy spent some of their seventeen years' exile at Iona; and there, where Columba was still a living memory, they learnt to know Celtic Christianity from the inside as no English ruler had hitherto known it. Oswald's conviction of the truth of the new religion when he regained his father's kingdom, was to be a far more potent force than the politic acquiescence of Ethelbert and of Edwin.

During the 'hateful year' (633–4) which followed the overthrow of Edwin, men relapsed into heathendom. The kings of Bernicia and Deira (the two kingdoms being again separated) acted ingloriously. Eanfrith, the king of Bernicia, the eldest brother of Oswald and Oswy, coming to sue for peace from the British conqueror, was struck down by him. The fury which the Britons had been storing in their hearts for two centuries was let loose. They took their last revenge.

Oswald returned from the land of the Scots with twelve faithful thegns[5] who had shared his exile and followed him to baptism. These, with a small force, withstood and defeated an 'immense' army of Cadwallon. At Heavenfield, where the Roman Wall crests a heathery hill before dipping steeply into the valley of the North Tyne, Oswald made a large cross of rough timber, and stood it up in a hole in the ground, holding it in both hands while others filled in the earth—the first cross, says Bede, to be erected in Bernicia. His army, at his bidding, prayed on their knees before this cross, Oswald himself invoking St. Columba. Then, at the first dawn of day, and somewhere[6] in that region of the Wall, Angle and Briton fought their last great fight; and Cadwallon was slain. This victory was but the first of innumerable miracles to be worked by Oswald's cross, planted on that same moor which from one dreary day to another had been scanned by Roman soldiers, confident in their discipline and asking for no miracle-working cross.

When Oswald had established himself as king of all Northumbria, it was naturally to Iona that he applied for Christian teachers; and in one of these, Aidan a Scot, he found (635) the right man for the work of converting his Northumbrian subjects. Oswald accordingly gave Aidan and his family of monks Lindisfarne, an island at high tide, situated near his fortress of Bamburgh. On that wind-swept headland, the bleakest spot of an inhospitable shore, a community of the regular Scoto-Irish type established itself, raising a collection of huts and an oratory within a defensive enclosure. From this 'island' members of the community year after year set out on foot across three miles of sand to preach, first in the neighbouring villages of Bernicia, and later in distant centres. Some of these were even hundreds of miles away in the south.

Bede[7] tells us how Aidan 'was wont to traverse both town and country on foot, never on horseback, unless compelled by some urgent necessity; to the end that as he went he might turn aside to any whomsoever he saw, whether rich or poor, and call upon them if infidels to receive the mystery of the faith, or, if they were believers, strengthen them in the faith'. What specially drew men to him was that he lived as he preached, and that he refused to accept any riches for himself or his followers. He was allowed to use the king's vills (which were probably the centres of local government) as the outposts of his journeys, and so he was able to cover wide tracts of Northumbria. The Scots were more successful than the Romans, not only because they perambulated the countryside, but because their mission was recruited by volunteers. Aidan's helpers did not wait to come till

Lindisfarne, drawing by J. M. W. Turner (1830). The ruins are on the site of the original monastery. Turner gives the spirit of the place, but distorts its details, especially the height of the Castle rock

Bradwell-on-Sea. Nave of the Church built by St. Cedd within the Roman Fort Othona (Ythancester)

By permission of the Controller of H.M. Stationery Office

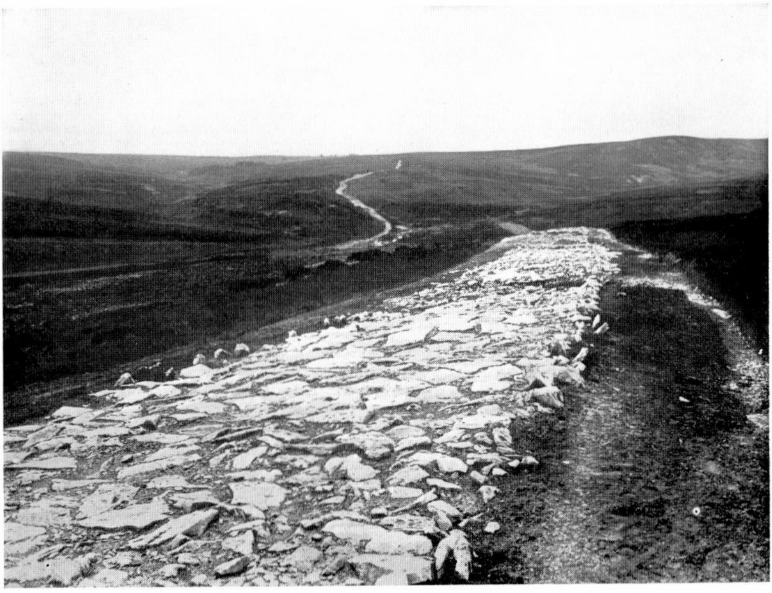

The Roman Road across the Wheeldale Moor, between York and Whitby

they were bidden.[8] 'Many came daily into Britain from the country of the Scots, and with great devotion preached the Word. . . . Churches were built in several places; the people joyfully flocked together to hear the Word; lands and other property were given of the King's bounty to found monasteries; English children as well as their elders were instructed by their Scottish teachers in study and the observance of monastic discipline.'

What made these seven years of Oswald's rule seem a golden age to Bede as he looked back at them from a distance of almost a century was the harmonious co-operation of the king and his missionary bishop. Oswald never forgot the lessons which he had learnt at Iona as an exile. When Aidan, who was not skilful in the English tongue, preached the Gospel 'it was a fair sight to see the king himself interpreting the Word of God to his ealdormen and thegns'. The harmony which existed between the king and the missionary saint is echoed in the familiar story about Aidan as he sat at table with the king one Easter Day, blessing the hand of Oswald, the hand which had just presented to the poor a silver dish containing the king's own meal—*Nunquam inveterescet haec manus*. For centuries the uncorrupted flesh of the king's right hand was preserved in the reliquary at Bamburgh, and the uncorrupted spirit of the king was immortalized in Bede's story for ever.

When this golden age was suddenly interrupted in 642 by the battle of Maserfield, and Oswald, like Edwin, became a victim to the enmity of the heathen Penda, the head and arms of Oswald were severed from the trunk. But the dead king was quickly canonized by the people. (It was characteristic of the Anglo-Saxons that their first native saint should be a king.) Miracles were said to be worked by his mutilated corpse; nay more, by the water in which his butchered limbs had been washed, and by a splinter of the stake on which his head had been placed. The corpse of St. Oswald, decapitated and dismembered, helped to propagate the new religion as effectually as Oswald the living king.

The Christianity of Oswy, Oswald's successor, was as firm as his brother's, if less effective; and Aidan till his death in 651 continued to receive the support of the monarchy in his work of conversion. The reign of Oswy was in fact the decisive period. Up to his accession, Northumbria had experienced only six years of official Roman Christianity under Edwin, and eight years of Scottish propaganda under Oswald. But Oswy's tenure of the throne (642–71)* was long enough for Christianity to take root and fructify throughout all the Anglian kingdoms, for the conflict between the Roman and Scottish churches to be brought to an issue, and for new personal conflicts, centring round Wilfrid, to be generated. The changing phases of the political situation which we have already noted—the growing power of Penda south of the Humber (642–55), the short supremacy of Oswy (655–8), the re-establishment of Mercian power under Wulfhere, son of Penda (658–75)—these phases in the political history did not greatly affect the progress of the Conversion. The great landmarks in its history at this stage are the sending of Scottish preachers to Mercia and Essex in 653, the Synod of Whitby (664), and after the Synod the coming of Archbishop Theodore to Canterbury. Little need be said about the first period of Oswy's reign. Aidan continued to preach in Deira as well as in Bernicia, being warmly encouraged by Oswin, a cousin of Edwin, who had re-established the House of Ælle on the throne of York. It was Oswin who gave Aidan a horse, and persuaded him to abandon the Scottish fashion of making his missionary journeys on foot. Then, when Aidan gave the horse to one of the first beggars he met, it was Oswin who, repenting of his first anger, fell down at Aidan's feet begging him for forgiveness. Aidan, as Bishop-Abbot of Lindisfarne, was, except for the theoretical authority of the parent church of Iona, sole ruler of the Northumbrian Church until his death in 651. Under him the monastery of Lindisfarne remained the training-school for preachers, and the centre from which the new learning radiated to distant kingdoms.

* Until 655 he was king of Bernicia only.

The methods of Celtic propaganda were traditional. In Iona St. Columba had trained twelve disciples; before him in Ireland St. Patrick had trained another twelve. Aidan accordingly followed the ancient custom and prepared twelve young men to continue and to extend his work. Thus was the idea of the *comitatus* applied to religion, and applied in such a way that the bands of trained followers could increase like a snowball.

The two of Aidan's pupils who were most prominent in extending his work after his death were the brothers Cedd and Chad.* They both took a part in preaching Christianity to the Mercians, but it is Cedd who first comes into the story—in the period before the Synod of Whitby. In the years 653–4 Cedd distinguished himself not only by being one of the first missionaries to the Angles of the Midlands, but also by reviving Christianity in Essex, where, as we have seen, it had died down since 617. Neither of these operations in the Scottish religious campaign need be told in detail. It is sufficient to remember that Christianity came to the Midlands in the same way that it had come to Kent and to Northumbria. When Peada, son of Penda, and under-king over the Middle Angles, wished to marry a daughter of Oswy[9] 'he could not obtain his desire unless he would receive the faith of Christ and be baptized with the nation which he governed'. Accordingly, Cedd and other disciples of Aidan, headed by Diuma, soon to be made their bishop, were sent to Penda's son-in-law with his Northumbrian bride.

Perhaps the most notable feature in this first step towards the Conversion of Mercia is the fact that the mission was arranged while Penda was still at the height of his power. The attitude of Penda to the new religion is an interesting contrast both to that of kings like Edwin, who came over slowly but surely, and to that of temporizing backsliders like Raedwald of East Anglia. We do not know how far Penda's earlier antagonism to the Christian kings of Northumbria had been dictated by religious motives. What Bede makes clear is simply this, that in his later

* OE. Ceadda.

years he remained a heathen, but no persecutor. 'Nor did king Penda forbid the preaching of the Word among his people the Mercians, if any were willing to hear it. But on the contrary, he hated and despised those whom he perceived not to perform the works of faith, when they had once received the faith of Christ, saying "They were contemptible and wretched who did not obey their God in whom they believed".' Though Penda had come to tolerate the preachers from Northumbria, he was not prepared to accept without challenge the increasing political power of Oswy. When Penda in the third of his great battles against the Northumbrians was killed, Oswy, for the time being all-powerful south as well as north of the Humber, 'converted the Mercians in the adjacent provinces to the grace of the Christian faith'. This battle of the Winwaed marks the final transfer of military and political predominance amongst the Anglo-Saxons from heathens to Christians. Paganism survived in out-of-the-way corners of the island, but never again could it openly challenge the new faith.

MISSIONS TO WESSEX (*c.* 635) AND ESSEX (653–4*)

Some knowledge of the conversion of Wessex and of the resumed conversion of Essex is needed to understand the situation of affairs in 664. The accounts in Bede of both events are short, and can therefore be given in his own words:[10]

'At that time the West Saxons, formerly called Gewissae, in the reign of Cynegils, received the faith of Christ, through the preaching of Bishop Birinus, who came into Britain by the counsel of Pope Honorius; having promised in his presence that he would sow the seed of the holy faith in the farthest inland regions of the English, where no other teacher had been before him. . . . On his arrival in Britain, he first came to the nation of the Gewissae, and finding all in that place confirmed pagans, he thought it better to preach the Word there, than to proceed further to seek for other hearers of his preaching.

'Now, as he was spreading the Gospel in the aforesaid province, it

* Cedd was not consecrated before 654, even if he began to preach in 653.

happened that when the king himself, having received instruction as a catechumen, was being baptized together with his people, Oswald, the most holy and victorious king of the Northumbrians, being present, received him as he came forth from baptism. . . . The two kings gave to the Bishop the city called Dorcic,* there to establish his episcopal see; where, having built and consecrated churches, and by his pious labours called many to the Lord, he departed to the Lord, and was buried in the same city.'

In this way there was established in Wessex a Church in communion with Rome, but at first not wholly under the control of Canterbury. The death of its patron, King Cynegils (641), caused the infant Church some growing pains, but its troubles are of no great importance. Turning to Bede's account of the revival of Christianity among the East Saxons,[11] we have a passage which describes how Oswy, when Sigbert,† the king of the East Saxons,

'came to the province of the Northumbrians to visit him, as he often did, used to endeavour to convince him that those could not be gods that had been made by the hands of men; that a stock or a stone could not be proper matter to form a god. . . . [After baptism] King Sigbert, having now become a citizen of the eternal kingdom, returned to the seat of his temporal kingdom, requesting of King Oswy that he would give him some teachers, to convert his nation to the faith of Christ, and cleanse them in the fountain of salvation. Wherefore, Oswy, sending into the province of the Midland Angles, summoned the man of God, Cedd, and, giving him another priest for his companion, sent them to preach the Word to the East Saxons.'

Cedd built several churches in Essex, notably that which may still be seen among the ruins of the Roman fort of Othona (Pl. 42 A). But even this second mission to the East Saxons was not a complete success. Some of the ground covered was to be again lost.

On the whole, however, it is true to say that some ten years before the Synod of Whitby every English kingdom except Sussex and the Isle of Wight had adhered to Christianity. The stage was set for a new act in the drama.

* Dorchester on the Thames.

† OE. Sigeberht.

THE SYNOD OF WHITBY (664)

Success brings its own difficulties, and with the assured victory of the new religion after the middle of the seventh century the interest of the story shifts. The conflict between heathenism and Christianity gave place to a conflict between one type of Christianity and another. Questions which had been of secondary importance now quickly became urgent; was there to be only one Church of the English? Was it to be Roman or Celtic? Or could both types of Christianity continue side by side?

Chaos there undoubtedly was before the Synod of Whitby. In Kent and in parts of East Anglia the Church was Roman and subordinate to Canterbury; in Wessex Roman, but independent of Canterbury; in Northumbria and in Mercia it was Scottish; in Essex the situation was uncertain. And this was not the only trouble. Other evils were threatening: that in each state the bishop and the local Church would be at the mercy of the local monarchy; that Christianity would remain disorganized, undisciplined, separatist; and that it would embitter the old strife between the kingdoms instead of fostering peace and unity. The history of the bishops of Wessex after the death of Birinus (651) is the best illustration of the consequences of a disunited provincial Christianity. The first successor of Birinus was a certain Agilbert, a Frank. The king of Wessex, finding that he could not understand this foreigner, created a new bishopric at Winchester, and gave it to a native bishop, Wini. Wini had at least the merit of speaking English. Agilbert took offence, and withdrew. Wini also quarrelled with the king, and was driven from Winchester. Later on (about 666–7) he succeeded in retrieving his fortunes by an act of simony, and bought the bishopric of London from the king of Mercia.

It was scandals such as these which brought home to some the need for a Church conference and for the appointment of a statesmanlike archbishop to control all the Heptarchic Churches, and to guide their first steps towards unity.

The controversy between Roman and Scot first became acute in Northumbria, when King Oswy's son, Alchfrith, fell under the influence of Agilbert, still nominally bishop of the West Saxons, and of Wilfrid, a handsome Northumbrian noble, newly returned from Rome. But the immediate occasion for the Synod of Whitby was the practical difficulty caused by the observance of Easter at different dates, the king calculating it according to the Scottish method of reckoning, and the queen (a daughter of King Edwin) according to the Roman.[12] In 664 Oswy foresaw that in the following year the difference between the two reckonings would be considerable, and that, while he was celebrating the Easter feast, his queen would be keeping her Lenten fast. No doubt he also realized that the adherence to the Romans of his son Alchfrith, whom he had made under-king in Deira, might revive the old antagonism between the two Northumbrian kingdoms in a dangerous religious form. It seems, however, that it was not so much considerations of policy which moved Oswy and his advisers to summon the conference as an uneasy feeling born of growing intercourse with the continental Church, that those who were following the usages of the Scots might be running in vain; that in spite of all their fastings and good works they might be failing to ensure their entrance to heaven. For these reasons, in 664, nine years after the defeat of Penda and five years after the successful revolt of Penda's son, Wulfhere, Oswy summoned to the place which before the coming of the Danes was called Streanæshalch the conference of leading Northumbrian Christians commonly known as the 'Synod of Whitby'.

This event, which is one of the great turning-points in the history of the race, deserves our special attention. We must think of the monastery where the conference met as one of twelve which had been founded by Oswy, as thank-offerings for his victory over Penda. The monastery was of the 'double' type, that is, it included a community of dedicated women, as well as a separate community of men for the services of the church. Men and women were alike ruled by the Abbess Hilda, who

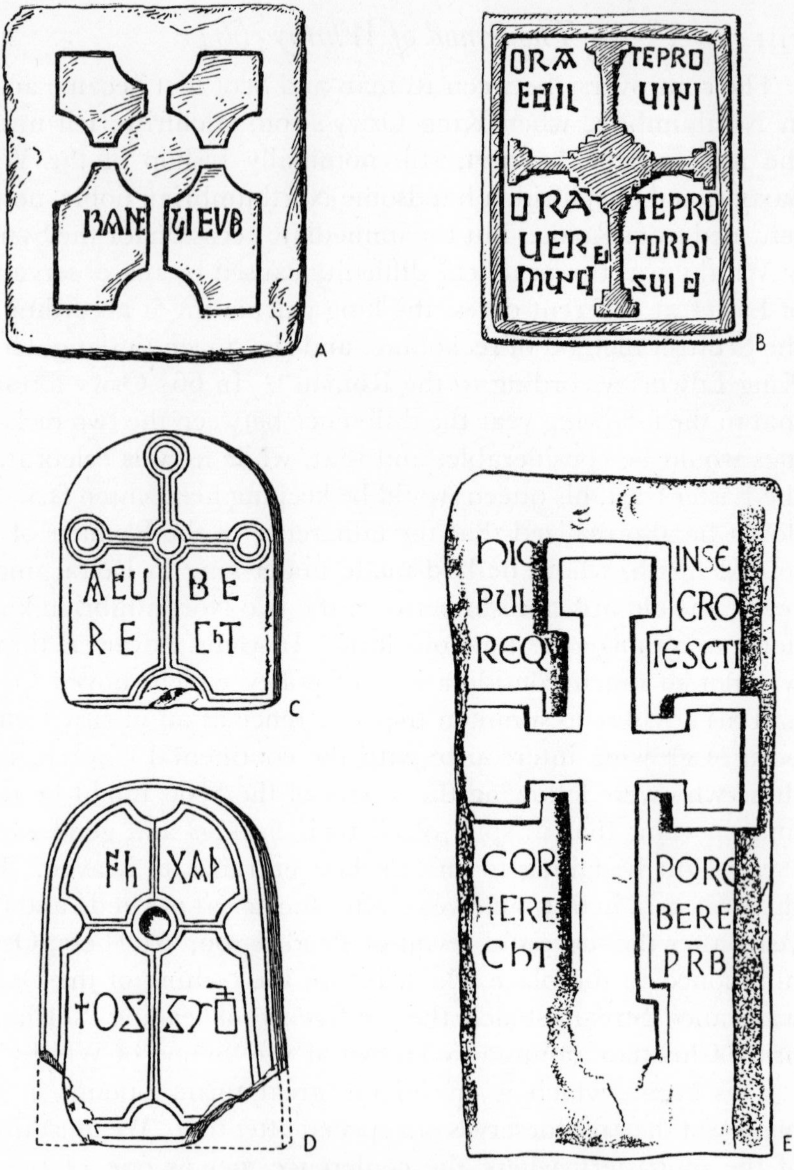

FIG. 48. Northumbrian Recumbent Gravestones.

A and B.—Hartlepool ($\frac{1}{5}$). A to the memory of (?) HANEGNEUB. B.—ORATE PRO EDILUINI ORATE PRO UERMUND ET TORHTSUID. C and D.—Lindisfarne. C (less than $\frac{1}{5}$) to the memory of AEDBERECHT. D (more than $\frac{1}{5}$) to OSGYTH (above in runes, below in Hiberno-Saxon characters). Since this is a woman's name, Lindisfarne may at one time have been a double monastery. E.—Monkwearmouth—a much larger slab ($\frac{1}{12}$)—probably of seventh century. The lettering is Roman with some Hiberno-Saxon characteristics.

thirty-seven years earlier had been baptized by Paulinus in the first days of Northumbrian Christianity. At Streanæshalch she[13] 'taught the strict observance of justice, piety, chastity, and other virtues, and particularly of peace and charity; so that, after the example of the primitive church, no one there was rich, and none poor, for they had all things common, and none had

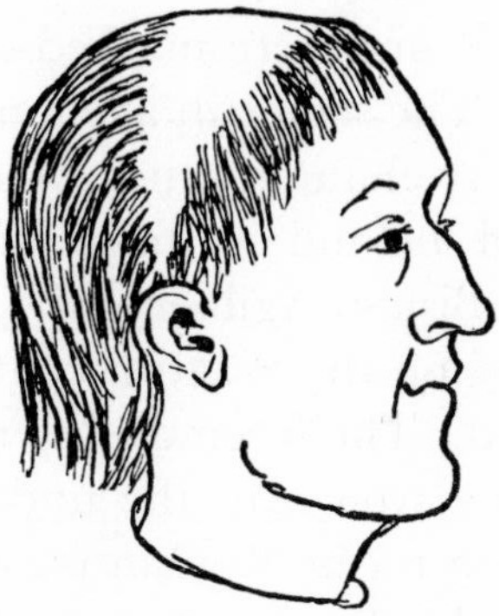

FIG. 49. The Celtic tonsure, probable appearance.

any private property. Her prudence was so great, that not only meaner men in their need, but sometimes even kings and princes sought and received her counsel.' Thus, under her wise discipline, the monastery was becoming the nursery of future bishops.

Thanks to Bede, many of the leading clergy who came to the conference are well known to us. There was Colman, the chief spokesman for the Celtic party, a Scot who had been sent only three years previously from Iona to become bishop-abbot at Lindisfarne; not yet able, it seems, to speak English, and therefore not effective as an advocate; but a prudent man and, like his clergy who accompanied him from Lindisfarne, a lover of simple ways and a despiser of money and wealth:[14] 'For the whole care of those teachers was to serve God, not the world—to feed the soul and not the belly.' There too, inclining to the Scots, was Bishop Cedd, Celtic by training and perhaps by descent, Celtic in his casual pluralism (he was now abbot of Lastingham in Deira as well as bishop of the East Saxons), Celtic also in his demonology: he had recently exorcized the evil spirits of the wilds of Lastingham by continuous prayer and extreme fasting throughout Lent.

Colman and the clergy who adhered to Scottish customs were a strange sight owing to their tonsure. Their heads were shaved from ear to ear: in front, it seemed, a wisp of hair; at the back of the head long flowing locks.[15]

The supporters of Rome were marked out from the Scots by their shaven crowns. The senior in age among them was James, the deacon and expert chanter, who, when Paulinus fled from Northumbria, stayed behind to teach and to baptize. The superior in rank was Bishop Agilbert, who, though a Frank, was no doubt well primed on the Scottish controversy, having himself studied in Ireland. The foremost in energy and ability, the man who had already won over the under-king of Deira, and was giving momentum to the Roman party, was Wilfrid, abbot of Ripon. He was by birth a Northumbrian, one of the fighting aristocracy, an enterprising restless fellow. He had not been happy as a boy at school, nor as a young noble in attendance on the queen at court, nor as an untonsured inmate at Lindisfarne. There, after a few years among the Scots, 'it came into his heart to pay a visit to the see of the Apostle Peter and attempt a road hitherto untrodden by any of our race'.[15a] During the five years (653–8) which he spent on his journey to Rome, he at last found in the cause of St. Peter the ideal for which he could fight with all the pugnacity of his thegnly ancestors. Some three years after his return to Northumbria, his patron Alchfrith, the under-king in Deira, made him abbot of Ripon, having first ejected those members of the community who refused to surrender their Scottish customs. And now in 664 Wilfrid had the great opportunity of his life; for Agilbert, the Frank, on the ground that he himself could not make a speech in English, asked him to plead the Roman cause. Wilfrid's speech was long and eloquent; but one of his sentences will suffice to show the line and the tone of his argument: 'All over the world the Easter which we observe is celebrated, except only by these and their accomplices in obstinacy, I mean the Picts and the Britons, who foolishly in these two remote islands, oppose all the rest of the universe.' Colman, speaking for the Scots, replied that they followed the usage of St. John, the Beloved of the Lord, the usage of Father Columba, and others who had worked many miracles. 'Who are these,' Wilfrid insisted, 'compared with the Apostle Peter, who keeps the door of Heaven?'

A memorable debate for us, if ever there was one! What if Ethelfrith, the heathen, the slayer of the twelve hundred monks of Bangor, could have returned to see his son presiding over these robed and shaven clergy, listening to the involved debate, whether Easter should be celebrated in the Scottish manner, from the fourteenth to the twentieth day of the moon, or in the Roman manner, from the fifteenth to the twenty-first. Oswy no doubt failed to follow the abstruse arguments as closely as he might. His decision at the end was certainly based on the simpler proposition, admitted even by the Scots. 'Peter is the doorkeeper, and he has the keys. Against him I will not contend.' 'The king, having said this, all who were seated there or standing by, both great and small, gave their assent, and, renouncing the less perfect custom, hastened to conform to that which they had found to be better.' The Conference broke up, and those who had taken part in it went their several ways.

'Colman, perceiving that his doctrine was rejected and his party despised, took with him . . . such as would not accept the Catholic Easter and the tonsure in the form of a crown (for there was no small dispute about that also) and went back into Scotland. . . . But Eata, who was abbot of the monastery called Mailros [old Melrose], a man most reverent and gentle, was appointed abbot over the brethren that chose to remain in the church of Lindisfarne when the Scots went away. It is said that Colman upon his departure requested and obtained this of King Oswy, because Eata was one of Aidan's twelve boys of the English nation, whom he received to be instructed in Christ.'

Colman and his followers then wandered from Iona to Ireland. They settled in Innisboffin, an island off Mayo. But those who agreed about the date of Easter found it difficult to agree about other matters. They might keep Easter from the fourteenth to the twentieth day of the moon, and shave their heads from ear to ear, but their ways of life were still discordant, and the thirty Englishmen who had accompanied Colman from Lindisfarne objected that 'the Scots, in the summer season, when the harvest was to be brought in, leaving the monastery, wandered about through places known to them; but returned again the next winter, and desired to use in common what the English had provided'.[16] Finally, a new monastery was established, and the English were transferred to it, to end the bickerings with the Scots.

Of the kings, Alchfrith the son, after securing the promotion of Wilfrid to a bishopric, disappears from history. All we know is that trouble developed between him and his father. At Bewcastle, in Cumberland, we may still see the cross-shaft probably erected to his memory by Wilfrid or some member of Wilfrid's party. It stands where it has stood for some twelve hundred years;* but the fate of this young king, who had taken the initiative in bringing about the discomfiture of the Scots, must remain a mystery.

Oswy survived till 671 and in the end became sufficiently devoted to his adopted Church to wish that Wilfrid should conduct him to Rome itself—a plan interrupted by his death.

Of the champions of Rome, Agilbert returned to France and became bishop of Paris; James, the deacon, lived on into Bede's own time, teaching the Deirans round Catterick how to chant in the Roman manner. Wilfrid at first went from one success to another. A few months after the conference he was, with the consent of King Oswy, made a bishop of the Northumbrians. He crossed to Gaul in great state with a band of clergy, and a troop of twenty fighting men. There he was consecrated by twelve Catholic bishops, who carried him aloft in a golden chair,

* See below, pp. 362 ff.

according to the Gallican rite. But success had come too early, and we shall see in the next chapter how the promise of his youth led to a middle and old age embittered by quarrels both with the rulers of Northumbria and with the archbishops of Canterbury.

The Conference at Whitby settled the question about Easter, but left behind a smouldering feud within the Northumbrian Church. Fifteen years later the Abbess Hilda still headed the opposition to Wilfrid, and laid an accusation against him before the Pope. By that time she had become an old lady of sixty-five, 'whom all that knew her called Mother'.

If we ask, then, what were the results of this so-called Synod, we find that, while in some respects the victory was limited, in the main it was decisive. It was limited because, strictly speaking, it only applied to one kingdom; because it only related to two diversities of custom; because it allowed other Celtic peculiarities to continue; and because it did not put an end to jealousies and ill feelings between the two schools within the Church. On the other hand, it was in fact decisive. Oswy still enjoyed prestige though he had lost supremacy in Britain. The other English kingdoms converted by the Scots quickly came into line. The neighbouring Celtic kingdoms followed more slowly: the northern Irish,* the Dumnonians, the Picts and Scots of Scotland, and the Strathclyde Welsh, changed one or two generations after the Synod of Whitby; but the Welsh of Wales not till 768, and the Cornishmen not till the ninth century. It is no exaggeration to say that the Synod turned the scales and decided that the English should take their religion and their civilization from the Roman world rather than from what Wilfrid called 'One remote corner of the most remote island'. Thenceforth their destiny was to be linked with that of the Continent. The Churches of the Anglo-Saxon kingdoms were to have the advantage of the unity, the organization, and the discipline, which the Roman Church had inherited from the Roman Empire. But while they were thus to escape the dangerous

* The southern Irish had changed their Easter some decades before 664.

liberty of Celtic Christianity they were long to retain the spiritual fervour, the originality, the zeal for learning and preaching, which the Scots had brought with them. The next two chapters will help to show how the characteristics of the parent Churches were combined in their English offspring.

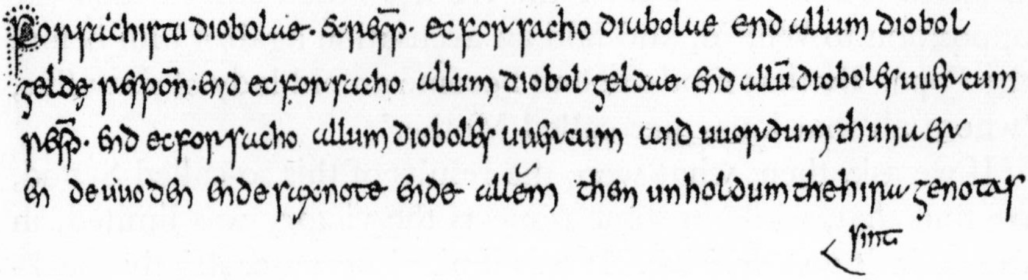

TAILPIECE.—The Old Saxon catechism (*Abrenuntiatio diaboli*) in which the German converts of St. Boniface were required to renounce heathenism:

Forsachistu diobolae? ℞. Ec forsacho diabolae.	[Dost thou forsake the devil? I forsake the devil.
End allum diobolgeldę? ℞. End ec forsacho allum diobolgeldae.	And all the devil's wage? And I forsake all the devil's wage.
End allum dioboles uuercum? ℞. End ec forsacho allum dioboles uuercum and uuordum thunaer ende uuoden ende saxnote ende allum them unholdum the hira genotas sint.	And all the devil's works? And I forsake all the devil's works and words, Thunor and Woden and Saxnote, and all the fiends that are their companions.]

MS. Vat. Palat. nro. 577.

IX

THE GOLDEN AGE

THEODORE AND HADRIAN

IN the first generation of the Conversion the Roman mission had established a base for Christianity in the south. In the second generation the Scots and their English disciples had tramped preaching through the North and Midlands, while another mission from Rome had founded a Church in Wessex. The third generation was to put an end to the confusion left by this earlier haphazard growth of Christianity. Its success was in a sense more remarkable than that of its predecessors; for Christianity was bound to spread to the English either from the south or from the north or from both; and the chances were all in favour of the English converts gravitating to the greater Church, to Rome rather than to Iona. But it was an extraordinary dispensation which sent Theodore of Tarsus to our island after the Conference of Whitby, just at the moment when it was essential that order should be organized out of chaos. By a happy chance the death at Rome of the Englishman who had been sent to Pope Vitalian to receive the archbishop's pall made it possible for Vitalian to appoint a successor, and all credit must be given to the Papacy for its selection of Theodore, who, even more than

HEADPIECE.—Aldhelm, Hildelith, and the Nuns of Barking.

Stephen Langton, that later nominee of Rome, brought the blessing of good government to the English people as well as to their Church. The choice of Vitalian had fallen first on Hadrian, an abbot of African origin, 'excellently skilled both in the Greek and Latin tongues',[1] and it was Hadrian who modestly suggested that the Greek Theodore would be a better man for the post, and offered to go in a subordinate position and accompany his friend to Canterbury. Though Theodore was 66 years old when he was thus chosen in 668, he ruled the Church with vigour until he was 87, and Hadrian, who was made abbot of St. Peter's (St. Augustine's) at Canterbury, survived till about 709. The lasting friendship and co-öperation of these two elderly men—the one an Asiatic, the other an African from a monastery near Naples—and the success of their joint work among the newly converted barbarians of the north, is one of the best testimonials to the cosmopolitanism of the medieval Church.

When Theodore, after more than a year's interval, arrived in England in May 669, the situation was critical. Though Oswy had recognized the authority of Rome and of Canterbury in the Conference of 664, for five years there had been no archbishop at Canterbury who could exercise that authority. These five years had moreover been years of plague; and bishops and clergy had been carried off by the disease. Theodore on his arrival found only three bishops in the land: Wini, who had committed simony by buying the see of London; Wilfrid, who had returned from a valid consecration in Gaul, to find that his diocese had during his absence been 'stolen' (that was the word used by his partisans) by Chad,[2] and whose quarrelsome disposition might render him more of a hindrance than a help to his metropolitan; and thirdly Chad, whose position as bishop of the Northumbrians was impaired not only by the charges of Wilfrid's friends but also by the participation of schismatic Britons in his consecration. Such was the situation in 669. Theodore's method of dealing with it, as described by Bede, may be summarized under six heads.

(1) His first business was to see that the bishoprics were filled with men who would co-operate with him. With this object he made a visitation throughout England: he consecrated a new bishop at Rochester, another at Dunwich for East Anglia; at London he allowed Wini to keep his see till his death; at York he removed Chad. Then, seeing the goodness of this humble man, he re-consecrated him according to Catholic rites, and installed him at Lichfield; he ordered him to be sensible and ride a horse in order to get round his diocese, and not to attempt it on foot in the Scottish manner—indeed, it is said that Theodore lifted Chad onto his horse with his own hands. The bishopric of all Northumbria was entrusted to Wilfrid. Thus, in the words of Bede,[3] 'Theodore visited all parts, ordained bishops in proper places, and with their assistance corrected such things as he found faulty'.

(2) His next concern was to enfold in a new unity the existing dioceses which had hitherto kept alive the particularism of the Heptarchic kingdoms. The visitation just mentioned was the beginning of this new policy; it was a visitation of all the island 'wherever the English inhabited'. Everywhere he instructed men in the Roman custom of celebrating Easter, so that, as Bede says, 'this was the first archbishop whom all the English Church obeyed'. Then, in 672,[4] he summoned to Hertford a council of bishops gathered from all the land, a visible symbol of unification; and the nine canons which Theodore persuaded the bishops to adopt were the first laws ever made for all Angles and Saxons. One of the canons provided that a similar synod should be held once a year on August 1st. This was carrying the idea of unity too far to be practicable, and it was not till 679[5] that a second synod was held, this time at Hatfield—a synod which formally declared its adhesion to the Catholic faith.

Thus we see that a united English Church was being consolidated in four different ways. It was acknowledging a common archbishop, it was being visited and reformed by him, leaders were assembling in council under his presidency, and together were formulating legislation to be enforced throughout every Heptarchic kingdom. In all this Theodore was preparing the way for the political union of the kingdoms.

(3) The unity of the Church was a means to an end, and the end was the reform of abuses. Theodore's programme of reform is best seen in the canons promulgated by his Council of Hertford in 672. By these a bishop was forbidden to 'invade' the diocese of another bishop, monks were forbidden to move in the Celtic fashion from monastery to monastery, and clergy were forbidden to wander at will from diocese to diocese. Thus the age of missions, the age of migratory clergy, was coming to an end; but this did not mean that the clergy were thenceforth tied down to small districts like modern parishes. There was an intermediate stage in which a group of clergy served a large district, often corresponding in size to a modern rural deanery. We shall see later that the parish system was to be a growth of centuries. Theodore assisted the growth, but here he was no creator.

(4) One reform discussed at the Council of Hertford was an increase in the number of dioceses. The need for it was obvious. Even after Theodore's division of the Northumbrian diocese, we find Bede still complaining that there were not nearly enough bishops, and that there were still many villages which had never seen a bishop. But vested interests were at stake. The bishops, assembled at Hertford, refused to endorse the proposal of their metropolitan. Theodore was left to act on his own initiative, and in the ensuing period he had to content himself with carrying out his scheme for the division of the dioceses gradually and partially, seizing opportunities as they occurred. On the retirement of a bishop of the East Anglians, Elmham was made a new see for their North Folk. Winfrith, the successor of Chad at Lichfield, was deposed for disobedience about 675; and then or later three new bishoprics were created in the Midlands—for the Middle Angles, for the Hwicce, and for the settlers in the district west of the Severn.* In 678 Theodore, with the consent of the

* Afterwards known as the bishoprics of Leicester, Worcester, and Hereford.

Northumbrian king, but without the consent of Wilfrid the Northumbrian bishop, began to carve out new dioceses, two in Bernicia with sees at Lindisfarne and Hexham, and one in Lindsey, for the time subject to Northumbria. This scheme led

to a long series of conflicts between Wilfrid and those whom he regarded as his persecutors, Theodore and the king of Northumbria. A reckless accusation of corruption was made against the archbishop by Eddius,* Wilfrid's chaplain, who narrated the quarrels at great length. All that need be admitted is that Theodore, though right in wishing to divide the vast bishopric of Northumbria, was irregular and high-handed in his treatment of Wilfrid. On the other hand Wilfrid, however much he might be within his canonical rights, showed in his stubborn resistance

* OE. Æddi.

more the fighting spirit of the thegn than the grace of the Christian. It is no small testimony to Theodore's own vigour that he was able to hold his own against such an opponent. Eddius tells us that the archbishop at the end of his life (686–7) was reconciled with Wilfrid, and puts into his mouth a humiliating and obviously fictitious confession of his past errors.

The result of Theodore's endeavours was that England at his death possessed fifteen dioceses, and though he had failed to apply his policy to Wessex, the omission was remedied by his successors.

(5) Another monument to the enterprise and good sense of Theodore is the Penitential which is known by his name. Though this treatise was written down after Theodore's death, it claims to give his replies to questions put to him about penance. Something will be said in a later chapter of the general attempt of the Church to discipline first its clergy, and later its lay converts, into ways of Christianity, morality, and decency, by requiring confessions from offenders and imposing fastings and other penances as the Church's remedy. Here we need do no more than notice the statesmanship with which Theodore in his Penitential adapts the customs of different branches of the Christian Church to the needs of the English people. The idea of substituting private confession for the public confession in church required in earlier centuries had been developed by the Welsh and Irish. Theodore recognized that the Celtic practice, though novel, was salutary. He revealed his wide experience of the Christian world by comparing the usages of the East and of the West; and he showed his judgement by recommending that which seemed to be the more suitable for his own province. Thus in the chapter on 'The Communion of the Eucharist or the Sacrifice', the Penitential says:[6]

'1. The Greeks, both clergy and laity, communicate every Sunday, as the canons require, and those who do not communicate on three Sundays, are excommunicated.

'2. The Romans similarly communicate, those who wish to do so; and those who do not wish to do so, are not excommunicated.

. . . .

'7. If necessary, confession to God alone is lawful.' [In some manuscripts the clause 'if necessary' is not found.]

Theodore was at times more tolerant than the Papacy. His book allowed an adulterous woman who had been divorced by her husband to re-marry after five years. But the permanent importance of his work is not in its details: it is his acceptance of the usage of private confession which is now recognized as a turning-point in the history of the Western Church.

(6) Last but not least among the services which Theodore and Abbot Hadrian rendered to the Church in England was the establishment of a school at Canterbury, where 'they gathered a crowd of disciples'. There they taught them such art of versification, and such astronomy, arithmetic, and music, as seemed suitable for clerics, giving them not only a sound education in Latin, but also some knowledge of Greek. Both men had come from lands where they had been in direct contact with Byzantine culture, transmitted without a break from the ancient world. Theodore, in particular, had been a student in the schools of Athens and, as a native of Cilicia, had lived in the neighbourhood of Syria, where learning and art had flamed into a wonderful sunset glow before the region was overwhelmed by the Arabs. The indifference of St. Augustine and his followers to learning, an attitude copied from Pope Gregory himself, now gave place to an enthusiasm more disciplined and purposeful than that of the Irish. The influence of the new school overstepped the boundaries of tribe and race. The Irish could not resist the strong attraction of its learning and its library. Aldhelm, a member of the royal House of Wessex, became one of its first students. Benedict Biscop, who had presided over the school in its early days while Hadrian was learning English ways, deliberately transplanted its traditions to Wearmouth and Jarrow in his own Northumbria. It is in the works of Aldhelm, and of

Bede the monk of Jarrow, that the value of the new education can best be illustrated.

It was altogether fortunate that the English converts of the third generation were sufficiently advanced in Christian culture to profit from the learning which Theodore and Hadrian brought them from Mediterranean lands.

When Archbishop Theodore died in 690, the Church of the English, ruled from Canterbury, rose with massive grandeur above the petty kingdoms in which the political energies of the nation were still confined. Under Archbishop Theodore's leadership it had become consolidated, learned, and influential, unmistakably the same Church as that which guided the destinies of the English people in the coming centuries. The miracle wrought by Theodore in uniting, organizing, and educating the Church was not the kind of miracle to win for him the title of Saint. He had not attempted to astonish the world by fastings and mortifications; what he had done was to rule his barbarians in the best spirit of ancient Rome; he had shown clearness of vision; he had formulated definite policies to meet definite needs; he had followed out his policies with skill and caution; he had been energetic and persistent. When the time came to assert the authority of the archiepiscopal church, he had asserted it—perhaps too unflinchingly—even against a prelate like Wilfrid and in the face of papal opposition. The Church canonizes its Saints: it is left for History to crown statesmen; and historians have long acclaimed Theodore as the first recognizable statesmen to appear in the story of England. If any one man was the founder of the English Church, it was Theodore.

The main thread of the story of the Conversion in the third generation is to be found in the work of Theodore, which we have now sketched. But this period, after the Synod of 664, is one of many-sided interest. From one point of view its most interesting feature is the interaction of the Roman and Celtic influences; from another it is the characters of the saints, which are as fresh, though not as varied, as those of men in more modern ages of transition such as the Renaissance. From yet another point of view, the wonderful efflorescence of various arts calls for attention. Yet all these aspects are connected, and it is well not to separate them too rigidly. It is the characters of the saints, and the sculptured crosses and illuminated manuscripts, which best illustrate the blending of the Roman and Celtic influences in the new Church.

Our arrangement of the subject must be determined by the fact that, in spite of the union of their Churches, the kingdoms were still so distinct that their contributions to the development of Christianity cannot well be brought into one picture. We must first study the kingdoms separately, and see the fruits of the Conversion produced in each—the saints, the new learning, the new arts. Then, in a later chapter, we shall collect some broader ideas about the general changes which followed the Conversion.

KENT

Our knowledge of the development of Christianity in the kingdom which had been its first home is disappointing. When we have studied the two great men whom Pope Vitalian sent to England, there is little to add. This may in part be attributed to the fact that Bede was too far removed from Kent to be specially interested in the doings of this Church; but, besides this, it seems that the Christianity of the Kentish-men was not of a specially vigorous kind.

On Theodore's death two years elapsed before a successor was appointed, and three more before that successor returned from his consecration at Lyons, to take up his duties. Whatever the cause may have been—whether it was this interregnum, or the disastrous wars of Kent against Mercia and against Wessex, or the characters of the archbishops themselves—it is clear that the successors of Theodore gradually lost the commanding position which Theodore himself had won. In the eighth century they interfered seldom in the ecclesiastical affairs of the other kingdoms; Northumbria in 735—Mercia also for a time (787–802)—legalized its emancipation by persuading the Papacy to give it an archbishopric of its own.

For the rest, we know that Bede had a high opinion of Albinus, the successor of Abbot Hadrian in the monastery and school at Canterbury; and further evidence that the monks kept alive its literary traditions will appear later in this chapter, when we survey the manuscripts of the age.

The Church in Kent was not lacking in monasteries; it enjoyed some intercourse with the clergy of the other kingdoms as they followed the highroad to Gaul; it secured from the Crown good laws containing clear statements of clerical rights; but we do not read of any notable zeal for religion in Kent. Its only well-known saint, Saint Mildred, though descended through her mother from Hengist, was a native of Mercia and a grand-daughter of Penda.

WESSEX—INE, ALDHELM, BONIFACE

The West Saxons had to wait till about the end of the seventh century to produce a saint of their own. Until then their Church had been much in the hands of foreign-born bishops: St. Birinus (635–51), who had baptized Cynegils, its first Christian king; Agilbert the Frank (651–62), who had given offence because he could not speak English; and later another Frank, a nephew of Agilbert, Hlothere (670–6). The Church had also suffered from the weakness of the West-Saxon State and the dearth of able kings. Wessex, owing to the rise of Mercia, lost control over its territories north of the Thames—those of the Hwicce about 628 and later those of the Cilternsæte (recovered only for a time in the age of Ine). Moreover, in what was left of Wessex south of the Thames there was little unity. Bede tells us that for ten years (674–84) *subreguli*, under-kings, divided the kingdom between them, and this was not a state of affairs without precedent. There is little doubt that the phenomenon of *subreguli*, common enough elsewhere, was specially a characteristic of Wessex, and there are traces of their existence in earlier times when the kingdom was nominally under the control of a single king.[7] For instance, a late version of the Chronicle says that when Edwin of Northumbria reduced Wessex in 626 he slew five kings. But the prestige of Wessex evidently reached its lowest point in the period just before and after the Synod of Whitby, for in 661 we find a Mercian king (Wulfhere, son of Penda) overrunning Ashdown, that is, the Berkshire Downs, and then making a present of the Isle of Wight and the Meonware to a king of Sussex. It was not till 685 that Cædwalla,* a mysterious descendant of Cerdic, unbaptized, though called by a Celtic name, and according to Bede 'a daring young man who had been banished his country', emerged with his war-band from the forests of the Chilterns and of Andred, where they had found shelter. Then in a two years' reign of unchecked success he removed the under-kings, and with much slaughter established the authority of the house of Cerdic over Sussex and the Isle of Wight, and even for a time also over Kent.

In the pages of Bede during the period before 685 we read of humiliations for Wessex; but a different impression can be obtained from the Chronicle and other sources. These give us no clear story, but they make it almost certain that the West Saxons were compensating themselves in the west for whatever they lost in the north and east. During long years of apparent weakness, turning their backs on their Teutonic neighbours, they were hard at work making their way westward among the Britons of Somerset, Dorset, and Devon—the 'West Welsh', as they were called—felling woods, building *tuns*, and reclaiming the heavy lands in the river valleys. A few stages in the process can be observed—enough to contradict the view that Wessex did not make much growth westward between the conquests of Ceawlin and those of Ine. We might speak of the westward advance being conducted on two, perhaps on three, fronts, if such a military metaphor were not unsuited to a process which was as much agricultural as military, being furthered by the felling axe of the woodman

* West Saxon, Ceadwalla.

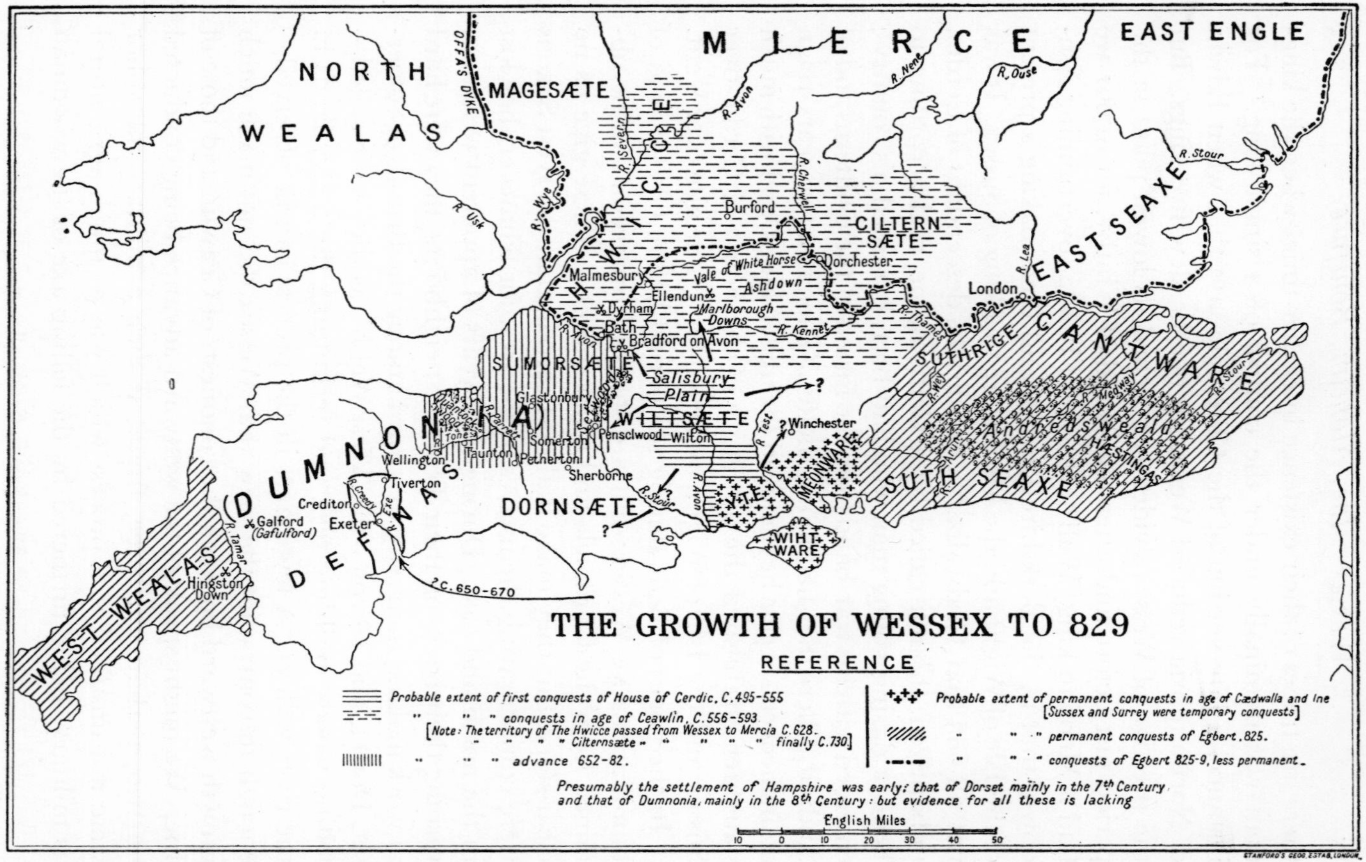
THE GROWTH OF WESSEX TO 829
REFERENCE
Probable extent of first conquests of House of Cerdic, C.495-555
" " " conquests in age of Ceawlin, C.556-593
[Note: The territory of The Hwicce passed from Wessex to Mercia C.628.
" " " Cilternsæte " " " " finally C.730]
" " " advance 652-82.
Probable extent of permanent conquests in age of Cædwalla and Ine
[Sussex and Surrey were temporary conquests]
" " " permanent conquests of Egbert, 825.
" " " conquests of Egbert 825-9, less permanent.
Presumably the settlement of Hampshire was early: that of Dorset mainly in the 7th Century and that of Dumnonia, mainly in the 8th Century: but evidence for all these is lacking
English Miles
10 0 10 20 30 40 50
NORTH WEALAS
MAGESÆTE
OFFA'S DYKE
MIERCE
EAST ENGLE
HWICCE
CILTERN SÆTE
EAST SEAXE
SUTHRIGE
CANTWARE
SUTH SEAXE
Andredsweald
HÆSTINGAS
MEONWARE
YTE
WIHTWARE
WILTSÆTE
SUMORSÆTE
DORNSÆTE
DUMNONIA
DEFNAS
WEST WEALAS
Salisbury Plain
Vale of White Horse
Ashdown
Marlborough Downs
Burford
Dorchester
London
Malmesbury
Ellendun
Dyrham
Bath
Bradford on Avon
Glastonbury
Somerton
Taunton
Petherton
Wellington
Sherborne
Penselwood
Wilton
Winchester
Tiverton
Crediton
Exeter
Galford (Gafulford)
Hingston Down
C.650-670
R. Usk
R. Wye
R. Severn
R. Avon
R. Nene
R. Ouse
R. Cherwell
R. Stour
R. Lea
R. Thames
R. Kennet
R. Wey
R. Medway
R. Arun
R. Test
R. Parrett
R. Tone
R. Creedy
R. Exe
R. Tamar
STANFORD'S GEOG. ESTAB., LONDON.

as well as by the spear of the warrior. The most northerly advance was that through the county which we know as Somerset. It was in full swing some twenty-five years after the conversion of Wessex to Christianity. Indeed, it was the fact that the West Saxons were Christians which no doubt accelerated the readiness of the West Welsh to submit. In 652 there was a battle at Bradford-on-Avon. In 658, after a battle fought apparently near Penselwood, King Cenwalch 'drove the Britons in flight as far as the Parrett', and from that time there is evidence in charters that Glastonbury was subject to the Saxons.[8] This was important, not only because south of the Avon it widened the separation between the Britons of Wales and those of the south-west—a separation begun by Ceawlin's victory at Dyrham eighty years earlier—but also because the traditions of Glastonbury made it a holy place. Its ancient wattled church, said to have been built by Joseph of Arimathea, continued to be venerated when it passed into the power of the Saxon king. The subjection to the conqueror and to the Saxon abbot, his nominee, were made tolerable by a tactful gift of lands, and thus,[9] 'Glastonbury never ceased to be a centre of Celtic pilgrimage, and as a temple of reconciliation must have played no small part in blending the two races'.

The next advance recorded in the Chronicle is in 682, when King Centwine 'drove the Britons in flight to the sea'. We shall probably be right[10] in interpreting this to mean a conquest of the country at least as far as the Quantocks, since we find the king enriching Glastonbury with lands near Quantockwood, within a few miles of the site of Taunton.

Of the southern advance through Dorset we know nothing; but the contrast between the place-names of Dorset and those of Somerset shows that the two movements were distinct.

What is most surprising is a settlement in Devon, which we may perhaps call a third advance. There is good evidence that the valleys of the lower Exe and of the Creedy were at this time occupied by the Saxons, for we are told in a Life of St. Boniface (*c.* 675–754) that this Apostle of Germany (then called Wynfrith) was educated at Exeter; and a later statement that he was born at Crediton receives some confirmation from a charter dated 739,[11] which speaks of the country round Crediton as if it had long been in the hands of the Saxons. We have therefore to account for the existence of a Saxon colony in the heart of Dumnonia (Devon) at a time when its British king was still an important, and apparently an independent, monarch. We can only guess what had happened. The situation is not what any one would have imagined were it not for the documentary evidence. An outpost so exposed to attack from Celtic neighbours would be unthinkable if we were dealing with warfare of a modern type. But it must be repeated that the expansion of Wessex was the result of gradual settlements rather than of scientific campaigns. The Saxons seem to have spread west much as did the Americans and Canadians in the nineteenth century. They occupied the lands they wanted, often those which they first cleared in the river valleys. The Britons on the higher lands were mostly content to let the new-comers alone; they presumably realized that if it came to open war they were likely to get the worst of it, and they may have consoled themselves with the thought that the Saxons were for the most part taking land which the Britons had not been in the habit of cultivating. They could live and let live. Even in Exeter there could be a Saxon and a British quarter without continual riots and bloodshed. In further explanation of the surprisingly early origin of the Saxon colony on the Exe and the Creedy, we may guess that the settlers in this region, the hardiest of all the Germanic pioneers, must for long have relied on the sea for their communications with the mother kingdom—Exeter was only a short sail from the older ports of the West Saxons. We may also give weight to the theory[12] that Dumnonia had been much emptied of its British inhabitants by the migration to Armorica.

Such was the situation of Wessex when its great men, first Aldhelm and then Ine, grew to manhood—Ine, who as king

(688–725) was to make Wessex again for a short time a powerful state; Aldhelm (*c.* 639–709) who was to be one of its most renowned saints.

With regard to Ine and his origin, we only know that he was the son of an under-king (Cenred, probably the ruler of the Dorsæte);[13] that he was fifth in descent from Ceawlin;* and that he was the only member of his branch of the House of Cerdic to be king of all Wessex until Egbert, a descendant of a brother of Ine, established the line which lasted until the eleventh century. If it be asked how it was that the succession passed to Ine from Cædwalla, a distant kinsman, we can only reply with the truism that authority came as a reward for personal prowess and ability. Who can say whether Ine won his position as a leader in the war-band of Cædwalla, or whether as the son of an under-king he gathered his own retainers round him? It is clear that when Ine obtained the monarchy he inherited three very different traditions: first, the memory of Ceawlin and of his short-lived West-Saxon empire, extending in the Midlands well to the north of the Thames; then, the separatist traditions of the under-kings, who neglected West-Saxon imperialism and contented themselves with the rule of small provinces, the later 'shires'; and lastly, those of Cædwalla, the enemy of separatism and the exponent of a new and more politic imperialism which found scope for its ambitions south of the Thames, and sought to plant Saxons in place of Jutes on the Isle of Wight and to conquer the Jutish *Meonware* and the South Saxons. The important point is that with the reign of Ine we have to all intents a new Wessex and a new monarchy within Wessex. It is a new Wessex because, while it has shed many of the districts north of the Thames, it is spreading east and west and beginning to absorb all the south of England. The process foreshadowed by Cædwalla was carried a stage further by Ine when, in 694, he defeated the men of Kent and made them pay compensation for burning a brother of the late king, 'thirty thousands' (presumably thousands of *sceats*).

* See genealogy, vol. ii, p. 721.

With regard to the westward extension of West-Saxon power, historians used to think that the *tun* of Taunton, built about this time, represented a notable encroachment on Dumnonia. But there is much to be said for the view that Ine's work in the west of England was chiefly that of consolidation. It is not until 710 that we read of open war between Ine and Geraint, king of West Devon. Ine's colonial policy has to be inferred from his Laws; these show how the government regulated the process by which new lands were planted with Saxon settlers. Men of the *gesithcund* class (in later times they would have been called thegns) were encouraged by a grant of land to become pioneers in the expansion of Wessex. Thus:[14] 'If a *gesithcund* man moves his residence, he may take with him his reeve, his smith, and his children's nurse.' But 'he who has a holding of 20 hides shall show 12 hides of land under cultivation when he means to leave'. 'He who has a holding of 10 hides shall show 6 hides under cultivation', and similarly out of 3 hides, $1\frac{1}{2}$ must be cultivated.

The only reasonable explanation of such regulations is that they relate to a scheme of settlement, state-directed and state-controlled. With the next law we turn from the gentry, who had grants of large estates, to dependent ceorls with their small holdings. 'If a man takes a yard [or virgate] of land or more, at a fixed rent, and ploughs it, [and] if the lord requires work as well as rent* he [the tenant] need not take the land if the lord does not give him a dwelling†: but [in that case] he must forfeit the crops.'

The policy of planting *gesithcund* men and their dependent ceorls in official colonies could clearly give rise to many disputes. What exactly were the obligations of the well-born settlers to the king above them, and to the ceorls who had followed them? Were they to be free to give up the undertaking at will? Might the king on his part evict them? Ine seems to have suggested reasonable compromises on all such points.

Accordingly, when we look at the map of Somerset or Devon

* OE. *gafol*.

† OE. *botl*.

and see Saxon *tuns* established in a country which so long remained British—*tuns* such as Somerton, Petherton, Taunton, Wellington, and the rest—we must remember that a *tun*, like a *burh*, was a fensible place, protected by a rampart or stockade.

The making of the Saxon outposts went on unnoticed by any chronicle. Apart from the Laws of Ine, the only reference to this all-important piece of history is an annal in the Chronicle under the year 722, which mentions a step back and not forward. It says that Taunton, which had formerly been built by Ine, was destroyed by his queen. The building of the *tun*—though in this case the work of the king and not of a noble—would have been too commonplace an incident to be mentioned if it had not been for its later (and unexplained) demolition.

It is scarcely necessary to point out that in this expansion of the power of Wessex east and west, the Church was as usual the ally and patron of the State. The establishment of West-Saxon authority to the east of Southampton Water and in the Isle of Wight is best illustrated by the mergence of the bishoprics of Sussex and of Wight in that of Winchester—facts reported by Bede; and the policy of westward expansion is equally well illustrated by the creation in 705 of a new diocese in Wessex west of Selwood, over which Aldhelm was to rule as first bishop. The West Saxons as they pushed onward into the lands of the West Welsh were the champions of Roman Christianity. It was no doubt the fact that the 'right' (that is the Roman) Easter and tonsure were identified in the minds of the West Welsh with subjection and dispossession, which made them cling longer than any other section of the Britons to their Celtic ways.

The alliance of Ine with the Church is also written prominently in his Laws. The first says that the clergy should keep their 'rule'; the second, that all children should be baptized within thirty days; the third, that Sunday should be observed as a holiday; and the fourth, that church dues should be paid at Martinmas.

But it is the Laws themselves, the fact that Ine moved the

West-Saxon *witan* to compile them, which really distinguished his reign from those of all other rulers of Wessex before King Alfred. The idea of issuing a Law Book was, of course, borrowed from the Kentish kings. One of the laws indeed is almost identical with a Kentish law of this same period. It lays down that if a stranger travels through a wood off the highway and neither shouts nor blows a horn, he may be assumed to be a thief, and slain as such—the kind of regulation about which it was well that the rulers of the kingdoms bordering on the Andredsweald should agree.

The note of violence does not recur so persistently in Ine's Law Book as in most of the barbarian codes. On the whole the tone of these West-Saxon laws is that of reason and reconciliation. In addition to the support of the Church and the regulations for the planting of lands by colonies headed by *gesithcund* men, we hear much about the rights of the Welsh, that is, of the subject Britons. It is true that their *wergelds* are only fixed at half the value of those of the Saxons—six hundred shillings for the Welsh holder of five hides of land, a hundred and twenty shillings for a free landowner* owning a hide. But the Welshmen's rights are at least definite;[15] even a Welsh slave cannot be scourged without a formal oath. The king clearly relies on the arms of 'Welshmen', both those who own their five hides and those Welsh horsemen who ride in the king's service.

The Laws of Ine, then, suggest that he deliberately depended on the support of the Church and in some measure on that of the subject Britons; but the main prop of his power was the aristocracy, the big land-owners, the *gesithcund* men. Their privileges and duties appear in sixteen out of the seventy-six decrees.

In these ways Ine's reign, coming a hundred years after Ceawlin and a hundred years before Egbert, shows evident signs of the greatness to which the West Saxons were ultimately to attain. For the moment his work seemed to be as ephemeral as that of Ceawlin. Before his death he had to battle against a

* OE. *gafolgelda*.

Mercian attack. His reign ended in revolts, and was soon followed by renewed anarchy. Provincialism was still to prevail.

None the less, the glimpse of Wessex which we have obtained in Ine's Laws is precious. It enables us to understand something of those processes working beneath the surface of history which were to make Wessex in the end a powerful kingdom, and it provides us with the proper background for the figure of St. Aldhelm.

Of Ine the man we have no information except the fact mentioned by Bede[16] that like his predecessor Cædwalla he resigned his crown and went his way to Rome, 'being desirous to spend some part of his pilgrimage upon earth in the neighbourhood of the holy places, that he might obtain to be more readily received into the fellowship of the saints in heaven'.

What is known about Aldhelm's life can also be stated in a few words. He seems to have been born about 639–40, that is within five years of the Conversion of the West Saxons. Like many other saints of the time, he was nobly born, akin to the royal House of Wessex. He studied first under an Irishman, Maeldubh, at Malmesbury, and then, though he was thirty or even older, at Canterbury under Hadrian and Theodore. Further facts recorded about him are: that after his studies at Canterbury had been cut short by ill health he returned to Malmesbury, where he lived, first as a monk, afterwards as abbot; that he made a journey to Rome about 693;[17] that about 705, when Ine divided the West-Saxon diocese, he chose Aldhelm to be the first bishop of Sherborne; that for four years he administered his new diocese with great energy, being a founder of new monasteries; and lastly, that he died in 709 at Doulting in Somerset.

Now it is easy to read these and a few other traditions about Aldhelm's life without at all comprehending the portent which had appeared in Wessex. Our eyes read the words that Aldhelm drew his learning both from an Irishman and Canterbury, and we give a formal assent to the fact that Aldhelm passed on to the West-Saxon Church a mixed tradition, Roman and Celtic; but do we conceive what was really occurring in the minds of Aldhelm and his fellow countrymen? Do we understand how these Saxons as they listened to the Irishman holding forth in his wattled hut were receiving glimpses of unplumbed profundities of knowledge? What mysteries were there half-opened to their astonished minds, what intoxicating draughts at the Hisperic founts of Celtic learning! This is certain, that we cannot begin to understand what was happening unless we make an effort of imagination to see the universe, with its mysteries and profundities, as these men saw it. We must begin by thinking of the scene of Aldhelm's life as a land of forests (those of Selwood and Bredon) so extensive that they were notable barriers. Selwood in particular was spoken of as the feature which divided the old Wessex from the new—that is from the far west where the Saxons were pioneers, scattered settlers among a population still fundamentally British.

The backwoodsmen of Aldhelm's middle west were separated from one another by wide tracts of scrub and forest, and were sundered from the centres of active Christianity—from Canterbury or Wales or Ireland—by gulfs which were hard to pass. In one of these isolated villages, now known to us as Malmesbury, the Irishman had appeared. He had come to these unknown parts in a spirit of adventure. He was seeking the perfect sanctity of an anchorite, but he was also ready to pass on his stores of the learning of the ancients to such pupils as gathered round him.

In order to gain an idea of Aldhelm's studies, let us glance at one or two of the books to which, as is evident from his writings, he had gained access. One of them was a *Lorica* (Coat of Mail), a poem of words intertwined like the rings of a byrny, the recitation of which was potent to protect a man from demons, as a steel coat could protect him from the thrusts of human enemies—to obtain perfect protection it was well to say it three times a day. It is known as the *Lorica* of Gildas, but is also ascribed to Loding, an Irishman who died in 661.[18]

1. Suffragare trinitatis unitas unitatis miserere trinitas	Help, O oneness of Trinity, have pity, O threeness of unity,

2. Suffragare quaeso mihi posito	I beseech thee to help me who am placed
maris magni uelut in periculo	in peril as of a mighty sea,
3. Ut non secum trahat me mortalitas	So that neither the pestilence of this year
huius anni neque mundi uanitas	nor the vanity of the world may suck me under.
. . . . . .	. . . . . .
15. Deus inpenetrabili tutella undique me defende potentia	O God, with thy inscrutable saving power defend all my parts,
. . . . . .	. . . . . .
18. Gigram cephale cum iaris et conas	skull, head with hair and eyes,
. . . . . .	. . . . . .

The rest of the poem enumerates the parts of the body which need protection.

Aldhelm knew also the works of Virgilius Maro Grammaticus,[19] who had probably lived at Toulouse earlier in the seventh century and had imposed his pseudo-learning upon a credulous age. Aldhelm therefore had heard of his twelve different kinds of Latin and of the controversy lasting fourteen days between the grammarians Galbungus and Terrentius about the vocative case of *ego*. He had taken to heart the recommendation of Virgilius that new words should be fabricated to replace those commonly used by the vulgar. He knew, it seems, the *Hisperica Famina*, the strange book which, setting out to glorify the schools of rhetoric, had provided Celtic stylists and their imitators with the rich artificial vocabulary admired by those schools in their decline—a new Latin compounded largely of Greek.

Even at Canterbury Aldhelm was in touch with Celtic thought, for Irishmen were among his fellow pupils in that school. Aldhelm caught from them or from Hadrian a thirst for learning which can hardly be appreciated by the modern world where education, universal and compulsory, is thrust upon men. This appears in the legend which tells how he went down to Dover and did hard bargaining with foreign merchants in his desire to purchase a Bible set out for sale among a number of other books on the shore. It appears too in a letter of his, in which he refuses an invitation of his bishop to attend some Christmas festivities on the ground that his work required all his attention—that work being the mysteries of Roman Law (a notable study, in a generation which produced Kentish and Saxon law-books), the hundred different kinds of metre, and the computations of arithmetic and astrology. To such studies as these, even Christmas festivities must give place. The Saxon must learn all the secrets in the wonderful books which were now being brought within his reach. He set about the work of mastering them in the spirit of the heroic age. It was a new adventure. With a determination not to be beaten he would storm the stronghold of knowledge, and when it was won, what then? What was it that Aldhelm acquired? Chiefly an immense store of curious words: words drawn from Gildas, from Virgilius the Grammarian, jaw-cracking words, manufactured from Greek, taken from the Hisperic vocabulary: words which would have astonished English, Romans, and Greeks, let alone Aldhelm's Saxon ancestors. And what was the learned man to do with these words? He might arrange them in intricate alliterative patterns. A letter[20] to Eahfrid begins: 'Primitus pantorum procerum praetorumque pio potissimum paternoque praesertim privilegio panagyricum poemataque passim prosatori sub polo promulgantes stridula vocum simphonia, et melodiae cantilenaeque carmine modulaturi, ymnizemus . . .' Aldhelm here was writing to a Saxon who had just returned from a six years' course of study in Ireland; he was showing off. He was having his heavy joke. He was outdoing Virgilius the Grammarian with his Galbungus. His P, P, P, P alliteration was a kind of password for savants.

Words were good playthings in other ways. They could be fitted together in double acrostics and in metrical lines. Aldhelm liked to expound the mysteries of the pithian metre or hexameter, the caesura pentimemeris, or the caesura trititrochaici.

He could fill parchment equivalent to thirty pages of modern octavo print with discussions about such things, giving illustrations from Virgil, Ovid, Lucan, Juvencus, Sedulius, Venantius Fortunatus, and other Latin poets early and late. It was an achievement, for no Saxon before him had made Latin verses.

In the end all these wonderful words acquired by Aldhelm were something more than playthings. The bent of the Saxon directed him to practical ends. His skill in rhetoric was calculated to impress men. He used it as an advertisement for the new schools of learning springing up in England.[21] 'The fields of Ireland are rich in learners . . . and yet Britain, placed if you like to say so at almost the extreme margin of the western clime of the orb, possesses as it were the flame-bearing sun and the lucid moon; that is to say, Theodore the archbishop . . . and Adrian his companion in the brotherhood of learning.' What need to go to Ireland when there were such teachers of Greek and Latin 'here on the fertile soil of Britain'? Aldhelm used his words also to reprove the Northumbrian clergy for their treatment of Wilfrid, and to better purpose he used them to reason with Geraint,* king of Dumnonia, and so 'persuaded many of those Britons who were subject to the West Saxons to adopt the Catholic Easter'.[22]

Above all, he devoted his rhetoric to the Praise of Virginity. His most famous work, *De Laudibus Virginitatis*—issued both in a prose and a verse edition—had a practical aim. It was composed for the edification of Hildelith, abbess of Barking, and her nuns (p. 303); for Justina, Cutberga (sister of King Ine), Osburga, Aldgida, Scholastica, and the rest. In the event, it long remained a popular book; and monks and nuns who had taken vows of chastity were for centuries strengthened in their profession by Aldhelm's recitation of the long roll of celibates, male and female, prophets, apostles, bishops, and all the noble army of the religious who had renounced the brass of married life and had been refined to the pure gold of Virginity.

* Geruntius.

Aldhelm can claim our interest not only as the most renowned of the saints of Wessex, but also as a typical West Saxon. For instance, he was an aristocrat who knew how to gain the sympathy and the love of the people. Tradition said that Aldhelm, presumably in his earlier years at Malmesbury, was in the habit of taking up his stand on a bridge by which the country people left or entered the town. There, like a professional minstrel, he used to sing to the people their own Saxon songs till he had collected hearers, and then from his songs he led them on to the serious matters of the Christian faith. This story, and the fact that Aldhelm's chief work in life was the establishment of Christianity in the middle west of Wessex, help to place his half-jocular 'conceits' in their proper proportion. He might be admired by the few for his literary style, but he was revered by the people for his saintly life. He was a man of action as well as a writer. While he made Malmesbury for a time the centre of the new learning, his influence overflowed into the neighbouring forest country. He founded new monasteries at Frome and at Bradford-on-Avon, and during the last four years of his life, as bishop of the new diocese west of Selwood, Aldhelm ruled, Bede says, 'most energetically'.

Another way in which Aldhelm may be said to typify the West Saxons is in his successful blending of Celtic, Roman, and Saxon traditions. His strength lay in his capacity to appeal with effect to the Britons, both those of the newly conquered districts, such as Glastonbury, and those in the neighbouring principalities, such as Dumnonia. He could argue like a Celt in the cause of Latin Christianity. What gave him his influence was his understanding of both points of view. Britons could not ignore a Saxon who spoke with such art. Never before or since has a literary stylist been so enthroned. He could write with authority to a king of Devon or a king of Northumbria; the rhetorician could do as much as the fighting-man to raise the prestige of Wessex.

Aldhelm's prodigies of style did not establish either at Malmesbury or at Sherborne a well-rooted school of learning. There was, however, some fruitfulness in the following generation, when Wessex contributed leaders for the conversion of the Germans of the Continent. Accordingly, to appreciate his influence, we must turn our eyes to Germany and study the career of Wynfrith, the West Saxon who, under the name of Boniface and with the help of a large band of his fellow countrymen, became the Apostle of Germany.[23] No Englishman has ever played so great a part in central Europe. He is the first Devonian of Saxon descent to appear in history, and he displays a spirit of adventure and determination which is not excelled by Gilbert or Drake or Raleigh. His labours form an important part of the history of Germany, France, and the Netherlands in the eighth century; but the greater part of his long life (he lived from about 675 to 754) was spent in our island, and he is a true representative of the school of Aldhelm.

From his biography, written by his follower Willibald, we learn that his father was a man of substance living near Exeter. Boniface—it is less confusing to call him from the first by the name under which he was to acquire his sanctity—was sent, when only six years old, to be in the charge of a friendly abbot at Exeter. He seems to have been some twenty-five years old before he realized that he needed a better education than was to be had in Devon. Then, migrating to the monastery of Nursling, near Winchester, he had the benefit of the full current of learning flowing from Aldhelm. Day and night he studied the liberal arts. He read in his course the acts of the martyrs, and it is significant that some ten years before he set forth on his missionary work, a friend dedicated to him a poem on 'The Pilgrimage beyond the Seas'. In time he became a teacher of repute. Everything pointed to his having a prosperous career before him in the English Church. He had friends at Ine's court; he was chosen to be the emissary of a synodal council and to take a message to the archbishop of Canterbury. Promotion was clearly within his grasp.

At this point, 716 (seven years after the death of Aldhelm), when he was some forty years old, he determined to give up his prospects in England in order to assist a heroic Northumbrian missionary, Willibrord, who had long been struggling against heavy odds to convert heathen Frisia. Boniface, having there acquired some insight into the conditions of missionary work on the Continent, returned for a short while to England; but the year 718 saw him set out on the road to Rome with schemes in his head for better organized work among the Germanic tribes. At Rome his zeal won the confidence of Pope Gregory II, and Boniface, having sworn fidelity to the successor of St. Peter, returned to Germany and Frisia, not as a free-lance like the Irish and English missionaries who had preceded him, but as one under the orders of a papal commander-in-chief. In the great work which he then began Boniface moved from one centre to another—Thuringia, Frisia, Hesse, Bavaria—and used to advantage all the many-sided traditions which he had inherited from the Church in England. Like Augustine, he obtained advice on details as well as general directions from the Papacy. Like Aidan and the Scots, he perambulated heathen villages, baptizing thousands of converts. Like Theodore, he established new sees and formed a disciplined army out of scattered clergy—the Franks and Irishmen who had long been dissipating their energies among the Germans east of the Rhine. The Papacy not only gave him metropolitan powers, but it also delegated to him the work of reforming the Frankish Church in Gaul.

What is the explanation of such extraordinary successes, obtained on the continent of Europe by this Saxon, who had been born in an out-of-the-way corner of Wessex? The explanation may be gathered from what has been already suggested. It was the spirit of enterprise, like that of an Elizabethan exploring new worlds, captivating the minds of his fellow countrymen and winning followers by the greatness of his projects; the persistence of a Saxon who made up for want of genius by the determination and practical sense of a man of affairs—qualities which taught him how to use the great forces of the Papacy and of the Frankish Mayors of the Palace, as well as how to obey them: these and other characteristics—adaptability, tact, and above all, an overflowing sympathy and friendliness, brought Boniface and his English mission to victory. Though raised to be the Metropolitan of Germany, he remained an Englishman, and continued to take an interest in English affairs. However, there was one change: at first he had sought advice from his English correspondents; later he was more inclined to give it.

The correspondence of Boniface and his circle of helpers and friends gives us an understanding of the minds and hearts of English men and women who had dedicated themselves to the service of Christ; an understanding more intimate than that to be found in the *Lives* of the saints or even in Bede's *History*. The letters show also how the mission of Boniface was supplied in many of its small wants by the gifts of friends, as well as supported by their prayers. A king sent a gold bowl; an abbot, knives or finely worked palls; nuns sent offerings of money, books of the Bible written in letters of gold, altar coverings, or clothing made with their own hands. It is the affectionate intercourse between the 'brothers' and 'sisters' in Christ which is the most beautiful flower of this correspondence, a happy sequel to the *De Virginitate* which Aldhelm had written for the nuns of Barking. It reveals a spiritual love which, in all simplicity and without harm, could accompany the spiritual warfare of these English Christians. The missionaries address letters to their 'beloved sisters';* Lul, the right-hand man of Boniface, in writing to an abbess and a nun in England, says:[24] 'I confess to your love; when . . . I departed from the famous kingdoms of Britain, leaving the fruitful soil of my native island whose craggy coasts the dark green waves of the foamy sea hem in on every side, . . . I longed to present myself at the shrine of the Blessed Apostles.' Almost all his kindred were dead, he says, and he was 'left alone and

* e.g. 'Venerandis et amandis carissimis sororibus' (ep. 67); 'Delectissimae ancille Christi' (ep. 66).

widowed in sad exile'; but the abbess had cared for him when he was sick and had shown him as a brother the unwearying affection which springs from the divine love. Boniface[25] tells his relative Lioba and other nuns of her company about his disappointments in his work. The women in reply pour out their troubles. Lioba, in her first letter to Boniface,[26] reminds him that except for her infirm mother she was now left alone in the world, 'and would that I could deserve to have thee in place of a brother, for in no one among men do I place such great trust as in thee. . . . I ask thee too, deign to correct the homely style of this letter, and to send me for a model some words of thine, which I crave eagerly to hear.' The letter was the beginning of a lifelong friendship. Lioba was one of the many English nuns who left England to take an active part in the evangelization of Germany; and when she died, abbess of a German nunnery, her body was laid at her request in the same tomb as that of Boniface.

We have dwelt on the spiritual love which helped to solace the men and women who, in dedicating themselves to the cloister, had surrendered the relationships of ordinary life; but this must not be allowed to lessen our sense of the gallantry displayed in their spiritual warfare. 'It would be difficult to exaggerate the praises of these valiant and devoted women, who faced the dangers of a distant journey, only to bury themselves in wild and savage regions, exposed to hardships from which even strong men had shrunk.'[27] It was Boniface himself who from first to last set the example of boldness. The courage which he required to hew down before the eyes of the heathen the sacred oak of Thunor at Geislar was not greater than that needed to speak the truth to the great personages of Christendom. Even the Pope had to be told that he ought to suppress the pagan customs still tolerated at Rome. Then, in 754, in extreme old age, Boniface won in Frisia what he had long courted—a martyr's death.

For enterprise of the more ordinary kind there is nothing in this age to surpass the pilgrimage of a kinsman of Boniface who later was welcomed by him in Germany and installed as a bishop. This man, a certain Willibald (who must be distinguished from the biographer of Boniface), not content with having travelled from Hampshire to Rome, then set out in 722 to visit the Holy Land.[28] In Sicily he saw Mount Etna. At Ephesus he visited the cave of the Seven Sleepers. Near Damascus he was shown the spot where St. Paul had been blinded; at Cana, one of the vessels in which water had been turned into wine; at Bethlehem, the house in which Christ had been born. The biography of this Hampshire man narrates with much detail the events of his long pilgrimage. It even tells how he smuggled balsam out of the Holy Land in a calabash, disguising its smell by smearing it with paraffin.

Of such stuff were the West Saxons of the eighth century. With enterprise like that of their forefathers, the men who had marched behind Ceawlin, they play the parts which now fall to them as Christians. They are pioneers. They are adventurers. They are fighting as *milites Christi* both in their own Wessex and on the Continent. They are not fighting simply against the sins of the flesh, as ascetics or anchorites. This West-Saxon warfare is well planned and well directed.

But at home, when the generation of Aldhelm's pupils had passed, the West Saxons found it increasingly difficult to understand the Latin writings of this saint who had been so formidable a stylist. When they copied them, they began to gloss them with simpler Latin and then with their own English words. Aldhelm had set his West Saxons too difficult a standard. It was unattainable; and therefore discouraged further growth.

MERCIA—GUTHLAC

The history of Mercia and of the Mercian Church in this period is little better than a blank. For the purposes of this chapter it will be enough if the reader remembers that the great Midland kingdom built up by Penda in the second quarter of the seventh century continued for the most part to hold together and to increase its power under those of his House who ruled after him; that is successively, two of his sons, then two of his grandsons, and finally a great-nephew. The bearing of the wars of these kings on the struggle for supremacy will be mentioned in a later chapter.

A succession of eminent German scholars[29] have countenanced a theory that the last of these kings, Ethelbald (716–57), is to be identified with a pupil of Aldhelm's who appears under the name of Ethelwald. If this theory could be accepted, we might at this point quote a letter of Ethelwald and some effusions of his in verse as the first extant literary productions of an English king, and as evidence that the new learning was affecting the royal House of Mercia. But the fact that this young man Ethelwald had to be reproved by Aldhelm for his love of wine and women (and at the same time commended for his songs), and the other fact that King Ethelbald forty years later was reprimanded at great length by Boniface and the bishops of Germany in conclave because he conducted himself scandalously instead of settling down in marriage, these are insufficient proofs of identity; for neither was the name Ethelwald uncommon among æthelings, nor unfortunately a life of immorality. It should be acknowledged, however, that the verses of Ethelwald show a royal licence in their disregard of rhythm and grammar.

Mercia in this age cannot produce its learned man but it can claim at least one notable saint; and him we shall treat as the representative of the Midlands.[30]

Guthlac (673–714), we are told, came of one of the oldest and noblest families of Mercia, which men called *Guthlacingas*. On reaching manhood, after being brought up in his father's hall, he thought of the mighty deeds of the heroes of old. Accordingly he collected a troop of followers and carried on petty wars of his own, devastating towns and villages and forts with fire and sword, and making a great slaughter through the land.[31] After nine years of this, his conversion came suddenly. Returning one night from a raid, he turned things over in his mind. His heart was suddenly filled with spiritual love. He thought of the old kings who forsook this world and its wealth; he thought of how every day brought him nearer to death; then signing himself with the Cross he vowed to become the servant of Christ, and told his war-band they must choose another leader. The first two years after his conversion were spent in the double monastery of Repton, which was ruled by a woman, the Abbess Elfrida. There his refusal to drink anything but water made him unpopular with the other monks. Afterwards, he longed for solitude, and went forth to the fens. The description of the 'immense marshes' formed by the rivers which drain into the Wash helps us to realize the great tracts of dark pools and reed-beds and winding channels which at that time penetrated far into the heart of the Midlands. Crowland, the small island on which he settled, could be approached only by a fishing skiff, and it was so lonely and haunted that no man had yet been able to dwell on it. The rest of the story of Guthlac, telling of his life as a hermit on this island, shows how his fastings and other austerities affected his brain. Devils appeared to him in the form of lions and wolves and bears. They came to him grunting like hogs, howling like wolves, croaking like ravens. One night, at a time when 'the Britons, the troublesome enemy of the Saxon race, were invading and harrying the English', he heard the devils speaking like Britons. The isolation which brought him his devils, brought him also, in true Celtic fashion, friendship with the animals round him. Swallows perched on him. Ravens restored the lost glove of a visitor. Men of all sorts visited him and testified in different ways to their sense of his sanctity. The bishop of Lichfield, it is asserted, begged Guthlac to reconsecrate him to the priesthood. The daughter of the king of East Anglia sent him a present of a leaden coffin and a winding-sheet. Ethelbald of Mercia, as a refugee before his accession, came to the saint to tell him of his troubles, and was comforted by the prophecy that God would destroy his enemies and raise him to the throne.

Many years later, after Guthlac had been long buried in his leaden coffin, Ethelbald (now become the most powerful king of the English), founded on the anchorite's small island the monastery of Crowland.

The story is typical. In similar ways other monasteries, both in Mercia and elsewhere, were springing up, monasteries which were to play a great part in the future of England.

Guthlac's story also reveals how much disorder and local strife, even within one of the greater kingdoms, remains hidden from us beneath the surface history of the Conversion. The devastations of the war-band which followed Guthlac in his youth read as if they were mere private warfare. The Britons who appear in the Fens and harry the English may perhaps be descendants of those who had fled to the forests at the time of the Conquest. Such incidents help to explain why Mercia, the last of the three great kingdoms to accept Christianity, was slow in making up for its bad start. The backwardness of the Mercian Church may be a reality and not merely an illusion produced by Bede's neglect. Guthlac seems to be an inferior imitation of Cuthbert, and his biography is admittedly modelled on that of the Northumbrian saint.

Mercia will make its contributions at a later stage. In the time of Offa and in the time of Alfred, Mercian Christianity will keep the traditions of good work alive when they are becoming moribund elsewhere. But that time is not yet. In the Golden Age the encounters of Guthlac with devils are a poor substitute for the literary feats of Aldhelm and the fine learning and art of the Northumbrians.

NORTHUMBRIA—CUTHBERT, WILFRID, BEDE

When we turn from Wessex and Mercia to Northumbria, we find its Church and the arts of Christianity in a much more highly developed state. Celtic and Roman influences are combining to produce a more abundant vitality. There are more saints, a richer variety of character, and there is a fresh and creative spirit in the works which men are carving in stone and writing on parchment.

The political background to the story is chequered. Seven years after the Synod of Whitby, King Oswy was succeeded by Ecgfrith (671–85), a strenuous king whose efforts to overwhelm the Picts in their fastnesses ended in the disastrous battle of Nectansmere, 685. During the next twenty years Northumbria was ruled by an illegitimate son of Oswy, Aldfrith (685–705), who had studied in Ireland and had become the best educated of all the early English kings, a writer of verse in Gaelic and a learned correspondent of Aldhelm in Latin. During this time Northumbria enjoyed unusual peace. But then, on the death of Aldfrith, it drifted into feuds over the succession to the crown which were to be continued for a century and a half to the undoing of the kingdom. For our purpose we shall do well to disregard this political history, and to concentrate our attention chiefly on the careers of three notable representatives of Northumbrian Christianity, Cuthbert, Wilfrid, and Bede, who represent three different monastic communities. The story of Cuthbert will take us to Melrose and Lindisfarne, where the Celtic tradition remained strong. That of Bede will introduce us to Jarrow and Wearmouth; that of Wilfrid to Ripon and Hexham—four monastic centres of exotic southern civilization. The lives of Cuthbert (*c.* 625–87) and of Wilfrid (634–709) span the period from the early days when Christianity in the north was revived through the teaching of Aidan, to those times when the Northumbrian Church bore its richest fruit after the State had been pruned by the defeat of Nectansmere. The life of Bede (673–735), a man of a younger generation, will bring us down to the period when political anarchy was beginning to exercise an injurious effect on religion.

We begin then with Cuthbert, and we see him first as a shepherd-boy among the rounded hills where the waters of the Tweed and its tributaries take their rise—a country of great lonely tracts of grassland and heather. Though of peasant origin (unlike most of the other saints) he none the less served as a young man in the ranks of some war-band, until he turned in disgust from the old heathen ideal of war service to the new ideal of Christian sacrifice which was being preached by the followers of Saint Aidan. Then we have a picture of Cuthbert riding up to the enclosure which surrounded the monastic huts of old Melrose. He goes as a free warrior, horsed and armed with a spear. He has chosen Melrose because he has heard of the sanctity of Boisil (St. Boswell), its prior. As he rides up, Boisil, looking at him, says to those who stand by: *Ecce servus Dei.* His character is clearly written on his face—men will say of him as of St. Columba, that he has the face of an angel. Thus was Cuthbert enrolled as a *miles Christi.*

The next stage in his life covers the thirteen years (651–64) in which, as monk and then as prior, he had his permanent home at Melrose. In this stage Cuthbert was Celtic in most, if not in all his ways: so Celtic, indeed, that after following his abbot about 661 to a new foundation at Ripon he withdrew before the abbey was handed over to Wilfrid the Romanizer. Until he became an anchorite on Farne Island, Cuthbert conformed to Irish tradition in his migratory habits. He made Melrose a centre for journeys to the most remote and poorest hill villages. The country-folk, in spite of their nominal Christianity, had remained heathen at heart. Cuthbert, we are told, used to wander among them for three or four weeks at a stretch;[32] 'and such was Cuthbert's skill in speaking . . . such a light shone in his angelic face, that no man dared to conceal from him the secrets of his heart'.

Like other representatives of Celtic Christianity, Cuthbert often exhibited a friendship with animals. Once, when passing through a moorland so desolate that there were no human dwellings where food could be had, the boy who was his companion found a fish which had been landed by an 'eagle' from the neighbouring stream, and brought it to Cuthbert. 'But why', said Cuthbert,[33] 'did you not give our hungry fisherman his share to eat?', and he insisted on the boy throwing half the fish to the bird. Cuthbert was thoroughly Celtic, too, in his asceticism. When he paid a visit to the abbey of Coldingham near St. Abb's Head, he spent two or three nights at a time in vigils on the shore. What was he doing? A curious monk followed him one night: and the story which he later told the brethren was that he had seen Cuthbert enter the sea up to his neck; he had seen him pray on bent knees on the shore; then, as the dawn began to break, he had seen two marine animals come and caress his feet and then disappear among the waves.

In 664, a few months after the Synod of Whitby, Cuthbert was transferred to Lindisfarne as prior. It was a difficult situation in many ways. The early Northumbrian monasteries could not cease to be the children of Iona.[34] The calculation of Easter was only one of many peculiarities; and while Colman, in withdrawing from Lindisfarne after 664, had taken with him those monks who were definitely opposed to the Roman Easter, many of the brethren who remained still sympathized with that and other Celtic ways. They objected to the reformed rule which Cuthbert wished to enforce. With infinite patience he reasoned with them. At conclaves, with perfect good temper he used the same arguments day after day until he gradually wore down opposition.

For twelve years (664–76) Cuthbert ruled the monks of Lindisfarne as their prior. He reconciled them to the Roman Easter. He enforced his new rule of monastic discipline. He persuaded them to wear simple clothes made of undyed wool. He himself, in the Celtic manner, still wandered round the shores of the island at night, or marooned himself on a neighbouring rock. Then, in 676, he escaped altogether from contact with his fellow men, and attained the perfect life of a recluse. He shut himself off from the world on the Inner Farne, seven miles from Lindisfarne, a small island reputed, like that of Guthlac in the Fens, to be the haunt of evil spirits. With his own hands he excavated a circular enclosure. He built up the walls with stones and turf to more than the height of a man. One half of his dwelling was an oratory, the other half was a living-room, and shut within these walls—where he could only see the heavens and only hear the sea breaking on his rocks—he fought his fight with the evil spirits, chanting his psalms and hymns, and brooding day and night on Divinity.

The victory of Cuthbert over his flesh was a triumph for all Northumbria. His fame was established in his lifetime. When a sister of King Ecgfrith lost the use of her legs and had to crawl on all fours, Cuthbert sent her a linen girdle which cured her in three days. The devout expressed their admiration of his sanctity according to the fashion of the age. An abbess sent him a linen winding-sheet; an abbot sent him a stone tomb; these he hid beneath sods of earth. His renown is best seen in the incidents which for a time put an end to his withdrawal from the world. In 684 Theodore, having deposed a bishop of Hexham, had a conference with Ecgfrith, in which Cuthbert was chosen to fill the vacancy. The following scenes were then enacted. Messengers arrive at the island telling Cuthbert that the archbishop and king have agreed to make him bishop. In vain. He will not leave his cell. King Ecgfrith himself comes to the island, accompanied by a bishop, a crowd of notables, and the brethren from Lindisfarne. They kneel, they weep, they entreat him to leave his oratory. Cuthbert also weeps. At last he yields; and the holy man, some months later, is conducted to the great church at York, and is there consecrated with pomp by Archbishop Theodore. This ceremony, performed on Easter Day, 685, is memorable. It is the climax which precedes the decline of Northumbrian greatness: it is a visible meeting-point of the old and the new, of Scottish and of Mediterranean religion. The cathedral church in which the anchorite is consecrated had been begun by Paulinus. It had been completed by Wilfrid, who had whitewashed its walls, refurnished its altars, covered the ridges of its roof with lead, and glazed the windows to keep out the birds. (That was Wilfrid's way. Cuthbert on his island had made it his custom to talk to the birds; on one occasion to condemn them: *in nomine Jesu Christi.*) The two men before the altar are a notable conjunction of the East and the West. Theodore, the native of Tarsus, once student at Athens, now emissary of Rome, statesman, successful administrator, maker of laws, placing his hand on the head of Cuthbert, once shepherd of Tweeddale, haggard and unkempt as on his lonely rock, an ascetic who has starved himself on a diet of barley and onions, and who, for all his Catholic orthodoxy on the Easter question, still has the soul of a Celtic anchorite. And around these two and the five other assistant bishops stand King Ecgfrith, his high reeves and his band of thegns. The minds of these are filled with thoughts of military glory and of conquests to be won in the north.

From the consecration in the church at York we must go on to another scene, two months later. While Ecgfrith and his army are campaigning against the Picts beyond the Forth, Cuthbert is visiting the queen at Carlisle.* He is being shown the Roman fountain of that city. Suddenly he stands still; his head is bent to earth. He raises it again with his eyes turned towards heaven, and he cries out: 'Oh, Oh, Oh! I think the battle is finished.' A few days later the news arrived that at that very hour the battle had been fought in which Ecgfrith and the flower of his army had been slain. Cuthbert's consciousness of the distant battle, though sceptics may say it is suspiciously like a similar story told of St. Columba, is a well-attested case of second-sight.

There is no need to dwell on the short episcopate of the Saint. His visitation of his diocese aroused unmeasured enthusiasm; but he was too much of a recluse to be a good bishop, and, at the end of two years, he returned to his cell on the Farnes.

A few months afterwards he was a dying man, and from the long story of his end told to Bede by an eyewitness, one last incident may remain in our memories. Cuthbert, in spite of his illness, had forbidden any one to stay with him on the island.

* Caer-luel.

Herefrith, the new abbot of Lindisfarne, after a five days' storm, sailed across to the island and found him in the hut near the landing-place. For five whole days Cuthbert had been unable to move, owing to an ulcerated foot. The only food he had had with him had been five onions; and pulling out these from under his coverlet, he showed the abbot that only half of one had been eaten. A few days later the dying man gave his last admonition: 'Ever keep peace and divine charity amongst you. . . . Have no communion with those who do not celebrate Easter at its right time. . . . Though I have been contemptible to some men during my life, you will see more clearly what manner of man I have been after my death. . . .'

It is evident that Cuthbert knew that his bones would be venerated, but not even he could foresee how his cult, enhanced by the fame of his miracle-working relics (relics carried in a coffin up and down the wilder parts of the north by monks in flight from the Danes), would remain the great binding force in what was left of Northumbria. When the kingdom had been torn to pieces by its feuds and by its Pictish, Scandinavian, and Scottish enemies; when Northumbria, even as an earldom, ceased to be a political entity, the bones of the Saint worked one of the great miracles of history and saved a remnant of independence for the north in the patrimony of St. Cuthbert, the County Palatine of Durham.

In view of the prodigious growth of the cult of St. Cuthbert, it is natural to question whether his fame was deserved. Undoubtedly there was an adventitious element in it; he outshone other saints who 'fought their fight' in the Celtic manner because of his ultimate orthodoxy on the Paschal question. Undoubtedly some of the admiration which he aroused was called forth by feats of mere physical endurance—his escape from the plague, his fastings, his immersions; and it was called forth also by the bodily strength which, for example, enabled him, in making his cell, to lift rocks on to his wall which would have needed four men of ordinary strength—deeds not unworthy

1. *O.* CARAUSIUS
R. CONCORDIA MILITUM

2. *O.* MAGNUS MAXIMUS
R. VICTORIA AUGG.

3. *O.* BISHOP LIUDARD
R. Double cross on globe

4. *O.* Copy of HONORIUS
R. SCANOMODV (runic)

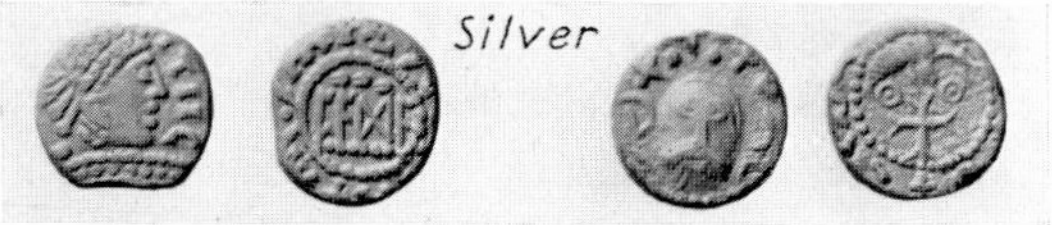

5. *R.* PADA (runic)
? = PEADA, 655–7

6. *O.* 'Woden' head

7. Four reverses of sceatta to show how the Roman standard types were debased; a head becomes a bird

8. *O.* ECGFRITH (671–85)
R. LUXX in angles of a cross radiant

9. *O.* ALDFRITH (685–705)
R. Anglian beast

10. *O.* Archbishop Egbert (732–66)
R. EADBERHT

1 and 2. Some coins of usurpers in the later Roman period.
3 and 4. Unique coins of the early Conversion period.
5, 6, 7. Sceatta, probably of the later Conversion period.
8, 9, 10. Northumbrian sceatta of the age of Cuthbert and Bede.

of a Beowulf. Undoubtedly also[35] 'Cuthbert's mind was unhinged by the austerities which he practised'. But when all is said, the fact remains that his primacy among the Christians of northern England was won by his spiritual gifts—by well-attested powers of second-sight, by complete disregard of self, by a patience which was inexhaustible, by love which overflowed, like that of St. Columba and St. Francis, to his fellow men and to his fellow animals.

Our second representative of Northumbrian Christianity is Wilfrid. When we last heard of him he had been expelled from his see by Archbishop Theodore in 678, presumably owing to his refusal to accept the plans of the archbishop and of King Ecgfrith for the division of his diocese. The years between his victory at Whitby in 664 and his expulsion had been the triumphant period of his life. They had seen him make his second journey to Gaul, attended by a retinue of a hundred and twenty armed followers, be consecrated by twelve Gallic bishops, and raised on their episcopal shoulders according to Gallic custom in a golden chair. They had seen him when driven by a gale on to the Sussex shore repulse the forces of the heathen South Saxons with his armed men, and secure the escape of his whole party through prayers which appeared to control the tides. They had seen him once show unusual moderation, and humbly return to Ripon when he found that during his long absence Chad, the pupil of St. Aidan, had somehow been insinuated into the see of York; and they had seen him finally, after the withdrawal of Chad, rule the diocese of all Northumbria—an ecclesiastic of the Wolsey type, living in almost royal state, and building churches in stone in the Roman manner at York, at Ripon, and at Hexham (Pl. 44).

In 678, when the blow fell, Wilfrid was driven from Northumbria, and most of the remaining thirty years of his life he spent in exile, contending for his rights. The authorities are unsatisfactory in their accounts of the quarrel. Bede is reserved:

Eddius, the biographer of Wilfrid, is an unscrupulous partisan. He blames the queen of King Ecgfrith, and says that she egged on her husband by harping on the 'secular glories of St. Wilfrid, his wealth, the number of his monasteries, the greatness of his buildings, his countless army of retainers decked out with royal vestments and arms'.[36] But Eddius discredits his own testimony when he alleges that Theodore's action was due to bribes.

Into the miserable wrangles which from this period until the death of Wilfrid filled up so great a part of Northumbrian history we need not enter. They were a blot upon the Northumbrian Church at the period of its highest vitality, but their permanent significance, either in political or ecclesiastical history, is slight. We need only mark the turning-points in the wearisome story.

Wilfrid, on his way to Rome to appeal against the action of Theodore, spent the winter of 678–9 in Frisia. He improved the occasion by preaching daily to the heathen Frisians, and according to his biographer he baptized almost all the chiefs as well as many thousands of the Frisian people. The winter of 679–80 was spent at Rome. He returned to Northumbria with a papal decree ordering the restoration of his bishopric, with a reliquary full of relics, and with baggage stuffed with ornaments for his churches.

It was something new in the experience of the Anglo-Saxons that the policy of a king and his councillors should be overridden by papal decree. King Ecgfrith had a short way with such opposition. The decree was rejected on the ground that it had been bought for a price, and Wilfrid himself was shut up in solitary confinement. So, for nine months in 681, while Cuthbert was chanting his psalms in his self-chosen island prison, Wilfrid, the champion of Roman customs, the bishop who had appealed to Rome 'as to a fortress and tower of strength', did his chanting in the custody of a king's reeve.

At the end of the nine months the queen 'became possessed with the devil' (she seems to have had a stroke), and since there was a suspicion that her seizure was a punishment for the treat-

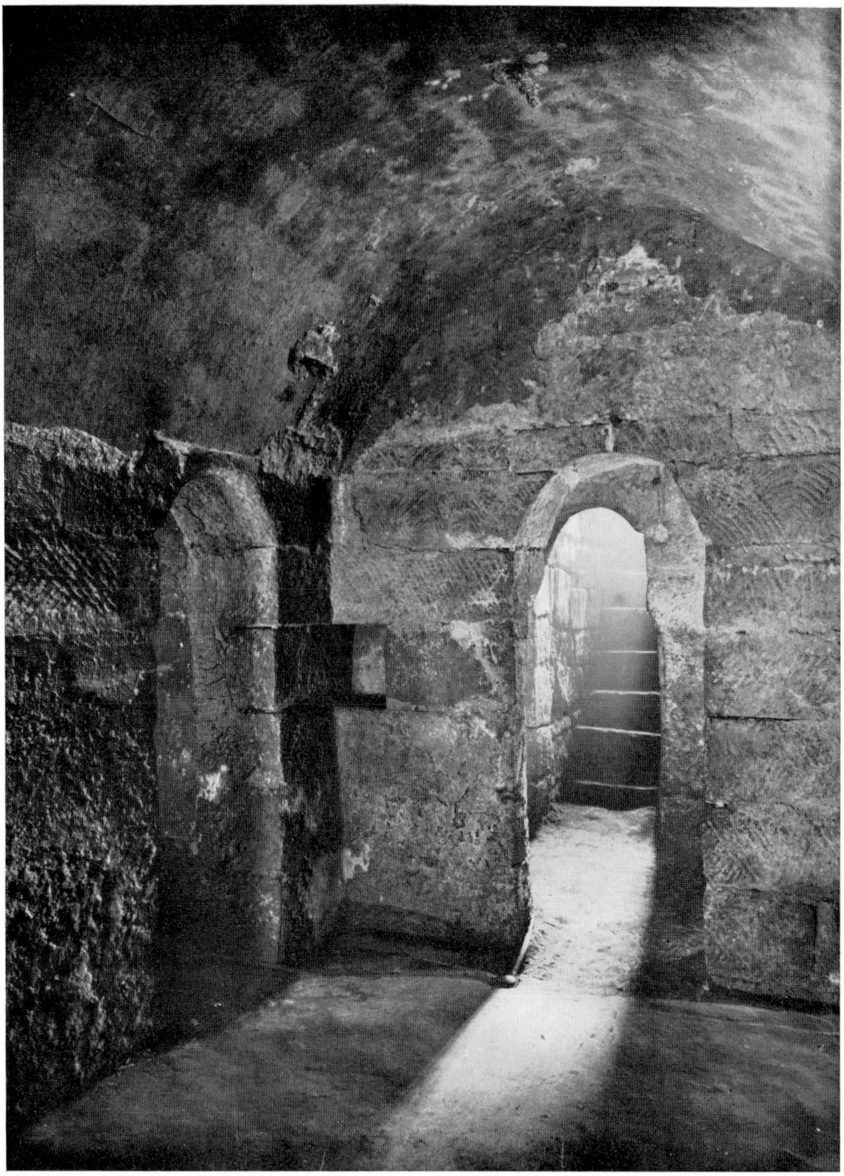

Hexham Abbey. The main chamber of Wilfrid's crypt

ment of Wilfrid, the bishop was released and allowed to depart with his relics and his retinue. There followed a second exile. Ecgfrith's influence was used against the fugitive, who was driven first from Mercia and then from Wessex. In the end he found a refuge in the kingdom of Sussex (681–6); he won the confidence of the South Saxons by teaching them how to catch fish in nets, and so took a leading part in the conversion of that kingdom and the neighbouring Isle of Wight, the two last strongholds of heathendom. (Cf. coin of Ecgfrith, Plate 43, 8.)

In 686 Wilfrid was reconciled to Archbishop Theodore and to King Aldfrith, the learned successor of Ecgfrith. He recovered his monasteries of Hexham and Ripon and a part of the Northumbrian diocese.[37] It was an acknowledgement of defeat, since he had to accept the division of the Northumbrian diocese against which he had so long fought. His administration of Cuthbert's bishopric for a year (687–8) at Cuthbert's death did not lead to a genuine reconciliation. The quarrel smouldered, till in 691–2 it once more blazed up. The old process began anew. Wilfrid departed for his third period of exile (*c.* 692–702). This time he found a home in Mercia, and for eleven years he did good work as bishop of the Middle Angles.

About 702, in a synod at Austerfield attended by most of the bishops of Britain, a new attempt was made to unravel the tangle of Wilfrid's affairs. But the decrees of Archbishop Theodore were again upheld in preference to those of the Pope, and Wilfrid for the second time appealed to Rome. Eddius, his chaplain and companion, says that he made the whole journey to Rome on foot—if true, a remarkable performance for an old man of nearly seventy. Soon after his return in 705 with fresh papal decrees, the death of King Aldfrith made it easier to end the long feud, and at the synod on the Nidd the final compromise was arranged. Wilfrid for the third time was restored—but restored only to his two best monasteries, Hexham and Ripon. All the bishops kissed and embraced, and Wilfrid had four years of peace within his restricted diocese before his death in 709.

Even this short summary of Wilfrid's career makes sufficiently obvious the contrast between him and his Northumbrian contemporary Cuthbert. Though Wilfrid won the devotion of his immediate followers, and kept a party of his own behind him, he stirred up more opposition than love. He had begun his career with every advantage: with great intelligence, unbounded vitality, with good birth, wealth, and friends at court; to these he had added a first-hand knowledge of Gallic and Roman ways, and the prestige acquired by his decisive part at the Synod at Whitby. But in spite of all his advantages he failed to assimilate the inner spirit of Christianity, and became more of a curse than a blessing to the Northumbrian Church. Never a popular saint, he has owed his place in history to the fact that Eddius, his biographer, was as great a fighter as himself. It may be said of Wilfrid that with his pomp, his large retinues, his buildings, his conflicts with the powers of this world, he was the first English ecclesiastic cast in the mould which afterwards produced Becket and Wolsey. He has not, however, the defence that can be set up for these later opponents of the monarchy. The cause for which he fought was primarily personal—his own position, his own rights, both of them obstacles in the way of the general welfare of his diocese. How little the cause of Wilfrid was the cause of Roman Christianity is shown by two facts: that Archbishop Theodore took the lead against him; and that Bede praised Wilfrid's chief opponents and omitted his miracles.

At the present day, as in the past, Wilfrid can well have his admirers. A good case can be made out for him on several counts.

It can be argued that the bitterness which so long pursued him came from those who sympathized with the Scots. Both the kings who persecuted him were in close touch with Scottish Christianity. Ecgfrith aimed at bringing the Picts within his empire; Aldfrith, his successor, had had an Irish education and possibly an Irish mother.

Then, if the actual performances of Wilfrid and Cuthbert are compared, there can be no doubt that Wilfrid accomplished more both for the Church and for the advancement of civilization. He himself, in making his defence in 702, claimed that he had been the first to introduce the Benedictine Rule as well as the first to root out the weeds planted by the Scots, and that he had also taught the Northumbrian Church to use double choirs, singing in alternation. And he might have claimed much more: outside Northumbria, some credit for the conversion of Frisia, of Sussex, and the Isle of Wight; for the foundation of monasteries, especially in Mercia; for useful work in administering a number of dioceses other than his own; above all, for transplanting to the north the artistic tradition of the Latin Church as well as its craftsmen, skilled in architecture and in sculpture.

Again, it may be held that Wilfrid, in opposing one king after another and in upholding the liberty of the Church, was ahead of his time; that he foresaw, as Theodore did not, the danger of the Church becoming a mere appendage of monarchy. Wilfrid may have been the far-sighted man of his age, realizing the evils which would come if kings and other laymen were allowed to treat their bishops and clergy like mere dependants. Arguing along such lines, we may defend Wilfrid's ultra-montanism as sound policy—a policy neglected by later generations of Anglo-Saxon churchmen to their own loss.

Or Wilfrid may be compared favourably with Cuthbert simply as a man. He was more clean, and 'made it his custom to wash his body during the night hours winter and summer alike, with blessed and holy water, until Pope John advised him to put an end to this rigour out of consideration for his age'.[38] The motives of Wilfrid were religious and not hygienic; but Cuthbert, acting also from religion, found, it seems, no mean between the extremes of standing for long periods up to his neck in the sea, and abstention from washing for months at a time.

There are no doubts about Wilfrid's sanctity in general; and his quarrels were only occasional eruptions. For long periods he was patient under rebuffs: from 666 to 669, when he found Chad in occupation of the see of York; from 681 to 686, when he was working in Sussex; from 692 to 702, when he was administering his Mercian diocese.

But when all has been said in his defence, can his admitted nobility and the heroic spirit which led him into so many encounters for what he conceived to be the right—or his rights—can these compensate for his glaring defects? The flaws in his character can be detected even in the panegyric of his biographer. Let us illustrate from two scenes Wilfrid's strong possessive instinct. The first scene is the dedication of the church at Ripon. It was celebrated with a feast organized by Wilfrid, lasting three days and nights. Before the feast[39] 'Saint Wilfrid, the bishop, stood in front of the altar and, turning to the people, in the presence of the kings read out clearly a list of the lands which the kings, for the good of their souls, had previously and on that very day as well, presented to him . . . and also a list of the consecrated places in various parts which the British clergy had deserted when fleeing from the hostile sword, wielded by the warriors of our own nation'.

The other scene is the last in his life—the division of his wealth.[40] 'A short time before his death, he ordered his treasurer to open his treasury in the presence of two abbots and some very faithful brethren . . . and to put out in their sight all the gold, silver, and precious stones: he bade the treasurer divide it into four parts.'

The emphasis on the acquisition of lands and treasure attributed to Wilfrid by his chaplain is significant. Cuthbert had gone to one extreme in the repudiation of worldly goods; Wilfrid went to the other. It is a memorable picture, that of Wilfrid, the *miles Christi*, the old warrior, surveying his hoard as did Beowulf before his death. But if, like Beowulf, he gloated over spoil, and like Beowulf, he fought till he was an old man, the treasure and the lands of Wilfrid were amassed with a purpose. The Church could scarcely have survived, and assuredly the monasteries could not have become centres of learning and civilization without endowments. This is true, but not the whole truth. It was the possessive instinct of the Church, even more than the interference of lay rulers, which was to be its undoing at the end of the Middle Ages.

Midway between Lindisfarne and Ripon, near the mouths of the Wear and the Tyne, were the twin monasteries of Wearmouth and Jarrow. These communities were prominent among others in England because their founder, Benedict Biscop (628–90), had concentrated all his energies on making them models of Roman Christianity according to the pattern of St. Benedict. For a short time the career of Biscop had coincided with that of Wilfrid. He had been the companion provided for Wilfrid when the latter, dissatisfied with Lindisfarne, first wished to go to Rome. The two men had then much in common. For Benedict Biscop was like Wilfrid a well-born Northumbrian, another of those young men belonging to the warrior class who had been disenchanted with the old ideal of bloodshed. Less precocious than Wilfrid, he had waited till he was twenty-five years old before 'he left his home, his kinsmen, and his country, for the sake of Christ and the Gospel'.[41] Unlike Wilfrid, Biscop pursued his pilgrimage to Rome without delaying in Gaul. This journey, equally decisive in the life of either man, clearly revealed the contrast in their characters. While Wilfrid, like a knight-errant of romance, was ever turning aside to make a friend or fight an enemy, Biscop never allowed himself to be deflected from his main purpose, that of studying at first-hand the culture and usages of the Roman Church in order to introduce them to his countrymen at home. That he might discover the monastic rule best suited to the English people, he compared the rules of seventeen of the most ancient of the monasteries in Gaul and Italy, and, on his second journey, following in the footsteps of St. Patrick and other Britons to the first great home of western monasticism, he had himself tonsured in the island of Lérins.

On his third visit to Rome (667–8) he was asked by Pope Vitalian to escort Theodore and Hadrian back to England. Then, at the request of Theodore, he presided for two years over the monastery of St. Peter's (later called St. Augustine's) at Canterbury, until the time when Hadrian was ready to take over its charge. Those two years in which Biscop was in contact with Theodore and Hadrian were all-important for Northumbria, for when he, with the help of King Ecgfrith, established a monastery at Wearmouth (674), and then, eleven years later, a sister foundation at Jarrow, this joint community between the Wear and the Tyne was almost an offshoot of the Church of Canterbury, and inherited the best traditions of the school of Theodore and Hadrian. Wearmouth-Jarrow became, as was intended, the model of what a monastery should be, the embodiment of all that Benedict had learned in Rome, Gaul, and Canterbury. It became, in fact, the most flourishing foundation in the island. Let us see wherein lay its superiority. Firstly in size, we know of no other monastery in England which could compare with its six hundred inmates. Then in buildings, if it was surpassed (as is probable) by the churches of Wilfrid, none the less it was largely built of stone 'in the Roman manner', with the help of masons whom Biscop brought with him from Italy. In equipment and ornament, it had the best that industry and money could procure. The windows were glazed by alien workmen; 'spiritual merchandise' was carried back from Gaul and Italy on each of his six continental journeys: books, relics, pictures of biblical history—these last to adorn his churches from wall to wall, 'so that all who entered the church, even if they could not read, wherever they turned their eyes might contemplate the lovable countenance of Christ and of His saints'.[42] Best of all, Biscop introduced teachers of crafts, and a famous singing-monk, John, arch-chanter of St. Peter's, Rome. Finally with regard to discipline, nowhere else in the island was the Benedictine Rule so fully realized. The details of this Rule we shall have to study when we come to the controversies of the tenth century. For the present it must suffice to remember that St. Benedict had aimed at stability (his monks were not to wander, but were to be cloistered from the world); at adaptability

FIG. 50. Monkwearmouth Church. The wall and two-storied porch are probably the work of Benedict Biscop (*c.* 675); the tower, tenth century.

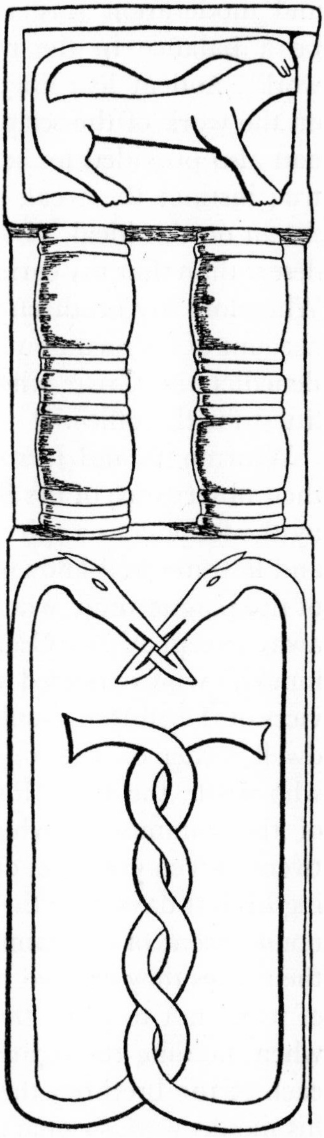

FIG. 51. Plinth of the porch with intertwined animals, surmounted by turned balusters supporting an impost with another animal in relief.

and moderation (instead of extreme asceticism, there was to be a balance in the monks' life between sleep, prayer, and work); and at learning (emphasis was placed by Benedictines on the work of the scriptorium and on teaching). St. Benedict had also provided for self-government; and Biscop, seeing with true instinct the weak spot of northern monasticism, was insistent on this ideal. 'I would rather that this place should be a desert than that my carnal brother . . . should become abbot. . . . Wherefore my brethren beware, and never choose an abbot on account of his birth, but seek out according to the Rule of Abbot Benedict the Great whoever for virtue and wisdom is proved fittest for the office.'[43]

Wearmouth and Jarrow are now remembered, not because of their observance of the Rule, but because of the spirit generated by the founders—a spirit beautifully reflected in the life of Bede and in some well-known stories. There is for example the story of the plague time, when all the inmates of Jarrow were swept away except Abbot Ceolfrid and the small boy (probably Bede himself) who struggled through the responses, so that the services of the church should still be maintained. Let us, however, dwell rather on the long story in which the anonymous monk who wrote the early history of the Abbey describes the grief of the community when Ceolfrid, after ruling as abbot for twenty-seven years, set off for Rome with the intention of spending his last days near the shrines of the Apostles. At the first announcement of his imminent departure, all wept and falling on their faces they clasped his feet and entreated him 'with torrents of tears' not to leave them so suddenly. Later, in the church, when, holding the lighted censer in his hand, he began to give each of the brethren the kiss of peace, he himself and many of his monks were so much overcome with grief that he could not finish the ceremony. Again, when he had seated himself in the boat which was to take him across the river, his deacons by his side —one holding the golden cross, the other, lighted candles—once more 'he could in no wise restrain himself from sobs and tears'.[44]

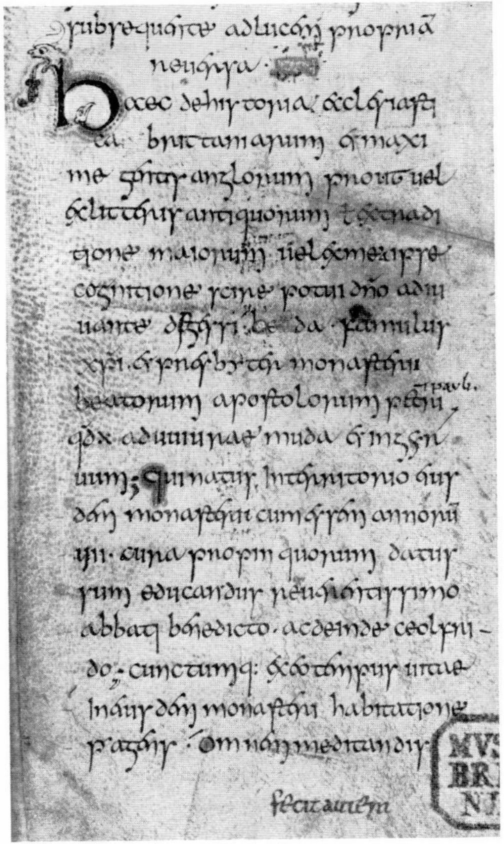

Haec de historia ecclesiastica brittaniarum, et maxi-
me gentis anglorum, prout uel
ex litteris antiquorum, vel ex tradi-
tione maiorum, uel ex mea ipse
cognitione scire potui, domino adiu-
vante digessi be[a]da famulus
christi, et presbyter monasterii
beatorum apostolorum petri (et pauli,)
quod est ad uuiuraemuda et in gyr-
uum; Qui natus in territorio eiusdem monasterii, cum essem annorum
vii. cura propinquorum datus
sum educandus reverentissimo
abbati benedicto, ac deinde ceolfri-
do; cunctumque ex eo tempus vitae
in eiusdem monasterii habitatione
peragens omnem meditandis

---

scripturis operam dedi; atque
inter observantiam disciplinae
regularis, et cotidianam cantandi
in ecclesia curam, semper aut
discere, aut docere, aut scribere
dulce habui.

Bede's record of his own life (Cotton MS. Tiberius C. ii, reduced)

It is in stories such as these that the change produced for the time being in the English character is best perceived. The men of religion (alike the followers of the Scots and those of the Romans) had become a highly emotional people. Many of the old characteristics of the race were turned into new channels. Loyalty, for instance, was still a leading trait. The devotion of the monk to his abbot could take the place of the devotion of the thegn to his lord.

The monastery of Wearmouth-Jarrow was of course pre-eminent above all by reason of Bede himself (673–735), and his writings, world-famous even within his own lifetime. A summary of his life can best be given in his own words, as it is appended to his *Ecclesiastical History*:

'I was born in the territory of the monastery, and at the age of seven years I was given by the care of kinsmen to be educated by the most reverend Abbot Benedict [Biscop], and afterwards by Ceolfrid. From that time I have spent the whole of my life within that monastery. I have wholly applied myself to the study of Scripture; and amid the observance of monastic rule and the daily charge of singing in the church, it has ever been my delight to learn or teach or write. In my nineteenth year I received deacon's orders; in my thirtieth, those of the priesthood. . . .'

Such was Bede's uneventful life at Jarrow—learning, teaching, writing; learning till he had absorbed all the knowledge preserved from the ancient world (including some knowledge of Greek); teaching till the tradition of classical education was established on a solid foundation; writing so unceasingly that his books fill twelve octavo volumes of modern print. At the end of the *Ecclesiastical History* he gives a list of his works, some thirty-six in number. Most of them survive. In his educational books—presumably among his earliest[45]—we see him teaching others as he himself had been taught. Thus in his *De Natura Rerum* he sums up what was known about natural phenomena. Most of his writings are commentaries on books of the Bible. Since the words of Scripture brought life to the souls of men and were deemed to be full of allegorical meanings, commentaries on them were labours on which a man might well spend a lifetime.

The *Ecclesiastical History*,* on which rests his fame in the modern world, was finished late in life, in 731. If we ask how it came about that Bede alone among the barbarians of northern Europe was moved to write the complete story of the Conversion of his nation, we see that various motives spurred him forward. From one point of view it was a sequel to his other historical works. In his *De Temporum Ratione*[46] he had looked at the history of mankind as a whole. Following Isidore of Spain he had distinguished Six Ages of the world, the Sixth Age beginning with the birth of Christ and continuing till the Day of Judgement. The *Ecclesiastical History* was the detailed study of Christianity in eastern Britain during this Sixth Age. With his co-ordinating and encyclopaedic mind, he was never happier than when he was collecting facts, and putting them into their right places. Just as he had expounded all that was known about 'The Nature of Things', so he determined to expound all that he could discover about the Conversion of the English people. Other monks had written eulogies of their own particular local saint. Bede's idea was to string the saints' lives together. The *Ecclesiastical History* was encyclopaedic hagiography. Consequently its chief aim was to edify. It was to supplement his commentaries on the New Testament. It was to show that the age of miracles was not yet past. It was to strengthen faith, and, as he says in his preface addressed to Ceolwulf, the king of Northumbria, 'If history relates good things of good men, the attentive hearer is excited to imitate that which is good'.

The characteristics of the *Ecclesiastical History* are familiar to all. Here, then, it will suffice to remind the reader of three of the most obvious merits of Bede as a historian.

The first is the high standard of accuracy which he set himself. This can be seen even better in his preface to his *Life of St.*

* *Historia Ecclesiastica Gentis Anglorum.*

Cuthbert than in his *History*. The preface of the *Life* is addressed to 'The father-bishop Eadfrith' of Lindisfarne (of whom we shall hear again when the wonderfully illuminated Lindisfarne Gospels come before us), 'and to all the congregation of the brethren'. He reminds them of the minute investigation which he has given to the deeds of the saint, and of his *subtilissima examinatio* of the credible witnesses. He says that in the next stage of the book he had submitted what he had written to the criticisms of those who had long been intimate with Cuthbert, and that finally, after some corrections had been made, the whole had been read aloud to the senior monks at Lindisfarne, and had been passed by them. Well might Bede claim that by intent he was a veracious historian,* and his claim cannot be better confirmed than by the testimony of Mommsen[47] that 'few writers have treated matters of fact with such laborious accuracy'. If then his stories are not always credible to us, the age in which Bede lived must obviously bear the blame.

The thoroughness with which Bede had prepared for the writing of his *Ecclesiastical History* is explained in his introduction: the questions which he put to Abbot Albinus the successor of Hadrian at Canterbury, and to the priest Nothelm about the south-eastern kingdoms, to Bishop Daniel of Winchester about Wessex, to the monks of Lastingham about Mercia and Essex; Nothelm's research, at his request, into the papal archives for letters of Pope Gregory: all this labour and care to tell the reader about the sources of his information, give Bede's great work a place apart from all other histories written in the Dark Ages.

The next characteristic in Bede which has always been singled out for praise is his 'fair-mindedness'. This, even more than his skill as a story-teller, is what has raised him above his contemporaries. It is illustrated by his whole narrative of the Conversion. Though he could be biased against the Britons as a race[48] and bitter about all error on the Paschal controversy, when he dealt with the schismatics as men he could be generous. Aidan is

* *verax historicus.*

praised as much as Augustine. He has love for Cuthbert, but also admiration for Wilfrid. With deliberate restraint Bede slurs over the quarrels within the Northumbrian Church. His function, like that of his monastery—placed as it was midway between Ripon and Lindisfarne—was to appreciate what was good both in Celtic and Roman traditions, and to help to reconcile those in conflict. Bede was always in close touch with Canterbury. He was devoted to Bishop Acca, Wilfrid's disciple and successor at Hexham. (It is to Acca that his works are often dedicated.) But at the same time he could see the beauty of the simple poverty of Lindisfarne. He visited the community on that island, and his name was inscribed in their *Liber Vitae*. The wealth of Northumbrian Christianity came from its fusion of the Roman and the Celtic traditions, and nowhere were the two more happily blended than in the generous mind of Bede.

And lastly, there is the miracle of Bede's good Latin style. How exactly he managed to escape the 'Hisperic infection' cannot be explained. Aldhelm had caught it, though he had studied under Theodore at Canterbury. The monastery of Wearmouth-Jarrow was not immune. Bede's own superior, the abbot who succeeded Ceolfrid, had succumbed to the fashion. And Bede, like Aldhelm, had read the rhetoric of Gildas and of Virgilius the Grammarian. None the less, thanks to his own good taste, to the sound Roman foundation laid by Biscop or Ceolfrid, to the influence of Pope Gregory's writings and to a northern feeling for simpler Latin, which is also apparent in the anonymous lives of Northumbrian saints, he somehow was able to set a new fashion of lucidity.

The strength and simplicity of his style reflect the character of Bede himself. His letter to Bishop Egbert of York, which will come before us when we deal with the Church of the eighth century, will show that he was not too much of a student to take a strong line on the public questions of his day. None the less, the picture which his own account of himself and of his thirty-six books leaves on the mind, is that of a monk who is for ever at his desk, writing and copying with his own hand, writing no doubt in winter (like another, a later, monk of Wearmouth-Jarrow) till his hand became so numb that he could no longer hold the pen. It was heroic labour. The story of its end is preserved in a long letter of his pupil Cuthbert which gives in the original Northumbrian speech the five lines of verse about 'the inevitable journey hence' which Bede composed on his death-bed; and describes how he was still at work even on the last day of his life, translating the Gospel of St. John into English, and making selections from Isidore. The fear of losing any moments from his precious writing had become an obsession. 'Write quickly', 'Write quickly', was his repeated entreaty to the scribe. One incident in the well-known story may be singled out to be placed in our memories with the picture of Cuthbert waiting for death on his lonely island, nursing his five onions, unable to move; and with the picture of Wilfrid dividing his hoard of gold and jewels. In this incident Bede, like Wilfrid, distributed his possessions. He said to his pupil, 'I have a few treasures in my casket, that is, some paper, napkins, and incense; run quickly, call the priests, that I may distribute to them such gifts as God has given me'. A few hours later he dictated his last sentence and died on the floor of his cell, singing the 'Gloria'.

Bede, like Theodore, was never canonized as a saint. But he was 'the master of the Middle Ages'.[49] From the first his writings were accepted as the standard works on history, natural science, and grammar; and now, while the earlier heroes of the Anglian race are mere names, or less than names, Bede's is the first English mind which speaks to the modern world fully and lucidly on a wide range of subjects.

THE ARTS

Before we leave the Golden Age of the Conversion, we must see what remains of its handiwork—some fragments of churches, some foundations and crypts, some mutilated crosses, bits of a wooden coffin, a few illuminated books. The list is not impressive, but the objects themselves have supreme interest for those who wish to know what manner of men were these English Christians. They are the best supplement to Bede in that they reflect the Christian mind from different angles.

First, let us look at the churches. There is no building of Theodore of which we can say, as before of Augustine, that here we have the work of Rome's emissary. But at Reculver, within the ruins of the old Roman fort, there were until 1805 substantial vestiges of a church built during Theodore's pontificate. A sketch made in 1805 while the building was being demolished shows one shaft still in place carrying a triple arcade, constructed of Roman bricks, between the nave and the chancel. This sketch* and the old foundations enable us to realize the continuity of the type of stone church which had become the fashion with Augustine and his followers in Kent. In Wessex recent excavation[50] has proved that Ine's church at Glastonbury was also laid out on the Kentish plan.

Mercia at Brixworth in Northamptonshire offers us something better than mere foundations. There are reasons[51] for thinking that the arches of the nave and the windows of the clerestory are the work of Wilfrid, who is known to have built churches in the Midlands when in exile from Northumbria. The architect certainly knew well the general appearance of a Roman basilica, but he was an amateur and in arch construction could only experiment (Fig. 52c) with bricks from some neighbouring ruin.

In Northumbria the only visible remains of Wilfrid are the crypts at Ripon and Hexham (Pl. 44), constructed with Roman-like solidity to hold the relics of saints. Many, though not all, authorities[52] believe that the west end and the porch of Monkwearmouth and the chancel (once the nave) of Jarrow

* Vide Clapham, *Romanesque Architecture I*, Plate 3. This and the other shaft may now be seen in the Close of Canterbury Cathedral. Fragments of the sculptured cross which once stood gaily painted to a height of nine feet at the entering of the choir are reproduced by Sir C. R. Peers in *Arch.* lxxvii (1927), 241 ff.

FIG. 52. Brixworth Church. A. The nave and west wall. B. Plan, showing the original aisles, now removed. C. Springing of an arch.

church go back to the days of Benedict Biscop and of Bede. But much imagination is needed if we are to see any of these churches as they appeared to the English men and women who first beheld them. Eddius declares that there were no churches on this side of the Alps built on such a scale as those of Wilfrid. He enlarges on their columns and walls, their winding passages and spiral stairs, the gold and silver and jewels of their ornaments, the purple and silk of their altars.

The large churches have almost vanished, but there is at Escomb in County Durham a minute church of about this period, one with squared chancel and absence of *porticus*, with high walls and narrow doors and windows, which gives a good idea of the type of building now developed in the north on different lines to the Augustinian churches of the south (Fig. 53).

North of the Roman Wall, in the region where Scottish influences predominated, there were at first no more churches built in stone in the Roman manner. The wattled or wood oratories and huts of Cuthbert's monks rotted away and left no trace of their existence.

But the Scotticized Northumbrians produced handiwork more remarkable than stone churches. The most wonderful of all is the Gospel Book which once adorned the altar of the church at Lindisfarne and which is now to be seen in the British Museum. There is general though not unanimous agreement that its colophon tells the truth about its origin.[53] This definitely states that the book was illuminated by the hand of Eadfrith, a monk who became bishop of Lindisfarne eleven years after the death of Cuthbert. Some of his full-page illustrations, those giving pictures of the Evangelists with their symbols, were copied straight from a manuscript brought from the south of Italy by a traveller, perhaps Benedict Biscop (Pl. 46); others contain the initial letters of the Gospels like the *Quoniam quidem* page (Pls. 47, 48; cf. Frontispiece of vol. II), and opposite each initial is a page of pure ornament centring round a cross (Pl. 49). These folios show that Eadfrith loved birds and dogs with something like

FIG. 53. Escomb Church. Interior and exterior. The chancel arch may have been taken from a building of the Roman period.

the love of which we read in the stories of Cuthbert, and he worked such animals, stylized, but not far removed from nature, into beautiful patterns. Eadfrith's art, when it is not copied from the southern book, is 'Hiberno-Saxon'. It is an Anglian variety—or rather, as some now think,[54] an anticipation—of Irish art. According to Baldwin Brown, it is 'Anglo-Saxon in its reticence and its instinct for keeping along a path once marked out, which contrasts with the volubility and waywardness of the Celt'.[55] We shall have good authority behind us[56] if we regard these and the other interlaced patterns of the age as no more than patterns, masterpieces of conventional art. But another view is possible if less probable. We may look upon the pages of the Lindisfarne Gospels as manifestations of the thoughts which passed through the minds of those under Irish influence. As Cuthbert and those brought up like him in the traditions of the Irish Church looked out on the world, contemplating interminably the elements of sea and sky around them, their minds were filled with adoration of the Creator and of His works, the earth and its living things. In their illuminations they gave expression to their love for the birds and the hounds whose necks they twisted and whose bodies they elongated into those tortuous designs; and through it all was a sense that living beings also were entangled into strange patterns, that life was twisted like these labyrinthine interlacements which crossed and turned, leading you out into puzzling complications and then bringing you back to the place or almost to the place from which you had set out. Life was like these pictures in the Lindisfarne Gospels. It was a maze; it was full of mazes; but in all there was design. The labour of these artist-monks was prayer—a form of worship. They expressed in colour and pattern, with plait and interwoven bird, the mysteries of this tangled world and the wonder of the universe.

As we look at these pages, we think of Eadfrith the monk working away in a hut, dark, draughty, exposed to the storms of wind and rain that sweep up from the North Sea. He works

Lindisfarne Gospels, picture of St. Luke and his symbol, copied from a book brought to Northumbria from S. Italy

Note the Greek legend : Ó ÁGIOS LUCAS

PLATE 47

Lindisfarne Gospels, beginning of St. Luke's Gospel

QUONIAM QUIDEM MULTI CONATI SUNT ORDINARE NARRATIONEM . .

Enlargement of part of Plate 47

Lindisfarne Gospels, cruciform page facing the beginning of St. Mark's Gospel

month after month, year after year, completing his one masterpiece, writing his bold half-uncial script, interlacing his birds and

FIG. 54. Ruthwell Cross.

hounds with unfailing accuracy and infinite patience, to the glory of God; illuminating his folios with colours that cannot be adequately reproduced by any mechanical process, colours which glow like the stained glass of medieval church windows.

Another form of art was developed by these northern Angles, once more manifesting a harmonious blending of Celtic and Roman influences—the tall stone crosses. These crosses, though in the end sporadic throughout Britain, were raised chiefly and in earliest beauty about the borderlands of Northumbria—in that human eddy caused by the meeting of the two cultures, the one coming from the Celtic West by way of Iona, the other from Rome and the Mediterranean lands.[57]

These tall stone crosses were made continuously from the seventh century until after the Norman Conquest. Then most of them were broken up and many were built into church walls. The reader will find in these pages illustrations both of some of the smaller fragments and also of the two more complete and better-known of the Northumbrian crosses. The shaft of that at Bewcastle still rises to heaven fifteen feet high where it was first set up, within the bounds of a Roman fort six miles north of the Roman Wall and on the edge of some of the wildest moorland of Britain. This shaft remains unchanged except for the weathering of its stone, but the cross-head is lost. The Ruthwell cross, some ten miles from Dumfries, has been partially restored and its general effect has been impaired by its removal from its original site. The two crosses are clearly the work of one sculptor or school. The figures and the spirit of the two are similar. That spirit is best expressed in the runic inscription which runs round one panel of the Ruthwell shaft, containing lines from a poem on the Holy Cross, better known in its later extended form, the *Vision* (or so-called *Dream*) *of the Rood.*

There is converging evidence for assigning the great development of the stone crosses to about the last quarter of the seventh century,[58] that is to the years following the Synod of Whitby and the coming of Archbishop Theodore. It was probably then that foreign sculptors made the cross for the church within the Roman fort at Reculver. It was about then also that the West Saxons

BEWCASTLE CROSS, North and West faces

The Runic inscription is below the figure of Christ, treading on the heads of beasts, and above that of a falconer (? St. John the Evangelist with his eagle,

A

B

RUTHWELL CROSS

A. The Magdalene wiping the feet of Christ with her hair. *B*. Christ treading on the heads of beasts

erected a cross at Glastonbury. And if these things were done in the south, it argues that the fashion must have been in full flower in Northumbria, the region where the art flourished like a native growth. The stages by which these sculptured crosses, standing three times the height of a man, came to be evolved, cannot now be traced. No doubt the first experiments in carving had been made with wooden crosses. Then Benedict Biscop or Wilfrid or Theodore introduced sculptors who inherited the traditions of later Greco-Roman art (their exact provenance cannot be determined); and soon the Anglian craftsmen became nearly as expert as their teachers.

Returning to the Bewcastle and Ruthwell crosses, we find a strong reason for dating them somewhere about 700 in the fact that high up on the Bewcastle cross there is inscribed in runes the name 'Cyniburug'. There can be little doubt that this stands for Cyniburg, the daughter of Penda, who married Alchfrith, son of Oswy. It seems that the lower half-obliterated inscription is a dedication to the unfortunate Alchfrith, the patron of Wilfrid, who disappeared from history mysteriously soon after the Synod of Whitby. Until the death of Wilfrid, there was good reason why Alchfrith should be commemorated in the region not far from Wilfrid's own Hexham.

Those who believe in the native authorship of the Ruthwell and Bewcastle crosses call attention to the crude carving of the Magdalene's hand in one panel (Pl. 51 A), to the traces of a Teutonic moustache on the face of Christ (Pl. 51 B), and to the characteristically English delight in birds and beasts. But whatever be decided about particular specimens, when we regard the Northumbrian crosses as a whole, there can be no doubt that the Anglian stone carvers did at this period quickly attain to a skill and artistry which lifted their works above all other sculpture of the age either in Europe or the Near East.

The Anglian is eclectic, but once more he is no mere imitator. In his crosses, as in his illuminated manuscripts, whatever he borrows he makes his own. From the Celts he takes the idea that a tall cross is the best kind of monument, a good memorial to a departed friend or an emblem round which country-folk may gather for worship; from the Byzantines or Romans he takes the pose of the figures and the design of the vine-scroll, from others the interlace. He takes Roman letters, but they are written in an Irish style. He takes runes from his Teutonic ancestors, on one border he inscribes a verse from the Vulgate, on another a stanza composed by a new Anglian poet. All these are fused harmoniously, and the 'Victory Beacon' (*sigbecn*) raises its shaft and cross-head aloft, every panel and almost every border on it enriched with ornament or lettering intended either to teach men about the new Judge and Saviour of the world, or to proclaim His triumph. At the top of the Ruthwell Cross is inscribed I.H.S.; XPS. On the Bewcastle shaft, above the figure of Christ is *Gessus Christus*. On either cross Christ is shown trampling on the snouts of animals—the *Bestiae et Dracones*.

That the victory was the victory of Love is shown by the panel wherein the repentant Magdalene weeps at the feet of Christ. But that the Christian triumph was regarded from the regular Anglo-Saxon standpoint as a victory of the old fighting instincts of the race is told in the verse which is given a central position at Ruthwell, the lines from the so-called *Dream of the Rood*:[59] 'Then the young Hero that was God Almighty, stripped Himself, strong and steadfast. Bold in the sight of many, He mounted the high cross when He would redeem mankind. I trembled when He clasped me, yet I durst not bow to the ground.'

The quotation must serve as a reminder that in our survey of the growth produced by Christianity from the soil of the English people we have said nothing about the efflorescence of Anglo-Saxon poetry. Every one knows Bede's story of how the first inspiration to compose verse came to Cædmon (*c.* 570–80), the diffident herdsman attached to the monastery at Streanæshalch; 'I cannot sing, and for this cause I left the banquet and retired hither, because I could not sing.' 'Nevertheless, thou must needs sing to me. . . . Sing the beginning of Creation.'

The present chapter has been devoted to the achievements of saints and others who can be conveniently assigned to the Golden Age of the Anglo-Saxon Church, from about 665 to 735. When we come to Old English poetry, except for the few lines assigned to Cædmon all else is treacherous ground, offering no certainty in its chronology. It is therefore safer to use the Christian poetry to describe the general changes in society produced by Christianity, rather than to illustrate the features of any one period. We shall therefore return to the poetry in later pages.

The present chapter has already led us on a far cry, from the coming of Archbishop Theodore. We have wandered by way of Aldhelm and of Guthlac to the Northumbrian saints and the vigorous life which both to the south and the north of the old Roman frontier wall was producing masterpieces in literature and the arts. Wherever we have gone we have seen foreign influences, if not foreign teachers, working on the raw material of Anglo-Saxon humanity. Whether it was produced by the stimulus of Celtic infusion coinciding with the Roman influence, or whether there is some other explanation, enough has now been told to show that this period was not only the most remarkable in the history of our pre-Norman ancestors, but that it can claim comparison with the ages of greatest vitality in medieval and modern England.

This period of the Conversion, more truly than the age of the Renaissance, gave Englishmen a new heaven and a new earth. It offered them also a new language, a new writing. It offered them books and an education based on books. It opened to them the literature of Rome, and a civilization gathered from all the Mediterranean world. It introduced them to all kinds of new ideas and new arts. What was impossible to a Christian people when old and young had their visions, and when signs and wonders were reported from every quarter? Even the relics of native saints were, it seemed, as efficacious as those imported from Rome. And the other miracles—the stone churches, Aldhelm's Latin style, Bede's *Ecclesiastical History*, the art of the

Lindisfarne Gospels, and of the sculptured crosses—are not these enough to demonstrate that the Anglo-Saxons, or at least a few of them, were as much alive and as gifted as the Elizabethans? It is true that there can be no comparison of progress where two generations start from quite different points. One thing, however, may be asserted, that while the Elizabethans were fascinated by plunder and the lure of Spanish gold, and were too often moved by new hatreds—hatred of Rome, hatred of Spain—the heroes of the Conversion were inspired by a great love for their fellow men. Their rivalry was to excel one another in good works.

Jedburgh. Fragment of Cross-shaft. About the end of the seventh century.

Scotland

NOTES

[*For the Abbreviations used in the Notes see vol. ii, pp. 712–17*]

I. THE ANGLES AND SAXONS IN GERMANY

[1] Bede, i. c. 15. Here and in other passages of Bede I have made use of Miss A. M. Sellar's *Bede's Ecclesiastical History of England, A Revised Translation.* (Messrs. G. Bell and Sons, 1907.)

[2] Wadstein, 29.

[3] For this controversy and further references see Chadwick, *Origin*, c. viii; Schmidt, ii. 22–33; Wadstein, 15 ff.; Siebs, 56 ff. Siebs, writing in 1931, concludes that the evidence of Tacitus and Ptolemy makes it 'certain' that the Cimbrian peninsula was not the home of the Angles; that 'Bede knew nothing about the continental peoples'; and that the home of the Angles cannot be fixed with any certainty.

[4] Chambers, *Widsith*, 194; La Cour, 131, 149, 188–9.

[5] For references to this controversy see Pauly-Wissowa, *s.v.* 'Saxones'. The question is still and may long remain *sub judice*. As is to be expected, the evidence of the urns is disputed. K. Waller (in *Mannus' Zeitschrift für Vorgeschichte*, xxv (1933), 40–59) identifies the urns of Plettke's types A1 and A2 as those of Chauci and not of Saxons. If he is right there was some continuity at least in the cemeteries of the Chauci and Saxons. He infers from the development of these types of urns in low-lying cemeteries that the Chauci gave way before the invading Saxons and fled to the marshes. Cf. Schütte, ii. 234.

[6] P. Zylmann, *Ostfriesische Urgeschichte*, 133 ff.

[7] For references to Roeder's writings see below, p. 371, note 15.

[8] Cf. H. Müller-Brauel, 'Sächsische Friedhöfe bei Stade' in *Praehist. Zeitsch.* xvii. 134–5.

[9] At Nesse near Wesermunde and at Galgenberg to the south-west of Cuxhaven. See F. Roeder's *Neue Funde* (Sonderdruck aus *Anglia*, lvii). Roeder thinks that the fashion of inhuming the dead was probably introduced into the Elbe-Weser lands by Saxon soldiers returning from north-east Gaul, 350–400. For archaeological evidence that Saxon soldiers served under the Empire in north-east Gaul see *Neue Funde*, 17–18, and references there given.

[10] Liber xvi (1), 1. Pliny's description is for the most part applicable to the terps of Frisia, though he applies it to a territory of the Chauci. See D. J. H. Nyessen, *The Passing of the Frisians* (1927), 268; P. C. J. A. Boeles, *Friesland tot de Elfde Eeuw* (1927), 123 ff.; P. Zylmann, *Ostfriesische Urgeschichte*, 142.

[11] e.g. J. H. Holwerda, in *R.G.K. XVI Bericht*, 135 ff.

[12] *Waldbäume und Kulturpflanzen im germanischen Altertum* (1905), c. 14. Hoops is here following Kluge in Paul's *Grundriss*, i. 336 and 349.

[13] F. Lot, *Rev. Hist.* cxix. 28 f.

[14] Bibliography in Pauly-Wissowa, *s.v.* 'Saxones'; also F. Lot, *ut supra*.

[15] Some historians believe that the settlements round Boulogne go back

to the time of Carausius in the third century: G. Kurth, *Clovis* (1901), i. 73 and 180; G. des Marez, *Le Problème de la colonisation franque* (1926), 36.

[16] See J. B. Bury, *Hist. of Later Roman Empire* (1923), 292.

[17] See T. Hodgkin, *Italy and Her Invaders* (1892), ii. 366–7; O. M. Dalton, *Letters of Sidonius* (1915), ii. 150.

[18] C. Blümel in *Germania*, xvii (1933), 29. Cf. P. Bienkowski, *De Simulacris Barbararum Gentium apud Romanos* (1900), 90.

[19] H. Shetelig in *Acta Archaeologica*, i (1930), 1–30.

[20] J. J. A. Worsaae, quoted in Engelhardt, 28.

[21] S. Müller, ii. 132 f.; Hastings, *E.R.E.* xi. 755.

[22] e.g. Schütte, i. 223–4; Philippson, 128–9.

[23] For *Widsith* and the following quotations see R. W. Chambers, *Widsith* (1912).

[24] Especially R. W. Chambers.

[25] E. Foord, *The Last Age of Roman Britain* (1925), 176–9, 190.

[26] i. 15.

[27] Wadstein, *Norden*, 3 f.

II. THE END OF ROMAN BRITAIN

[1] The general reader will find an up-to-date bibliography at the end of R. G. Collingwood's *Roman Britain* (1932). A full bibliography of the works of F. Haverfield is in Haverfield and MacDonald's *Roman Occupation of Britain* (1924), 38–57. Sir G. MacDonald's *Roman Britain 1914–1928* (British Academy Supplemental Papers, No. VI) gives a useful summary of recent excavations, &c., which will be found reported in more detail annually in the *Journal of Roman Studies*.

[2] D. Atkinson, *Romano-British Site at Lowbury Hill*, 25.

[3] Cf. D. Atkinson in *Essays, James Tait*, 6–11.

[4] J. Bushe-Fox, *Richborough Castle, Official Guide* (1930).

[5] Wheeler, *Wales*, 261–8, 291–2, and *Trans. Soc. Cymmrod* (1920–1), 83.

[6] Haverfield, *Roman Occupation*, 263.

[7] Statement of Dr. R. E. M. Wheeler.

[8] *Antiquity*, iii. 271–2.

[9] Cf. Kendrick and Hawkes, 294.

[10] *J.R.S.* xviii (1928), 204 ff.; xix. 202–3; R. E. M. and T. V. Wheeler, *Report on the Excavation of the . . . Site in Lydney Park* (1932).

[11] Claudian, *De Consulatu Stilichonis*, i. 253–5.

[12] *M.G.H. Auct. Ant.* ix. 652–4 as emended by the editor, T. Mommsen.

[13] *Historia Nova*, vi, §§ 6–10, in *M.H.B.*, p. lxviii.

[14] J. B. Bury, in *J.R.S.* x (1920), 130 ff. In support of Bury—E. Stein, in *R.G.K.*, xviii *Bericht* (1928), 92, note 2; H. S. Schultz, in *J.R.S.* xxiii (1933), 36–54, with references to recent articles. In opposition to Bury—R. G. Collingwood, in *J.R.S.* xii (1922), 74 ff.; F. S. Salisbury, in ibid. xvii (1927), 102–6, and xxiii (1933), 217–20; and *Num. Chron.* (1927), 108 ff. Cf. also MacDonald, *Roman Britain 1914–1928*, 67–73.

[15] Schultz, art. cit., and *Antiquity*, vii (1933), 381.

[15a] An alternative expansion is: *Felicium Temporum Reparatio*. Cf. *Num. Chron.*, 1933, 182.

[15b]. T. D. Kendrick, in *Antiquity*, vi (1932), 161 ff.; and E. T. Leeds, *Celtic Ornament* (1933), 144–64.

[16] c. 62, ed. Mommsen, 205–6. Cf. Welsh genealogies in *Cymmrodorion*, ix. 170; Lloyd, in *R. Irish Acad.* xxxvii (1926), 132; Chadwick, *G. of L.*, 309–11.

[17] Bibliography for St. Germanus in Kenney, i. 163.

[18] Text and trans. of N. J. D. White, in *P.R.I.A.* (1905), 260 ff.; ibid., *St. Patrick, His Writings and Life* (1920). For general bibliography for St. Patrick see Kenney, i. 165–70.

[19] The authority of the *Annales Cambriae* is sometimes quoted in support of 428; but (1) the *Computus* which, in Harleian MS. 3859, gives this date may be really the end of the *Historia Brittonum* and not the beginning of the *Annales*; and (2) in any case it is probably only an echo of the *Historia*.

[20] *M.G.H. Auct. Ant.* ix (ed. Mommsen), 660.

[21] e.g. R. Thurneysen, in *Englische Studien*, xxii (1895), 174; F. Lot, *Bretons et Anglais, P.B.A.* xvi (1930), 327–45, and *La Fin du Monde Antique* (1927), 236. For a criticism of this view see R. V. Lennard, in *History*, xviii (1933), 204–15; and for an eccentric interpretation A. Anscombe, in *Brit. Num. Journ.*, 2nd ser., ix (1927–8), 20–1.

[22] See passages collected in E. K. Chambers, *Arthur*, 237–8. Also Plummer, *Bede*, ii. 27; Thurneysen, *ut supra*, and E. W. B. Nicholson in *Zeitschrift für Celtische Philologie*, vi (1907), 439 ff.

[23] Migne, *P.L.* li, col. 618, *Carmen de Providentia Divina*, line 38; col. 612, *Poema Coniugis*, line 30.

[24] At least the *De Vita Christiana*. Cf. R. Morris, in *Trans. Soc. Cymmrod* (1914–15), 43–6.

III. THE CONQUEST OF KENT

[1] Bibliography for Gildas, in Kenney, i. 150–2. Note specially F. Lot, in *Mediaeval Studies in Memory of G. S. Loomis* (1927), 229–64.

[1a]. 547 or 549. Cf. E. K. Chambers, *Arthur*, 13–15, on the *Annales Cambriae*.

[2] e.g. by F. Lot, in *Mélanges*, 1 ff.

[3] Some writers think that the Hengest of *Beowulf* and Hengist, the Conqueror of Kent, have more than the name in common. M. G. Clarke, *Sidelights on Teutonic History during the Migration Period*, c. v, esp. 186–7; cf. Chadwick, *Origin*, 53; R. W. Chambers, *Beowulf* (1932), 443 ff.

[4] H. Zimmer, *Nennius Vindicatus* (1893); Faral, i. 56–73. Cf. F. Lot, in *Mélanges*, 9–14; F. Liebermann, in *Essays to Tout*, 25–44; Chadwick, *G. of L.*, 153–8, 297, and *passim*. Bibliography in Kenney, i. 152–5. R. Thurneysen's

article on 'Zu Nemnius (Nennius)' in *Zeitschrift f. Celtische Philologie*, xx (1933), 97–138, is valuable. It not only corrects the reading of the author's name; but it accords with Liebermann's view that Nennius (or rather Nemnius) himself produced different versions of his *Historia*, and explains how he came to do so. He believes that the first version, that of the Harleian MS. 3859, was compiled *c.* 826. To the above must now (1934) be added a new critical edition of Nennius by F. Lot (*Nennius et L'Historia Brittonum*).

5 Wadstein, 36.

6 Chadwick, *Origin*, 97–107; Schmidt, ii. 26, and 510; J. Hoops, *Waldbäume*, 585–6; F. Lot, in *Rev. Hist.* cxix. 23–34. Cf. also Schütte, ii. 297–312.

7 *M.G.H. Auct. Ant.* vol. iv, *pars prior* (ed. F. Leo), Carminum liber IX, i. line 73 f.

8 Inferences are made from a fourth, and even more unsatisfactory, passage —this time from the anonymous geographer of Ravenna (*c.* A.D. 650)—by Oman, 209; Chadwick, *Origin*, 47; and others.

9 Cf. R. W. Chambers, *Beowulf* (1932), 8–10, 260 ff., 272 ff., 333–45, 401–9, 417–18; ibid., *Widsith*, 237–41. Siebs (p. 61) suggests that the Eutii or Euthiones may be localized in the Ems-Weser region by a phonological connexion which he traces with the modern name Iade, a river of that region.

10 e.g. in the territory of the Gyrwe between Norfolk and Peterborough (*V.C.H. Northants*, i. 250) and at Girton near Cambridge (E. J. Hollingworth and M. M. O'Reilly, *Anglo-Saxon Cemetery at Girton College, Cambridge*, 13). E. T. Leeds, in *Ant. Journ.* xiii (1933), 234 ff.

11 Cf. R. G. Collingwood, *Archaeology of Roman Britain* (1930), c. 15; Schetelig, *Cruciform Brooches*; B.B. iii. 248–64; Åberg, 28 f.; *B.M. Guide*, 23 ff.

12 Cf. E. T. Leeds, in *Ant. Journ.* xiii. 240. Note that part of Cambridgeshire is reckoned as East Anglian.

13 Leeds, cc. 6 and 7. For what follows in addition to Leeds see B.B. iv. 690–6, 742–4; Åberg, *passim*; Brenner, 342–6.

14 Åberg, 30–1, and 2.

15 *Antiquity*, vii (1933), 429–52.

16 E. Brenner, in *R.G.K.*, vii *Bericht*, 344.

17 Cf. H. Kjaer, *Ligbraendingen i Danmark i Oldtiden* (1931), 73 ff.; H. Schetelig, in *Praehist. Zeitsch.* iv (1912), 351 ff.

18 J. E. A. Jolliffe, in *Pre-Feudal England, The Jutes* (1933).

19 H. L. Gray, *English Field Systems* (1915), c. vii, esp. 415; and G. Slater, in *V.C.H. Kent*, iii. 323 ff.

20 It is worth mentioning that the contrast between the Kentish fields and those of the Anglo-Saxons reproduces a contrast which had once existed between the enclosed rectangular fields of west and north Jutland and the open fields with strips of the Elbe lands. This is a point which has only recently been indicated. (See G. Hatt, 'Pre-historic Fields in Jylland', in *Acta Archaeologica*, ii (1931), 122–56.) What makes it difficult to use this as

an argument for the Jutland home of the Jutes is that the evidence at present available assigns these rectangular Jutland fields to the early rather than to the late Iron Age. In a private letter Professor Hatt reports that he has found reason to think that certain fields of this type (south of Marager, Jutland) may have been occupied till the fifth century A.D. Compare also a note on ancient fields in Holland apparently similar to the 'Celtic' fields of England, by van Giffen in *Antiquity*, ii (1928), 85.

[21] Note, however, J. K. Wallenberg, *Kentish Place-Names* (1931), and *The Place-Names of Kent* (1934).

[22] Ekwall, *E.P.N.I.* 34, 107; Karlström (1927).

[23] Ekwall, *E.P.N.I.* 107.

[24] See Leeds, 116–20; B.B. iv. 744–51.

[25] A recent contribution to the subject is that of Schütte. Arguing from the river names of Kent, Holstein, and Mecklenburg, he concludes (ii. 238) that 'the large majority of Hengest's . . . followers were not Jutes but Saxons'.

IV. THE FIRST STAGE OF THE SAXON AND ANGLIAN CONQUESTS

[1] *E.P.N.S.* vi and vii (1929–30), esp. xxiv; Ekwall, *E.P.N.I.* 109; A. Mawer, *Problems*, 15–19.

[2] B.B. iv. 674.

[3] See in *E.P.N.S.* vi. xiv, some arguments of H. M. Stenton for accepting Cissa as a son of Ælle.

[4] *V.C.H. Surrey*, i. 260–2; *V.C.H. Sussex*, i. 345; Leeds, 45–9; B.B. iv. 688–90; *Arch.*, 2nd ser., liv. 369–82; lv. 203–14. Leeds, in *Ant. Journ.* xiii (1933), 229 ff., explains the typological development of the floriated cross design of the round brooches differently from the development indicated in my Pl. 22.

[5] Leeds, 56; B.B. iii. 261; Åberg, 13.

[6] *Archaeology*, 60.

[7] *History*, x. 105.

[8] Leeds, 58–9; also in *Arch.* lxiii (1912), 159–202; Åberg, 16–24; B.B. iii. 274–8; R. Smith, in *B.M. Guide*, 33–6.

[9] *P.S.A.*, 2nd ser., iii. 136; *Arch.* xlii (1869), 417–85, and xlv. 405–10; *Ant. Journ.* i (1921), 87–97.

[10] Leeds, in *Arch.* lxiii. 173; B.B. iii. 52; iv. 645, 662 ff.

[11] *Arch.* lxxiii (1923), lxxiv. 73–105. Cf. E. T. Leeds, in *History*, x (1925), 101.

[12] *Ant. Journ.* viii (1928), 177 ff.; F. Roeder, *Typol.-Chronol. Studien*, 54.

[13] *History*, x (1925), 97 ff.; and in *Ant. Journ.* xiii (1933), 229–51. Cf. Leeds, 54–5.

[14] For what follows see Leeds, *Archaeology*, 78–82; *Ant. Journ.* xiii. 229–51; B.B. iv. 621–2; Fox, 237–96, esp. 276 ff.; E. J. Hollingworth and M. M. O'Reilly, *Anglo-Saxon Cemetery at Girton College, Cambridge* (1925); Lethbridge, 76–7.

[15] F. Roeder, *Die sächsische Schalenfibel der Völkerwanderungzeit* (1927); 'Die sächsischen Fenstergefässe', in *R.G.K.*, xviii *Bericht* (1928), 149 ff.; 'Die Henkelgussurnen', in *Mannus, Zeitschrift für Vorgeschichte*, Ergänzungsband, vi (1928), 190–201; *Typologisch-chronologische Studien zu Metallsachen der Völkerwanderungzeit* (1930).

[16] See G. H. Wheeler, *E.H.R.* xli. 497–503; R. W. Chambers, 94–6; E. K. Chambers, *Arthur*, cc. 1 and 6; de la Borderie, in *Rev. Celt.* vi (1883), 1 ff.

[17] For an excellent summary of this subject see E. K. Chambers, *Arthur*.

[18] By W. G. Collingwood, in *Antiquity*, iii (1929), 292–8.

[19] T. C. Lethbridge, in *Man.* xxxi (1931), 247; E. K. Chambers, *Arthur*, 197–204.

[20] Lot, in *Mélanges*, 19.

[21] W. H. Stevenson, in *E.H.R.* xiv (1899), 32–46.

[22] A. S. Napier, in *Modern Language Notes*, xii (1897), 110–11.

[23] Cf. Plummer, ii. 14; W. H. Stevenson, art. cit.; and O. G. S. Crawford, in *Antiquity*, v (1931), 457.

[24] Plummer, *Bede*, ii. 28.

[25] *Bretons et Anglais au Ve et VIe siècles* (P.B.A. (1930)), p. 6.

[26] Cf. R. W. Chambers, *Beowulf* (1932), 411–17.

[27] See H. Sweet, *Oldest English Texts* (E.E.T.S. lxxxiii (1885), 169–71). For Wessex cf. G. H. Wheeler, in *E.H.R.* xxxvi. 161 ff.; H. M. Chadwick, *Origin*, 23–5.

[28] To these may be added Cerdices-beorh (Cerdic's barrow) mentioned in Kemble, *C.D.*, no. 1077.

[29] In *Antiquity*, v (1931), 441 ff.

[30] Oman, 225.

[31] *History*, x (1925), 108.

[32] To see that heathen cemeteries are not a reliable test of heathen settlements, first look at a map of the Saxon cemeteries (that of the Ordnance Survey when published will be the best). Then note (1) that the Severn valley was apparently conquered in the years following 577, about two generations before the Conversion of Wessex; (2) that the West Saxon conquest had advanced so far into the south-west of Britain that by 658 they pretty certainly had overrun Somerset and, according to the learned editors of the English Place-Name Society, also the Vale of Taunton; (3) that sometime before 663 Winchester was made the see of the bishop of the West Saxons, and that the district must presumably have been settled by the Saxons for some generations before that event. (Cf. *E.H.R.* vii. 438, for evidence from church dedications.) It seems therefore that in all these three directions there must have been large tracts of territory settled by heathen Saxons who left no trace of themselves in heathen burials. It is not enough to say that grave-furnishing went out of fashion shortly before the Conversion. The fashion could just as well have changed at an earlier date.

[33] See Mrs. M. E. Cunnington, 'Wiltshire in Pagan Saxon Times', in *Wilts. Arch. and Natural Hist. Mag.* xlvi (1933), 147–75, esp. 152–7, and references there given to recent excavations.

[34] Coins of Honorius (A.D. 395–423) have been found under the dyke. For references see Kendrick and Hawkes, 295.

[35] Two of the facts which must be weighed by any one wishing to speculate on this subject are:

(1) In Roman times Hampshire had been a land of 'villas' in contrast to Salisbury Plain, a land of native villages.

(2) The reason for this contrast is probably that the chalk of Hampshire is overlaid with non-calcareous soils, and that when left to nature it produces scrub. The scrub which had deterred cultivators before the Roman period may also have deterred Saxon invaders at this first settlement.

[36] In order to avoid confusing the reader, I have in these and in subsequent pages accepted the statement of the Alfredian Chronicle as it has come down to us that Cynric was the son of Cerdic. The probabilities are, however, that the name of Creoda has dropped out, and that Cynric was really Cerdic's grandson and not his son. See Stevenson, 159; Chadwick, *Origin*, 24.

[37] E. Ekblom, *Place-Names of Wiltshire*, 19; Grundy, in *Arch. Journ.* lxxv (1919), 187–8.

[38] O. G. S. Crawford, *Air Survey and Archaeology* (1928), esp. 7–8; and *Wessex from the Air* (1928).

[39] E. T. Leeds, in *History*, x (1925), 107 ff.; O. G. S. Crawford, in *Antiquity*, i. 251. Cf. also A. Major and E. J. Burrow, *Mystery of Wansdyke* (1926), esp. 138 ff. and bibliography; O. S. Taylor, in *Trans. Bristol & Glos. Arch. Soc.* xxvii. 131–55. Sir C. Oman, in *Quarterly Review*, vol. 253 (1929), esp. 297–8, assigns the dyke to the sixth century, and thinks it was thrown up by Constantine of Dumnonia against Aurelius Caninus.

[39a] Cf. R. E. M. Wheeler, in *Antiquity*, viii (1934), 290 ff.; also the forthcoming London Museum publication, *London and the Saxons*.

[40] *Ant. Journ.* x (1930), 387–8.

[41] In *E.P.N.S.* I. i. 52.

[42] Leeds, 43.

[43] *J.R.S.* i. 170.

[44] See R. E. M. Wheeler's Introduction to R.C.H.M., *Roman London*, 64–6. The substance of what follows was written before the publication of *Roman London* noticed above.

[45] Sweet, in *Englische Studien*, ii. 310; W. H. Stevenson, *E.H.R.* xiv (1899), 38, n. 29.

[46] e.g. Oman, 230.

[47] *The Roman Occupation of Britain*, 278.

[48] See Hübner, *Inscriptiones Britanniae Christianae, passim.*

[49] See Gordon Home, *Roman London*, 150–2.

[50] R.C.H.M., *Roman London*, 65.

51 *Bede*, ii. c. 7.

52 Ekwall, *E.P.N.I.* 114–15.

53 *Bede*, ii. c. 3.

54 References in *V.C.H. Essex*, i. 316; Chadwick, *Institutions*, 276, and *Origin*, 59.

55 *Origin*, 87–8.

56 F. M. Stenton, in *Essays presented to R. L. Poole* (1927), 139.

57 *A Handbook of the Pre-historic Archaeology of Britain* (1932), 64.

58 So F. Elgee, *Early Man in North-East Yorkshire* (1931), 219–20.

58a Leeds, 71.

59 For the beginnings of Bernicia see Leeds, 71–2; B.B. iv. 752–61 and 810–13; Oman, 188–92; *Northumberland County History*, x. 12–13; Watson, *Celtic Place-Names of Scotland*, 127 ff.

60 Information supplied by Mr. R. C. Bosanquet.

61 Leeds, 72.

62 *Bede*, v. c. 24.

63 *Nennius*, c. 61, 201.

64 Into Chronicle A (the Parker MS.). Thence copied into E (Peterborough MS.).

65 B.B. iv. 760.

V. GENERAL CHARACTER OF THE SAXON CONQUEST

1 D. C. Whimster, *Archaeology of Surrey* (1931), 177; Hollingworth and O'Reilly, *Girton*, 15–17.

2 Oman, 213–14; cf. R. V. Lennard in *History*, xviii. 204–15.

3 e.g. E. T. Leeds, 17; G. Sheldon, *The Transition from Roman Britain to Christian England*, 54.

4 *Origin*, 88–9, see also 296–302. Cf. Hoops, i. 89–90.

5 I owe these remarks on the dialects to Mr. C. L. Wrenn.

6 Leeds, 73 ff.; B.B. iv. 597 ff., 617, 626; Fox, 284–95.

7 Cf. B.B. iv. 570 and 581. Leeds, in *Ant. Journ.* xiii. 238.

8 Quoted from Widukind (i. 1) by Chadwick, *Origin*, 92.

9 Zachrisson, 76 ff.

10 *J.R.S.* xviii (1928), 118.

11 e.g. E. C. Curwen, in *Antiquity*, i (1927), 261 ff.; ii (1928), 168–72; A. M. Raistrick and S. E. Chapman, in *Antiquity*, iii (1929), 165 ff.; R. Eckford in *P.S.A. Scot.* (1928–9), 110–18; H. E. K. Jones and M. E. C. Mitchell in ibid. (1932–3), 70–81.

12 See B.B. iii. 51–2; 130 ff.; iv, 643, 683, 695, 732, 741, 802, &c.; *V.C.H. Essex*, i. 319–27; Rolleston in *Arch.* xlv. 4.

13 *J.R.A.I.* xlv (1915), 107.

14 See Mawer, *Problems*, 2–5.

15 Ibid. 3–4. See also the prefaces of the *E.P.N.S.* volumes, *passim*; also Zachrisson, 47 ff.

[16] See E. Ekwall, *English River-Names* (1928), esp. xlvii and lxxxix.

[17] *E.P.N.S.* viii. xx.

[18] M. Förster, in *Texte und Forschungen* . . . 119–243.

[19] For what follows see J. Beddoe, *The Races of Britain* (1885); Ripley, *Races of Europe* (1900), 319 ff.; Fleure, *Races of England and Wales*, 98 ff.; G. M. Morant in *Biometrika*, xviii. 75–104.

[20] It should, however, be noted that Beddoe's results are in part confirmed by an independent inquiry conducted by W. Bradbrooke and F. G. Parsons (*J.R.A.I.* lii (1920), 113–26), who compiled statistics about applicants at Bletchley for employment on the L. and N.W. Railway.

[21] Morant, 181–2.

[22] G. Des Marez, *Le Problème de la colonisation franque* (1926), 82 ff.

[23] *Germania*, c. 33.

[24] Bede, iv. c. 16.

[25] Ibid., ii. c. 20.

[26] H. J. Randall, in *Edinburgh Review*, vol. 242 (1925), 355.

[27] Zachrisson, 64; referring to Fox, 282, 320, &c.

[28] Stevenson, 241.

[29] H. D. Buxton, in *Ant. Journ.* i (1921), 95–6.

[30] Gildas, c. 21.

[31] Ibid. c. 6.

[32] See Cabrol, xi. 960 ff., for theories and bibliography of this migration.

[33] Nennius, c. 56.

VI. THE SECOND STAGE OF THE CONQUEST

[1] Eddius, c. xlii.

[2] *E.P.N.S.* III (1926), xiv; G. H. Wheeler in *E.H.R.* xli (1926), 501–2.

[3] *E.P.N.S.* iii. 155–6. Cf. article on this campaign by W. M. Hughes in *Antiquity* (1931), 291–314.

[4] *Op. cit.* xiv and ii. The reasons for questioning the judgement of the editors in this case are (1) the spelling of the name by Ethelweard, *M.H.B.* 504, a point which I owe to Mr. Lethbridge, and (2) the opinion of W. H. Stevenson. Even if the opinion of the editors of the *E.P.N.S.* is accepted, the argument in the text is scarcely affected, since they suppose the battle to have been fought 'in the district east of the Middle Thames'.

[5] *E.P.N.S.* IV. xiv, note; cf. Chadwick, *Origin*, 5–6.

[6] Oman, 286.

[7] Grundy in *Arch. Journ.*, 2nd ser., xxv (1918), 175–8.

[8] See vol. ii, p. 721; and cf. G. H. Wheeler in *E.H.R.* xxvi (1921), 161 ff., and xli (1926), 497 ff.

[9] E. Ekwall, *Place-Names of Lancashire* (1922), 231. Cf. the same author's *Scandinavians and Celts in the North-West of England* (1918), 6.

[10] c. 63.

[11] Cf. A. P. Forbes, *Lives of St. Ninian and St. Kentigern* (1874), lxxv, lxxvii,

212 ff.; H. Zimmer, *Nennius Vindicatus* (1893), 78 ff.; Chadwick, *H.A.* (1912), 105–9; *G. of L.* i. 151, 156; &c.

12 Chadwick, *G. of L.*, i. 109, 102 ff.

13 Lloyd, 162–71; Chadwick, *G. of L.*, i. 527; Skene, *Four Ancient Books of Wales*, i. 374–409, especially 376–7.

14 The authorities differ about the date of Ælle's death. I have followed Bede, *De temporum ratione*, in *M.G.H. Chron. Minora*, iii (ed. T. Mommsen), 309, as against the *Saxon Chronicle*, which assigns it to 588.

15 i, c. 34.

16 E. Ekwall, *Scandinavians and Celts in the North-West of England*, p. 2, thinks that the northern part of Cumberland was probably conquered by Ethelfrith but that 'the southern part perhaps remained British till the time of Ecgfrith (671–85)'.

VII. HEATHEN SOCIETY

1 i. 76. 2 *Origin*, 154-8.

3 Jolliffe, 71; cf. Chadwick, *Institutions*, 167, 347; Brünner, ii. 14 n.

4 *Laws of Wihtred*, c. 21; *Ethelbert*, c. 25. Here and in other quotations from the Laws, I generally follow, with permission, the translation of Mr. F. L. Attenborough, *The Laws of the Earliest English Kings* (Cambridge University Press, 1922).

5 Chadwick, *Origin*, 78; *Institutions*, 105–14 and 156.

6 c. 51. 7 c. 42.

8 For the controversies surrounding the poem see R. W. Chambers, *Beowulf* (2nd ed. 1932), giving in Part V an account of 'Recent Work on *Beowulf* to 1930', and on pp. 538 ff. 'Additions to the Bibliography to 1930'. See also the annual summaries given in *The Year's Work in English Studies*. The best summary of modern views for the general reader will be found in W. Lawrence, *Beowulf and Epic Tradition* (1928).

9 Chadwick, *Origin*, 157.

10 Chadwick, *Institutions*, 288.

11 Oman, pp. 357–8.

12 See Liebermann, ii. 424–30, for references; also Brünner, i. 186–95; A. G. Little, in *E.H.R.* iv (1889), 23–9; M. Larsen, *The King's Household* (1904), 76–88; Beck, in *E.H.R.* xxvi (1911), 555.

13 Chadwick, *Origin*, 160.

14 *Kindred and Clan* (1913), esp. cc. 7 and 8; cf. Pollock and Maitland, ii. 240 ff.; Chadwick, *H.A.* c. xvi. For the Germanic views of the nineteenth century see Kemble, i. c. ii; Stubbs, *C.H.* i. 87 f. See also P. Vinogradoff, *G. of M.* 135–40, 241–2; Seebohm, *T.C.* esp. cc. 3 and 15; Liebermann, ii, *s.v.* 'Sippe'; Brünner, i (1906), 110 ff.

15 Mawer, *Problems*, 115–16.

16 See *E.P.N.S.* i, Part ii (1924); G. B. Grundy, *Saxon Charters of Worcestershire* (1931), iii–viii.

17 *Archaeologia*, lxxiii (1923), 147; lxxvi (1926), 59–80. For other house-sites cf. Kendrick and Hawkes, 323–4; T. C. Lethbridge and C. F. Tebbutt, in *Proc. Cambridge Ant. Soc.* xxxiii (1933), 133–51.

18 *Ant. Journ.* vii (1927), 141; Lethbridge, 84. 19 So Lethbridge, 84.

20 Lethbridge, 80. For English dress in the heathen period see B.B. iii. 372 ff. Cf. also Hoops, iii. 58–64; iv. 345–6.

21 *V.C.H. Bucks*, i. 199–204; *B.M. Guide*, 63–5; Åberg, 10–1. Also Lindqvist, 130–3, and T. D. Kendrick in *Antiquity*, vii (1933), 437, pointing to an earlier date.

22 E. T. Leeds, in *Ant. Journ.* iv (1924), 113–25.

22a This brooch is admittedly the finest piece of Anglo-Saxon jewellery in existence and is in the Museum at Liverpool. I must warn my readers against paying a visit to the Museum in the hope of seeing the brooch, since it is not exhibited to the public but is kept locked up in a safe.

23 B.B. iv. 517. 24 *Boethius*, 40.

25 'The foe' may be the ox. Tupper, *Riddles of Exeter Book*, 115; Gordon, 327.

26 Grein-Wülker, i. 338–52; Gordon, 341–7. Here and in other quotations from OE. poetry, I generally follow, with permission, the translation of Professor R. K. Gordon, *Anglo-Saxon Poetry* (Everyman's Library, Messrs. J. M. Dent & Sons).

27 Wihtred, c. 28; Ine, c. 20.

28 A. J. Wyatt and R. W. Chambers, *Beowulf*, 158–9.

29 For the following section on Anglo-Saxon heathenism see Philippson, with bibliography of the subject. The English reader may be recommended P. D. C. de la Saussaye, *The Religion of the Teutons* (1902); E. K. Chambers, *The Medieval Stage* (1903), cc. v and xi; Chadwick, *Origin*, cc. x and xi; and the older classics, Kemble, c. xii, and J. Grimm, *Teutonic Mythology*, 4 vols., ed. J. E. Stallybrass (1880–8).

30 Mawer, *Problems*, 59–61.

31 *Opera* (ed. Giles), vi. 139–342, c. 14.

32 Quoted from Chadwick, *Origin*, c. 11, where the subject is fully discussed. See also R. W. Chambers, *Beowulf* (1932), 68–86, 314–22.

VIII. PART I. THE CONVERSION, TO 633

1 For general bibliographies of Celtic Christianity see *C.M.H.* ii. 791–2; Gougaud, xviii-lv; Kenney, i, *passim.*

2 *Vita S. Samsoni*, c. 7.

3 Rhygyfarch's 'Vita Davidis', in *Y Cymmrodor*, xxiv (1913), §§ 22 f., trans. by A. W. Wade-Evans, *Life of St. David*, 15; J. Vendryes in *Rev. Celt.* xlv (1928), 140–4.

[4] Bede, ii, c. 2. [5] H. C. Lawlor, *Monastery of St. Mochaoi* (1925).

[6] See preface of J. T. Fowler in his *Adamnani, Vita S. Columbae* (1920).

[7] See reasons for identifying this book with that in the Museum at Dublin, in *P.R.I.A.* xxxiii. 241–436.

[8] Adamnan, *Secunda Praefatio*.

[9] Adamnan, i, c. 3. [10] Ibid., ii, c. 22.

[11] *Irish Liber Hymnorum*, ed. J. H. Bernard and R. Atkinson, ii. 49–51 and 208–12. Translation by N. J. D. White in his *St. Patrick* (1929), 61–71; L. Gougaud in *Bulletin d'ancienne littérature et d'archéologie chrétiennes*, i. 271–2; ii. 38–41, 101–7; Kenney, 272–4.

[12] *Life of Gregory* by a Monk of Whitby, extract in Plummer, *Bede*, ii. 390. Emendation of P. Ewald in *Historische Aufsätze . . . an G. Waitz gewidmet*, 48.

[13] It is still reasonable to follow Bede rather than Gregory of Tours in the chronology of Ethelbert's reign. For other views see G. H. Wheeler, in *E.H.R.* xli (1926), 501–2, and H. H. Howorth, *Augustine the Missionary*, 39–40.

[14] Note on the maps showing Supremacies. It will be convenient to notice here some unsatisfactory features of the map on p. 261 and of similar maps on later pages. To illustrate the element of guesswork in these maps, it should be understood that the only reasons for showing the territory of the Hwicce as part of the *imperium* of Ethelbert are the inferences that Ethelbert's safe-conduct protected Augustine when he travelled west to confer with the Welsh, in Wessex, and that the Hwicce were a dependency of Wessex.

Bede's patriotism or his admiration for the first Christian kings of Northumbria leads him into some exaggeration when he speaks of the empires of Edwin and Oswald. In Book ii, c. 5, he says that Edwin had 'the overlordship over all the peoples who inhabit Britain, alike English and British, except only the people of Kent'. If this is taken literally it means that all the princes of Wales and the other Celtic princes from Cornwall to the Clyde bowed to him—a claim which can scarcely have corresponded to the facts. His statements about Oswald are less clear and less probable. He says that Oswald was the sixth who held *imperium*—'et ipse Nordanhymbrorum rex Christianissimus hisdem finibus regnum tenuit'. Since, as Plummer rightly points out (ii. 86), Bede carefully distinguishes between *regnum* and *imperium*, this passage tells us nothing about Oswald's *imperium*. But in Book iii, c. 6, Bede says of Oswald 'Denique omnes nationes et provincias Brittaniae, quae in iv linguas, id est Brettonum, Pictorum, Scottorum, et Anglorum, divisae sunt, in dicione accepit'. This statement accords ill with what little we know of Wulfhere's power in the Midlands and of the power of the Welsh princes both before and after Oswald. It also seems at variance with the statement in Book ii, c. 5, which implies that Oswy was the first to reduce the Picts and Scots and make them tributary. However, some support for Bede comes from Adamnan, who says (i, c. 1), 'Postea totius Britanniae imperator a deo ordinatus est'.

Again, Bede's information is incomplete. For instance, he makes no mention of the kings of the Lindisware (i.e. of Lindsey). I have, with some hesitation, followed F. M. Stenton's view in *Essays... to Tout*, 136–50, that the list of these kings preserved by 'Florence' of Worcester indicates that Lindsey was, till the extinction of its monarchy in the eighth century, probably part of the *imperium* and not of the *regnum* of one or other of its two neighbours.

The existence of a local dynasty is a good but not a sufficient test for distinguishing *imperium* from *regnum*. Thus there were kings in Kent and Essex throughout the reign of Offa; but the Kentish charters of the period and the inscriptions on the coins suggest that the effective power in Kent was exercised by Offa himself; and if this was true of Kent, it was also in all probability true of Essex and of the other south-eastern kingdoms. When a king delegated power in a sub-kingdom to a son or near kinsman (e.g. Penda to Peada or Egbert to Ethelwulf) I have generally assumed that the effective authority remained with the overlord.

In most Anglo-Saxon institutions there was little that was well defined, and one may therefore infer that there was also an absence of logical distinction between *regnum* and *imperium*.

Names of lesser principalities (e.g. of the Gyrwe in the Fen district), and especially those in Wales, are omitted from the maps so as not to crowd them.

The political conditions existing in the west of the island from the Mersey to the Clyde are especially obscure.

To conclude, though my maps correct those of Green in many particulars, I cannot pretend that they are satisfactory. Here as elsewhere it is better to make mistakes than to leave complete blanks.

15 Bede, i, c. 23.

16 Bede, i, c. 25.

17 *Greg. Ep.*, ii. 304.

18 Ibid., i. 431.

19 *Bon., Ep.* 3, 271–2; Kylie, 52–4.

20 Bede, i, c. 27.

21 Cf. vol. ii. 427–9.

22 Bede, i, c. 30.

23 Ibid., ii, c. 20.

24 The date of Augustine's death may be 605. Cf. Plummer, *Bede*, ii. 81.

25 Bede, ii, c. 5.

26 *Laws of Ethelbert*, cc. 21, 27, 54.

27 See Sir C. R. Peers in *Antiquity*, iii (1929), 65–74, and in *Arch.* lxxvii (1927), 201–17; B.B. ii, 2nd ed. (1925), c. 4; Clapham, 16 ff., 85–6.

28 Bede, i, c. 33.

29 Clapham, 33.

30 Watson, 340–1.

31 Bede, ii, c. 16.

32 Ibid.

33 Ibid. iii, c. 1.

34 J. B. Lightfoot, *Leaders in the Northern Church* (1890), 11.

35 Cf. Bede, *Hist. Abb.*, c. 3 in Plummer, i. 366.

VIII. PART II. THE CONVERSION (*contd.*)

1 Bede, iii, c. 24.

2 Or perhaps the lower Trent. It is doubtful whether Lindsey passed to Mercia in 658 or later. *V.C.H. Lincoln*, ii. 247.

3 Eddius, c. 20.

4 Bede, iv, c. 21.

5 So Adamnan (i, c. 1). Bede says 'with a large band'.

6 Bede, iii, c. i, implies that the battle was fought and Cadwallon killed at Denisesburna. The burn later known by that name, some three miles south of Hexham, is strangely far from Heavenfield.

7 Ibid. iii, c. 5.

8 Ibid. iii, c. 3.

9 Ibid. iii, c. 21.

10 Ibid. iii, c. 7.

11 Ibid. iii, c. 22.

12 The complicated points at issue are well summarized in Plummer, *Bede*, ii. 348–52; and in Gougaud, 185–201.

13 Bede, iii, c. 23.

14 For the Conference of 664 see Bede, iii, cc. 25 and 26; and Eddius, c. 10.

15 Authorities differ on this point. For a summary see L. Gougaud, 201–6.

16 Bede, iv, c. 4.

IX. THE GOLDEN AGE

1 Bede, ii, c. 1.

2 Eddius, c. 15. For different views about the positions of Chad and of Wilfrid see G. F. Browne, *Theodore and Wilfrid*, 34–50, 94–9; R. L. Poole in *E.H.R.* xxxiv (1929), 8–10; J. L. G. Meissner, *The Celtic Church in England* (1929), c. ii. The reasons why it is impossible now to discover the rights and wrongs of the situation are (1) that Bede and Eddius do not agree, and while Bede was the more truthful, Eddius, having long been in close contact with Wilfrid, may have been more fully informed; and (2) that there was, no doubt, genuine confusion at the time, owing partly to quarrels between Oswy and his under-king Alchfrith, the special patron of Wilfrid, and partly to the fact that the Northumbrians as yet were more accustomed to Celtic than Roman ideas of episcopacy. Oswy, in having Chad consecrated bishop as well as Wilfrid, probably did not realize that according to Roman ideas each should have a clearly defined diocese.

[3] Bede, iv, c. 2.

[4] The date is usually given as 673. For its correction see R. L. Poole in *J.T.S.* xx (1918), 22.

[5] Usually given as 680. Ibid. 33.

[6] I, c. xii in *H. and S.* iii. 173–203. For bibliography on the Penitentials see Kenney, i. 228–9, 239. Note also P. Fournier and G. le Bras, *Hist. des collections canoniques en occident* (1931), 50–65.

[7] See Chadwick, *Institutions*, 282–90.

[8] J. A. Robinson, *Somersetshire Essays*, 28–9.

[9] Ibid. 35.

[10] Ibid. 30; cf. *E.P.N.S.* VIII. xvi.

[11] *Crawford Charters*, pp. 1 and 44; W. Levison, *Vitae Sancti Bonifatii* (1905), xxix.

[12] *E.P.N.S.* VIII. xix–xx.

[13] Chadwick, *Institutions*, 286.

[14] Ine's Laws, cc. 63–8.

[15] cc. 23, 24, 32, 54.

[16] Bede, v, c. 7.

[17] Some of these statements rest on post-Conquest biographies and have been questioned. For the life and works of Aldhelm see bibliography in Schubert, 280–1; and Manitius, i. 134–42. The best Life in English is G. F. Browne's *St. Aldhelm* (1903).

[18] C. Singer, *From Magic to Science* (1928), 123 and 115. See also L. Gougaud in *Bulletin d'ancienne littérature et d'archéologie chrétienne*, i. 268.

[19] References in Manitius, i. 119–26.

[20] Ehwald, 488. Cf. Kenney, i. 227.

[21] Ehwald, 492; trans. of G. F. Browne, in *St. Aldhelm*, 263.

[22] Bede, v, c. 18.

[23] For bibliographies see Manitius, i. 142–52; Schubert, 281. The English reader will find a good biography in G. F. Browne's *Boniface of Crediton and his Companions* (1910).

[24] Ep. 98; translation of E. Kylie, *The English Correspondence of St. Boniface*, 99–100.

[25] Ep. 67; Kylie, 149–50.

[26] Ep. 29; Kylie, 110–11.

[27] E. Bishop, in *Transactions of the Devonshire Association for the Advancement of Science, Literature, and Art*, viii (1876), 512.

[28] *Vita Willibaldi*, in T. Tobler, *Descriptiones Terrae Sanctae ex saeculo VIII*, &c., p. 76; C. R. Beazley, *Dawn o Modern Geography*, i. 140–57.

[29] E. Dümmler in *Ep. Bon.* 238, note 2; Manitius, i. 141; R. Ehwald, *M.G.H. Auct. Antiq.* xv (1919), 522. Cf. L. Traube, *Carolingische Dichtungen* (1888), 132; H. Bradley in *E.H.R.* xv (1900), 291–2.

[30] See *Vita S. Guthlaci*, by Felix (composed 716–49), edited together with

the early OE. rendering in P. Gonser's *Das angelsächsische Prosa-Leben des Hl. Guthlac* (1909). Earlier editions by C. W. Goodwin (1848) and W. de G. Birch (1881).

31 A versified version of the *Life* (Grein-Wülker iii. 98 ff.) makes the young Guthlac a mere plunder-seeking outlaw.

32 Bede, iv, c. 27.

33 *Auct. Anon.* § 18.

34 J. L. G. Meissner, *The Celtic Church in England* (1929), c. x, argues that 'Lindisfarne remained outside the Northumbrian Church and under Celtic discipline' till 721. Cf. J. A. Duke, *The Columban Church* (1932), 103–5.

35 Plummer, *Bede*, I. xxx.

36 Eddius, c. 24.

37 With his see either at Ripon or at York. Cf. R. L. Poole in *E.H.R.* xxxiv (1919), 13–16, and J. L. G. Meissner, *The Celtic Church in England*, 70–5.

38 Eddius, c. 21.

39 Ibid., c. 17.

40 Ibid., c. 63.

41 Bede, *Hist. Abb.*, §. 1, in Plummer, i. 365.

42 Ibid., § 6, in Plummer, i. 369.

43 Ibid., § 11, in Plummer, i. 375.

44 Plummer, *Bede*, i. 396–8.

45 For the Life and Works of Bede, see Plummer's excellent introduction, *passim.* Bibliographies in Kenney, i. 230; Hoops, i. 189; Manitius, i. 70–87.

46 Edited by T. Mommsen in *M.G.H. Chronica Minora*, iii. 247.

47 Quoted by R. L. Poole in *E.H.R.*, xxxiv. 2.

48 Bede (ii, c. 2) speaks of the Britons as *gens perfida.* Cf. Faral, i. 513.

49 Quoted from Wattenbach by C. J. B. Gaskoin, *Alcuin* (1904), p. 32.

50 Peers in *Ant. Journ.* x (1930), 24–9.

51 B.B. ii. 105; Howorth, *G.D.* ii. 187–96. Cf. Clapham, 32–5.

52 B.B. ii. 128–32; Clapham, 38.

53 B.B. v. cc. 15, 16. See refs. there given to those who hold different views; also Brønsted, 92–3; F. Henry, *La Sculpture irlandaise* (1933), 62 ff.

54 Clapham in *Antiquity*, viii (1934), 43–57.

55 B.B. v. 375–6.

56 e.g. R. H. S. Macalister, *Archaeology of Ireland.* Cf. F. Henry, *La Sculpture irlandaise* (1933), *passim.*

57 References to the literature on the subject will be found in B.B. v. cc. 1–12; W. G. Collingwood, *Northern Crosses of the Pre-Norman Age* (1927); see also Brøndsted, 16–86; C. R. Peers in *P.B.A.* xii and in *Arch.* lxxiv (1923) 253–70; Clapham, c. 3.

58 Clapham, 61–9. Cf. W. G. Collingwood in *Antiquity*, vi (1932), 35–54.

59 Following mainly the translation in B.B. v. 219–20.

ADDITIONAL NOTES

P. 9, *Map of the Saxon Migration.*—The coast and forests of the region now known as Belgium are based on the map of G. Des Marez, in his *Le Problème de la Colonisation Franque.* The coast and water-ways of Frisia are based on the map of J. C. Ramaer, given in J. de Vries' *De Wikingen*, p. 17. The map represents the supposed conditions of the first centuries of our era; by the fifth century the sea had, no doubt, gained on the land. For the conditions of the coast of North Germany west of the Weser I rely on information kindly given by Dr. H. Schütte. He tells me that he is preparing geological maps of the region, showing the changes made from early ages. It seems that owing to the gradual sinking of the land the sea began to encroach about the first century of our era, and more considerably about the fourth century. But the serious inroads which in time formed the Zuider Zee, the Dollart, and the Jade Bay, only began in the Carolingian age. Dr. Schütte believes that the forests of North Germany extended up to the marshes, and that only the sandy districts were free of wood. For the forests in the middle of Germany I have used a map of O. Schlüter, given in Hoops's *Reallexicon*, I. Tafel 29. For the distribution of woodland in Angel (shown in more detail on the map on p. 5) we have careful studies by V. La Cour in his *Sønderjyllands' Historie*, vol. i, and in F. Mager's *Schleswig.*

The regions occupied by Foederati are those shown in E. Stein's map in his *Geschichte des Spätrömischen Reiches.*

P. 109, *Map of Mid-Britain.*—The course of the Ouse and the Cam and some other features of this map are based on the work of Major Gordon Fowler, who kindly lent me a map and articles of his now printed in the *Proceedings of the Cambridge Antiquarian Society*, vols. 33 and 34, and elsewhere. Major Fowler points out that in my map the coast-line of the Wash between the Welland and the Nene should have been shown two or three miles (sometimes more than that) inland of the existing coast-line. He also says that his investigations have not yet proved to what extent the Romans straightened out or diverted some of the natural rivers and streams of the Fenland.

The features of the Norfolk Broads I take from the maps of the *Cambridge Medieval History.* Mr. R. Rainbird Clarke, who is now studying these matters, points out that while the reconstructions of these maps are not improbable, they are not proven. I have also used B. Willson's *Lost England* for the coast-line south of the Broads.

All historians of this period must acknowledge their debt to the Ordnance Survey Map of Roman Britain for its attempt to mark the distribution of dense and sparse woodland. At the same time some of the uncertainties in the method adopted are brought out in the recent controversy about the loam terrains of South-East England in *Antiquity*, vii–viii.

The distribution of cemeteries and the dates assigned to the early grave-gear are based mainly on *The Arts in Early England* of Baldwin Brown and the articles of Reginald Smith in the volumes of the *Victoria County History*. I have, of course, attempted to bring their results up to date.

P. 129.—With reference to my guess that Cerdic's father may have been called in to help some local British leader against the Jutes among other possible enemies, it should be mentioned that this runs counter to some modern speculations. For example, Mr. O. G. S. Crawford, in *Antiquity*, v (1931), 444, calls attention to Asser's statement that Alfred's mother was descended from Stuf and Wihtgar, and that they were Jutes; and from the relationship between these two heroes and Cerdic, recorded in the Chronicle (anno 534—cf. above, p. 126), he infers that Cerdic was also a Jute. Where all is so uncertain it would be idle to labour the question, but the following are reasons which make me hesitate to accept Mr. Crawford's theory.

1. The word *nefan* of the Chronicle need only imply that a sister of Cerdic had married the father (? a Jute) of Stuf and Wihtgar.
2. Wihtgar with a name resembling the Latin *Vectis* seems, like the Port of Portsmouth, to owe his existence to the antiquarian speculations of Alfred's circle. He is not nearly so well authenticated as Cerdic, whose genealogy comes down from an earlier century.
3. 'The Jutish elements' in the cemetery at Harnham Hill are too slight to be a valid archaeological argument.

Some linguistic affinities between Kentish and Old West Saxon, noted by other writers, present a complex problem. They do not necessarily prove any original kinship between the peoples. The traditions of antagonism between the House of Cerdic and the Jutes are strong.

P. 137, *The fate of London and its hinterland.*—See three interesting articles on this subject by Dr. R. E. M. Wheeler and Mr. J. N. L. Myres in *Antiquity*, viii.

P. 149.—The map for the beginning of the Northern Kingdoms is based on Elgee, *Early Man in North-East Yorkshire*, and on his *Archaeology of Yorkshire*; also on an article by M. K. Clark in the *Yorkshire Archaeological Journal*, xxxi (1931); and on references kindly supplied me by Mr. W. F. Hedley. Since the map was drawn a new article by C. W. Phillips in the *Archaeological Journal*, xci (1935), 97–187, has shown that in Lincolnshire there were many more cemeteries, including some with cremation urns, than I have shown. In the other counties also intensive local studies are certain to increase the numbers of cemeteries on a distribution map.

The coast-line of southern Yorkshire I have copied from a map in T. Sheppard's *Lost Towns of the Yorkshire Coast*.

P. 154, *Head-piece. Detail from the Utrecht Psalter.*—This and other details from the Psalter have been taken from *The Illustrations of the Utrecht Psalter*, edited by E. T. Dewald (Princeton University Press, 1932). A complete facsimile of the Psalter was published privately. It is necessary to caution readers of this History against the idea which has often existed in the past that the Utrecht Psalter illustrates the fashions of the Anglo-Saxons. It seems to have been brought to England some time before A.D. 1000, but, as was shown by P. Durrieu in *Mélanges Julien Havet*, 646 f., it was produced in or near Rheims about the second quarter of the ninth century. It would therefore be much better to call it the Rheims Psalter than the Utrecht Psalter, since this last name only indicates the place where it has been for the last two centuries. It has been long obvious that the book derives from a Greek or Greco-Latin archetype of the fourth or fifth century.

A good modern account of the Psalter, with notes on previous discussions about it, will be found in articles by Mrs. G. R. Benson and Mr. D. T. Tselos in the *Art Bulletin*, xiii (1931), 11–79. These authors hold that the archetype must have been copied and certain western features introduced into the copy about the seventh or eighth century. 'The fusion of the Greek and Latin elements whether at one or two points certainly must have been done in the West,' probably by a Greek artist. This artist was, it seems, the master who gave life to his figures and well-balanced proportions to each crowded scene. The Utrecht Psalter itself was a copy in line technique of this intermediate work, and at least three, perhaps more, persons had a hand in it.

Several features in the drawings appear to be later than the fifth century, and there is at least one, 'The Globe-Mandorla,' in which the Christ-logos is surrounded, which must be a Carolingian addition. As a whole, however, the fashions and objects depicted are those of the fifth century or earlier. This being so, I am better justified in using the Psalter to illustrate my early than my later chapters.

It may be asked why drawings deriving from a Greek original should have any place whatever in a book about Saxon England. To this I can only reply that they are better than nothing, and for my purpose far better than the illustrations of the other manuscripts produced during these centuries in the West. Though they do not portray the fashions of Anglo-Saxon society, they do give vivid sketches drawn from men of the Dark Ages. They render them as living and moving beings; and a group of spearmen like that on p. 154 or a hunting scene like that on p. 539 gives the reader some idea of what was to be seen, whether in Britain or Gaul or the Eastern Empire.

Moreover, the Utrecht Psalter has a connexion with Anglo-Saxon England, even if it is only adventitious. From the influence of the Utrecht Psalter on another book of the Psalms (Harley MS. 603), made at Canterbury early in the eleventh century, it is commonly inferred that the Utrecht volume was brought to Canterbury during the Reform movement of the tenth century. The reason for placing its arrival so late is that Harley MS. 603 is the earliest English manuscript to reveal its influence. The argument is by no means conclusive. Few English illustrated manuscripts of any kind survive from the previous period, and it may be that the Utrecht book had been long in England before men were ambitious enough to try to copy its skilful drawings. The occasion of its arrival can only be conjectured, but to my mind the intercourse between the province of Rheims and England which occurred in the ninth century gave likely opportunities for the book to be brought to our island. When Ethelwulf visited the court of Charles the Bald and was married to his daughter by Hincmar, archbishop of Rheims, the Utrecht Psalter was nearly a new book. It is quite possible that Hincmar gave the book either to Judith or to Ethelwulf (we know of other books which he gave away). Or it may have been brought to England later on, when Grimbald became an intermediary between the churches of Rheims and England. In either case its pictures may have been seen and admired by Alfred. But however it came to England, my excuse for reproducing so many drawings from it is that they, though wrong in their details, give the best general idea of what men looked like in the Dark Ages.

P. 172, *Beddoe's statistics*.—A question which I put to Dr. G. R. de Beer, Jenkinson Lecturer in Embryology, about the value of the evidence of nigrescence received the following interesting reply:

'. . . The point raised is a very interesting one, and your remarks on p. 172 on the necessity for accepting Beddoe's conclusions with caution are well founded. I am bound to go further, and to say that the "evidence of nigrescence" is no evidence at all, for or against the survival of the Romano-British race.

'These are my reasons:

'1. The 13,000 deserters are not a representative sample of the whole population, but only of a particular small portion, socially undistinguished, probably economically unsuccessful, and almost certainly morally weak. Whatever statistics Beddoe may have got from a consideration of his deserters must be subject, either to confirmation, or to complete reversal, when compared with a truly representative sample of all classes of the population.

'2. When Beddoe wrote, the biological concept of heredity was still that of "blending inheritance", according to which the variance (visible effect of parental characters) was supposed to be halved at each successive generation, and the effect of any new infiltrations would be rapidly swamped into the general type of the stock which remained for that reason conservative.

'But it is now known that inheritance far from being blending is particulate, the characters being controlled by discrete factors (Mendelian genes) which can be shuffled about between one generation and the next, independently of all the other factors. Thus a man may have all the characters of a Nordic except that he may have black hair, just as a negro may be an albino. Here, therefore, the effect of variance is jealously conserved, and small infiltrations of new blood from other groups may be maintained in the population instead of being swamped. This constitutes a source of error so very much greater than it would be under the idea of blending inheritance that evidence of the original source of a population based on a few of its present characters may be very misleading.

'To establish the persistence of any racial type, therefore, it would be necessary to take into consideration not one but all the characters. This is unfortunately impossible, owing to the very complex mode of action of Mendelian factors in the human race, and to the extraordinarily mixed and "heterozygous" nature of almost all populations.

'3. (A corollary of (2).) There have not been wanting occasions since the Saxon Conquest on which persons carrying the factors for dark hair could have "inoculated" these factors into the British population. Libertine Spanish seamen or prolific Jewish women may well be expected to have produced "evidence of nigrescence" during fourteen centuries.'

P. 198, *Sketch of Bamburgh.*—The small hill in the left foreground of the sketch is one of two unexcavated pre-Anglian *tumuli* marked on the Ordnance Map (about 400 yards south of the main gateway). I am confident that the sea penetrated in the eighth century to near this spot. Its meanderings are a contribution of the artist.

P. 357, *Brixworth Church.*—A plan of the church in Clapham's *English Romanesque Architecture*, i. 34, shows less of the original building in the apse and in the wall of the South Chancel.

PRINTED IN
GREAT BRITAIN
AT THE
UNIVERSITY PRESS
OXFORD
BY
JOHN JOHNSON
PRINTER
TO THE
UNIVERSITY

Review by J.N.L. Myres in Arch. Journ. XCII. Pt One

Town names 163-164

THE ISLANDS

BOOKS BY STAN STEINER

The Islands: The Worlds of the Puerto Ricans

La Raza: The Mexican Americans

The New Indians

Co-editor (with Shirley Hill Witt)
The Way: An Anthology of American Indian Literature

Co-editor (with Luis Valdez)
Axtlan: An Anthology of Mexican American Literature

THE

ISLANDS

THE WORLDS OF THE PUERTO RICANS

STAN STEINER

PHOTOGRAPHS BY GENO RODRIGUEZ

HARPER & ROW, PUBLISHERS
NEW YORK
EVANSTON
SAN FRANCISCO
LONDON

1817

The following verses come from Roy Brown's songs from his long-playing record, *Yo Protesto* (Disco Libre Inc., Puerto Rico), translated by Maria Lopez Kelley and Stan Steiner: in Chapter 16, page 212, "The Stockholder," and page 213, "The Mind"; in Chapter 18, pages 259, 260, "Monon"; in Chapter 19, page 263, *"Paco Marquez."*

FIRST EDITION

Designed by Sidney Feinberg

Library of Congress Cataloging in Publication Data

Steiner, Stanley.
The Islands: the worlds of the Puerto Ricans.
Bibliography: p.
1. Puerto Rico—Civilization. 2. National characteristics, Puerto Rican. 3. Puerto Ricans in the United States. I. Title.
F1960.S74 917.295'03'53 72-9157
ISBN 0-06-014079-8

Grateful acknowledgment is made for permission to reprint excerpts from the following:

Lines of poetry in Chapter 5 come from "Black Dance" by Luis Pales Matos, originally published in Spanish in *Tuntún de Pasa y Grifería,* Biblioteca de Autores Puertorriqueños, Puerto Rico, 1937. Reprinted by permission.

Excerpts of mask maker story in Chapter 5 and *jíbaro* song in Chapter 7 come from *¡Hablamos! Puerto Ricans Speak* by Henrietta Yurchenco. Copyright © 1971 by Praeger Publishers Inc. Reprinted by permission.

Lines of poetry in Chapter 6 come from "Battle Hymn of the Republic (Brought Down to Date)" by Mark Twain from *Mark Twain: Social Critic.* Copyright © 1958 by Mark Twain Company. Published by International Publishers. Reprinted by permission.

Lines of poetry in Chapter 9, pages 112, 113, 125, and 134, come from "Pamphlet" (*Panfleto*") by Luis Muñoz Marín, translated by Muna Lee de Muñoz Marín from *The Anthology of Contemporary Latin American Poetry,* edited by Dudley Fitts. Copyright 1942 by New Directions Publishing Corporation. Reprinted by permission.

Lines of poetry in Chapter 9, page 134, come from "Umbrella" by Luis Muñoz Marín from *Poetry,* December 1924. Copyright 1924 by The Modern Poetry Association. Reprinted by permission.

Excerpt of news story in Chapter 29 comes from the New York *Daily News,* May 19, 1970. Copyright © 1970 New York News, Inc. Reprinted by permission.

Lines of poetry in Chapter 30 come from "The Library" by Felipe Luciano from *The Puerto Rican Poets,* edited by Alfredo Matilla and Ivan Silen. Bantam Books, Inc., New York. Copyright © 1971 by Felipe Luciano. Reprinted by permission.

Unless otherwise noted, translations from Spanish poems have been made by Barry Luby and Stan Steiner.

Contents

BOOK ONE

BOOK TWO

Illustrations

There is not one Puerto Rico. There are four Puerto Ricos. There is the Puerto Rico of the island. There is the Puerto Rico of San Juan. There is the Puerto Rico of the United States. And there is the largest Puerto Rico of all—the state of mind.

—An aged *jíbaro* on Calle Cristo
in Old San Juan

I would be Puerto Rican if I were born on the moon.

—A leader of the Young Lords Party
in New York

BOOK ONE

Prologue: Every Man Is an Island

"On the island a man may make love to a fruit. With his eyes. With his senses. With his hands."

He cupped his hands. In his palms he held two hands full of air, as in a bowl, that he molded and he fondled as though the warm and heavy air of the tropics were a clay to be shaped into an imagined fruit or a carved stone head of a Borinquén goddess or the face of his beloved.

The stone steps that he sat on had been worn by hundreds of men who for hundreds of years had sat and said the words of his dream: "On the island a man may make love to a fruit. . . ."

In the street the cobblestones were uneven as an old man's teeth. Christ Street, Calle Cristo, was one of the oldest built by Europeans in the Americas. On the hill of Old San Juan the street began at the plaza of the Church of San José, where the bones of Ponce de León lay by the altar and stood guard over La Perla, the Slum by the Sea, where the whores of the conquerors had lived for centuries; from there, the street ran down the hill to the Palace of the Governor, La Fortaleza, half a dozen streets away. The history of the island was in the street, in the sun.

The man sitting on the stone steps nodded at the passers-by. He was not silenced or embarrassed by them. In the old days, he said, Governor Luis Muñoz Marín often walked up the street but that would not halt a Puertorriqueño from sculpting his dream of the island out of the air with his hands.

"Life is real here," he said. "It has a taste, a shape. Even the air we breathe has a taste.

"If you hold life in the hand, can't you feel its shape?" he said. "Let us say a fruit; it has a feeling, it has senses of its own. The body of a fruit helps to define it, to give it meaning. But you have to hold it in your hand before you eat it. To feel it. To sense it. To enjoy it. To love it.

"And that is what I missed in New York City," he said. "In New York there is never time to hold anything in your hand."

He was a refugee, who had come home to his island as to his love.

In the Galería de Casa Blanca, the White House Gallery he owned on Calle Cristo in Old San Juan, halfway between "the whores and the tourists," he sat on his stone steps and remembered his youth. He had grown to boyhood in the days when the verandas were shaded with palm trees in Santurce, now the downtown shopping center of the city, no longer with verandas, no longer with palm trees. One day he had become a wanderlusting young man. "To be born a Puerto Rican is to be born a refugee," he said; and he had gone to New York to seek his fortune and awoke in Korea. In his muddy uniform he dreamed of walking on Madison Avenue in a clean Arrow shirt.

"So after the war I became an advertising man."

José Antonio Olivo Ferrer was an artist. In the advertising agency he became a spiritualist and a sorcerer. He became a connoisseur of a surrealist beer, as well.

"We invented reality. In New York everybody does.

"Let us say some corporation came to us with a beer. To advertise their beer we had to differentiate their beer from all other beers. So I would drink their beer. I would drink twenty beers, to taste the difference. There would be no difference. So we had to invent a difference. I would then illustrate the reality we had invented.

"It was unreal," he said. "New York was exciting. So many things were always happening. But they were not real things."

As he talked, a friend walked by. He was too nervous to sit. He was a writer and he asked: Who was I? Why was I writing this book?

To capture the cosmos of the island, I said.

"Cosmos?" He laughed. "We do not have a cosmos. We only have an island. Every man, here, is an island. Every man is his own world."

I remembered what a high school teacher, Ishmael Pérez, in the mountain town of Utuado had said to me: "If you live on an island, with the sea on all sides, you are alone. Not lonely, but alone. To live on an island is to be isolated. Everyone comes to us. Everyone uses us. They are powerful and we are small. We are a small island in the sea.

"But," said Ishmael Pérez, "no one can lift us out of the sea."

Every day, at dawn, the sea gave its shape to the island, as surely as the artist's hands molded the life they held. The sea defined the map of the island. There was a saying: *If you walk in any direction, you come to the sea, so you have to turn around and meet yourself walking in the other direction.*

What did that mean?

The writer said: "Nowhere on the island is any more than fifteen miles from the sea! The island simply is. It exists, as it is. You have to accept it, and you have to accept yourself.

"A man can hold the island in his hands."

He said this without sorrow or regret. Since he had come home "out of the cold"—he, too, had worked in New York—he sometimes wondered why he had come. But he was not unhappy; he was merely uneasy at being at ease.

"Life here is very sensual. It is too human, too sensual, too beautiful to think. That's why our thinkers have always gone into exile." He himself often went back to New York. "I need nervousness," he said, for he worked hardest "in a gloomy, dim, filthy, cold room somewhere in New York. The cold! It's what makes the Anglo-Saxon work so hard. Every Puertorriqueño has those two selves—warm and cold, Latin and Anglo.

"In the sun, everything is in the open. Every pore is open. Every thought. Our bodies are naked, even when we are dressed. Here it is always summer.

"We are too happy digesting life to eat it," and he laughed.

And yet had not the Japanese philosopher of the weather, Watsuji Tetsuro, in his book *Fudo* written of the hidden energies of the people on the islands of "eternal summer"? "Everyone thinks here at last is the place where summer never ends." *Summer never ends!* On these tropical islands "the monotony of [life] does not stem from emptiness. Rather it is a monotony full of content, of power," wrote Watsuji Tetsuro. "The monotony is not that of empty feelings on the part of men who take no interest in anything. Rather it is that of people who are ever agitated and burning with violent passions. Indeed, there would be startling changes if some way were found to break this mold and set this teeming power in motion."

I quoted this. The writer shrugged and walked away from the words.

José Antonio Olivo Ferrer stood up. He nodded with a quiet vigor. "Yes, it is so. When I came home, I thought I would be bored on the island. The island is so small. So I said to myself: Let's see what happens. But I have been here for eight years now. And I am not bored. It is a funny thing. An island is as small or as great as a man himself.

"Man is small," he said. "How much space on earth does a man need? As much space as he can hold in his hands."

1

The Lost Tribes of Borinquén

In the mountains a man could be free. He had the look of a man who had lived in the mountains for a long time. The squint in his deep eyes was full of distance. In the river, at the foot of the hill, the half-naked boys were swimming, but he saw instead the dead Borinquén Indians.

Was he an Indian? The Indians of Borinquén,* their name for Puerto Rico, had vanished hundreds of years ago. He could not be an Indian.

In the jungles of tropical flowers, where the two mountain streams came together, the water was clear as the sky. There was a fragrance of orchids.

"In the mornings they washed themselves here. They washed every morning. They were very clean," said the man from the mountains. He spoke of the dead Indians, who in the sixteenth century had bathed in the river. "A little ways down the river is—how do you

* The Indians had named the island *Boriquén*. When the Spaniards came, they mispronounced the name. For like all Europeans they had difficulty with the Indians' tongue. In his writing, Dr. Chanca, the physician on Columbus's second voyage, wrote it as *Burenquen*. And later chroniclers spelled it *Burinquin, Boriqui, Boricua, Burichena, Borichen, Borriquen, Boriguen, Boriquer,* and *Boluchen*. From these misspellings came the popular and equally incorrect modern form of Borinquén, used on the island today, which I, too, use.

According to the storyteller the real name of the island was none of these, but was *Tierra del Valiente Señor,* the Land of the Valiant Lord.

say?—a rapid water where to go to relieve themselves. So they do not dirty the water where they washed, they go there, where the river is bent," he said.

No one remembered these things. They had happened hundreds of years ago, before the Indians had abandoned their village by the river. Who had told him where the Indians had bathed and shit?

"It is something that I *know* by memory," he said.

When he spoke, each of his words was like a stone, hard and true. He talked about the rivers and trees and rocks on the island, as though they were his brothers. He talked like a man who had learned to live in the twentieth century reluctantly.

"If God had asked me," he said, "I would have liked to live in the fifteenth century. He did not ask me what I wished."

He had been born on a mountain not far from the river. In his village his family was one of the oldest and most respected, but he did not wish to use his name. I called him "the storyteller." That was what he really was, anyway.

On the river bank there was a *bija* tree. He picked a handful of its berries. The small red seeds were once used by the Indians to make a dye with which they painted their skins. "Not for decoration," the storyteller said, "but as insecticide." He squeezed the seeds and the red juice of the *annatto,* or *achiote,* dye ran into the crevices of his hand.

"Ay! You see!" he triumphantly said. "How red it is! It made our ancestors look redder than they were. So the Spaniards thought our people were red-skinned. *La gente colorada,* they called them. But actually the Indians were like us. They were light-skinned. How do you say?" He searched for the word: "They were light bronze."

"Like a lion's mane, the color of the Indians is reddish blonde," Father Bartolomé de las Casas wrote in his sixteenth-century *History of the Indies.* "And if they had worn clothes they would have looked almost as white as we [Spaniards]." Besides, the priest wrote, "they bathe frequently and keep very clean." It seemed a peculiar custom to the man from dry Iberia. When the women of the island gave birth, the priest went on in amazement, "they bathe in the river and are as clean and healthy as before giving birth." An early chronicler of these curious habits of the Indians of Borinquén noted the daily washing "before they put the red paint on their bodies." He thought the morning bath may have been a religious ritual, like the morning mass. If not, why else would they bathe *every* morning?

"On the island we still use the dye of the *achiote* seed religiously," the storyteller said. "We use it to dye our food. So inside we are still red as Indians."

In the meadow by the river the grass climbed the slope of the hill in green waves. Where it was greenest were the ruins of the Ceremonial Grounds of Caguanas. "This was one of our largest villages of Indians," the storyteller said. He pointed at some nearby fields. "And those fields were where the Indians grew their *maíz* and *tabaco.*" He spoke the words in the old tongue of the Indians, now called Arawak.

"Listen! Do you know how many words in the United States come from Puerto Rico?" he asked.

"No! You do not. I will tell you," he said. "Our people gave the world the names for many things, in Spanish and in English. *Canoa* for canoe. *Hamaca* (*amaca*) for hammock. *Maíz* for maize, the corn. *Tabaco* for tobacco. *Sabana* for savanna. *Cacique* for Indian chief. the *yucca* (yuca), the *papaya,* the *iguana,* the *key,* the *huracán* (hurricane). All those words come from the Indians of Borinquén.

"Even today we eat the fruits and the roots our Indians grew. So you could say our history is living inside our bodies. In our bones and in our blood. That is why I make the saying 'If you scratch a Puertorriqueño, inside of him you will find a Borinqueño.' Our history is only skin-deep."

On the mountain road from Lares to Utuado, the Ceremonial Grounds of Caguanas were the history book of the storyteller. They were his sanctuary. He often would come there to read about the past, in the rivers and trees and rocks, as a young man may go to a library to study. As a priest may go to a monastery to meditate.

All that day the storyteller had walked about the Indian ruins of the Ceremonial Grounds. The meadow was a vast, flat field that was fenced by rows of oblong slabs of rock. On some of these were the carved and painted moon-faced gods of the *piedras pintadas,* the painted rocks, of the Indians. In the fields there was a *batey,* a plaza, that had been unearthed by Dr. Ricardo Alegría, the director of the Institute of Puerto Rican Culture. He believed it was an ancient ball court, where the Indians had played a ceremonial game like soccer, using balls made of the resins of native trees, the first time any European had seen any kind of rubber, he said.

The culture of the Borinqueños was as gentle and diminutive as the island, thought Dr. Alegría. Nothing here was as "grandiose as the Aztecs or the Mayans," Dr. Alegría said. He did not believe that the ball courts were the ruins of a great Indian village.

"No! I disagree with what Señor Alegría says," the storyteller said. "In this place was the *yucayque* (*jucayque*), the village, of our great *cacique,* the Chief Guarionex. That is why the fields are here. That is why they built the *batey* so big. That is why there are so many Ceremonial Grounds here. How do I know this? I have been told this. That is why I know. Wherever there was a big *batey,* there was a big village."

The works of many learned men seemed to agree with the unlearned storyteller. In his *General and Natural History of the Indies,* written in the sixteenth century, Gonzalo Fernández de Oviedo (y Valdés) observed that "near each village there was a *batey,* or ball game." If there was a *batey,* there was also a village. Four hundred years later, one of the most famous anthropologists of his time, Jesse Walter Fewkes, who came to the island in 1899 on the heels of the U.S. Army, observed the same thing. In Utuado, wrote Fewkes, he found "several large villages," and near each was a *batey,* "where the Indians assembled for ceremonial and other dances."

The ball courts of Caguanas may not have been the scene of as innocent sport as it seemed. In the old chronicles of the Conquistadors there was evidence that the ball games played there were religious rites, in which victory or defeat decided not only the nature of messages to, and from, the gods, but the fate of sacrificial victims whose lives depended on the scores, as among the Mayans. Religious offerings of the dead, at the ball courts, continued *well into the twentieth century*. In 1903, when the anthropologist Fewkes revisited the Caguanas site, he was disturbed to discover: "The ground was very damp, not at all suitable for the preservation of the bones or any fibrous material. Nevertheless, we found ten skeletons of both adults and children with funeral vessels so distributed that they were very evidently offerings of the dead."

Even after the conquest of the island by the United States, the religious rites of the Borinquén Indians seemed to have survived at Caguanas, near Utuado. The "pagan rituals" of the dead caused the first American Governor to order the immediate building of modern cemeteries.

One wondered, in seeing the ancestral ball courts, how many of the sacred beliefs in ball games had reappeared in the fervent, almost religious devotion of the islanders to the game of baseball. When the idol of the islanders, Roberto Clemente, died in an airplane crash at sea, off San Juan at Christmastide of 1972, thousands gathered on the beaches to mourn him. The island was swept by a hurricane of grief, prayers, eulogies, and religious services. Even the newly elected Governor memorialized the sports idol in his inauguration speech, and canceled all the inaugural festivities, in his mourning; an unusual homage even for a baseball player.

"In the Institutes they do not know this history of the Indians," the storyteller said. "Who knows the history of the Indians? No one knows but the Indians." As long as the Indians lived, history was a living thing. He did not need books to know these things. Was history written in books, or in the blood of his ancestors who had lived it?

"Let me tell you the story of the cacique *Guarionex," he said. "It is not historically recognized. But it is what I have gathered out of the stories of the old people of this land, where I was born, and where my forebears have been born for five, or six, or more generations.*

"All of this land of Utuado, Adjuntas, Jayuya, and Lares was known as the lands of Otoao, in the beginning when the Spaniards came. The story goes that it was the name of an Indian chief, Otoao. In the Indian language Otoao means a 'valley between mountains.' That is appealing to geography. But, appealing to technology, it means Otoao was the ruler of

the 'valley between mountains.' So Otoao happens to be the name of the Indian chief in the land known as Otoao itself.

"In the beginning, as I said, Otoao was the ruler. So take it that way. Our Indians were very hospitable. They were people of peace. And they were not skeptical of the Spaniards. But the Spaniards came to conquer. In fact, they came after riches. The Indians did not think it that way. So they made friends with the Spaniards."

In the beginning, the Indians thought of the Spaniards as gods. At least, the Spaniards thought they thought so. "They entertain the idea that I have descended from heaven," wrote the delighted Admiral Cristóbal Colón, "and on our arrival at any new place they announce this, crying, 'Come, come, and look upon beings of a celestial race.' " Since the Admiral admittedly did not understand their language, they may have been crying something quite different. He may have confused the Indians' "astonishing affection and kindness" for the homage of the medieval peasants that he was familiar with in Spain.

"They are very simple and honest and exceedingly generous with what they have; none of them refusing anything he may possess when he is asked for it, but on the contrary inviting us to ask for it," Colón wrote in disbelief; for "They exhibit great love towards all others in preference to themselves."

"Whether the people possess any private property" was vague to the Admiral, "for I observed that one man had charge of distributing various things to the rest, especially meat and provisions and the like." It was all very strange. They behaved "like idiots," giving away "objects of great value," but they were not "slow or stupid, but of very great understanding."

The Admiral, who had come "in the name of Christ," decided that the Indians "might be led to become Christians."

"Among the Indians there was a sacrament that we call compadrazgo *in Spanish. In the Catholic way. In the Indian way it was named* guaitiao. *By the way of* compadrazgo *two people become related by a church sacrament. By way of* guaitiao *two people become related by blood. They cut a small cut in the wrists, under the wrists, and they cross both wrists, so the blood of one mixes with the blood of the other.*

"In that way, by the sacrament of the guaitiao, *they become* guaitiaos. *That means brothers of blood.*

"The Indians believe in this. But the Spaniards looked at it as a way to gain control of the Indians, morally and spiritually. In that way Otoao became the guaitiao *of Ponce de León. He changed his faith to the Catholic faith. He changed his name to the Christian name of don Alonso."*

Juan Ponce de León, dapper and goateed, looking more like Don Quixote than a Conquistador, came to govern Borinquén in 1508. He was befriended by the old *cacique* Agueybana the Elder, who could not have known that his new friend had come on orders of the King of Spain to conquer the island, and to denude it of its wealth.

On the banks of the Río Grande de Loíza the Spaniards discovered gold. In a joyous frenzy they forced the startled Indians to work in the placer and underground mines they established. By 1510 a smelter had been built, which on its first day refined 100,000 pesos' worth of gold. Ponce de León, who had become the first Governor of the island, celebrated by building a villa of stone, sending for his family, and changing the name of his settlement from Caparra to Puerto Rico, the Rich Port.

But the Indians, who must have thought the Spaniards had gone mad, kept running away from the mines. In an attempt to force the islanders to work, the Spaniards set up an *encomienda* system, in which the Indians were "given," by royal decree, to *patrones* who held them as half serfs, half slaves. The *cacique* Agueybana the Brave, a nephew of the old chief who had befriended Ponce de León, was "given" to the *patrón* Sotomayor, to work in his *encomienda* as a servant.

Soon there would be war. . . .

"And the Indians became skeptical of the Spaniards. They have been mistreated. They have been robbed of their land. They have been abused of their friendship. They have been made to work in the mines as a slave. But, more than that, their women have been abused by the Spaniards.

"So the cacique *Otoao fell in the estimation of the Indians by changing his name and his religion.*

"It was then the Indians had a new leader by the name of Guarionex. He had come to Borinquén from Santo Domingo, where he had experi-

enced fighting against the Spaniards. He had to flee there. So he came and established himself in the land of Otoao, where Caguanas is, actually. The yucayque *of Guarionex has never been discovered. But, if you study the geography of Caguanas, you have to concede this was the place the old people talked about. Anyway, Guarionex became the chieftain of the whole land that had been the domain of Otoao. That is how Guarionex was accepted as the leader of the Indians and was recognized by the Spaniards as their true foe.*

"Guarionex was the one who led the Indians in their battle against the town of Sotomayor. They burned the town."

The revolt of the Indians failed. Yet it was not a failure. Within a few days the Indians had killed "more than half of the Spaniards" on the island. Led by the *caciques* Guarionex, Urayoan, and Agueybana the Brave, they burned not only the town of Sotomayor, but other settlements. The mines were halted. The battle reports of the Conquistadors boasted of no more than a few hundred dead Indians. Most had safely escaped.

In 1511 the revolt began. In 1512 the Council of Catholic Bishops met in extraordinary session to reconsider "the rights of the Indians."

Not long after that, in 1521, the King of Spain, Emperor Charles V, issued his famous decree freeing all Indian slaves in the Indies. He may have acted for moral, as well as military, reasons. The *encomienda* system was doomed in Borinquén. It was exported to Mexico.

In the meanwhile, Guarionex had disappeared. . . .

"But he did not die in warfare in Puerto Rico. As a matter of fact, there is no tale of Guarionex being killed in battle. He was captured and taken on a ship to Spain, to show to the King that the rebellion had been finished. While the ship in which he was being taken to Spain was anchored outside the port of the Ozama River in Santo Domingo, a hurricane blew out. The ship was wrecked in the hurricane. All the crew and passengers drowned, except Guarionex and two Indian chieftains from Borinquén, prisoners like him, who escaped. They swam to safety. They gained the shore. They escaped.

"They escaped to the Virgin Islands and escaped capture. And that's about all that can be known about the great cacique *Guarionex."*

There was nothing more the storyteller wished to say.

His remembrance of history was a tribal memory. The details he knew—"Guarionex was a man *close* to six feet," he said—had come from the dim, unrecorded past, that was 460 years ago, almost to the day he told the old stories.

"All these stories I heard from old people. Who are already dead. Who have died," he cautiously said. "My grandfathers. I recall them. As a little boy I heard some of them. As a grown man I heard some. The old people used to tell legends and stories, I recall. From these things the old people tell me I gathered these stories about our history.

"Our Indians did not die away the way some people think," the storyteller said. "If you look in the faces of the *jíbaros,* you know somewhere the Indian history is living."

The scholars did not agree with the storyteller. His myths were not their myths. If "history is a fable, generally agreed upon," as Napoleon had said, the history of the Borinquén Indians was agreed upon by everyone but the Indians. It was said the Indians had vanished from the island by the sixteenth century. They had left behind their language, their music, their architecture, their crops and fruits, their style of cooking, their diet, their morality, their family life and structure, their belief in spirits and their gods. But they were gone.

Folk arts of the Borinquén Indians were popular with tourists and museums. In the folk arts the aboriginal culture is still alive, Dr. Alegría said. "Like weaving hammocks and baskets." And there were native foods that were uniquely Borinqueño. "That was about all" of the Indian way of life that was left.

The Indian population of the island "*disappeared* as a cultural group in the first century of the Spanish conquest," he said, and he mourned the death of the Borinqueños. Disease from Europe and Africa caused epidemics that killed thousands of Indians. The mines killed thousands more. When the King granted freedom to the Indians, in the sixteenth century, the Bishop of Puerto Rico could only find sixty still alive.

"Unfortunately there are no more Indians on the island of Puerto Rico," said Dr. Alegría.

The same requiem has been enshrined in popular book and scholarly tome. "Indians, as a civilization, were wiped out centuries ago by the conquistadors," wrote former *New York Times* reporter Kal Wagenheim, in his matter-of-fact *Puerto Rico: A Profile.* In his study of studies, *Puerto Rico: Freedom and Power in the Caribbean,* the British Borinqueño, Gordon Lewis, did not bother to mention the existence of any Indians at all. Nor did they exist in *The Modernization of Puerto Rico* by Henry Wells; the people of the island were all "whites, mulattos and Negroes," Wells said, as far back as 1765.

It has been estimated that thirty to fifty thousand Borinquén Indians lived on the island when the first Conquistadors came. No one knew the exact number. There may have been one-tenth of that, or ten times that many. Not until the dead Indians became a statistic of moral guilt debated in the Church councils of the Vatican and Valladolid did the Spaniards try to count the living. Then it was too late. A man hiding in the hills from the swords of the Conquistadors was not likely to report his wife and his children to the census taker. The official censuses of the Indians grew smaller and smaller. Any count of the conquered by the conquerors was always about as meaningful as a census of rabbits made by wolves.

The elusiveness of the invisible Indians was depicted with an unwitting and perhaps unconscious irony in the historian Arturo Morales Carrión's otherwise precise *Puerto Rico and the Non-Hispanic Caribbean.* The King's decree freeing the Indian slaves "after eleven years of contact, came too late to preserve the aborigines as a distinct ethnic group," he wrote. But a few pages later, the Bishop was quoted as saying, seventy-five years after their "extinction," that the Indians were ill-concealed heathens. "Nothing is more likely," declared the Bishop, in 1586, "than that the Indians, induced by the promise of liberty of conscience, which the English profess, should leave the Catholic Church [and] fall back into idolatry."

Later still, the "extinct" Indians reappeared in Puerto Rican history. When the Earl of Cumberland, who had captured San Juan, fled the island, the King of Spain sent an armada, commanded by General Don Francisco Coloma, to reconquer the colony in 1599. The surprised General found the city of San Juan inhabited almost entirely by Indians. He reported that the settlers had fled to the mountains, from the city, and the Indians had fled to the city, from the mountains. In the harbor the departing English had dismantled the ramparts of the fort of El Morro. Some Indians returned to the city and began to reconstruct the fort, the historian Carrión wrote; but most hid in the mountains.

And yet, had not the Governor of Puerto Rico reported seventeen years before, in 1582, that "not one Borinqueño remained on the island"? It was all very strange.

Father de las Casas witnessed the aftermath of the Indians' bloody slaughter by the Spaniards. "Once the Indians were in the woods, the next step was to form squadrons to pursue them; they pitilessly slaughtered everyone, like sheep in a corral. It was the general rule of the Spaniards to be cruel; not just cruel, but extraordinarily cruel." They would "test their swords" by "slicing off heads and cutting bodies in half." They would sever an Indian man's hands and "leave them dangling by a shred of skin," saying, " 'Go, now, spread the news to your chiefs.' "

In fear the Indians who had not been captured dispersed into the mountains and valleys as "young birds flee when they see a hawk," and had hidden *"in the entrails and subterrain paths of the earth."*

On the mountainous island there were hundreds of deep caves and hidden valleys. In these the Borinqueños hid and lived for generations. They became even then, as they were to become again, exiles in their own land. A writer of contemporary Puerto Rican history, Marianna Morris, has said: "They escaped by the hundreds, making their way into the hills at night." It was the fleeing Indians who were the ancestors of the *jíbaros,* the men from the mountains, she has written: *"Jíbaro* is an old word meaning 'one who escapes from civilization.' The exodus of the Indians, heading for the high places, is remembered as 'The Flight of the *Jíbaro.*' "

At the end of the nineteenth century there were still entire villages of Indians in the mountains. One of these, known as the Barrio de los Indios, had three thousand inhabitants.

Of all the islands in the Caribbean the influence of the Indians has been the strongest and most lasting in Borinquén. In the traditional words and music, dishes, and dances. And some say the ways of the Indians are visible in the easygoing way people look at the earth, the life of the family, and the life of the spirits of the dead.

"The way I look at it is this," said the storyteller: "Yes, we are Latins, but we are more Borinqueños than we are Latins, and we are more of Indians than we are Spanish.

"Look at our faces! Where have you seen more beautiful Indian faces? Spanish blood and Indian faces! People look in the mirror in the morning and they do not see themselves. They do not know who they are. They do not see they are Indian.

"I will tell you a story. Have you heard the legend of the *granadillo?* The *granadillo* is a big tree that grows in our mountains. Some say it is the tree of the passion flower, but it is not exactly. Once, I wrote a little something on *'La Cuesta del Granadillo,'* 'The Road Uphill to the Passion Flower.' Which is the story of a Spaniard who in the beginning of the colonization ventured himself into these lands. And he got acquainted with an Indian girl. And they lived together in love.

"And then, with the invading of the land by other Spaniards, the lover had to decide: Was he an Indian or was he a Spaniard?

"So the lovers pacted a suicide.

"The Indian girl and the Spaniard did die. But their burro and their dog did not die. In the night, when the moon shines through the branches of the trees and their *ánimas,* the souls or ghosts of the lovers, appear, you can hear their burro braying and their dog barking in the countryside.

"In the rural *barrio* of Caonillas, where my family has lived for hundreds of years, there was and still is a site known as La Cuesta del Granadillo. Long ago it was an Indian trail. And later it was a pack trail. Now it is a paved road. The legend takes place at the foot of a very lofty *granadillo* tree. And the tree is still there. So you see the legend does not lie, about the suicide of the lovers.

"We are the children of that suicide."

A man may not know that he is Indian. A man may know and may not admit he is Indian. "But it does not matter. The ignorance of your father and mother does not change who you are," he said. "No matter what a Puertorriqueño decided he is, it already has been decided for him.

"So if I did not have Indian blood in my heart, my heart would not beat. Yes, it would kill me not to have the blood of an Indian," the old man said.

2

The Earthly Paradise

"I am convinced this is the spot of the earthly paradise," Cristóbal Colón, Admiral, Viceroy, and Governor of the Ocean Sea and Islands and Mainland of all "You have Discovered," wrote to the King and Queen of Spain. The rough-fingered, self-educated Genoese sailor searched in the memories of his *machismo* for the most romantic and idyllic simile he could think of—"a woman's nipple on a round ball."

The world was not round, the Admiral said. It was like the breast of a woman, shaped in the "form of a pear." Where the pear's "stalk grows" there was a "prominence like a woman's nipple," he told the court. And on that nipple were the islands of the Indies. These islands were that part "highest and nearest the sky," "the eastern extremity [of the earth] where the land and islands end." In sailing "westward of the Azores," had he not noticed that "the ships went on rising smoothly towards the sky"? Clearly, he was at the Gate of Heaven.

Colón, known better, but not so well, as Christopher Columbus, confessed that he was tempted to stay forever. This country, "most serene Princess, is of such marvelous beauty that it surpasses all others as day surpasses the night."

It was a land of perpetual summer. The "nightingales were singing in November," and the "trees retain their foliage in all seasons," he had written in wonderment after his first voyage. Of all the islands the most beautiful was the one that he named San Juan Bautista. The Indians called it Boriquén, "a very beautiful and fertile" place.

But it was the "gentle and friendly" Indians who convinced the Admiral by their behavior that he was nearing heaven. Were they not almost Biblical in their innocence, giving "all they have" to strangers, offering "great love towards all others in preference to themselves"? Europeans did not behave like that. Nor were Spaniards that Christian. Like Eve and Adam, before the Fall, the Indians seemed to be without evil or guile or bodily shame. "The inhabitants of both sexes on this island," he wrote of Española, "and in all other [islands] I have seen, go always naked as they were born, with the exception of a few women, who use the covering of a leaf."

A leaf! He had surely discovered the new Garden of Eden, or the Garden of Eve, at the very least. So the Conquistadors imagined themselves to be the new Adams, in a wholly "New World."

"New islands, new lands, new seas, new peoples; and, what is more, a new sky and new stars," exulted the Portuguese writer, Pedro Nunes, in his celebration of the New World, the *Treatise of the Sphere,* in 1537. The historian Francisco López de Gómara, in his *Historia General de las Indias,* proclaimed the popular awe of the day: "The greatest event since the creation of the world, excluding the incarnation and death of Him who created it, is the discovery of the Indies."

In the Old and New Testaments the scholars of the sixteenth century had hoped in vain to find a divine prophecy of these unknown lands. At the birth of Jesus, it was written, three Wise Men came "from the east"; but popular religious belief had them coming from the "three corners of the earth"—Africa, Asia, and Europe. One was black, one was yellow, one was white. The *Santos* of the Wise Men, in Puerto Rico, depict the Wise Men in this way, to this day. Nowhere was there word of a Wise Man coming from America, an Indian. There was no fourth corner of the world on the Biblical compass.

Saint Augustine, beloved by the Spaniards, thought that there may have been a land to the west, but he thought of it as shrouded in mist, a vague "swamp." In the books of the medieval geographers there was not even a mist. So it had to be a "New World."

In this way, the Europeans did not "discover" America, they "invented" it, commented the Mexican historian Edmondo O'Gorman. They "invented" it with their dreams and desires. They wished to fill the void in their maps and knowledge and treasuries with the nations and empires they created. They created a mythology of Biblical Indians, and tried to force the inhabitants to fit their myths. O'Gorman wondered, in *The Invention of America,* whether the conflict between the European dream and the American reality may have been the origin of some of history's recurring nightmares, ever since.

Some of the critics of Colón's fantasies may have thought his experiences were "little else than fables," but on his "voyage to the new heaven and new earth," the Admiral knew he had discovered a dream: "All I have related may appear wonderful and unheard of." He reminded them that he had done what "the powers of mortal man had never hitherto attained." To say this was a fable, a dream, a fantasy, was to tell the truth.

But America was no fantasy.

On the island of Puerto Rico, as in all the Americas, the coming of the Admiral has never been celebrated as "Columbus Day." The day was not his alone. It was, and is, El Día de la Raza, the Day of the Race, the New Race, the people of the Americas. For on that day the dream of "the earthly paradise" and the reality of life on the islands were wedded, to create Puerto Rico.

3

The Daughters of Eve

The daughters of Eve may have been "gentle and friendly," but they were well armed.

When the ships of Admiral Colón landed on a small island in the Caribbean during Easter of 1496, the long boats of the sailors were attacked by the women warriors of an Indian tribe: ". . . a multitude of women armed with bows and arrows and with plumes on their heads rushed out of the woods and assumed a menacing attitude."

The sailors, hungry for food and love, begged the women to let them go ashore so that they might barter for a few loaves of Indian bread. All they wanted was something to eat, they said.

Go! Go! the women warriors told the Spaniards contemptuously, according to the account of Fernando Colón, in his biography of his father. If they were hungry, let them go "to the northern shore of the island where their husbands would furnish them with what they needed," the women said. And, saying that, they refused to let the sailors ashore.

Infuriated by this feminine insult to their *macho,* the frustrated Conquistadors opened fire on the women with their Lombard guns. The women and their families fled their villages, "which the Christians entered, looting and destroying all they found," in the words of Colón. In one hut the men came upon some cassava dough, but once they had eaten, they set forth to find the women, who had both infuriated and intrigued them.

One sailor, a "courageous Canary islander," captured "a lady *cacique,"* a woman chieftain—much to his regret. She almost killed him. She could have escaped, wrote the young Colón, but "seeing he was alone, she tried to make *him* prisoner; she grappled with him, threw him to the ground and would have choked him [to death] if the other Christians had not come to his aid."

"The whole island belonged to women," the "lady *cacique"* told the Admiral. He believed her. The men of Spain, and the Admiral himself, had observed that the "women seem to work more than men," and they fought with "strange fury," sometimes beside their men and sometimes without them. On one island the arrow of a woman warrior pierced the armor of a Conquistador; the Spaniards soon became accustomed to such surprises.

Not only the island, but the men, were ruled by these women. That was, at least, what the women told the Spaniards. When they so desired it, they would ask their husbands to "lie with them"—and then only "for certain periods," when it pleased them. It was a state of marital affairs that seemed to deeply impress itself upon the *macho* of the men of Spain.

"The Admiral believed it on account of what he had seen of these women, and because of the energy and strength they displayed," his son wrote. He had read of "what certain books tell of Amazons." So, to the Conquistadors, the women warriors of the Caribbean were no more unbelievable than the tales of sea monsters or visions of lost continents that the European sailors of the sixteenth century knew to be the truth.

On the island of Borinquén, too, there was a "lady *cacique."* The Spaniards renamed her Loíza. She ruled the region known as Hayamano; her domain was the fertile land at the mouth of the island's largest river, the Río Grande de Loíza, where some of the most powerful spirits and gods on the island lived. And still do. Like all the women of Borinquén, the "lady *cacique"* of Hayamano had to be respected; she could invoke the spirits.

In the seas along the coasts of the island lurked a male god, Juracán, whose violent hurricane winds brought death and destruction. But it was the goddess of fertility who brought the warm rain and the crops. She was the creator of life. It was woman, not man, who was the source of human survival in the New World.

The "Mother Goddess" was ruler of the waters and winds, of the earth and life, "the female complement of the male fire god, Yocahu." For the native Jehovah, unlike his Biblical counterpart, was not all-powerful. He was merely a male deity. In the matriarchal society "the extraordinary importance of the female as the source of creation, common in the Antilles [was] probably due to the matrilineal organization of the indigenous clans," wrote the Puerto Rican anthropologist Eugenio Fernández Mendez, in his lively and brilliant evocation of *Art and Mythology of the Taino Indians of the Greater West Indies*. His work richly described the humanity and grandeur of life on Borinquén when the island was ruled by "the earth mother concept."

A matriarchal society was rarely simplistically sexist. The sophisticated insights of the Borinqueños into the psychology of human nature was evident in the "dual male-female nature" of their gods. Life was symbolized by a circle; it was "the union of the two generating principles, masculine and feminine." Unlike in male-dominated societies, the women of Borinquén did not use their strength to demean their men.

On the religious ball courts of the villages, the sacred *bateys*, women played beside, or against, the men. The games were "usually played by teams of men, or of women, and sometimes teams of both sexes," wrote Fernández de Oviedo. "On still other occasions women played against men and married women against the unmarried"; for these games were homages to powerful spiritual, and sexual, gods. The virgins wore nothing at all, "whether they were playing ball or not," but the married women all wore a mantle, that was "very fine, white and handsome," to hide their genitals, not from the eyes of the men, but from the eyes of the gods, whose faces were carved, or painted, on the stones surrounding the ball courts.

Neither the men nor the women overwhelmed one another in these games. "It is amazing to see the speed and agility of both sexes," wrote de Oviedo.

No doubt what surprised the men of Spain most about the women of Borinquén was not their strength but their social power and boldness. They did not hide behind a veil, as did the Moorish women of Andalusia. They were not servile and shy, like the Catholic women of Castile. Nor did they seem to fear their men. It was the woman who chose the man she wished to love. It was the woman who ended a love, at will. And the men seemed to have few rights of love, or even to their own children. But they did not protest. For the "gentle and friendly" women of the island behaved as if they were its natural masters. The *macho*-minded Conquistadors had never met women like this.

It was these women of Borinquén who had originally guided the Conquistadors to their island. On the second voyage of the Admiral his fleet came to a small island in the Lesser Antilles he renamed Guadalupe. The island was inhabited by Carib Indians, who were said to be man eaters; when they captured a young man, it was said, they castrated him "to fatten him like a capon before eating him." But the hungry Spaniards (not quite man eaters, yet) after their long voyage hurried ashore in the hope of finding food. They found a group of "female captives [who] were taken of their own consent, and other women of the island [Carib women] who were surprised and carried off," reported the ship's physician, Dr. Chanca. Later, Father de las Casas said it was only six women and two boys who were taken aboard ship for the amusement of the sailors.

The women did not try to escape, but they offered to guide their newest captors to a far richer and larger island to the north which they called Borinquén. This was their home and, if the Spaniards would let them, they would take them there.

In the balmy harbor of Guadalupe, the Spaniards enjoyed the captured women for eight days, while they waited for a landing party "lost" deep in the interior of the island. In time the ships set sail, blown to the north, through a necklace of islands that the Admiral renamed the "Eleven Thousand Virgins." On the nineteenth of November, 1493, they came to the "very beautiful and fertile" island which the women said was Borinquén.

When the women of Borinquén saw their island, they jumped into the sea and swam to shore. It was night, but they "could not wait till dawn," one of the island legends says. In the morning the men went ashore to recapture the women. But they had fled. And so the ships of the Admiral sailed away, womanless again.

The Indies became known for their "great lure of licentious women," Cervantes later wrote. "Marriage laws are nonexistent," Father de las Casas thought; "men and women alike choose their mates and live as they please." To the Conquistadors, bound by the feudal codes and wedding canons of sixteenth-century Europe, like their brothers-in-arms in Puritan England, the New World became a symbol of the attainable.

The Dean of St. Paul's Cathedral in London, the Canon John Donne, composed a most lyrical of hymns to the "Virgin Lands" of the New World. In "To His Mistress Going to Bed," Donne had wedded the dream of geographic discovery to erotic conquest:

> Licence my roving hands, and let them go,
> Before, behind, between, above, below.
> O my America! my new-found-land . . .
> My mine of precious stones, My Empery,
> How blest am I in discovering thee!

Four hundred years later, Charles Allen, the first United States civilian Governor of Puerto Rico, lamented what Donne and Cervantes had celebrated. He was appalled, so he said, by the "loose relation of the sexes" on the island.

And yet all of these opinions were those of men. The women of the island had a different view.

Nowhere was the status of women more boldly displayed than in the psychiatric practice of the Arawak Indians, among whom the men of the tribe suffered the pangs of afterbirth for their wives. It was the men who experienced the postnatal trauma. And it was the men who had to be nursed back to health by the old women.

As late as the 1880s, a tribe of related Arawaks of Guiana still practiced this birth therapy. The woman worked until a few hours before birth, then went to the forest with some women. In a few hours she was up and at work again. When the child was born, the father took to his hammock, and abstained from work, from eating meat, smoking, washing, and above all from weapons of any sort. He was nursed and cared for by the old women. The practice was reported in *Among the Indians of Guiana* by Sir Everard F. Im Thurn (London, 1883). In the old mountain villages of Puerto Rico, to this day, women seven months pregnant sleep on the outside of the marriage bed so that they do not have to climb over their husbands to get out of bed; for if they do that, it is believed, their husbands will suffer the pains of birth.

On the island it was the sex of the male, not the female, that was sacrificed to the gods. The chronicler of such an ancient Borinquén ritual, Francisco Aguado, described this sacrifice: "They [the Indians of Puerto Rico] took this gentleman, and, having removed his clothes, tied him to a tree with heavy ropes, they then began their rejoicing with music and dancing . . . bringing their bows and arrows in their hands, *each one shot at him,* almost without missing a shot, making a great shower of arrows, *striking him in the part of his body that gives him the greatest pleasure.*" The blood of his phallus was an offering to the gods of fire and fertility. In the Yucatán, Bishop Diego de Landa observed a similar phallic rite among the Mayans, near Chichén Itzá, where the priest *"wounded the victim with an arrow in his parts of shame."*

It is curious that so much has been written of the Aztec rituals of sacrifice, wherein a young virgin, the very word being synonymous with young woman, was dismembered, her heart and her blood offered to the gods, but so little has been written (by historians and anthropologists, who were mostly men) of the phallic rites of the Mayans and Borinqueños, in which the sex and blood of a man, not necessarily a virgin, were offered as a sacrifice to the gods.

The men of Spain could not conceive of a world where women were not merely the equal of men, but often were their masters. In Spain the man was the patriarch of the family, and the titular ruler of Church and state; he soon overthrew the memory of matriarchy of the ancient tribes. Centuries of Roman and Islamic domination had imposed the patriarchal order upon the tribes of Iberia. "Family" itself was a Latin word that had come from the archaic Oscan *famel,* which meant a slave, a servant, a possession. The word "father" or *"padre,"* had come from *pater,* the owner, master, possessor. So the father of the family, paterfamilias, literally meant the "owner of the slaves."

Roman law, which governed Spain for hundreds of years, decreed that a father could legally sell his chattels, who were his children. His wife was by law his "daughter," and he could sell her, too. In the early Roman provinces, such as Spain, so many men did sell their wives that the Senate of Rome had to pass a law prohibiting the practice. The *macho** of the Spanish man was influenced by the heritage of these Roman laws. And it grew under the invasions of the Visigoths and Arabians, until with the rise of knighthood, and the chivalry of the *hidalgo,* it flowered into that peculiarly Spanish quality that became known as *machismo.*

The Lord of the Spaniards was a man. In the heaven of Catholics, and Mohammedans, there were no feminine gods. Neither religion had that much faith in women. If a woman entered heaven, she was likely to be a saint, or a whore. Preferably both. It depended on the religion.

It would never have occurred to a Conquistador that there could

* In the Velázquez Dictionary *macho* is defined as being, among other things: "1. A male animal; in particular, a he-mule or he-goat. 2. A masculine plant. 3. A piece of some instrument which enters into another. 4. Hook to catch hold in an eye. 5. Screw-pin. 6. An ignorant fellow. 7. Pillar of masonry to support a building. 8. Sledge hammer. 9. Block on which a smith's anvil is fixed. 10. A square anvil. 11. Masculine, vigorous, robust; male." The noun *macho* is related to the verb *machacar,* "To pound or break anything into small pieces," and the verb *machar,* "To pound. Firmly, strongly. [As in] *Creer en Dios a macha martillo,* To believe in God firmly and sincerely," and the verb *machetear,* "To beget more males than females."

be a religion in which the God of creation was a woman. He did not worship the mother earth. He conquered her.

A man was his own master. He may have served the Lord, and the King, but he was no man's, or woman's, servant. If he was the "servant of the Lord," that ennobled him, it did not humble or diminish him. The old proverb of the Conquistador was *"Tiene su alma en su armario,"* "He keeps his soul in his closet"; for the man of the Spanish Renaissance believed, as the dramatist Calderón de la Barca had written, "We owe the King our fortune and our life, but honor is the *patrimony,* the father, of our soul."

The Conquistador was fiercely individualistic. If his *machismo,* at times, seemed foolish bravado, he saw it as evidence of his own God-given uniqueness. In Spanish the word meant more than manhood; it meant that he had *Irish;* he had *chutzpa;* he had courage; he had honor; he was a true man of God; he was a Spaniard.

On the island the *macho* of the Conquistadors came into conflict with the matriarchy of the Indians. For the women of the island had a *macho* of their own.

In the galleons of the Conquistadors there were no women; unlike the English Puritans, who settled in New England with their wives and children, and the burghers of Amsterdam, who came to New Amsterdam with their entire families, the Spaniards who populated New Spain were all men. On his second voyage, when Admiral Colón first came to Borinquén, at least seventeen hundred men were on his ships, but not a single woman.

"The sea of the sixteenth century belonged to men and to men alone, and their possession of it was proclaimed by ritual and ceremony, as well as by fact and skill," wrote Charles Ferguson, in his study *The Male Attitude.* "The very vastness of the waters formed a kind of universe with Man at its center. Ships were little domains under the reign of kings called captains, whose control was unmolested by any feminine restraints that on land might have to be considered, even if they were disregarded."

Even the imaginary Conquistador of La Mancha, Don Quixote,

knew better than that. He had advised Sancho Panza, who longed to be the "governor of an island," to be sure to bring his wife. "It is not well for those in government to be long without their women," the old knight told his squire.

It was a matter of time, and not too much time, before the Spaniards and the Indian women were wedded in conflict. As early as 1501, the Governor of the Indies, Juan Ovando, Knight Commander of Lares, ordered that Indian women could not be held in concubinage by the Conquistadors against their will. The codes of chivalry and canons of Catholicism decreed that if a man loved, and lived with, a woman, he had to marry her; and "this had to be done voluntarily on both sides, and not forcibly," said the Knight Commander.

The sexual rights of the women of Borinquén were recognized more strongly by the King's Royal *Cédula* of 1505. It ordered the colonial officials to treat the "sexual offenses" of the Indian women with leniency, but to punish the offending Spanish men harshly. And, in 1516, the Cardinal Cisneros, Regent of Castile, enunciated the imperial, if not the moral, reasons. He instructed three Hieronymite monks who were being sent to the Indies to advise the Spanish men to marry their Indian mistresses, most especially if they were the daughters of *caciques,* when, as His Eminence said, they were "successors of their fathers, in the absence of a son—because that way all the *caciques* would soon be Spaniards."

"Intermarriage was good for the colonization," Dr. Alegría, director of the Institute of Puerto Rican Culture, told me. Spanish men married the Indian women. And the Spanish women married the Indian men, he said.

By 1539, so many Spanish men were living with Indian women that they were ordered by the King to marry, at once. If these passionate Conquistadors did not marry their Indian lovers "within three years," they were to be punished by the loss of the royal title to their lands, and their *encomiendas* of Indian serfs and servants as well.

In years past, Roman and Arabian conquerors of Spain had conquered the native women as well; the rulers of Spain had learned that lesson of history. Now history would be avenged, and the men of Spain would be the conquerors.

The Borinquén women were (and are) deprived of their sexual right to the island. In Spanish (Roman) law the ownership of the land was in the hands of the men; and that legal *macho* was written into the laws of the island, with a few words destroying the ancient birthright of the women, by which the land was inherited through matriarchal rule.

One remnant of that old Spanish law is still upheld. Article 91 of the Civil Code of Puerto Rico decrees that land is "community property" of husband and wife, but if the marriage ends, for any reason, the man assumes the ownership of the land. Not only that, but "the husband as administrator of the community property can spend his wife's income freely," said Baltasar Corrada del Río, president of the Civil Rights Commission of Puerto Rico. The woman "is limited to purchasing items used for family use." The island legally belongs to the men.

But the Conquistadors were to discover, as have their descendants, that the historic and spiritual power of the women was not easily nullified by a piece of legal paper. The law of the land was more an illusion of the *machos* than a reality to the women: for "this law really isn't adhered to by most families," as Ellen Gonzáles, an island journalist, has casually commented.

In the mid-twentieth century the matriarchal rights of marriage, and of property, were observed by Oscar Lewis in *La Vida;* but the anthropologist seemed to be unaware he had observed a persistent, and old, Indian way of life. "Women feel that consensual union gives them a better break; it gives them some of the freedom and flexibility men have," Lewis wrote of the San Juan *barrio* women of 1965. "By not giving the fathers of their children legal status as husbands, the women have a stronger claim on their children if they decide to leave their men. *It also gives women exclusive rights to a house or any other property they may own*" (emphasis added).

The *caciqua* of Loíza would have understood and approved this exercise of matriarchal rights. Lewis saw it as evidence of his theoretical "culture of poverty," and a rejection of "middle class [male] values." He did not see it as evidence of male "poverty."

Borinquén was, and still is, in many ways a matriarchal society. When the Conquistadors landed, nearly five hundred years ago, the village and family life was ruled by the women; the family name, the ownership of the land, and the tribal leadership were inherited through the women. Not the men. That life style of the agricultural people still persists in the industrial suburbs. Although the *caciques* on the island were most often men, proud of their *macho,* as they still are, the women ruled and overruled the men, as they still do.

On the island the percentage of women lawyers, professors, doctors, politicians, and spiritual leaders exceeds that of most Latin-American countries, and certainly the United States. In recent years there have been no fewer than three women on the Supreme Court bench in Puerto Rico, while the Supreme Court of the United States has yet to seat a single woman justice.

"In a way, the Spanish conquest of the Americas was a conquest of the women," wrote the historian Magnus Morner, in his *Race Mixture in the History of Latin America.* But his was the man's view. The men of Spain may have thought they had conquered the Indian women, but the women of Borinquén undoubtedly thought the conquest was theirs. In their own ways the *machos* and the matriarchs may have both been right.

4

The *Machos*

Convent of the Conquistadors

In the courtyard of the convent the old men were playing dominoes, the clicks of the ivories like the sound of rosary beads. There was no other sound. On four sides of the courtyard were rows of white arches built with an absolute grace. The convent of the Dominican monks on Calle Cristo, the Street of Christ, in Old San Juan is one of the serene and perfect buildings in the world.

The old men, their brooms at their feet, played dominoes in the convent religiously. No matter who was ruler of the island, the caretakers of the convent would sweep the courtyard. And then, what else was there for the descendants of the Conquistadors to do but play dominoes?

The stones of the stoic plaza were worn by the descendants of the Conquistadors, who had sunned themselves there for 450 years. By the sea wall, on La Caleta Las Monjas, the Little Street of the Nuns, stood the Casa Blanca, the White House, built of stone by the son-in-law of Ponce de León for his family in 1523: the year the convent was begun.

San Juan was the oldest European city of the Americas. In 1971, the city celebrated its 450th anniversary. One hundred years before the English Puritans had landed on the rock, the Dominican brothers of Don Quixote were building a miniature Renaissance town on the tropical island.

The monks built the convent and the church stone by stone, hand by hand, with few tools and with simplicity and honesty.

In the Chapel of the Holy Virgin of Belen is the fifteenth-century Flemish painting of the Mother of Christ, "The Virgin of Bethlehem," suckling the Infant Savior. Many miracles are attributed to this Virgin. On the day in 1898 when the United States Navy bombarded San Juan a cannonball was fired into the Church of San José. The Chapel of the Virgin and the crypt and the convent were not touched. No sign of the cannonball could be seen. In the Christmas season of 1972 someone stole the Virgin.

The convent and the church were built as a sanctuary. In fear, the early Spanish settlers brought their children and women there. For years the convent was a barracks for the colonial soldiers of the Spanish Army. When the Army of the United States conquered the island, the sanctuary became the headquarters of their Caribbean Command.

It was the soldiers who replaced the crosses with the swords and the whores. In later years Old San Juan became the red-light district of the city. The brothels of the Spanish and then of the American soldiers lined its historic streets. In the elegant old houses, being restored now to their original beauty, the young girls were kept in decaying rooms with the barest decency. On the narrow side streets, built for the carriages of the aristocrats, were the off-limits bars and the sexual circuses for the tourists. The walls of the churches peeled and crumbled with neglect. The convent, once one of the first universities of the Americas, had become a slum of the Renaissance.

And yet, the heritage of Old San Juan was preserved not by historical restoration, but by its neglect. It was ignored by progress and was preserved by this irony.

On the cobblestones of the narrow streets there was not enough room for a bulldozer.

"And for many years the doors of the convent were locked to the people of Puerto Rico. It was in the hands of the Army. In 1955 the convent was restored. Those who came to the opening ceremony were surprised. They had not known that the convent existed. They did not know their history. It had been here since 1523. But they had never been inside.

"Colonialism had closed the eyes of our people to their history. It was a locked door."

A small man with the eyes of a grandfatherly owl sat in an old Spanish colonial chair with a high-throned back. He was Dr. Ricardo Alegría, an anthropologist and the director of the Instituto de Cultura Puertorriqueña, the Institute of Puerto Rican Culture, established by the government to restore Old San Juan, and to rediscover the lost history of the island. His office had been the office of General Brooks, Chief of the Caribbean Command of the United States Army. The scholar had replaced the soldier in the convent.

"If you were a colony, it is not easy to recreate your country's history. Some of our historical documents were taken to Spain and to the United States. We have tried to get them back," Dr. Alegría quietly said. "We have a few of them back. One by one, you might say stone by stone, we are rebuilding our own history. To do that we study our Indian ancestry, our African ancestry, and our Spanish ancestry. So our people will *know* who they are. So our people will feel proud of their great heritage.

"Puerto Ricans suffer from the complex of inferiority. One reason is because our island is small. One reason is because we have been a poor island, economically. But the main reason is because of colonialism our people know very little of our history. In our schools the teaching of our history is limited to one year, in the first grades. So, right now, you can graduate from the University of Puerto Rico without ever having really studied the history of Puerto Rico.

"We have no history!" Dr. Alegría smiled bitterly.

His fascination with the Indians had led him into the caves and mountains, where he had unearthed some of the relics of the Indians' life. In a romantic way, Dr. Alegría thought that the culture of the Indians had given the island its sensual and "material things," its fruits and hues, its lushness and beauty, that were, in the way he spoke of them, almost feminine.

The *macho* of the Conquistadors had made a deeper imprint upon the Puerto Rican mind, Dr. Alegría thought. Its élan, its vitality, its heritage were more forceful. The culture is mostly Spanish, he said, its values, language, religious ideas and most of the customs.

And the culture of Spain was one of the oldest in Europe. Its "rich and complex history," Dr. Alegría said, might be compared to the great Mediterranean cultures of Greece and Rome.

In the Roman Empire the lands of Spain were known as the "Old Dominion." The legions of Rome had invaded the country in 206 B.C., to cut the invasion route of Hannibal, and to drive the army of the Carthaginians, whose soldiers were mostly Spaniards, from Europe. For six hundred years, until the collapse of the Roman Empire, the fertile fields of Andalusia and the rich mines of Toledo made Spain "the Peru and Mexico of the Old World," as Gibbon remarked. In the beginning, as in the end, history was to repeat itself; the victims were the victors.

Roman soldiers not only conquered. They loved and they mated. In this way the men of the Caesars were not unlike the Conquistadors. Sons of "the Roman men and native women of Spain" were known as "Spanish Romans," much as the progeny of the Conquistadors were known as *"españoles"* and later *"españoles mejicanos."* Many of the most famous leaders of Rome itself were born of the progeny of these conquests.

The Emperor Trajan, who conquered the Eastern Empire, was born of Spanish ancestry. So was the Emperor Hadrian, thought by some historians to have been the wisest and greatest Caesar of them all.

Seneca, the orator and philosopher, who as Minister of State crystallized Roman thought, was a Spaniard. He was born, as was his father, in Córdoba. In philosophy and literature the Spanish Romans had their own province: the poet Martial, the jurist and writer Quintilian, and the satirist Lucan were men of Iberian blood.

In the Roman Legions the Spanish Romans were triumphant. The Caesars came more and more "to depend on men of the western provinces" (Spain). Consuls and military commanders of the Empire, in Britain, in the German provinces on the Rhine and in Syria were at one time all born in Spain.

Before the birth of the Spanish Romans other men had come and taken the land, and the women. The Phoenician sailors had conquered the tribes of Iberian Celts along the coast of Andalusia, as early as the eleventh century B.C., where they built mines and factories. It was they who gave Spain its name. *"Span,"* or *"Spania,"* in the language of the Phoenicians, meant "the far off," or "the hidden and remote" land.

The men of ancient Greece came in 230 B.C. And they too settled along the coast of Andalusia, where they built Hellenic colonies. It is thought that the Greeks brought not only the first vineyards and olive orchards to Spain, but their literary heritage.

Later, when these conquerors of the Mediterranean had become Spaniards, the wandering bands of Visigoths conquered, and were conquered by, the land. Inheriting the Roman clergy and Roman laws, the Kings of the Visigoths ruled Spain for three centuries (A.D. 409 to 711). Unlike in Europe to the north, where the "dark ages" reigned, in Spain a humanist feudal tradition began to emerge, that was voiced in the writings of Saint Isidore.

It was the "Moors" of Africa who were the last of the conquerors. The horsemen of the Islamic Empire invaded the land in the seventh century, and they ruled the land for seven centuries. Not until the Battle of Granada, in 1492, the year Cristóbal Colón sailed for the New World, were the Moslem philosophers, Arabian poets and mathematicians, Berber warriors, Moorish knights, Sephardic Jews, and princes of Islam ousted from Spain. By that time the poetic romances, singing language, advanced sciences, and moral sensuality of the Eastern civilizations had become wholly embodied in the Spanish soul. And these remained long after the "Moors" were gone.

Like the Greeks and Romans before them, the men of Mohammed had settled most deeply in Andalusia. And this was "perhaps more important for Spain and Spanish America than has ever been stated," wrote Charles Chapman, in his monumental *A History of Spain.*

"The Spanish colonization of the Americas passed almost wholly through the ports of Seville and Cádiz, and was confined in large measure to Castilians," Chapman noted. "At the time, however, Andalusia was considered part of Castile, and it was only natural that the Andalusian 'Castilians' should have been the ones to go [to the New World]." So it is that many Latin Americans "pronounce their Spanish in the Andalusian [Castilian] way"; and, "in other respects, too, one finds Moslem-descended Andalusian traits in the Americas."

On the island of Puerto Rico these men, the Castilians of Andalusia, gave the people their "gentle, sensual and soft-hearted nature," Governor Luis Ferre said. "It was not simply our Spanish inheritance. The Spaniards can be hard and cruel. Our *serenidad,* the serenity in the souls of Puerto Ricans, is not a Spanish trait. It comes from Andalusia, for that is where most of the Conquistadors came from."

Who were these Andalusians? They were the sons of the Celts, Iberians, Phoenicians, Carthaginians, Greeks, Romans, Visigoths, black Moors, Arabians, Syrians, Mohammedans, Berbers, and Sephardic Jews.

In the courtyard of the Convent of the Dominican monks, on Calle Cristo, the Street of Christ, in Old San Juan, the old men who sat playing dominoes in the shade of the graceful arches were the descendants of some of the oldest civilizations in the world. They no longer knew. They had forgotten.

The Rock of Gibraltar

Where the land ended on the edges of the island the fortress stood.

It had risen from the sea, the horn of a bull jutting into the waves, on a sullen and brooding mass of rock hauled to the land's end by African slaves to build El Morro. Enough rocks to build an Egyptian pyramid. For three hundred years it was the unconquerable bastion of Spain: the "Gibraltar of the Indies."

It hung on the farthest point. No man could go farther without leaving the island. Built as a symbol of Spanish power, it was empty like the wreck of a Spanish galleon.

Many of the rocks of El Morro had been brought from Europe as ballast in the ships of the Conquistadors. On the tropical island of Borinquén there had been no dark knights before the Spaniards came. No Gothic thoughts. The fortress was built with foreign stones, amid the palm trees and wild orchids.

No medieval castle in Spain was more formidable. It towered 160 feet above the sea, higher than the palm trees. In the six tiers of parapets and battlements, dungeons and tunnels, the Conquistadors could, and did, hide from the sun for months. The walls were twenty feet deep. So impenetrable and dense were these fortifications that the bombardment of El Morro by the invasion fleet of the United States Navy, in 1898, hardly damaged the man-made mountain. It was invulnerable.

In the Castilian, *"andar al morro"* meant "to come to blows." Whoever held the fortress was the master of the passage to the Indies and all of the Americas.

The island was more than a lovely "green jewel in the necklace of the Antilles." It was the first port reached by the Conquistadors coming to the New World. It was the last port of call of the armadas of the *Situado,* that carried the gold of Mexico and Peru to the royal treasury of Castile. As the most easterly island of the Greater Antilles, it lay "halfway between the Old World and the New World, halfway between North and South America," strategically the military doorway to the Caribbean.

"Since this Island is the key to the Indies," wrote the royal officials to the King in 1529, "it must be rendered safe." They meant safe from the other Europeans. They petitioned the King "to build a fortress here." But the young Charles I of Spain, who had inherited the reins of the Holy Roman Empire at the age of sixteen and had been crowned Emperor Charles V, was somewhat busy seeking to establish Spanish hegemony over Europe, which he titularly ruled from the banks of the Danube to the North Sea, to St. Peter's in Rome.

The Emperor seemed uninterested in the insignificant and tiny island. After all, the Pope had given him almost all of the Western Hemisphere for his private domain.

The buccaneers and corsairs of France landed in 1528, and again in 1538, attacking the town of San Germán, burning it to the ground, sacking its church and monastery. Once more, the royal treasurer of the island, Juan de Castellanos, appealed to the crown: *"This island is the key to all who come to these regions."* But the Emperor Charles V, whose armies had just conquered Rome, was now engaged in a war with Francis I of France. The island was on its own. And in 1543 the French corsairs again attacked San Germán. They looted and burned the town for the third time in a decade.

Led by François le Clerc, "one of the most French Corsairs of his era," whom the Spaniards called "Pie de Palo," "Wooden Leg," the French raided and pillaged at will. Their attacks severed Castile's trade routes to the New World and endangered Spain's rule of the Indies.

The work on "the fortress of the bull" had begun in 1539. So huge were the fortifications of this "Christian Rhodes" that the work took fifty-two years. "The forte," wrote the jubilant Governor, Diego Menéndez de Vargas, in 1590, "when it is ended will be the strongest that his majestie hath in all the Indies.

"And now, the people of the country sleepe in security," the Governor wrote.

No sooner had the fortress been finished than it was under siege. Sir Francis Drake, a favorite of England's Queen Elizabeth, whose boldness and heroism had contributed to the defeat of the Spanish Armada in 1588, had set sail with a fleet of 33 ships and a force of 4,500 men, to loot and conquer the island of Puerto Rico.

The "pirate prince" of England had heard that a royal *Situado,* laden with two million pesos of Spanish gold and silver, was anchored in San Juan's harbor. Storms had driven the ships to port, and while they were being repaired, the gold, thirty-five tons of gold, was stored in the cellars of La Fortaleza. Drake decided to besiege El Morro, and capture the city. He lost five hundred men in one attempt alone. The uncanny gunners of the fortress shot a cannonball into his cabin—knocking "the stoole from under him." Drake, wounded and dismayed, sailed away on his limping flagship to die at sea in 1596.

Infuriated by this humiliating defeat, Queen Elizabeth dispatched an army, under General George Clifford, the Third Earl of Cumberland, to conquer the island. Cumberland was a knight exemplar, his armor etched and painted with scrolls of lacelike delicacy now displayed in the Metropolitan Museum of Art in New York. He had been victorious eleven times in fighting for England; his invasion of the tropical island, in full armor, was to be his twelfth triumph.

The English landed in 1598 on the Condado beach, where the tourist hotels now stand. They surprised the Spanish, captured the city, and laid siege to El Morro from the rear. Cumberland had learned from the boldness of Drake to be cautious. He besieged the fortress for 155 days. Although he won, he lost, for his soldiers were decimated by tropical diseases and guerrilla attacks. The Earl had to abandon El Morro. He left the island on his ship, the *Malice Scourge,* grumbling as his chaplain, Dr. Layfield, was to say, "that it was not Gods pleasure that yet this Iland should bee inhabited by the English."

The iron cannon left behind by the English were melted and remolded by the islanders into the statue of Ponce de León that stands in the plaza of San José.

In the dungeons and tunnels, the underground passages and dark chambers of the fortress, the invaders and defenders of the island disappeared from sight. The rocks were neutral. They did not know, or care, who manned their parapets.

On the beaches of the island the soldiers of the European armies dragged their armor in and out of the sea. Seldom were those who fought for Puerto Rico Puerto Ricans. The wars fought under the palm trees were begun in the cold shadows of parliaments and chambers of state thousands of miles away.

In 1625, one year after they had peacefully conquered the island of Manhattan, the Dutch tried their hand at the conquest of El Morro. They too captured the city of San Juan, and they raised the flag of the Prince of Orange over La Fortaleza. But the gunners of El Morro turned their cannon on the castle. In a few weeks La Fortaleza was a ruin. The walls had fallen on the Dutch soldiers. Seeking to rescue his crumbling position, General Bowdoin Hendrik of the Netherlands, in a rare act of valor, tried to breach the gate of El Morro by fighting a hand-to-hand duel with the Spanish Captain, Juan de Amezquita. Hendrik was to die from the wounds he suffered, within the year. The Dutch withdrew.

Persevering in all things, the English then tried again. In 1779, during the American Revolution, a plan for the invasion of Puerto Rico was drafted by Major General Vaugham, but the defeat of the British armies by the Yankee revolutionaries had weakened the English and they were unable to conquer the tiny island.

Lord Ralph Abercromby attempted an invasion in 1797. His soldiers had just taken Trinidad, and with ten thousand triumphant troops he landed near Condado Beach. To this arrogant aristocrat Spain was a "decaying nation." Trusting, as he did, "in the weakness of the enemy," he was taken aback by the "powerful artillery" of El Morro. Not only that, but as Colonel Flinter later wrote, the English were "cut off by the armed peasantry, who rose *en masse,* and to the number of not less than 20,000 threw themselves into the fortress."

England decided to conquer El Morro by purchase. Better yet, to trade the Rock of Gibraltar, which it had previously taken in its war with Spain, for the man-made rock of the "Gibraltar of the Indies." In London, the cabinet agreed to the barter, as did George III. Lord Shelburne had advised the King that Puerto Rico "may be catch'd at," and the British spokesman at the peace negotiations with the Americans, Richard Oswald, had told Benjamin Franklin "that only an equivalent territory, such as Puerto Rico, would ever satisfy the English nation in return for Gibraltar."

But the Spaniards were reluctant to agree to the trade. Edmund Burke tried to demean the offer. After all, he declared in the House,

"Puerto Rico was in every sense an unclothed territory. All the wealth of Spain had not been equal to its cultivation." Surely it was beneath English disdain, for it was not a "post of honor."

Thus, the parapets of El Morro were not to be conquered by the Anglo-Saxons for one hundred years. Its cannon were silent through the nineteenth century. Its defenders slept within its walls until 1898, when the invasion by the United States rudely awakened them.

It had risen from the seas. Not as an Aphrodite rising from the foam, feminine and serene, but as that bull of male mythology, Zeus, the abductor of Europa. The fortress had neither beauty nor grace. Once its military uses had ended it was useless: a relic that reflected not its glorious history, but its ugliness. The Yankee tourists are the new invaders. By the tens of thousands they climb in and out of its dungeons. They picnic on the grass where the Dutch General Bowdoin Hendrik and Captain Juan de Amezquita dueled. They photograph their girl friends straddling the rusted cannon. And they stand on the parapets, shooting at the sea with Polaroid cameras.

One sunny day, in November, 1971, a little boy whose parents had taken him to visit the fortress fell to his death from the parapets. He was not the last tourist who would die on the rocks of El Morro.

The Don Quixotes of San Germán

On the old bench an austere man sat upright as a young man. He looked more than eighty. The bench on the ancient plaza of San Germán faced an abandoned seventeenth-century monastery of the Franciscan monks. It was a museum piece. So was the old man. In the torrential sun he wore a tight collar, knotted black tie, and a business suit.

If he had owned a suit of medieval armor, he would have worn it. He was not bothered by the tropical heat. An aristocrat did not sweat. With a silky large white handkerchief he wiped the dust of the cobblestoned street from his face. Dirt soiled his sense of decorum; it was a personal insult to his dignity. His white skin was like a pair of white gloves. His alabaster face had the faint patina of rum and old age and eau de cologne.

The old man stood up. It was time to stride across the plaza on his way to his shop, as he always did at the noon hour.

"A sixteenth-centuryer! It's what we call men like him. He thinks he lives in the sixteenth century. He thinks he is a Conquistador," said a neighbor. "But I think he is a Don Quixote."

In World War II the elegant old man had made a fortune by selling safety pins. On the island, which had been blockaded and isolated by German U-boats through the war, there had been a shortage of safety pins, and the latter-day Conquistador had "made a killing," his neighbor said, by selling the scarce and high-priced safety pins to the frantic mothers of the middle class. He obtained them, it was said, as contraband. A ship laden with the priceless safety pins had braved the enemy's submarines, one moonless night, and had unloaded its clandestine cargo at an atoll near the shore where Cristóbal Colón had landed, in 1493. It sounded like a folk legend.

No one could prove the tale, but everyone knew the old man had become mysteriously wealthy during the war. He was admired for his good fortune. Since the war he had become wealthier. He was admired even more. As one of the town's distinguished citizens he sat on the bench of the old and noble families. One of the few critical things said about him was that his family coat-of-arms was a gold safety pin; he was the Knight of the Diaper, some said.

"If your family did not come here with Ponce de León, you cannot sit there," a neighbor cursed. "If you do not have the right name, you cannot sit there. If you do not wear a tie, you cannot sit there. Of course, I am exaggerating," he said, "but not much."

The bench was reserved, though not by law or city ordinance. It was the seat of authority, by archaic and antiquated traditions as old as the codes of chivalry of the poor *hidalgos,* the Conquistadors of Puerto Rico, whose descendants had become the lords of the once-rich sugar plantations, the landless landed gentry, the keepers of shops, the provincial lawyers and intellectuals, the manufacturers of tourist trinkets, and the new used-car salesmen.

All the towns on the island had their own hierarchy of old men who sat on their patriarchal benches. They sat in judgment on everyone who walked across the plaza. They had little legal power, but they behaved as though they had great moral authority. Perhaps they did.

In the Spanish colonial years the shopkeepers, provincial lawyers, and country gentry had governed the day-to-day life of the towns. They had possessed the beneficent absolutism of *patróns*. Even then, the real political and economic power on the islands was in the hands of the colonial officials, and the absentee landowners across the sea. But, if others ruled in matters of imports and exports, the *patróns* ruled in matters of birth and death.

These little old men hardly seemed descendants of the Conquistadors. But they were the remnants of the Renaissance.

In the year that Cristóbal Colón had anchored off the coast of Puerto Rico, the man who was the symbol of Renaissance man, Leonardo da Vinci, was at the height of his genius, at forty-one; while Michelangelo was at the beginning of his, at eighteen. Raphael was ten, and Titian was sixteen, and Dürer was twenty-two. Copernicus, the scientist of his era, was twenty, and Erasmus, the conscience of his, was twenty-seven. The master of the house of de Medici, Lorenzo, the Magnificent, had just died, and the new master of the house of Borgia, Cesare, was seventeen. His mentor, Niccolò Machiavelli, was twenty-four. In England, the secular saint Sir Thomas More was fifteen. In Germany, the young theology student Martin Luther, had not yet at ten become an Augustine monk. In Italy, the Dominican monk and martyr Savonarola was forty-one. While in Spain, the Saint Ignatius Loyola, who was to be founder of the Society of Jesus, was barely two years old.

Of all the ages of man this was one of the most luminous. In Europe there were as many brilliant minds at work as there had ever been, and perhaps would ever be again.

Erasmus, in his moral guide to Renaissance warfare, *Military Christians,* had advised the conquerors, as good Catholics, to read Saint Augustine and Plato before a battle. They did not. They did read, if they could read, the works of Erasmus. Diego Mendez, a Conquistador who had sailed to the Indies with Colón, on his death in 1536 left no fewer than four books by Erasmus, one of them, *The Art of Well Living.* He bequeathed to his heirs, as well, the *Moral Philosophy* of Aristotle, and a book titled *A Treatise on the Complaints of Peace;* the library of what every Conquistador should know about his conquests.

On his flagship, the Admiral himself kept a small library. He had an unruly and inquisitive mind, as befitted a "discoverer." A self-educated man, he had read widely in ancient and medieval literature. So had the first Governor of the Indies, Ovando. In spite of their reputations as illiterate and brutish men, many of the early Conquistadors were finely educated for their day. Hernán Cortéz, for one, had studied law and theology at the University of Salamanca, one of the centers of Renaissance thought.

In later years, the Conquistadors could not be quite like these early "discoverers." The conquest required a different man. Often these new men were nothing but outcasts and thieves. It was the impoverished *hidalgos,* not the noble lords, who came to the Indies. Hard-minded, tough, resilient, brutal, dream-eyed, and hungry soldiers and criminals replaced the visionaries and "sublime madmen" who sailed with Colón.

The Admiral despaired. On his fourth and last voyage in the summer of 1503, the very sight of these new Conquistadors was "a great insult to my honor." His heavenly islands of the tropics were being desecrated by "boorish" libertines and land speculators. "Many of the men who have come to the Indies did not deserve baptism in the eyes of God, or men," the melancholy sailor wrote. "For seven years I was at [the] Royal Court, where everyone thought my plans were a joke, but now even the tailors beg to be discoverers." These men were not fit to enter his dream.

On the island everything was "extremely good and healthful," wrote a settler in 1582. If there had been gold, "nothing would be lacking." But the gold was long since gone. The island was bucolic, a pastoral nirvana of "perpetual spring," Diego de Torres Vargas said, in his *Descripción de la Isla y Ciudad de Puerto Rico* of 1647. "It is all very fertile and green; fertile for whatever crop one wishes to plant." The King cajoled, implored, and ordered the settlers to farm the land. But, as one old Conquistador was to say cynically, *"Lo que el Rey manda, se obedece, no se cumple"*—What the King orders is obeyed, but not executed.

After all, the Conquistadors had not sailed across the ocean to plant beans. The conquest of the kingdoms of the Aztecs persuaded many of them to leave the island for Mexico. And then came word of Inca gold in Peru.

The cry of "May God take me to Peru!" echoed through the island. Hundreds left. In San Juan, the Municipal Council wrote to the King: "The news that reaches us from Peru and other places is so extraordinary that it encourages not only the young men, but also the old, to move." Governor Francisco Manuel de Lando went personally to San Germán in hope of calming "the people agitating to go to Peru." He was unsuccessful. In dismay, the Governor wrote to the King:

"Many crazy people have secretly left from small ports far from the towns; of those who remain, even the most firmly rooted think of nothing else. . . . Day and night I maintain a vigil so that no one can leave, but I cannot guarantee that I can contain them."

On one occasion his soldiers fought a grotesque battle with the restless Conquistadors. "It was necessary to kill three of them," the Governor reported. "Some were whipped, others had their feet cut off." Even that did not halt the exodus. The Governor implored the King: "If your Majesty does not provide some remedy soon, I fear that this island will be fully emptied."

All men who were caught seeking to leave the island would have their feet cut off, the Governor ordered. It was, by far, the severest emigration law in history.

The wars of conquest by the European empires, from time to time, swept the island's shores, but they blew out to sea, leaving the island as it was before. It became the backwater of the Spanish Main. The Conquistador's suit of armor rusted in the warm rain. There was nothing on the island to conquer.

In the land of illusion between the dream and reality was the very terrain where Miguel de Cervantes was to discover his *"Ingenious Gentleman, Don Quixote de la Mancha."* He was the quintessence of the Conquistador. He was Cristóbol Colón, without so much as an oar. And his darker shadow, Sancho Panza, was one of the earthy, "boorish" men whom the Admiral so sadly deplored, but depended upon.

The bumptious Sancho dreamt of being "governor of an island." All through the book, as he rode his ass, he begged his master "for that island you promised me." Had not Don Quixote told him "that among knights-errant of old it was a very common custom to make their squires governors of the islands they won"?

A man on the road asked Sancho how he intended to govern his island. He could not read.

"To govern islands [one] must at least know grammar," the man said.

"I have seen governors," Sancho replied, "who are not to be compared to the sole of my shoe, and yet they call them 'your Lordship' and serve them on silver plate." Surely, he too could do that.

One night, in a vision, Sancho went to heaven. He peered down from on high on the insignificance of the island of his dreams, and he decided he did not want it.

"Since I have seen the earth from up there and have seen how little it is, I am not as anxious to be governor as I was," Sancho said. He preferred to have "a bit of heaven" to the "biggest island in the world."

"My friend," Don Quixote told him, "I cannot give anyone a bit of heaven. It is reserved for God."

"Very well," sighed Sancho, "let me have the island, and I'll do my best to be such a governor that in spite of the rascals, I'll go straight to heaven."

In the end of the fantasy, when Don Quixote at last discovered an island for him to govern, he was disappointed. The island was nothing but an ordinary Spanish village, full of ordinary Spaniards. In spite of all their efforts to discover paradise, neither Don Quixote nor Sancho Panza could find any other world but the one they carried in their minds.

Sancho felt betrayed. He cried out in anguish: "What they call luck is a drunken wench, who does not know her own mind. She is blind."

"You are quite a philosopher," Don Quixote chided him. He disdained his squire's lusty self-pity. "There is no such thing as luck in the world. And whatever happens, be it good or bad, does not occur by chance, but by a special providence of Heaven; hence the saying that man is the architect of his fortune." The old knight was proudly emphatic: "I was the architect of mine!"

In the true Spaniard's belief that birth and death, joy and sorrow, hope and despair, were one and the same, the Knight of Sorrowful Countenance had not been defeated by his defeat. It was "the typically Spanish trait," as Salvador de Madariaga said, "the coexistence of contrary tendencies."

"Our Lord Don Quixote, the Spanish Christ!" the philosopher Miguel de Unamuno had christened him in *The Tragic Sense of Life*. "The greatest thing about him was his having been mocked and vanquished, for it was by being overcome that he overcame; he overcame the world by giving the world cause to laugh at him. Perhaps the passion and death of the Knight of Sorrowful Countenance is the passion and death of the Spanish people. May it not perhaps be that the philosophy of the Conquistadors was, in its essence, none other than this?"

So armed the Conquistadors did conquer. They had the strength to laugh at themselves, "with a bitter laugh," to "see [themselves] from without." For they were many men in one.

On the old bench in the quiet plaza of San Germán there was no sign of the blood of the Conquistadors. No sign of the blood of the Borinqueño Indians, or of the African slaves, whipped through the ancient streets by the thousands in chains. The plaza is now immaculate.

And the old men sitting in the sun are immaculate, too.

René Torres looked down upon his neighbor from his rocking chair on a balcony above the plaza, on "the bench of dreams." He was the owner of the Cemi Gallery of Folk Art. On the far end of the plaza, overlooking the stone steps of the monastery of the Franciscan monks, now the Porta Coeli Museum of Religious Art, his gallery was itself a small museum of the sacred and the profane art of the *jíbaros* and Indians; he was a connoisseur of Puerto Rico's aesthetic past, which he sold to the tourists.

The irony of the Conquistadors delighted him. René Torres had come to the town of San Germán from the City of New York. It was not his birthplace, except "in spirit." He had come in search "of what everyone else is looking for," he said, "my roots"; for though he had lived in New York for most of his life, he "was a Lugo," and his family was old and well known in the neighboring *barrios*.

As a Lugo, he said, he "had been honored" with a seat on "the bench." It did not matter that in his youth he had been a seaman who had known wars and revolutions. The aristocrats of the town were not interested in his career on Madison Avenue. They knew his family. He "was a Lugo," and he would always be a Lugo. He was pleased, yet puzzled, to discover that he indeed "had roots."

"Here," he said, "every man has his place. And he keeps his place. As his father did, and his father's father did, before him. Sometimes it seems almost un-American."

"And those old Don Quixotes on that bench! They like to think they are living in the sixteenth century. Maybe they are. In an old town like this it doesn't matter what you do, or say. All that really matters is your family name, your traditions, and if you have the *serenidad,* the serenity, and manners of a gentleman."

René Torres looked pensively at the town. "When I lived in New York, I never believed in traditions. There are no traditions in New York. I never believed in the aristocracy. I still don't. But I will tell you something strange. Here, in this old town, where there is very little of the kind of democracy you have in New York, there is more of a feeling of democracy than I ever experienced in New York." He shook his head. "I do not understand it. I am not sure that I even like it. Maybe it is just an illusion."

In the sun the old men, the Don Quixotes of San Germán, sat stiffy as knights without armor.

5

The African Masks

Calabo and bamboo
Bamboo and calabo
The grand cocoroco cries: tu-cu-tu—
The grand cocoroca cries: tu-co-to.*

The stately woman danced barefoot on the plaza.

The African soul is vibrating
In deep rhythms of dark dancing

She was so dark her skin was almost black. On her head she wore a bandana as women did in West Africa and Haiti. The women on the island did not wear their hair that way. Nor did they have such eyes, haughty with laughter and conceit. She hopped like a bird. A man on the sidewalk walked around her, his eyes avoiding hers. She laughed.

Now, the black woman surrenders
To the dance that dances her

She danced by herself, without sound.

In a shop window on the plaza of Loíza Aldea there was a sign: ¡PELUCAS! The latest fashions in wigs. Lilac, pink, white, silver, gold,

* From the poem "Black Dance" by Luis Pales Matos (1899–1959), one of the poet laureates of Puerto Rico, and an intimate friend of Governor Luis Muñoz Marín in his youth.

red and orange wigs, shimmering in the sun. The black woman halted her dance and peered at the shop window of headless hair.

"Ah, for the *locas* [the crazy women]," she cried, laughing.

Under a frayed palm tree two old black men sat. And watched her. They nodded. One of the old men said: "It is true. We wear the American wigs and Spanish faces. But I tell you a secret. In our hearts, on the Fiesta de Santiago, there is dark music. *¡Grifo!* Very dark. Very *indio.*"

Yet it was not the day of the Fiesta de Santiago. Why then was she dancing?

"On the day you dance, that is the day to dance. In our village we do not tell time by the calendar," the old man said. He paused. "Besides . . .

"She is a spiritualist woman," he said. He said no more.

A naked child danced around the woman, then he became embarrassed and ran away. The old men sitting in the shade of the palm tree, their faces worn as stones, nodded appreciatively. In the single grocery store and dry cleaner on the plaza the elderly women shoppers scowled with tolerant amusement.

The village was "the village of the blacks," they said. Some said its inhabitants were the descendants of African slaves. But its name said something more. Long ago, it was said, Loíza was the christianized name of the *caciqua,* the Indian woman chief, who ruled the village of Hayamano when the Spaniards came; and Aldea was an Arabic word, borrowed from the Moors, that meant a small village. So it was "the small Arabic village of the Indian woman chief."

It was a fabled place of dark and ancient beliefs and mysteries, known throughout the island. Nowhere were there more spirits than in Loíza Aldea. The Cave of Maria, where the oldest skeletons of the archaic Borinquén Indians had been unearthed, was nearby, and the village was a graveyard of living history.

On the banks of the Río Grande de Loíza, the houses stood in between the mangrove swamp and the blue sea. The river was full of fishes and spirits of the dead. It flowed out of the rain forests on the mountain of El Yunque, on whose peak lived the goddess of fertility that the Borinqueños worshiped. Her waters nourished their fields. They still did. The lands were fecund with the odors of sugar cane and mangos and coconuts. "Our river is as fertile as our women," the old man said.

In the old days the Borinquén Indians had built an altar of carved rocks, the *piedras pintadas,* in the midst of the river to calm the passions of the water gods. The stone altar had stood guard over the village for hundreds of years. When the Americans invaded the island in 1898, the altar mysteriously disappeared. It was a bad sign, the old men of the village said.

The fishermen of the village believed in signs of the gods and spirits. If the signs were not favorable, they did not fish, even when it rained and it was good to fish. And it rained every day.

In the doorway of a hut a young black man waited out the rain. I asked him: Wasn't he a fisherman? Sometimes, he said, I am a fisherman.

Sometimes?

Yes.

When are you a fisherman?

When I fish.

Isn't this a good time to fish? When it rains?

Yes.

Then why don't you fish?

It is not a good time.

Didn't you just say it was?

Yes. But not for me.

The fishermen of Loíza Aldea knew there were two times to fish: when there were fish and when it was the time to fish. It was a time told by signs, by omens, by the spirits. Every man had his own spirit; it was as personal as his name, and as old as the river. It never changed.

For hundreds of years the road to the village had been an ox trail. No one complained. It was paved, but the villagers were still isolated by history and by preference. There was running water now. Some of the huts had light bulbs. But the river was the same. The spirits of the dead had not changed.

The smaller villages of Medianias (the Place of the Mild Ones, the Spaniards had named it, perhaps because the Indians had lived there) and Colobo (an old Indian word that may have meant "the Place Where the Black Men Live") looked like the island of centuries ago. Huts were thatched with palm leaves. Children were naked. Old people remembered the stories of black slavery.

An old woman of Colobo said: "No, we have no water in pipes. We have nothing modern here. We are too poor."

Her mouth grinned: "All we have is the beautiful ocean. It has running water, don't you think? And the sun is as bright as the light bulbs, don't you think?"

An old man of Medianias said: "I like the country. Here we feel happy as the birds in the skies. No troubles, no fears—we live in the open air. In the city, we live like in a jail. Here we hold the customs and the feeling of our forefathers. In the city, we lose everything."

San Juan was barely fifteen miles away, but hundreds of years away.

In 1508, when the Don Quixotes of Spain first came to the villages, they did not come seeking the birds in the skies, the sun, the river, the fishes, the fertile women, or the spirits. They came in search of gold. Along the Río Grande de Loíza were the richest deposits of yellow stones on the island. Enough for the Spaniards to build a smelter, some of the first placer mines in the Americas, and to try to enslave the Indians.

When the armored men sought to enslave them, the Borinqueños fought. And they ran away to the mountains. To enslave a tribal man in his own homeland was never wise, or too successful.

The tribal peoples of Africa were then brought to the island as slaves. So that they would not run away they were branded and chained and brought to a strange island, thousands of miles from their ancestral homes. Those who could escaped to the mountains to join the Indians. In the early years of slavery it was the Jelofe

(Wolof) tribesmen of Senegal who were most often shipped to Puerto Rico. Later came the slaveships of Yorubas, Ashantis, Ibos, Fantes, Congos, and Mandingos; but in the beginning it was the Jelofes who led the way into the mountains, to freedom, where they joined the Borinqueños in their hidden caves and villages.

As tribal people the Jelofes and the Borinqueños lived in somewhat similar ways. They had common beliefs. They knew similar trees and gods and spirits. They ate roots and fruits that were familiar, for both were men and women of the tropics. So they understood one another better than either understood the behavior of the Europeans.

Love, too, united them. Slaves and Indians were free, according to the Spanish "Laws of the Indies," to mate and marry. The African men on the island outnumbered the black women by four to one; so it was natural that these men sought Indian women as lovers. And the children born of these matings created the strongest bonds between the slaves and the Indians.

Uprisings of the Jelofes and the Borinqueños became common. In 1527, the first large slave revolt swept the island, when these Jelofe tribesmen joined the Indians in guerrilla warfare against the Spaniards. In their mountain villages the tribal warriors gathered and swept down on the Spanish settlers. Plantations were burned. The mines of Loíza Aldea were wrecked. And the yellow stones were thrown back into the river. Year after year the uprisings went on.

The Don Quixotes of San Juan were going bankrupt. In 1530 the city council lamented in a message to the King that to be free of debt they too had to flee into the mountains, like escaped slaves: "All the residents of this island are very much in debt as they have taken Negroes on credit with the hope of mining a great deal of gold, and because they have not found it, many of them are in the jails; others have fled to the mountains, and others are in ruin."

By 1532 the colonial officials were begging the King to outlaw the importation of Jelofe and Berber slaves. And the King so ordered: "Be very careful in the Casa de Contratación [The Trading House] that you not allow into the Indies of black slaves called Jelofes."

Slavery in Puerto Rico was unlike that on any other Caribbean island. Its history, from the beginning, was unique and ironic. The first slaves on the island were white, not black. In 1504 five slaves were shipped in iron chains from Spain, by order of the King. All were white and all were women. For a decade these "Christian female slaves," who were sent to be sexual servants of the Conquistadors, constituted the largest part of the slave trade.

The first black man to come to Puerto Rico was a free man. He was Juan Garrido, born in Angola, a Christian soldier who had fought with Ponce de León in Española, and who was one of the Conquistadors of 1508. Later he sailed with the island's first Governor on his voyage of exploration to the "island" of Florida, becoming the first African to set foot on the future United States—one hundred years before the coming of the Puritans.

Not until the first sugar mill, an old-style *ingenio,* was built in the vicinity of San Germán in 1523, by the lawyer and scholarly slave-owner Licenciado Tomás de Castillón, were black slaves brought to the island in large numbers. Even then, the blacks and the Borinqueños worked together in the sugar fields and mills. An old *higüera* gourd, painted by the *jíbaro* folk artist Israel Porrata of San Germán, depicts one of these *ingenios.* Porrata drew black men flailing the raw sugar stalks by hand onto hard wooden posts. And the Indians sifting the sugar through cane screens. And black women stirring the "white gold" in huge caldrons. In the plantation scene, where the *ingenio* is surrounded by the *bohíos* (huts) of the *caciques,* Porrata shows the blacks and Indians living side by side. "It is as my grandfathers had described it to me," said the aged *jíbaro* painter. Wherever there was sugar, there were slaves. The cultivation of sugar cane was introduced to Puerto Rico by the first colonizers. It was sown, at first, in a village of free Indians, named Tao, and later it was planted in San Germán, in Guayama, and in Loíza Aldea.

And yet, the Spanish did not bring the blacks. In 1518 King Charles V licensed a Flemish merchant and nobleman to transport four thousand slaves from Africa to the Indies. In the years slave traders came from England, France, Germany, Holland, Belgium, and Portugal, they grew wealthy selling black slaves to the Spaniards, who grew guilty buying them.

In the "Laws of the Indies" the Spanish jurists and theologians had agreed that slavery was an evil necessity of conquest. But it was evil nonetheless. Enslavement of the Indians had been forbidden years before. As Catholics and humanists, the Renaissance Spaniards were never at ease with the "peculiar institution" of slavery. The civil rights of slaves had been protected by law, in Spain, as long ago as the thirteenth century, in the *Siete Partidas* of King Alonso, the Good.

The earliest European abolitionists were Spaniards. In the sixteenth and seventeenth centuries eminent men like Father Diego de Avendano, in his *Thesaurus Indicus,* Father Benito de la Soledad, the scholar Alfonso de Sandoval, and the writers Molina, Soto, and Mercado, all condemned the slave trade and urged its abolition. So did Father de las Casas, who had originally advocated the enslavement of Africans to protect the Indians, but who later contritely confessed his error: "The Africans have as much right as the Indians."

"Among the slave traders there was a joke," said Dr. Ricardo Alegría, of the Institute of Puerto Rican Culture. "It was a joke they used to tell about the Portuguese, because the Spaniards were not involved in the slave trade. The joke was that in Africa, in the eighteenth century, every time the Portuguese took a cargo of slaves, the first thing they did was to baptize them. It was the Catholic idea that the slaves were human beings. Even when they were selling them, for money, they tried to save their souls.

"That was the joke," Dr. Alegría said. He did not smile.

On the island the black slaves were treated "more humanely" than elsewhere in the Caribbean, he said, citing the eighteenth-century journals of travelers to Puerto Rico, especially English travelers.

In his journals, written in the early 1800s, Count von Humboldt had said: "It cannot be denied that the mildness of Spanish legislation [concerning slaves] stands out when compared with the *Code*

Noir [Black Code] of the majority of the other peoples who have possessions in the two Indies." Spanish laws gave four rights to black slaves that no other nation granted them: the right to marry as they wished, the right to legally petition for a "new owner" if they were mistreated, the right to purchase their freedom "at the lowest market price," and the right to purchase the freedom of their wives and children, even though they could not afford to purchase their own.

Slaves may have thought less of these differences. As Count von Humboldt himself wrote, "Nothing is more illusory than the extolled effects of laws which prescribe the model of the whip, or the number of lashes to be given in sequence."

"There *was* a difference here," Dr. Alegría insisted. "It was the Puerto Rican slaveowners who fought for the abolition of slavery. They granted freedom to *most* of their slaves, even *before* slavery was officially ended. They went to Spain to demand that slavery be abolished, with or without indemnity. I think that was one of the most glorious pages in the history of the conscience of mankind."

When the Spanish government at last abolished the remnants of slavery in 1873, there was a great fiesta. People danced in the streets all over the island. There were good economic reasons for celebration, Dr. Alegría said. Slavery in Puerto Rico had always been limited by the island's geography. On the coastal plains there was little more than fifteen miles of flat, arable land. There was simply not the land for the vast slave plantations that were cultivated in the rest of the Caribbean, and in the Southern United States.

"Here, we never had the great plantations and landowners," said Dr. Alegría. "Our island has always been the country of the small farmer, the individual landowner. It is a mistake to say that Puerto Rico was part of the slave 'plantation system.' Whoever says that doesn't know enough about our history. In Cuba slavery was important, but in Puerto Rico it was not."

In all of the Spanish Indies there were fewer blacks "than in the single State of Virginia," Count von Humboldt said in 1803. In Puerto Rico there were 127,287 "Free People of Color" and only 34,240 slaves (in 1827). Nowhere else in the Caribbean did the free dark-skinned men and women outnumber the slave population, as they did on Borinquén, by four to one!

Early in its history the island was a refuge for runaway black slaves. One of the first recorded instances occurred in 1664, when four men, escaping from slavery on nearby Santa Cruz (St. Croix), reached the shores of Puerto Rico and begged for sanctuary. It was granted by Governor Juan Pérez de Guzmán on the condition that the refugees agree to baptism into Catholicism and that they swear allegiance to the crown of Spain; evidently the ex-slaves thought it a small price for freedom and they agreed. Henceforth, the Governor ordered, all *gente colorada* who agreed to those conditions would be accepted as "free people of color."

By 1714 so many black slaves, men and women, had escaped to Puerto Rico that they founded the town of San Mateo de Cangrejos (Crabs). It is now known as Santurce, one of the central districts of San Juan.

In every slave society the exploitation of man's labor was coupled with the exploitation of woman's sex; for men have always used slaves to satisfy their psychic needs and sexual fantasies. The men slaves may have suffered death, but the women slaves suffered sex. It was this "duality of slavery" that the Don Quixotes of Spain created, where the Puritans only condemned it. And this gave birth not only to the mestizo and mulatto body, but to the mestizo and mulatto mind; the "black skin, white faces" of Fanon's "orphans of colonialism"; where Christianity and bestiality, the whip and the phallus, created the divided self of love and hate.

In the mountain villages of the *jíbaros* the Spanish word for dagger, *daga,* came to mean the *machete.* But in the poor barrios, such as Loíza Aldea, the word *daga* meant the penis.

The life in the Indies offered "no barriers, no inhibitions" to the men of Spain. "Why should there have been?" Oxford University's Professor Ronald Syme asked in his *Colonial Elites:* "The Spaniards were heirs to that Mediterranean civilization that knew no colour bar. How indeed could it have? Dark pigmentation is frequent in the Mediterranean. Indeed, it is recorded that some of the natives of the

New World were paler in complexion than a number of the Castilian Spaniards." For "Spain itself was a blend of races." After seven hundred years of Moorish occupation it could not have been otherwise.

"Our ancestors in Spain were accustomed to mixing with people of different ideas and customs and religions and skin colors," said Dr. Alegría. "The secret of this was in the nature of the Spaniards' wars against the Moors," where brothers often fought brothers. It was not a matter of color, or race, that made a man a slave, so much as a matter of conquest; there were Christian Moors and Spanish infidels who at different times enslaved one another.

"In the Americas they merely did the same as they did in Spain. They continued the same traditions."

Slavery in Puerto Rico might have been determined by conquest, rather than by race, but the Spanish were nonetheless intensely conscious of color. The letters and journals of the Conquistadors were full of reference to the hues of the *gente colorada,* the People of Color, or the Red-Skinned People, whom they were forever comparing to the Moors. In his journals, the Admiral Cristóbal Colón meticulously noted whether the inhabitants of the islands he came to were as "dark as Moors," or "lighter than Moors." To be a Moor was to be at the mercy of the Inquisition; for the Berbers and black slaves who were "brought up among the Moors" were barred from the New World, not because they were dark-skinned, but because they were Moslems, the vanquished enemy. Color became not a measure of race, but of status. It became, as well, a measure of caste.

The "castes of color" that the royal officials of Spain, in the eighteenth century, listed included no fewer than sixteen subtleties of shade:

Spaniard and Indian beget *mestizo.*
Mestizo and Spanish woman beget *castizo.*
Castizo woman and Spaniard beget Spaniard.
Spanish woman and Negro beget *mulato.*
Spaniard and *mulata* woman beget *morisco.*

Morisco woman and Spaniard beget *albino.*
Spaniard and *albino* woman beget *torna atrás.*
Indian and *torna atrás* woman beget *lobo.*
Lobo and Indian woman beget *zambaigo.*
Zambaigo and Indian woman beget *cambujo.*
Cambujo and *mulata* woman beget *albarazado.*
Albarazado and *mulata* woman beget *barcino.*
Barcino and *mulata* woman beget *coyote.*
Coyote woman and Indian beget *chamiso.*
Chamiso woman and *mestizo* beget *coyote mestizo.*
Coyote mestizo and *mulata* woman beget *ahí te estas.*

Simón Bolívar cruelly voiced the painful *grito,* the cry, of these mestizos: "We are the abominable off-spring of those raging beasts that came to America to waste her blood and to breed with their victims [the Indians] before sacrificing them. Later the fruits of these unions commingled with slaves brought from Africa." In his letter to the Congress of Angostura, the Liberator of Latin America sought to offer the "new breed" created by the Spaniards' conquest of the Africans and the Americans their place in history.

> We must bear in mind that our people are neither European, nor North American; they are a mixture of Africa and America rather than an emanation from Europe. Even Spain herself ceased to be European because of her African blood, her institutions and her character. It is impossible to determine with any degree of accuracy to which human family we belong. . . . Europeans have mixed with Americans and Africans, and Africans with Indians and Europeans. While we have all been born of the same mother, our fathers, different in origin and in blood, are foreigners.

In the village of Loíza Aldea, the human paradoxes of the conquest came to life in the Fiesta de Santiago. Every year, on a day in July, the villagers, the descendants of black slaves and Borinquén Indians and the Don Quixotes of Spain, put on the ancient masks of the conqueror and conquered, Catholic and pagan, sensualist and spirtualist, lover and rapist. They exhorted their defeat and celebrated their triumph. They had survived their fate.

Santiago, or Saint James, was the patron of the knights of Castile who drove the Moors from Spain. In the Indies, as everywhere in the Americas, "Santiago!" was as well the battle cry of the Conquistadors in their slaughters of the Indians.

Ay, tibiri, that black were
white! How devilish!

On the day of their Fiesta de Santiago the quixotic children of the *gente colorada* celebrated their own conquest. It is an exorcism by which they expurgated the sins of their history.

The revelers wore masks. Some appeared in white face, dressed as the *caballeros,* the Don Quixotes of Spain, the Conquistadors. Some were *vejigantes,* who impersonated the Moors, "the Devils against the Christians," in beautifully grotesque masks carved from the husks of coconuts, and adorned with horns. Some were the *locas,* the clowns, the crazy women.

It was the *locas* who seemed to be the happiest. The crazy women were men, wearing dresses, stuffed with rags and pillows for breasts and hips, who laughed with that high-pitched hysteria of men impersonating women. A gay transvestite way of mocking the Santiago. On a fiesta day, not too long ago, one of these men ran through the village streets, his pillow slipping from his dress. "*¡por favor! ¡Por favor!*" he shrieked in falsetto laughter at the startled tourists, "Please! Please! I'm pregnant! Take me to the Bronx Hospital!"

In the coconut groves of Medianias lived the maker of the masks. His name was Castor Ayala, an elderly man, delicate and fragile. His large eyes seemed full of innocence and remembrance. In his long life he had been a carver, painter, businessman, and manufacturer of souvenirs for the tourists. But he was known mostly as the maker of the mysterious masks of the Fiesta de Santiago.

He remembered black slavery. It was a memory his grandparents had given him. He talked of the instruments of torture and the instrument of love.

"My second grandfather told me the Spaniard like very much the black race," the old man told Henrietta Yurchenco, who wrote his words in her book *¡Hablamos!* "And they mix the race. That's the reason there is no pure black. Nobody here is pure black. There is many mixes, Spanish race, Indian race, and black race. Nobody can say, 'I am pure.' If one say that, I say, 'Where is your grandfather, and your second grandmother?' Everywhere there is mixture.

"And that is the reason there is no racial problem," the old man said. "We live like brothers."

Señor Ayala was black. He was not an American black, nor an African. He was a black Puerto Rican. But his "spirit" was Indian.

His artistry was inspired by the "spirit of the Indian." And he told this story: "One morning, about five o'clock, my neighbor saw an Indian standing at the gate, his hands across his chest. He was smoking a pipe and had great feathers in the back of his head and part of his head was shaved. She called her sister and she saw the same thing. They couldn't work that day, because they were shaking and had a fever. They told me and I joked, 'Ha, don't worry. That's my watchman, don't get afraid.' Then I went to Guayama, and the spiritualist there say she see the same thing. About five different [spiritualist] ladies in different parts of the island say the same.

"One of them told me, 'The Indian was your father in ancient times, and he is by your side always. Don't you feel him by your side when you are alone?'

" 'Yes,' I said, 'I don't see him, but I feel he is there.'

"She said, 'Everything you design is not from you. Your hand is directed by him.' "

Were his African masks really the masks of the Indians? The forgotten faces of the Borinquén tribes of Loíza, the *caciqua* of Hayamano, hidden beneath the feathers and plumes and spiny horns, like the tentacles of a tropical lobster, that adorned the coconut disguises of the *vejigantes?* It was not too strange to be true. No one knew.

In the Fiesta de Santiago the beliefs and the bloods of the black slaves and the Borinqueños and the Don Quixotes of Spain were mixed beyond reason. But one thing was clear: the Spanish *caballeros* were not the heroes of the fiesta. Nor were they the villains. They were ornamental figures. And the *locas* were simply the clown dancers of all sacred tribal rituals. They acted as the buffers between the gods and men. It was the masked *vejigantes* who were the heroes of the day, wearing the faces of Castor Ayala to symbolize "the Devils against the Christians," the heathens, the Jelofes, the Africans, the Indians.

Ay, tibiri, flowering tree!
Ay, tibiri, that's no biri!
Ay, tibiri, that black were
white! How devilish!

One summer day, as he sat on the veranda of La Fortaleza, the Governor's palace in Old San Juan, admiring his gardens of tropical palms and orchid trees, the then Governor of Puerto Rico, Luis Ferre, who was a conservative Catholic, mused about "the Calvinist hypocrisy of the English" toward the children of black slaves. He laughed: "In our Spanish blood we do not suffer from *that*. On the island we do not have the kind of racial problem that you have on the mainland.

"In Puerto Rico we have solved the problem with our sins, that you have preserved with your virtues," said the Governor.

6

The Americanos

The Tropical Indian War

An old man, so old that he was ageless, remembered the day when they landed. That was seventy-three years ago. He was thirty-three then. Was he one hundred and six years old now? He thought so. It was difficult to know, it was so long ago, when he was born in the mountain town of Jayuya. Was that in 1865? No man could remember an entire century. And yet he remembered how the people ran into the streets, crying, "The Americanos have come!" on the day of the Fiesta de Santiago, the twenty-fifth of July, 1898, when the United States of America invaded Puerto Rico.

"Let's go to the mountains!" people cried. "The Americanos have come!" It was an ambivalent *jíbaro* cry of joy and fear.

He did not see the landing of the Yankees himself. At the time he was in jail again. The Spaniards had locked him up again.

The old man said: "I used to drink a lot of rum. And raise hell." And so, "the Spaniards kept putting me in jail." It was the way that the colonial government had of humiliating the *jíbaro* men, he thought. "They would kill the *machos*. So they could marry our women." He despised the way the Spaniards treated Puerto Ricans. Like little children. It insulted a man's pride.

In the old-age home in Ponce, he sat in striped blue pajamas, and thought of those days. The old man had been hospitalized because of a painful auto accident: one evening, while he was out for a stroll, he had been run down by a hit-and-run driver. But, he had lost none of his *macho.* "I am dying to have a girl friend," the one-hundred-and-six-year-old told a reporter. "But," he confided, "let me tell you, women only want money. They don't want the man." Some said he had been married eight times. He denied it. "Oh no," he said, "I've only been on that trip five times." There was no denying that his *jíbaro* love of life had not been weakened by Spanish jails or American autos.

When he was a boy he had lived in an Indian cave in the green hills of the little *barrio* of Magueyes, near Coamo. The forest life of the old Borinqueños was not new to him; his home town of Jayuya had once been the *yucayque,* or village, of an Indian tribe. That may have been why he became El Coquero, the coconut cutter; he would wander free when he was not in jail.

"I am Juancito, El Coquero de Magueyes," he said: Little John, the Coconut Cutter of Magueyes. The old man rarely used his Christian name, Juan Candelario García. He preferred to be El Coquero: "The oldest *coquero* alive," he boasted.

The cave of Magueyes was not far from the old Spanish military road from Ponce to San Juan. On that dirt road the young boys of the 16th Pennsylvania Regiment marched under the coconut palms on their way to conquer San Juan—which they were destined never to conquer. He remembered the wandering Americanos not unkindly.

"They came to the jail. And freed me."

The old man did not lift his *machete* against them. Nor was he one of those who went into the hills to join the *macheteros* or *guerrilleros.*

In years past the *jíbaros* had fought alongside the Spaniards to defeat the invading armies of the English and the Dutch. Some of the *jíbaros* fought the Americanos too, in 1898; they fought "in the Villodos revolt, at Monte del Gato [the Mountain of the Cat], around Guayama and Salinas, at Asomante, Guánica, Yauco, and Guayanilla, and withdrew to the center of the island with the mass of the Spanish army, always harassing the enemy," recalled Miguel Meléndez Munoz, in his *El Jíbaro en el Siglo XIX* (*The Jíbaro in the Nineteenth Century*).

But not El Coquero. He waited and he watched. He thought, perhaps, as did many of the *jíbaros,* that it was wiser to sit by the road than to march with a new, or old, conqueror.

In the villages very few of the country people had ever seen a Yanqui before. The old *patrones* and young intellectuals of Ponce and San Juan knew that the United States had declared war against Spain, to "free Cuba" and force the Spanish empire out of the trade routes of the Caribbean; but the villagers hardly knew there was a war on.

Who were these men? Why were they here? Where did they come from? What did they want of us?

When the soldiers of General Nelson A. Miles landed on the twenty-fifth of July on the beach of the peaceful and remote village of Guánica, they surprised the stunned villagers and themselves as well. They had landed on the wrong beach of the wrong town on the wrong side of the island.

At the time, the Army had had little experience in overseas wars. Nor had the Navy. The officers had "a lack of knowledge of steamships," said Senator Henry Cabot Lodge, and less knowledge of tropical islands. "The vast majority of our people did not know [Puerto Rico] existed," Colonel Theodore Roosevelt, Jr., was later to write; and, as his father, President Theodore Roosevelt, wrote at the time, many of the men in his Rough Riders "had never seen a larger town than Santa Fe [New Mexico], or a bigger body of water than the Pecos in flood." So they "trusted the Navy" to get them to Puerto Rico, wherever that was.

In Washington, when the plans for the invasion of Cuba were drawn up in the spring of 1898, Puerto Rico was evidently thought to be too insignificant to be considered. The war fervor which swept through the newspapers and the Congress rarely, if ever, even mentioned the island.

The colony of exiled Puerto Rican patriots in New York resented the slighting of their century-old struggle for independence. Ever since 1869, when Dr. Ramón Betances and Eugenio María de Hostos, the "George Washington and Thomas Jefferson of Puerto Rican independence," met in New York to organize support for Cuban independence, the national leaders of the two countries had worked together to overthrow the Spanish colonialists. In 1892, when the Cuban Revolutionary party of José Martí was founded, the Puerto Rican exiles were among its leaders: Sotero Figueroa, the secretary of the party's council, was Puerto Rican. And, in 1895, the Junta Revolucionaria de Puerto Rico (the Revolutionary Council of Puerto Rico) was established as a section of Martí's group, with Dr. Julio J. Henna as its chairman.

It was Dr. Henna who journeyed to Washington on March 10, 1898, in an attempt to convince Senator Lodge of the need of "carrying the war to Puerto Rico if a Spanish-American conflict broke out." The elder Lodge, a distinguished member of the Senate's Foreign Affairs Committee, and one of the prominent "War Hawks," advised Dr. Henna to talk to Theodore Roosevelt, the young and rambunctious Assistant Secretary of the Navy.

"We have not given your island a single thought, and I have no information whatsoever on the place," Roosevelt was reported to have told the doctor. "All our activities are concentrated in Cuba."

The doctor promised the future Rough Rider that "the entire country would rise up *en masse* against the Spanish government, in the vanguard of the American forces." Whereupon, "The Under Secretary of the Navy got up, threw his arm around the doctor's shoulders and said, '. . . From this day forward Puerto Rico will figure prominently in the war plans we are preparing,' " according to an account of that conversation, retold in the *Crónicas de Puerto Rico* (*Puerto Rican Chronicles*) of Angel Rivera. In the days that followed, Dr. Henna and Roberto Todd, another Puerto Rican exile leader, met with the Navy chiefs, the War Committee, and President McKinley himself, urging that Puerto Ricans be permitted to lead the invasion, "with authority to sign proclamations"; as it had already been agreed the Cubans do. But their suggestions were graciously ignored.

Instead, the eager and inexperienced Roosevelt and Leonard

Wood, a former Army surgeon who had served in the wars against the Apaches and the capture of Geronimo, were commissioned to form the 1st United States Cavalry, the Rough Riders, to lead the attack. Roosevelt was to be colonel; Wood the lieutenant colonel.

On seeing Wood in the corridor of the White House, President McKinley would ask, "with a smile," "Have you and Theodore declared war yet?"

"No, Mr. President," Wood said, smiling back, "but we wish you would."

The impatient Colonel Roosevelt grumbled: "McKinley has no more backbone than a chocolate éclair." He wished to "get on" with "the splendid little war." If his Rough Riders did not get into action quickly, he feared he "might not even have had the consolation prize of going to Puerto Rico"; in fact, he never did.

His Rough Riders were made up of Indian fighters, bounty hunters, western sheriffs, tough old cowhands, former U.S. marshals, ex-preachers, professional gamblers, mountain men and a few Ivy League football heroes from Harvard, Yale, and Princeton; but most of the men were "wild riders of the plains" who "had taken part in the killing of the buffalo herds and had fought the Indians when the tribes were still on the war path," said Colonel Roosevelt. He boasted: "The captains and lieutenants were sometimes men who had campaigned in the regular army against the Apache, Ute and Cheyenne. . . .

"My men were children of the dragon's blood," he said. "They were to a man born adventurers."

There were "Rattlesnake Pete," who "had lived among the Moquis" (Hopis), "Cherokee Bill," "Happy Jack" of Arizona, and "Smoky" Moore. There were Ben Franklin Daniels, who had been "Marshal of Dodge City," and Sheriff "Bucky" O'Neill, of Prescott, Arizona, and no fewer than three sheriffs from New Mexico—Curry, Llewellen, and Ballard, "who had broken up the Black Jack gang of ill-omened notoriety." "Some were men whose lives in the past had not been free from that taint of those fierce kinds of crime into which the lawless spirits who dwell on the border land between civilization and savagery so readily drift," the Colonel said, not without a certain pride.

In the regular Army too these "lawless spirits" of the frontier filled the ranks. Congress authorized the raising of three cavalry regiments from among "the wild riders and riflemen" of the Rockies and the great plains, the Colonel explained. The Officers Corps and the General Staff were composed of such men, who had been fighting the Indian tribes for thirty years.

General Nelson A. Miles, an old Indian fighter himself, commanded the invasion. He had directed the campaigns against the Apaches, and he had forced the surrender of Chief Joseph's heroic band of Nez Percé, after the Army had mercilessly pursued the tribe halfway across the West, reducing the women and children to near starvation. It was for these triumphs that Miles was appointed Commanding General of the Army. In that honored post, on the twenty-fifth of July, 1898, Miles personally led the attack on Puerto Rico.

He issued a proclamation, as he often had before, in the wars against the Indians:

". . . in the cause of liberty, justice and humanity, [the] military forces [of the United States] have come to occupy Puerto Rico. They come bearing the banner of freedom. . . . We have not come to make war upon the people of a country that for centuries has been oppressed, but, on the contrary, to bring you protection, not only to yourselves, but to your property, to promote your prosperity, and to bestow upon you the immunities and blessings of the liberal institutions of our Government."

The landing on the island had been planned at Fajardo, on the extreme northeast corner, near San Juan, but it took place instead at Guánica on the extreme southwest corner near the island's desert. Some military tacticians later said that General Miles had wisely changed the landing site, because the Spanish Army was waiting at Fajardo. But some were dubious. The village harbor of Guánica had no docks large enough to berth any boats larger than a rowboat; as Senator Lodge politely said, "Guánica was very deficient." If there were few Spanish soldiers on hand to oppose the landing, there were few Americanos who could get ashore.

One correspondent wrote: "It was a hell of a way to fight a war."

The masses of the Spanish Army were on the distant coast. So it was difficult to fight at all. One thing that had apparently been overlooked by General Miles was that there was only one military road that crossed the mountainous island. In the intense heat of summer and the dense foliage of the jungles the Americanos never reached San Juan. The armies of Spain and the United States never were to meet in battle on Puerto Rico.

Even so, after nineteen days of marching about with little resistance—from July 25 to August 12, when Spain surrendered Puerto Rico—the somewhat confused Americanos had advanced a mere twenty miles up the western shore, to Mayagüez, and about thirty miles along the southern shore, to Guayama, and not much further than that on the road to San Juan, before they were stopped by the Spanish fortifications at the mountain town of Aibonito. Little more than one mile per day.

In the military annals of the campaign in Puerto Rico that brief encounter is often termed a "picnic." The truth was that the United States never conquered the island, nor occupied more than one-tenth of it, before Spain surrendered.

The war had actually ended before it had begun.

On July 22, three days before the troops of General Miles landed, the government of Spain had asked for peace. The cablegram of the Duke of Almodovar del Río, the Spanish Minister of State, had not reached President McKinley until July 26. It was odd because most of the cablegrams during the peace negotiations were delivered in one or two days; but this, the most crucial of them all, took four days to reach the President's desk. Spain's plea that the war be "terminated" at once had arrived, some thought conveniently, the day after the invasion fleet of General Miles had safely landed. It was then, of course, too late to recall them. So the United States, which in the beginning had not given "a single thought" to the island, could now demand "the immediate evacuation by Spain of the island of Puerto

Rico." The Duke of Almodovar del Río mournfully replied, "This demand strips us of the very last memory of a glorious past." And then surrendered.

In fighting the Indian tribes General Miles had had considerable experience with treaties of peace. The Army, in those wars against what Colonel Roosevelt called "the most bloodthirsty and wildest of all the red men of America," were not inhibited by the usual codes of war between nations. Nor was there an obligation to adhere to the protocol and terms of peace negotiations with those "wild beasts," the "savage Indians." To many of the military men the Spanish-American War must have seemed to be a continuation of the Indian Wars—merely a tropical Indian War.

"Warring against the colored nations was more dangerous and more exciting than big-game shooting, but still more or less in the same category," the son of the Rough Rider, Colonel Theodore Roosevelt, Jr., who was to become Governor of Puerto Rico, later wrote, in the *Colonial Policies of the United States.* He explained: "Destiny seemed to point to an entire world ruled by white people. . . . The general attitude of mind of the white people at that period was that no nation with any pretense to importance should be without colonies. We decided that we, too, would be an empire, and shoulder 'the white man's burden.' "

In the debate in Congress on whether or not the country should declare war, Senator Thurston of Nebraska had defined "the white man's burden" with refreshing self-interest: "War with Spain would increase the business and earnings of every American railroad, it would increase the output of every American factory, it would stimulate every branch of industry and domestic commerce." The "Saving of Civilization Business," as Mark Twain called it, was not without its material rewards; for "the white man's burden" consisted largely of highly profitable products for the export market. "God and commerce," to the minds of the war's more eloquent advocates, were partners in the conquest. In defending the war Senator Albert Beveridge of Indiana thundered in the Senate chamber: "[God] has marked the American people as His chosen nation to finally lead in the regeneration of the world. This is the *divine mission* of America."

As for the war booty, the Senator was as righteous: the islands "are ours forever," he intoned. "We will not repudiate our duty. . . . We will not abandon our opportunity. . . . We will not renounce our part in the mission of our race, trustee, under God, of the civilization of the world."

The eloquence of Senator Henry Cabot Lodge reiterated this theme, but with a patriotism that was literally fiery. "War is fire, and when it begins no one can tell where it will stop, or what will be burned away," declared the "Senator from the United Fruit Company," as his critics dubbed him. And, "this war has brought unimaginable results," said Lodge; it made the United States "a great world power."

In vain reply to the euphoria of conquest Senator George Hoar of Massachusetts, addressing his fellow Senators as "my imperialistic friends," told them: "You have sacrificed nearly ten thousand American lives, the flower of our youth. You have devastated provinces. You have slain countless thousands of the people you desire to benefit." His words were to re-echo in the Senate years later in the debates over the war in Vietnam. But he, too, was voted down.

The War against Spain was condemned by many as the most blatantly self-aggrandizing that the country had fought since the war against Mexico. It was a "miserable business," wrote ex-President Grover Cleveland. "I am ashamed of the whole affair." Carl Schurz, former Secretary of Interior in the Cabinet of President Grant, was so convinced that the "American people thoroughly opposed the policy of imperialism" that he called for a national plebiscite to reject the colonialization of Puerto Rico, Cuba, and the Philippines. He was wholeheartedly supported by Andrew Carnegie, perhaps the leading industrialist and steel baron of his day, who believed that if the plebiscite were held the "Government would be drowned."

In opposing the war Cleveland, Schurz and Carnegie were voicing the peace movement of the time, the Anti-Imperialist League, of which all three were officers. Unlike the peace movements of recent years, these nineteenth-century "doves" were representative of some of the titans of industry, the distinguished old banking families, and the most conservative liberal statesmen of their time; men who adhered to a belief in old-fashioned individualism and Jeffersonian democracy. "We are mostly Republicans," said Senator George Wellington of Maryland.

Founders of the Anti-Imperialist League of 1898 had been such national figures as ex-President Grover Cleveland, John G. Carlisle (Secretary of the Treasury), David Starr Jordan (president of Stanford University), William Graham Sumner, Moorfield Storey (Dean of the Yale Law School, the first president of the NAACP, and president of the American Bar Association), Episcopal Bishop Henry C. Potter, T. J. Conaly (Rector of the Catholic University), Reverend Edward Everett Hale, Simeon E. Baldwin (president of the American Social Science Association), Thomas Wentworth Higginson (descendant of a leader of the Puritan colony of 1629), Samuel Gompers (founder of the AFL), and a score of United States Senators. These men were the moral, if not the civic, leaders of what the nation had been. Like Andrew Carnegie, they fondly quoted the Lincolnian dictum, "When the white man governs himself and also governs another man, that is more than self-government; that is despotism."

In dismay and disgust the "doves" had attracted such intellectual luminaries as William James, William Dean Howells, and Mark Twain, who rewrote "The Battle Hymn of the Republic" to fit the war spirit of the day:

> In a sordid slime harmonious, Greed was born in yonder ditch . . .
> As Christ died to make men holy, let men die to make us rich—
> Our god is marching on! . . .
>
> Let the faithless son of Freedom crush the patriot with his heel;
> Lo, Greed is marching on!

Even as the government was demanding the possession of Puerto Rico at the signing of the Treaty of Paris, Senator George Vest of Missouri was introducing a resolution into Congress that declared: "Under the Constitution of the United States no power is given the

Federal Government to acquire territory to be held and governed permanently as colonies." His anticolonial resolution was one of half a dozen offered in the Senate. "The colonial system can exist in no free country, because it uproots and eliminates the basis of all republican institutions," said the Senator from Missouri. His plea was supported by the Anti-Imperialist League, with its 700,000 claimed members. But it was ignored by the pro-war Senators and Congressmen.

Lamented Charles Francis Adams, grandson of John Adams and son of John Quincy Adams, in a speech given at Lexington, Massachusetts, where barely a century before the American colonists had taken up arms against the British Empire: "On every one of the fundamental principles discussed (in the Declaration of Independence, the Constitution, George Washington's Farewell Address, the Monroe Doctrine) we abandon the traditional and distinctively American grounds." In his oration "Imperialism and the Tracks of Our Forefathers," the descendant of two Presidents sadly eulogized the passing of the "spirit of liberty" for which his ancestors had fought.

Once the war had been won it became more popular, as triumphant wars do. In his witty commentary on the war Finley Peter Dunne's not-so-comic character Mr. Hennessy said to Mr. Dooley about the island booty, "I'd take in th' whole lot iv thim"; to which Mr. Dooley mockingly replied, "An' yet 'tis not more than two months ago since ye learned whether they were islands or canned goods."

In the battle of "Americanism versus Imperialism," as Carnegie had termed it, to the victor went the spoils—Puerto Rico.

The independence of Puerto Rico from Spain had never interested the United States. Earlier in the century everything in its power had been done by Washington to make certain the island remained a Spanish colony, and that the black slaves on the island were kept enslaved.

After the defeat of the Spanish empire in Latin America by the armies of Simón Bolívar, the young republics of Mexico and Colombia had urged "the liberation" of Cuba and Puerto Rico. Many of the Spanish monarchists and colonialist officers from the continent had sought refuge on the islands, particularly on Puerto Rico. Until the Spaniards were driven from the Caribbean the newborn nations felt uneasy and threatened; *"Cuba y Puerto Rico Libre"* was the cry of the liberators.

In 1826 the Congress of Panama was convened by the newly independent nations of the Americas, to celebrate and consolidate their freedom. At that jubilant meeting Mexico and Colombia proposed their plan to free the islands; but the United States, invited to join the celebration of liberty, did so by demanding that the Spanish monarchy and black slavery be preserved in the Caribbean—much to the shock of the admiring Jeffersonians of Latin America. Secretary of State Henry Clay, in the Cabinet of President Adams, sent delegates to the Congress with instructions that the liberation of Puerto Rico and Cuba, advocated by Mexico and Colombia, was "by all means to be discouraged."

Slavery had to be protected, our government insisted. "If Cuba and Puerto Rico were to be revolutionized, slave insurrections would follow, and the insurrectionary spirit would be likely to communicate itself to the slave population of the Southern States," commented Carl Schurz in his *Life of Henry Clay*. The slaveowners dominated "not only [the] home policy, but also the foreign policy of the Republic. . . . It was therefore thought best that they [Cuba and Puerto Rico] should remain in the possession of Spain."

On the island the naïve *jíbaros* and *patrones,* who greeted the Americanos with flowers and flags, thinking they would "free them from Spain," knew none of that undiplomatic history. "Some of them thought that we were merely going to push the Spaniards out and then turn over the conduct of affairs to them," Colonel Theodore Roosevelt, Jr., cynically said. But the Puerto Rican exiles in New York knew better. They had heard the demands for the annexation of the islands that began during the presidency of Ulysses S. Grant. At that time, the Secretary of State, Mr. Fish, "reverted to the old idea of purchase [of the islands] and brought the proposition to the attention of the Spanish government." Senator Lodge noted that it was the "silly passion which Spaniards call pride" that ruined the cash sale. Ever since, the United States had been trying to replace Spain's imperial interests with its own.

His fear of such duplicity was what caused Eugenio María de Hostos to seek, futilely, to undo the work of Dr. Henna, and to halt the invasion. In Paris, Dr. Ramón Betances, on learning the American "war plans," wrote a desperate and prophetic letter to Dr. Henna:

> What are the Puerto Ricans doing? Why do they not take advantage of the opportunity afforded by the [naval] blockade to stage a mass rebellion? It is essential that, when the vanguard of the American Army lands on the shore of Puerto Rico it be received by Puerto Rican forces under the banner of independence, and that they be the ones to welcome them. Cooperate with the Americans . . . but do not help them annex our country. If Puerto Rico does not act promptly it will always remain an American colony.

It was too late. Once the military occupation of the island had been secured the Congress of the United States, on April 12, 1900, passed the Organic Act (or Foraker Act), which placed control of Puerto Rico harshly in American military hands. An "Executive Council" was set up, to be appointed by the President of the United States. Of its eleven members, six were American colonial officers. There was to be an elected "House of Delegates," or "Lower House"; but the "Upper House," composed of the appointed "Executive Council," in "clear violation of the principle of separation of governmental power" (*Americanization in Puerto Rico* by Aida Negrón de Montilla), had the "dominant position in the affairs of the Island." The Civil Governor was not to be elected, but was appointed by Washington. Freedom from monarchical colonialism had brought legislated colonialism.

The irony of all this was that Spain had granted Puerto Rico autonomy before the war began. In 1897, the Liberal party, then in power in Madrid, had reached an agreement with the island's leading statesmen, led by Luis Muñoz Rivera, in which "Puerto Rico was given not only a Government and Parliament of its own," but a large degree of control over its internal and foreign affairs, "plus exemption from military service and other dispensations which even today seem extraordinary" (*Enciclopedia Puertorriqueña*). On February 9, 1898, six months before the invasion of the island by the United States, Puerto Rico had become an autonomous state.

In the name of liberty the Foraker Act destroyed the liberty of the people. "The idea of self-determination had not been born," explained Colonel Theodore Roosevelt, Jr., "and altruism took the form of a firm belief that the best a white country could do for a colored one was to take it over and let the superior whites administer the affairs of the inferior indigenes. Besides all this," he added, "colonies were a badge of importance as far as a nation was concerned."

After the war the first Civil Governor of Puerto Rico, Charles H. Allen, called the people "unfitted to at once assume, without careful training and preparation, management of their own affairs." His words echoed those of the Military Governor, Brigadier General George W. Davis: "I have found it necessary to assert in strong terms the general unfitness of the great mass of the people [of the island] for self government. . . . Puerto Rico, unlike Dominica, Haiti and Venezuela and many other republics, never was, is not, and probably never will be independent."

General Hanna, the United States Consul in Puerto Rico, had testified with military simplicity: *"In the providence of God, she* [*the island*] *is ours today; she will be ours forever."*

Years later the freighter S. S. *Daniel Pierce* was shipwrecked in the harbor of Guánica. The old boat ran aground on a sandbar. In its hull was a cargo of sulphuric acid. On the waterfront of Guánica, near the wreck, there was a monument to the United States Army that had landed in that harbor on the day of the Fiesta de Santiago, the twenty-fifth of July, 1898. The tourists who came to see the monument were puzzled by words written on the rusting hull of the old freighter: *"Su Patria o Su Muerte":*

OUR COUNTRY OR OUR DEATH!

One dark night some youths had rowed out to the precarious wreck and had painted the patriotic words on the side of the ship. Whenever an American tourist would take a photograph of the monument to the American soldiers who had died on that beach, the words that paraphrased Patrick Henry's cry of "Liberty or death!" would appear in the background.

The town fathers of Guánica decided something had to be done about the unsightly wreck. It was suddenly discovered that the sulphuric acid was "eating through the tanker's hull"; the ship had to be disposed of for the safety of the harbor. So it was towed out to sea and sunk.

Somewhere on the bottom of the sea, the S.S. *Daniel Pierce* lies proclaiming to the fish: *"Su Patria o Su Muerte."*

"Let Us Construct a Water Closet!"

On the antiqued loveseat in his office, in the recesses of a corridor on the fourth floor of the Longworth Building of the House of Representatives, Jorge Córdova Díaz, the Resident Commissioner of Puerto Rico in Washington, D.C., and its spokesman in Congress (he could speak all he wished, but he could not vote), recently recounted the invasion of his island by his American friends with gentlemanly disdain: The Yankee Conquistadors were small-town imperialists, "the inventions of Mark Twain."

"America was a very provincial nation in those days," he said. "It was not prepared for the type of imperialism upon which it embarked at the turn of the century. It was not prepared to take over Puerto Rico.

"But it embarked on a policy of taking over all these islands—the Philippines, Guam, Hawaii, and Puerto Rico. And as a result a great deal of damage was done." It was not the conquest of Puerto Rico that he objected to; he deplored the lack of grace with which it had been done.

A man of handsome austerity, he came from an old and elegant family and had been a Supreme Court justice on the island before becoming a reluctant politician. Even now he had a haughty attitude toward the necessities of politics, which he thought of as "uncultured." The severest curse Señor Córdova could think of was to say someone was "uncouth." His conservatism was not so much the "Goldwater conservatism" his opponents accused him of as his inbred sense of what was proper; just as he was not so much pro-American as American-bred, having grown up as a boy in Washington, D.C., when his father was Resident Commissioner before him, from 1917 to 1932.

"It is hardly necessary to remind a people of Spanish ancestry," he had once written, that it has "nobility in its blood." The unforgivable misfortune of those Yankee Conquistadors was that they had no such nobility, but came from an "inferior culture"; that is, "It was inferior to our Spanish culture." He admired the Spain of Generalissimo Franco not because it was fascist but because it was Spanish.

Of the conquest of Puerto Rico he said with sadness: "In those years the people of the United States were far too provincial. So were their leaders. They knew of nothing beyond their borders. They thought the rest of the world was either semicivilized or savage. They believed no culture was of any worth but the culture which then prevailed in the United States.

"And they thought Puerto Rico was in deepest Africa."

The naïveté of the conquerors was humbly evident in the report of the Military Governor, Brigadier General George W. Davis (1899–1900), who voiced his befuddlement at discovering that the Puerto Ricans were not at all like New Englanders: "The laws, customs, language, institutions and aspirations of the people were all *strange, and in many respects, very difficult of comprehension*" (emphasis added). If the surprised General was baffled by these "strange" people, his successor, the first Civil Governor, Charles H. Allen, was less confused than confounded. In his official *First Annual Report of Charles H. Allen, Governor of Porto Rico* [sic], *submitted to the President of the United States, William F. McKinley, May 1, 1901,* he wrote with annoyance:

"American occupation found the island inhabited by a race [*sic*] of people of different language, religion, customs and habits, with no acquaintance practically with American methods."

It was decided that a body count of everybody and everything on the island was needed. But first the island had to be located on the map. That way the new Conquistadors would at least know where they were geographically.

"Porto Rico [*sic*], the loveliest island washed by the ocean's waves, lies between the Atlantic and the Caribbean, 1,380 miles from New York City," Governor Allen wrote to President McKinley. He compared the island to several states for size: "Porto Rico is approximately three times as large as Rhode Island, one and eight tenths larger than Delaware, three fourths the size of Connecticut, nearly one seventy eighth the size of Texas."

And then Governor Allen (he was an Amherst man, who had been Assistant Secretary of the Navy, along with Teddy Roosevelt) offered an early version of what was later to become known as "the Puerto Rican Problem." It seemed to him that the most urgent and immediate of the many obstacles facing those who hoped to Americanize the islanders was the problem caused by the lack of latrines: "this neglect in the use of modern [water] closets."

On the island there were "153,305 dwellings inhabited by the people," but "only 1,181 have modern appliances used in latrines," the Governor reported to the President; while "34,829 have old-style Spanish cesspools, and the remaining 114,295 have no provision made for such necessary conveniences." At the turn of the century, a fascination with bathroom plumbing and toilet fixtures had swept the

United States. To be a "civilized man" one had to have a toilet that flushed. Seventy years later, two-thirds of the homes still did not have "modern appliances used in latrines."

Years later, the *Caribbean Review* wryly quoted James Joyce's sardonic aside in *Ulysses* concerning the Roman conqueror who "brought to every new shore on which he set foot his . . . cloacal obsession. He gazed about him in his toga and he said: *It is meet to be here. Let us construct a watercloset.*"

In the eyes of Governor Allen there was another severe deficiency in the public welfare: the cemeteries were "crowded to overflowing." He lamented: "Military orders were issued that new cemeteries be opened, but poverty prevented their immediate enforcement." The Governor was hopeful that this blessing of civilization would soon be bestowed upon the island: "The time may yet come when some insular necropolis may rival Greenwood, or Arlington."

Once these sanitation problems posed by feces and death had been disposed of, the Governor turned to another problem which disturbed his New Englander's morality perhaps even more, what he distastefully referred to as "loose" sex.

As his Official Report to the President of the United States put it, rather indelicately: "On account of the loose relations of the sexes" more than one-third of the men and women who were living together as man and wife were not "legally married." His census takers had discovered that "upon this island [there are] 148,605 illegitimate children." It was true, the Governor wrote to the President, "that those people living in concubinage are generally quite as faithful to each other as those who are legally married," and that they had "just as much affection for their children." He hoped that with more "liberal laws," such as a "reduction of the fees" for marriage licenses, the "faithful" poor would be able to afford, and purchase, his standards of morality.

The Governor came at last to what he thought was the most immoral of all the sins of the Puerto Ricans. On the island not one person in ten worked at a regular job. There were 535,235 Borinqueños of "marriageable age," that is "over 15 years old." And yet, in all the manufacturing and mining, commerce and transportation industries there were no more than 51,591 workers. It was true there were said to be 197,761 "agriculturists," and 64,818 "laborers, who are supposed to be engaged in pursuits other than tilling the soil"; but he seemed to have his doubts about how hard they really worked. But, worst of all, there were a mere 2,194 citizens in the "professional classes," less than one-half of one percent of the population. That left 218,871 Borinqueños who did not seem to be working at all.

The exasperated Governor said: "These children of the sun have learned to rely too much on the kindness [of nature]"; it had encouraged "their natural ability to slumber." To a man who had come from a country where vagrancy was a crime and loafing was a sin, he knew at once there was something wrong with a country where leisure was a way of life.

Were not the *jíbaros* "like the Indian," as an officer of the United States Army had complained? In those missionary and government Indian Agent reports of the nineteenth century there was no more calamitous and self-righteous unease with the life style of an American Indian tribe than in Governor Allen's chastisement of the "children of the sun," the "idle," "lazy," and morally "loose" Puerto Ricans. He might have been writing of an Indian reservation, rather than a tropical island. The old colonialist attitude of paternal benevolence that had been nourished for over a century toward the Indians was about to be exported to the new colony.

In the Governor's tale of the island's woes he expressed faith in the "indomitable thrift and industry which has always marked the pathway of the Anglo Saxon." That lonely hope was his sole optimistic note. He believed that they alone would "make at least five spears of grass to grow where one had grown before." In time, the spirit of American industrialization would bring to Puerto Rico riches "sufficient not only to support in comfort the million of people which we have now [on the island], but five times as many." That is, five million people; an interesting prophecy in light of the dire predictions of overpopulation of his successors.

All that was necessary was "the introduction of fresh blood," Governor Allen concluded, ". . . the American capitalist."

After more than half a century the memory still embittered Resident Commissioner Córdova. He was an ardent supporter of the United States, an advocate of statehood for Puerto Rico; "so-called independence" was akin to "treason" in his view. It was "being imposed on Puerto Rico by the puppets of the Cuban dictator" and the "public enemies" of the island. Still, history was history. He blamed the colonialist attitude of early officials on "the arrogance they inherited from the British empire," and the ignorance of the United States.

Córdova recalled the attitude toward Puerto Rico among members of Congress in the twenties and thirties. "When my father was in Washington most of the politicians didn't know, or care, enough about Puerto Rico to have an attitude. And that extended to our Presidents!" Only President Woodrow Wilson was respectful of Puerto Rico in his father's day. Those who followed him—Harding, Coolidge, and Hoover—were "horrible."

"But we have gotten over that," said the Commissioner. "Now it is a rare Congressman who hasn't visited Puerto Rico. And many of them have a good idea where Puerto Rico is. They do not think it is someplace in deepest Africa, or in the farthest reaches of the less cultured spots in the world's oceans."

On the wall as he reminisced was an autographed photograph of Vice President Spiro Agnew; beside it was a thank-you note from President Richard Nixon.

7

The *Jíbaros*

The man with the broom came onto the plaza. He swept up the cigarette butts.

One by one, with a round, straw broom, he cleansed the cobblestones. A man ought to walk with dignity in the plaza of his own town. No matter how poor he was, or the town. The country people of the mountains, the *jíbaros,* were too poor to be without pride. In every town, on every morning, the man with the broom swept up the night.

In the mountain town of Utuado the plaza was as clean and quiet as the sky. There were none of the noises of the city. Nor smog. Nor tensions. Nor garbage clogging the gutters. The poorest *jíbaros* had respect for the town. Long before the coming of the Spaniards, in the 1500s, the native islanders had lived in the villages of the mountains. And Utuado, like the neighboring towns of Jayuya and Adjuntas and Lares, was a sanctuary and symbol of the "soul of Puerto Rico"; it honored the old ways.

The man with the chickens then came into the plaza. He came singing to his chickens.

A wiry man, his neck as scrawny as an old cock's, he wheeled his wire cages ahead of him with ceremonial step. The uneasy hens cackled, as though they knew the old women were waiting to fondle their breasts and wring their necks. In his disdain for the old women who asked him, "How much for this one?" and "How much for that one?" the man wheeled his cages to the public market, but did not enter; he stood outside talking to his cronies and pretending to ignore the old women. He would get higher prices that way.

Now it was time for the old man with the cross to enter the plaza. He came with his young God dangling on a chain around his neck.

On the steps of the Church of Saint Michael he stood stiffly as an arthritic Conquistador. He opened the heavy wooden door of the church slowly, for he was old. At last the door swung open. He thanked God. He blessed the town. The bells tolled for the mass. The workday could now begin.

For hundreds of years the day had begun this way. Why should this day be different?

Buenos días. Good day to you. If a man had no time to be polite, he had no time for God, or man. He was no longer a Puertorriqueño.

The *jíbaros* said: A man should live each day as though it were his entire life. That is because each day was a lifetime.

On the mountain roads, said the *jíbaros,* a wise man walked as though the day had forty-eight hours. That was because it did.

Horses pranced into the plaza with the fast gait of the delicate *paso finos,* the Fine Steppers, sometimes know as the *fino finos;* for these graceful and small horses were said to have such perfect balance that they could trot up a steep hillside so smoothly that their riders holding a glass of water would not spill a drop.

In the hills of Utuado, at the *jíbaro barrio* of Caonillas, there had been a *potrero,* or horse farm, where the *paso finos* had once been bred. The brothers Asencio and Blas de Villahueva had built the *potrero* in the early 1500s. And from the Arabian and Spanish horses that the Conquistadors had brought to the island they developed the unique *paso finos* of the *jíbaros.* Later the horses were taken by Cortéz and Pisarro and De Soto for the conquest of Mexico, Peru, and the United States. Don Pedro Matos, whose family had lived for centuries in the hills of Caonillas, said to me. "So it was Puerto Rican horses that helped conquer the Americas." He told me that the Southwestern mustangs and cow ponies were descended from the *paso finos.*

Into the plaza rode the young men in their *jíbaro* hats, straw-brimmed *pavas,* tilted back with jaunty *macho.* They had come into the town at dawn to show off their horses and themselves to their girl friends. The schoolgirls merely smiled behind their hands.

The cars then came out of the hills, the alleyways, and the *barrios* into the quiet plaza. A policeman, who was gossiping with the chicken man, pretended not to see or hear the noisy traffic jam. He knew better than to interfere. The *jíbaros* drove their old cars with the same bravado that they rode their horses; it was safer to stay out of their way.

¡Jíbaro, Sí! ¡Yanqui, No!

A melodious chant of the newest political slogan chorused into the plaza. The singers were young, and their voices were sweet and angry.

¡Jíbaro, Sí! ¡Yanqui, No!

Into the traffic students of the local high school rushed, in mini-skirts and bell bottoms, crying out *Ahora,* the name of the newspaper of the Puerto Rican Independence party, and *Claridad,* the newspaper of the Puerto Rican Socialist party, admonishing the *jíbaros* in their stalled Fords and Chevies that the "imperialist culture" of the Yanquis was invading the town. The policeman smiled. The old padre scowled. A loudspeaker blared forth the latest "Latin rock" hit song from New York. The students danced. The man with the chickens lifted a Coca-Cola bottle to his lips. In the bottle was island rum. The shop windows reflected the morning sun like mirrors, as did the gray screens of color television sets, amid displays of religious amulets and spiritualist herbs and plastic crucifixes made in Japan and transistor radios and St. Joseph's aspirins and Day-glo bumperstickers that proclaimed "PUERTO RICO, MI ENCANTO"—"MY ENCHANTED ONE, PUERTO RICO."

The day spanned the centuries in a few moments.

On the benches of the plaza the old *jíbaros* were silent, but their eyelids wrinkled in delight. The boys and girls crying their *grito* of defiance in the streets were their grandchildren. In their own youth the old men and their wives had cried out in the plazas, too. But with *machetes* in their hands.

Lean, taut, quiet, taciturn, soft-spoken, articulate but illiterate men, the *jíbaros* had been the foot soldiers of every revolution on the island since the uprising of the Utuado Indians against the Spaniards, in 1511. It was they who united the mountain tribes of Borinqueños and the escaped African slaves in guerrilla warfare against the Spanish plantations and mines through the sixteenth century. They joined the Spaniards to defend their island against the invading armies of the English and Dutch.

In these mountain towns lived the *guerrilleros* and *macheteros* who had fought the Spaniards in the revolts of the early 1800s. On the Plaza of Lares it was the *jíbaros* (many had come from neighboring Utuado) who raised the flag of Puerto Rico in the Revolution of 1868. When that revolution was lost after the Spanish repressions of 1887, the "Terrible Year," many of its intellectual leaders had to flee the country, but it was the illiterate but knowing *jíbaros* who kept the independence movement stubbornly alive. By 1891 they had become so strong that the colonial police arrested seventy members of the Asociación Liberal Separatista de Utuado on the charge of "conspiracy" to drive the Spaniards out. They were defended by the statesman and poet José de Diego. Not even his eloquence could help them, though, for several of the accused proudly proclaimed their guilt in court.

"A man ought to say what he believes for everyone to hear. He ought to be proud of his beliefs," said one of their descendants. "If I have to choose between my life and my conscience, I choose my conscience."

The grandchildren of these *jíbaros* came out of the mountains a century later to die in the aborted revolts of the 1930s and 1950s, when the Nationalists led by Don Pedro Albizu Campos fought to oust the Americanos from the island.

In the old days the folk saying was *"¡Para un jíbaro, otro jíbaro, y para dos, el diablo!"* ("One *jíbaro* equals another *jíbaro,* and yet two *jíbaros* equal the devil!")

"If it were not for us, the *jíbaros,* there would be no Puerto Rico," said Don Pedro Matos Matos. "The heart and soul of Puerto Rico is in the heart and soul of the *jíbaros*.

"For hundreds of years we have resisted all the foreigners—the Spaniards *and* the Americans. You know how? It is no mystery. On the coasts, in the cities of San Juan, Ponce, Mayagüez, when the foreigners came, they assimilated the Puerto Ricans. Not here! In Utuado, in the mountains, the foreigners were assimilated by us. *¡Sí!* They marry our women. And our women they make Puertorriqueños out of them. The *jíbaros* are very stubborn. Especially if they are women. I think our women may be a little more Indian than our men.

"Anyone who wishes to know the Puerto Rican must know the *jíbaros,*" said Don Pedro. "Or he knows *nothing*. We *are* Puerto Rico."

In the muted town of Utuado, the voice of Don Pedro was as clear as the church bell. On the plaza he often had spoken of what it meant to be a *jíbaro*. A man of passionate words, intense but gentle, he breathed the "*jíbaro* spirit," though he in no way looked like the stereotype of the poor country man. He drove an American car; he used an electric typewriter. He wore no *pava* or any hat at all. Yet he was a *jíbaro*. "In my bones," he said, "and in the bones of my ancestors, who live on this island."

The son of a poor *jíbaro,* he had been sent to an orphan home after his father's death, his family was so destitute; then he enlisted in the U.S. Army, lived by his wits in Harlem, cut cane in the sugar fields, worked at construction jobs, was a journalist and an independence activist.

"I am a simple man," he said with barely a smile. "Just a typical *jíbaro*."

Don Pedro sold life insurance. "For the dead," he said, laughing. In his air-conditioned office on the Calle George Washington, near the plaza, he leaned back in his push-buttoned lounging chair bought at J. C. Penney, and deprecated his success. "That," he said, "is what I do for money. It does not fill my heart."

"Ah, Don Pedro, he is in love with the *jíbaros,"* a friend said. "Some men have a mistress. Don Pedro has Puerto Rico. And he is jealous of his love as a *jíbaro* is of his *querida,* his beloved."

On the wall above his desk was a large portrait of Dr. Betances, the "Father of Puerto Rican Independence." In the bookcase at his side was an eleven-volume set, in frayed leather bindings, of the *Messages and Papers of the Presidents of the United States,* the last volume incongruously devoted to the Rough Rider Theodore Roosevelt. Beside it was Eisenhower's *Crusade in Europe, Lyndon B. Johnson: The Exercise of Power,* a thumbed file of electronic catalogues, and Ian Fleming's *You Only Live Twice.*

"Jíbaros are not simple-minded, as you may think. We understand the paradoxes of history. We have lived with them for so many centuries. We are more sophisticated than it seems. I have little education, but I learn everything I can about history. So I can teach the young. So they will outwit history."

The *"Patrón* of the Youth," he was called by some. His office was always full of students—the boys and girls of the streets—who listened to his tales of the *jíbaros,* of how it was "before the Yanquis," and to the history that he alone seemed to remember.

"In the early years of the Conquistadors, that is in 1509, or after, the Spaniards came to Utuado from the sea. They came on a short cut through the jungles. It was an Indian trail. They arrived, first, at where Caonillas is today. Where my family lived. They started to bring horses and cargo into the mountains around 1519. Those were the horses of Cortéz."

So he began. The bored teachers at the local high school would have been dumfounded by the rapt attention with which their bored students listened to the words of Don Pedro.

"Who lived here before the Spaniards?" he went on. "The Indians lived here. In this area there is evidence of many Indian villages."

In the mountain valleys the Indians "were rich" in those days, he said. "The land was rich, and all the land was theirs. The water was clean. The crops of corn grew plentifully. The fruits grew on the trees like flowers. Even the men of Columbus remarked how sturdy the villagers were." And, "They had none of the disease, ugly behavior, prostitution, and slavery that the Europeans brought to our island."

Life was serene. "Then, around the year 1553, one Asencio de Villanueva requested from the King of Spain authority to found our town of Utuado. It was to be called La Villanueva del Otoao, which is 'The New Village of Otoao,' in honor of the Indian chieftain who ruled the land. But the King had a requisite poor Villanueva could not meet: he had to bring fifty families from Spain and pay the costs of bringing them, to settle a town. For this reason of poverty Utuado was not founded until almost two hundred years more."

And still the Spaniards came. They conquered the Indians. When they caught them, they killed them, or "made love to them. So, you see, we, the *jíbaros,* were born of love and war. We are the children of that paradox of history.

"Jíbaro was the name of a tribe of Amazonian Indians, related to the Tupi-Guarani family. They are known as the most hostile to 'Western' cultural assimilation," Don Pedro said. In his opinion, the Borinquén Indians were "relatives" of the Jíbaro, or Gíbaro tribe.

In adopting the name of *jíbaro,* the Spaniards used it to describe the Indians, and later the mestizos and the Blacks who escaped to the mountains, fleeing servitude, Don Pedro said. Later, it came to identify the *criollos* or Puertorriqueños in the rural zones "who kept the rustic way of life and who were free of assimilation." In the central highlands, the Indians and Europeans mated, as did the Blacks and Indians and Europeans on the coastal lowlands. "That is why there are two types of *jíbaros* in Puerto Rico," said Don Pedro. "Some say they are 'pure Spanish,' and some resemble Africans, pale black, with curly or kinky hair." Both were "morally and spiritually Puerto Rican."

"The *jíbaro* is uniquely Puerto Rican," Don Pedro said. "He exists nowhere else on earth."

In the *Nuevo Diccionario Velázquez* the word "*jíbaro*" is said to be of Cuban Indian origin, meaning to "run wild." The historian Coll y Toste, in his *Prehistoria de Puerto Rico,* doubts this: "Our provincial word *jíbaro* [derived] from the root *jiba* [a native bush]," he writes, and was "indigenous"; although he notes that in Cuba it was used to "designate a wild dog." And the historian Salvador Brau, in his *Historia de Puerto Rico,* writes that the Spaniards used the word fearfully to describe "the countryfolk of Puerto Rico," because of "their rough and wild habits." He too insists the word was of Indian origin. There is no Spanish equivalent for *jíbaro*.

So deeply embedded were the Indian ways in the life of the *jíbaros* that when the Spaniards officially founded the town of Utuado, in 1733, they gave it the Indian name of Otoao. "Not until the year 1745, in the parochial baptismal book, on page three, on February 27, was the word 'Utuado' used for the first time," said Don Pedro. "In the beginning Utuado was just a small village. With no church. Just a few houses. And mostly Indian inhabitants.

"And that is why the *jíbaros* are so stubborn, so silent, so humble, and so independent. Because we are so Indian. That is why we resist assimilation."

"We say, Yes! to the conquerors. In our hearts we say, No!" said a cane cutter, Luis Pérez.

It was the Indian way. And it was the *jíbaro* way. The colonialization of the land by the Spaniards and then the Americans, into a one-crop economy, was resisted by the *jíbaros.* "At first, we grew cocoa beans for the conquerors, then we grew ginger, which grows wild along the riverbeds, then we grew coffee, then we grew sugar cane, and then tobacco," said Don Pedro. "But in Utuado we always managed to grow many crops simultaneously—the tobacco, the coffee, and our own food. So, though in the lowlands they had a one-crop economy, in the mountains we boasted a diversified agriculture. That accounted for our more sound economy in our towns. In our land we raised corn, all kinds of beans, rice, and roots—the old Indian food. Even our land had an independent spirit."

The land had once belonged to the *jíbaros,* as it had to the Indians. "Of all the farms fully 93 per cent are tilled by their owners," wrote the first American Governor, Charles H. Allen, in 1901. Hardly "7 per cent are renters." Their farms were small, averaging 45 acres. Even their coffee "plantations" averaged no more than 27½ acres; while the sugar "plantations" were barely 35 acres.

On his small plot of land, that was his not by deed but by inheritance, the *jíbaro* grew all the food he needed for his family. He freely picked the wild tropical fruits growing about his *bohío,* or hut, to sweeten his diet. On the island there were no droughts, no crop failures, and the growing season lasted all year. The *jíbaro* had little money. But he was a free man.

"Nature has done so much for these people and has required so little in return that the problem of life has been free of those terrible anxieties which possess the soul of toilers in other climes," Governor Allen wrote in envy and awe of the *jíbaro*. The soul of his Protestant ethic was threatened by the sight: "In a climate where the temperature ranges between 70 and 85 degrees, day and night, week in and week out, where little clothing is required and shelter means protection from the tropical sun rather than climatic changes; *where a man can lie in a hammock, pick a banana with one hand and dig* [*up*] *a sweet potato with one foot, the incentive to idleness is easy to yield to*" (emphasis added).

So rich was the island, the American Governor wrote, that a ten-acre orange grove could support a family "in the best country style of Virginia, or Ohio." He thought the ease of life of the *jíbaros* was so pleasant as to be sinful.

"Like the Indian," an officer of the U.S. Army of Occupation said in 1899, the *jíbaro* "is not given to labor; in his resistance to civilization he confines his efforts to the strictest necessities." His complaint was echoed by the Post Commander of Humacao, a Captain Swift. "They are inferior to the cotton field hands of the United States. They are weaker physically, less ambitious, more shiftless and idle." And the Commanding General of the U.S. Army, Brigadier General George W. Davis, summed it up: "They are without ambition and see no incentive to labor beyond the least that will provide the barest sustenance. All over the island they can be seen, sitting beside their ruined huts [after the hurricane of San Ciriaco, in 1899] taking no thought of tomorrow."

Such words re-echoed the eighteenth-century lament of an Irish soldier of fortune, who as an emissary of the King of Spain called the *jíbaros* "lazy and unsuitable men" whose "habits of indolence were encouraged by the sweet climate." Marshal Alexandro O'Reylly foresaw no way of forcing the *jíbaros* to "better themselves," but by "the levelling of the forests."

If the Spaniards of the eighteenth century lacked the will, and the technology, for "levelling the forests," the Americans of the twentieth century possessed both.

Don Pedro believed that the invasion of Puerto Rico by the United States led to the ruin, almost total ruin, of our farms. Coffee exports were halted. By commercial agreements with other countries, "the United States destroyed our coffee markets in Europe. And, in mountain towns like Utuado, we produce the best coffee in the world."

After recovering from the hurricanes of 1928 and 1930, the *jíbaros* had managed to maintain a stable economy all through the Depression. Then, in the late 1930s, Don Pedro said, the governments of the United States and Puerto Rico began to create artificial lakes in the mountains to produce electric power for urban industrialization. "They dug up our towns. They flooded our best farmland. They made the *jíbaros* homeless in their own land.

"Fields were abandoned. Farms were abandoned. When those dams and lakes and power plants were built everyone wanted to work there. There were good jobs. And money. So everyone looked to the power plants for work. No one wanted to work on the farms. So the food producers from the United States absorbed local markets. And we, who has always grown our own food, had to import food. We couldn't compete with your giant food companies. They ruined the last production we had, which was food." Nor did the farms benefit from the power plants: "After the dams and lakes and power plants were completed we had no farm economy and we had no work. The electricity was not for us, anyway. It was for the cities. So we started down. We lost our way of living to progress. Progress brought us hunger."

In *The Pauperization of the Jíbaro,* the economist Raymond E. Crist said that the original landowner usually moved to town to become part of the meager middle class; a few of his *peones,* or workers, "uprooted and landless—their shadowy birthright sold for a lean mess of pottage," took jobs, but "the many, now landless and displaced, formed a great reservoir of cheap labor."

Everywhere on earth it has been the same, the trek of reluctant refugees fleeing from rural towns, as from a battlefield devastated by technological war, into the urban ghettos. One by one they came at first. Then by entire families. On the island by the late 1940s it was an exodus.

In the cities the barefoot *jíbaro* was a country buffoon. He was likened to a stubborn burro or a rare tropical bird. The motif of ridicule was foretold by the Chief of the Insular Police, an American officer, who in 1920 declared: "We divide the people of Porto Rico [sic] into four categories for purposes of [criminal] identification according to the shape of their feet. The minority, mostly townspeople, wear shoes. Of the great mass of countrymen, those with broad flat feet, live in the canefields around the coast. The coffee men [*jíbaros*] have over-developed big toes, because they use them in climbing the steep hills. In the tobacco districts, where the planting is done by foot, they are short and stubby. It beats the Bertillon [police identification] system all hollow." To the Chief of Police, the urban *jíbaro* did not have an identifiable face, just a foot; though that may have been an American conceit or joke.

The scholarly scions of the older colonialism of the island—the wealthy *criollos*—viewed the *jíbaro* more solemnly, but no less contemptuously. He was "barefoot, ignorant and sickly, superstitious and dreadfully inefficient," wrote the eminent sociologist José C. Rosario, in *The Development of the Puerto Rican Jíbaro and His Present Attitude Toward Society,* in the 1930s. The *jíbaro* was "the Island's greatest social problem."

"A unique pre-industrial character type," the contemporary anthropologist Gordon Lewis said in his book *Puerto Rico: Freedom and Power in the Caribbean.* "The decadent seminatural economy" of the *jíbaro* was inherited from "the descendants of" the Indians. He was a peripheral man, archaic and quaint, who had "inherited, to begin with, the anti-social individualism of the early Spanish settlers, many of whom were common soldiers." Still, the *jíbaro* was of "some importance," the anthropologist conceded, for better or worse, the beginning of "the peasant class so typical of Puerto Rican society, even today."

Don Pedro remembered: "When I was a boy *jíbaro* used to mean a man who was rustic, uncivilized, rough, ordinary, stupid. He was thought of as a hillbilly. It was an insult for a man to be called *jíbaro.*

"Not any more!" he said.

Once the *jíbaro* had lost his land and spirit, and been forced into the ghettos of the cities, to be relegated to the urbane refuse heap of the "culture of poverty," then, ironically, his image was elevated to the status of a "folk hero." He was hailed as the romantic, if not always noble, common man. Governor Luis Muñoz Marín founded his Popular Democratic party in 1938 upon "the image of the *jíbaro.*" His party symbol was the profile of a *jíbaro,* wearing a *pava.* And Governor Luis Ferre, the advocate of statehood, in 1970 assured his followers that his New Progressive party was really seeking merely a "*Jíbaro* Statehood." It amused Don Pedro. "Nowadays, any Puerto Rican, rich or poor, white or black, educated or illiterate is proud of being called a *jíbaro,*" was Don Pedro's wry comment, "even Governor Ferre."

The newest image of the *jíbaro* was eloquently evoked by a writer. "What is the *jíbaro?*" María Teresa Babin asked in *The Puerto Rican Spirit.* "The *jíbaro* represents that which is most intimate, resistant and pure of the Puerto Rican nationality," the "essence" of "*Puertorriqueñismo.*"

On the benches of the plaza of Utuado the old *jíbaros* sat silently. They neither laughed nor cursed. They had heard many things. They had seen conquerors and saviors come and go. They would *sentarse y esperar*—sit down and wait.

Each was the ruler of his *batey,* his yard. He ignored the world beyond. And his neighbors and his family treated him with the dignity of a king, though he was poorer than the poor. A man was a man. He was not a dog. He was not a chicken. He might be a cock, but that was different. A cock had style.

His sitting was not idle. It was not a time of rest between his labors. The Spanish word for that was *huelga.* In the modern world of industry *huelga* had come to mean a strike. The word was old, going back to the days when the peasants would enjoy a *huelga,* rest in the fields of the Lord. A man who was thinking about life was not idle. "He may be looking at things, or studying them, or enjoying life, or doing what is the hardest and most important thing of all—learning *serenidad*—serenity," said a *jíbaro* on a coffee farm in Jayuya. "That takes a man a lifetime to learn."

To sit with *serenidad* a man had to believe in the eternity of everyday life. Nothing changed, though everything changed. "The soul of the *jíbaro* has not changed as much as you may think," said Don Pedro. "He has changed the clothes he wears, but the soul of a man is not something he buys in a supermarket."

In the eyes of these *jíbaros* on the benches there was a bright blasphemy that viewed the twentieth century as an absurdity, rather than an inevitability. There was none of the hopelessness that deadened the eyes of old men on the benches of the cities. Like Indians, the *jíbaros* seemed to know a joke or a truth they kept to themselves.

"Even in the cities the office workers are the sons and daughters of the *jíbaros,*" a shopkeeper in the town of San Germán told me. "Some say they are lazy. They are not lazy. They do not work for the sake of working, the way you Anglo-Saxons do. To do that would be 'uncivilized.'

"Our people on the island are essentially still hunters and gatherers. Like the Indians. If the *jíbaros* need work, they work. They work hard. They go and get a job the way they used to go and pick fruit off a tree, in the *campos,* the countryside.

"Like the Indians," he repeated. "Why work if you don't have to?"

So the *jíbaros* sang:

Le, lo, le, le, lo, le,
I have nothing to do,
I have nothing to do.
I pursue this life
For it gives me joy;
Everything is mine,
I don't have to save,
I don't have to think,
The way of life loves us,
Everything is in my hand,
Without having to work.

In the words of Luis Marcano, a *jíbaro* singer of Cidra, a poor village in the mountains, the impoverished life of his countrymen had became a dreamlike idyll. The song mocked itself. Everyone who listened to such a song laughed at himself.

Le, lo, le, le, lo, le,
I am become a wastrel,
I am become a wastrel.
I drink a little beer,
And if there is a small guitar
I also sing a song,
And if I get a nickel
I spend it on billiards.
I may win or lose,
Why should I get angry,
If I can enjoy myself
Without having to work?

And yet there was a sorrow in the words. The journalist Mariano April once wrote: "In the Puerto Rican countryside a deep sadness reigns, reflected in the vague melancholy of the people's songs, a sort of nostalgia for a pleasanter, happier, freer life."

Evening came, warm and cool, like the tropical rain. On the plaza the lights darkened by nine o'clock. The shutters of the shops and houses were shut to keep out the lizards and the sudden rains. A few young men talked loudly in the one bar and poolroom that stayed open until midnight. But by then the old padre had put down his book and his last glass of wine. The old *jíbaros* on the benches of the plaza had gone home. The policeman had gone to sleep.

Then the jungles awoke. The small frogs or *coquís,* whose song was like their name—*¡Coquí! ¡Coquí!*—became a symphony. Even in the suburbs of San Juan the *coquís* interrupted the late news on TV. Here in Utuado their voices sounded like the spirits of the dead.

At midnight all the cocks began to crow, as they do when the moon is high. The old man, *el viejo,* went out of his hut to piss down the mountain, as he often did at 2 A.M. The cocks crowed again. As the false dawn lit the mountain ridges at 4 A.M., the cocks crowed once more. They crowed for a last time at 6, though their hearts were no longer in it. By dawn, when it was time to wake up the town, the cocks were too tired to do anything but go to sleep.

Soon it would be time for the man with the broom to come into the plaza.

8

The Bittersweet Sugar

Grasses grew three times as tall as a man and they tasted sweet as sugar. In the wind the grasses were becalmed as the green waves of an inland sea. The long, sweet grasses were, indeed, canes of sugar. They grew wildly as weeds, billowing in the wind like a surf against the sky. It was easy to forget they had nurtured empires of rum and molasses and slavery.

The long grasses grew tall; some were known to have grown as tall as a four-story building, but they swayed as delicately as palm trees. The knives of the sugar mills were disrespectful of the majestic grasses, they knifed and crushed them and ground them down into teaspoons of sugar. In the mills the barracuda-sharp rows of cane knives, the crushers and the mechanical grinders shrieked like the cry of a tortured man caught in the gears.

Los viejos, the old men, with limbs like roots, remembered the day it had actually happened. A man, maybe a little drunk, had lost his footing; he was torn to pieces by the cane grinders. In every sugar *central* the old men remembered when that happened. It happened in every mill. Once or many times, so they said.

A *viejo* suggested the new advertising slogan for the sugar industry: "Just a little sugar in your coffee. Just a little blood in your sugar," he said.

The Gothic offices of the sugar mill of Guánica were the relics of another era, of plantation owners in white suits, but the old man who appeared wore his hair crew-cut, businesslike.

"Mister" Oliver was his name. He was not the *patrón* or the owner of the mill. He was a "pretty good *gringo,*" they said, but no one fondly called him a *don*. Nor was he a *señor*. In "almost" retirement he had become the mill manager to "see what I can do to help the government, which runs this museum piece now, revive the dying sugar industry," he said; but, still, a Yanqui was a Yanqui, and he was always "Mister" to the men who worked in the mill.

All his life he had been the manager of sugar mills. Maybe he had lived too long, he said with tight lips—as though the taste of the sugar has turned bitter in his mouth.

Once the mill of Guánica had ground one million tons of sugar cane a year. No more. Like a colonial palace it had stood amid the graceful palms on the tranquil harbor of Ensenada. Now the white paint had peeled from the verandas, its machinery was archaic and rusted. The mill was a memory of the days when "sugar was the King of the Yanquis."

The cane was piled in dry and rotted heaps, in the yard. So far that year there had been four breakdowns of machinery. "And so the cane lies there and dries out. It's just like a mess of *bagasse." Bagasse* was the waste; the dried and squeezed husk of cane left after its sugar had been extracted, from the Spanish word *"bagasa,"* that meant a whore, a dried-up woman.

The poor yields of the sugar troubled Arturo Riollano, one of the island's leading agronomists and coordinator of the University Agricultural Experimental Station sugar cane programs in Río Piedras. He sang a dirge for "the rhythm of the industry's rapid deterioration"; the sugar production had suffered from a "downward trend [that] has been continuous and implacable," he said; it was "disastrous." The government had been forced to assume the management of practically the whole sugar industry.

In 1952, when the sugar cane harvest reached an all-time high of 1,300,000 tons, there were some 36 sugar mills, or *centrales,* on the island, and more than 19,000 sugar plantations. They employed almost 150,000 cane cutters alone. But by 1972 more than 7,000 of the sugar plantations and 16 of the *centrales* had been abandoned. There were fewer than 25,000 cane cutters.

By the spring of 1969 the island's sugar crop had fallen to a fifty-year low. By 1971 it threatened to be even worse. In his despair, the Secretary of Agriculture, Rivera Brenes, had appealed to the heavens: "God willing, if the weather, which has been good since Holy Week, continues to hold up, all the cane will be cut," he hoped.

"Blame the weather," said the Secretary of the low sugar yield of the cane.

Mister Oliver did not blame the weather, or God, but his fellow Americans in the sugar-refining industry. "For years the mill was run by the South Puerto Rico Sugar Company," he said. "They ran it well. And they took out good profits." Then the old mill was bought by the conglomerate Gulf and Western. It was rumored that they intended to use its losses as a tax write-off. The officials of the company denied this.

"The management cut all of our fields of seed cane and fed it into the mill. Cut the seed cane!" he said in dismay. "Well, how can we improve the quality of the cane when all the seed is gone? Let men go. Let the machinery go to ruin. They didn't care about things like that. They didn't want to invest any money. The mill went bankrupt, and then they sold it to the government."

If only the old machinery was fixed, "we can bring it back," the manager said; he had faith in machinery.

On a nearby farm, in Yauco, a sugar-cane farmer was not as forgiving: "The sugar companies have ruined my sugar crop," he accused. "It was the Americanos who brought the sugar industry to the island. And it is they who have destroyed the sugar crops."

In 1897, before the invasion of the island by the United States, the annual sugar production was a mere 68,328 tons. The long, sweet grasses were not native to the island. Spain had brought the first sugar-cane seeds, and had built the first mills, the *ingenios,* by order of the

King, in 1529. In the sixteenth century, however, sugar was an exotic and rare spice in Europe; the apothecaries sold it by the ounce, as "a medicament."

The *ingenios* were gracious and cruel. In these mills were several hardwood poles, turned by oxen. Cane was fed in between the revolving poles by Indians and black slaves. The yield was meager.

It was the rich, dark coffee of the island that was really prized by Spain. Puerto Rican coffee was a great delicacy in Europe; in 1895 alone 60 million pounds of coffee had been exported to the continent; the crop covered 200,000 acres, or 40 percent of the cultivated farm land on the land. The land was hilly and the *jíbaros* independent, the Spaniards reasoned; so coffee was the natural crop for the island. For it was grown by "free labor."

The European coffee market was lost "with the coming of American sovereignty," noted the economist W. E. Packard; the sugar companies were "powerful in Washington" while "the coffee grower had no friends at court" to protect him with tariffs and subsidies.

In 1899 the hurricane of San Ciriaco devastated the coffee trees. The coffee farmers appealed for a loan from the Executive Council set up by the Americans to rule the island. The six Americans of the Council rejected their pleas, twice, overriding the request of the five Puerto Rican Council members. "It was the death blow to the coffee economy," said Juan Antonio Corretjer, "the ruin of the industry which afforded work for half the population."

A *jíbaro* whose family had farmed the land for generations told me that coffee was the natural product of the highlands. "In growing the coffee always we have the wood from the coffee trees and the food growing with the coffee. Because on the coffee farms we have the banana, the plantain, and crops of food you cannot grow on the sugar plantations.

"The Americans planted sugar instead. And with their sugar they established new *centrales,* the big sugar mills, but did not replace them. For fifty years they kept the same old machinery. So the sugar declined. And what is left for us? Nothing!

"They wanted us to be dependent," the old *jíbaro* said. "So they forced us to have a one-crop economy, to keep us under control. And that was the policy of Spain, too. It was not an invention of North America. It was an imperialist policy."

In the early 1920s, Santiago Iglesias Pantín, then leader of the sugar strike which swept the island, and head of the Socialist party (he was later to become Resident Commissioner in Washington, in the administration of President Roosevelt), spoke of the effect of these agricultural changes, as he saw them: "Formerly all our wealth went to Spain. Now it goes to the States, but with this difference,—under Spanish rule wages were low, but the employers were paternal; they thought occasionally about their *peones*. At least the workers had enough to eat. The corporations that have taken their place are utterly impersonal. No, they sit tight in their comfortable church pews giving thanks to the Lord with a freer conscience than ever did the Spanish Conquistadors, for they are too far away to see the suffering of *their peones*. . . . There has been a vast improvement in personal liberty, under American rule," Iglesias said. "But the island has been surrendered to Wall Street, to the heartless corporations that always profit most by American expansion."

Santiago Iglesias was then a Senator. He was a powerful man in the history of the island, but at the time he felt powerless: "Now, there is not corn meal and beans enough to go round, because the big sugar *centrales* hold all the fertile soil. They have bought all the land around them, even the foothills, so the people cannot plant anything, but *must* work for the companies. But what can we do? The politicians, the high officials, are all interested in sugar. They and the corporations form the *invisible* government. They are the law, the police, the rulers, the patriots." He may have smiled, for he repeated the word, "Patriots!"

"Eighty percent of the population goes to bed hungry every night," he said, yet "sixty percent of Puerto Rico is uncultivated. Do not let [them] tell you about 'anemia.' The anemia of Puerto Rico comes from no worm, but from the fact the people are always hungry. It is the sordid miserliness of corporations, bent on keeping our people reduced to the level of serfs, that is the fundamental cause of the naked, barefoot, hungry, schoolless, homeless desolation of the working classes."

The sugar plantations reaped high profits, but, "the corporate form drained away all the profits," Governor Tugwell wrote in *Changing Colonial Climate*. "In the case of Puerto Rico much of the profit went to the mainland and so the injury was intensified." Of the three largest sugar corporations, only one-fourth of their $81 million in profits was left on the island in a fifteen-year period (1920 to 1935).

In the cane fields as late as 1940 the wage of the *agregado* was 15 cents an hour. He averaged $3.48 a week. That was more than the tobacco-field worker received, $1.48 a week, but less than the $5.31 a week paid to factory workers that year. Since work in the fields lasted only a few months a year, the average wages were even less. It was better than the 50 cents a day paid in 1920.

Samuel Gompers, president of the American Federation of Labor, had written in 1904: "The salaries being paid now in Puerto Rico are 50 percent under those that were paid under Spanish rule in most industries and in agriculture, and sometimes less." More than forty years later, in 1946, the United States Tariff Commission reported in its study *The Economy of Puerto Rico:* "Most of the inhabitants still lack the means to feed themselves properly, clothe themselves adequately, house themselves decently."

The social decline of rural life, caused by the one-crop sugar economy, shocked economist W. E. Packard. "My surprise was great," he wrote, that after a half a century of American rule and example, Puerto Ricans had the "same miserable standards of living for the great mass of the people that characterize so many areas of Latin America. Yet the American sugar baby in Puerto Rico, fat, dropsical and spooned [fed], still sits high in the chair." He quoted Luis Muñoz Marín, who once was reported to have said: "Like a cow, the sugar industry was fed by the government and milked by the corporations."

The *Report on the Sugar Industry,* Document No. 1 of the first session of the Legislature of Puerto Rico, put it succinctly: *"Sugar was everything and everything was sugar."*

In the early days an attempt had been made to limit the power of the sugar corporations through the Organic Act of 1900, sometimes called "the Constitution of Puerto Rico." The old Populist movement and the new antitrust Congressmen of the day reflected "a fear widely expressed that corporations in the United States would own all the valuable land in Puerto Rico within 'the shortest period of time,' unless the Congress took steps to prevent it. . . . Giants in corporate form had an insatiable appetite." (*The Land Authority and Democratic Process in Puerto Rico* by W. E. Packard.)

"If such concentration of [island farmland] holdings shall become the case," Congressman Jones had said during the debate on the Organic Act, "then the condition of the population will, I believe, be reduced to one of absolute servitude." Because of such fears the Congress, by a joint resolution of both houses, decreed that "every corporation hereafter authorized to engage in agriculture [on the island] shall be restricted to the ownership of not to exceed 500 acres."

The law was clear, but meaningless; it provided for no enforcement procedures and no penalties. "No one paid any attention to it," observed Henry Wells in *The Modernization of Puerto Rico.*

Two generations later the Supreme Court of Puerto Rico adjudicated this federal law. When it did in 1938, it was promptly overruled by the Circuit Court of Appeals in Boston—the home of some of the largest corporations on the island. The case went to the United States Supreme Court, which on May 25, 1940—forty years after the five-hundred-acre law had been passed by Congress—finally affirmed it.

The Supreme Court was explicit, as well as compassionate: "To prevent the development of an agrarian monopoly which would own and control the best lands on this small and densely populated Island," read its decision, "and which might eventually *convert the Island into a large sugar factory, served by a half-slave proletariat*, and to encourage the division of lands into small tracts, owned, controlled and cultivated by their owners, the Congress enacted Joint Resolution No. 23 [the Organic Act]" (emphasis added).

By 1940 some 580,788 acres of the richest land—about four-fifths of all the farmland—was owned by the large corporations and plantations of over 500 acres, even though they were but one-fifth of the "farmers." The small farmers and *jíbaros,* who constituted 73.2 percent of the farming population, owned barely 15.7 percent of the land—an average of fewer than 7 acres per farm.

The land monopoly covered the island. It forced the small farmers into bankruptcy and drove the *jíbaros* down from the hills. Unable to feed their families, they became *agregados,* landless farmworkers, on the vast sugar plantations. Sometimes it was said that the Puertorriqueños were landless peasants when the United States invaded the island. But they were neither landless nor peasants. The government census of 1901 listed 197,761 independent farmers and only 64,818 farm laborers. The landless *agregados* were a creation of what Governor Tugwell termed "the inevitable development of technology" by the sugar industry.

It was small wonder that "technological efficiency looks frighteningly like a gargoyle to the more far-seeing Puerto Ricans," commented economist W. E. Packard. Unable to grow their own food on their farms, the people had to "starve or migrate."

Coffee, once the pride of the island and the "taste of leisure," had to be imported. On the tropical island that was sacrilege. But the native crop satisfied barely two-thirds of the Puertorriqueños' thirst for "coffee and conversation"; only 200,000 of the 350,000 hundredweight consumed yearly. The humiliated government in 1971 brought in 75,000 hundredweight of coffee beans from the Dominican Republic.

Yet the coffee market of Mayagüez, one of the oldest, was closed by the Department of Agriculture in the midst of the harvest season in 1971.

Banana and plantain crops were in a "crisis situation." Some of the richest banana-growing lands had been bulldozed for urban suburbs and shopping centers. The banana and plantain were the "potato of the people"; for they were cooked, fried, baked, served as plantain chips like potato chips, and even eaten raw. In the old days they grew wild on the hillsides, free for the plucking. Puertorriqueños, it was estimated, had "a per capita consumption of eighty plantains per year" in the 1970s; but there were enough plantains for only three months of the year in the local supply, complained Eduardo Carro of the Rico Banana Company in the hilltown of Orocovis.

Miguel A. Rodríguez Rivera, of Congelados Criollos, Inc., the largest processor of bananas and plantains on the island, said that his plant's new stainless-steel assembly line for the making of *tostones* had not been used for a year. The plantain plant operated at 10 percent of capacity; he could process eight million plantains, but could find only two million.

So severe was the shortage that one manufacturer had to import 5,879 cases of "foreign" plantain chips, "bagged, labelled and boxed, from Santo Domingo." In 1970 the island imported 250,000 plantains, he said in disgust; it was ridiculous.

"Yes We Have No Bananas," commented the San Juan *Star*.

In San Juan the wits were saying that soon the island would have to import everything: mangos from Mexico, pineapples from Hawaii, oranges from Florida, and Puertorriqueños from New York.

Governor Ferre, in his Palace, was confident that the island's "ailing agriculture" would be healed by infusions of government funds. Loans to farmers had reached $488 million, he informed a meeting of the Credit Association in the San Geronimo (St. Jerome) Hilton; not only that, but the government had insured the crops against hurricanes, had given "incentive payment" to 5,559 sugarcane planters, paid more than one-third of the wages large-scale farmers gave their field hands, and, besides, the pigeon-pea crop was at an all-time record of 90,000 hundredweight of pigeon peas.

An old-time planter who once had been the Popular party's gubernatorial candidate was less confident. Luis Negrón López said the government money had gone mostly to the sugar mills and big planters, while small farmers "had received the most promises, but had received the fewest benefits."

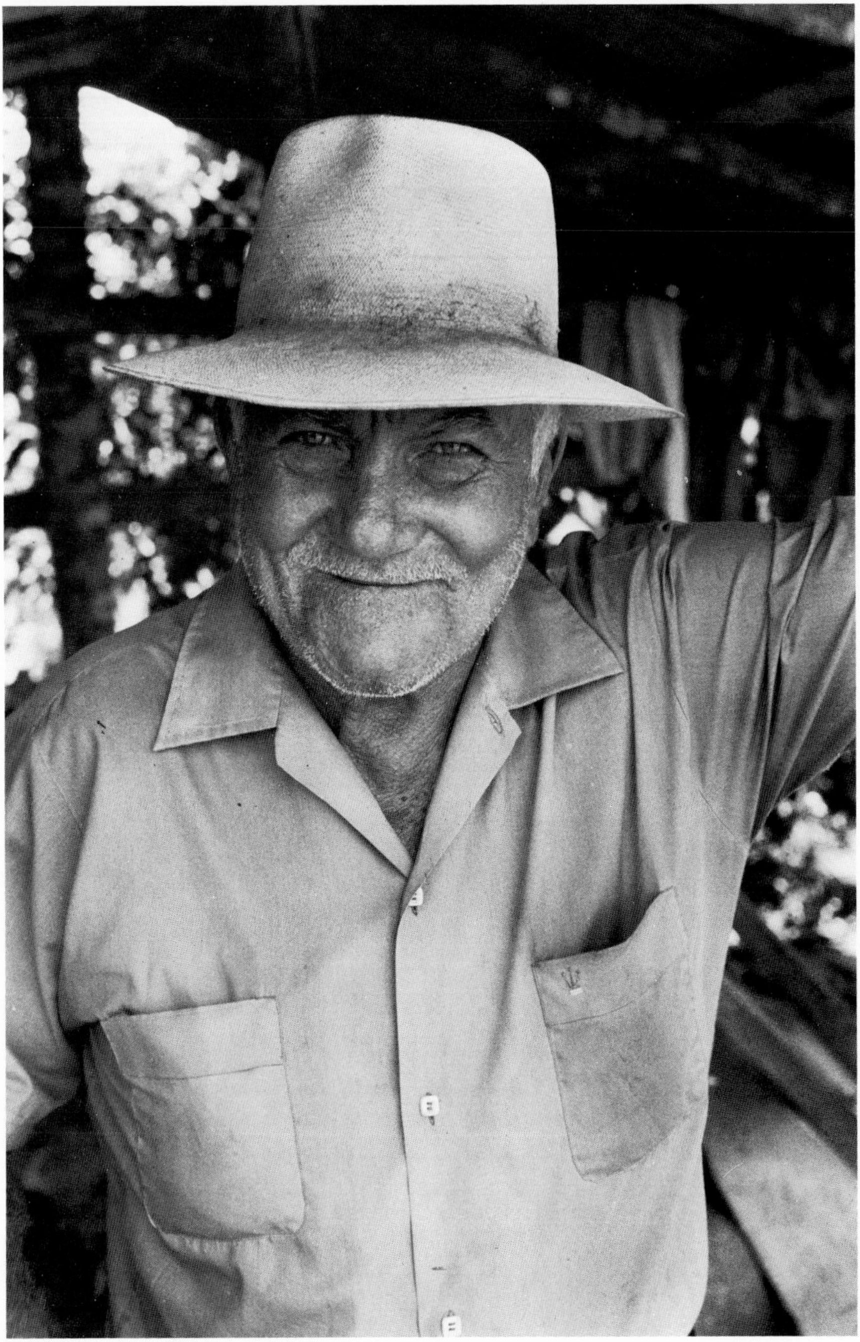

An old *jíbaro* in the hills of Utuado

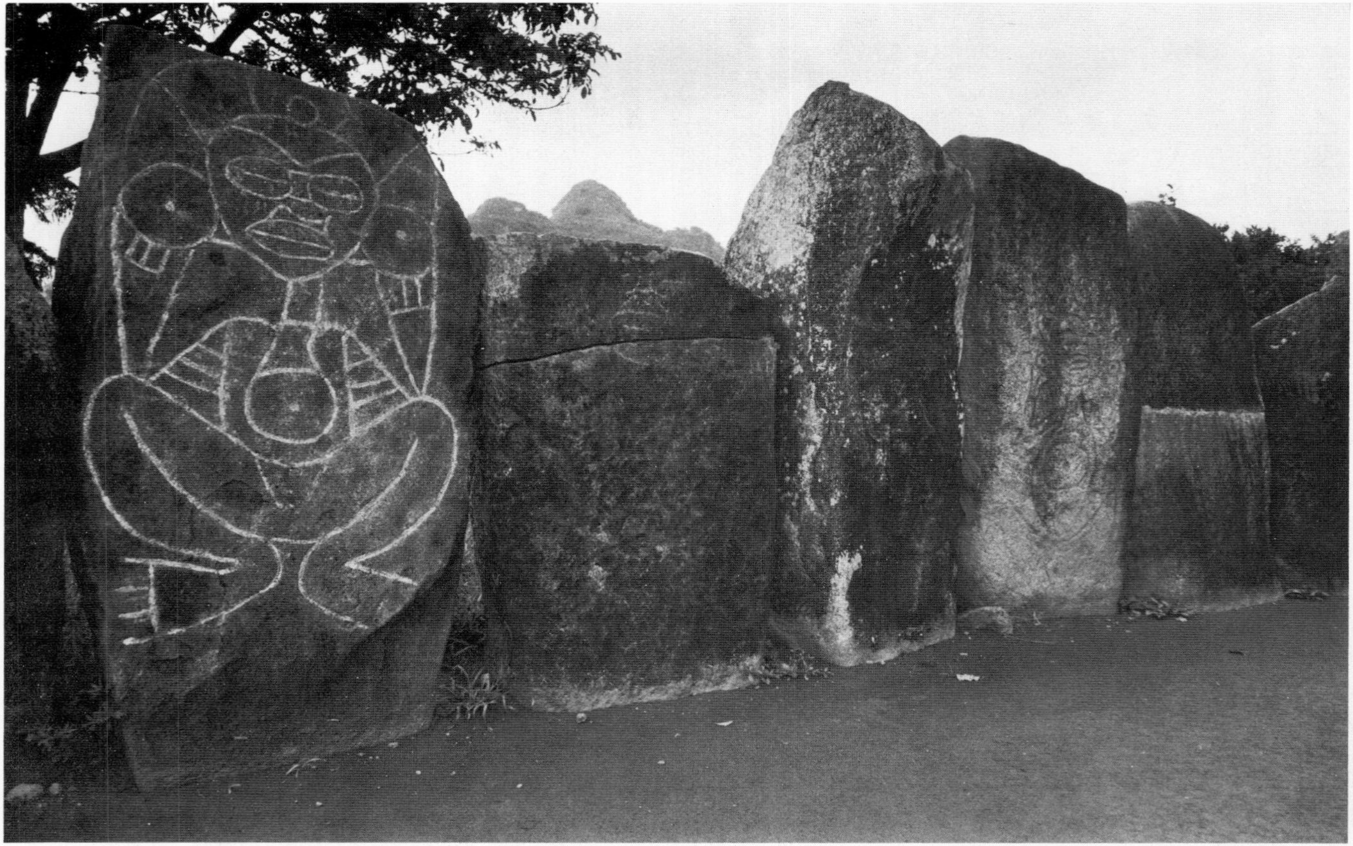

The stone of Caguanas—an ancient Indian ball court carved with Borinquén gods

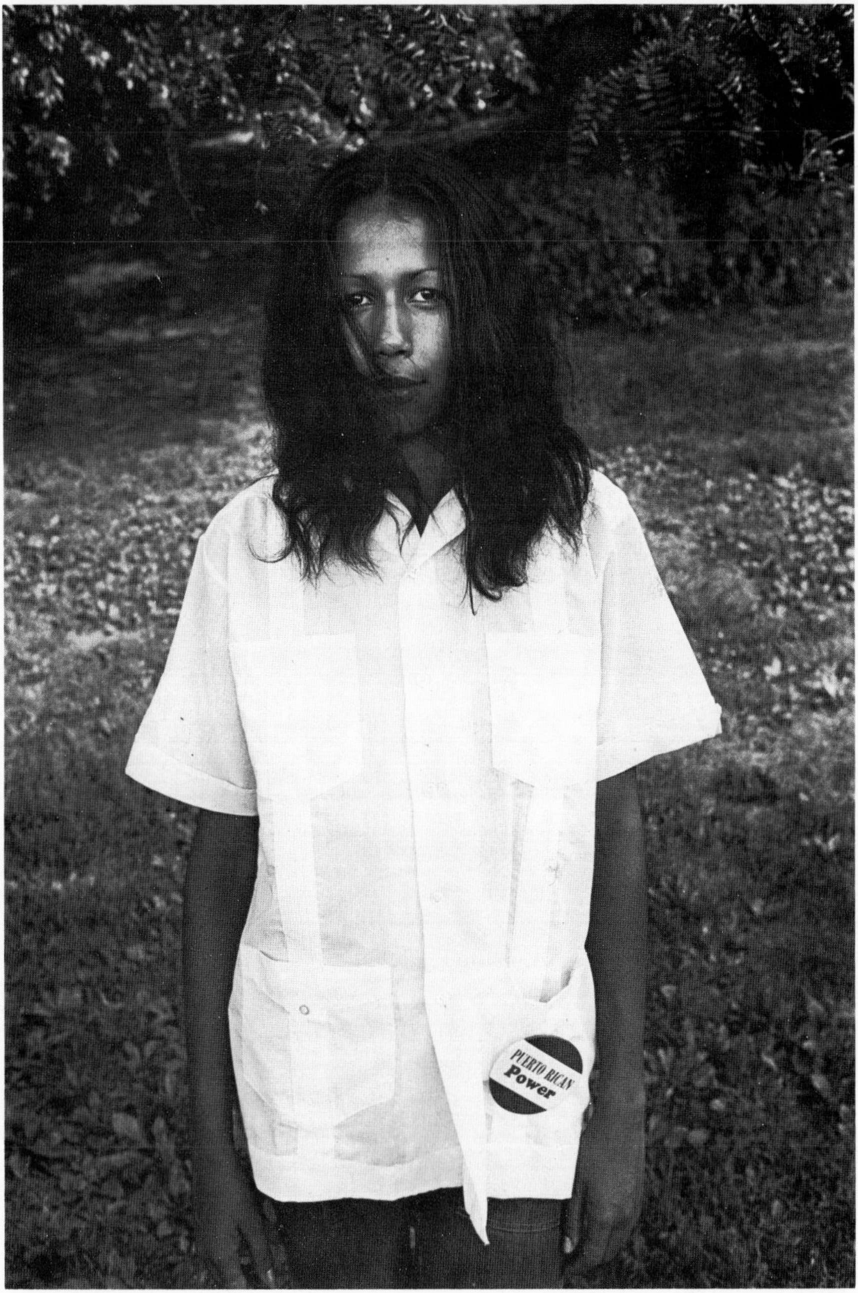

A contemporary Indian girl of Jayuya

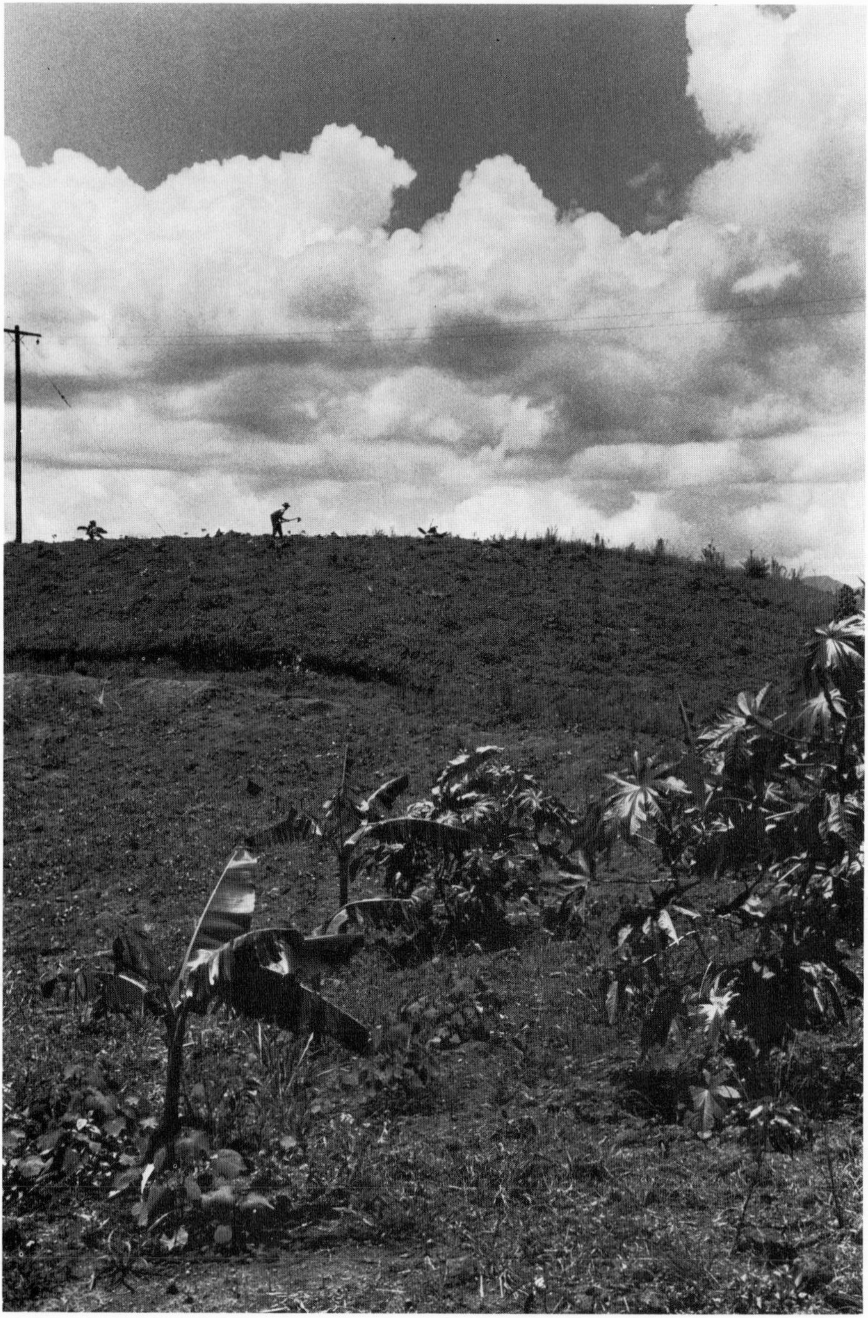

Under the tropical sky—hoeing a field of young banana trees

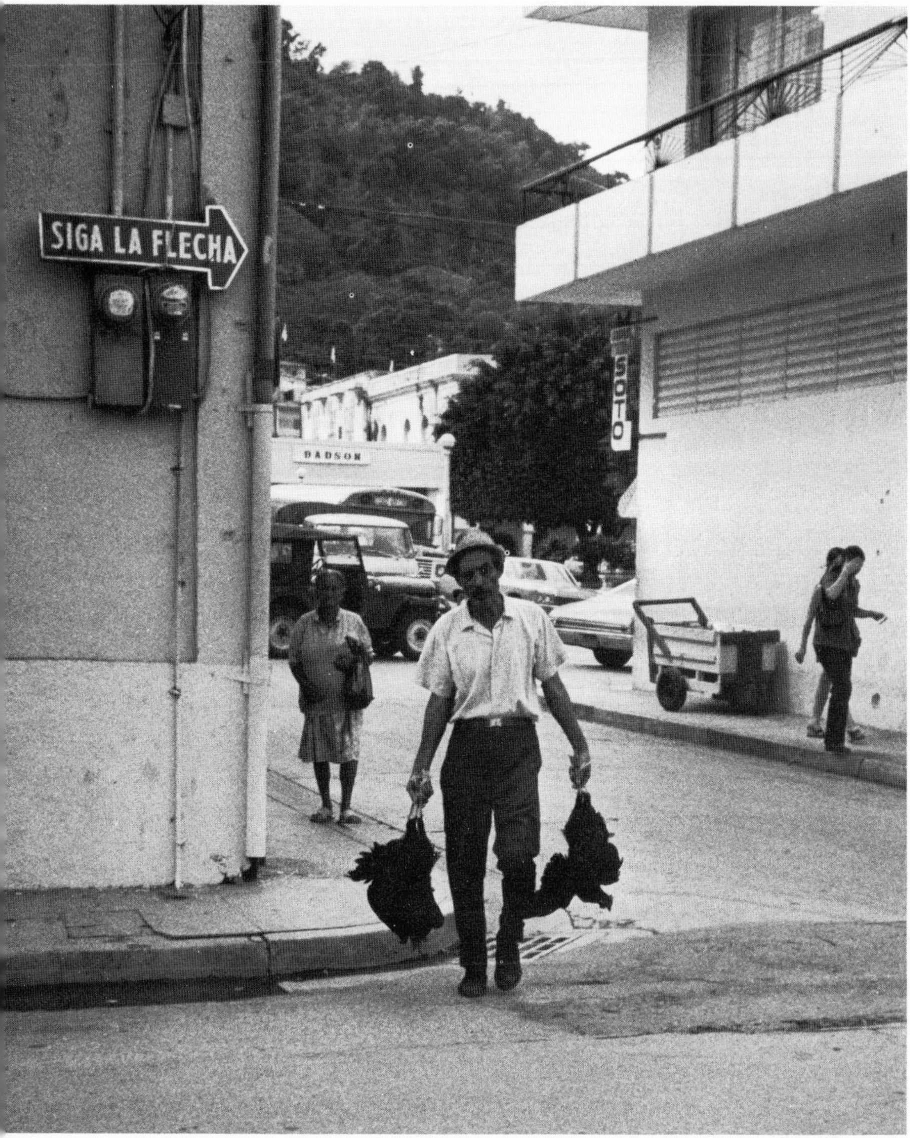

The man with chickens, going to market in Utuado

The *paso finos* of Borinquén—horses of the Conquistadors

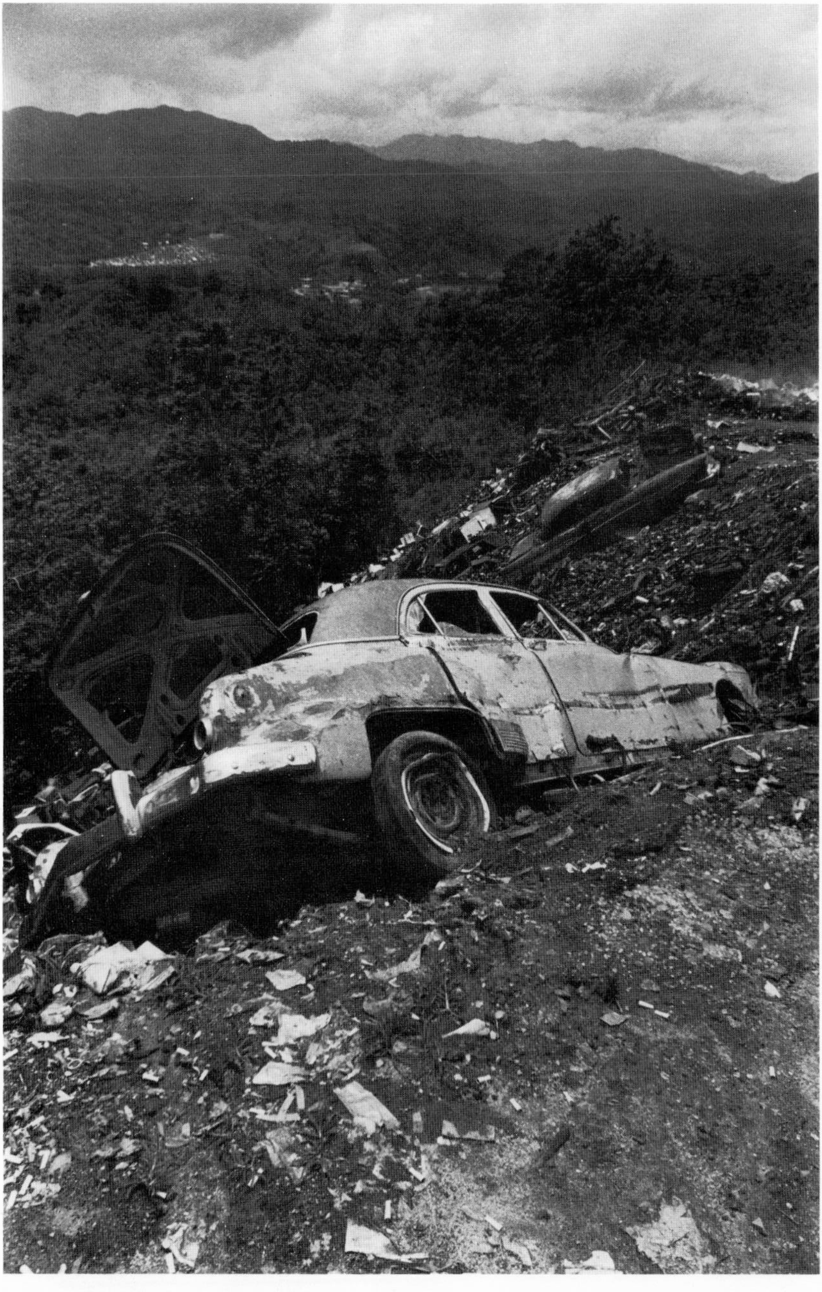

The chariots of the new Conquistadors—a junkyard of American cars

La negrita vieja—an old black woman in Old San Juan

Long ago, the young Luis Muñoz Marín prophesied: "In the old days most Puerto Rican peasants [*jíbaros*] owned a few pigs and chickens, maybe a horse and cow, some goats, and in some way had the use of a patch of soil. Today this modest security has been replaced by a vision of opulence. There are most things they can't get. The margin between what they have and what they imagine has widened enormously." He wrote that in 1929 in the *American Mercury*.

On the edges of the country roads the long sweet grasses still grew wild, surrounding the houses and the schoolyards and the suburban towns. The mangos and the coconut palms and the banana trees still flowered on the hills. Was it possible to uproot them? There were *jíbaros* who thought that if every cane field on the island was bulldozed and cemented for a factory or a highway, the odor of the sugar cane still would permeate the island.

In the fields where the cane was gone, even the humidity tasted sweet. The intoxicating aroma of the raw, burnt sugar was everywhere: a candied, acrid odor that penetrated the *bohíos* of the *agregados,* and the houses of cement in the new Levittowns. Even in downtown San Juan.

The sweet odor of the sugar has gotten under our skins, the *jíbaro* said; it has sweetened our blood, but it is bittersweet.

9

The Pamphleteer of God

The Dream of Bare Feet

I am the pamphleteer of God,
God's agitator,
and I go with the mob of stars
and hungry men
toward the great dawn. . . .

Even in his youth there was darkness in his eyes. His eyes did not yet have that brooding, heavy-eyelidded look of tropical *dolor,* of sorrow and of pain, of his later years; but the sadness was already there. He seemed too wise, or too devious, for a man so young.

In the baleful eyes of the young poet there was a way of looking at the world as though he were about to invent it. In the eyes of his countrymen he was a god. *Padre, papá* and *el hombre dios,* the man-god, they reverently said of him. He was older and wiser by then, and he told them that it was horrible, *horroroso,* to hear a man called god in a democracy. As a young man he had not yet been humbled by the devotion of the poor *jíbaros* and the wealthy industrialists to the "miracles" they said he performed as Governor; his ideas were then no more than the words of his dreams:

the dream that dreams in stomachs strangled by hunger
　　(A bit of bread, a bit of white bread!);
the dream of bare feet
　　(Fewer stones of the road,
　　Lord, fewer broken bottles!); the dream of trampled hearts
　　(Love . . . Life . . . Life!)

Luis Muñoz Marín wished to rewrite his world with his words. And he did.

On the island the older gods were dying. The gods of the Spaniards had died long ago, they had become plaster saints, and the gods of the *jíbaros* were dying too—their memory flickered in the spiritualists' candles. Was it not time, the young poet thought, for men to become godlike again? He would be "the pamphleteer of God," the savior of his island and the *jíbaros*.

He went to live in Greenwich Village, where so many of the young gods lived in exile in the 1920s. In time he came to know the cow-licked poet Carl Sandburg; the blasphemous H. L. Mencken; the oracle of Harvard, Archibald MacLeish; the grey eminence of the prairies, Edwin Markham; and Vachel Lindsay; and the greatest bullfighter of them all, the *bello* Belmonte. It was a dream come true to the twenty-two-year-old poet. His father had warned him, "Reality does not correspond to a dream." But the son did not believe that. As a writer he knew that an intellectual creates his own reality, in his words. "In the theatre of [his] dreams," the youth once wrote, his visions were always a "great success." After all, he was "God's agitator."

In musty Greenwich Village the handsome, intense, dark-eyed poet from Puerto Rico lived with his bride, Muna Lee, a child-faced sprite from Mississippi, the vivacious, dark "free spirit" of the bohemian world of letters, who seemed to have been recreated from a romantic poem by Sidney Lanier. Yet he was full of longing for the "hunger and memory" of his "lost island." In cocktail parties and Sunday afternoon soirees he prophesied the resurrection of the poor, hungry *jíbaros,* whose symbolic deaths fed "the roots of gathering spring," to the acclaim of literary critics; for his dreams appeared in English, in the *Smart Set, The Nation, The New Republic,* and Mencken's *American Mercury.* His beloved *jíbaros,* who did not read Spanish, much less English, did not know of the prophecies he was proclaiming in their name. They soon would.

He was celebrated by the rebellious rich, the joy seekers who had stepped from the novels of F. Scott Fitzgerald. The god seekers, the "weekend Freudians," who worshiped "the great yea-saying of Nietzsche, the passion of life," in literary sex—as Max Bodenheim recalled the Greenwich Village literati—wrote of him as a "Caribbean Adonis." And he was hailed by the utopia seekers, refugees from Babbittry within Babbittry, who talked of revolutions, "Not, to be sure, the fighting Marxism of the East Side ghetto, but nevertheless the literary proletarianism of the *Masses,*" as Caroline Ware wrote of those years, in *Greenwich Village: 1920–1930.* Were they not, Max Bodenheim asked, the true bohemians "who live between two worlds," seeking "through the magic of art, or drink, or politics, to find the Blessed Isle in an age that is disintegrating before their eyes"? The young Luis Muñoz Marín was one of them, for in that armistice between World Wars he was more of an exiled seeker of the "Blessed Isle" than any of them.

He had been exiled from his island, at the age of three, with his father, who had fled as a political refugee to live in New York. Of the first thirty-three years of his manhood the young poet was destined to live for twenty-two years in nostalgia, within the land of his conquerors. He was born José Luis Alberto Muñoz Marín, the son of the "Prime Minister" of Puerto Rico, in February of 1898, ten days after the island had been granted its autonomy by Spain, in the fading twilight of nineteenth-century colonialism. When he was five months old, the island was colonized again, by the invasion of the United States. Even as an infant he was fated to live "between two worlds."

His father, Luis Muñoz Rivera, was "the father of his country," a patriarchal don, not merely the most prominent statesman on the island, but "a giant to embrace these mountains," in his son's words. He was a man of the nineteenth century, whose Balzacian enthusiasms were zestful contradictions; he was the colonialist leader of

Puerto Rico, under both the Spanish and American flags, and yet he was a fervent believer in independence; he was a brooding poet of *La Bohème* and the scion of the provincial bourgeoisie, whose own father had been a landed *patrón* and Mayor of Barranquitas; he was the loyalist leader of the Autonomist party and the editor of *La Democracia,* whose fiery rhetoric was the voice of "Puertorriqueño dignity" and "independence of spirit"; he was a gentleman of the old school, who would have defended his honor with a sword in a duel at dawn, and did.

El León, the Lion, as he was known. A man of powerful build, robust and gregarious, with a majestic and awesome mustache, in the shape of a *machete* that fitted his larger-than-life manner. He was a man of *macho,* not with women, but in the older and truer sense of *macho,* with men—and with himself.

It is said that Don Luis Muñoz Rivera single-handedly negotiated the "Treaty of Sagasta," with Spain, by which the island won its autonomy in 1897. On the beach in Andalusia, where he met Práxedes Mateo Sagasta, the leader of Spain's Liberal party and soon to be Prime Minister, he had hinted he might join the Cuban Revolutionary Committee in New York if autonomy was not granted. Led by José Martí of Cuba and Eugenio de Hostos of Puerto Rico, the revolutionaries had been fighting for several years to free Cuba from the dwindling Spanish empire. Once Cuba had fallen, the guerrillas had planned to free Puerto Rico. Some thought that threat had, in part, provoked the United States invasion of both islands.

"And what," Sagasta reportedly asked, "if I reject your ideas?"

"I will go home by way of New York," replied Muñoz Rivera. He left Spain with a promise of autonomy in his hand.

On the sudden conquest of the island by the United States, Muñoz Rivera traveled to Washington, D.C., to seek a status of autonomy similar to that he had won from Spain. He had been appointed titular head of the Cabinet of Ministers in the colonial government of the new conquerors, in 1899. And he had faith they would listen to him in "the spirit of true democracy" of America, "where the liberty of man and the dignity of the people [were] inviolate." "We, from the small islands, must be equal to those of immense continents," he said; for that "equality of unequals" was the basis of "true democracy." He had read Jefferson.

In response, the Congress passed the disastrous Organic Act of 1900, which established a "democratic dictatorship" over the island. Muñoz Rivera was enraged by what to him was a betrayal: ". . . we believed there was drawing near an era of liberty and we attended to the spectacle of territorial absorption . . . we supposed, at least, we would be declared a territory and we have not even been declared a colony . . . nothing of what was promised has been granted . . . our condition is that of serfs belonging to a conquered island."

"We dreamed of the law and the sword appeared," he wrote in his new daily paper, *El Diario de Puerto Rico;* ". . . the liberty for which Washington and Lafayette struggled remains on the continent without reaching the colony." His newspaper was attacked by pro-American mobs, his presses were smashed, and his life was threatened. El León went into exile to the mainland.

Still, the elder statesman had faith in his political belief in the "equality of unequals." He thought that conflicting loyalties might be resolved by mutual loyalties: "to be good and loyal Puerto Ricans [and] good and loyal Americans." In later years, when he was Resident Commissioner in Washington in 1917, his hope ended abruptly with the passage of the Jones Act—a World War I measure aimed at hemispheric defense that was to arbitrarily extend American citizenship to Puerto Ricans, "without the voice, without the vote" of the island's people. Anyone who refused to accept the decree of citizenship was to be denied the right to vote entirely. It was a law, one wit said, "written by Gilbert to disenfranchise Sullivan."

One last time, a saddened and weary elder Muñoz went to Congress. He had a deep voice that was "impetuous, swift, enslaving and persuasive." "My compatriots are generously permitted to be citizens," he ironically told the House of Representatives, "of the only country they possess, but they are eliminated from the body politic: the exercise of political rights is forbidden them." By a "single stroke of the pen they are converted into pariahs," and the island was being divided "into castes like the Brahmans and Sudras of India." As eloquently as he could he pleaded with Congress to "permit the people of Puerto Rico to decide by their votes whether they wished the citizenship of the United States, or whether they prefer their own natural citizenship." He was at fifty-seven not an old man, but he was losing hope. He wept.

"Give us our independence," declared Muñoz Rivera. He quoted from the National Platform of the Democratic party of 1902: "Imperialism abroad will lead rapidly and irreparably to despotism at home." There was prolonged applause. And then the Congress, controlled by the Democratic party, passed the Jones Act.

On the sixteenth of November, 1916, six months after his speech, El León died. If faith in his political reason was lost, he had no other. He was one of the old *patrones* of politics, who devoted a lifetime to leading the people because he thought they were helpless as children without him. "This people doesn't want to save itself," he once wrote. El León had faith in himself. When his own strength was gone, he died.

Long ago, in his poetic testament, *Minha Terra,* he had written:

Puerto Rico, you pallid Puerto Rico
You cannot break out of your jail
Because you lack—long live Christ!—
Much nerve in your character,
Because in your fields there is no people;
Because in your veins there is no blood.

And again, in his book, *Retamas, The Brooms,* in 1897, he forecast his own tragic despair and his defeat:

Decadence is coming.
You can feel it now.
The once proud people
Has degenerated.

Of the passing of his father the son said: "Muñoz Rivera's death closed what we may call our Puerto Rican heroic period. It is gone forever." His father was a giant who embraced "the mountains that shelter his countrymen, the *jíbaros*."

"If only I were a giant to complete the work of Luis Muñoz Rivera," the son cried.

But the son was a rebel. In the early twenties he had come home to the island not to join the "millionaires' club" of the Senate but to be among the poor *jíbaros.* The sugar-cane cutters were on strike and young Luis became a street-corner orator. He had come "too late," as a biographer wrote. Old Santiago Iglesias, the venerable *caudillo* of the Socialist party, was growing tired of jails and defeats. He thought that by statehood, as his AFL cohorts had convinced him, the island's workers would inherit the labor laws of the mainland. So the aging radical (his daughters were *Libertad, Igualdad,* and *Fraternidad*) was about to merge his movement with the Republican party, the statehood party.

In dismay, Don Luis left the island and the Socialist party. He was not disillusioned by socialism, which he never understood, a friend said, but by the Socialists, whom he understood too well.

And the old men who remembered the poet in the Socialist party of the post–World War I years, men like Jesús Colón, remembered him as "a quiet man with a tongue of fire, but a man of many silences. He was not a leader. He was a dreamer."

"Come back!" demanded Antonio Barcelo, who had assumed the leadership of the Unionist party of Muñoz Rivera and the editorship of *La Democracia.* "Take your father's place!" The poet returned home again, though not wholly for these political reasons. He knew from his childhood that politics was rarely a matter of politics alone. "Once there was a prince," he had told his children in a bedtime story, "who wanted to find the most beautiful thing in the world. He traveled everywhere. To every land. He saw the most beautiful jewels and the most glorious work of men's hands. He searched high and low. But he never found anything of which he might say, 'This is it. This is the most beautiful thing in the world!' At last, tired and discouraged, the prince returned to his own land. Suddenly, he saw something round and bright. It was like translucent ivory with a glow of gold. 'This is it. This is what I have been searching for. This is the most beautiful thing in the world,' the prince said. He picked it up. It was an onion."

The story of the prince was a fable for children. Except that Don Luis *was* the prince. He was "the son of Muñoz Rivera," as long as he lived. On the island, "the sons of the well-to-do were taught that they were inherently superior," commented that puritanical critic of the *patrón* tradition Governor Rexford Guy Tugwell. "They did not question it. Muñoz was a pampered boy and he had no more reason to adopt a critical attitude than any of his contemporaries." And yet the "boy" did not merely "question"; he was intensely critical. He was a rebel. He dreamt of transforming the onion into gold.

At the very least he had two reasons. One was that he was a poet; and he thought he had experienced the hunger of the *jíbaros* with more fragile pain than did men to whom hunger pains were more ordinary. The poet's conceit! Then, too, he could not forget he was his father's son. He was born with a legacy. When the boy was three years old, his father had dedicated his *Tropicales* to him with the admonition: "To my son: When you reach the age of thought and action read these stormy pages and remember that your father passed through life working, struggling. You shall know better times. Work, struggle!"

So the prince went home again. It was the time of Depression; the year was 1931. The island had been ravaged by hurricanes and economic disasters. Puerto Rico was "the poorest land in Latin America"; a "hellhole of misery worse than the Black Hole of Calcutta"; "the stricken land" of "helpless peasants."

One-third of the workers were "permanently unemployed" in 1934, estimated the Puerto Rico Policy Commission—150,000 "heads of families." Some one-fourth to one-third of the rest of the population were unemployed for most of the year.

"What the unemployed eat is a mystery, though it is a common sight to see them scavenging in garbage pails in the cities and begging their food from garbage trucks," wrote Earl P. Hanson, of the National Resources Committee, later a planner and Executive Board member of the "New Deal" Puerto Rican Reconstruction Administration (PRRA). "The prevalence of malnutrition in Puerto Rico," Hanson said, contributed to the "nearly 90 percent of the rural population and 40 percent of the urban inhabitants [having] hookworm in their intestines." The death rate from gastrointestinal diseases was 360 per 100,000 population, compared to 25 per 100,000 in the United States. The death rate from tuberculosis was 325 per 100,000, compared to 60 per 100,000 in the United States; it was "higher than in any other civilized country."

"The problem is primarily economic, not sanitary," said the earlier Brookings Institution study. But the economic planner Hanson thought "the problem is also political."

"Puerto Rico, as a colony of the American empire, is organized and managed primarily for the benefit of the few powerful commercial interests on the mainland, and not for the benefit of the Puerto Ricans," Hanson wrote in *The Dilemma of Puerto Rico*. "Under the existing social-economic structure, millions are drained from the island every year, while Puerto Rico itself is virtually bankrupt."

In the mountain villages the *jíbaros* were suffering a "living death" in the ruins of their rural way of life, which had collapsed beneath the burden of the sugar companies' one-crop economy. Don Luis's romantic image of the *jíbaros* was just that. He was betrayed by reality. The "ghastly spectacle of wealth being drained from a starving population into the richest country on earth" so angered him that he decided to challenge it with his words. He had no other weapons. He was not an economist or a revolutionary, and he was not yet a politician.

On the dying island, "Poverty was widespread and hunger, almost to the verge of starvation, common," wrote Colonel Theodore Roosevelt, Jr., the appointed Governor from 1929 to 1932. Every city or large town had its slum, "where the squalor and filth was almost unbelievable." As a result, "the island was disease ridden," Governor Roosevelt wrote. "Financial conditions were in bad shape."

The economic experts had offered several schemes to lessen the depression. "One original suggestion," the Governor thought, "was that canaries should be obtained and given to the poor, who should teach them to whistle 'The Star-Spangled Banner' and then sell them to the American tourists." Whether the Governor thought this funny, or grotesque, was not clear.

Not all of the economic ideas were as imaginative as that. But all had one thing in common. They came from the universities and government on the mainland. Ever since the conquest of the island the experts and academics on the mainland had been attempting to manage its economy. The domination of the island's agriculture by the sugar companies had been planned and administered under the guidance of such men as J. H. Hollander of Johns Hopkins University, "an expert in public finance," in 1901 the first colonial Treasurer. His successor was a fellow professor of renown, W. F. Willoughby, who was instrumental in "Americanizing the island's economy"—he later became president of the American Political Science Association; while the island's Commissioner of Education from 1902 until 1904, the distinguished Samuel McCune Lindsay, was better known as professor of social legislation at Columbia University. Even the earlier Governors, Charles H. Allen and Beekman Winthrop, were graduates of Amherst and Harvard (*magna cum laude*) respectively.

From the beginning, the island was thought of as a "perfect laboratory" for economic policies and social experiments. The new colonial policies of the United States might be applied, tried, revised, and tested with little fear of rebellion or international repercussion. It was the paradise of economic planners, social planners and family planners. (Later, in 1956, the island became the first "laboratory" for "The Pill." The birth control experiments were so successful that by 1971 they had resulted in the "voluntary sterilization" of one-third of all "fertile" women in Puerto Rico, according to Dr. Samuel Lugo, director of the Health Department's Family Planning Program—about 225,000 of 670,748 women.) One of the planners explained: it had a "docile" and "captive" population.

One of those who had stereotyped the people as apathetic was Calvin Coolidge. In response to a plea for economic aid, sent to the White

House via Carlos Lindbergh, who had visited the island, the President solemnly informed the people that their misery was their own fault, not his. "This lethargy of body and soul is the offspring of moral and physical vices that drag down the spirits and lead peasants to such a stage of social degradation," Coolidge had said.

In 1930 the scholarly study of the prestigious Brookings Institution in Washington, *Porto Rico* [*sic*] *and Its Problems,* echoed these sentiments: "The passive helplessness of the rural community" was the main obstacle to "progress." On the island "There is a degree of submissiveness to misfortune and a lack of class feeling that to an outsider is difficult to understand. Perhaps," the experts thought, "it is the widespread illness." In any event, as long as the Puertorriqueños acted like stoic Indians, the study concluded, the solving of the island's problems would have to be done by the mainland, not the people of the island.

At the advent of the "New Deal" the old colonialist attitudes were inherited by anticolonialist social reformers. In no time more experts on government commissions and university study groups descended upon the depressed island than ever before in its history, each intent on analyzing the miseries of San Juan and prescribing for them in Washington, D.C.

In his mildly critical *Puerto Rican Politics and the New Deal,* the scholarly Dr. Thomas Matthews was exceedingly circumspect: "Thirty years of neglect and *even* [my emphasis] economic exploitation were to be undone by government planning and regulation. However this new [*sic*] policy had its drawbacks. Neglect was exchanged for excessive management. The idea that the Puerto Rican had to be watched, directed, and managed was apparent. He had to be shown what was to his benefit."

Colonialism assumed a beneficent paternalism. In practice, it was racist. The new *patrones* and the old *patrones* in Washington differed not as much as they imagined. In his appointment of Governors of the island, President Roosevelt did not differ appreciably from the appointments of President Harding. As the fury of Muñoz's words had been responsible, in part, for the removal of President Harding's happily and brusquely racist Governor, E. M. Reily, so now young Muñoz's editorial wrath was partially responsible for the removal of President Roosevelt's first choice as Governor, the dictatorial R. H. Gore: "A damn liar," Don Luis called the Governor, among other things.

On the inauguration of the new President, in 1932, Don Luis had hopefully written, not to the President, but to his wife, Eleanor, offering his solution to the misery of the island: "Not with doles, but with social justice, operating under an economy that shall be as far as possible planned and autonomous." The planners of the "New Deal" were more responsive to the idea of planning by Washington than to any plan for autonomy. Nothing had changed but the promises.

"A society of despair produced, finally, a literature of despair," the anthropologist Gordon Lewis lamented. It was typified in Antonio S. Pedreira's popular doctrine in the thirties of melancholy *insularismo*. The island was "soft" and "feminine," wrote Pedreira, unlike the presumably "hard" and "masculine" United States; for the tropical climate "melts our will" and the Puertorriqueños were, as a result, "docile by nature." Even our *danza* was a dance of "sadness, meditation, tranquillity," Pedreira wrote. The "culture of old" had died, and no new culture had replaced it.

Into that "era of melancholy" came the young poet, full of dreams. He argued with his friends and foes, the "sons of the well-to-do," the old elite who sat on the verandas of the *haciendas* and languidly embraced the ideas of *insularismo*. Socialism might be a romantic idea, Don Luis said, but independence was an economic and political necessity. Let it be renamed planning and autonomy—the words did not matter. Until the Puertorriqueños managed their own affairs, nothing and no one would help them. He had learned from the death of his father that one paid a price for appealing to the colonial experts for the autonomy of a colony; it was too high a price to pay again. Instead, he advocated using "the threat of independence" against the United States, as his father had used it successfully against Spain.

The elderly political *patrones* welcomed him, but not his ideas. In his youthful impetuosity they saw vigor but danger. Life in the colony had taught them that no sugar company would permit any Puerto Rican to plan its economy; and they had seen no sign in Washington that any President even considered the idea of autonomy. He was a bohemian, this young poet; he knew nothing of life in a colony.

"He was still dreaming," an old *político* of that day remembered, with a tight grin—"fortunately!"

For a decade Don Luis reasoned and argued with the fearful *patrones*. In 1937 he at last left the Liberal party, and one year later, with a roomful of followers, founded the Popular Democratic party, the PPD—his Populares. (The year before, in 1936, Don Luis had set up the Acción Social Independentista, Social Action for Independence, "to defend the independence of Puerto Rico"; his closest colleagues—Rafael Píco, Jaime Benitez and Felisa Rincon, who was to become Mayor of San Juan—were all, at that time, *independentistas*. So was Don Luis.) His was to be the "party of the poor," of the *jíbaros*. Not of the *patrones,* the *políticos,* the elite. And so the Populares adopted the *pava,* the straw hat of the *jíbaros,* as their party symbol, and their slogan became "Bread! Land! Liberty!" in the tradition of nationalist and revolutionary movements.

"*¡Vergüenza contra dinero!*"—Honor, not money!" It was perhaps an ironic cry for the "party of the poor." But it echoed in the mountains. The *patrones* laughed at him.

Up in the mountains what would the *jíbaros* think of him, who spoke to them in the name of their unspoken thoughts? Who was he to think he knew what they had hidden in their hearts for centuries? He did not know the *jíbaros,* and they did not know him. He was not one of them. He was the son of a *patrón,* a man "between two worlds," a poet from New York. Who would vote for a poet?

I Have Broken the Rainbow

I have drowned my dreams
to glut the dreams that sleep in me in the veins
of men who sweated and wept and raged
to season my coffee. . . .

¡Jalda arriba! Up the hill! It was more than the motto of Don Luis. The man, his style, his romanticism, his charisma, and his triumph were told by those words.

Up the hill to every *barrio* in every mountain village that he could reach Don Luis walked. He walked for 837 days. "I have seen more Puerto Ricans than any other living person," he said. He talked to the *jíbaro* face to face. Was there any other way?

On the plazas, in the cafés, on the streets, in the *bateys,* the yards of their huts, their *bohíos,* he cajoled, he joked, he provoked, he lectured and he listened. In the past, no *patrón* came to the *jíbaros.* The *jíbaros* came, hat in hand, to the *patrón.* The country people were suspicious; who was he and what did he want, this man in his white suit who pretended to be their brother? If Don Luis had walked naked in the plazas he would not have shocked the *patrones* and delighted the *jíbaros* more; he was defying the codes and castes upon which the mystiques of the older colonialism rested.

He could talk a lame and blind burro into walking up a steep hill backward, they said of him. It was not quite true, but these legends of his charisma did him no harm.

Always his words were the same: The poor have power. In your hands your vote is your *machete.* You must not throw it away.

Don Luis told the *jíbaros:* If you sell your votes to your *patrón,* as hungry men often do, then you are selling him your *macho,* your manhood. Would you give away your *machete* to an enemy in the midst of a fight? No sane man trusts a politician. Good! Don Luis said; I do not ask you to trust me. I do not ask of you to give me your vote. Lend it to me. And in return I will give you bread! land! and liberty! But if I am shown to be untrustworthy, take your vote back at the next election.

El Vate, or the Bard, the *jíbaros* called him. They knew that a man who talked the way he did was not an ordinary politician; he had to be a poet.

Year by year he went into the hills. As Cesar Chavez later would walk on his pilgrimage to Sacramento, behind the Virgen de Guadalupe, and as Reies Tijerina walked to the sanctuary of the sacred *Cristo negro,* the Black Christ, of Chimayo, so Don Luis walked to the *bohíos* of the *jíbaros*. His political followers were worn out by his "tireless campaigning," but to Don Luis it was a personal pilgrimage, a poet's pursuit of his dream, more than a politician's search for "a popular base of power among the powerless." True, it was said that he was no longer a poet; had he not burned his old books of young poems in the kitchen stove as "junk?" But could a man burn up his youth?

The *jíbaros* began to wonder if they could unseat the *patrones* of the Senate; he had convinced them, as he had convinced himself, that a "democratic and legal revolution" was possible, even in a colonial country. But was it his political logic or his "Byronic romanticism" that inspired the poor, apathetic, and suspicious of voting, to trust "revolution by ballot"?

On election day, November 5, 1940, the Populares became the leading party on the island. They won a majority in the Senate. Don Luis was elected its president. He sat, at last, in his father's old seat on the podium.

"The sun rose on November 5 burning ropes and melting chains," El Vate said.

Still, the poetic politics and romantic economics of El Vate did not greatly impress the sugar companies or the government bureaucracy. He was merely another colonial leader of "a government that could not govern and a legislature that could not legislate." In the seat of power he was powerless as a *jíbaro* in the hills.

On the eve of World War II the world powers were preparing to battle for the mastery of the earth. Who would listen to a lesser poet on a little island in the Caribbean Sea?

Colonialism, which had ruled the world for four hundred years, was being threatened. "We are face to face with the greatest tragedy that has ever overtaken mankind. The collapse of Europe," W. E. B. DuBois was later to write caustically; for World War I "had loosened the seams of imperialism," and World War II was about to tear them asunder. He prophesied the ascendancy of the nations of Asia, Africa, and Latin America. In a few years these colonial nations were to "emerge," as the dark star of Andromeda, into the galaxies of world history. Puerto Rico too would be swept up in this emergence.

Once more, Puerto Rico became the Gibraltar of the Caribbean. The island was transformed by the World War into one of the largest military bases for the defense of the hemisphere. The government began the construction of huge air bases, such as Ramey Field, and vast naval installations. It was an irony that a poet might enjoy: the wars in Europe and Asia had forced America finally to notice the "island on its doorstep."

In September, 1941, three months before Pearl Harbor, President Roosevelt appointed Tugwell, one of his close advisers and a former "New Deal" brain truster, as Governor. Puerto Rico was "more or less in the position of Pearl Harbor, and we expected something of the sort in the Caribbean," Tugwell recalled. "We had German submarines patrolling in the deep water, 200 yards off our north coast." Ships were sunk "approaching our shores. A number [of ships] were sunk within sight of the waterfront." The plans for the invasion of the island had been drawn up by the German Admiralty. On any day, it was expected, Puerto Rico would be under siege and bombardment.

The island's food supplies from the mainland were cut off by the German blockade. With its own farm economy destroyed, the hunger of the *jíbaros* grew into an epidemic of starvation. Conditions which had been bad enough in the Depression years became steadily worse.

"I complained to the Army representatives about no food coming into Puerto Rico" to feed the people, Tugwell said; but "the Navy didn't have any intention, at that point, of establishing convoys for civilians." The food was for the American soldiers, now hundreds of thousands. The starvation grew worse.

"My duty as the representative of my country in Puerto Rico was to shape civil affairs so that military bases which might soon, before they were ready, have to stand the shock of attack, were not *isolated in a hostile environment*" (emphasis added), Tugwell wrote in his memoirs, *The Stricken Land*. The "hostile environment" was the people of Puerto Rico.

If there was an invasion, what would the starving *jíbaros* do? In 1934 had come the Revolt of the Sugar-Cane Cutters, that had begun with an island-wide strike, and led to four years of uprisings and repressions, assassinations and police reprisals. The memories were still alive. In those prewar years the anticolonialists of Roosevelt's New Deal, like the Interior Department's Director of Territories Ernest Gruening, reacted with threats and terror; in his *Diary,* Secretary of Interior Harold Ickes wrote: "Gruening, from being a liberal, has apparently decided that the mailed fist is the proper policy in dealing with these subject people." Leaders of uprisings, like Pedro Albizu Campos, the Nationalist party chairman who had been asked by the sugar-cane workers of Fajardo to lead their strike, had been jailed by the hundreds. In 1940, from his Leavenworth cell, the fiery Albizu wrote a public letter condemning the brutality of the German and Japanese fascists toward the Jews and Chinese, but warning his fellow countrymen to expect no better from the democracies. Not until "the Japanese have defeated America, will Puerto Rico have her independence," he told his armed followers. Governor Tugwell had reason to feel the island was "hostile."

Yet the new colonial policy of the New Deal anticolonialist was based upon rural reform and "relieving distress." Tugwell shunned the "mailed fist." In this he pioneered the concepts and methods that Senator John F. Kennedy was to enunciate twenty years later, in advocating the Alliance for Progress. Latin Americans "will not accept these conditions of existence," Kennedy told the U.S. Senate. "There will be changes. A revolution is on the march. A revolution that will be peaceful if we are sufficiently intelligent, moderate if we take the necessary care, successful if we are fortunate, but a revolution that will come whether we want it or not. We can influence its character," Kennedy said, "but we cannot modify its inevitability."

So, too, Tugwell worked to influence the "character" of the independence movement and "moderate" its armed methods. He could not, obviously, do it alone.

A man was needed whom the poor *jíbaros* trusted. He had to be a man who understood the paradoxes of history and who was sympathetic to the conflicting ideals of United States hegemony. But, most of all, he had to be a man who would be able to maintain peace on the island in the midst of a world-wide war.

Luis Muñoz Marín, alone of the island's leaders, had won the faith of the *jíbaros,* and yet had faith in the democratic ideals of the United States, his "second home": "Latins can have Anglo-Saxon psychology," he said.

Several years before, Tugwell had come to the island with a governmental group to study land reform and had "interviewed" Muñoz. Tugwell's probing had the quality of a job interview. He wanted to know if Don Luis was genuinely the leader of the *jíbaros* or merely a *político*. Tugwell was blunt, as always: "The question I had to ask him was, I said, whether his interest was in doing something for the landless farm workers and impoverished farmers, or whether what he really wanted was to do something to the advantage of the large farmers, or *colonos*. I was rather disappointed that I failed to get a clear statement from him."

The liberal Brahmin from the New Deal treated the rebellious son of the *patrón* with "condescension"; he was a "pampered boy," Tugwell complained. For his part, Don Luis treated the patronizing New Dealer with aloofness; he referred to him as the "appointed Governor," and "offered to cooperate," if Tugwell supported "his" land-reform ideas. And thus began the strange alliance between the two men, the man who was to be the last appointed American Governor, and the man who was to become the first popularly elected Puerto Rican Governor. As in the dance between the *toreador* and *toro,* the bullfighter and bull, each man thought he was *el otro,* the other one.

In his conceits Tugwell was a man of vigorous egotism. He thought he knew Puerto Rico's problems as well as any Puerto Rican. "Its problems were largely agricultural," he explained. "I had been in charge of sugar economics in the Agriculture Department, when I was Undersecretary." So he knew the solutions to the problems as well as, if not better than, the island leaders. "Even though they were my friends," he said, "they were still politicians and they weren't interested in good government." He would teach them.

"His boys" he called the men he selected. "The whole group that were attracted to government service . . . during my governorship were under thirty," Tugwell said proudly. Rafael Píco, a young professor of geography, was to become the first chairman of the Puerto Rican Planning Board and the chief planner of the island's industries. ("I'm sure you don't know anything about the job," Tugwell told him, "but you'll learn.") Teodoro Moscoso, a druggist from Ponce, was to become the director of Operation Bootstrap, and the chief administrator of the industrialization program. Roberto Sánchez Vilella, a civil engineer who had worked on the hydroelectric dams of Utuado, was to become the executive secretary to the Governor, and the Governor himself, Jaime Benitez, who was Tugwell's choice as chancellor of the university, was to become the ideologue of the commonwealth idea. And then there was Don Luis. One and all, he thought of them as "his boys." . . .

These brilliant and ambitious young men were, it happened, the most intimate lieutenants of Don Luis. It was they who had founded the Popular party, and it was there that Tugwell "found" them, running the government. If he sought to use them to lead the colony away from independence, into industrialization, they sought to use him as an opening to the West, to the capital for industrialization. Before the starving agricultural island, without an agriculture and "devoid of natural resources," as Jaime Benitez believed, could hope to attract industries, the threat to foreign investors of independence had to be laid to rest, and a "formula" of political compromise had to be conceived. That formula was the Commonwealth of Puerto Rico.

"Commonwealth is not a brilliant formula conceived and brought about by a flash of genius. It is rather an imperfect affirmation of the middle of the road approach," said Benitez. He termed it "an evolving, flexible, elastic form of association." Neither an old-fashioned colony nor an independent state, the Commonwealth was a "Free Associated State" that merely institutionalized the existing "way of life."

"We have made a virtue out of necessity," Benitez said.

The origin of the commonwealth idea was perhaps in a speech given by Edmund Burke to the English Parliament on the eve of the American Revolution. In 1775 he had pleaded with the Parliament that the colonies be granted "similar privileges and equal protection" as in England, lest they rebel. "Magnanimity in politics is not seldom the truest wisdom; and a great empire and little minds go ill together," Burke advised. The Lords did not listen. It was the "fatal war" that followed that convinced "two visionaries of a still more radical turn of mind, Granville Sharp and John Cartwright," to suggest "an association between Britain and her colonies in a free commonwealth," noted Edward Grierson in *The Death of the Imperial Dream.*

Lord Rosebery revived the word, and the idea, in 1884. But it was not until the old British Empire had begun to fall that the modern concept of commonwealth was to arise. In 1917, during the colonial upheavals which shook England in World War I, General Smuts, of South Africa, gave the phrase its new meaning. That year the Imperial War Conference officially recognized that the colonies were, after all, dominions—"the autonomous nations of the Imperial Commonwealth," as the general said. It was not a euphemism; rather it was a recognition of the strength of the independence and revolutionary movements that had erupted in revolts in Ireland and the English protectorates in China, and were threatening to do so in

Egypt and India. Lord Balfour reasoned that by loosening the reins of empire Britain might hold on to them.

In 1926 the Imperial Conference of the British Empire, led by Balfour himself, formally defined the status of colonies within "the Commonwealth" as one of "autonomous communities within the British Empire," which were to be "freely associated." Similarly, the Commonwealth of Puerto Rico was described as an Estado Libre Asociado, a Free Associated State.

It may have been a historic coincidence, but in the post–World War II years, when the Commonwealth of Puerto Rico was established, the British Commonwealth, for the first time, admitted "brown [skinned] dominions," to use historian Grierson's phrase. Prime Minister Nehru, of India, had announced his intention of "throwing off direct allegiance to the crown and becoming a Republic in 1949." And so, the concept of commonwealth was loosened a bit further, to embrace independent brown nations. Puerto Rico, like India, was conceived of in those Cold War years as "a bulwark against Communism."

Many have accepted credit for the idea. The status of Puerto Rico, it may be presumed, pleased President Roosevelt; he thought well of the liberal form of the British Empire. As his Governor, Tugwell, said, "Roosevelt felt in the British tradition" when dealing with colonial problems.

Governor Muñoz, in arguing for a popular referendum on the commonwealth form (Senate Bill No. 600), had appealed to the Congress in explicit historical terms: "If the colonial system were abolished [in Puerto Rico] it would be a long step toward reaffirming the world leadership of the United States . . . especially in Latin America." Commonwealth would be "a model of trusteeship for the whole world."

When the island overwhelmingly voted for the status of Commonwealth in 1951—387,000 to 119,000 (many *independentistas* did not vote)—Don Luis was jubilant. "We can proclaim to the world that the last juridical vestiges of colonialism have been abolished," he said. Governor Muñoz saw it as a practical compromise that recognized "the co-existence in Puerto Rico of the two great cultures of the American Hemisphere," as the new constitution declared; but the poet, Don Luis, could not resist seeing poetic visions in which commonwealth went "beyond nationalism," to embrace "the universal soul of humanity."

The candid Assistant Secretary of State for Interamerican Affairs, Adolf A. Berle, Jr., was more precise: "Puerto Rico has independence in everything except economics, defense and foreign relations." Congressman Joseph Mahoney, a veteran of the Interior and Insular Affairs Committee, was coldly legal-minded: "The U.S. Constitution gives Congress complete control [of Puerto Rico] and nothing in the Puerto Rican Constitution could affect, or amend, or alter, that right."

One of Don Luis's old admirers wrote: ". . . the retreat from independence meant a fatal return to the old game of appeasing Washington." The judgment of *independentista* leader Juan Mari Bras was even harsher: "In 1945, or 1946, Muñoz made a deal with Washington. He traded his belief in independence for the promise of economic aid, capital investment and the industrialization of the island, not for our people, but for foreign corporations, in the United States. He betrayed the independence movement. He betrayed himself. He sold Puerto Rico to the highest bidders in the United States." An epitaph for Don Luis's independence hopes was written by the former *New York Times* correspondent Kal Wagenheim, in *Puerto Rico: A Profile:* "His politics were consistent with a long line of Puerto Rican reformers, who flirted with independence, and finally settled upon the middle road—autonomy—when confronted with what one might call the 'realities' of dealing with a large colonial power."

Even his friends said that in politics he was "two men." He was a *caudillo,* a witty tyrant, who ruled by the charms of his *personalismo,* his charisma, when he could, and by rude power when he could not. "On paper Muñoz is very democratic, but in practice he is something else. He is the law," said a former Popular leader. To such accusations Don Luis disarmingly answered, "Now, I am not to be blamed too much for being somewhat persuasive along certain lines and along certain problems." It was not his fault. "Would you ask me to be deliberately unpersuasive?" he would say, smiling.

It was said that an English journalist once asked Muñoz: "Now that you have the Commonwealth, when will Puerto Rico get economic freedom from the United States?"

"About the same time Britain does," Don Luis answered.

Don Luis had the last word, as always. He had written it years ago in his poem "I Am the Pamphleteer of God":

> I have broken the rainbow
> against my heart
> as one breaks a useless sword against a knee.

To Govern Is to Invent

> Tell me,
> Umbrella mongers,
> When has an umbrella ever
> Kept the rains and the mist
>   from entering a heart
>   and shaping it
>   with dreams?
> When has it kept the rains
>   and the mist
> From entering a heart
>   and breaking it?

One night, after working late on official papers, Don Luis and a friend, who was a poet, walked out of the Palace of the Governor to a little café in Old San Juan to have a quiet drink.

Don Luis was restless. In the elusive night air "the spirits of the water" hovered over the harbor; he suggested they visit the home of his cousin Mercedes, the poetess, in the Old City near his Palace. Her house was as historic as it was dilapidated. Amid the books and memories of the bohemian life he once had known, the Governor was at ease. They talked for hours of the status of poetry and lesser matters. The hour was late. The Governor invited the poet: "Come to La Fortaleza. You can stay in the guest room."

"I am not of that world, Luis," the poet said.

Don Luis sighed with the weariness of his life. "Neither am I."

He went home to the Governor's Palace, alone.

And yet he was Governor for sixteen years, from 1948 to 1964, elected overwhelmingly by the people for four terms. He was politically "the master of the island" for a generation. In that time, "Puerto Rico was changed, forever. There is no question of what Muñoz accomplished," said his lifelong opponent and successor, Governor Luis Ferre. Even those who would not grant him that historical niche, men such as the *independentista* writer and editor Cesar Andreu Iglesias, a man of sharp opinions and severe insights, unhappily had to acknowledge his eminence: ". . . for better, or worse, Muñoz is the key man of the times."

In one generation Don Luis inspired, and Governor Muñoz guided, the metamorphosis of the poorest land in Latin America to the richest, per capita, in the colonial world. He was to be hailed as the "miracle man of the Americas" by one newspaper—one of the more modest accolades. The "poet in the fortress," as a biographer called him, was to do what no economist or politician had been able to do. And he did it by ignoring, or violating, the accepted rules of political and economic development. "People think too much of ideology, and too little [of] global truth," he said.

On the first days of the first session of the Senate that Don Luis had chaired as majority leader, in February, 1942, the bill to form PRIDCO—the Puerto Rican Industrial Development Company—was passed. It was, in the beginning, a wartime "emergency measure" to provide the island with government-built factories to supply the essentials of "civilized life" (shoes, cardboard boxes, glass, dishes, and cement) that had been blockaded by the Nazi submarines. In the beginning it was more than that.

In those years Don Luis still believed in independence. PRIDCO's "inspiration and guidance came, to a considerable extent, from the autonomy faction in the island's politics," thought economist David Ross; for it was a time "in which Puerto Rico might have been economically able to be independent," as Don Luis later said.

Little money was to be had on the island for the building of factories or anything else. In the forty years of its domination by the United States the yearly profits of the sugar crops had almost all been exported, as had the profits of four hundred years of Spanish colonialism. The island was a classical case of colonial impoverishment. What had once been an incredibly lush and rich tropical economy had been "milked" like a cow, as Don Luis had said.

But the war had diminished the domain of the sugar companies. It was difficult, if not impossible, to export sugar through the Nazi blockade. The need for peace on the island in the midst of war enabled the Populares to secure tens of millions in New Deal funding for industrial development, and to loosen the hold of the one-crop sugar economy.

After the war these factories were sold to the industrialist Luis Ferre. In the colonial economy they could not compete with mainland industries. It did not matter if the island's industry was a "celestial operation," said Governor Muñoz, somewhat bitterly, as long as there was industry.

"You cannot have celestial," Ferre said, laughing, "but the next best is private [industry]."

No one wished to invest in the "tropical hellhole," however. In 1947 there were a mere thirteen factories of U.S. origin on the island, providing no more than two thousand jobs. "There is no possibility *whatsoever* of any more capital [investment] in Puerto Rico," one corporation had advised Teodoro Moscoso, as late as 1950. Something had to be done to entice foreign investors. What if the colonial prejudices of businessmen could entrap them in their own myths?

"To govern is to invent," said Don Luis.

On the island the living conditions were desolate and the towns were impoverished. Fine, that meant industrial costs were low. "On the mainland you're met with inescapable wage hikes, increasing taxes and narrowing profit margins. An overseas operation might loosen the purse strings somewhat," read the new government's propaganda. On the island the Puertorriqueños were "docile" and "humble"; fine, there would be few union problems and strikes; the workers were "loyal" and there was "low turnover, low absenteeism." On the island, the *jíbaros* were accustomed to squalid poverty; fine, any wage would be a high wage; the "average industrial hourly [wage] of $1.76 compares with about $3.30 on the mainland and fringe benefits are lower." By 1972 the average industrial worker's take-home pay was $65.05 a week, one-half to one-third that of his counterpart on the mainland. "Most [of the island's employers] will tell you they're getting more than their money's worth.") Unemployment was as high as 85 percent in some towns: One, "Your operation will never be affected by a manpower shortage." The tropical climate made people "lazy"; fine, there were year-round "plush golf courses" and "new, high rise, luxury condominiums and spacious townhouses," where "you can expect *The New York Times* and *Wall Street Journal* to be on your desk by early morning."

"And your wife will rejoice to hear that domestic help is abundant," said a full-page advertisement in the *New York Times* during the 1950s, written by the economist Beardsley Ruml for the Commonwealth of Puerto Rico's EDA office.

Most of all, though, there were no taxes. "We want *new* and *expanding* industries. To get them, we promise freedom from all taxes, local and federal," Governor Muñoz wrote, in the same advertisement. The Commonwealth offered "freedom from all taxes, income and property, for periods of 10, 12, 15 or 17 years, depending on the location of the plant," according to a government release; it was "PUERTO RICO'S FINEST HOUR," one headline declared.

". . . as close to paradise as man will ever see . . ." said the vice-president of the St. Regis Paper Company, H. L. Christensen.

"Puerto Rico Is the Most Profitable Address in the U.S.A." was the slogan thought of, it was said, by Teodoro Moscoso. To the "independent soul" of Don Luis it may have seemed an impertinence, for he ordered the words "in the U.S.A." removed. Not until the regime of Governor Ferre was the original wording revived. But, no matter what the political status of the island, the "tropical hellhole" had indeed become a "financial paradise," in the words of the *Wall Street Journal.*

The success of Operation Bootstrap, as it was called before it was renamed Fomento, meaning to "stir up," was beyond even Don Luis's economic dreams. In 1950 there had been 82 factories on the island, the EDA estimated. In 1960 there were 717; in 1968, 1,684; in 1970, almost 2,000. The income of the people, per capita, increased just as dramatically. In 1950 it was $279. In 1960 it was $577. In 1968 it was $1,313. And by 1970 it had reached almost $2,000—the highest in Latin America.

It was "an epic of a society which achieved greatness," the old Populare Jaime Benitez said. "From 1940 to 1960 a tremendously significant social and human revolution happened in Puerto Rico. The pathos and drama of that achievement was largely unwritten, untold and in many ways unknown," he said, "because it has lacked the people to express it, to sing it, to honor it." No colonial country in history had ever been industrialized so quickly and so completely.

The "model" of the island's industrial boom was to become the "model" of the Alliance for Progress, for all of Latin America. Soon after the election in 1960, President Kennedy asked Adolf Berle, Jr., to lead the Latin American Task Force that was to plan the Alliance. As Juan de Onis and Jerome Levinson described it in their history *The Alliance That Lost Its Way* (Brookings Institution), Berle had "maintained close contact over the years" with his friend Muñoz, whose counsel he now sought in setting up the task force. Puerto Rico's "political stability," he felt, was "a model for democratic development throughout the hemisphere."

On the Latin American Task Force were mostly professors from the United States. Exceptions were Arturo Morales Carrión, the international affairs adviser of Don Luis, and his old Populare colleague Moscoso, of Operation Bootstrap; their job was to provide "a Latin feel for political issues and personalities." These two Puerto

Rican leaders became Berle's principal aides in defining the Alliance; de Onis commented, "Berle's idea, supported by Moscoso and Morales Carrión, was to identify the forces in each Latin American country that were comparable to the AD [Acción Democrática] in Venezuela, and help organize them into political parties" to defeat "the challenge of Cuba." The President was anxious to extend his New Frontier to the parliaments of Latin America, having failed to establish it on the beaches of the Bay of Pigs.

At Punta del Este, the delightful Uruguayan beach, the first Alliance for Progress conference was held in the summer of 1961. Che Guevara, in his green Army fatigues and combat boots, worn for the occasion, and C. Douglas Dillon, the Wall Street investment banker, whom Kennedy had appointed Secretary of the Treasury, in his blue pin-striped suit, faced one another across the conference table. Guevara chided the banker that funds for the Alliance "bear the stamp of Cuba," for without the existence of Cuban socialism the Alliance would not exist; and Dillon coolly replied by promising $20 billion to "countries of Latin America [who] took the necessary internal measures" (Juan de Onis).

Moscoso, who had become coordinator of the Alliance, had the hopeless task of maneuvering between this economic Charybdis and political Scylla. He failed. Later, in 1968, when he had resigned his position, Moscoso condemned the hemisphere program "modeled" on the island, and suggested it be abolished, along with the CIA establishments in Latin America.

In the ironic mind of Don Luis these contradictions were challenges. He thought of economic progress as an "American" rather than a "Latin" phenomenon. "My position involving the economic realities," the poet explained to the Status Commission in 1965 was "based on economic progress [that] seem[ed] to be functioning more on the line of the Anglo-Saxon mind." If the material wealth of industry and the human traditions of island life were wedded, there would be a flowering of *jíbaro* culture, Don Luis thought, that would "free the human spirit."

The "flowering" of urban life on the island created quite unexpected blossoms. In the *urbanizaciones,* as the suburbs were more accurately called, the new middle class sought to forget their *jíbaro* past. On the cement homes of Mayagüez an iron grille guarded each man from his neighbor; in the suburbs of San Juan the crime rate burgeoned and heroin addiction, almost unknown on the island before, became an epidemic. The poor furnishings of the past were discarded. In the living rooms ("Aren't all rooms to live in?" an old *jíbaro* asked), there were plastic sofas and color television; and artificial fruits were left on the dining-room sets at night to feed the "spirits of the dead." The fresh fruit in the *supermercados* was too expensive to leave out of the refrigerator, and there were no mango trees in Levittown, an *urbanización* of San Juan.

A man had to own a car to get to work on time. In tranquil Old San Juan the decibel level of noise was 90 to 110, higher than New York's din of 85, and higher than the "threshold of pain," at 100. "San Juan may well hold the world's record in noise pollution," said a local paper.

Once the success of Operation Bootstrap was achieved, Don Luis began to fear that it had failed. "I began to wonder—was Puerto Rico turning materialist, losing its traditional graciousness, abandoning its soul?" he asked himself. And he answered: "The human being should have a passionate wish to be free, rather than a passionate wish to be a possessor. In the old days you lived a good life, served God, and went to heaven. What are we living for? To beat the Russians? To own an automobile? Two? Three? Four?"

He remembered a folk saying of the island that he was fond of: "Every man must do three things in his life, plant a tree, write a book, and have a son."

"I wish they would plant more trees and write more books," sighed Don Luis.

Now it was the time, he suggested, for Operation Bootstrap to be succeeded by Operation Serenity. In a lecture at Harvard University he elaborated: "The first task we have called Operation Bootstrap, a large effort with little means; the second we named Operation Commonwealth, working at a new form of human freedom; the third, I believe, I would call Operation Serenity"; for its goal would be to help "the spirit of man in its function of leader of, rather than servant to, the economic processes. . . .

"Serenity through an efficiency placed at the service of understanding," Don Luis called it. "In Puerto Rico we are trying to develop the art of being wide awake without developing insomnia," he had once said.

In the new suburbs of the new middle class that the Populares had created, the people needed money to pay the finance charges on their old dreams. Not new dreams. They voted Don Luis's intimate and hand-chosen successor, Governor Roberto Sánchez Vilella, who had been El Vate's trusted executive secretary, out of office in 1968. They ended the twenty-year reign of the Populares, when Don Luis's protégé divided the vote by establishing his own People's party. They elected the most adamant opponent of the Commonwealth, industrialist and statehood advocate Luis Ferre.

On the crowded superhighways of San Juan "the spirit of man" may have seemed of dubious inspiration. Who needed the old poet of the *jíbaros?*

"The Death of Poetry" was how the defeat of the Populares was described in the *Caribbean Review* by the directors of the Instituto Psicológico de Puerto Rico, the Psychological Institute, Charles Albizu and Norman Matlin: "To the voter worried about where his next paycheck was coming from 'Operation Serenity' seemed anything but relevant. It seemed like a retreat to the poetry of the forties.

"In the process of trying to alleviate the *jíbaro's* economic misery, Muñoz has created the middle class," the psychologists wrote. But it had "not turned out as he had hoped. Muñoz visualized a middle class composed of *jíbaros* with money, loyal to tradition, freed from economic pressure so they could express the latent poetry of the *jíbaro*. It has, of course, not turned out this way." For the middle class was "simultaneously the end of all his labors and a menace" to all he envisioned. It was, to Muñoz, "a kind of Frankenstein monster" he had created, but rejected. To the psychologists, it seemed that Don Luis had created his own political pallbearers: "For the middle class, Ferre is more than just a successful businessman, he is Mr. Middle Class himself."

It was an irony that would have delighted the poet, Don Luis, but Governor Muñoz could not enjoy it. He could not even talk to reporters about it. "For a week he said nothing. He refused to congratulate us," fumed Luis Córdova Díaz, a friend of the newly elected Governor Ferre, who had himself been elected Resident Commissioner; his father, when he was Resident Commissioner in 1917, had employed the young Muñoz as his secretary. "It was typical of the man," the insulted Córdova said, "to be so ungracious"; but to Don Luis it was not a matter of grace or manners. The "Era of Muñoz Marín" was over.

His old *compañeros* of the early days had become leaders of the establishment of the society they had established. The geography professor Rafael Píco had become chairman of the board of the Banco Popular, the largest bank on the island. In 1970 he was chosen the "Boss of the Year." While the druggist from Ponce, Teodoro Moscoso, had become chairman of the board of the Commonwealth Oil Corporation, one of the largest in the Caribbean. He was a regular in the inner circle of Governor Ferre. "Commonwealth" and "Popular" were now corporate names, instead of the battle cries of the *jíbaros*.

El Vate, of all the old leaders, had nothing. He had few financial interests and fewer financial holdings. It was said that, like his father, all he had was "the glory and the debt": for it was impossible to imagine *el hombre dios* in a business office.

Soon after the ending of the reign of his Populares, Don Luis left the island. He went into exile, to live in Rome as a recluse, courteous but curt to visitors, granting few interviews. He was in exile as an old man, as he had been as a young man. For four years there were rumors that he would return to the island. He did not, although the *jíbaros* waited.

When he had resigned from the governorship, Don Luis had said, "I am leaving the burdens of office to come back to the roads along the mountains and through the clearings where we first met. I am not leaving you. I am returning to you." But he left the island.

His beloved *jíbaros* began to turn away from El Vate. It was a sad and reluctant disenchantment, but had he not deserted them?

Once the party of the *jíbaros,* the Populares had come to represent the elite of the *barrios.* In town after town it was the schoolteachers, the merchants, the professionals who ran the town committees of the Populares; and to the *jíbaros* these people were the local establishment, the new status quo of middle-class success created by Operation Bootstrap, Fomento, and *La Nueva Vida.* The *jíbaros* were rarely represented, if at all. In Utuado, at a meeting of the town committee of the Populares, there were a dozen well-groomed men in business suits, looking like any respectable group of salesmen in Des Moines, Iowa. The meeting was held, interestingly, in the offices of the Lucky Seven Supermarket. Not a man wore a *jíbaro*'s *pava.*

In one mountain town a *jíbaro* talked about Don Luis as he would not have dared a decade ago. He was a "stranger," said the coffee farmer of the former *hombre dios,* the man-god. He was not one of us—not a "true" Puerto Rican—said the *jíbaro,* with no anger, but with cold eyes.

"Yes, the Muñoz family, it came from Venezuela. The grandfather of Don Luis Muñoz Marín was one of the captains in the Spanish Army, who was defeated by Simón Bolívar. He bought the title of Mayor of the town of Barranquitas with Venezuelan gold. That's historic truth.

"So these people came here always thinking of Spain to protect their stolen privileges. And why did they come? To escape the independence of Latin America.

"They came from Spain to Latin America, where they became the owners of most of the wealth. They dispossessed the Indians. And when the Indians and the mestizos won independence, these Spaniards fled to Puerto Rico. By that time they were not Spaniards any more, and they were not Puerto Ricans. No, they did not have in mind the interests of Spain, or the interests of Puerto Rico, but their own interests. They had money and education. They took over everything. It is these families, the exiles from independence, who are the Muñoz, the Sanchez, the Ferre families. All those who are uppermost in the politics of Puerto Rico.

"And we, of the old families of Puerto Rico, we became just peasants. Just poor *jíbaros*. People without a trade. People without a land. People without anything.

"It is true that Don Luis has true Puerto Rican blood by the side of his mother. But his grandfather came here in 1859, I think. So recent! He was a stranger to us."

The old *jíbaro* knew he would not have said these things before. He would have held his tongue, even if he had thought them; and even now when he spoke he was uneasy, his voice barely audible. But, he said, he was "speaking the thoughts of others," so it had to be said. *El hombre dios* was after all just an ordinary man—"like me," the *jíbaro* said, laughing. "Maybe I cannot go on vacation to Rome, like he goes. Maybe I can go on vacation to East Bronx. That is all."

"The pamphleteer of God" had suffered the fate of all apostles.

The poet in politics was a man who walked on a tightrope of his own words. Don Luis was such a man. He was alone in the midst of a crowd, bowing to the mob, "the man of the people," who seemed untouched and aloof, most of all when he was lifted to their shoulders and looked upon them from above.

In the Governor's Palace, it was said, he had hidden his youth-filled dreams under his gregarious ambitions. He "looked" lonely, said a friend, when he would sit hunch-shouldered at his massive desk, even when surrounded by the noisy business of government. One of his former associates reminisced: "Don Luis was a great actor. He convinced everyone with his performance as 'the man of the people.' But sometimes I wondered, when I caught him unawares, if he ever convinced himself?"

Once, when he was younger and in exile, he had glimpsed that paradox within himself, in a poem of wry insight and bemusement:

How can I take you seriously, martyr?
Did I not once surprise the bottom of my soul
In the act of hugely enjoying
The renunciation of the surface of my soul?

Year by year Don Luis had gone less often among the *jíbaros*. He did not have the time. Don Luis had to be, he thought, the *patrón* of his own dream. That left him little time to dream.

Governor Muñoz no longer read the poetry of Don Luis; he read reports on economic growth and the imbalance of trade. An ex-poet could not administer the "industrialization of paradise" by recitations of the ironies of Cervantes or Neruda or himself over a cup of coffee in the cafés of Old San Juan. Some of his friends thought he had become "the prisoner of his own dream." They told this story, a modern fable:

The office of the Governor was in the throne room of La Fortaleza. He sat not where the King would have sat, but at the other end of the long, corridorlike room. In his white suit, within the high white walls, he worked at his great desk, talked to visiting dignitaries, signed official papers, and chatted with friends. Often he was seen looking, with a wondering eye, at the empty place at the far end of the room where the throne of the would-be kings of America had once stood, in a splendor even more lonely than his own.

In meetings his mind sometimes wandered away from the talk. His eyes were lost in thought, in memories, in fantasies. Who could say? As if those eyes had been searching for something, and had lost their way, they would become clouded by a brooding look of *dolor* that darkened his entire face. Once, his old friend Teodoro Moscoso was discussing an industrial-development matter with the Governor. He looked up from the statistics he was reading to see, to his surprise, that Don Luis had been staring across the room at a bust of Gandhi. Where were his thoughts?

On the crystal chandelier that hung from the twenty-foot ceiling of the throne room that was his office two little bananaquit birds had built a nest. The French doors to the patio were always opened so that the birds might fly to and fro. On the elegant glass doors Governor Luis Muñoz Marín had posted a sign.

> TO ANYONE WHO IS ABOUT TO
> CLOSE THESE DOORS: A PAIR
> OF BIRDS (BANANAQUITS) HAS
> LEGALLY CONSTITUTED A NEST
> ON THE CHANDELIER IN THIS
> ROOM AND IS ENTITLED TO
> FREE ACCESS AT ALL TIMES.
> PLEASE DON'T CLOSE THE DOOR.

The little birds enjoyed the courtesy. For they stayed quite a while. In the throne room no affair of state was permitted to disturb them.

In the mornings, when the Governor went to work, he first would make certain the doors were open. The breezes of the warm sea cleansed his offices. He was soothed by the cries of the freighters in the harbor, the sounds of the sea, the voices of the vendors in the streets of Old San Juan, the perfumed flowers in the gardens of his palace, but, most of all, by the songs and flutterings of the bananaquits which nested in the chandelier of the throne room; it was one of the few poetic ironies that he still permitted himself to enjoy.

One morning the birds flew away. . . .

He waited. He waited for one day, for two. In sadness, the Governor reluctantly ordered the French doors closed and locked. He ordered that an air conditioner be installed in the throne room.

10

The Baroque Computer

As the evening sun was setting in pink and orange upon the sky-blue waves of San Juan harbor, the talk of the guests turned to computers.

On the promenade of the Palace of the Governor, beside the relics of Spanish cannons, the potted and unpotted palms and the orchid trees that sweetened the night air, the business executives were trying to look like grandees. The waiters in formal jackets flitted about with ubiquitous grins and silver platters heavy with hors d'oeuvres. In the twilight there was an air of colonial mannerisms, genteel and servile. Though the beige-skinned waiters were not the only Puertorriqueños on the promenade—there were half a dozen members of Governor Ferre's Cabinet present—the guests, who had come at the special invitation of the Governor, were mostly the senior executives of North American corporations—Gulf Oil, Pittsburgh Plate Glass, Phillips Petroleum, Du Pont, Ford Motors—dressed stiffly in business suits and ties in the balmy tropical air. In the leisurely and yet official atmosphere they sipped their cocktails like *patrones* on the verandas of their own *haciendas*.

"It's the main reason my wife and I stay on the island," said a man from Pittsburgh Plate Glass.

"What's that?" he was asked.

"Ah, the Spanish style of life," he said, smiling. "So gracious."

The moon had risen. Under the silhouette of dark palms along the shore a ship began to navigate the calm waters of the harbor.

"Oh, it looks passive. But it's one of the trickiest harbors in the world," a yachtsman who was a banking executive said. "The tide is slippery. You can't do more than ten knots, and you have one minute to get in."

"Sounds like some women I know," his junior officer said, laughing.

At that moment, the Commissioner of Public Works, Antonio Santiago Vázquez, who was known as "the most powerful man in the government, next to the Governor himself," strode onto the promenade. Santiago was the chairman of the Mining Commission and the Environmental Quality Board—"a flagrant conflict of interest," his critics said—as well as the chairman of the Highway Authority, the Water Resources Authority, the Sewers Authority, the Conservation Fund, and the Road Safety Commission. In all he was a member of fifteen commissions and chairman of seven of them. "A Renaissance man in a technological society," said the San Juan *Star*.

"Oh, it's you," said one of the corporate *patrones*. "When do we get water for our plant!"

The stooped shoulders of the overworked Commissioner slumped. "Ah, yes, yes, yes." His eyes brightened vaguely as he replied, "Tell me, how many Puerto Ricans will be working in your plant?"

"Ninety percent!"

"Ah, good."

"We need the water by July."

Santiago sighed once more. "Let me see, this is April. Yes, you should have your water. [The island's environmentalists were loudly opposing the water project of the chairman of the Environmental Quality Board and the Water Resources Authority, at the time.] Now, if you will pardon me, I have to see the Governor." He hurried away.

Now that the Commissioner had come the evening meeting could begin. The cocktail hour had ended.

It was a "very crucial meeting," the Governor had said in his invitations; for he had summoned "seventy of the most important community leaders on the island"—the executive officers of the largest corporations—to discuss his plan "for computerizing the Government of Puerto Rico with the latest computers." And not only Puerto Rico, but "Latin America, too."

In a pilgrimage led by Governor Ferre, the executives walked, cocktails in hand, through the corridors of La Fortaleza, to the "petite theatre." Ferre, an energetic and lithe man, who was nearing seventy (he did fifty leg-ups, fifty situps and thirty squats every morning), spoke at once and enthusiastically, without a microphone and without sitting down. He lectured the businessmen on the meaning of money: "We should not think only of making money. It is important to make money. But make money for what? Another war? Our country made a great mistake with the war in Asia. We have wasted a lot of money. We have wasted ten years.

"Our problem is not in Asia, it is in Latin America," he said. "That's why I want the North-South Center for Technical and Cultural Exchange here in Puerto Rico. I want to make Puerto Rico the center of technology between North and South America."

The idea was not new. Federico Degetau, the founder of the Republican party of Puerto Rico, in 1899, and the first Resident Commissioner in Washington, in 1900, had advocated the use of the island as a "communication link" in a speech at the University of Pennsylvania on December 19, 1900: "If it [the United States] wants to express its ideas and methods of government, it may do so through Puerto Rico, which communicates with the Latin peoples. . . . The experiment with Puerto Rico is a far-reaching experiment with the Latin people." Degetau wished to accomplish this through a Pan-American University on the island. But it was Ferre who had added the idea of technology to the dream of Degetau, at the First Inter-American Conference of Accounting in 1949. And it was Ferre who had sent to the legislature the bill establishing the North-South Center, in 1971 when he had become Governor. Now he asked the corporate executives for financial contributions for his "technological dream." Some had already contributed.

In his dream the Governor saw the Center as a technological laboratory, an institute for the "engineers of government"—"To use the language of science. To use the latest computers. To use Puerto

Rico as a 'testing ground' for programs to help America, and Latin America."

On saying this, Ferre impatiently excused himself. He turned the meeting over to his Commissioner, Antonio Santiago Vázquez.

Santiago, like Ferre, was an engineer (he had been the chairman of the civil engineering department of the University at Mayagüez), and like Ferre he spoke brusquely and forthrightly ("As a matter of fact," he said, "I don't like politics").

"I like to look at Puerto Rico as a nice laboratory," he said.

"Here ideas can be tested that cannot be tested on the mainland," the Commissioner told the executives. But he did not elaborate, except to say: "We have an outstanding laboratory [on the island] for this." Of course, the acceleration of technology might result in some "estranged people," but with "science and technology we can overcome our lack of resources" and solve these problems eventually.

And with that Santiago bade the guests of the Governor good night and thanked them for coming. He apologized that the evening was not "more cultural."

On the charming balcony of the "petite theatre" in the Palace no musicians had played for years. In that royal chamber of La Fortaleza, where the *elegante* ladies and gentlemen of the Spanish Court once had been entertained, there was now the control center of Governor Ferre's computers. He had hidden his mechanical minds, for aesthetic reasons perhaps, behind the drapery that shrouded the walls of the theatre. Under the musicians' balcony, where the Governor and his Commissioner had spoken, there was a screen for the projection of computerized wisdom on closed-circuit television.

It was an intimate chapel of technology. Small as a sanctuary, the perfect room in which to listen to the cello of Pablo Casals or to Bach. "Bach has been upstaged," an *ayudante,* one of the young aides-de-camp of the Governor, said, laughing. The asthmatic hum of the computers was the only sound.

The Governor was known to be a classical pianist. He had earned his degree from the Boston Conservatory of Music the year he graduated from MIT. Even now he was practicing the religious music of Franz Liszt.

"My dream," the Governor said, "is to bring self-respect to technology. Our people think technology has ruined their lives. But technology is neutral. It depends on how it is used. And why. And on the culture and morality of the engineers."

He wished to "humanize technology," the Governor said. He wished to "computerize the Latin soul," said his critics.

"Oh, what innocence!" scoffed Benitez, the former president of the University of Puerto Rico; "What simple innocence! for a man to have such faith in computers. Computers are useful, so are typewriters and cakes of soap. But they will not solve the problems of life of man. Ferre! He is not an illusion as some people think. He is merely illusory. He believes his fantasy world is the real world."

In the businesslike office of the Governor—he worked in the small anteroom to the throne room of the Palace—"No, I will not use the throne room. It is not comfortable to me," he said—Ferre always had a computer control panel at his elbow. "Let me see," he said, beaming, "what would you like to know? At my fingertips is every important item of information about the island. The computer knows everything." He affectionately fingered the key for "Bank Deposits." In seconds the average cash value per Puertorriqueño as determined by deposits appeared on the screen.

"So what shall we see next?" His fingers had poised at "Beer Consumption." They moved on. Instead, he touched a key for "Citizens' Feedback." Onto the screen clicked the numbers of telephone calls, letters, telegrams and/or visits by irate or loyal citizens. If he had touched a different key, the statistics would have been subdivided into the types of complaints people had about whatever sector of the economy, or morality, had disturbed them. "You see, I know at once exactly what people think," the Governor said. "The computer is politically objective."

The *patrón* of the technological Palace no longer had to hold court in the throne room. *Peón*, penitent, and protestor no longer came as often as during the reign of Don Luis Muñoz Marín to seek the Governor's benediction. "My door is always open," Ferre said; but entry seemed to be by computer card.

Yet the Governor's belief in technology was not his faith. He was "a Renaissance man in the twentieth century," his *ayudante* said; for "he combined the techniques of modern industry with the philosophy of Saint Augustine and Cervantes." In his restoration of La Fortaleza the Governor had tried to engineer that unlikely harmony.

On the far side of the Palace overlooking the harbor was the great room where formal dinners were held. It was a majestic room, with a banquet-length table and high heirloom chairs and glittering chandeliers; but, unlike the computerized "petite theatre" up the corridor, there were no electric lights in the dining room.

"We use candles. Even for the state occasions," said the Governor. "I believe in keeping the old traditions wherever possible."

La Fortaleza was no ordinary governor's residence. It had been restored by Ferre himself in the baroque style of its origins, the medley of Renaissance Gothic and Spanish *colonialismo* that was to his own taste. The thought of computers in its romantic interiors, amid the opulence of its gilded fixtures and Louis XIV loveseats, was as incongruous as the presence of computers in the Louvre or the Prado in Madrid.

From the portrait of Queen Isabella II in the foyer, to the "Kennedy bed" in an obscure guest room, where the late President had slept, history pervaded La Fortaleza. After all, its walls, thicker than the length of a man's arm, were originally built as a fortress, in 1533. And there was an unreality in its restored history; for it resisted modernization in the name of tradition.

In the sumptuous bed where tourists were told that "Jackie Kennedy once slept" the incongruous wedding of past and present were beautifully grotesque. Here was a gloriously gaudy and gregarious bed of high brass, garish with metallic curls and shiny balls, that conjured up a fantasy in the eyes of the young *ayudante* as he fondly peered at its fluffed pillows. "I see a 'royal playmate.' Lying naked with long black hair, golden-skinned and sunburned to her navel, almost brown, with dark and dangerous eyes, her figure very, very ample."

On hearing of his lieutenant's fantasy the Governor merely laughed.

The fantastic remembrance did not seem improper in the tropical Palace built as the castle for the would-be kings of the New World. It was a royal mansion of the elected aristocracy, in a constitutional democracy—the "most beautiful governor's residence in America"—where the grandeur of the Empire of Renaissance Spain and the technological expertise of the United States were being mated by a millionaire manufacturer of cement, The Governor Luis Alberto Ferre Aguayo del Rey—"the King."

A gentle man, with a pensive and at times thoughtfully vague look, Luis Ferre had a grandfatherly manner. He was deceptive. He was a businessman, to whom politics had been a philanthropy. Like his private collection of sensual and religious baroque art. The elder statesman of the island's industrialists, he had a disdain for politics and a contempt for politicians, whom he thought not only inefficient but uncultured. (One day, after a state meeting, the aging Governor was discovered on his knees in his music room, admiring an unhung painting of nymphs cavorting in the forests, which he had recently bought.) In his rich and flamboyant restoration of the Palace, his *ayudante* said, the Governor may have wished to protect himself, in his private hours, from the ugliness of politics with the "beauty of his art collection."

In Ponce, the "most Spanish city on the island," where he built his cement factory and his Museum of Art, Ferre resided in gracious seclusion. His estate was a dreamlike *hacienda,* set in a palatial garden. It was his "private monastery," said a friend; for in his leisure life Ferre preferred to be alone with his piano and his library; he was "a meditative man by nature," the friend said. Politics was merely his newest interest; it did not interest him deeply. In his heart the Governor longed to be a philosopher or teacher. "If I had not been what I am," he told a journalist, "I would have been a university professor." Later he added: "I am the thinker. I am the philosopher. A man is important because of what he feels and thinks. Not merely because of his political beliefs."

Now that he had to be Governor, however, he ran his administration as he had directed his industrial empire, with personal force and single-minded purpose—with "a gloved hand, but firm objective," he said; he believed in a "strong hand." He was determined that Puerto Rico would become a modern technological state. "As part of the great American economic structure," Ferre declared, "we must be technological. We must be equal citizens. We must have statehood. And we will have all these things. It is just a matter of time." The days of *"¡Ay bendito!"* were gone.

Luis Ferre was a "new force" in the tradition of *patrón* politics on the island. He was neither a poet-lawyer nor the scion of one of the old families of the plantation aristocracy. "I am an engineer," he said, almost defiantly. "Engineers have always been in the family." The Ferre family had made their fortune in heavy industry—cement, iron, construction, petroleum—businesses that the older families had always considered somehow "un-Puerto Rican." His ancestors had in fact come from France, by way of Cuba. (In *Standard and Poor*, brother José nostalgically listed one of the lost Ferre enterprises, in Santiago, Cuba.) Some of his opponents still referred to Ferre as "the Cuban."

On the island he had become one of the wealthiest industrialists, if not the wealthiest, as well as the symbol of *La Nueva Vida,* the New Life—the slogan of his political party, the New Progressive party, of which he was the founder, the financier, and the leader.

"I am *the* leader," he said, with no false modesty.

He was accustomed to having his own way. When the government had built several factories and had jarred his concept of private enterprise—under the governorship of Luis Muñoz Marín—he had bought them. When the Republican party had refused to listen to his advice, he had established his own party and not only won the election but eliminated the Republicans.

In a sense, it was his disdain for politicians that made him a politician. One of his closest associates and friends, Luis Córdova Díaz, then Resident Commissioner of Puerto Rico in Washington, D.C., described the irony of that "political accident":

"Our friends in the Republican party, the statehood party, refused to participate in the Referendum of 1967—to decide whether the people wanted commonwealth, statehood, or independence. They wanted to abstain. 'No,' they said, 'the Referendum will be weighted for commonwealth.' So, they said, there was no use in fighting against that. They were practical politicians.

"But a group of us, led by Ferre, decided we could not abstain. We had to fight for statehood. We went to the polls."

The old détente of the *político patrones* was disrupted by the brash upstarts. "We had to fight both major parties, the Republicans *and* the Populares," Córdova recalled. "We had to fight both political machines. We were people without a political machine and without political experience. Ferre had some. I had none. And so it was a surprise to everyone in Puerto Rico—including us—when we pulled nearly forty percent of the vote for statehood.

"I remember the night before the Referendum, I went to Ferre and said: 'Look, we're going to do pretty well. We have to organize a political party. We cannot afford to let our people disband.'

"He agreed with me. Ferre had pledged that we did not intend to form a new party. Now he agreed to do it, as long as he had the support of people like myself. So that's how I got myself into my present office and how we won the election."

Statehood! The "time had come" for the improbable dream of half a century. The urbanization of the *jíbaros,* the Americanization of Puerto Rico's economy, and the migrations of millions of people to the mainland had strengthened the island's ties with the United States. In the past the Congress had been reluctant to admit any state into the Union until its population became primarily *anglo*—New Mexico was a crass instance of this.

"Now things had changed," said Córdova. "The Congress was

much more understanding of cultural differences. And then the admission of Hawaii was the shot in the arm that changed our statehood dream into a reality."

In his speech to the National Press Club in Washington, D.C., the following year, Governor Ferre elaborated on this: "Statehood for Puerto Rico will not mean assimilation; will not mean the disappearance of our cultural tradition or the abandonment of our Spanish language. This, as you know, is anthropologically impossible and constitutionally unnecessary." Besides, he thought: "The United States is moving away from the illusion of the 'melting pot' and towards the reality of democratic pluralism."

Córdova, too, believed this: "In my lifetime I have seen racism to Puerto Ricans diminish," he said. "The State of Puerto Rico will enter the Union as an equal, but culturally different, member state. That is what we are fighting for.

"So in February of 1968 a handful of us formed the New Progressive party. In November of 1968 we went to the polls. And we won! Who thought we would win? No one. When we won by a plurality of 44 to 45 percent, and the Populares got only 41 to 42 percent, it was a surprise to everyone. Myself, too! For forty years I had been practicing law. I was senior partner in a substantial law firm. Now I was elected Resident Commissioner. But I was not ready. I had made no preparations. I never in my life had held a political office. I was, as you may imagine, a bit surprised.

"So was Ferre," Córdova said, laughing. It was "like a dream."

The "nonpolitical" engineers and lawyers suddenly discovered that the government, that "bureaucracy of do-gooders and ideologues" they had railed against, cursed, and ridiculed for years, was in their hands. But what to do with it? It seemed logical to them to reorganize the government along the technological lines of their ideal, the United States itself. After all, technology worked efficiently and successfully in their own businesses. So why not "computerize the bureaucracy"? Ferre had said: "I wish to see if technology can be applied to the methods of government."

On becoming Governor, Ferre had inherited an island economy

that was dependent on the fads and fashions of the mainland. Hundreds of factories were engaged in the production of brassières, lingerie, dresses, infants' nighties and panties, shoes and sports clothes. Ferre's own business experience had been primarily with heavy industry. And the new Governor had a definite distaste for Puerto Rico's reputation as "The Brassière Capital of the World."

Ferre and his engineers decided to build heavier industries. The efforts were "centered on, but not limited to, capital-intensive heavy industry such as fabricated metals, transportation equipment, petrochemicals, plastics, and electrical equipment," commented the Morgan Guaranty Trust Company, in its *Puerto Rico and the Foreign Investor.* So successful was the heavy-industry program that the petrochemical refineries alone, in which $450 million were invested before Ferre took office, reached $750 million hardly two years later; they were "expected to reach $2 billion by 1975," reported the Morgan Guaranty bank. The zooming production of the island's industry had surpassed $4 billion, in 1970, but it was the technological industries that led the way to *La Nueva Vida.*

"In a few years we have done what it took the United States one hundred years to do," Commissioner Santiago said proudly.

The "Quiet Revolution" of industry, the bankers of Morgan Guaranty called it. But on the island it was often harsh and intrusive.

On the lovely southern shore, where the green hills of sugar cane met the sea, the little towns still dozed, as they had for centuries. Here was the city of Ponce, the beloved home of the Governor, known as "the last refuge of *serenidad* and gracious living." And it was here, under the sky, on the virgin beaches of the Caribbean, that the belching smokestacks of the petrochemical refineries were concentrated. They darkened the sky and the water with grimy soot and gaseous fires that burned night and day. After his election, Governor Ferre had promised, in 1969, "We're going to have an island that's spotless."

In the bay of Guayanilla, near Ponce, the oil refineries lined the shore, like an endless inferno. Not only the fumes of the oil but the stench of the chemicals polluted the beaches. On the road, within a few miles, stood the surrealist giants of technology—UNION CARBIDE, ESSO, CORCO, OR COMMONWEALTH OIL, HERCULES' HER COR CHEMICALS, OXOCHEM CORP., OLEFINS, FLUOR WESTERN, ZACHRY INTERNATIONAL, PEERLESS PETROCHEMICAL, and other such technological anagrams. Few of the workers lived near the refineries. It was too ugly.

In a field wedged between the huge refineries across the road from Union Carbide and Corco the sugar cane still blew in the wind. A flamboyant tree grew nearby, its bright red flowers oblivious of the fires.

Up the road, in the village of Tallaboa, a few farmers tended the cane fields as if the refineries did not exist. The hard-armed men, with faces turned to burnt sugar by the sun, laughed bitterly. "It is the best land for sugar. And for growing everything. Everything grows here." One farmer in Tallaboa Poniente viciously kicked the rich, thick dirt with his boot. "Soon the earth will look like the floor of a garage. Why have they come here? Why don't they go?"

The employment supervisor of one large corporation, Juan Cardono, replied: "Why in this area? I think mostly because of the cheap labor cost. And the low cost of the land. The land was cheaper than somewhere else because it was planted in sugar cane and the workers were sugar-cane workers.

"So," the supervisor said, "it was cheaper to come here."

One plant in the nearby town of Guánica had been closed by the Mayor, Jaime ("Jimmy") Rosas Martínez. Rosas was an enthusiastic supporter of Governor Ferre, a leader of the New Progressive party on whose ticket he had been elected. In Chicago, where he had lived, he had become a baseball player, boxer, trumpet player, and "All-American boy." He described himself as a "200 percent" American. "I don't want Puerto Rico to become independent or Communist," he said. He was "gung-ho for Ferre's industrial programs," the Mayor said, "but not in my town!"

In the beginning he had not opposed the Caribe Nitrate plant in Guánica. "We needed jobs," Rosas said. The unemployed *jíbaros* swarmed into the town from the fields. "Our people were so poor they had to sleep on dirt floors. I have seen babies sleeping in the mud." But the nitrate plant did not help the poor. "They employed 104 people and 72 of them came from outside the town. They told us our people didn't have the necessary technical skills."

One morning "the wind changed," the Mayor said. The fumes of the nitrate plant blew over the town. Hundreds of people became sick. "In one barrio we had maybe four hundred, maybe five hundred, children sick. They were poisoned by the nitrate fumes. In one night we had forty-five children in the hospitals," he recalled. Even as he said it, his lips tightened with anger.

"We closed the plant," said the Mayor, "and it stays closed."

"Let them keep those plants, with their pollution, over there. I don't want any chemical plants on the Guánica beach. Yes, it would mean jobs and money for us. But I don't want it!

"In Guánica we want to have our beautiful beaches clean and pure as the sky." (Up the coast, the world-famous Phosphorescent Bay at Parguera was "growing dimmer, day by day" in the polluted sea.) "If they talk of 'development,' I say, Sure! Let us develop bathing beaches for the people of Puerto Rico. Not for the tourists, or summer resorts for the managers of the petrochemical plants, but inexpensive, nice beaches where Puerto Ricans can go. We need 'clean industry' that doesn't destroy our island. We don't want our sugar cane poisoned. We don't want our children poisoned. We have learned our lesson.

"I will tell Ferre," said the Mayor of Guánica, "no more poison in our sky. That's not progress!"

In the once "eternal paradise" the jungles were being denuded by the new industries. "Puerto Rico is rapidly losing [its] trees," warned San Juan's meteorologist Ed Miller, a veteran of two decades on the island. When Ponce de León landed, his companions noted, "the island is very pleasant, with many abundant watering places, because of the many luxuriant trees"; but now, Miller said, "only 15 percent of the island is covered by trees.

"We know that wiping out the forests and the trees destroys the soil," Miller said. So it was no surprise "that 48 percent of our land has severe to very severe erosion, and that an additional 22 percent has slight to moderate erosion"—more than two-thirds of the island.

"This island," the meteorologist said, "is facing the grave loss of her limited natural resources through the indiscriminate cutting of trees, soil erosion from overconstruction, and poor soil and water management practices, thoughtless sand and gravel extraction, industrial dumping and the unconcerned littering of her cities, beaches, rivers and countryside. . . . As our capacity to destroy our environment grows every day, our resources are gradually disappearing."

So much sand was being taken from the beaches for the cement to build new suburbs, factories, and highways that the famous beaches were vanishing. From the beach of Boca de Cangrejos "so much sand was extracted to build the international airport," said Jaro Mayda, author of *Environment and Resources,* that the beach "collapsed" into the sea.

Mayda, a professor of jurisprudence and international law at the university, recommended an immediate "U-turn in social planning" to restore "the ecological and social balance of the island, which has been disturbed by the one-sided industrialization of the last 25 years." But to some it seemed almost too late. The director of the Environmental Quality Board, Cruz A. Matos, was dismayed to see "all my beautiful memories of the island covered in concrete."

In the cement of the parking lots surrounding every new shopping center and petrochemical plant were the shimmering white sands of a tranquil tropical beach. "See that parking lot?" said a young worker in the Bacardi rum factory in Cataño. "That's the beach where I used to swim."

Even the spirits of the dead—the *jipia*—were fed plastic fruits. In the night the *jipia* were said to wander from house to house, visiting relatives and eating tropical fruit. This was an old belief of the Borinquén Indians. But in the suburbs and *urbanizaciones* the fruit in the *supermercados* was too expensive—much of it was imported from Florida—to serve to spirits. On the dinette-set tables were bowls of polyfoam pears and delicious apples. None of these fruits were any more native to the island than the polyfoam. They were imported from Hong Kong. On the television sets were bouquets of tiny kumquats, miniature grapes, and toy pineapples made of glass blown in West Germany. In the modern kitchens there were bunches of plastic bananas from Japan on the refrigerators.

The housewife in Utuado, seeing a guest eying her plastic offering, was embarrassed. "It is so hot, you know, that a real fruit would rot in a few hours. These fruits will last forever. Besides, they don't bring flies in the house."

"Someday the *jipia* will die of indigestion," said a university girl in a condominium in Hato Rey. "Then they will leave Puerto Rico for Nueva York, where the tropical fruits are cheaper."

"Discontent is the mood of all of Puerto Rico," the political analyst Juan M. García Passalacqua commented; the people troubled by the way of life and alienated by the government. He blamed it on the "failure" of the government's policies, but he might just as well have blamed their "success." The adulation of statehood, technology, and corporate growth by Ferre had led to a "polarization of angers." "The stage is set for confrontation," García Passalacqua wrote.

"Terrorism, the systematic use of force as a means of coercion, is being used by persons of both pro-independence and anti-independence ideology. . . . Bombings of continental firms are now followed by burnings of MPI [*independentista*] offices. Puerto Ricans confront Puerto Ricans, at the university, at the Caribe Hilton, in the Condado area. An eye for an eye is the new rule."

"We are certainly becoming barbaric," Commissioner Córdova agreed.

So sharp and antagonistic were the social and political divisions created by the policies of Ferre that on the island of *serenidad* there were warnings of "civil war." The young leader of the Populares, Senator Rafael Hernández Colón, thought it "unbelievable." But he feared the "blind policies of Ferre" had ignored the "ordinary needs of ordinary people" and had caused "the polarization of the political and social life that was creating the threat of civil war." Unless the

Populares were returned to power, with a "middle of the road government," declared the Populares leader, "civil war might become the inevitable consequence" of the Governor's policies.

Even the philosophical engineer in La Fortaleza feared "they" might kill him! The Governor had become so weary of the picket lines that chanted beneath his windows that he had lost count. "I have at least two picket lines each day," he sighed. "There are so many of them. Sometimes I wonder how many picket lines I have had since I became Governor. At least a thousand!"

In the Palace of the Governor, on his glass-enclosed, sunny veranda, in the perfumed air-conditioned air, Luis Ferre lounged in a high-backed, thronelike, Spanish colonial chair, and he mused about the changes being wrought by his "technological dream." He, too, was deeply troubled.

The engineer had become philosophical and meditative. "Science is not an absolute," he said, almost angrily. "Contrary to what many people think, science is just an approximation of the truth. It is constantly changing in accord with new ideas. So this idea that science is the absolute truth, and nothing that is not scientific is the truth, is completely mistaken." He never believed technology was the answer to all man's needs; it was "but a small, very small, part of truth, of life." He struck at the air with his fist. "We are beginning to learn today that maybe we have been discarding some areas of knowledge that are basic to the emotional balance of the human being. The young people have sensed this more than the older people," said the Governor. "And they have made us alert to this. Because they are the ones who have been suffering from this misunderstanding of the concept of knowledge.

"For two hundred years, since Descartes, we have believed that reason is the only way to knowledge. Whatever was not reason was not knowledge. In this belief we have discarded all the irrational knowledge of the human being, the cultural, the emotional, the subconscious. The technological societies of today have become completely rational and have lost their faith in cultural values.

"In America, when we have a society where everyone is a rationalist, we will have destroyed the basis of our culture."

He was talking philosophically. If he was referring to anything that was happening in Puerto Rico, he gave no indication of it.

"Man is the most irrational of all the rational animals." The Governor laughed to himself.

On the wall there was a serene portrait of a forgotten lady of the court. He gazed thoughtfully at her lanquid eyes. The baroque computers in the "petite theatre" seemed centuries away. Were his thoughts lost in the corridors of his Museum of Art in Ponce?

If he thought this way, why did he go on with his "technological dream," the Governor was asked. What would he do when his political career had ended and he was defeated?

"Ah," the Governor sighed, "I will return to my museum."

Soon after the conversation on the veranda, Luis Alberto Ferre Aguayo del Rey, the engineer, was defeated in his bid for re-election as the Governor of *La Nueva Vida,* the New Life, on Puerto Rico.

11

The "Man-in-the-Middle"

The little man knelt at the podium as he sewed the drapery. In the hushed excitement of the ornate yet austere building of archaic grandeur that had been the old colonial capitol of the island, the little man, on his knees, sewed with a deft, intense reverence. He believed his work was essential to the inauguration of the new Governor. When he was done, the drapery would be hung, and the Governor of Puerto Rico could take his oath of office with dignity.

So the little man sewed, ignoring the talk of civil wars.

And thread by thread the intent tailor finished his work. He admired his skill, with a satisfied smile, knowing that governors would come and governors would go, but without his drapery hung in its traditional way the inauguration of any government would not be official.

He stood up importantly, as if to say: "*I* am indispensable."

Who was he? Charlie Chaplin, or Cantinflas, or Juan Bobo, the Everyman of Borinquén. He was simply a *jíbaro* with a needle and thread. He laughed at the confused *ayudantes* who were running about like young cocks in heat, the secretaries too busy to be seductive, the nonchalantly nervous plainclothesmen, the benign capitol police, whose eyes pleaded with suspicious onlookers to leave, and the newspapermen looking for trouble, at least an unsuccessful attempt at assassination.

In the cafés on the plaza there was talk of revolution, in between sips of coffee. No one seemed too disturbed by the talk. The politicians threatened one another, however, with dire predictions of what would happen if the other fellow, *el otro,* was to win the elections.

Day by day the police had been jailing the leaders of the opposition *independentista* parties. The accusations varied from possession of marijuana to "conspiracy" to overthrow the government; from illegal pasting of posters on the walls to murder of the head of the riot police. None resisted arrest. In the face of what they termed "provocations" the Armed Commandos of Liberation called off their bombing of "Yankee businesses and installations." In the truce the streets were unusually quiet. There was no pre-election street fighting. There were no political killings, as in other years.

In the ominous quiet the island seemed to be in the eye of a political hurricane. The enemies faced each other at the polling booths, with restraint, as if waiting.

"If we do not win the elections, there might be civil war," had been the calm, matter-of-fact warning of Rafael Hernández Colón, the candidate of the Popular Democratic party, the Populares. He was known as a cool young man. That seemed to be so. In his office as president of the Senate, he had talked of civil war with a straight, almost cold, face, his tight-lipped voice barely acknowledging his own words. The threat of upheaval came, he thought, from the polarization of left and right, in the independence and statehood parties. "Politically these bitterly opposed forces feed on one another," he said; if either one triumphed, "Puerto Rico faces a long, dark night of economic ruin and Balkanization, in which we, and the United States, have everything to lose.

"We represent the middle of the road between the two extremes of independence and statehood," he had said. "We represent reason amid emotions. We alone can bring stability and peace to the island. We represent the reality of commonwealth."

Rafael Hernández Colón was the man-in-the-middle, by choice. He had determinedly decided to make his political stand between the two extremes, both outside and inside his party. It was a tenuous position, but he hedged it meticulously with friends and enemies, who owed him political favors with which he had carefully paved his path to La Fortaleza, and the governorship. "My husband's decision to run for Governor wasn't something that happened overnight," quietly said his wife, Leila Hernández, a petite woman with a knowing smile, like a sigh. "I've had years to get used to public life."

The "upcoming, young, rich-but-not-so-rich president of the Senate, with good looks and a beautiful family," as journalist Ismaro Velásquez described him, knew he could not depend upon the aging political *patrones* of the Populares, of which he was also president, to satisfy his ambitions. He was one of "the new breed" in politics. He turned his Romanesque profile, with its considerable appeal, to the youth. "It's natural for the youth to identify with youth," he said. And there were 478,000 potential voters on the island between the ages of eighteen and twenty-four. He was the youngest candidate for Governor in the history of the island. He was thirty-six.

"Cuchin," as his *aficionado* José Torres, the former light heavyweight world champion, familiarly called him, wished to be the candidate of the new generation. He cultivated the Kennedy image, consciously and well. Once he was introduced to Norman Mailer by the professional fighter. "He's smart," Mailer said, in giving his blessing. "Somehow he reminds me of Bobby Kennedy."

"He creates a super reaction in people," said Torres. "Like Bobby Kennedy [he] has trouble conveying to the always screaming crowds the issues of importance. It always reminds me of the time I spent with Kennedy in Indian reservations and in the ghetto areas in the U.S.

"In Hernández Colón we had the beginning of a new mentality in Puerto Rico," said the boxer.

Like George McGovern, whose nomination he had supported by casting the votes of Puerto Rico for the South Dakotan at the Democratic Convention of 1972, he hoped "to reach and inspire and motivate the youth," to convince them "the system worked." He campaigned too for their beliefs, as much as their votes. He urged a new program of "radical reforms" that would "end poverty" forever. "If this society made a decision of conscience to eliminate and eradicate poverty," he said, it could "wipe out poverty in Puerto Rico in ten or twelve years."

In his speeches he often spoke of "the dignity of being Puerto Rican," and condemned the American "assimilationism" of his statehood opponents. Let there be, he said, *"absolute control* by Puerto Ricans of immigration, coastal shipping, culture and the draft"; but he did not mention an independent economy. He proclaimed himself an "autonomist" in the great tradition of Luis Muñoz Rivera.

On arriving at the San Juan airport on election night he was greeted by a youth who cried: "Hello, Mr. Governor!" A newspaperman who was there reported: "Grinning his tight-lipped smile, the thirty-six-year-old Popular party president stood quietly, laughing, as if to himself.

Someone told him, 'And they said Puerto Rico was assimilationist!'

" 'No!' Hernández Colón replied, 'Puerto Rico does not surrender.' "

It was the voice of his "new Puerto Rico," confident, defiant, independent, and a bit arrogant.

In his youth he may have dreamt of independence. When he was twenty-six, a young lawyer in the Bar Association, he had been coauthor of a status resolution that strongly stated: "Puerto Rico will not enjoy true sovereignty until Congress renounces *all its powers* over the island" (emphasis added). But what good was a dream that Congress would not pass? He was a practical man. "Most meaningful legislation depends on the availability of funds," he said. Why talk of a dream that no one would fund? "Where others were ideologues," a critic commented, "he was a realist."

So he now thought of independence as a "foolish dream," and he had fought it. The smallness of the island and its "meager resources" made independence unrealistic, "as I dream it," he once had cryptically said.

The family of Rafael Hernández Colón may have been his school for practical politics. His father was a Supreme Court Justice, who advocated statehood, as did his brother José. His younger brother, Cesar, who had been his law partner in Ponce in earlier years, was an adamant *independentista*. Even in his family he was the-man-in-the-middle. "We talk politics when we get together," he said, "but never in a disagreeable way." He disliked passion in politics.

On election day the man-in-the-middle was elected Governor of Puerto Rico by nearly 100,000 votes. "LANDSLIDE!" the headlines cried in disbelief. When he had challenged the venerable Governor Ferre, the prophets and the polls had given him little chance. He was "too young." He was "too modern." He was "too unemotional." He was "too un-Puerto Rican." In his triumphant sweep the Populares won control of seventy-three of seventy-eight municipalities and both houses of the Legislature. It was "the victory of the new generation," proclaimed the dazed prophets; perhaps "the young one" was, as his campaign slogan said, *"Un Hombre Para Nuestro Tiempo"*—"A Man for Our Time." But there were some who thought he had been elected by his enemies, and one old man.

"It was a common sight the day after the elections to see 'victory caravans' floating by with both PDP [Populares] and PIP [*independentista*] banners from different sides of the same car," one political commentator noted. "Thousands of *independentistas* opted to vote against statehood, rather than for independence." And so they voted for the man-in-the-middle.

The "vast majority" of *independentistas* "opted to defeat Ferre," said Mari Bras, the Socialist party leader. In this the election was "clear evidence of the Puerto Rican people's repudiation of unconditional assimilation," urging the new Governor "to end once and for all the colonial system and return to our people their sovereign power."

In his post-mortem press conference the defeated Governor Ferre voiced rare agreement with the Socialist Mari Bras. Ferre blamed his loss on the *independentistas* who had voted for the Populares. He thought there had been a "coalition," if not a "conspiracy," of the minority parties to defeat him. If the ex-Governor was correct the

Populares increase of 255,000 votes was composed primarily of *independentistas,* more than they themselves claimed.

On the mainland the youth vote was disappointingly small. But on the island it was very strong. In Puerto Rico more than 82 percent of the registered voters had cast their ballots. The youth more so than other age groups. Pre-election polls, taken by Governor Ferre's staff, had indicated that one-third of the young voters were *independentistas.* And yet, though they stated their belief in independence, they evidently had voted for the Populares candidates.

Yet it was not the victory of audacious youth over cautious age. In the months before the election the elderly Don Luis Muñoz Marín had, at long last, returned to the island, to campaign for the "young one" and to see that his old nemesis, Ferre, was graciously retired. "MUÑOZ MARÍN IN EL BATEY, in your front yard," the notices of his radio talks beckoned. There was the fatherly, now grandfatherly, white-mustached face of El Vate, looking into the eyes of his countrymen; the kindly but severe stare of a disapproving *patrón,* chastising the *jíbaros* for behaving foolishly while he was away.

"The Godfather has come home!" a young man said.

In his baronial baritone old Don Luis intoned the lost virtues. The "personification of the good old days" fondly remembered now that they were nostalgic memories rather than day-to-day realities, the aged *patrón* of everyone's youth evoked a fatherly aura of paternalism upon the noisy voices of the politicians; as only *el hombre dios,* the man-god, could have done. And, though the effect of Luis Muñoz Marín's rhetoric on the voters could not be measured at the polls, his power was no less than if Franklin Delano Roosevelt's voice had returned with his radio "fireside chats," to haunt Richard Nixon's rehearsed posing on television. In the election Don Luis "was the decisive factor," a political journalist said flatly.

But the dream that the voice of Papá had evoked, "softly cooing" to the "*jíbaros* of yesteryear," at his welcome-home rally outside of J. C. Penney's in the parking lots of the Las Americas shopping center, was just that. The bucolic bliss of his pretechnological era was gone;

it had never existed—except in nostalgia. "Big Daddy at La Fortaleza is dead. Forever," wrote the journalist. And yet the triumph of the dream at the polls was real enough.

The Governor-elect had a popular mandate. But a mandate to do what? Populares enthused: the elections settled the dispute about political status once and for all by endorsing commonwealth. Still, nearly 48 percent of the ballots were for parties opposed to the commonwealth. No, it was not that simple, wrote another San Juan political commentator; the people wanted "a return to the good old days." The island "dreams of a past where there were no great upheavals, no protracted labor conflicts," he wrote; no pollution, no traffic jams, no heroin, no urban decay, no crime waves, no commercial vulgarities imported from America. The symbol of the old *jíbaro*, the *pava* hat, was still the most politically powerful on the island; for it represented Puertorriqueñoismo.

Up in the hills the joke was told of how the old Muñoz, while campaigning with the young Hernández, had come to a mountain stream and had calmly walked across on the water. In his wish to imitate whatever the old man did, the young man splashed about, vainly, trying to walk on the water. On the far bank Don Luis watched with amused tolerance for some time, then yelled impatiently: "Jesus! Don't you know you are only a disciple?"

On his election the new Governor had some debts to pay to "the old guard of the Populares." He obliged by promptly appointing Teodoro Moscoso as director of Fomento, the industrial-development agency, his old post under Governor Muñoz. The genial white-haired Moscoso was at once the center of controversy, charges of "political payoff" and the outcries of the ecologists. "After years as a top executive of Commonwealth Oil," editorialized the San Juan *Star,* could "Moscoso re-adjust to . . . an era marked by antipollution and environmental sentiments and a questioning of the concept of all-out industrial promotion?" Undaunted by the criticism of "political payoff," the Governor appointed his close friend and Populares campaign manager, Victor Pons, as Secretary of State. Pons, a corporate lawyer and former "legal adviser to Kennecott Copper," which for years had sought government approval for a vast mining operation, was immediately accused of conflict of interest; but his appointment was confirmed quickly by the Populares majority in the Legislature. In similar fashion, a Populares *político* in the rural hill country, Damian Folch, whose commercial expertise seemed to consist in his ownership of the Lucky Seven Supermarket in Utuado, was appointed Secretary of Commerce. Folch, like Moscoso and Pons, was a wealthy supporter of the Populares campaign and a vocal advocate of the copper-mining project that was bitterly opposed by the *jíbaros* and ecologists, who had voted for a "return to the good old days."

Still more controversial was the selection of the island's former Chief of Police, Salvador Rodríguez Aponte, as the governmental Chief of Staff. The insurance and real-estate executive had been a political appointee to the police force, which he had attempted, not too successfully, to reform. He became known for his personal arrests of prostitutes in front of the tourist hotels, and for "the most oppressive persecution of *independentistas* since the early 1950s": a portent of the future.

The youthful Governor, it seemed, was ensnared by "the old fossils, the new professional politicians, and the big contributors" to his campaign, San Juan columnist Tomás Stella declared. Had the Populares returned to the past, when "cronyism and expediency were often more important than quality in public service?" he asked.

Once his campaign debts had been paid Governor Hernández Colón began to fashion his administration in his own image. For the most part, he appointed men and women of the new intelligentsia and the professions—scientists, doctors, lawyers, university professors, and social workers—to direct the government agencies. His desire to surround himself with the island's intellectuals was reminiscent of President Kennedy's reign over "the Court of Kennedy Intellectuals" in the early years of the New Frontier. If the new government seemed imitative of that era, it was because Rafael Hernández Colón greatly admired the style and goals of the War on Poverty.

"I wish to restore our faith in ourselves," the Governor said, "and to create a new Puerto Rico, where we will maintain our material prosperity, but we will distribute more equitably and with a greater justice to the poor, the landless, the jobless, to all."

His hope for a "new Puerto Rico" of "equal opportunity for the poorest citizens" rested on a tax-reform program; for it was to be financed, in part, by new corporate taxes. It was not unexpected that his critics predicted that the "radical reforms" would be beset by the paradoxes that led to the frustration and demise of the New Frontier and the War on Poverty.

No sooner had the young Governor taken office than he was burdened with the unsolved problems of the old regime. The sugar harvest was at a new all-time low; his Agriculture Secretary, Gonzáles Chapel, who had declared his intention "with an administrative *machete* in hand, to slash at the roots of Puerto Rico's agricultural problems," morosely announced that anyone who thought sugar production would return to the "old days" was a "dreamer." In the abandoned fields and city suburbs the homeless squatters increased; his Housing Secretary, José Enrique Arrias, former chancellor of the University of Puerto Rico, at Mayagüez, announced a "firm, but humane" policy of evictions. At Guayanilla eight hundred residents, enraged by the second leak of lethal chlorine gas from the Pittsburgh Plate Glass chemical plant, one of the island's largest factories, brought suit in the courts demanding the entire plant be shut down, and asking personal damages of $10 million because of the threat to their health, "the peace of their homes and the joy of living." The Governor's younger brother, Cesar Hernández Colón, an *independentista,* was one of the lawyers for the irate villagers.

"Let them, our colonial reformers, continue with their fairy tale," fumed the *independentista* newspaper, *Claridad.* The reforms of the Governor were a "bag of promises, something for everyone," it chided; the "Yankee capitalists" would not permit them. "We are no longer content with stopgap measures. The irreconcilable and painful reality has dealt a powerful blow." If the *independentista* voters had supported his election, their leaders now condemned him as a "prima donna."

In the days before his triumph the Governor-to-be was asked what he thought of the lines in Shakespeare's *The Tempest:*

> I' the commonwealth I would, by contraries,
> Execute all things.

"Are you playing with words?" he asked, scowling.

Not I, but Shakespeare, he was told.

"Well, of course, there may be some truth in that," said Governor Rafael Hernández Colón afterward, with a slight smile.

12

Casiano, Go Back to the Bronx!

The revolver had a white handle. In the executive offices, on the highest floor of the skyscraper, the armed guard sat by the elevator, his revolver in an open holster on his hip. He was reading a comic book. A gray-haired, distinguished-looking man wandered into the reception room. In his fingers he held an empty coffee cup. "Where are the secretaries? Where are the secretaries?" he muttered. "Is there no one who will bring a man a cup of coffee?" The guard looked up from his comic book in alarm.

He jumped up, his hand poised at his revolver. The young secretaries and their *independentistas* sympathizers of the Boilermakers Union might decide to raid the executives' coffee break or bomb the water coolers. Had they gone crazy? On every floor of the building there was an armed guard. The secretaries of the Puerto Rico Industrial Development Company, the financial arm of Fomento, the government's agency of "progress and industry," were on strike. It was unheard of. . . .

San Juan newspapers were awed and appalled: "It was the first such strike in history." The shock was no less than if the computer analysts of the Central Committee of the Communist party, in Moscow, had gone on strike, or the Papal Guard of the Vatican. Sacrilege.

On the steps of the office building, under a garden of lavender and pink and yellow umbrellas the secretaries sat drinking cups of coffee and eating *pasteles.*

A line of men, led by the *independentista* leader Pedro Grant, who was secretary of the Boilermakers Union and head of the United Labor Movement of "more than a hundred unions," he said, marched back and forth. Singing. The lounging secretaries marched with them occasionally, in the shadows of their umbrellas, as if simply strolling in the tropical sun.

On a folding chair by the curb a young girl sunned herself in a beach outfit of floral short shorts and a jaunty *jíbaro* hat. Her legs were crossed elegantly. The bumper-to-bumper midday traffic on the Avenida Ponce de León paused noticeably as it passed. Her fingers, tipped with bright orange nail polish, held a picket sign that greeted the motorists with the words:

CASIANO, GO BACK TO THE BRONX!

The crowds of lunchtime office girls who poured out of the nearby bank building laughed. She sat, as if on the beach, relaxing in the warming sun. Uncrossing and recrossing her long legs, she wiggled her picket sign seductively:

CASIANO, GO BACK TO THE BRONX!

Manuel Casiano was the director of Fomento. He was a New York–born Puerto Rican who had made a small fortune in the rags-to-riches Horatio Alger tradition. The government had brought him to the island as administrator of its heavy-industry programs, where his talents as a go-getter had achieved more success than popularity.

Her picket sign was impolitely political. She was asked: Are you saying, Yankee Go Home?

Yes, she said, smiling.

But Casiano is Puerto Rican.

Ah, maybe he is Puerto Rican. But Fomento is for the Yankees, she said of her employer.

On the Avenida Ponce de León one of the motorists had stopped to admire the picket sign, or the girl. He tooted his horn. He whistled. The traffic, which was always tied up at that hour, came to a standstill. The secretary smiled happily at her admirer. Leaning back in her folding chair, she uncrossed and recrossed her long legs and wiggled her picket sign:

CASIANO, GO BACK TO THE BRONX!

Fomento, for the first time in its history, was being ridiculed and criticized on the island, not only by *independentistas* and radicals, but by businessmen and government officials. The new irreverence to what had been called the "holy of holies of Puerto Rico's progress" was typified by the strike of its own employees.

An island newspaper reported: "Fomento's industrialization program, often hailed as a model for developing nations, has a factory closing rate of one for every three plants opened." In "an obscure report," never officially released, the government's economists estimated that of the not quite 3,000 factories that had been opened since Operation Bootstrap began, 1,083 had closed their doors. Even these statistics did not reveal the extent of the crisis, thought economist José Antonio Herrero, of the School of Business Administration at the University of Puerto Rico. He calculated that "many" factories closed merely to reopen under a "new name," in order to receive a renewed government tax exemption. The "new" plants were really "old" plants. So, much of the industrial boom was a statistical charade, he thought.

But the bankruptcies were real enough. Sergio Camero, a well-known industrialist and past Fomento administrator, estimated that bankruptcies "exceeded 100" in 1970. He termed it a "disastrous year."

Economists for the government, attempting to paint the rosiest possible picture that year, admitted that, of a labor force of 850,000, at least 100,000 were unemployed and approximately another 150,000 were underemployed. The rate of unemployment and under-employment was officially set at 29.4 percent in 1970. Unofficially it was higher.

"In the *barrios* the unemployment rate is always higher than it is in La Fortaleza," said a San Juan union leader.

"Puerto Rico is at a crossroad. The constant growth of the industrial sector has come to a halt," said Amadeo I. D. Francis, director of the Puerto Rican Manufacturers Association. Not merely had industrial growth halted, but in some industries it had retrogressed. He cited the shoe manufacturers who had "reduced employment by 32 percent between 1968 and 1970." In the garment industry the decline in jobs was even more drastic—62 percent in a few years.

The end of the "economic miracle" was explained by government officials as an "echo of the economic slump in the U.S." Roberto de Jesús Toro, president of the Bankers' Association, was matter-of-fact: "The Puerto Rican economy has become more and more integrated with that of the U.S.," he said. "Nowadays [any] change is felt in San Juan the same day the change appears in the *New York Times* or the *Wall Street Journal.*"

No one had thought of the possibility of a recession in the postwar boom years. If the well-being of the country was born of the mainland economy, it would be subject to its whims. The risk was known. "Because the impetus of rapid growth is being given through the use of imported capital there exists the danger," said a Puerto Rican Planning Board report of 1958, "that withdrawal of income received from this investment may slow down the overall rate of growth of the economy." But few had believed in the possibility. The possibility had become a reality.

One of the smallest countries in the world, Puerto Rico had become the fifth-largest market for the merchandise of the United States. More than $2 billion worth of exports were shipped to the island in 1969–70 alone. It ranked just behind Canada, West Germany, Japan, and England as a consumer of American goods and food. Since the island sold much less to the United States than it bought, its yearly balance-of-trade deficit had reached half a billion dollars. "It is no exaggeration to state that a considerable amount of industry has been saved for the U.S. by Puerto Rico," said Amadeo Francis, and the "balance of payments has served [the U.S.] well in this process"; for the Americanos had an unbalanced balance of trade of its own, and its deficit was reduced by virtue of Puerto Rico's "captive market."

And yet this was more than an inheritance of economic genetics. The child was born of the father: a resemblance was to be expected. But in encouraging American investments Fomento had discouraged Puerto Rican initiative. One economist estimated that 78 percent of the island's industry was American-owned, while another estimated 83 percent.

"It's been said that you can walk across Puerto Rico, from Mayagüez to Fajardo on the roofs of the buildings owned by mainland American companies, never touching the ground," wrote an editor of *Nation's Business,* Sterling G. Slappey.

The resentment of the island industrialists and businessmen was slow to surface. But it had reached public print. In Aguadilla, one of the poorest cities, a group of manufacturers held a press conference to condemn the "lack of effective cooperation" they received from Fomento, which had forced them to close down factories and lay off workers; for, they complained, the government's industrial-development program "has shown a preference for giving large contracts to non–Puerto Rican firms." Local businessmen of the Northwest (Coast) Manufacturers Association, led by their president, Ferdinand Rivera, protested "the unjust manner in which the government is carrying out its bids."

In Carolina, near San Juan, a manufacturer of doors made of native woods declared his business was being ruined by the government's encouragement of door imports. He asked: What good is it to say, "Develop native industry," when local manufacturers are being "put out of business" by their own government?

"To import oil from Venezuela and Algeria so it can be refined to be exported to the United States? I ask you, how does that help us?" fumed one local manufacturer, who wished to be nameless. "I love

America. But sometimes I wonder does America love me, when my business, it goes bankrupt." He manufactured a native wood product that was being priced out of the market by a plastic made from a petroleum-refinery by-product.

"It is not just the money," he said. "The plastic is so ugly. The wood of our trees is so lovely."

Even the advocates of the government's foreign-investment program had begun to express disquiet. "The hippopotamuses of money," said Senator Ruben Ramos Rivera of the conservative New Progressive party, were "seeking excessive gains." On the floor of the Senate he accused the "extreme capitalists" of trying to squeeze larger subsidies and profits out of the island at the expense of the economy. Ramos Rivera said the banks, breweries, petroleum, and rum companies, most of them American owned, were destroying the economic stability of Puerto Rico because of their "egotism."

None of these businessmen were *independentistas*. They supported the commonwealth and statehood political parties. They wished to maintain close economic ties with the United States. It bothered them, however, that after twenty years of industrialization so much of the economy was controlled by outside companies, and so little island-owned industry had been developed, or even encouraged, by the Fomento programs.

"In Latin America today there is a growing current of new nationalism," Galo Plaza, the Secretary-General of the Organization of American States and the former President of Ecuador, had told a hemisphere conference. "The new nationalism is a phenomenon that is almost universally misunderstood outside Latin America," he said. "While the countries require increasingly greater amounts of capital and technology, they have the right to make sovereign decisions as to which kind of capital should be welcomed, in which sectors, and under what terms. They prefer greater participation of foreign investment in joint ventures and complete exclusion of foreign capital from certain sectors of vital national interest." In "discarding imported patterns under familiar labels, both to the left and to the right," he said, they are discarding "obsolete patterns of outside tutelage." And in this way they will seek "to chart the course for development without foreign interference, or well-meaning paternalism."

That did "not mean that Latin America is assuming a hostile attitude toward any country," Plaza said. "Nevertheless, the countries of Latin America are becoming increasingly disillusioned in their relations with the wealthy countries, and particularly with the United States. This reaction cannot be explained in economic terms," he had said for, "There are strong emotional overtones connected with the foreign ownership of key industries."

On the island, too, these "emotional overtones" were evident. The unease of the local industrialists was not a criticism, either of industrialization or of the profit system. Rather it was an expression of their sense of trepidation and misgiving about the nature and ownership of the industries, which were increasingly threatening the *serenidad* of island life. Was it all too fast, too large, too successful? Was Puerto Rico beginning to resemble New York?

On a summer day a torrential tropical rainstorm hit San Juan. The deluge came in waves, flooding the streets of the banking district of Hato Rey. In years past the rain would have drained into the mangrove swamp and flowed out to sea. Now the inlets lined by flowering reeds and mangrove trees had been cemented. Instead of coconut palms there were skyscrapers. The rainwater had nowhere to go. It flooded the streets, and rushed, like a surrealist river, past the Fomento offices.

A banker, his trousers rolled up to his knees, stood in the midst of the street of water that lapped at his calves. He laughed, like a boy caught swimming in his Sunday clothes. In his left hand he held his attaché case. In his right hand he held his shoes and socks high above the flooded street. He waded from gutter to gutter in the knee-deep river, on which floated a mailbox, several morning newspapers, a woman's high-heeled shoe of pink silk, a Coca-Cola bottle, and the debris of the secretarial lunch hour. In the lobby of the National City Bank, his trousers dripped and his bare feet left a wet trail on the floor.

13

The Cement Gods

On the road from the mountain town the young girl wrecked her car. Her mouth was bleeding. Her puppy on the seat beside her had affectionately jumped onto her lap and she had swerved off the road and her car had become skewered on a stump and now she was slumped over the steering wheel.

"The girl is bleeding!" cried my friend. "Wait! Wait!"

He leaped from my car before I could stop and ran to the bleeding girl. A crowd had gathered from the neighboring *barrios,* the houses nearby, children going to school, and the passing motorists on their way to work, who had stopped to help. One turned off the sputtering motor. One calmed her puppy. One held her hand, a motherly woman, who began to weep. And soon there were many weeping women; the young girl wept too.

My friend gently lifted the frightened girl from her car into ours. He sat her beside me, saying, "Go! To the hospital! Hurry!"

The crowd stood sadly about as we drove away. One could feel the sorrow and warmth of their concern for the girl. It had almost a physical weight.

In the emergency room of the town hospital, which was no bigger than a clinic, no attendants were in sight. No nurses. No doctors. But the waiting room was full of neighborly people who soothed the girl. One offered her a drink of coffee. Another told her God had protected her; she was fortunate that "it had not been worse." Her weeping and her bleeding began to subside.

By now the girl was pale with shock. She fainted.

On the table in the examining room, the girl awoke and began to weep once more, this time for her puppy. Someone brought the puppy to her and she hugged him, weeping louder. A nurse came with forms. A doctor came in a sport shirt; he decided she was no emergency case, after all. She began to weep again. He suggested that she visit a private doctor who had more time for weeping girls than the town hospital. This doctor had a hospital of his own. And I drove her there. In the waiting room there was the by now customary crowd of medical penitents. One man had a broken arm in a shabby cast. He had been waiting for three hours, he said. And there were several very pregnant women, who waited with heavy faces for the private doctor to emerge from behind his closed office door. The girl retold her story of the accident, which had become rather dramatic with her retelling of it. And the pregnant women comforted her, their bellies large with sympathy; as if to say, "So you think you have troubles!" The girl relaxed.

The hospital was dingy. And it was boring. We grew impatient and took the girl to the doctor's private examining room. The door had no door knob. Just a hole. An orderly stuck his finger into the hole and opened the door. The girl lay on an examining table under a lighting fixture with four sockets, two dangling on broken wires. One bare bulb worked. In the next room, where the oxygen tanks were stored, a hole in the wall the size of someone's head went through to the alleyway. The sewage and water pipes were exposed. Piles of refuse lay in the corners of the wards. In all, the gloomy hospital was like an old print of a lunatic asylum of eighteenth-century England.

"Oh, that hospital is in violation of every building and health law," said my friend. "It should be closed. But the doctor has political influence."

And yet in a few minutes the examining room was full of cheerful and noisy people. Her boy friend appeared. So did her sisters and brothers. Her mother came, weeping loudly. Her father came quietly.

By the late afternoon the girl had eleven visitors. No matter what her injuries were, her severe shock had been overcome without the help of a single social worker or psychiatric nurse.

When we left her the girl was sitting up in bed, laughing bravely through her tears and biting her bleeding lip. She kissed us. In the morning she would be ready to drive down the mountain to the city, where she was a student at the university.

Later that day, on the highway back to San Juan my car was trapped in one of those traffic jams that have turned the roads of Bayamón into an endless parking lot. The bumper-to-bumper cars seemed to stretch all the way to New York. In a way, the urban blight on the highways of San Juan seemed worse than that of New York, perhaps because of the incongruity of the coconut palms swaying above the traffic lights and the mangos that fell on the windshields of the stalled cars.

In the far lane of the divided highway a young girl was waiting for the light to change. Suddenly a car bludgeoned her car from behind, backed up, and drove away. She slumped over the steering wheel. Her mouth was bleeding. The blood was running down her lip and chin. No one helped her. No one even stopped his car. No one could. If anyone had halted on the highway, the traffic would have been snarled for miles. In the mountain town the young girl's accident had involved dozens of people, most of whom tried to help her. But, on the highway into the city no one wished to become involved. It was like any city. There was no human contact. People were helpless to help.

And so I too drove off, looking back at the girl in the rear-view mirror. . . .

The story of the two bleeding girls was told to Governor Ferre. He became quite agitated and apologetic. "No! No!" he exclaimed. "It was not the fault of the people. Our people are compassionate. Very compassionate. If they did not stop to help her, that was because they could not.

"Who can stop on a highway!" the Governor said.

In the winding mountains near Lares there was a little roadside café. The driver of a diesel truck had stopped there for coffee and a pastilla;

his giant vehicle, as large as a railroad car, blocked the road. A jíbaro *on horseback galloped up to the café. He sat on his horse and yelled for a drink of rum, which he swallowed, without dismounting, from a glass the café owner handed him. The diesel driver and the* jíbaro *horseman began to argue, in a friendly way: which was better on a mountain road, a horse or a truck. As they argued the traffic jammed the road, unable to pass them.*

On the country roads and city highways of the island there were more than half a million cars. The registered motor vehicles surpassed 530,000 in 1969. If they had been lined up bumper to bumper across the island, these cars would have formed a one-hundred-mile-long Chinese Wall ten cars high, from the beaches of Mayagüez in the west to Fajardo in the east.

Not too long before, in 1960, there were hardly 172,000 cars on the whole island. The adults still outnumbered them by ten to one. Now the cars had closed the ratio to three to one. And "the auto population grows five times faster than the human population," warned Jaro Mayda, a teacher at the Law School of the University of Puerto Rico, who advocated automotive "birth control" to halt "the wildest laissez faire in car importation" from the United States.

The plague of auto fumes and noise had not yet brought a visible increase in illness. But the auto accidents, which had reached 59,556 by 1970, had begun to equal the incidence of tropical diseases such as malaria and yellow fever that had ravaged the population the century before. In 1970 there were 214 Puertorriqueños who died on the roads because of the traffic.

It was the "Dio Quiere *Hypothesis," the God Wills Hypothesis, wrote a reader of the San Juan* Star: *"The traffic jam must be God's will. Nobody else wants it."*

In a valiant determination to contain the runaway traffic a vast highway program had been begun by the government. "Puerto Rico already has the highest, or one of the highest, ratios of roads to land areas," was the comment of Professor Mayda. "We have relatively more roads than anyone, or almost anyone, in the world." And "The First Law of Motodynamics" decreed that "unless the automobile population is controlled, automobiles always grow faster than highways can be built for them," said Mayda. So he looked with dubious eye upon the "new highwaymanship and bulldozership" that was moving across the island like "a major geological force, on the order of a glacier, irreparably destroying the land" and covering the tropical forests with a patina of cement.

At the fabled Luquillo beaches the "graying of Puerto Rico" that he feared had begun. In the groves of coconut palms, where the wild orchids adorned the roadside trees, the highwaymen had built Route 9990, though Professor Mayda said the "estimated hourly traffic in this place [was] 2.7 cars and 5.12 cows."

In most communities the cars had driven the islanders off the roads. The residents of the *barrio* Tortugo, in Río Piedras, sought to recapture their tropical peace of mind by ripping up the concrete roadway with pneumatic drills, and building mounds across the path of the traffic. "Cars use the road as a racetrack," one of the local people complained. And several children had been killed by the wild drivers. When the police were summoned to halt the work of the *barrio* "Highway Destruction Department," the residents insisted, "No law forbids building the mounds" in the road. They were arrested. They immediately filed suit against the Secretary of Public Works. And two weeks later they rebuilt the mounds in the middle of the neighborhood road.

The "plague of concrete" had begun to spread "far beyond metropolitan San Juan," wrote a journalist in the capital. He lamented the day when the suburban highways and villas would stretch for sixty miles along the northern shore, in one vast *"villa concreto."*

None of these concrete fears unduly troubled J. Raymond Wilson, the optimistic director of Puerto Rico's Highway Authority. In heralding the Las Americas superhighway, the island's largest, which would bisect the island from Ponce to San Juan, he spoke confidently of the computers that would control the flow of the traffic. The superhighway, built at the cost of $200 million, would be uniquely Puertorriqueño, he promised. Along the cement roadway the highway director proposed the construction of "100-foot-tall allegorical cement statues" that would "help prevent drivers from falling asleep." These statues would be of patriotic figures. He had requested the Institute of Puerto Rican Culture to help in selecting the patriots to be cast in cement. The "cement gods" were necessary, the highway director thought, because the superhighway was "so straight" it would bore the individualistic island motorists. He suggested, as well, that "ornamental" flowers be planted by the roadside, to replace the tropical forests that had been destroyed to build the highway.

"Is the island going to be covered entirely with cement?" a prominent leader of the opposition independence movement was asked.

"Yes, I think so," he said laughing. "Our Governor is in the cement business, you know. The Ferre family owns the biggest cement factory on the island. It is our largest native-owned industry. So, if Governor Ferre has his way, we may become the largest tropical parking lot in all of the Caribbean."

On the Los Angeles Freeway, or the Ryan Expressway in Chicago, or the Belt Parkway in New York City, a man may feel like an ant on wheels. He drives as the man in front of him drives, and the man behind him. He obeys the traffic signs even when there are no signs. He is the perfect urban man.

But not the Puertorriqueño. If the ordinary man was dehumanized by the traffic, the Puerto Rican man had found a way to humanize the traffic. He mocked it.

On a one-way street a man may go the wrong way, wind in and out among parked cars, elude the traffic by riding on the shoulder of the road, cut across the grass or a gas station to avoid a red light, and park his car on the sidewalk. If he did it boldly, and got away with it, those who cursed him laughed at his audacity, barely resisting the temptation to stand up in their stalled cars and cheer him on. But he must do all this with verve. With grace, With élan. To bulldoze through the traffic, like George C. Scott in a Patton tank, with the loud-mouthed, bull-necked, and lovable viciousness of the New York cab driver would bring him no praise for bravado on the island. He would be ostracized as a Yanqui.

A man had to handle his car as he would the body of his lover. Or, better yet, as though his car were his own body and the car in front of him was his lover. He had to be tender and intense, gentle and insistent. He had to cajole, soothe, and insinuate his way through the traffic, gliding into the smallest openings between the cars with skill and a smile. He must never force his way. That would be a sign of Yanquismo. And would be un-Puertorriqueño.

"Look at her . . . Take her! Try her! Make her perform!" read the new car advertisement in the San Juan Star. *Beneath the seductive headlines there was a photograph of the car, with the legs of a young girl nakedly dangling out the window. "If you want more . . ." the enticement read.*

If a man drove into the path of traffic going in the opposite way, the other drivers might let him in. But not all the way. They would play with him. They would open a hole large enough for him to get his car into the traffic jam, but not large enough for him to get through. He had to outwit them. Not until he showed his *macho,* preferably with a flourish, would they let him go in or out or through.

In the city the *macho* of a man was exhibited by his hands on the steering wheel of his car. Where else could he express it? Not in his office. Not in the supermarket, pushing a shopping cart behind his wife. Not in the neat, boxed, look-alike house in the suburbs where even the *coquís* were silenced. Not in the voting booth. His driving was a definition of his manhood. To be cursed, to be admired, to be chastised, to be praised. It did not matter what he said, as long as he felt free to be himself.

On the road from the Muñoz Air Guard base, just beyond the San Juan airport, to the highway to the city there was a sign that warned the air guardsmen:

DANGER
DRIVE CAREFULLY
YOU ARE ABOUT TO ENTER
THE MOST DANGEROUS
PLACE IN THE WORLD
A PUBLIC HIGHWAY

Even the traffic cops did not interfere too often. In San Juan there was a saying: *If a man took an examination for the police force and failed, they gave him a uniform!* But it was more than that. When the traffic cops took off their uniforms, they, too, donned the *macho* of the ordinary man. And so they understood. The way a man drove was an extension of his self. To criticize the way he drove was as much an insult as to criticize the way he made love.

Not all of the motorized macho *occurs on the highways. In the central mountains, at the one-time cigar-manufacturing center of Caguas, the professional drag-race drivers, such as "Chiquí" Fonesca in his souped-up jalopy "Hot Pepper" and Luis Bolívar Cruz in the Garage Barrica's "Fireball," perform on the race track every Sunday the extraordinary feats that the ordinary commuters demonstrate daily on the roads of San Juan. Asked why he risked his life in this way, one driver shrugged: "I guess it's what you might call* machismo.*" One of his buddies replied philosophically: "The car might be considered an extension of a man's masculinity."*

In the Age of Machines one could tell as much about a man by the way he drove his car as by the way he made love. And since the urban man probably spent more time in his car than in the arms of his lover, one probably could tell more.

One young girl in Río Piedras, at the University of Puerto Rico, laughed at that: "We drive too fast. We eat too fast. We talk too fast. We make love too fast."

"Who does?"

"Everybody does."

"Men and women?"

"Yes," she said. "It's one of our national characteristics. It's how we express ourselves."

But the strange thing was that there was nowhere to go. On the island the main highway was a squared circle; the faster you drove, the faster you were back to where you had begun. It took less than a day to circle the island. The entire trip was no more than three hundred miles, from one end of the island, squaring the circle, and back again.

"Why do you drive so fast?" I asked a young boy.

"I don't know," he said, shrugging.

"Are you really in a hurry to get somewhere? Is your girl friend pregnant?"

"No." He giggled. The thought amused him. He was seventeen, a high school student who lived in Levittown near San Juan. "When I get in a car, I go crazy," he said. "Everybody on the island does."

"If you drive as fast as you do, you will drive right off the island," I suggested, "into the sky."

"Ah!" he laughed. "That may be why we do it."

14

La Turista: Without Jesus or Marx

"I never had been on a plane like that. Everyone was high!

"On that flight we had this sweet-assed little stewardess, who was swaying up and down the aisle, even when the plane wasn't. She was higher than a hippie. You know, she was giving out those little bottles of booze they have on planes. And this fellow, he yells: 'Baby! I got a bigger bottle than that.' And he waves a quart of Scotch in her little, sweet-assed face. 'Baby! You keep your baby bottles,' he yells. 'If you're a good girl, I'll let you have a drink from my bottle.'

"Wooie! That flight was the highest trip to San Juan ever. I bet they could have run the engine of that jet just on the air in our cabin."

The man sitting in the aisle seat had the boyish, and sheepish, grin of a middle-aged man on his way to a weekend in San Juan with his wife's secretary. He may have been. He was too nervous, and he talked too much. In his crisp suit, buttoned-down shirt and anonymous gray tie he looked as if he were on a business trip. He was incognito, disguised as himself. On his lap he had the *Wall Street Journal,* which he had begun to read; he yawned and immediately fell asleep; until a stewardess in red hot-pants coaxed him awake with the offer of one of those little bottles.

On board *La Grande, The Great One,* as the Boeing 747s were nicknamed on the island, there was an atmosphere of excitement.

Eastern Airlines had worked strenuously to make its gigantic planes seem frivolous. It enticed the *turistas* with the promise of the "music of our island on every flight," *"En Mi Viejó San Juan"* and similar night-club ballads; *Comidas Criollas,* native dishes, that featured a "Puerto Rican hamburger" renamed "Chopped Sirloin *a la Criolla."* "We want to be most Puerto Rican in our service," said the airline, offering its waiting passengers *Piña Colada* in its *Su Casa* lounges at the John F. Kennedy Airport.

"I like going to Puerto Rico," the man said, "because it's not like going to one of those foreign countries which are foreign."

He seemed like a respectable small-town businessman. Or perhaps a local politician who owned a highway night club, featuring divorced, topless go-go waitresses, who had several children at home to support. It happened that he was both.

In the New England town where he ran a "couple of night clubs" he was "primarying the mayor." When he was asked what "primarying the mayor" meant, he laughed tolerantly at such political ignorance and said, "I *run* him." Politics was like running a night club to him: "No matter what you do the name-of-the-game is the same. Cash on the line. The only difference is the size of the denomination."

Was he going to Puerto Rico on business? "Oh no, this trip," he said, grinning, "is going to be strictly happysville.

"I was going tapioca. So told the wife I had to get away from it all for a while." Somewhere in a suburb of New England he left "the wife," willingly, behind. "She agreed I better work off some steam. And so I decided to go on a junket."

On a junket?

"Junkets are the greatest."

What's that?

"A junket? You never been on a gambling junket?"

No. How does it work?

"Everything is arranged by the hotel. Room, food, plane tickets, chips at the casino. Everything."

And the girls?

He laughed. "No one 'arranges' for girls in San Juan. Don't have to. The hotels are lousy with them. In the casinos you can practically get a girl every time you get some chips. It's beautiful."

Gambling was legalized on the island in 1948. It was done "after long and careful deliberation on the part of government officials," recalled the brochure handed to bettors in the casino of the Caribe Hilton; for it was thought that Craps, Roulette, and Blackjack might be an added "attraction for the increasing tourist trade." Ever since then the "junkets" had been coming. The island was host to only 32 "Groups and Conventions," with fewer than 2,000 *turistas,* in 1955. By 1970 there were 722 of these "Groups and Conventions," that brought 82,397 *turistas.*

In the ornate casinos of the resort hotels—some of them look like redecorated sets of the *Gold Diggers of 1935*—formal attire, tie and jacket, and country-club manners, are *de rigueur*. The gamblers have no fear of being "fleeced," the Caribe Hilton's brochure reassured its patrons: for "the croupiers and dealers are fine young men. They are all graduates of the School of Croupiers." Gambling was "formerly frowned on by Puerto Rican government officials fearful of drawing too many professional gamblers and underworld figures," reported *Time* magazine.

"Of what value is it for a hotel to have full occupancy, let us say with teachers, if they don't gamble at the casino?" said Abrán Pena, president of the Musicians Union. He reflected the growing feeling that it was not the hotels that controlled the casinos, but rather the casinos that controlled the hotels.

Not all of the *turistas* had come to gamble, of course. Some were content to lie on the sunny beaches, or beneath the shade of the coconut trees. Or even to venture forth into Old San Juan to buy souvenirs made in Haiti—the Japan of the Caribbean trinket trade. These vacationers have increased so enormously that their yearly arrivals have equaled half of the native population. Back in 1948 the visitors to Puerto Rico were fewer than 50,000; but by 1970 the statistics on regular and "special" visitors, estimated by the Puerto Rican Planning Board, soared to 1,384,632.

Schoolteachers, newlyweds, the Jet Set, businessmen, and politicians (the island had become a balmy favorite of governors' conferences) had inundated the beaches. In spite of the recent recession in tourism that forced several hotels to close (the grand Condado Beach Hotel, dowager of the luxury resorts, closed so suddenly that guests coming down for breakfast one day were told "to clear out" by the desk clerk, and had to carry their own luggage; the bellhops had all been dismissed in the night), and despite the gloom of the hotel managers ("Right now the lobbies look like undertakers' parlors between funerals," said Roberto Bouret, director of the Hotel Association, during the summer of 1970), the tidal wave of *turistas* continued to flood ashore on the tiny island.

If the quantity of *turistas* had risen, some thought that their quality had fallen. The man who came on a "junket," said one hotelier, was not unlike a "paying Rough Rider."

"The *turistas* have changed," said a clerk in Don Roberto's gift shop on Calle Cristo, one of the oldest on the island. "A different type of *turista* comes these days. You know, they save all year for a week in a beach hotel. And they've spent their savings on the package deal, before they get off the plane. So they have nothing left. They are not wealthy. They are secretaries."

He peered somberly about the colorful shop: "In the old days people would spend three or four hours in looking at things. Then they would say, I would like that! and that! and that! Maybe a few hundred dollars of fine things. We don't have *turistas* like that any more. Our biggest sale all day has been fifteen dollars. No, it was only twelve.

"Look at the cheap wood that we sell, from Haiti. Five years ago we wouldn't have anything in the store from Haiti. We make our own mahogany things. It is our own design. Our mahogany is the finest made in Puerto Rico: grown here, cut here, dried here, carved here. But we can't sell it. I haven't sold a twenty-five-dollar bowl in years. I tell you, these *turistas* do not really come to see Puerto Rico," the clerk said. "They do not even know where they are. They might as well be anywhere."

Luxuriant as new suburbs, the high-rising resort hotels were self-sufficient little cities unto themselves. In the Caribe Hilton a *turista* may go to the casino, a theater, see several movies a week, dine in half a dozen restaurants, shop in a score of boutiques and gift shops, swim in the pool, dream beneath the palms, the trees each spotlighted by a different hue, or visit the historic ruins of Fort Gerónimo, without ever leaving the hotel grounds. He simply takes an elevator from floor to floor. Easter Week at the hotel begins with mass (English) and ecumenically goes on to a fashion show, Ping-Pong contest, scuba and skin diving, underwater egg hunts, bingo, judo and jousting demonstrations, and a rum party.

And, since almost every hotel has an "Olympic-size" pool, it is no longer necessary to get sand inside one's bathing suit. Not many of the *turistas* go near the ocean.

Condado Beach, where the huge hotels have encircled the sea, has been called no-man's land by the *independentistas.* The university activists will not go there. Even to visit a friend. It was along the sidewalks of Ashford Avenue in the Condado section, with its cheap tourist shops, coffee houses that advertise bagels and lox, drugstores and gaudy boutiques, that there were a series of "terrorist bombings."

A few years ago the students at the University of Puerto Rico began to clamor that the *turista* hotels "give the beaches back to the people." One day they invaded the lobby of the Caribe Hilton, climbing the fence by the sea. The protesters won a great deal of publicity and a few civic resolutions that proclaimed that the beaches did indeed belong to the people. Now even the Holiday Inn has a high fence separating its beach-chair-lounging guests from the beach.

"The people of Puerto Rico have never been properly oriented to understand the importance of the tourist industry," complained José Davila-Ricci, the former editor of San Juan's *El Imparcial;* the *turista* should be revered as "the No. 1 breadwinner." He surpassed the "traditional products [of the island] like sugar, bananas, coffee, meat."

But one student leader vigorously disagreed; "The *turistas* look at us like freaks. We ought to confiscate their hotels as resorts for *jíbaros* and *barrio* people. Let the *turista* stay, if they want, and wait on us like servants. Let the *turista* wash out our latrines for once. If I see one on the street, that is what I would like to say to him."

On his previous junket to San Juan the man on the Boeing 747 had rarely left his hotel. He had been to the island four times, he recalled, but so far he had "never seen Puerto Rico."

He remembered that he had taken a taxi from the airport directly to his hotel. As he always did. In the hotel he had paused at the bar for a few drinks, then had gone up to his room. When he stepped off the elevator, there was a girl standing there in a bikini.

"This girl had on a bikini's bikini," he said. "I mean it hardly covered anything worth covering. It was a leopard-skin bikini, but there wasn't hardly room on it for a leopard's spot.

"I did a double take. 'Are you for real?' I said.

"She smiled and she said, 'Hi! I work for Senator So and So.' I mean she was even higher than I was. And I was pretty high.

" 'No kidding?' I said. 'Know old Buzz well.' That isn't his name, but I don't want to use the Senator's right name. Right? So I say, 'He's a good friend of mine. I worked for him in the last primary. Why don't we go to my room and have a drink on that?'

"And she said, 'I don't mind if I do.'

"So we go to my room. We have a couple. Like a cat she sits down on the couch, with her legs up, so that her leopard skin goes up. It wasn't a real leopard skin. But it was furry.

"To get my mind off it, I say, 'What are you doing here?'

" 'Legislative stuff,' she says, 'for Congress. The Senator likes to see things for himself.'

"I think to myself, 'I bet.'

"After a while my partner, who I'm supposed to meet, comes in. He sees this girl sitting there like a cat in her leopard skin, and right away he leaves. He figured he was in the wrong room. So he goes down to the lobby and he calls me up, 'George, you been in this hotel five minutes, and you got a girl in your room already. How come? You ain't no lady killer like that back home.' He was jealous. Of course, I couldn't tell him it was Congressional business.

"That's what I like in Puerto Rico. That's the way it always is." He grinned. "Anything goes in Puerto Rico."

On Ashford Avenue, the busiest thoroughfare of the *turistas,* there has for years been an unending parade of young girls with conveniently cool see-through blouses, too-tight toreador pants and visibly suntanned bodies. They are most often easily distinguishable from vacationing schoolteachers.

These "Ashford Avenue girls" do not usually come from the island. Most of them are foreigners. In spite of the books of recent years that depict *La Vida,* or the life style, of prostitutes in Puerto Rico, few of the working whores on the island have been native born. Examination of the arrest records of the San Juan police has shown that the prostitutes tend to come from pre-Castro Cuba, Argentina, Brazil, Santo Domingo, and, during the off-season in Miami Beach, from the United States.

"A man who goes to the whore loses face," a labor-union leader in Santurce explained. "He loses *macho.* He may have a mistress, yes. A woman may be a mistress, yes. But a whore? That is not our style. So most of the whores are foreigners. So most of their customers are foreigners too."

In the winter of 1969 police in San Juan began one of their periodic sweeps "to clean up" prostitution on the Condado. The raids became a nightly tourist attraction on Ashford Avenue. Some 1,100 young women were arrested in less than one year. And yet merely 97 women were convicted of violating City Ordinance No. 112, which frowned on the selling of sex to *turistas.* No *turistas*—of course—were arrested.

La Rivera night-club impresario Anthony "Tony" Tursi recalled that in his waterfront cabaret alone the vice squad had arrested 363 women. It was a farce, he said. All that the police raids accomplished was to frighten the whores off the streets into the resort hotels. "The girls have moved into the casinos and bars of the big hotels," said Tursi, where they were more conveniently available to the *turistas.* "Anyone who wants to verify this can walk into those places and soon be surrounded by Ashford Avenue girls."

Tursi scoffed: "Vice squad agents believe I invented prostitution in San Juan." He denied the honor. Instead he credited King Charles V of Spain with importing the European cultural innovation to the island; whores were unknown to the Borinquén Indians. The Emperor of the Holy Roman Empire had "sent a letter to the Governor of Puerto Rico, in the year 1593, telling him to establish two houses of prostitution on the San Juan waterfront to [help] eliminate sex crimes against the good women of the young colony." In his night club, the reputed "Vice Czar of the San Juan waterfront" seemed to imply he was merely obeying the King's command. The whores who had been arrested in his bar were protecting the virgins of the island from the *turistas*. On the Condado, the beautiful "Playground of Puerto Rico," the men on flying "junkets" had inherited a historic tradition.

"Like a stone tossed into a pool, causing an immediate splash, and ripples that spread widely," José Davila-Ricci lyrically wrote, the blessing brought by the *turistas* was "new money infused into the national bloodstream." He meant no pun. In the island's hotels the registered guests (the Tourist Development Corporation had counted 714,900 in 1970) provided jobs, and discontents, not only for about 10,000 bellhops, waiters, maids, janitors, and clerks, but for thousands of others who catered to their pleasures.

As the waves of *turistas* grew, so did the hotels. Each new hotel was more majestic than the last, until the skyline of San Juan was dominated by "the pleasure domes of Condado." They towered over the banks.

The most opulent and lavish of all was the Cerromar Beach Hotel. Its opening in the winter of 1972 had the pomp and ceremony of a state occasion, attended by Governor Luis Ferre; Chi Chi Rodríguez, the island's most illustrious golfer, and his friend Jack Nicklaus; the astronautic hero Colonel Frank Borman; the chairman of Eastern Airlines, Floyd D. Hall; and Laurance Rockefeller, of the Rockresorts Corporation, which owned the new tropical "Xanadu amid the palms."

In the Salon Grande, the evening festivities began with "a party to end all parties" in the rhapsody of the San Juan *Star*. "The grandest buffet ever seen" on the island was spread before the guests "as far as the eye could see." Caviar and oyster and rare game hens, stuffed with pâté, had been flown in for the feast, that was adorned with petit fours, served in boxes sculpted of chocolate, and tropical fruits. Luxuriating guests, who "literally couldn't pull themselves away from the spread," were entertained by Andy Williams's crooning of "the theme from 'Love Story' "; while the Tuna de Cayey, a Puerto Rican night-club group, sweetly sang the humble folksongs of the *jíbaros* in homage to the Christ Child, for the feast took place soon after Twelfth Night. The Christmas songs bored the guests, however: "We already heard them," wrote a piqued society writer for the San Juan *Star,* "a month ago."

Host for the gala evening of bicultural folksinging was entrepreneur Laurance Rockefeller. In dedicating his family's newest emporium of tourism the hotel's publicists indicated that the "cultural diversity" of the feast was calculated. The Cerromar Beach "was designed to accommodate large groups of businessmen" from the mainland. For this reason its décor was "rather masculine," with "warm brown tones prevailing." And yet the Cerromar Beach, though a bit more ostentatious, was no less exclusive than its dignified sister Rockresort down the coast, the Dorado Beach, where a single room was $75 to $95 a night. It was rather that the new-style *turista,* the businessman on a "junket," preferred a little more flamboyance to decorum. The crowning of Miss Universe was to be held within its "rather masculine" interior in a few months. Even then, the reigning Miss Universe was waiting in her bikini, to be dethroned, in one of the older Condado Beach hotels.

Not long after the opening of the Cerromar Beach Hotel, the first "Caribbean Seminar on Lasting Tourism" convened in San Juan to discuss the new-style *turista.* The guest of honor was philosopher Jean François Revel, whose best-selling book *Ni Marx, Ni Jesus* (*Without Marx or Jesus*) had caused a sensation in some political circles. Revel, at the tourism seminar, enthralled the gathering of resort owners, travel agents, and manufacturers of souvenirs with his visionary promises of an era of "new internationalism" among *turistas.* He prophesied that "the abandonment of the nationalist stance," especially in the United States, would "in turn permit the growth of cultural diversity." The *turista* of the future would be the child of that era; he would be a man of "cultural diversity." He would respect all cultures, even the Puerto Rican. He would be a true citizen of the world of tourism.

The political writer of the San Juan *Star,* Juan Manuel García Passalacqua, commented that Revel's "arguments are relevant particularly to Puerto Rico." He did not say why.

Soon after the seminar had ended the Cerromar Beach Hotel was bombed. It happened on the day of the Miss Universe pageant.

On the land near the hotel were squatters' huts. The homeless *jíbaros* from the hills and the jobless of the urban *barrios* had been invading the empty fields and coconut groves for months. Here, amid the splendor of the *turistas,* the poor built makeshift villages of crates, abandoned cars and Coca-Cola signs. In pots, hung on open fires, the destitute families cooked wild fruits and grasses, with rare scraps of meat, to feed their starving children. From time to time the police raided the squatters' colonies and burnt them to the ground. The squatters, having nowhere else to go, would come back and rebuild their huts.

The squatters' huts were not visible from the balconies of the Cerromar Beach Hotel. But the beautiful hotel, rising like a palace by the sea, its five hundred rooms with windows shining in the sunlight like jewels, was clearly visible from the squatters' huts.

On the day the gossip columnists, travel writers, fashion photographers, Hollywood starlets, and the Governor were to pay homage to Miss Universe the resort hotel was bombed, by "unknown terrorists," who terrified the heralds of the "new internationalism" of tourism. In the squatters' huts the poor just shrugged.

15

On the Mountain of Wild Strawberries

On the mountain were fields of wild strawberries. They were red as tiny roses, delicate and fragrant. In my mouth they tasted sweet as elderberries and fragile as raspberries. Unlike the tart and pulpy commercial strawberries, these bright flowers of the jungle, on the high ridges of the coffee plantations of Utuado, were not to be chewed, for they dissolved on the tongue, soft and aromatic as a tropical orchid.

Beneath the wild strawberries was a mountain of copper, worth $3 billion or more, to those who prized electric wire.

"It is always there," a *jíbaro* said. "We have old mines there. Very old."

Why wasn't it mined?

"They don't need it. They had mines in Chile. They don't have that any more."

So now the copper of Utuado would be mined.

"No! They wish the copper. We wish the mountains."

The mining engineers had come to the scent of the copper. In the fields of wild strawberries they had gashed a road up the mountain to the mine pit with bulldozers. In the offices of Kennecott Copper and American Metal Climax executives talked of a "copper find" worth hundreds of millions in profits. And coming after the loss of their mines in Chile to the government of Allende, it was a godsend. (In the cathedral of Santiago, Chile, at a *Te Deum,* it was said the late

President Allende had prayed, *"Gracias a Dios porque el cobre nos pertenece"*—"Thank God the copper is ours.") No one knew exactly how much copper was beneath the mountain of the wild strawberries, but the talk was of the island becoming "the mining center of the Caribbean." It was "one of the richest deposits in the world," exclaimed a somewhat too enthusiastic local official.

Wasn't this a poor island?

"No more!" he smiled broadly. "It is good as gold. Better!"

Up the mountainside the road was a cliff-hanger. It ran along the edge of the ridges, two ruts of dirt on top of the precarious slopes upon which the coffee and plantain trees grew. In the high jungles of the *jíbaros'* land, the mining pit was hidden by thick bushes. The wild strawberries had grown into the empty pit once more. And it was abandoned.

In the mists, the green valleys drifted by far below. The huts of the *jíbaros* were bright as flowers of the fiery *flamboyan* and yellow tropical elder and lavender myrtle and purple fern trees. Poverty was idyllic, from a distance. The mines of Barrio Consejo, the Place of the Village Meeting, were in one of the poorest and most deeply traditional regions of the central highlands. So were the mines of Vegas Arriba Adjuntas, the Meadows of Upper Adjuntas, and the Barrio Santa Isabel, near Lares. Life here was serene and untouched, almost, by the nervousness of the electric cities.

"Our beloved mountains," sighed the Right Reverend Francisco Reus-Froylan, Episcopal Bishop of Puerto Rico, were the heart of "our precious Puerto Rican culture." It was "the area that has produced the sweet music of *le lo lai;* the terrain of the uncomplicated serene men of integrity; hospitable, of natural warmth; of the tradesman's instinct for his own business. His values are of the earth and the work of his own hands. He is the man who, until a few years ago, fed Puerto Rico. For many he is still the principal fountain of inspiration for our own 'Puerto Ricanism'—with its customs, its attitudes, its proverbs, its religious expressions—in other words, an entire culture, one reaching back centuries."

The mines would be a "cultural disaster," the Bishop said. "I am opposed!"

He had told this to the Kennecott Copper board of directors. For the heart of Puerto Rico "will be wiped out, once the mining operation, with its gigantic technology and overpowering financial impact, is implanted in the region," said the Bishop; he begged the company not to "destroy our precious culture." They listened politely.

In the *barrios* of Utuado words not of compassion but of anger were being spoken. There was violence. A jeep used by those who opposed the mines was mysteriously burned one night. Equipment was damaged and destroyed. Unseen by the police or the newspapers, the violence was silent and nameless; it was a war of shadows.

And yet upon the mountain it was quiet. The wild strawberries were sweet as ever.

"Beautiful, isn't it?" a *jíbaro* said. He had come up the mountain with one of the Mining Brigades of university students who were fighting the mining companies. He plucked a wild strawberry. And, savoring it in his lips, he swallowed it whole, like a mouthful of rum.

"If they dig the mine, they dig away the mountain?" he simultaneously asked and answered. "*¿Sí?* Then our coffee and plantains will be destroyed? Our life!

"So," he said, grinning, "we stop them."

And how would he stop the bulldozers of the mining companies?

"You will see," he said.

By lying down in front of the machines?

"No! We will not lie down. We will stand up to them," he said. "I tell you, not one shovelful of copper will be taken from our mountains by the Yankees. We know these mountains, these valleys, these caves, these hidden places, better than anyone in the world. We have lived here for hundreds of years. So I tell you again, not one shovelful of copper will be taken from our mountains by the Yankees. We will stop them."

In a Jesuit sanctuary, walled and still, on a middle-class street in a suburb of San Juan, one of the five bishops of the Catholic Church of

Puerto Rico, the Monsignor Autulio Parrilla Bonilla, was asked about the vow of the *jíbaro*. He believed the resistance was more than a threat. The stalwart Bishop, a formidable and stolid-faced man, who had been rector of the seminary for priests and chaplain of the National Guard ("He is a conservative in religion and a socialist in politics," one of his fellow priests said), nodded and repeated the threat in his own words:

"Not a single pound of copper will be taken out of Puerto Rico!" the Bishop intoned, as though he were damning a mortal sin.

"We are going to prevent the exploitation of those mines," he declared. "I can assure you that as far as the independence movement is concerned not a single pound of copper will be taken out of Puerto Rico! This has been said in a very solemn way and repeated many times by the leaders of the independence movement. And they're going to do it."

The Bishop was asked: Now what does that mean?

"It means," he reiterated, "that not a single pound of copper will be taken out of Puerto Rico!"

But how will it be prevented?

"Physically!" Bishop Parrilla replied quietly.

The "Battle of the Wild Strawberries and the Copper" had reached into the farthest corners of the island. It was a symbolic struggle but a very practical one. Ever since the negotiations of the government with the copper companies had begun in 1961, they had been kept secret, for fear the issue would explode upon the public, as it eventually did. In the Fortaleza four governors had come to power in that time, promising a white paper and a decision on *las minas*—the mines; but none had dared defy the public outcry by deciding in favor of the mining companies, and none had dared defy the mining companies by deciding in favor of the public outcry.

Into the impasse the Episcopal Church had come, to convene a Church Panel on Copper Mining in Puerto Rico during the winter of 1971. The public hearing, open to all sides of the controversy, was held under the auspices of the Board of Missions of the United Methodist Church, the Board of Social Ministry of the Lutheran Church, the Inter-American Affairs Committee of the Presbyterian Church, the American Baptist Home Mission Society, the United Church of Christ, and the Episcopal Church. As stockholders of 143,000 shares in Kennecott Copper and 60,000 shares in American Metal Climax, the churches were represented by Robert Potter, lawyer for the *Wall Street Journal,* who had arranged for the hearing in the courtlike chambers of the austere Colegio de Abogados, the Bar Association of Puerto Rico.

Both mining companies were invited, but "both companies refused to be present at the hearings," reported the churches.

Pedro A. Gelabert, the director of the Mining Commission, testified with an odd mixture of *gusto* and *apologia.* He talked hopefully of perhaps 2,000 jobs being created in the construction of the mines, and 800 jobs thereafter. It was a bonanza; for, he said, only 38 families would be dispossessed on the 3,500 acres that the copper companies would use. And the government had been offered a dazzling royalty for the copper that came to $231 million in thirty years. If it looked like the benefits were small, "the government probably won't go ahead with it," he said.

He was accused of lying. Scholars and scientists of the Institute of Consumer Research said the figure of 3,500 acres was false. The mining companies had asked the government for 36,000 to 40,000 acres. Besides, the "social costs" of the mining that the government would have to bear were estimated at more than half the royalty offered—$125 million. Even that cost did not include the price of the huge environmental damage that would be done.

Jíbaros and professors talked of their doubts about the promise of thousands of jobs. An economist had estimated that only "600 jobs would actually be created at the mines, and many of these would be for North Americans." Ramón Ororio, a member of the student Mining Brigade, said, "Much of the employment in the mines is of a highly technical nature and would be given to technicians brought in from elsewhere." Father Benjamin Ortiz Belaval of the Puerto Rico Industrial Mission recalled the petrochemical companies had "promised 35,000 jobs, but only 5,000 developed."

"Too seldom has the dream come true," said Bishop Reus-Froylan. "The poorest somehow remain poor and suffer more. It is those already part-way up the ladder who get the technicians' jobs and begin to own two cars instead of one. Those who are the poor of the 'copper region' of Lares-Adjuntas-Utuado are not going to get the jobs . . . they will migrate and become the casualties of a socio-cultural upheaval. What will surely happen is a repetition of the classic pattern of urban slum building from which Puerto Rico has suffered so much in recent years."

And the earth, too, would become a casualty. Dr. José Francisco Cadilla, a professor of geology and former chief geologist of the government, testified there would be "permanent damage done to the environment." He knew of a number of government studies that opposed the mines, for this and other reasons, and which had therefore been suppressed. In 1965 the Planning Board study of the mines recommended the project be rejected; the study was "repressed." In 1967 a government report, by the Johnson Committee, stated that because of "water and air pollution possibilities" the mining "was not feasible"; the report "was taken out of circulation." Later, a study prepared by the Aqueducts and Water Commission that forecast "changes in acidity and taste of the water" was "withdrawn from circulation." The geologist concluded that the government knew the mines would destroy the land, the water, and the air of the island. It was acquiescing, said Dr. Cadilla, to a "political situation dictated by American capital."

Even the sea around us will die, testified Dr. Maximo Cerame Vivas, director of the Department of Marine Sciences of the University of Puerto Rico, if the mining wastes were dumped into it, as planned. These wastes, or tailings, were poisonous; and they would "smother 5,000 square miles of the ocean bottom in the Caribbean Sea." Neither fish nor ocean organisms could "escape or survive." And the beaches of the island would be washed by a sea of death.

It was a sociologist of Utuado, Irvin Torres Torres, who voiced the fears and angers of the inhabitants of the mountains. "What is at stake is the whole culture of Puerto Rico," he began. "The coffee and mountain culture are the hub of the Puerto Rican identity. No price can be put on the culture that would be disrupted by this mining. How will subeducated farmers adjust their very beings and way of life in an alien surrounding?" They won't! he said.

"When the U.S. needed sugar, we grew sugar. When it needed cheap labor, we were cheap labor. Now, it needs copper.

"Men in dark suits will come telling how they will provide jobs for every man, woman, and child on the island. They have come before in the name of the industrialization program, the migrant-worker program, the Army and Navy bases, and the petrochemical industry. None of these promises ever came true. And in the meantime Puerto Ricans have been drafted, immigrated, urbanly renovated, educated in the American way of life, their family structure 'modernized' and they have been conspicuously consumed.

"And why does this situation exist? Because Puerto Rico is a colony and colonies are made to be exploited.

"The hearing itself is a manifestation of colonialism," he said. Instead of a hearing, let the poor people act on the proposal of the Agricultural Experimental Station of the University that 2,350 self-supporting family farms be set up in the *barrios* of the mountains. He said: the government "has its hands tied." It was up to the poor themselves.

And so in the end the churches contritely recommended: "That American Metal Climax, Inc., and the Kennecott Copper Corporation postpone mining on the island of Puerto Rico because of the danger such mining will be to the health and well-being of the people of Puerto Rico." It was this message that Bishop Reus-Froylan took to the meeting of the Kennecott Copper stockholders in New York. "As a Christian," he said, he had come to beg that "our culture, our people, our rich and fecund island" not be seen by the stockholders merely in "terms of money."

The Bishop was "un-Christian!" said Rafael Píco; he was advocating poverty!

Píco, the chairman of the Banco Popular and former "father of the Planning Board" that had guided the industrialization of the island

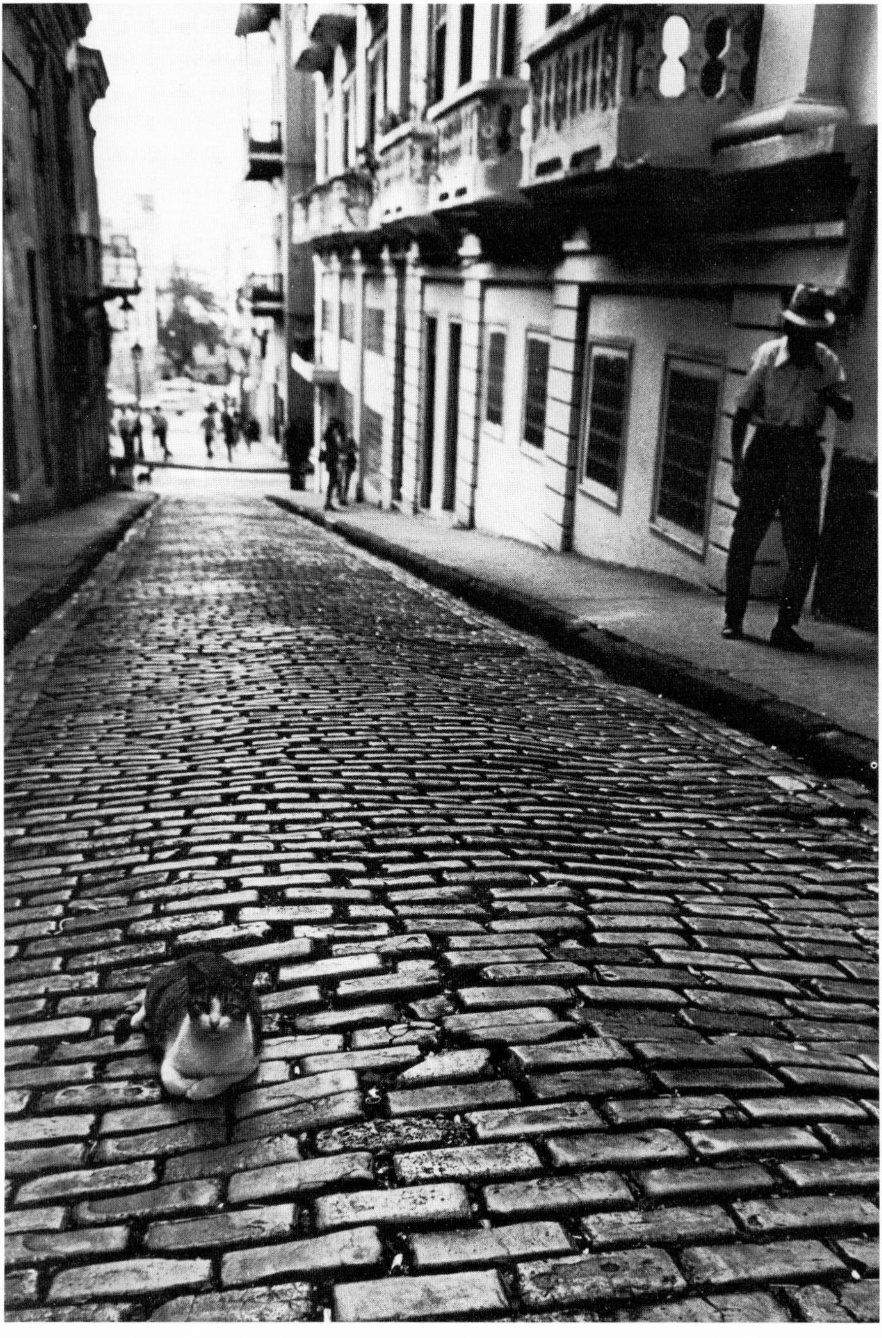

Once the cobblestones of Old San Juan were still.

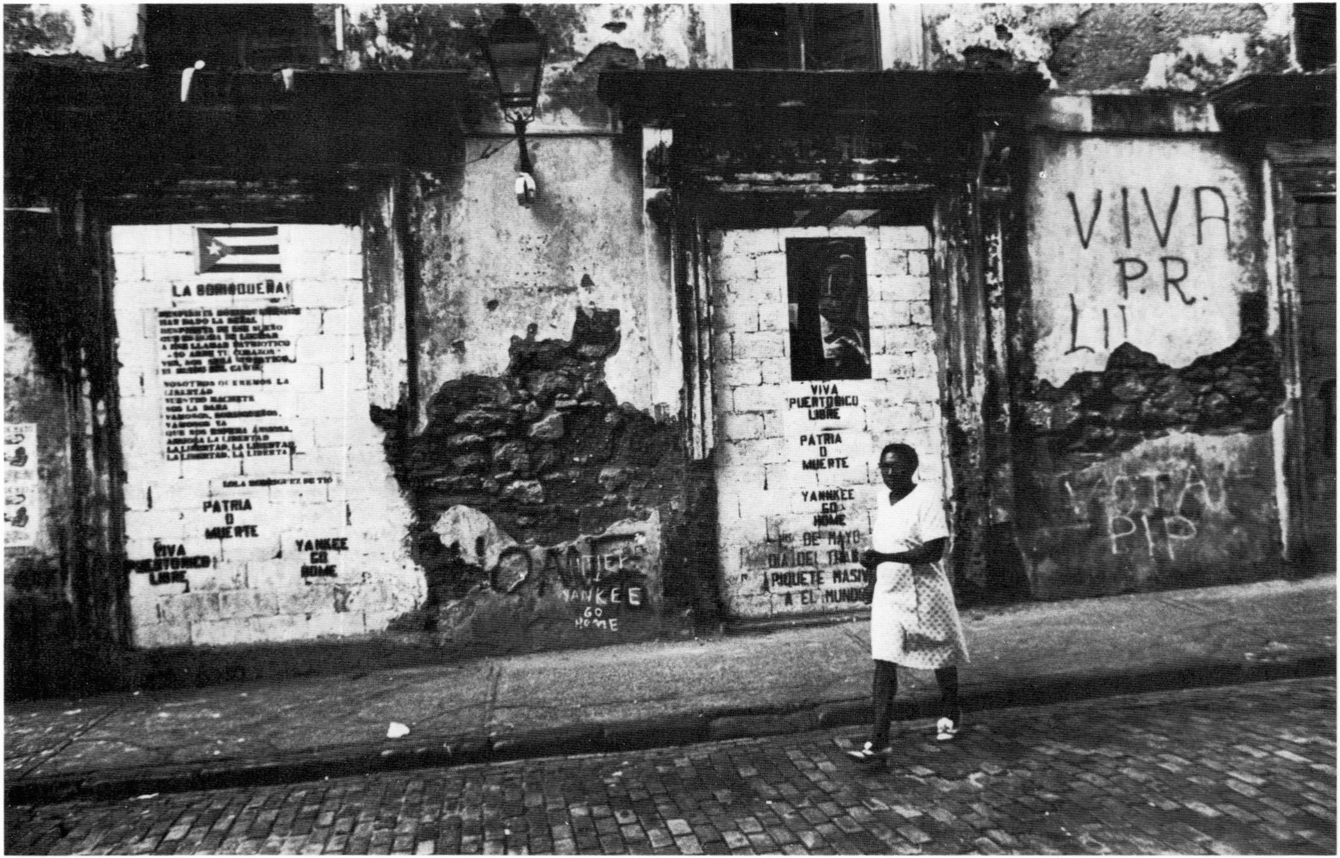

The wailing wall of an island *barrio*

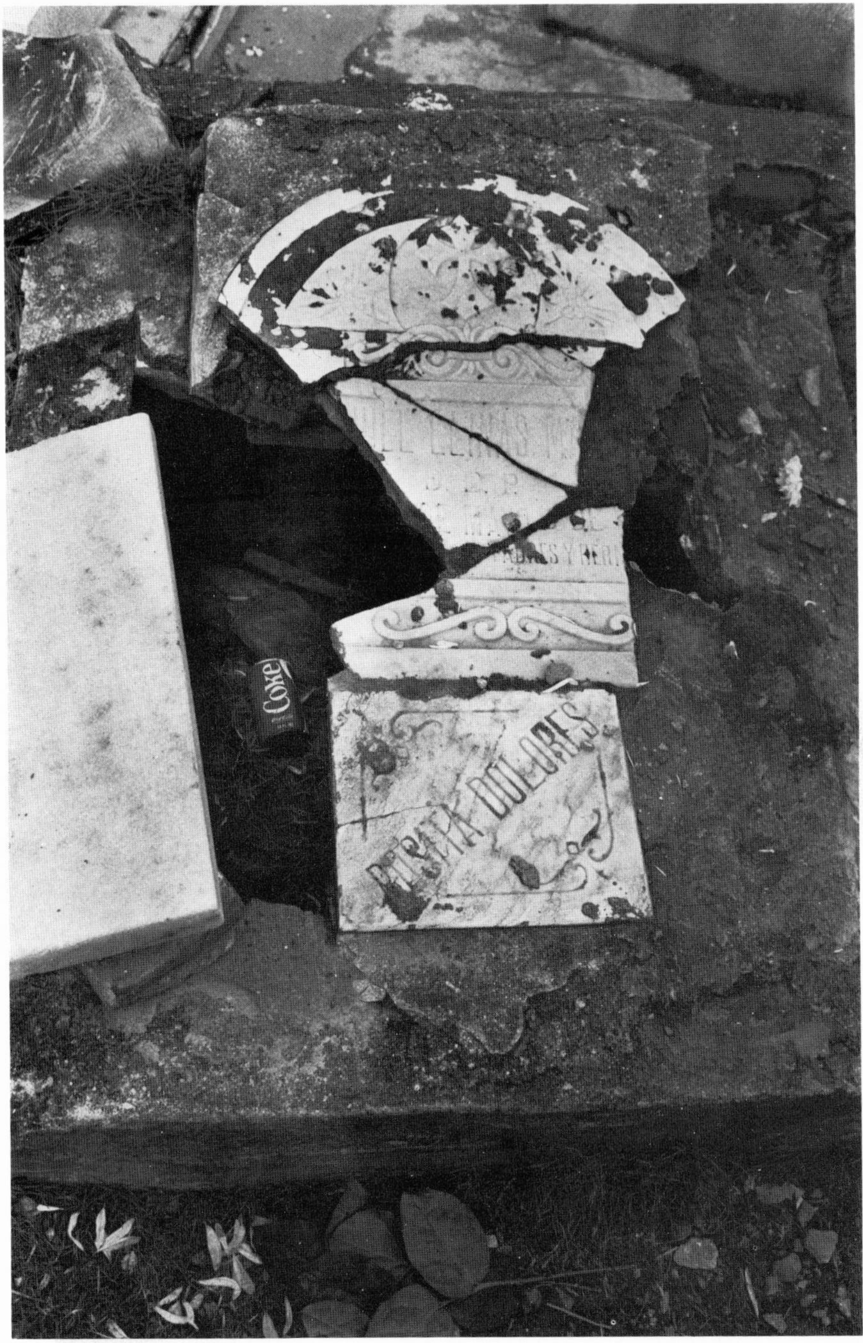

Coke in a broken crypt of the Old San Juan Cemetery by the sea

The statue of Ponce de León raises a Puerto Rican flag before his Gothic sixteenth-century church.

The dark eminence of an oil refinery on the way to Ponce

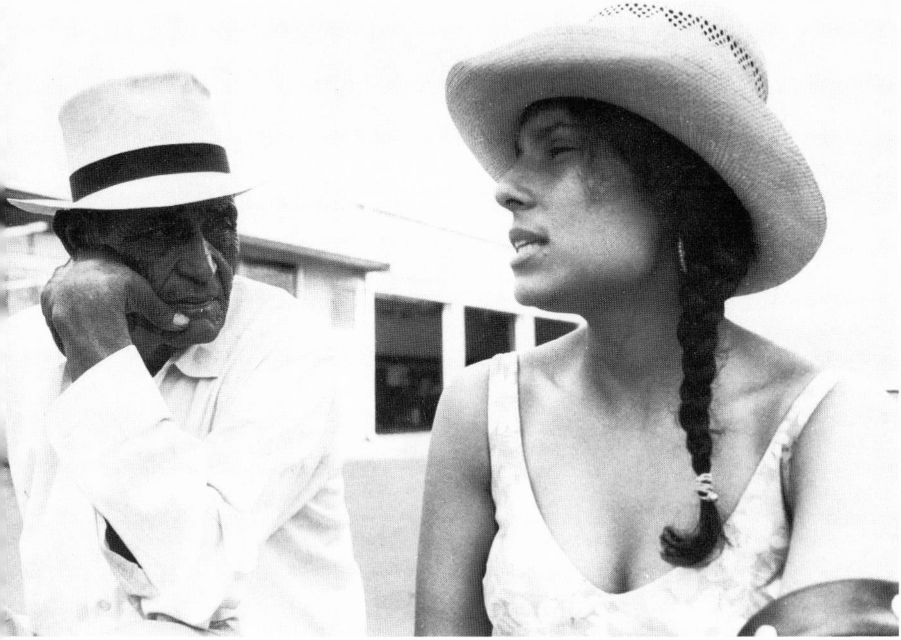

The old and young Borinquén

The "400 percent Americano" poses near La Fortaleza

Tourists on the steps of the Cathedral of San Juan

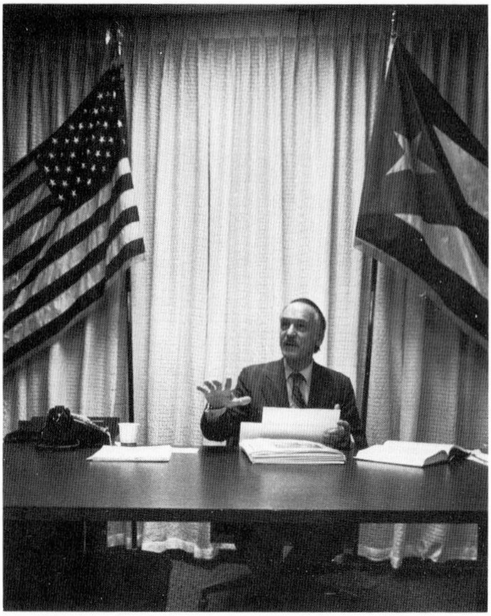

Former Governor Luis Antonio Ferre

Juan Mari Bras, leader of the Puerto Rican Socialist party

Governor Rafael Hernández Colón and Luis Muñoz Marín, on façade of the Popular Democratic party headquarters

Ruben Berrios Martínez, president o the Puerto Rican Independence party

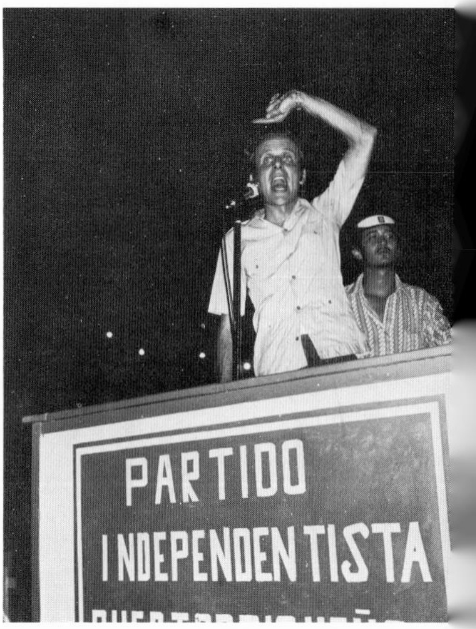

under Governor Muñoz, had come to the meeting to reassure the copper company, "You're welcome in Puerto Rico." He replied to the churchman with surprising wrath: "My friend Bishop Froylan talked about the peasant culture up in the hills. . . . I submit that to try to protect that cultural poverty that exists there, abysmal poverty, is the most atrocious mistake to make. The cultural poverty doesn't have any merit by itself, and I think we should abolish it, wherever it exists. It is really un-Christian to try to preserve, as has been said here, a peasant cultural poverty that exists in central Puerto Rico.

"If you really want to preserve their culture, you should leave Puerto Rico," he told the Bishop. The *jíbaros* were Catholic and "really alien to Protestantism," Píco went on, with the gracious afterthought, "which is, of course, welcome. . . . But to rejoice in the poverty, in the adversity, in the backwardness of that area is something that is un-Christian."

Píco said in anger: those who fought the mines were either "misguided conservationists" or, worse, "the soul brothers of the Communists of Chile; yes, they are the same breed who would like to get rid of all outside capital, that brings so much good to all of this area."

"The projected mining of copper is a highly explosive political issue in Puerto Rico," said the report of the church panel. It ruefully commented that the "allegations of political imperialism" seemed to come from both sides at once.

"Copper, like oil, is one of the world's most politicized commodities," noted the *New York Times* financial page. "Nationalization of U.S.-owned copper facilities [in Chile] has led to more international problems for the volatile metal." It quoted Kennecott's general counsel, P. N. McCreary, as warning that his company's agents would "seize copper wherever we find it" that was shipped from El Teniente, the Kennecott mine expropriated by the Chilean government. One ship, a German freighter loaded with Chilean copper, was seized in a Dutch harbor because of an injunction the American company obtained in a French court. It was as if international war on the high seas had been declared.

On the island, the "specter of nationalization" caused the American copper companies to proceed cautiously and politely. The Puerto Rican government was offered, at the start of the negotiation, a 2 percent royalty on the copper, and then a 20 percent share of the profits, and then 33.5 percent. And then, when the agitation of the *independentistas* became more effective and threatening, an offer of 50 percent of the profits was made, reportedly coupled with a 51 percent share in the control of the mines by the government.

Even this did not persuade the *independentistas*. "Japanese companies will give more," said Bishop Parrilla, "with less risk of pollution"; these Japanese businessmen were "lurking in the background," said the *New York Times* of the corporate yellow peril. But the government would not consider the offers from Japan, charged the Bishop. "See, they are Japanese. They are not Americans. It's not the companies that want the copper. No! It's the Pentagon that wants the copper." Copper was indeed "bedeviled by politics," as the *New York Times* had observed.

"This question of copper is a question of the Pentagon, because it is needed to continue the wars. It's not needed for electric toasters," said the former chaplain of the Puerto Rican National Guard. "I know! And they know they are losing the mines in Chile, the mines in Africa, and the mines everywhere in the 'third world.' Soon, their only 'safe' source of copper will be Puerto Rico. And they will bargain, and they will wait as long as they have to wait, and they will try to take it.

"But we're going to prevent it!" the Bishop said. "We're going to prevent it physically! We are going to do it *that way!*"

No factory on the island had ever been opposed with such vehemence and violence by so many people as the copper mines. The *independentistas* and environmentalists, conservatives and socialists, *jíbaros* and scholars had joined in a strange alliance. It was as if in these remote mountains of the rural highlands a desperate and last-ditch stand were being made against the promiscuous industrialization and Americanization of the island's Puerto Ricanism. And it was this sense of *"¡Basta!"*—"Enough!"—that had created the adamant resistance.

And so the wild strawberries grew sweetly as ever on the mountains of copper. On the fragrant hills of the *jíbaros'* lands no more engineers were to be seen. In February of 1972 the director of the Mining Commission, Pedro A. Gelabert, declared that, after ten years and $8 million spent on "studies for the proposed mining in the Jayuya-Lares area," the copper companies were "delaying the start of mining operations."

"Kennecott may be cooling off on the Puerto Rican venture," Commissioner Gelabert had reportedly told a San Juan newspaper.

In the history of the island it was the first time that public opinion had halted, and seemingly had stymied, a massive foreign-owned industrial development. There was something else that had happened. There was the beginning of public knowledge that the "poor island" was enormously rich in natural resources. Nothing was to have so profound an effect on the self-image of thousands of Puertorriqueños.

Myths die hard. But a myth of colonialism's self-depreciation of the island was dying.

There was a "paucity of natural resources, especially minerals," on the island, Oscar Lewis had written in *La Vida*. It was widely believed. In the green hills "natural resources are limited, or nonexistent," agreed Ralph Hancock in *Puerto Rico: A Success Story.* "Lack of resources," said Clarence Senior, a United Nations consultant and director of the Social Science Research Center of the University of Puerto Rico, in *The Puerto Ricans,* was a major "handicap" in the island's development; he believed Puerto Rico's mineral deposits to be so insignificant that he did not bother to mention them.

Imagine a land, mused the newly elected Resident Commissioner, Jaime Benitez, where "all available mineral resources were eliminated." That land was Puerto Rico in 1960, just one year before the copper "discovery" was to be made.

"Puerto Rico is a small, poor island," the former chairman of the

Planning Board, Rafael Píco, had said, inviting "outside capital and techniques and management" of Kennecott Copper. He saw no "practical" recourse. The aggressive young Governor, Rafael Hernández Colón, drew the obvious political conclusion from that "practical" fact: "We do not have the natural resources for an independent nation. And without the economic resources, independence is a political impossibility." It was "an illusion," he said, to talk "rhetorically of self-determination for a poor island."

And yet the copper had been known to exist on the island since its "discovery" by Columbus. In seeking to impress the rulers of Spain with the riches he had found, Admiral Columbus had brought "abundant samples of gold and copper," which he laid before the King and Queen. These proved, he boasted, "the existence of extensive mines of these metals" on the islands. Although the Admiral was prone to exaggeration, the copper ore that he "discovered" in 1494 was real enough.

In the nineteenth century Spanish officials wrote of these copper deposits, which remained unmined. They detailed the location of the ore, its quality and its abundance. "Copper has been found in sufficient prospects to justify application for the location of some claims," Governor Charles H. Allen reaffirmed in his official report to President McKinley in 1901; he emphasized that there were large deposits not only of copper but of iron.

Once the wealth of the island had been "rediscovered" a conglomerate of mining entrepreneurs of Canada came bearing gifts, and a floral float in the Carnaval de Ponce. They wished to impress the populace with their good intentions in seeking leases for mining exploration of 70,000 acres adjacent to the Lares-Utuado-Adjuntas mine fields. "Some of the most prominent industrialists" of Canada participated in the negotiations; for mining engineers had unearthed rich deposits in "plentiful proportions," not only of copper but of "molybdenum, gold and silver."

Then, in the winter of 1971, the United States Geological Survey released a startling mineralogical map of the island that detailed 184 sites of major ore deposits. It revealed an abundance of nickel, zinc, iron, magnesium, cobalt, gold, silver, copper, and perhaps uranium.

So the colonial myth of "the poor island" was laid to rest. In its program for "Independence, Socialism, Democracy" the Puerto Rican Independence party enthusiastically embraced the new-found euphoria. Lyrically it proclaimed that the copper alone "was worth more than $10 billion." The "poverty-stricken" Puertorriqueños were suddenly the possessors of vast natural resources. No longer was "economic dependence" an argument that could be convincingly used against political independence, they said; history had ended the controversy, not with bullets of steel, but with copper wires.

In a *barrio* high in the mountains a young girl said: "They will have to kill me before I will let them come up this road with bulldozers. Yes, I will die here. They will not pass.

"The copper is ours. Soon the island will be ours," she said.

16

On the Road to Lares

On the Road to Lares

On the grass of a wooden hut on the mountainside that sloped steeply from his remote village to the road down below, the little boy danced barefoot beneath the *yagrumo* trees, in and out among the banana and coffee plants, waving his clenched fist at the passing cars. The boy was eleven. At most he was twelve. He sang in a small voice that was innocent and lyrical: *"¡Jíbaro sí! Yanqui, no!"*

The boy would not have known a year ago what a clenched fist was, but now he was a "revolutionary."

Under the *flamboyan* trees that flowered in the village schoolyard two young women teachers in a country school were eating their lunch in the shade. They jumped up and lifted clenched fists upward to the brilliant red-flowering branches of those trees. In the midst of the road that unwound through the mountain village the school boys and girls began to dance. Hips swaying, elbows undulating, with casual grace, they joyously danced to songs of the troubadour of independence, Roy Brown, the poet of *"Yo Protesto"—"I Protest,"* —whose lilting voice came from a loudspeaker on the roof of a passing car:

> And if the Borinqueños will awaken
> It is the eve of people who hunger
> To scream and to scream. . . .

His songs were revolutionary, it was said. Were they not songs of joy and death, love and pain? And yet they had the lift of dance music. So if he sang of sorrows, the feet would not be still, or sad, for long.

So the troubadour sang:

> A man is a rebel who weeps
> when he confronts a dream
> by nailing himself to the Cross—
>
> But, no, no, I can't comprehend
> pain, the mirror of love. . . .

An old man sitting on an old crate in a roadside café, sipping a cup of coffee, lifted a clenched fist, gnarled as a knot of aged wood. He shouted:

> *¡Viva Puerto Rico Libre!*
> *¡A Lares!*

"On to Lares!" he grinned with toothless abandon. "Long live a free Puerto Rico!" He held on to his cup of coffee, his eyes squinting happily, for despite his revolutionary fervor the old man had not spilled a drop from his cup.

It was like that all day on the road to Lares. On mountainous slopes so steep they would have defied goats, in the *bateys* of *jíbaro* huts, and on the verandas of country houses, thousands and thousands of people sang and shouted and waved Puerto Rican flags and happy clenched fists at the passing cars; while the young people danced to the tune of patriotic and revolutionary songs on the loudspeakers. Even *"La Borinqueña,"* the national anthem, was sweet on the lips. "A gentle ballad, composed not after the triumph of war, but in a nostalgic mood, which speaks of Puerto Rico's discovery and its natural beauty," said one listener. It, too, had a lyrical sadness.

"If we ever have a revolution our children will dance to the barricades," said a priest that day. "But why not?"

So the troubadour sang:

> The mind is a sleeping soul,
> dreaming and wishing one day
> truth will be known—

But, no, no, I can't comprehend
pain, the mirror of love. . . .

The day was the twenty-fourth of September, the celebration of El Grito de Lares, the "Declaration of Independence" of the island. Or, translated with more truth, it was "The Cry of Lares." On that day every year the people celebrated the revolution of 1868 in the town high in the mountains where the *jíbaros,* with their *machetes,* and the merchants, schoolteachers, and village intellectuals, with their antique rifles, had driven the Spanish garrison from Lares, and had proclaimed their "Republic of Puerto Rico," for one brief day or two in that summer of one hundred years ago. In the plaza they had unfurled the flag, with its remembered words, "Liberty or Death! Long Live Free Puerto Rico! Year, 1868," a banner of strange purity for revolutionaries, with its white cross and single white star.

"Citizens: to want to be free is to begin to do so," proclaimed the revolutionary Comité del Sur, with simple dignity.

The tranquil island had suffered from a succession of brutal and authoritarian Spanish colonial governors. After the victories of Simón Bolívar and his nationalist armies on the continent, Puerto Rico had become the refuge of the fleeing monarchists and slaveowners from all over South America. In fear of any liberal reform or revolutionary idea, these Latin bourbons influenced the appointment of "the parade of Caesars" who governed the island after 1825.

First came General Miguel de la Torre, who had been defeated by Bolívar in Venezuela, and who was so frightened of the Puertorriqueños he prohibited meetings after dark, but for cockfights and card games. His governorship was called the reign of the "three B's"—*baile, botella y baraja*—dance, drink and dice. Then came General Miguel López de Baños, whose paranoia caused him to outlaw beards and goatees, because "he felt they were too suggestive of revolution." Then came Marshal Juan Prim, the Count de Reus, whose historic fame rested on his *Bando Negro*—Black Edict—which decreed that a dark Puertorriqueño who insulted a white Spaniard would be imprisoned for five years, and if a black attacked a white the sentence was death, a decree quite incongruous on the multihued island. Then came Lieutenant General Juan de Pezuelas, who thought "too much education spoiled Spain's colonists and made them subversive." He instituted the Ley de Libreta, a law that forced everyone to carry a passbook that listed his name, his place of work, his salary; if someone was caught without his *libreta,* or was not working, he was sent to do forced labor. General Pezuelas went further; he forbade Puertorriqueños to change their residences, to travel from town to town, or even hold parties, without government permission. And then Governor Juan María Marchessi, who had been so frightened by the revolutionary uprisings in Santo Domingo and Cuba, and the rebellion of his own garrison of Spanish artillerymen in San Juan, that he exiled the liberal leaders Dr. Ramón Betances and Segundo Ruiz Belvis (who had advocated the abolition of slavery and the institution of civil rights for Puertorriqueños); the government began a reign of terror that turned the reformers into revolutionaries.

The uprising was long and well planned. Village after village, town after town, was to rise up upon the signal of the revolutionary junta. Led by Dr. Betances, the exiles had arranged for a shipload of rifles and cannon to be sent to the island from Santo Domingo. Once the revolution was successful and the Republic of Puerto Rico had been established, several Latin American governments had agreed to recognize the new nation.

An informer revealed the plans to the Spanish authorities. The Camuy revolutionary junta was seized. Hundreds of patriots were arrested and imprisoned in the cities of Mayaqüez, Ponce, Arecibo, and Aguadilla. In the hills of Adjuntas the secretary of the revolutionary junta, Baldomero Bauren, and the adventurous military leader Matias Brugman, an American citizen, were hunted down by the Spanish troops and executed, their bodies riddled with bullets. The guns of Betances never reached the island's shores.

On the whole island the *jíbaros* of Lares fought alone. In their hands betrayal had placed history.

Lares was the Bunker Hill and the Bastille of Puerto Rico. It was a shrine of the war of independence that had been lost, not won. The pilgrimages to its memory were full of grief and nostalgia, as though the Battle of Lexington and Concord had been lost by the American revolutionaries and the Fourth of July was the memorial to the death and defeat of George Washington. El Grito de Lares had to be celebrated with a fiesta, lest the memory of the loss of liberty become unbearable.

All that day the caravans of cars passed on the roads to Lares. It was thought that forty to fifty thousand people gathered in the little town every year. Miles on miles of cars crowded the winding mountain roads and the precarious villages of the *jíbaros*.

In one of the cars there was a farmer. He was a *jíbaro* from the hills of Utuado, who had the name of Arturo Chabriel. "My great-grandfather was the second-in-command of the revolution," he quietly said, and with a wry grin added, "On the other side of my family, my other great-grandfather was a commander of the Spaniards who joined the revolution." Evidently he was amused by the irony of history.

Arturo Chabriel was a man of few words. Lean and elegant, as were many of the *jíbaro* farmers, his reticent and modest manner was jarred by the intensity with which he relived the fighting of the Revolution of 1868, as the car neared Lares. He became volatile.

Once more he fought the battle in his ancestral memory. By the roadside, house by house, he pointed to where the revolutionaries had lived and had met. He knew them all by name, by family. He fought not only the soldiers of Spain, but the battle of local pride between the town of Lares and Utuado, his home town. "Most of the revolutionaries were from Utuado," he said. "Our farms were more populated than those of Lares. Everyone thinks that the revolutionaries all came from Lares. That is not history"; as if to say, "I am history."

When a revolution is not won, it has no end. The presence of the past was in his voice. It seemed to be as real, to him, as the reality of the world that passed by the windows of the car. "History does not die," a younger *jíbaro* said.

"The battle goes on," the farmer said. He was an *independentista,* just as much "as were my great-grandfathers." But "times had changed," he said, nodding. "The Spaniards were not so cruel with the prisoners of the revolution as the United States is now cruel with the prisoners of the independence fight. So we have to now be more quiet. Who knows what in the future will happen? Life is unexpected as this road."

On the road to Lares from Utuado, there were huge holes where the rains had washed the pavement into the valley. The road hung on to the mountainside like a broken rope. Where the road had not been wide enough for two cars it was hardly wide enough for one. A fence of old boards, at times, stood between the cars and the oblivion of the beautiful valley in the tangled jungles hundreds of feet below. Sometimes there were only a few bamboo poles.

The road had always been an adventure. It took as long to go from Utuado to the sea as to cross the sea to Europe, an early traveler had written. When the U.S. Commissioner Henry K. Carroll came on his fact-finding visit for President McKinley in 1899, he was told not to go on the Utuado-to-Lares road without first "writing his will."

If anyone had paved the road since that day, it was not visible. "Who in the government would pave the road to revolution?" the *jíbaro* who was driving said.

Deep in the jungle a car lay where it had fallen from the road. Cradled in a hammock of greenery, it lay in a bower of fern and of vines. The car looked content, not wrecked. On its hood a cock pranced happily. Lizards had squirreled a nest in its upholstery. In the windshield a wild orchid bloomed. Within a few years the jungle would cover the car with oblivion. And the metal carcass would be invisible beneath the lush tropical foliage. And everything would be peaceful.

"Sooner or later," laughed the *jíbaro* who was driving, "you see what happens. The island conquers its conquerors."

And the troubadour on the roof of the car sang, through the loudspeaker of the eight-track tape:

> But, no, no, I can't comprehend
> pain, the mirror of love. . . .

And the troubadour sang:

> But, if it is true that every man
> defines himself, I define myself in a vision—
>
> My sacred hand, I extend to a friend,
> My noblest kiss, I give to my woman,
> And I offer my country my devotion. . . .

And the troubadour sang:

> But, yes, yes, I can confront
> pain now, I can feel love. . . .

The mountain road descended into the little town of Lares, where fifty thousand people waited to dance to his song.

Los Gritos

In the Cementerio de San Juan, under the old city wall by the sea, the mourners sat amid the tombs and crypts on folding chairs beneath silk umbrellas and a canopy of canvas, as if at a melancholy garden party. The sea was fierce upon the rocks. The wind moaned through the tombs of the dead heroes buried on the precarious edge of the island.

"Long live José de Diego!" a man at the tombstone vainly cried to the sea.

The day was the day not of the death but of the birth of the great patriot. One wondered: how many dead heroes were buried on the island to be mourned, and how many lost causes to be celebrated?

His tomb was completely covered with flowers. There was a wreath of white lilies, in the lovely shape of a Greek lyre, from the Nationalist party—in memory of the comrades of Don Pedro Albizu Campos still imprisoned for their "attempted assassination" of President Truman. There was a wreath from Puerto Rico's House of Representatives—José de Diego had been President (1907–17) and Speaker (1917–18) of the House. As one of the leading statesmen of his time, he was a member of the Cabinet in the autonomous government, under Spain, in 1897—as Assistant Secretary of Government and Justice, he served as the equivalent of Attorney General—and he was appointed to the Executive Council of the colonial government of President McKinley in 1900. There was a wreath from the Institute of Puerto Rican Culture. He was one of the island's most beloved lyric poets and political philosophers. In Spain he was known as the "Knight of the Race," though in his student days the government had imprisoned him in their jails of Barcelona, Tarragona, Valencia, and Madrid. There was a red wreath from the Partido Independentista Puertorriqueño—PIP, the Puerto Rican Independence party. He was a principled *independentista,* one of the few leaders who had refused to accept the citizenship of the United States under the Jones Act in 1917. One of the orators at his tomb was the youngish and buoyant Ruben Berrios Martínez, the president of PIP, who had just been released from his three-month imprisonment by the government for defying the U.S. Marines on the island of Culebra—a living "target range" for naval "war games." He passionately cried: "If José de Diego were alive, he, too, would have been in prison with me!" And there was a wreath from the Masonic Order of San Juan businessmen.

It was a national holiday. The offices of the government had closed. And yet no government officials had come to the tomb. Not even an *ayudante* of the Governor.

An orator, with the lean demeanor of a retired Shakespearean actor, waved his arms as he recited a romantic and patriotic ode by José de Diego.

"*¡Patria!*" cried the orator, weeping.

The mourners applauded. Gathered at the grave were the aristocracy of the *independentistas.* "Lawyers, doctors, professors," Berrios said, "are the leaders of our party." And the eulogy was literary.

There were muffled sounds of footsteps on the cobblestoned path of the cemetery. In moments the dignified mourners were overwhelmed by two hundred youths, who swarmed over the graves and surrounded the tomb. A boy wore a Venceremos Brigade tee-shirt, from Cuba. His companion wore a purple beret of the Young Lords of New York. One university girl was fashionable in bell bottoms with leopard spots, and a *jíbaro* straw hat bought in a *turista* shop. There was a delegation from the Boilermakers Union. Led by the lawyer Juan Mari Bras, then the leader of the Movimiento por Independencia (MPI), now the Partido Socialista Puertorriqueño (PSP, the Puerto Rican Socialist party), these were the self-styled "militants" of the independence movement. They had not come to mourn dead heroes.

In his conservative gray suit with the genteel look of the "*patrón* of the Marxist revolution," as one of his admirers fondly called him, the *socialista* lawyer lectured the elderly mourners without notes, without gestures, his hands in the pockets of his jacket.

"De Diego forever illuminated our path to independence by his sacrifice, by his courage," Juan Mari Bras intoned in the oratorical Spanish of such occasions; he was paraphrasing Don Pedro Albizu Campos: "De Diego has prophesied the triumph of our cause. The moment of our liberation is coming! It has come! The time has come when Puerto Rico is prepared to join the socialist revolutions of the twentieth century.

"And then," he quietly said, "the spirit of the dead de Diego will live again."

On the rocks below the old cemetery walls the surf thundered. It had heard the words before. Each year at the tomb of de Diego someone spoke the same words with the same passion. The sea was no more shocked by the cry of revolution than were the wealthy mourners at the crypt—who, one by one, politely clasped the hands of the orator.

The sea sighed.

The words of the new "*patrón* of the revolution," Juan Mari Bras, may have been an echo of the past. He and his movement were something very new to the elite traditionalists of the *independentistas* —these bearded veterans of the war and the intense-eyed young women from the university, and the modish young workers from the factories, who had the determined look of ideological revolutionaries—ardent, blasphemous, and vigorous. In a pocket of the blue Levi's of one young girl there was a little red book, *The Thoughts of Chairman Mao.*

Some of these youth may have been members of the Commandos of Armed Liberation (CAL). They were a secret army on the style of the IRA, which had bombed hundreds of American-owned stores and commercial enterprises. None, they said, had ever been caught. It was unlikely that urban guerrillas would come to so public a ceremony. But whoever knew who they were would hardly say.

Or they may have come from the island of Culebra, on whose shores the young *independentistas* had been bodily standing in the path of the U.S. Marines. The island of farmers and fishermen was being used as a target range by the U.S. Navy. And dozens of Puerto Rican pacifists and patriots had been arrested that spring when, obeying the dictum of Jean-Paul Sartre and their beliefs, they had lain "like seashells in the sand," as one said, while the Marine Corps terraced the beach with barbwire. No one in the history of the island had ever before physically defied the armed forces of the United States in that way.

Or they may have been university students back from the mountains of Utuado, where they served in the Volunteer Mining Brigades, pledged to fight and die rather than permit the copper companies to "take a single shovelful of copper" from the island's rich mountains.

Whoever they were, and wherever they came from, they were a new kind of *independentista.* They had no fear of the "giant in the north."

An eminent Puerto Rican writer who has been a lifelong advocate of independence said of them: "I feel that the young revolutionaries may be willing to kill many. Even me, if they thought that I was in the way of their ideology." She winced. "No! I do not wish blood. I wish independence. But not blood."

Her unease was that of an old teacher who wondered why her beloved students had not learned to believe as she believed. There was no anger in her words, merely sadness. It was an expression of that sense of frustration, and fear, that had come to separate the generations whose worlds no longer seemed to be the same worlds, though they were members of the same *familia*. The young and old *independentistas* reflected that familial schism of history.

"They are not gracious," said a well-known lawyer. "They do not behave like Puertorriqueños." He was a respected leader of the independence movement who admired the youth, who admired him. But he too was disturbed by the "loss of grace" among the young revolutionaries. It was not a style of life, but a way of life, to him. "Living in these cities one does not learn to be gracious," he sadly said. "And so our youth have become a little harsh, but it is perhaps necessary to be harsh to survive in this modern life.

"After all, in many instances they have learned this in New York, and in the United States Army—in Vietnam," he said.

The old *independentistas* were the poets and *patrones,* the intelligentsia and shopkeepers, of the island. In their patriotic fervor there was always the moderating influence of social caste and *hacienda* etiquette. And their devotion to independence tended to be romantic; it was not unaffected by a spirit of *aplanamiento,* of drowsiness and the melancholy of *insularismo,* that vague and not unpleasant sense of decadence, of Don Quixotism, of tropical *angst* and lassitude, that was a cultural pride of the Creoles of the upper classes of the island.

In the nineteenth century, the romantic poet José Gautier Benitez had written of the island "rising like Venus from the waves," as in an erotic reverie. "I feel like kissing/the sand of your shores!" he wrote. On so dreamlike an island, the poet thought, independence would come as in a dream. It would "conquer liberty" without a bloody conflict that was un-Puerto Rican. The island would not be a

. . . prophetic ship
armed in war, daring the hurricane,
conquering port and waves
and men, dauntless and brave;

but will be a peaceful, tiny boat
on the perfumed breeze. . . .

As if in reply to this dream Lola Rodríguez de Tio, the author of the national anthem *"La Borinqueña,"* wrote with angry compassion of "the sad souls who dream":

Is a country to be born
or a race to be raised
where hearts to offer
their blood are lacking?

The romantics had often been revolutionaries. But with a difference. In the reality of island life they were scions of the political hierarchy of colonialism who might plead with, or oppose, the policies of Spain and the United States as social equals—arguing for the autonomy and civil rights of the island as Roman Power y Giralt had, as the island's representative in the Cortes of Spain in 1813, and as Luis Muñoz Rivera had before the Congress of the United States in 1917. For they were not *jíbaros,* the outcasts of colonialist society, but were members of the elite, who knew the modes of political etiquette.

In the town of San Germán, as throughout the island, the tradition of social caste had long dominated the *independentistas.* One of the leading lawyers in that ancient town was an *independentista,* with "Marxist leanings," it was said, that were "so far left" the security police kept his office under surveillance. But the conservative lawyers for the local landowners and bankers laughed about "The Revolution of Don ———."

One of the provincial elite said: "If he and his *compañeros* ever have their revolution, we will settle matters amicably at the country club over cocktails."

So it was that an opponent of Juan Mari Bras, who thought his politics were "treasonous," could say nothing worse about the independence leader than "He was a gracious man. Now! he is not gracious!" He was a traitor to the elite not because he advocated independence or revolution, but because he no longer "respected" his social position as a lawyer. *That* was "unforgivable."

In the old days, the elite of the *independentistas* came from the old families. So did the heroes and martyrs. The heirs of those landed *patrones* and plantation owners had inherited the Spanish love of honor—in *serenidad y benignidad,* serenity and graciousness—and a disdain for the "materialist culture" of the United States that went beyond politics. It was a heritage and conceit *a la española;* as the writer María Teresa Babin noted: "In the presence of love, pain and death we behave *a la española,* in the Spanish way, perhaps with a *slight tinge* of Indian or African origin" (my emphasis).

Now she said, "Each new Creole generation increases its love and affection of its Puerto Rican home, growing further away from its [Spanish] sources, to the point that the distant sparkle of the Hispanic origin fades away from the majority of the inhabitants."

Among the young *independentistas* in tee-shirts and blue Levi's the "tinge" of their Borinqueño origin was not "slight." The sons and daughters of the poorest *jíbaros* in the squatters' huts of the cities, who had begun to attend the high schools and universities, and the first generation of workers in the Fomento factories, with the luminous Borinqueño faces of *indios* and *grifos,* held whatever *serenidad* was hidden in their souls behind the masks of *urbanizaciones.* Beneath the masks there was a new way of thinking.

They were neither *patrones* nor *peones;* they were neither Hispanic nor American; they were the modern Puertorriqueños. They had a pride in being themselves.

If their Hispanic origins had faded, the presence of their twentieth-century existence was psychedelically self-evident in the style of their clothing and beliefs. In the suburbs of San Juan and the *barrios* of New York, *benignidad* was more of a gracious memory than a day-to-day fact of life. Unlike the elderly *independentistas* who mourned yearly at the tomb of José de Diego, for a dead hero and a dead era, these youth were the spiritual contemporaries of Mick Jagger and Frantz Fanon, Roberto Clemente and Che Guevara, Marilyn Monroe and Bernadette Devlin. They had never known the *serenidad* of rural life. They were would-be revolutionaries who were attempting to combine independence and socialism in what Juan Mari Bras had called "an uniquely Puerto Rican style of revolution for national liberation."

"Once the independence movement was very romantic," said Ruben Berrios Martínez, the Puerto Rican Independence party leader. "It believed in romantic nationalism of the Simón Bolívar and George Washington type. It had no ideology. It had no organization among the common people. It had no scientific analysis of society.

"Now we have an ideology. And a scientific program for independence," Berrios said. "And socialism!"

The scion of an old family of the landed aristocracy, who had come to the island with "the exiles of the Bolívar Revolution of 1820," Berrios had been educated by the Jesuits and had graduated from Georgetown ("Where boys of good families go," he laughed) and Yale and Oxford. His "John Kennedy–like charisma" was enhanced by his boyish bravura, his oratorical brilliance and the innate charm of his *hacienda* upbringing. "My family was rich. Is not any more. But still preserves their old customs," he said. Four of his uncles on his father's side had been Senators from the Popular Democratic party of Governor Muñoz. "On my mother's side they belong to the Republican party, the statehood party of Governor Ferre." In the University of Puerto Rico, where he had been a professor of international law—which he had studied at Oxford—he had led his colleagues in reorganizing the elitist Independence party in a "politically scientific way" to appeal to the poor, the *jíbaros,* the squatters, the youth, the factory workers, the outcasts of society, with a program of "democratic socialism."

In the past, "all independence movements were just that," commented former Governor Roberto Sánchez Vilella. "They did not have well-defined social and economic programs. Now, for the first time, we see them working for a socialist republic."

Berrios pondered that thought: "The struggle for independence of the nineteenth century and the struggle for socialism of the twentieth century have joined here in Puerto Rico. We have been waiting for the right moment in history. The moment has come."

"Yes," Berrios said, grinning, "I am a traitor to my class."

Pedro Albizu Campos—"When Tyranny Is Law, Revolution Is Order!"

On sunny Palm Sunday afternoon, a young Puerto Rican dragged his dying body over the hot pavement of a Ponce street. It was March 21, 1937. Summoning all his strength, he reached the sidewalk. His finger moistened in his blood, he wrote:

¡Viva la República!
¡Abajo los asesinos!

Long Live the Republic!
Down with the assassins!

He was one of 21 [people] who were dying at this same moment. His name was Bolívar: Bolívar Marquez. The coincidence of names evokes Neruda's poem:

I met Bolívar on a long morning.
"Father," I said, "Are you, or
are you not, or who are
you?"
And he said:
"I rise every hundred years
when the people awake."

Around Bolívar Marquez, rifle and machine gun fire (by the police) were wounding 150 more—men, women and children. This was the Ponce Massacre.

The words were written by the poet Juan Antonio Corretjer. In his eulogy to the dead, *Albizu Campos and the Ponce Massacre,* Corretjer told how members and adherents of the Nationalist party had come from all over the island to parade on that Palm Sunday; as one survivor remembered, "We have a party there celebrating the freedom of the slave." It was to be a festive day. When the police and the soldiers opened fire, before the parade had even begun, the celebrants and passers-by fell by the hundreds on the bloodied pavement between the Josefina Convent and the Protestant church on the corner of Marina Street. Everyone within sight was a target of the uniformed machine gunners.

A young man strolling down Jobos Street saw a policeman come toward him, gun in hand. He cried, "I am not a Nationalist! I am a National Guard! I am—" His death silenced his cries. José Delgado was his name. He was a member of the National Guard, who that very morning had been drilling with his regiment a few streets away.

His death was typical. The socialite Don Luis Sánchez Frasqueri, the father of the Governor-to-be, Roberto Sánchez Vilella, had parked his car on the next street in time to prevent the police from killing one man but not another, whose corpse was "filled with holes." The dying man had begun to write the word "VALOR"—"courage"—in his own blood on the sidewalk, but was able to write no more than "VAL" before the blood had obliterated his word. The father of the Governor had witnessed this.

Who was responsible? In Berlin, in Rome, in Tokyo, the propagandists of the Axis powers chortled at the "hypocrisy" of the democracies.

In an editorial a few days later, the New York *Post* reflected on the mood of dismay and disbelief that had swept through the Americas: "We expect Congress to make an independent investigation of the increasing unrest in Puerto Rico. The suppression of the Nationalist Party seems to become bloodier. . . . If Puerto Rico wants independence our answer should be to grant it. To answer her demand with machine guns is dishonorable for a people who love the memory of [their] own seditious nationalists of 1776."

Congress did not act. The American Civil Liberties Union (ACLU) did. Led by its respected lawyers Arthur Garfield Hays and

Roger Baldwin, after a lengthy investigation the civil liberties body concluded the "Ponce riot" had indeed been a "Ponce massacre," that had been planned by the government. The report of the ACLU, of which the Secretary of the Interior, Harold Ickes, was an officer, reluctantly placed the blame for the massacre directly at the door of the Governor of Puerto Rico, General Blanton Winship, who had been appointed by President Roosevelt and who served under Secretary Ickes.

"So the President of the United States ordered General Winship to make the massacre in Ponce just to make an example and stop our movement for independence," exclaimed one incredulous Nationalist leader. It was more, Corretjer thought, than one of the most brutal assassinations of innocents in the history of colonial government on the island. On that day, in some hearts, the hope for a bloodless path to independence ended.

"Apparently, all was darkness," Corretjer wrote. "In political life, what is real is often not visible. The doors of history were opening wider for what was, and has been, the core of Albizu Campos' life: the independence of Puerto Rico."

Seven years before, in 1930, Don Pedro Albizu Campos had come home to the island after his years of study at Harvard and service in the U.S. Army. The Nationalist party had "disintegrated" into a "debating club" led by its older intellectuals. At a conference in the spring of that year, Don Pedro, with the younger Nationalistas, captured the leadership of the party and proclaimed that henceforth it was a "revolutionary vanguard" of a yet nonexistent "powerful mass movement." He was elected its new president.

A few words have to be said of the nature of this man. He was small, delicate in body and manner. But his eyes were burning stones, his high cheekbones seemed carved of dark rock, hard as obsidian and unbending. It was said that his voice was as fiery as his words, for Don Pedro had none of the calm gifts of persuasion; when he spoke, his words were like electric shocks—jarring, accusing, and unforgiving.

The memories of his friend and long-time intimate, Juan Antonio Corretjer, tell something of the kind of man he was:

Pedro Albizu Campos was born at *Barrio de Tenerias,* a rural area in the neighborhood of Ponce, on "the Day of Saint Peter and Saint Paul," as he was fond of repeating, in 1891. He was seven years old when the U.S. invaders went through his native city, late in July, 1898.

He received his early education in the public schools of Ponce, up to high school. At the time a scholarship offered to the brilliant teenager by the *Logia Aurora* [Ponce's Free Masons] enabled him to go to college at the University of Vermont.

It was during his studies at Vermont that two Harvard professors, while teaching a summer course there, took note of his talents. Because his scholarship did not cover his full college education, the Harvard professors got him a small job at Cambridge, explaining to him it would be easier for him to advance his studies in the Harvard environment. . . .

He graduated from Harvard's College of Sciences and Letters and the Harvard Law School.

It was in Harvard that two powerful influences in his life developed: his conversion to Catholicism . . . and Irish nationalism. A Catholic priest, Father Ryan, appears to have been his guide to communion; while a Catalonian sage, an astronomer that was for many years to be the director of the Ebro Observatory, Father Luis Rodes, apparently gave him the peculiar clue to combine faith and science, mysticism and common sense. The Irish rebellion, during this period, further raised the prestige of Catholicism; since, in Ireland, at least, it was an oppressed church and appeared to favor national revolution.

At the outbreak of the First World War, he joined the Harvard Cadet Corps. . . . As a commissioned officer, Albizu asked to serve with Puerto Rican troops. . . .

So, as he came back to Puerto Rico after the war, and after graduation from Harvard, all the elements combining the personality he was to project into Puerto Rican history were present: the blend of Catholicism and patriotism, mysticism and self-sacrifice, typical of Irish nationalism.

One year after the homecoming of Don Pedro, in 1931, Don Luis Muñoz Marín had returned to the island. He, too, found the political situation had "disintegrated." The Liberal party, led by his father's old Unionist colleague Antonio Barcelo, was so weakened that it was proposed that even the word "independence" be dropped from its platform. In anger, the young Don Luis threatened that if the Liberals did so he would vote for the Nationalist party of Albizu, though he disagreed with what he termed the "narrow, single-minded" belief in independence or nothing. The threat was a back-handed recognition that the revitalized Nationalist party had come to symbolize an alternative for those who believed in independence.

In its political beginnings the Nationalist party had been the spokesman for many of the island's leading statesmen and patriots of the post–World War I era. These men had often sought accommodation with the United States, whose democratic ideals they deeply admired. But the colonial wartime policies of Washington were arbitrary and authoritarian: the island was in effect a military protectorate, ruled by military men in the guise of civil governors under the War Department—as it remained until 1934. In a sense, these military men were responsible for the founding of the Nationalist party.

One of the younger leaders of the Nationalists, Carlos Feliciano, put it harshly: "The United States government had a military government there [in Puerto Rico]. In a violent way they break in there. In a violent way they break all kinds of our laws there. So the only way to fight [military] violence like that was with violence. This was the only way."

Love of quiet debate was not one of the traits of the military governors. Nor was constitutional democracy. They crassly misapplied, and misunderstood, the colonial directives from Washington, that were stringent enough to begin with. One blatant example of this was the imprisonment of Santiago Iglesias Pantín. In 1901 the Socialist party and labor leader had gone to Washington to meet with Samuel Gompers, the AFL president, who introduced him to President McKinley at the White House. Encouraged by this cordial reception, Iglesias returned to the island hopeful of organizing the sugar workers into unions with governmental approval, or at least sympathy. He was promptly arrested by the Military Governor and sentenced to three years, four months, and seventeen days in jail for violating an imperial *Spanish law* that declared the organizing of Puerto Ricans into labor unions to be a criminal act!

Not until a lengthy campaign, led by Luis Muñoz Rivera, was the labor leader freed. Theodore Roosevelt, upon being elected to the presidency, convinced the Congress to repeal the sentence and end the use of Spanish laws, much to the displeasure of the military.

In World War I, the enforced U.S. citizenship for Puerto Ricans, decreed by the wartime Jones Act, "a military necessity," further threatened the peaceful relations between the two countries—as Luis Muñoz Rivera had warned Congress it would. He was ignored. In 1917 the majority of the Puerto Rican House of Representatives, convened under the Jones Act, requested the law be repealed. They, too, were ignored. Feliciano said: "They give us what they call United States citizenship. They don't give us this because we have beautiful faces. No! They give us this because they [were] already planning the first war and they want Puerto Ricans [to] fight in that war. We repeal this law. They impose it anyway. They force us to accept it."

Some of the leaders of the old Unionist party acquiesced. Some were as outraged as Muñoz Rivera had been. "The compromise entered into by the Unionists [after the death of Muñoz Rivera], to the detriment of their original ideals, led to the formation of the Nationalist party," the historian Federico Ribes Tovar wrote. Feliciano noted: "In 1920, the Unionists took away from the platform the issue of independence. And they split the party. From that split came the Nationalist party."

The Partido Nacionalista was established on September 17, 1922. The Nationalists were often condemned later as an aberrant group of political malcontents and "extremists," but in their origins there was no justice for such an accusation; the party was created, and built, for the political and intellectual leaders of the island, who voiced the independence sentiment and style of their time. Its founders included the distinguished lawyer and writer José Coll y Cuchi, editor of *Las Antillas,* and son of the then president of the House of Representatives, Don Cayetano Coll y Toste. One of its early presidents was José S. Alegría, the writer and journalist who at the time headed the Society of Publishers, father of Ricardo Alegría, director of the Institute of Puerto Rican Culture. Among its members were the revered writers Angel M. Villamil, Francisco Matos Paoli, and Juan Antonio Corretjer. Its vice president was Don Pedro Albizu Campos.

In the Depression years the strength of the Nationalists grew, led by Don Pedro. "*The majority* of Puerto Rican voters are now committed to independence," the New Deal planner Earl P. Hanson wrote in 1936. But the colonialism of the time was so rigid and undemocratic, that as the Puerto Rican Reconstruction Administration official said, "a single sugar company . . . can exercise more political power in Washington to *maintain* the status quo, than can the entire island to *alter* it" (emphasis in original).

And so Don Pedro Albizu Campos turned his ideological wrath on the sugar companies, hoping to cripple them with strikes and neutralize their power. Under his leadership the Nationalists organized the Asociación de Colonos de Canas, the Association of Cane Planters, the small sugar farmers, in 1932. By 1933 the cane fields were swept by "spontaneous" *huelgas*. In January, 1934, the cane workers in the sugar *central* of Fajardo went on strike, rejecting their AFL union and publicly asking that Don Pedro lead them. He did. The romantic "mystic patriot" from Harvard found himself chosen by the *jíbaros* and *agregados, colonos* and mill hands as their savior; he was no longer a visionary intellectual, but a "workers' revolutionary," the "Puerto Rican Zapata."

To regain their dignity as men, he told the *jíbaros,* they had to "act like men." "Imperialism of the Yankee has caused us to despise ourselves," Don Pedro said. "From landlords it has transformed us into *peones;* from *peones* into beggars condemned to death."

"Nationalism is the only salvation," he had said in 1932, "because it revives in each of us the conscience of a free man, for whom dignity is without price, and who cannot understand why he should not have the right to control the destinies of his children and his country. . . . Puerto Rico represents a picture of a shipwreck of the most prized human values: honor, patriotism, sacrifice." More than a mere strike, he demanded the "restitution of man."

In the offices of the sugar companies there was a wave of hysteria. At Christmastime, as the strike began, the Citizens Committee of One Thousand to Preserve Law and Order was formed. It cabled President Roosevelt: "State of actual anarchy exists. Towns in state of siege. Police impotent. Business paralyzed." The Fajardo Sugar Company's vice president and manager, Jorge Bird Arias, urgently wired the Secretary of War: "Existing conditions, both economic and political, demand an exceptionally good, *strong,* and capable man." In the War Department there were many who agreed with both the urgency and nature of the demand. The former Military Governor of Puerto Rico, Colonel James Beverly, a "Texas sugar corporation lawyer," sent a memo to his friend General Cox:

"I strongly favor an ex-army officer for the next governor . . . [to be] appointed at once, one who has sufficient experience . . . and one who has the courage to do his duty whether it is popular or not. Is not General Winship available for a position of this kind?"

The "strong man" was found. On January 1, 1934, the military recommendation of Colonel Beverly was dispatched—the day that the Fajardo strike began. On the twelfth night of the sugar strike, the twelfth of January, on the advice of the War Department President Roosevelt appointed as the new Governor General Blanton Winship, later to be accused of being instrumental in planning the Ponce massacre. The retired Army General was a Southern bourbon "who regarded the island as an extensive Southern plantation with the sugar men as his foremen and the people as good or bad folks" depending on whether they worked "without complaint"—the comment of a Puerto Rican leader quoted by Governor Tugwell. To Winship the bad folk were the Nationalists. He treated them as severely as rebellious slaves, and he set about to destroy their independence movement.

In 1935 the police of San Juan, under the command of Colonel E. Francis Riggs, a counterinsurgency expert who as Chief of Police had "semimilitarized" the local officers, invaded a political meeting at the university and publicly "executed" five leaders of the Nationalist party. One year later two young Nationalists "executed" Colonel Riggs, while he was on his way to church. The police then beat the youths to death.

All that year, and the next, the guerrilla warfare went on. In self-defense, and to prepare for the "patriotic revolution," Don Pedro ordered his youthful followers to form a uniformed and armed Cadet Corps that he was to model upon the Harvard Cadet Corps he had belonged to and the Irish Republican Army.

"For the strong to hear the weak their ears have to be opened with bullets," Don Pedro said. "The motherland's right to independence is not open to discussion. And if it is to be discussed—it will be by bullets!"

The journey from a political strike to guerrilla warfare had been abrupt but not unexpected. It was the path traveled by reformers who became revolutionaries in every colonial country when faced with military opposition. Nor was it an unwelcome path to Don Pedro; had his beloved Irish rebels done less, and did not his absolutist Catholicism demand as much? At the funeral of the martyred murderers of Colonel Riggs—Hiram Rosado and Elias Beauchamp—Don Pedro offered the eloquent rationale for what was to come. He held their "precious ashes" in his hand. And he cried to the mourners:

"A tyrant has fallen, who was named Colonel Riggs, whom may Heaven forgive for the crimes he committed in Puerto Rico. We say this without hatred, nor rancor, but with the purest Christian certitude, as if we looked him straight in the eyes, as we did that day in El Escambron [where he fell]. The murder [at the university] at Río Piedras was his work, and his guilt in that slaying [of our leaders] is shared by a number of misbegotten Puerto Ricans. Responsible, together with them, is General Blanton Winship, who occupies La Fortaleza. Cold-blooded murder, to perpetuate murder as a method of government, is being carried out by the entire police force. . . .

"In this case, the police, under the command of General Winship committed a murder worse than those of the gangsters of Chicago. Worse! for the gangsters have a code of honor and do not kill a kidnaped man. General Winship has based his policy on the suppression of the laws, the courts, the attorneys, and the judges. For what need is there of such officials when, with a half-dozen brigands, armed with machine guns, with an army at his beck and call, with a fleet, and with a tyrannical government that dispenses justice in the name of foreign despotism, they can murder, at police headquarters, all who are taken there?

"There are no laws, no courts! Nothing! Tyranny is not interested in any of that." And yet, Don Pedro said, General Winship "is doing us a supreme favor. They can kill Albizu Campos. They can kill ten thousand Nationalists. A million Puerto Ricans rise up. For the surest and fastest way to recreate a proud and patriotic nation is for the Yanqui government to continue its 'school for murder.' "

It was in this atmosphere that the Ponce massacre happened. On March 14, 1937, the Nationalist Committee of Ponce notified the city officials that they wished to hold a parade on Palm Sunday. On March 15 Mayor José Tormos Diego granted permission, a formality under the law. On March 19 Colonel Orbeta, the Insular Chief of Police, came to Ponce "to study the situation"; the Colonel was a Spaniard whose brother-in-law, Dionisio Trigo, was Generalisimo Francisco Franco's representative on the island for the Falangist party. (Later, when Trigo died in Berlin, his body was given a Nazi Luftwaffe escort to Madrid.) On March 20 Colonel Orbeta reported to General Winship in San Juan. The Governor ordered the parade halted. He sent the Colonel back to Ponce to carry out his order, using select squadrons of the "semimilitarized" police, armed with machine guns, to halt the paraders by whatever means he thought would be "most effective."

On Good Friday, Father Orjales, a Catholic priest, intoned from his pulpit: "Centuries ago Jesus, the Son of Nazareth, was crucified by 'civic justice,' and in the streets of Puerto Rico 'civic justice' crucifies defenseless children, men, and women." The passions of that Easter Week have not yet been forgotten. In churches throughout the island candles are lit for the dead by thousands who never knew them, and do not agree with them.

In spite of a secret Interior Department report (the McCaleb Investigation), which like the report of the ACLU placed the blame for the mass murder on the military tactics of General Winship, neither Secretary of Interior Ickes nor President Roosevelt removed him from office. General Winship ordered the survivors indicted for murder. Rather than obey this surrealist command, the District Attorney of Ponce, R. V. Pérez Marchand, resigned. And yet within one year the government had arrested, convicted, and imprisoned nearly all of the leading *independentistas* in the Nationalist party. The party was all but destroyed. The Cadet Corps dispersed. One of those who escaped imprisonment—many were sentenced to life terms—estimated that his jailed *compañeros* "numbered in the hundreds, maybe thousands."

Almost all were eventually released or pardoned, or vanished.

It was surreal that Don Pedro Albizu Campos was imprisoned twice in federal penitentiaries, convicted of conspiracy to overthrow the government of the United States; for his Cadet Corps was neither capable of, nor created for, such political fantasies. The rebellions of his followers were as much moral as military acts to Don Pedro. He envisioned the uprisings as purgations of the soul, acts of exorcism by which the enslaved mentality of a colonial people might be ennobled and freed. If he had been a priest urging an ordeal of religious faith by fire, rather than a politician urging a revolution of sacrifice by gunfire, he might have been better understood.

"Precious ashes [of the dead martyrs] bear witness to the immortality of Puerto Rico," he said. "They told us that courage was dead in our land. And when they said that courage was dead, they then condemned our motherland to slavery. But, gentlemen, the lie has been given to the accusation that we Puerto Ricans, as a people, are docile cowards."

The myth of docility had been propagated for centuries; it was believed by islander and non-islander alike. It was, after all, comforting to imagine a lovely and tranquil island in the midst of a cruel, war-ravaged, tumultuous world; the "Blessed Isle" of gentle and "child-like" people of peace. Puerto Rico was "never able to organize a revolutionary struggle for freedom," said Oscar Lewis in *La Vida;* the men did not have the *machismo* of "Mexican men," and the "absence" of a "great revolutionary tradition" cursed, or blessed, the people with docility. "Puerto Rico never fought for its independence except for a two-day skirmish at Lares in 1868," Arthur Liebman, a Harvard University research fellow and specialist in the island's struggles, wrote in an essay. There was, Liebman thought, a "weak sense of national identity." "Puerto Rico *never unfurled* the banner of revolution," the caustic Luis Muñoz Rivera had told the Congress of the United States in 1917. "What bitter irony!" His words voiced a greater irony than the Congress understood.

For the history of the "gentle" island had been the history of rebellions. The Indians had attacked the Conquistadors of Spain in 1511 to begin *their* wars of independence; since that time the island had been torn by unending uprisings and revolts. The Borinquén Indians attacked the Spaniards again in 1513, and in 1520, and in 1526, and in 1530. Soon after that the islanders, joined by runaway African slaves in the mountains, formed guerrilla bands that raided and ruined the European settlements through that century and the next, attempting to drive the invaders into the sea. In 1527 the earliest of the large-scale slave revolts occurred on the island. The Blacks' wars of independence, chronicled by Dr. Díaz Soler in his *Historia de la Esclavitúd negra en Puerto Rico, 1493 to 1890,* were to continue unceasingly for four centuries. All these native and slave rebellions were in fact wars of independence, not only for the Indian and African, but for the island itself.

Carlos Feliciano spoke of this history in his own way: "The truth is that they push through the eyes and through the ears of the people a lie. That the Puerto Ricans never fight for independence. That we were 'docile.' Because the truth is that the Puerto Rican people start the war against imperialism hundreds of years before. First, the Indians fight for their independence against Spain. And then the black slaves fight for their independence against Spain. You know, the slaves, the black people, the Indians and the *jíbaros* go in rebellion against Spain hundreds of times.

"The struggle for independence begin when Columbus landed. And the first Indian fight against him," said Feliciano.

Once the Puertorriqueños' modern national identity was formed and proclaimed in the nineteenth century, the rebellions became island-wide. In the early 1800s the slave rebellions had a great deal to do with the nature of the military regimes imposed by Spain. And the revolts of the *jíbaros,* both of overt and passive resistance, were now eulogized, and often led, by the Creole intellectuals. Even the garrison revolts of the Spanish troops reflected the fight for independence. In 1835 the Puerto Rican liberals joined with the Granada Regiment in San Juan in an unsuccessful revolution aimed at island autonomy. When the "Revolt of the Sergeants" erupted again, in 1838, its aim was to proclaim a Republic of Puerto Rico. Similarly, the "Mutiny of Artillery Men" in 1867, which preceded the Grito de Lares by one year, had strong overtones of the fight for independence, for it was preceded by the Betances "Call to Arms" in 1862, and once again in 1865.

As late as 1901, when "Premier" Luis Muñoz Rivera was threatened with death by pro-American mobs, he was secretly visited by *independentista* leaders who told him that a guerrilla army of eight thousand *jíbaros* was waiting "to march on San Juan" to defend him. Muñoz refused the offer. "There must not be bloodshed," he said. In the mountains the *jíbaros* waited for another day and another leader.

Still, the legend of the docile and submissive *jíbaros* persisted. It seemed more a historical wish than a historical fact on the strife-torn island.

"This is a legend that frightened men have used to traffic with the life of the nation," said Don Pedro Albizu Campos. "Our people is an heroic people. Our people is courageous."

Not by rhetoric but by "sacrifice" he sought to deny the curse of the myth of docility. "He is not even a man," he said of any man who would not "give his life to the motherland." In the "Byronic romanticism" of the Nationalists' "Revolution of 1950" Don Pedro expressed his belief in sacrificial death—"dying for her," the motherland—as an act of absolution, as the "path to immortality," that was inevitable, self-evident to anyone with his military training. But the revolt was not planned to triumph. His was the sacrifice of a John Brown, not the triumph of a Lenin.

Love of one's country was not an ideology. It was a passion. "As a woman is loved, so the motherland must be loved, spiritually and physically," Don Pedro said. "Whoever is not ashamed when she is violated is no patriot. He is not even a man." For, he taught his young Cadets, "The motherland is founded on the emulation of heroism. She belongs to no one. Not even to the patriots. She belongs only to those who have won her by dying for her." His was the violence of a lover who vowed to die, not live, for his beloved. "Before they can take our country, they will have to take our lives," he said.

In telling how the revolution began and ended, Carlos Feliciano gave flesh to these ideas. He fought as heroically as anyone. As a lieutenant in the Cadet Corps he knew the Nationalist party was "not ready" for the revolution. The fighting had been provoked by the government of Don Luis Muñoz Marín, he said. Using the Smith Act enacted by the United States Congress, "They want to break down the Nationalist party. They use this unconstitutional act. They start arresting our brothers," Feliciano said. "On that morning, October 30 [1950], about 10 o'clock, they break in the house of our brother, Muniz, the [Nationalist] leader of Ponce. He dropped down and he started shooting. Many of the Nationalists joined him. You know, they speak about this on the radio. So we decided to fight. And the revolution started.

"After that, in Jayuya, in Utuado, in Arecibo, in Río Piedras, in San Juan, in Mayagüez, in many other towns we begin to fight. It's true the Lares revolution was big; but that was just in Lares. This time, in a dozen towns we start the real struggle for independence and open revolution.

"We free Jayuya at that time. The police run away, you know. They can't fight us. But the United States Army was another thing.

They use the 296th Infantry against us, that they used in Korea, after that. Five thousand soldiers! They use the tanks, the airplanes, the bombs, the bazookas. They have the machines. They have everything. Everything! We have just a few rifles and 45s. So in the end they take back what we win. They arrest Albizu Campos and our brothers and sisters. They arrest hundreds.

"I was arrested too, in my town, for the Smith Act. After one month, they indict me for 'conspiracy,' " he said laughing, "to overthrow the government of the United States, but not *in* the United States. In Puerto Rico!"

Feliciano had spoken proudly. He seemed less concerned with the defeat of the revolution than with the nature of his act of "sacrifice," of his *macho,* of his patriotism.

The uprising in the hills was a heroic and archaic event. In a time of mechanized warfare the *jíbaros* with their *machetes* and rifles were no more than Roman gladiators who fought futilely against "the machines" of the Army and Air Force of a technological state. One man in Jayuya sorrowed for his cowardice of that day: "I wanted to go into the plaza and fight," he lamented twenty years later. "But how could I fight a tank. With what? With my bare hands? With my *machete?* With my *grito?* No! with my death!"

In the countryside the uprising of the peons was superseded by the terrorism of displaced peons in the city streets. The urban guerrilla tactics of the Cadet Corps preceded those of Uruguay's Tupamaros and Palestine's Al Fatah by more than a generation. Unlikely as it seemed, in this form of resistance by rural-type armed groups within the cities Puerto Rico offered an unexpected "model" to Latin America and the dispossessed peasants and tribal people of the colonial world.

Governor Muñoz thought the armed *jíbaros* of Don Pedro represented a "lunatic quirk" in politics. In the hearings of the Status Commission in San Juan in the summer of 1965, there occurred this curious conversation between an advocate of statehood, Abidam Archilla, and the former Governor of the Commonwealth of Puerto Rico:

MUÑOZ: *Didn't you hear that some Nationalists drove into La Fortaleza and shot* [*at*] *me 13 years ago? Didn't you hear that they drove to the Blair House and shot* [*at*] *President Truman?*
ARCHILLA: *Oh, yes.*
MUÑOZ: *Thirteen years ago.*
ARCHILLA: *Oh, yes.*
MUÑOZ: *Well, this is nothing new in Puerto Rico. It's just a minority lunatic quirk with no influence on the politics and the people of Puerto Rico. . . . The unpeaceful are a very little group. . . . The number is negligible.*

A "madman," Don Pedro Albizu Campos was a "fanatical genius," whose ideas were based on "political megalomania" and "perverted idealism," Gordon Lewis was later to write. The Nationalist leader was "interested not so much in a genuine struggle for independence as in fomenting a neo-fascist attack upon democracy itself," Lewis said. Although sympathetic to the *independentistas,* the writer nevertheless condemned Don Pedro as the leader of a "Creole-Fascist-Nationalist movement," guided simply by his "virulent hatred of the Americans."

Carlos Feliciano thought such judgments absurd. He had known Don Pedro intimately. They had been imprisoned together after the "Revolution of 1950."

"In La Princessa, the prison in San Juan under the city wall near La Fortaleza, I have the honor, the privilege, to live with Albizu Campos in the same cell," Feliciano said. "Here we live together for several months, like brothers.

"Oh, he was a beautiful man. He was the most beautiful man I ever know. Never in my life I see a man like Albizu Campos. You know, his sister used to come to the prison, once or twice a week, to bring him things. He used to give them away to people in the prison. Nothing he owned. Nothing he wanted. Nothing belonged to him. One day the prisoners, they make a party for Albizu Campos with music and things like that. 'No!' he said. 'This party is not for Albizu Campos. This party is for everyone here.' I don't have words to say how Albizu Campos was. Never I saw a man like that.

"A sweet man," Feliciano said. "He was something sweet. There was something sweet inside him.

"If I tell you this, you won't believe it. But in the five years I was in prison, I never was so free as the time I spent with Albizu Campos. I *feel* free. That was the truth."

The frail revolutionary leader grew ill in prison. Don Pedro was taut and highly tense. In his more than a decade of imprisonment, in federal penitentiaries and prison hospitals, his health deteriorated. For years the fiery-tongued Nationalist had accused the prison authorities of trying to murder him by electric shock and radiation treatments; he was said to be "hallucinating" and ranting in "mental delirium."

His cellmate remembered how he had seen Don Pedro tortured in La Princessa prison. "They kill him there. They burn him," Carlos Feliciano said. "I see this. I see Don Pedro Albizu Campos, half his chest, his arm, his leg, his back, all burned. Complete. All his body was burned. Complete. Swollen up, all his body. We put towels and cold water on to relieve his pain, because he was very bad burned. That's what I saw. We have pictures of this.

"In prison, three or four doctors examine him. They give different kinds information about what he have. But they all agreed that he was treated with some kind of radioactivity. Like cobalt or X-ray. He have the same burn as people who have cancer, and are treated with radioactivity, or X-ray. This is a thing we make public at the time. This is a thing we never want to speak of too much, because this is too much for the mind of some people. But the truth is what I saw."

At Christmastime, 1964, Don Luis pardoned Don Pedro. The man he once had threatened to vote for as the symbol of independence was dying. He suffered a cerebral thrombosis that caused partial paralysis, loss of speech and his senses. On the twenty-first of April, 1965, he died and a leading newspaper in San Juan, *El Imparcial,* said in a eulogy:

> Albizu Campos, like many of the great men of history, always moved by highest passions and most beautiful ideals, one of which: the inde-

pendence of his country Puerto Rico, he defended with patriotic intransigence that won him international renown. If he had been born at the beginning of the XIX Century, instead of its close, his dynamism and his efforts, his combative energy and his selfless and impassioned devotion to the cause would have produced the Republic of Puerto Rico, and he would have been its indisputable national hero in the sublime struggle to complete the work of Simón Bolívar.

But Don Pedro had written his own eulogy:

> Courage is all that makes it possible for a man to step firmly and calmly through the shadows of death; and it is when a man passes serenely through the shadows of death that he enters upon immortality.
>
> It had been my wish to go to my grave untainted with gold, which corrupts men, and unstained with the blood of my fellow man; but independence, like every supreme good, demands the sacrifice of the wisest, the most noble, and the most pure of the nation.

So the man died, and the legend was born.

17

The Making of a Martyr

On the crisp and bright afternoon of an autumn day—just past two o'clock on the thirty-first of October, 1950—two young Puerto Rican revolutionaries, with guns drawn, attacked the official residence of the President of the United States, Harry Truman. The newspapers reported the ensuing gun battle on the streets of Washington, D.C., in doomsday-size black headlines:

ASSASSINATION ATTEMPT
ON PRESIDENT TRUMAN!

An unsigned document given to me twenty years later tells the personal story of these two young revolutionaries. One died that day. One was imprisoned for life. No one can say, for sure, who wrote this description of the bloody events of that day nor if it is wholly true, but the story has the emotions and the details of reality. It is a story that has never, to my knowledge, been told before:

October 30, 1950. Nationalist rebellion in Puerto Rico. Early that morning the radio stations in New York begin to transmit news of armed confrontations between the Nationalists groups and police. The first newscasts bring rumors, unconfirmed news. As the day goes on the number of reported incidents grow, there are interruptions in communications between New York and Puerto Rico, the fragmentary reports began to be completed. The afternoon papers carried descriptions of the events; in the streets the Puerto Ricans began to discuss and comment on the events;

by nightfall it is obvious that the Nationalists have raised arms against the yankee empire.

Two Puerto Rican patriots, members of the Nationalist Party Directive in New York, had previously made an agreement: in case of any incidents occurring in Puerto Rico, they would meet on the bridge at Willis Avenue, the bridge connecting the Bronx and Manhattan. That night they met.

For a long time they discussed the events occurring in Puerto Rico that day. During the discussion they agreed on the necessity of placing the event in Puerto Rico in international terms. It was necessary to show that the occurrences in Puerto Rico were not a "riot," or local problem; that it was the confrontation between the oppressed people of a nation against the oppressor. Therefore it was urgent to place the act in its correct historical and international context. The two patriots decided that the most effective way of doing so was by taking the struggle to the president of the oppressor's government, the residence of the president of the U.S. In no instance did they think of killing the president. Their objective was to use the symbol of the presidential house as a stepping stone to an international forum.

In their action, the two Puerto Rican patriots knew they would die. Oscar Collazo and Griselio Torresola understood that when it comes to the life or death of their nation they must also fight in terms of life or death.

That night they separated to complete the details of the trip to Washington. Griselio Torresola was in charge of getting the weapons. That night they said goodbye to their families.

Who were these patriots?

Oscar Collazo was born on January 20, 1914, on a coffee plantation outside the town of Manatí. He was the youngest of 14 children. His childhood was spent in Ciales, Jayuya, and Manatí. At the age of 13 he attends a conference given by Juan Antonio Corretjer during the celebration of José de Diego's birthday. Corretjer speaks eloquently about the love of country, the history of great Puerto Ricans and the Antillean heroes. The speech awakened in Oscar a love for his country and for his people; love that was to stay within him all his life and was his strongest point. At 17 he goes to San Juan to participate in a rally with the Nationalist Party at the Baldority de Castro Plaza. There he listens to the words of Don Pedro Albizu Campos. The next day he joins the Cadet Corps of the Nationalist Party. His youth was spent in San Juan, Ciales, Manatí, and Jayuya, where he meets the Torresola family. For his dedicated work and his leadership qualities he is promoted to Lieutenant in [the] Cadet Corps. The economic situation in Puerto Rico forces him to come to the United States. The Ponce Massacre finds him aboard a ship at high sea, on board the ship *Borinquén*. In 1943, he becomes president of the Nationalist Party Directive here in New York. During all this time and up to 1950, Oscar distinguished himself in the party for his dedication to work and love of his family.

The life of Griselio Torresola is very similar to that of Oscar Collazo. He is born in Jayuya in 1925, youngest of a family that would distinguish itself for its love of country and dedication to work. At a very young age he joins the Cadet Corps. At the age of 20 he was to come to the United States. Griselio was known for his firmness of character and faithfulness. In 1950 he was 25 years old.

That night both patriots silently said goodbye to their families. Not even their most intimate relatives knew of their plan, they did not want them in danger. Both families understood that the patriots were off to a very important mission. Griselio Torresola said goodbye to his wife; they had been married six months. Oscar Collazo said goodbye to his wife, but didn't say a word to his only daughter. The only thing he carried beside his clothing and money were guns and a picture of his daughter. They left their homes early in the morning knowing they would never return.

On October 31, 1950, Oscar and Griselio leave for Washington. They reached Washington where they stayed in the Harris Hotel under fictitious names. That night they familiarized themselves with the weapons and discussed the action that was to take place the next day. Griselio was an exceptional shooter. He was one of the better shooters in the Nationalist Party. Oscar knew how to use rifles but his knowledge of pistols was limited.

In the morning they had breakfast and walked around the town. They returned to their rooms and later left toward Blair House, temporary residence of President Truman. They took a taxi.

At about 2:15 they reached the vicinity of Blair House. So as not to call attention to themselves, they separated and approached Blair House from different directions. When Collazo was near the entrance hall he drew his pistol; he waited until the agent on duty turned to face him and then he shot. The pistol didn't fire.

In his rush to fire, he had forgotten to take the safety off. He took the safety off and fired. He wounded the agent in the knee. Oscar Collazo did not want to kill the man, he just wanted to put him out of action. Meanwhile, pistol in hand, Griselio was approaching from the west side of the entrance; he began to fire. A policeman fell mortally wounded, another fell with lesser wounds. No one knows who killed the policeman.

The American government has not presented evidence to this effect. On the policeman's body were found bullets from Griselio's gun and also bullets from a policeman's gun. It has never been said as to which bullet caused death.

Meanwhile, Oscar was maintaining a duel with another policeman. Torresola's bullets were spent, which gave a policeman time to aim and shoot him through the head. Oscar, fighting various policemen, was wounded in the chest and put out of combat. Collazo was arrested and taken to a hospital.

Never in their plans did they intend to kill the president. As it has been stated, Griselio was an exceptional shooter and it was a known fact that President Truman was to use the presidential residence as a base for an international act.

Griselio Torresola, dead, was accused of killing the policeman. Since it was impossible to punish a dead man, Oscar Collazo received all the weight of repression. He was sentenced to the electric chair. Meanwhile all his family had been arrested, interrogated and photographed. For more than a year his family was persecuted. Once Oscar was sentenced to die he was placed in a cell next to the electric chair. He was in that cell for two years. While he was there 14 people were executed. In his cell they installed a phone connected to the white house. At any time Oscar could call the president and plead for mercy, knowing it would be given. Oscar never pleaded clemency. A person of principles never pleads or kneels. Two years of torture and pressure, even his lawyers recommended that he ask for clemency.

The work of the Nationalist Party, the pressure and reaction on an international level forced the president to grant a stay of execution. Oscar was instead sentenced to life imprisonment. The U.S. government has offered Oscar the possibility of getting out of jail; all he has to do is sign a petition for probation. But Oscar Collazo has rejected this offer of probation. His is a political case. He is a political prisoner, a prisoner of war. The only way he will accept getting out is if the U.S. government grants amnesty to all Puerto Rican political prisoners. Oscar Collazo has repeatedly manifested his intentions and desires to participate in the political life of his people [once] he is out of jail. Oscar Collazo is part of his people and his country.

Griselio Torresola continues to [live] as Don Pedro said, "He has never been absent." To us he is a symbol of struggle, a revolutionary symbol.

[The poet, Juan Antonio] Corretjer, speaking of these two Nationalists, says: ". . . those that sacrifice themselves, those that turn their backs on the conveniences of life, that give their lives when at [their] peak, facing the enemy . . . that [turn] their backs on material things to go on a mission, surely not to return, as was done by Griselio Torresola and Oscar Collazo, they have not lost contact with reality, they have made contact with the weapons of the enemy, they have realized that the sacrifice of their lives is the love of the nation."

18

¿Qué Es Socialista?

The little balcony looked down on the quiet plaza. He nonchalantly pointed to where the machine guns had fired at his windows.

In the plaza of Río Piedras the pink-and-blue church was an ethereal fairytale castle. On benches old men played dominoes. A young woman walked by with a yellow silk umbrella. *Serenidad* was everywhere. There! He pointed to where the mobs had attempted to break down the door of his office. "These walls," he said, indicating the new paneling, "have twice been set fire to!"

"I may be assassinated at any time." He smiled faintly.

He stood on the balcony above the plaza like a *patrón* of an urban plantation. He was wearing an embroidered and pleated white shirt, informally opened at the neck in the old style of the island, but nonetheless there was a formality about him. As a few men did, very few men, he had a dignity within him. It was difficult to imagine him in the mountains in Army fatigues, leading a band of guerrillas, as had his friend Fidel Castro. In no way did he resemble the stereotype of the "revolutionary extremist" described in the newspapers.

"We are different," he mused, in reference to nothing in particular. "We are Latins. To be Latin is to be cultured, they say."

The calm and elegance of Juan Mari Bras had that graciousness of a gentler time, when the island had not been divided by the harsh, straight lines of highways and skyscrapers, and "class consciousness." And yet he was the leader, first, of the militant Movement for Independence, and now of the Puerto Rican Socialist party. He resembled a genteel don, a Marxist *patrón;* in the movement his followers called him Mari, in the way others said Kennedy.

Mari Bras was a man of grace. But not in his politics. His ideas were factual and direct and stolid; his oratory was unsubtle and simple, with little hint of irony or of humor. It may be this was the way he thought of "reaching the masses," as he repetitively urged his adherents; for as an intellectual and lawyer, his Marxism advocated a concise, if uninspired, "scientific analysis of society" as the path toward the "solution of its contradictions." He had faith in reason.

And yet there seemed to be a contradiction between the manner of the man and the logic of his politics. He was genial, not at all harsh; warmly courteous, not coolly abrasive; old-fashioned in tastes, not technologically modern; and sensitive to nuances he did not publicly voice.

Once he had mildly criticized a political group in New York that had supported him and which he supported. He grimaced: "They do not *act* like a Puerto Rican should."

What did he mean?

"Ah, they are not gracious."

In his poor office, he folded his hands in his lap and talked of death. He had the manner of an understanding teacher and the patience of a *padre*. He spoke of threats to his life, of students killed by the police on the university campus, of youths beaten bloody in the prisons, of hundreds of *independentistas* arrested on charges varying from "bombing plots" to smoking marijuana, of the houses and cars of sympathizers burned, of leaders shot at, of tens of thousands of *jíbaros* whose huts had been bulldozed, of villages set ablaze by "government orders." All of these were signs, he quietly said, of "the coming revolution."

"We are in a prerevolutionary situation," he said; "not exactly in a revolutionary situation yet."

In past years the independence movement had been provoked into "premature revolutions," he said. This was what happened to the Nationalists of Don Pedro Albizu Campos. "We will not be provoked. The provocations are an attempt to create a climate of hysteria. But we are calm. We have learned. Now we are deeply rooted throughout the island. If the government puts everyone in jail, or assassinates all of us, it will not stop us. Now it is too late for them.

"The independence movement is more massive today than it ever has been in history," he said. "Colonialism is no longer an abstraction. It is seen more easily, by more people, because of the growing contradictions between the imperialists in the United States and the people of Puerto Rico. So independence is no longer an abstract idea; it is real.

"Look at Culebra!" This was the little island of fishermen and farmers off the coast, where the U.S. Navy had bombarded the land and beaches every year with millions of shells, using the island as a target range. "Always there have been military and naval and nuclear bases in Puerto Rico. But in Culebra we have a situation where a whole community is menaced. It is impossible for the fishermen to go out and fish, because of the bombardment from the sea by the navies that maneuver there." The people of the island were up in arms. Even the government said, "It is opposed to the Navy. But every year the Navy says it will stop the bombardment and every year the bombardment of our island goes on," he said. "And that is how you, not we, demonstrate the need for independence.

"Imagine," said Mari Bras, "if we had a navy and used Central Park, on the island of Manhattan, as our target range!"

On Culebra pacifists and *independentistas* had built a chapel on the beach within range of the shelling. And in Puerto Rico there were endless protests and picket lines. So intense was public pressure that the then Governor Ferre, and Senate President Hernández Colón, secured promises from Washington that the naval bombardment of the island's pastures would cease. Secretary of Defense Melvin Laird personally assured the Governor by letter, in August, 1971, that the use of Culebra as a naval "practice range" would be halted by the end of 1972. The Pact of Culebra was signed.

Jubilant, then Governor Ferre used the promise all through his re-election campaign as evidence of the sincerity of the United States, and of his influence with his "good friend" the President, Richard Nixon. When Ferre had lost the election, Washington reneged on its promises. Just four days before the bombardment of Culebra was to have halted, on December 27, 1972, Secretary of Defense Laird announced that the U.S. Navy would continue to use the island as a target until 1985!

The Pact of Culebra was a "farce and betrayal," charged one *independentista*. It demonstrated "an absolute lack of respect for the people of Puerto Rico, a complete disregard of international law and utter ignorance of the most elementary principles of human fellowship," said Mari Bras. Once more the cry was heard, "Force the Navy not only out of Culebra but out of Puerto Rico."

In apologia, or as near to it as he could come, Secretary Laird promised the United States would reconsider its decision to renew the shelling of the island "as soon after 1985 as possible." By then the pastures of Culebra would be unfit for animals or men.

On the beaches of Los Pinones, lined by coconut palms and the blue sea, there was another island community "menaced by complete destruction by the imperialists," said Mari Bras. It was "one of the most beautiful of all our beaches," within sight of San Juan, where "the government has ceded [the beaches] to an American hotel corporation for a tourist complex. No one asked the Puerto Ricans who live there, who have lived there for hundreds of years. To the four hundred families on that, their ancestral beach, colonialism is not an abstraction. They understand it. We do not have to explain it."

Unfortunately, the *jíbaros* on the beaches of Los Pinones owned no deeds to their houses and lands. As the natives of the island they innocently, and historically, believed the earth was theirs simply because they lived on it, grew their crops, bore their children, raised their families, and buried their dead, as their ancestors "always have lived," for centuries. That traditional and Indian way of land tenure could not withstand the bulldozers of the government planners and tourist-complex operators.

"And this is happening everywhere throughout the island," said Mari Bras, "in endless ways, every day, to our people."

The suburbs and *supermercados* and factories and highways had dispossessed thousands upon thousands of these so-called "landless *jíbaros.*" From hundreds of *barrios* the rural by-products of industrial growth began the trek to the cities' slums. On the edges of garbage dumps and the sewage canals, along the polluted waterfronts, in the purgatory between the suburbs and the factories, the refugees built entire cities, where they lived freely as they had always lived, in the hills. "Squatters" the newspapers called them, for they did not pay rent as workers did, nor did they have mortgages, the membership cards of the middle class. No one knew how many Puertorriqueños lived this way.

One estimate was that 200,000 people lived in these homeless homes. But another expert thought they might number 300,000. The computers of the census could not count all of the homeless, jobless, nameless *jíbaros* whom Francisco Aponte Pérez, president of the Bar Association, had "legally" characterized as "the new landless urban peasants."

There soon were battles between the government and the *jíbaros.* Weren't they violating the property laws by building homes and living on lands that were not legally theirs? Hundreds of huts were bulldozed and burned every month. The eviction of the squatters of Villa Kennedy, a self-made village amid the palm trees near the beach of Bayamón, was so brutal it was condemned as "inhuman" by Governor Ferre; when the bulldozers were done, all that was left of the village was heaps of broken furniture and dolls. Ironically, the land of Villa Kennedy was reportedly owned by Governor Ferre's brother.

In Canóvanas, near San Juan, a dawn raid by "unidentified men" with police escorts razed and burned more than one thousand squatters' huts in a single day.

Socialistas of the new party of Mari Bras went to the squatters' huts to organize. The activists of Ruben Berrios's Independence party went too, with their lawyers and their new cry, *"¡Arriba de los Abajo!"*—"Arise! Those of the Bottom!" It was the first time since the Depression years of the early thirties that the intellectuals of the independence movement had offered the poor more than the rhetoric of patriotism.

"We tell them the land belongs to those who live on it. Not to those who own it," a young middle-class activist explained, "Puertorriqueñoizing Marx." She did not say "to those who work on it."

That was not a new idea to the *jíbaros*. That was the way they always had lived. A man lived in harmony with nature; he did not manipulate it, nor change it. The earth belonged to God. If the spirits of a man were in harmony with the earth, the trees, the *familia,* then God and nature would give him a good life. The ideas of tribalism and Marxism met, and joined, in the squatters' huts, though from different views of man and God.

In their mountain villages the *jíbaros* were never unemployed. Even when they were jobless. There was always something to do. A family to be cared for. A child to be loved. The chickens to be tended to. The crops to be picked. The *bohío* always needed repair. And if there was nothing else, there was the long walk to the plaza, where the problems of the world waited to be solved.

But in the squatters' huts of the city there was nothing for the *jíbaro* to do. He could not sit amid the bankers' secretaries, on their lunch hour, in the plaza. There was no plaza in Hato Rey.

The unemployed man was nobody. He was a statistic, at best. At worst he was treated as though he had some social disease by the social workers and welfare investigators and the newspaper editorialists. He had to eat the surplus foods grown by someone else. He was surplus, too. He could not grow his own crops. Like the tropical rains in the cement gutters of San Juan, he had no place to go but deeper into the urban sewers of society. He lived on his own sewage.

On the Martin Pena Channel, in the shadow of the glass skyscrapers of Hato Rey, the huts of the squatters clung to the banks of refuse. The huts on stilts were decayed and flimsy, perfumed by the stench of the sewage; a sweetly sickening odor of death. The water where the children played was ugly with feces and filth. If a child fell into the water, he would not drown even if he could not swim; they said: "The water is too thick with shit."

When the office girls of Hato Rey held their noses and complained, "It is like a cesspool in those *barrios,*" that was the literal truth.

"What [has] our progress cost us in human suffering?" lamented the journalist Luis Muñiz.

The poorest were poorer than ever before. In a time of industrial prosperity the penniless *jíbaro* was a pariah; he was an outcast, an embarrassment, to be displaced and discarded. His "impoverished reality" seemed like an accusation to the more affluent, who dared not "believe it really exists." Luis Muñiz chided the "progress intoxicated leaders" for ignoring not only the poor, but their own statistics. Since World War II poverty had increased faster than affluence, said Muñiz. The economic share of the top 20 percent of the people had risen from 50 to 55 percent of the island income, while the share of the poorest 20 percent had fallen from a pitiful 5 percent of the island's income to a pitiless 4 percent. Even the share of the new middle class had not risen, but had fallen, from 45 to 41 percent, since Operation Bootstrap had begun—according to the government's own surprising figure.

On the tropical "Island of Paradise" one-fourth of the people subsisted on handouts of surplus foods from the mainland. The neglect and ruin of the farms had forced 660,000 to 700,000 islanders onto a dole of imported beans, rice, and powdered milk. In the *barrios* the squatters' huts of the cities there were 325,000 refugee *jíbaros* on welfare. More than half of the hungry, it seemed, received no welfare at all.

And those who were paid by the government "for being poor"—in the early 1970s—received precisely $8.77 per month per person, if they had "dependent" children. If they were both poor and disabled, they received a little more—$13.38 a month. The blind and poor were rewarded the most, for they were given $13.53, blindness being worth 15 cents more than an ordinary disability.

The poor were doubly cursed by poverty and affluence. Prices of most foods imported from the mainland were higher on the island, while wages were lower than on the mainland. Incongruously, in the typical year of 1969 the Food Price Index was 125.5 in the United States, but was 145.9 in Puerto Rico. Beans, a staple of the diet, not to mention rice, milk, and fruit, were higher priced in the rural towns of the island than in New York.

In Utuado a *jíbaro* cynically remarked: "We survive because hunger has always been part of our diet."

"The myth of the Puerto Rican miracle" no longer enthralled these hungry and jobless *jíbaros,* who had been discarded by society, suggested Luis Muñiz. He wrote bitterly: "How much longer before [the people] face the reality of Puerto Rican poverty? How much longer do our political leaders feel they can fool us, and themselves, by ignoring our social problems and trying . . . to hide the brew so long as that brew doesn't boil? And how much longer are we going to act as a developed country when thousands of Puerto Ricans have never seen a doctor? . . ."

Mari Bras said: "The false illusion of progress" has been "limited to the well-being of a small clique of bureaucrats and servants of American capitalism. For at most it has enriched a minority of the middle class. The society of consumption which they enjoy they project in their propaganda to the United States, in their publicity, saying this is the reality of Puerto Rico, but it is the reality of a small minority. And the majority of the people never have tasted this consumption society.

"So it is not exactly a polarization of left and right we see on the island," he said. "It is a polarization of poor and rich."

Into that gap the *socialistas* and *independentistas* plunged, hoping to create a political crisis. Mari Bras said, "I think independence will come as a result of a crisis in the colonial structure." And so the *independentistas* turned to organizing the employed and unemployed *jíbaros.* The investment of American capital had built vast industries and a working class. By 1971 the Movement for Independence had proclaimed "The Year of the Worker." By 1972 several determined, hard-fought, politically-led strikes had shaken the island. In the *huelga de teléfonos,* the strike of the telephones, the violence—Mari Bras called it "militancy"—was so widespread it required three pages, single-spaced, to list all the disrupted and destroyed equipment. By 1973 the United Labor Movement, led by Boilermakers Union leader and *independentista* Pedro Grant, had at least forty member locals; some said there were one hundred. The once-quiescent island unions had become one of the strengths of the independence movement. When 100,000 *independentistas* marched through San Juan, in a mass of humanity a mile long, most of the demonstrators were neither intellectuals nor *jíbaros,* but workers.

"Everything is changing. And it is not always for the better," lamented the veteran AFL-CIO representative on the island, Augustín Benitez. "Soon I expect to see people walking *naked* in the streets. I don't know what's happening to people. Yes, they will be walking naked in the streets very soon."

The change in the *jíbaros*' way of life had led to the change in the independence movements. Socialism, too, was a symbol of *La Nueva Vida,* the New Life, on the island. "In a neo-colonial society independence, by itself, is no guarantee of freedom," said Mari Bras. "Socialism is the only road to national liberation in the underdeveloped world. Before the Cuban Revolution socialism was associated with the Soviet Union or China. After the Cuban Revolution it was inspired by nationalist ideas, especially in Latin America." That was why his party had a "double nature." It advocated both "independence and socialism": "First independence," he said, "then we will concentrate on gaining power.

"So the struggle for independence, which is the struggle of the nineteenth century, retarded here in Puerto Rico, has joined with the struggle for socialism, which is on the agenda of the contemporary world. And that is why the Independence party of Ruben Berrios now calls itself 'socialist' too."

And yet, "Socialism in Puerto Rico will not be Cuban! or Chinese! or Soviet! It will be Puerto Rican," Mari Bras emphatically said. "It will never lose that humanness we have. Never, I think, will we lose that. That is a philosophical matter. For if a man believes in the freedom of man how can he be a chauvinist to any man? We are not chauvinists."

"Socialism in Puerto Rico" had become an active topic of discussion, if not political practice. In student circles it was "the 'in' thing," said a university activist. The pragmatic and brusque leaders of the United Labor Movement increasingly endorsed, and were endorsed by, the campaigns of the Puerto Rican Socialist party. Even the conservative leaders of the New Progressive party, the Nixon Republicans, talked, with no visible hostility, of the possibility of "modified socialism." The "moderate form of socialism" might be economically helpful, according to Senator Juan Palerm, an NPP legislator. And the staid Ramón Mellado, whose stern policies as Secretary of Education had represented "the archetype of reaction" to the student radicals, shocked everyone by blithely commenting, on resigning from the government, that capitalism "is out of style." He thought that an "intermediary between the two extremes" of capitalism and socialism was "on the horizon" for Puerto Rico.

The stubbornly individualistic *jíbaros* in the hills may have been curious but dubious about the books by Mao and Che that their sons and daughters brought home from school. Still, even in the quiet plaza of Utuado, the old men talked, with furrowed brows, of these strange ideas.

"¿Qué es socialista?"

"¿Un ángel?"

They laughed. One man, whose family had farmed the hills for hundreds of years, shook his head at his cronies.

"¿Socialismo?" he scoffed. "It is nothing new!"

"Without knowing it the *jíbaro* is a socialist," he said. *"¡Sí!* He is living in socialism, in his habits and in his way of life. The small farmer in Puerto Rico has to share everything with his neighbors. Always. His tools. His horse. His car. His food. Always it has been like that for us in the hills.

"So it will not be hard for the *jíbaro* to understand socialism. It is the only way he will survive. He will become *politically* a socialist, as well. Like the peasants of China."

The idyll of *jíbaro* life had changed not only in the squatters' huts and urban slums. In the remote *barrios* and silent villages of the mountains the revolutionary ideas of Che Guevara and Frantz Fanon had come to the conservative plazas, not written in books the *jíbaros* could not read, but in the atmosphere of the times, the very air they breathed. Strangely, or not so strangely, the thoughts had been brought home by the children of the *jíbaros,* educated in the American schools, and by the *jíbaros* themselves, who had gone to the cities seeking work in the American factories.

"*¡Ay bendito!* is a sigh of the romantic past," said Don Pedro Matos Matos. "It is not representative of our thought, our mood, of today. More accurately the *jíbaro* would say *¡Basta!* Enough!, or maybe even *¡Fuego, Yanqui!;* literally, that is the military command to fire!"

In the plaza, on the loudspeaker, there played a song of Roy Brown:

And the children are frightened
And dying men are dying
in silence—
And the Indian of the Andes,
And the Indian of Father Hidalgo,
still wait
for the man of fate
the one who never came
who walks with science—

And a young man in penance
cries in anger:

FIRE! FIRE!
  the World is on FIRE!
FIRE! FIRE!
  the Yankees want FIRE!
FIRE! FIRE!
  the Yankees want FIRE!
FIRE! FIRE!
  the Yankees want FIRE!
FIRE! FIRE!

the Yankees want FIRE!
FIRE! FIRE!
the Yankees want FIRE!

"Romantic?" Don Pedro smiled. "Our youth are idealistic. But very realistic. It is the youth who are the strongest in this revolutionary way of thinking, of course. They will turn Puerto Rico into the Ireland of the United States," he said. "Look at what those Commandos of Armed Liberation [CAL] are doing already."

If the islands of Ireland and Puerto Rico were to be compared, so might the IRA and CAL. The courageous and brutal guerrillas of the old Irish revolution were portrayed by the mass media of the United States with more romanticism (the IRA, after all, was fighting British soldiers), but the young Puerto Rican guerrillas, who had bombed hundreds of American banks, *supermercados* and military recruiting posts, had the same élan and a similar rationale. Even history cast familiar shadows on the two movements.

The great-great-grandfather of the IRA was the Fenian Brotherhood. It had been founded by self-exiled Irish patriots in Paris in 1832. But not until hundreds of immigrants to America came home to Ireland at the end of the Civil War, in which they had served in the Union Army, and "put their military skill at the service of Ireland," were the Fenians able to begin guerrilla warfare on their island.

So, too, it was said that many of the young members of the Commandos were battle veterans of the United States Army in Vietnam. They had been taught all they knew about guerrilla tactics and use of incendiary bombs by the Army of the United States. They had "medals on their chests and hatred in the hearts," it was said. Evidently they were excellent guerrillas, for after two years of operations on the island, not one had been caught.

One high government official in talking of the Commandos asked somewhat apprehensively if I would write about them. "Everyone on the island, from those who throw bombs to those who catch the bombers will be in the book," he was told.

"We catch the bombs," he said, sourly smiling, "but not the bombers!"

The bombing raids became so widespread that Governor Ferre had to appeal to the people: "Help us to isolate these terrorists, no matter what your own political beliefs may be. They are not a group of men with a political belief so much as a group of persons who are potential tyrants. They want to destroy our democratic institutions.

"Each bomb that explodes in Puerto Rico," the Governor charged, "means less industry and less tourism, less opportunities for happiness and property. Each bomb that explodes in Puerto Rico means more factories closed, more closed hotels, and less job opportunities."

The independence groups disavowed knowledge of or responsibility for the young Commandos. But Ruben Berrios and Mari Bras both spoke of the need for "diversity of struggle." "The Commandos are part of that diversity of struggle of the people in pursuit of independence," Mari Bras said rather stiffly. "When open and legal struggles are repressed, when there is official and institutional violence against the people, then the clandestine forms of struggle become more prominent. So far it is only a small part, but it is significant already, among the youth.

"After all, the young are more victims of colonialism than the old. They face obligatory service in the armed forces of the U.S., not the old. They are sent to die in Vietnam, not the old. They go to jail for refusing to be killers, not the old. From the beginning of the war in Vietnam this has been a rallying cry for the independence movement.

"Violence generates violence," he said. "That is unavoidable."

That did not mean there would be a violent revolution on the island. No! he had not meant that. He startled at the thought. "It could be something like in Chile," Mari Bras thoughtfully said. "Or it could be *something* violent. We cannot anticipate what the means to power will be. The important thing is that imperialism is not as powerful as it used to be. So the intervention in the Dominican Republic or Vietnam cannot be easily repeated after Indochina." His tone was not of prophecy, yet it indicated his hope.

In Washington, D.C., at one of the peace marches, Mari had said: "We don't want to fight with the American people. We don't have anything against the American people. We want to live in harmony. But the polarization of forces in the world today is such that either the American people defeat imperialism from within, or you will be faced with an international struggle in which the people of the world, the whole of humanity, will unite to destroy the United States." If that happened, the "majority of the people, who are innocent, will pay for the errors of a small minority." He hoped that would not happen. "But," he said, "that is the course of history.

"We are growing stronger and you are growing weaker every year," Mari Bras reassured himself.

"Come to Lares!" he suddenly enthused. "There you will see how strong we are. There you will see tens of thousands of Puerto Ricans who support independence from throughout the island, young and old, poor and, yes, even a few rich, now are patriots." He did not laugh, but smiled in that full-cheeked, jovial way that he had. Even in the midst of politicizing his round and gentle face seemed about to smile.

"Yes! Come to Lares!

"I will see you there," he said, "if I am not dead. No, I don't think the United States government would like to see me dead. They know what reaction that would cause in Puerto Rico. But there are always the potential fanatics."

He smiled once more, but he did not seem to be joking.

19

The Flowers of the Field

On the plaza of Lares, in the perfect sun, a troubadour sang with the voice of a child and the words of an old man:

> The banner is unfurled
> and the people sing,
>   and dance,
>   joyously;
> but wait, enough of
>   poetry,
> tomorrow they bury him.

Lares was the *Santuario de la Patria,* the Sanctuary of the Nation. It was an almost holy city, a shrine not of religion but of politics. On the plaza there was a white obelisk inscribed with the names of the *Héroes de la Revolución.* The plaza itself was named the Plaza de la Revolución; for it was here, on the steps of the church, that the Republic of Puerto Rico had been proclaimed on the morning of the twenty-third of September, in 1868. In the cemetery those who had died to win that brief moment of glory lay in graves to which patriots came, yearly, to kneel.

"To Lares—one goes on one's knees," said El Maestro, Don Pedro Albizu Campos, quoted by the Committee to Celebrate El Grito de Lares, of which Bishop Autulio Parrilla Bonilla was president.

In the plaza there was a tree planted by Don Pedro Albizu Campos at the pilgrimage to Lares that he led in the early thirties. The tree has grown large and full of leaves. On the trunk there was an old photograph of Don Pedro, nailed to the tree much as the image of a saint.

The tree was a shrine. An old woman touched the bark and crossed herself.

Every year on the day of the defeated revolution thousands came as on a pilgrimage to a dead saint. And to hear the orations, intoned in a mass, that offered absolution and salvation, with the promise of independence next year.

It was like a fiesta, in a way. The little boy with a small flag of Puerto Rico tied to a stalk of sugar cane, who marched back and forth before the speakers' stand, mimicking a wooden soldier. And the dapper old men, with neatly trimmed white mustaches and ruffled shirts limp on their gently sloping bellies, who reminisced of years spent in jail for causes that were lost. One young girl of fifteen, with a sunny brown face, her long blond hair flowing from beneath a Pinocchio hat, and a belt of bullets hugging her childish hips. The young men from factories of Cataño, who offered a small paper cup of rum, golden in the sun, to friends who passed. Activists from the university wearing pins of the Mining Brigades and "YANQUI, GO HOME!" buttons on their psychedelic bell-bottom jeans, while they munched on hot dogs *a las Puertorriqueño,* and sipped Coca-Cola. The bearded guitarist who strolled through the streets, singing an old *jíbaro* song of love, like a village troubadour.

The bumper stickers on the cars were as human as the people. In Spanish one said:

SOY BORICUA
EN SANGRE Y CORAZÓN

I AM BORINQUEÑA
IN BLOOD AND HEART

In English, there was another, on a Volkswagen whose hood was draped with a Puerto Rican flag:

I LIKE YOU BEST
NEXT TO MYSELF

And then there was a tribute to the political power of baseball:

PUERTO RICAN POWER
IS ROBERTO CLEMENTE

The crowd was young, mostly. It seemed to grow a little younger every year.

In the midst of these youth was a lanky young man in his shirt sleeves. He was older, but not much. He gesticulated, with theatrical waves of his long arms, to the circle of admirers who listened as though spellbound by what had been called his "poetry of politics." Ruben Berrios, the president of the Puerto Rican Independence party, was the idol of these youth; he spoke their language, but he did more than talk: he had been jailed for his beliefs and his *acts*.

"Most of the activists of our movement are young," Mari Bras had said. "It makes one feel young too. The young always are more generous, more free of strings and obligations, and so are more free to fight for an idealistic cause."

But the effervescent Berrios called them "the flowers of the field."

"Like the flowers of the field no one knows where the fighters for independence grow. They grow wild," he said. "In every high school and college there is now an independence youth group. These youth are not the hope of the future. These youth are the hope of the present. Nowadays, our youth no longer question their Puerto Rican identity. It is a fact of life to them. Like the sun. Like the flowers."

As always, Ruben Berrios and Mari Bras came to Lares to declare comradeship and unity. They embraced on stage, as they always did. They symbolized the two largest independence groups on the island. Berrios scoffed at the rest. "So small they meet in Volkswagens for general assemblies," he said, laughing. He was not opposed to the united front that Mari Bras perennially proposed. "It is only people who are not sure of themselves who are not willing to enter into temporary alliance with people who are not sure of themselves," said Berrios; but in the same breath he added, "People assume that it is good to be united. Who said that it's good to be united? Maybe it's not."

"He is not scientific," retorted Mari Bras. "We are more radical. We are not elitist."

If Mari was calm, Berrios was volatile; if Berrios was charismatic, Mari was fatherly. The men were as personally different as they were thought to be politically similar. Not that their philosophies or ideologies were the same. Berrios was a "democratic socialist," and he emphasized the "democratic" as much as the "socialist"; while Mari was the more "orthodox Marxist," as he said with firmness, "in the traditions of Puerto Rico"; his ideas more rooted in the economic conditions of the island than in the intellectual ones, it was said. On Berrios's desk were books by Martin Luther King and Mao Tse-tung, while on Mari's desk there was only a photograph of Don Pedro Albizu Campos and a flag.

But it was more than that. In a crowd Berrios personally stood out. A thin, tall, ascetic young man with his hair blowing on his high forehead, boyish and vigorous, he had the limbs of a dynamic male ballet dancer, which he used dramatically when he gesticulated to a crowd. He either sought the crowd or the crowd sought him. It did not matter. In his manner there was an energy that attracted the eye. "Ruben was always on a stage," recalled a college classmate. "Not just *on* stage, but up front, in stage center. He always was the star performer. He still is."

In the plaza of Lares people gathered around the stage. On the far side of the square, with his wife, Juan Mari Bras stood quietly, talking with friends and well-wishers. His father and mother were at his side, beaming at the occasion and at their son, embarrassed and proud.

Berrios, as always, was in the heart of the crowd. He talked with fervor, even if his audience was not much more than himself. In the eloquence of his oratory he reflected the poetic style of the romantic *independentistas,* as much as Mari Bras reflected it in his manner. And yet both men had proclaimed their belief in the "scientific socialism" of the contemporary revolutionary movements. Both men, though they offered homage to Don Pedro Albizu Campos, publicly shunned his mysticism, his religious devotion to sacrifice and purification of the soul, his Byronism, his *machismo*.

"We are very scientific," said Berrios. "The patriots of the past were *too* romantic.

"Socialism has come to the Independence party like small rivers coming to the Mississippi," he said. "It has been a historical process of trial and error that, unfortunately, even the scientific approach to politics requires. We have a very mature ideology. We are the most mature independence movement in the world. We have received the most shocks. We are cured. We are immunized. That is why we are not pure in a historical sense. Nobody in a revolutionary movement is pure. We have gone through hundreds of years of defeats, of treasons. So we are very mature. In Puerto Rico we have a very strong nationality. We have a very compact, well-defined, strong culture. Within every Puerto Rican is the feeling that, since we have been suppressed for more than four centuries, he has to compensate. Maybe this explains why a country so small as ours has been so outstanding in so many areas. And why, after seventy-five years of economic, political, and cultural domination by the most powerful empire in the history of the world, we have tens of thousands of people fighting for independence. It sounds absurd to some people! But it is the truth!"

Long ago had not Luis Muñoz Rivera said: ". . . if it were possible to open the heart of every Puerto Rican, and if it were possible to see the collective soul of the million beings who inhabit this forgotten rock, we would see there written, in indelible letters, the word 'independence.' "

If this was so, why was it that the *independentistas* received barely enough votes to elect a single Senator, Ruben Berrios himself, and two Representatives in the 1972 election? They received barely 5 percent of the vote, enough to survive as an electoral party. On his retirement from La Fortaleza in 1964, Governor Luis Muños Marín had spoken of the "independence ideal" as a fantasy that had become history: "The data is that the number of people in Puerto Rico opposed, peacefully or unpeacefully, legally or illegally, to permanent union between Puerto Rico and the United States, in one form or another, is less than 3 percent of the population." That was the vote then. Now the vote was a little more.

"Elections!" Berrios exploded. "Democracy does not mean going to the elections every four years. That is a little part of democracy, but is it the last stage? In elections votes are stuck with saliva to the wall. We will win the election when the Americans want us to win the election. We won't fool ourselves. We know that when it is profitable for the Americans to offer us autonomy offers of autonomy will come. We will wait. We are willing to negotiate. We are willing to bargain. We are reasonable.

"It is necessary only to wait for the right moment in history," he said. "That moment is here.

"Now we are ready to be free. If ever there was a country in the history of humanity that was prepared for independence, it is Puerto Rico. Compare us to the United States as it was in 1789. Or to any of the African colonies. Some people say, 'That is because the United States itself has prepared us.' My answer is: So what! What are they going to do with these highways? Roll them up like linoleum and take them home to the United States?"

Berrios was jubilant with the thought. He inspired himself by his beliefs, much as a poet or a prophet will by his faith.

"If ever a human being has to choose between the slavery of the senses and the freedom of the spirit, it will be death," he said. "He does *not* have to choose between these. He does *not*. The whole concept of democracy has been discredited by the United States, and the whole concept of socialism has been discredited by some of the socialist countries. That is horrible for mankind. But I *know* the senses *and* the spirit, the freedom *and* well-being of mankind can be met in a true democracy of socialism.

"Not only in Puerto Rico, but the men of the world have the obligation to seek that type of society. And create it. We want an elite society. We want a society where everyone is an elite. In this sense we are *utopians! Of course!* We are *utopians!*"

On the hill that sloped steeply from the plaza to the river was the foulest slum of Lares. It was a rural Casbah, like the squatters' huts of San Juan. The urine ran down the precipice of stone steps into the river. Like 60 percent of the houses on the island, these still had no sewage system. In recent years the sanitary engineers had induced some of the urine into a pipe that ran through the alleyway until it emptied into the river "hygienically." But the children, barefoot and hungry-eyed, still waded in the stream. The poor families of five, or ten, or fifteen lived as they always had, in wooden shacks of one room or two, clinging to the hill, above the stench of the river of urine.

In the last shack by the abyss the Spirit Woman lived. Her Templo Espiritista, as the sign over her door invited the sufferers, was dank and shuttered. The Spirit Woman sat in the darkness promising cures and casting spells for a small fee.

A *flamboyan* tree was flowering gloriously over her shack.

Not everyone in Lares went to the plaza to hear the politicians. Some heard but did not listen. Some listened but did not believe.

On the balcony of a building across from the church there was a banner:

THE SUPREME BENEDICTION
OF THE HUMAN SOUL IS LOVE
AND THE MOST NOBLE LOVE
IS LOVE OF OUR COUNTRY

An old *jíbaro* woman looked up. "Tell me what it says," she begged. "I cannot read."

In the afternoon the sun had begun to dissolve the crowds. When the sun was at the epoch of its ascent in the skies, at noon, a solstice and stillness had suddenly come upon the people.

One by one they had begun to leave the plaza. The clenched fists rhythmically arose to punctuate the speeches and the hips swayed to the rhythms of the revolutionary guitarists; but there were no more than a few hundred listeners in the plaza, while tens of thousands wandered up and down the streets, singing to themselves and chanting their own slogans, with flags flying in an unending procession of faith and good-humored defiance. By two o'clock in the afternoon the crowds had wandered away.

They sat on the sidewalks, in shaded siestas. They slept in the side streets and alleyways, young and old, boys and girls, deep in contented dreams. They rested along the walls of the church, with babies and lovers in their arms.

Who listened to the speeches of the politicians? The other politicians.

Enjoying the beauty of a hillside, under a tamarind tree in a field far from the hot sun of the plaza, a group of boys and girls lay in the grass in the cool shade, with cups of shaved ice, drinking Coca-Cola while they listened to the speeches of patriots on a portable radio. The young revolutionaries of Lares were sensible. Why sweat on the hot cement when you can lie in the sweet shade? It was a beautiful day to lie under a tamarind tree. And what was more important for a revolutionary than to enjoy beauty?

"I cannot really tell whether my thirst for liberation is a consequence of my search for the real beauty of life or whether my search for that beauty is a consequence of my urge for national liberation," Berrios had said.

"From the depths of the mountain, from the cries of the forgotten children in the ghettos, from the silence of our waters without colors, from the fear of freedom of those who have always been enslaved, from the hope of those who trust humanity, from the dichotomy of the *yagrumo,* from the shallowness of cement, and from the deepness of our natural consciousness, you will hear and you will understand. When others in your nation hear and understand, liberation will advance one step further," Berrios said. "Nobody can be free until each human being is also free."

In the church sanctified by the Revolution of 1868 Bishop Parrilla Bonilla intoned a solemn mass. He was assisted not by one but by six young priests, who stood by his side. So that the Holy Ghost was invoked by seven voices in unison, and the worshipers were seven times blessed.

On the altar, draped upon the holy cloth, was a Puerto Rican flag. In between the altar and the communion rail stood the Bishop in the resplendent gold-and-green robe of his bishopric; his deep and masculine voice booming as he appealed for the mercy of God, crying out, "*¡Dios! ¡Dios! !Dios!* Oh, help us free our beloved country."

Not on Holy Thursday, at Easter, nor on the Birth of Christ, at Christmas, was the church so crowded. In the mass of worshipers, who filled every pew and every aisle, so tightly no one could move, two flags of Puerto Rico mysteriously appeared, huge banners at least thirty feet long, held at arm's length by young men above the bowed heads of the worshipers in the pews. The youthful hands that held the flags were clenched into fists.

A young man wearing a dirty tee-shirt and Levi's and a Castro army hat pushed his way into the church. He faced the altar. Bishop Parrilla had ended the mass. In silence, as the churchgoers murmured, "Amen," the young man lifted a picket sign he had hidden between his legs. It was in the form of a crude wooden cross upon which he had nailed the drawing of a clenched fist. He did not speak. He had no written message. He offered no words. A hand, clenched into a fist, nailed to the cross, that was all.

Always there was the drama of the morality play. The politics of revolution was not enough; it had to offer the heroic act of sacrifice and glory; it had to exalt the pain of being Puertorriqueño; what Mari Bras had called "that humanness we have."

Once someone said: The difference between politics in Mexico and Puerto Rico is this: In Mexico when a man says he will kill you, you better watch out. In Puerto Rico when a man says he will kill you, it is conversation. Revolution was a song to be sung. To be danced to. To be prayed to. To be enjoyed. Had not Governor Ferre said: "It is the poets, not the people, who talk of revolution"? The people came to be entertained by the rhetoric of revolution, as to the religious drama of the mass or the television morality play of good and evil.

"Let them think that," said Berrios, laughing. "If that is how they think, they are bigger fools than I thought. When the revolution comes, like the Czar of Russia they will be looking for their summer palace to go to after their winter palace has fallen. They do not understand what has happened in Puerto Rico. They do not know the poor people of Puerto Rico. In this sense, they are fools, historically. But I do not think they can afford to be fools and ignore life much longer."

Berrios exulted, his lucid eyes lighted as if by a vision: "We mean what we say. And they better realize we mean it!"

In the plaza of Lares, in the sun's warm glow, a folksinger, a petite and pretty young woman on the stage, swayed her hips to the Puertorriqueña rhythm of her lilting song:

Ta, ta, ta, ta, ta,
Revolución . . .
Ta, ta, ta, ta, ta,
Revolución . . .

Epilogue: The Bird Lost in the Sanctuary

The small bird was perched on the altar. Suddenly it flew into the nave. It soared and circled above the altar, like a butterfly enticed by the light coming through the circle of windows around the dome of the nave. The dome was painted blue, a false sky. On the ceiling there was a fresco of white clouds. But to the bird the sky looked real. It flew upward to the dome. And it was trapped.

No one was in the church to see the bird but one old man. He merely smiled. On his lips there was a voiceless sigh:

¡Ay bendito!

Blessed be the Lord!

In the pews the old man sat alone. He was not praying. He was resting in the shade. The sun was hot in the plaza at noon, but in the church it was always cool. So the old man had come inside to sit for a moment and shade his eyes. He sat with his hat in his lap.

What could the old man do to help the bird? He could not climb into the dome at his age, four stories or more above the altar, to break open the windows with his fists. He could not call the *padre* and say: Oh, Father, ring the bells! Summon the fire department with their ladders! There is a bird in your belfry! At that, the parish priest, tired by the furor of yesterday, would have dismissed the old man as drunk.

So the old man slept. In the church the one small sound was the wings of the little bird.

It was a large church, but poor. The wooden altar was simple and austere; rising thirty feet, at least, toward the dome of the nave, it was a plain structure of unadorned colonnades with bare niches for the statues of the Virgin and saints. Here were none of the silver and gold Madonnas that beckoned the poor in the churches of Mexico, or the stolen treasures of the cathedrals of Europe.

The church was quiet as a sanctuary. On the balconies of the plaza the flags and banners had been taken down, folded lovingly, to be stored away for another year. The celebrants who had come from all over the island, fifty thousand of them, in homage to the shrine of independence, to celebrate the day of El Grito de Lares with revolutionary speeches and music and rum, had all gone home again.

On the wall of the church there was a modest plaque, old as history:

IN THE PARISH CHURCH OF LARES
AND OFFICIATED BY FATHER
JOSÉ GUMERNIDO VEGA
ON THE MORNING OF THE DAY
OF THE 24TH OF SEPTEMBER, 1868
THERE WAS CELEBRATION
OF A SOLEMN MASS
FOR THE PROVINCIAL GOVERNMENT
OF THE REPUBLIC OF PUERTO RICO
THANKS BE TO GOD ALMIGHTY
FOR THE PROCLAMATION
OF INDEPENDENCE

At noon, the *turistas* came with Japanese cameras. They photographed one another, posing by the worn plaque.

Lares was somnolent in the noonday sun. Once more it was nothing more than a little mountain town, drowsing on a hillside. A few of the *jíbaros* sat on the plaza. It was just an ordinary day. The fiesta was over.

In the church the old man was awakened by four young girls. The schoolgirls, who were twelve or thirteen years old, had come in their starched uniforms to pray to their favored saints, for the usual blessings young girls need. On their lunch hour the schoolgirls came every day. Kneeling at the altar, they did not look up to see the little bird flying in the nave. They went on their way.

The old man alone heard the wings of the bird. It flew desperately, faster and faster, dashing its head against the false clouds on the ceiling. But it could not break out of the painted sky.

In a sudden swoop the bird flew out of the nave, and, excited by its apparent escape, darted from the altar to the choir loft, from the choir loft to the altar. Still it could not find the doors of the church. The bird's chirp soon grew to a cry of fear, then a *grito* of terror.

¡Ay bendito!

Blessed be the Lord!

The old man sighed. He got to his feet slowly. Nothing could be done for the bird. So he, too, left the church.

In the glass crypt by the altar, like a glass-enclosed cart of a *pastiles* vendor, the life-sized plaster body of Jesus lay asleep.

That evening, by the time the parish priest came to say his evening vespers, he may have found the bird lying dead upon the altar, or upon the crypt of Jesus.

Or had it escaped and flown away?

BOOK TWO

Prologue: *¡Ay Bendito!* The Night the Lights Went Out in New York

It was the fiesta of the darkness. The lights went out all over New York. The city had lost its power. A miracle had happened: the hand of God had struck Consolidated Edison blind, and the television sets were dumb, and the refrigerators were warm, and the stoves were cold. The city was coming to an end, without a whimper, without a bang, because someone had turned off the lights. It was human, after all. The Puertorriqueños rejoiced: the Lord was just and life was a joke.

¡Ay bendito!

Blessed be the Lord!

Children of the *barrio* danced in the street that night. On the Lower East Side the failure of the power was celebrated with the darkest humor. In their hands the children held torches of milk containers, burning like votive candles on Holy Thursday in the Cathedral of San Juan, as they danced in the gutters; for the street lamps were unlit and there seemed to be no moon in the smog. At midnight they lit piles of old tires in the middle of the street. The police would not come into the *barrio* that night; later it was said there was no increase in crime in our street, for everyone was dancing. So they poured gasoline on old tires until the bonfires burned high as the fires on the beaches of Puerto Rico on San Juan Bautiste Eve, when the supplicants plunged into the midnight waves to cleanse themselves of their sins in the dark seas.

¡Ay bendito!

Blessed be the Lord!

Who else danced in the darkened street? In the suburbs the people locked their doors.

In the better neighborhoods the people stayed indoors, behind their apartment walls and window bars. And in the dark they stared at their television sets, that were frighteningly black, waiting for the announcer to tell them all was well.

The moment the power stopped, everyone and everything stopped. In the city everything and everyone was plugged into the power system.

¡Ay bendito!

Blessed be the Lord!

On Seventh Avenue in garment factories, and in sweatshops in the Bronx, the sewing machines were silent, at last. The women could hear themselves sing in Spanish; for the machines "speak in English." In every factory the machinery was powerless. The lathes and grinders and buffers and borers and punchers and platers and stitchers and riveters were nothing more than oversized metal toys that would not work.

In the supermarkets the shopping carts full of milk and butter and ice cream and frozen meat were left to rot in the aisles. The girls at the checkout counters could not open the cash registers without power; every one was run by electricity. And it was against the rules to count money by hand. Shoppers had to buy in the candlelit *bodegas.* In the office buildings the elevators were suspended in the air. Even the elevator men had to walk down the stairs. The electric typewriters were still. The electric water coolers were warm. Silence filled the subway tunnels, as the dumfounded commuters waited on the platforms for trains that never came. On the stages of Broadway the theater curtains would not rise or fall. The theaters were dark. The lights no longer lit up on the pinball machines in Times Square. The traffic lights were black. And the "DON'T WALK" signs went out, so that walkers on the streets were forced to walk.

¡Ay bendito!

Blessed be the Lord!

And the men in the dirty movie houses and the women in the beauty parlors and the children being watched by television stumbled into the streets, with eyes blinking at the world, wondering where they were.

On the tenement stoops of the *barrio* the fathers and mothers sat, laughing encouragement to the children who danced from sewer to sewer, in the middle of the darkness. Running up and down the sidewalks with their torches made of milk containers, the children celebrated. In time someone brought out beer and wine. The fiesta of the darkness continued late into the early morning: it was darker inside the tenements than outside, so why go to bed?

¡Ay bendito!

Blessed be the Lord!

In the morning all the newspapers pontificated and piously accused the scientists for the failure of the God of power. Everyone on our block knew it was a gift of God. The Spanish-language newspaper, *El Diario,* mocked the darkness of the night with two words, quixotically printed on a totally black page. "¿POR QUE?" it read.

"WHY?"

And on the street of our *barrio* the Puerto Ricans laughed in relief, for maybe Nueva York would become like Puerto Rico someday. The night of the tenth of November, 1965, would be remembered.

¡Ay bendito!

Blessed be the Lord!

20

In the *Barrios* of the Mind

In softest Spanish she talked to her parrot.

The bird sat in its locked cage in the tropical garden of fake flowers and plastic fruits in the tenement parlor and stared at her with one sad and silent eye. One of its eyes had fallen out. Its useless wings were painted onto its hollow body. The parrot was made of papier-mâché. It could not hear her words.

Carmencita Colon was a woman of forty, small and plump, barely five feet tall. But she had the vigor and tense vitality of a larger woman. She worked, at times for ten hours a day, in a garment factory, coming home to cook supper for family in the traditional manner of a Puerto Rican wife. In her life there was little time, or room, for fantasy; so she talked to the parrot as if it were alive, and she tended lovingly the flowers and fruits that bloomed with brilliant artifice all winter long.

On her television set there was an enormous bouquet of paper flowers. In the bower of polyfoam fruit on the table were mangos, bananas, and apples that looked as if they had been polished with floor wax. The green water in the fish tank was alive with goldfish and seaweed; but a bulb illuminated the water, and the serene green light bathed the room in unreality.

"We forget the city here," Mrs. Colon said. Her living room was her private tropical island.

In the street below the window was one of the desolate corners on the Lower East Side of New York. Police would not walk down the street if they did not have to. The winos and addicts had the hallways and gutters to themselves most of the time. The kids from *"los projectos,"* who snatched the purses of old ladies on the corner, were "home free" if they made it into the labyrinth of the housing project across Avenue D. One evening I was mugged a few steps from the corner by two children who were not more than fourteen. The smaller had an old revolver as large as his face. Some neighborhood candy stores sold almost as many drugs as the drugstores, but the families were too poor to give the children enough pocket money.

In the hallways on cold nights, the addicts roamed like rats, seeking warmth. The scratching on the doors at night sounded the same. On the stoops the speed freaks sat, becoming thinner and thinner every day. They were runaway children from suburban homes whose parents came to visit, on occasion, with gifts of money and guilt.

There was no hint of the ugly and dirty street up in the Colons' tropical garden. In the tenement apartment it was bright and sunny. The green plastic furniture was covered with clear plastic slipcovers. Like oil on water, it slipped when one sat on it. The floors were washed clean as the walls, and the walls were radiantly blue as the island sky. Families on the block all painted their walls in the gayest tropical colors to hide the gray tenements. José Colon, under the eye of his wife, had painted their living room vibrant red, the bedroom walls sky blue, the kitchen cabinets leafy deep green, and the window frames sunny yellow.

Wherever the tenements had been torn down the apartment of a Puerto Rican family was known by the rainbow of hues on its walls, glowing with the colors of the island.

Of all the families in the tenement the Colons were the most respected, not because of their tropical apartment but because of their urban son. Joseph was in college. He was born in New York, and so was named Joseph, not José. A single child, he may have eaten better and he may have been loved more singularly than if he'd had a dozen brothers and sisters. Some said he was spoiled. But if he was it showed to no disadvantage. He was a tall and handsome youth.

Joseph dressed neatly and walked with a fresh bounce in his step. He was clever and quick. He had eluded the hatreds and sorrows that trapped so many young men on the block.

At eighteen, Joseph married and moved away. He never came back except to visit his parents. He planned to be an architect, among other things.

"Someday," he said, "I'm going to come back and build a real garden on the block. My mother won't need a fake one."

In the window of the PUERTO RICAN BARBERSHOP down the block there was a hand-lettered sign:

LET'S MAKE
7TH STREET
A DECENT
PLACE TO
LIVE

On the sidewalk, under the sign, two shivering boys huddled with their heads between their knees, listening to silent music they alone could hear, swaying to its secret rhythms and rifes. The older boy was perhaps fourteen. His companion was not that old. If they were cold, or high on dope, it did not matter.

A barber, with manicured black hair, sleek and shiny, glowered at the boys through the window. He was angered by their indifference to his civic sign.

The candy store next door had a sign in the window, too. It said CANDY STORE FOR SALE. It had been there for years.

As long as anyone on the block could remember, Leah was selling her candy store and moving to Florida: "To live in peace." Leah said it was not because she was afraid of the *schwarze,* the Blacks, as she called the Puerto Ricans. In Leah's eyes anyone who was not Jewish was black. The Puerto Ricans were blackest of all. She was not afraid of anyone. Not even her shapeless husband, in his smelly underwear, who had waddled up and down the cellar steps for forty years, grunting like a bear as he carried cases of soda for the egg creams, frightened her. He frightened the little children. To them he was a Jewish bogyman. But to Leah, he was her *schlemiel,* "Worse than a *schwarze.*"

Leah sold candy and cigarettes and anything else they would buy to the children on the block. For forty years she had prepared egg creams for her neighbors and for forty years they had been repaying her with stories of suffering. She was tired of all the suffering. "In Florida who suffers?" she sighed. All her friends were long since in Florida—the Jewish families she had known as a girl when her father died and left her the candy store. "May he rest in peace!" Leah said. "I curse the day! Who wants to buy a candy store? On pennies who gets rich?" Her pennies had bought several tenements on Avenue D, the old people on the block said.

In the back of the candy store stood the worn wooden booth of the community telephone. The neighbors, too poor to own telephones, had been using Leah's booth for generations. Once the language had been Yiddish, now it was Spanish.

Leah nodded, as though in prayer. "If that telephone could talk, the stories it could tell."

A young child had come from the booth; her brown face was pale, her English confused by fright. "If the hospital call me, Leah, you call me? *¡Por favor!* you call me! My father, they say, he is dying. He is dying."

"So if he is dying why don't you go see him?" Leah shrugged. "All right! All right! I'll call you."

"I cannot go," the girl said.

"Why not? How many times does your father die?"

"My baby is sick. My boy friend will go."

The girl turned away. She left the store. "Her boy friend is fifteen. And she?" Leah intoned in her Mother Courage voice, full of sorrow and damnation, "And she is maybe fourteen. I tell you. It is not easy to be a *schwarze.*"

Once a year the white truck of the Department of Health would park on the corner. A kindly man in a white smock would hand leaflets to the women. In English and Spanish it was the same message every year: "Let's Get Rid of the Rats." *"Acabemos con las Ratas."*

KEEP YOUR BABY'S CRIB CLEAN.
WASH YOUR BABY'S FACE AND BODY
BEFORE PUTTING HIM TO BED.
RATS FOLLOW THE SMELL OF MILK.

As an afterthought the leaflet would say: "WATCH YOUR BABY AFTERWARD." Someone always asked the kindly man: "You mean we should sit up all night? And get bitten?"

In New York City the rats did not outnumber the people, the Department of Health said reassuringly. There were no more than two million rats. But every year an estimated three thousand ghetto residents were bitten, mostly children. The epidemic of rats had begun in the post–World War II years, when from 1945 to 1950 known rat bites had increased by 238 percent. Since then, as the tenements had deteriorated, the rat population had prospered. The tenements were infested by poverty.

Poverty had been brought to the Lower East Side by the Irish peasants of the earlier nineteenth century. It had been inherited by the Jewish peasants of the latter nineteenth century, whose odor, the pungent sour and sweet aroma of the poor, saturated the hallways, woodwork and rooms. For poverty has a peculiar odor of its own. It is neither ugly nor foul, but intoxicating as lethargy, a heavy burden in the air. The newcomers from the tropical island could smell it immediately.

Once in a while there would be a new face on the block. In the morning a man would sit on the stoop sleepily, peering at the passer-by or the garbage or the gray sky. If he was a new refugee from home, he often wore a borrowed coat, too large for him. What did he see? And what did he think of the city?

In the morning of the first day in the city it was a shock to see how cold the world had become. *¿Frio?* No! It was not just the cold, but that the cold was so gray. The morning sun squinted at the people, and the people squinted at the sun, with cold eyes, as if the morning was their enemy. On the island the morning was blessed as birth. Here everyone squinted at everyone else, as if their neighbors were the *policía,* the landlords, the *brujas*—the witches—of their dreams.

And why did they walk with lips half opened and mouths half shut? Was breathing that difficult in the city? So many people seemed to be talking to themselves, and saying nothing. They hurried by the hundreds to work, or God knows where; for they talked to no one as they passed. No man or woman said, Good morning! Even the children did not say, Good morning! Yet they looked like Puertorriqueños. But how could they be if they did not begin the day with God, and say *Buenas Días?*

The young girl's hair was dyed red. Her eyes, blue as the sea in the Bay of Guánica, were exaggerated by mascara; and her lips stiff with orange lipstick. She who talked so happily at the party in his uncle's apartment last night, to welcome the stranger, walked past him like a spirit of the dead, her lips cold, her eyes frozen.

In the island he had known the silence. But this cold and poverty were strange to him.

On Seventh Street, between Avenues C and D, some of the tenements had been built before the Civil War. The block looked like any block. But it wasn't. Its people were not only poor and hard-working Puerto Rican families and old Jews who clung to the neighborhood like barnacles, but long-hair rebels, poets, refugee intellectuals, and a self-defrocked priest who was guru and holy junkie of the addicted, and a vice-president of Standard Oil, who owned, but did not live in, one of the fourteen townhouses that once had belonged to sea captains. In the days when four-masted schooners docked at the foot of the street, where the river had been filled in with garbage to build *"los projectos"* this had been a busy waterfront. Now, the busiest trading houses on the block were two tenements that looked like any others but for the large cars from Connecticut and New Jersey that parked outside every Friday night, while their owners rushed up the rickety stairs to buy their weekly supply of dope. One regular was a Rolls-

Royce that double-parked ostentatiously, but was never ticketed by the police cars that meticulously, and with some difficulty, drove around it.

The block had a distinct odor. It was slightly sweet, slightly sour. Some thought it was a combination of garbage, incense, and marijuana. But it was the smell of an underground river. A subterranean stream flowed beneath the tenements, the remnant of the days of sailing ships. When the river backed up every spring, a dank odor rose into the cellars of the tenements, as from the tomb of history.

On hot summer nights, when the young men who sat on folding chairs in front of the Puerto Rican social clubs played dominoes by the light of the street lamps, the odor of the hidden river was especially pungent. The games of dominoes were one of the rituals of the block. On any night when the weather was warm—for dominoes had to be played in shirtsleeves, its official uniform—the groups of men played on crates, bridge tables, or stoops, deep into the dark. One night, an amateur thief who was a newcomer to the block snatched a purse on the corner and tried to escape down the crowded sidewalk. The domino players rose up, stoop by stoop, like a gantlet. If the police car had not come they would have stoned the poor thief with their dominoes.

At the far end of the street, on the corner of Avenue C, there was a thieves' market, where every Sunday the neighborhood burglars and addicts sold the odds and ends of their week's work. It was a wondrous place for children and a bargain bazaar to shoppers, for everything was available on the sidewalk, from brassières to television sets. The officers at the local police precinct knew about it, but "It was impossible to stop," one of them said. "When they hear us coming, everything disappears."

On the streets, nothing was hidden. On the stoops lovers fought, in emotional performances equal to any dramatic stage, with a rapt neighborly audience, if not applause. The younger lovers, too, courted on the stoops, for it was too crowded in the tenements for intimacy. The infants knew the world, for the first time, and the old, for the last time, on the stone steps. In the evenings the men sat with cans of beer, settling world affairs, or if a young man had a guitar he serenaded the street lamp, or the moon if it shone through the smog. At midnight, on summer nights, the stoops were as crowded as beaches, as families tried to escape the heat of the tenements.

"The Puerto Ricans behave like they were in front of their huts on the island," a local police inspector complained.

And then, one summer day there was dancing in the street. It was not a holiday, or a saint's day. The long-hair boys and girls had simply decided to dance. Several years ago they were the Love Children, who later became the Flower Children. In the spring of 1968 they had sat in the trees in Central Park throwing flowers at the police below. In the summer they announced a celebration of life. They sat on the tenement fire escapes, with feet dangling, playing flutes and whistles and drums; while in the street the new youth in ancient dress, the collegiate tribesmen resplendent in embroidered vests and silk headbands, the worn-clothed addicts, and the little Puerto Rican girls, in party dresses, all danced. The mothers on the stoops beamed. It was a *fiesta de amor,* a fiesta of love, they said. In the afternoon someone painted all but one of the fire hydrants gold and silver; that one was painted lavender. The undercover agents among the dancers were too dazzled by the joyous atmosphere to interfere.

No one had blocked off the street, but the neighborhood police did not dare disrupt the outburst of brotherhood. The *fiesta de amor* in those gutters was not mentioned in the morning newspapers. It was a year of ghetto riots, and dancing in the streets, for love, was not news.

On the wall of the supermarket on Avenue D a message had been painted inside a heart: "MARÍA Y JOSÉ MARRIED FOREVER," dated "JUNE, 1969." The fires of the ghetto riots burned the vow of love away. In the wake of the massacre at Attica Prison, where many Puerto Ricans were among its victims, the Grand Union supermarket was bombed and burned. Instead of the heart, and vow of love, the words on the hollowed building said "AVENGE ATTICA."

In an abandoned tenement, with broken windows, its hallways

littered with garbage and junkies, smelling of urine and semen, the neighborhood rebels had written on the boarded-up storefront in the basement:

BOURGEOIS
ELEMENTS
MUST
GET OUT!

It was signed "Red Guards." And a few stoops down the street another prophecy was scribbled on the door of what may once have been an Irish café or a Jewish candy store or a Puerto Rican *bodego:*

REVOLUTION!
1966

Someone crossed out the year. Underneath a latter-day prophet had written:

OR
WHEN WE ARE READY!

As though in reply, a gutter Unamuno had written in large letters of rebuke:

FREEDOM IS THE CRIME
THAT CONTAINS ALL CRIMES

Of all these words on the wall none spoke the thoughts of the Puertorriqueños of Seventh Street more eloquently, and simply, than a single phrase in white chalk barely visible on the dirty window of an empty store:

I CAN'T BREATHE

And there were other signs of the times: "TOME WINSTON . . . RICO SABOR . . . BUENO . . . SABROSO." "Rich-tasting, good, and savory." It was second only to the entreaty: "SCHAEFER BEER . . . CUANDO TENGAN DESPOSDE TOMAR MÁS DE UNA." "When you're having more than one."

One of the ads for beer or cigarettes, the wine and roses of the poor, had been slashed with red paint, its siren-faced ethnic model defaced. Beneath it the unknown sign painter had proclaimed the most prevalent message of all with his revolutionary spray can:

¡VIVA PUERTO RICO LIBRE!

Up on Eleventh Street and Avenue C the tenement murals of the children had been desexed, not defaced. Underneath the words "VIVA LA PAZ"—"Long Live Peace"—there had been a childish painting of a young and innocent girl, with her thin brown arms flung open to the world, like Christ. Her abdomen had been painted white. The penis and testicles of a white man had been crudely drawn between her thighs. Nearby was the scrawl "FUCK THE SPIKS!" It was not a Puerto Rican block.

The street fighting with words was as old as the block was old. Long ago the Yankee sea captains of Seventh Street welcomed the Irish peasants with signs: NO IRISH NEED APPLY. The descendants of the Irish peasants now welcomed the Puerto Rican peasants in kind. Not far away, on Ninth Street and Cooper Union Square, the antiwar draft riots of the Irish had terrorized New York during the Civil War. But that had been forgotten. Still nearer was the birth bed of the rebellion of the Jewish peasants. On Rivington Street the messianic Marxists of *Jews Without Money* by Michael Gold had preached the gospel of "O workers' Revolution. You are the true Messiah. You will destroy the East Side when you come and build there a garden for the human spirit." But that too was forgotten. And it was still nearer that the Irish and Jewish peasants had joined hands, to march in the first May Day parade in Tompkins Square, hardly one block away.

None of this seemed to touch the block. The Irish and the Jews had long ago moved away from their memories, to the suburbs. The block was not a block in a ghetto or a borough of the city. It was a world. Reminiscing about the block he had lived on when a boy, Felipe Luciano, once a leader of the Young Lords, said: "Like the only thing we knew was the block. You never went out of that block."

A few old Jews had been left behind in an old-age home on the corner of Avenue C. The granite building looked like a morgue. It had actually once been a bank, before decay overcame it. On sunny days, which were few beneath the gray fumes of the Consolidated Edison plant by the river, two old women sat outside the living cemetery on a wooden bench. They sunned themselves. They talked, but not to each other. They had forgotten the little English they had known, and in Yiddish welcomed the Puerto Ricans who walked by their home.

The old Jews were fed by a jovial fat Puerto Rican woman, who bought them *cuchifritos*. She was blessed in Yiddish.

One by one the old Jews died. Even old Jews die. The synagogues changed their religions. Instead of Passover they celebrated Easter, a change no greater than from the Hasidic congregations who were replaced by the Pentecostals. In one Iglesia de Virgen Negra, the Church of the Black Virgin, the evangelical minister did not remove the Jewish star from the nave; he simply placed the cross beside it.

The kosher butcher shops became *carnicerías puertorriqueñas*. And the naked chickens were replaced by fresh pork for the holy holidays. Like the store of the Brothers Colon, where their sign of the times offered *Carnes Frescas, Frutas, y Productos Tropicales*—Fresh Meats, Fruits, and Tropical Products—though the sign painted on the windows still proclaimed, "HARRY'S KOSHER CHICKENS."

Many of the merchants remained in their stores, where they had spent a lifetime, or tried to. Until one summer day in 1969 . . .

The quiet riot that erupted on Avenue C, in the summer of 1969, was a neighborhood affair. It was dubbed the "mini-riot" by the newspapers; for the singing teenagers who danced down the middle of the street did a great deal of yelling in Spanish, but little damage. One of the riot leaders was said to be Carlos Aponte, a serious-eyed student, who was given a job with the Northeast Neighborhood Association as a "street worker" for his efforts. He later became a rhetorical revolutionary, joining the Young Lords, who soon expelled him, on the advice of their "friends in the Police Department," who informed them that mini-riot leader Aponte was an undercover agent for the law-enforcement agency.

One store was looted by rioters that day. It was a bakery, known for the aroma of its Jewish pumpernickel. The rioters broke the bakery's windows and stole armfuls of bread.

The bakery was owned by a nameless Jew. He had no name he was willing to share with his customers. On his wrist were the tattooed numbers of a Nazi concentration-camp bookkeeper; he may have thought that was name enough. A sallow man, his face shadowed by an uneven stubble, the silent Jew seemed to detest his bakery. He seemed to have pride in just three things: a young son, who helped out on Sunday, wearing a velvet *yarmulke;* the bread that glistened as though it had been scrubbed; and his new white Oldsmobile, in which he delivered bagels, cornbreads and pumpernickels to his shop from the wholesaler downtown. Of these it was the new white Oldsmobile, his symbol of America, that was his most visible pride. He watched it like a protective hawk, so "the hoodlums on the street should not make a scratch on it."

On the day of the riot someone smashed the windows of his car. It was a trifle, but the tortured Jew became hysterical. He boarded up his bakery, swept the glass from his car seat and drove away. He never returned. Where the bakery had been, on the corner of Avenue C and Seventh Street, was a television repair shop, REICINO TV REPAIRS. And on the corner of Avenue C and Eighth Street the BORRIQUEN BAKERY opened.

21

The Exiles

Is There Life after San Juan?

The sign in the San Juan airport taunted the exiles:

IS THERE LIFE AFTER SAN JUAN?

It was an advertisement for Hertz rental cars: "Hertz Reveals All, and All Is Free. . . ." Enticing as it was cryptic, did the sign mean that the flight to New York was not the direct path to Heaven, after all? Or did it mean that life in San Juan was death in paradise?

One hot, moody tropical morning, with the sweet smell of rain falling on the palm trees in the parking lot of the airports, thousands of people sweated as they waited for flights to the cool world. In long lines of joyous children, sad little grandmothers, young fathers with eyes alerted for insults, and women with their lives in bundles, whole families waited. They stood at the ticket counters of Eastern Airlines, waiting to fly away on "The Wings of Man."

Where are you going? To a job in Denver, to my family in Boston, to visit with my aunt in Hawaii, to stay with my son in the Beautiful Bronx. Was it possible to tell of a Biblical exodus with statistics? It was recorded in the computers of the Tourist Development Corporation of Puerto Rico that within ten years, from 1960 to 1970, exactly

13,902,773 digits, representing people, had departed from the island. During that single decade, 13,539,748 digits had arrived on the island. Since the island had fewer than three million inhabitants, those departing outnumbered the native population by more than four to one. Surely a statistical miracle. It seemed even more so when one considered that this was almost equal to the entire population of the United States west of the Mississippi excluding Texas and California.

The Wandering Jews of the Caribbean. It was a joke: there were more Puerto Ricans up in the air, at any one time, than on earth.

In the past, Puerto Ricans had been taken to work in the sugar-cane fields of Hawaii, of Louisiana, of Texas. The *barrio* in Hawaii had been settled in the early 1900s. There were now Puerto Rican *barrios* in all fifty states. In Seattle, in Los Angeles, in Phoenix, in Denver, in Houston, in Omaha, in the prairies of Middle America, in all the cities along the Great Lakes, from Duluth to Chicago to Cleveland to Buffalo, up and down the Atlantic Coast from Florida to Maine, wherever there were jobs no one else wanted to do there were Puerto Ricans.

"Soon we will go to Alaska," a *barrio* leader in Neuva York said, laughing, "As soon as it gets a little warmer up there." In the census of 1970 there were actually 566 Puerto Ricans reported living in the "Land of the Midnight Sun."

In the tropic heat of the San Juan airport there was an uneasy air of excitement, a mixture of Ellis Island and the Yankee Stadium. Everyone in the waiting room seemed expectant and uncertain. There was none of the fear of crossing a foreign border, the forbidding silence of waiting, the apprehension of denial of visas, the dread of the power of customs officials; but there was nonetheless a tension. Why am I going? Where will I be when I get there? Am I a tourist or a refugee?

"RELAX IN SU CASA LOUNGE," invited a sign, but there weren't any seats.

In the waiting room there was still another sign that enticed the travelers to feel at ease:

EN NUEVA YORK VISITE EL
CLUB CABOROJEÑO
145 ST Y BROADWAY
AMBIENTE FAMILIAR!!

Cabo Rojo was the town where Dr. Ramón Betances, the Father of Independence, had been born. It was still, as it had been, a rural town amid the sugar cane, decorated by *flamboyan* trees and flowers as bright as the sunset at sea. The advertisement for the Club Caborojeño portrayed the night club against a background of tenement windows, pink, peach, green, and red as the tropical night, on the Upper West Side. Here was the *ambiente familiar,* the familiar atmosphere of Cabo Rojo, in Neuva York. On Broadway, the street of fantasy.

In the overheated, overcrowded womb of *La Grande,* the Great One, as the superjetliner 747 was called, subdued silence descended. Unlike most flights, that brought lonely men from office to office, the flight from San Juan was a family affair; the whole of a rural town seemed to be in the plane. Little boys in long pants of Sunday suits, and little girls wrapped in much lace like dolls on wedding cakes ran up and down the aisles. A white-haired grandmother held a huge framed, tinted photograph of her family upon her lap. Her husband watched his *vieja,* his old lady, fumble with the three shopping bags full of gifts, *pasteles* and remembrances that she was bringing to Nueva York, "Ah, *vieja,*" he told her fondly. "You are *loca.*"

Someone asked the stewardess: "How many children on this flight?"

"About four thousand," the girl shrugged helplessly.

In the stereophonic earphones a program of Puerto Rican music was offered, featuring *"Yo Soy el Gallo,"* "I am a Cock," and songs of *amor* galore: *"Sin un amor,"* and *"En nombre del amor,"* and *"El que siembra amor,"* and *"Love Story"* by Chucho Avellanet. There were programs of Now Sounds, and Popular Sounds, and Songs & Stories for the Children from San Juan, like *Land of Billy the Kid.*

The sea was blue. The sky was green. The clouds were a rainbow of lavenders and purples. And the sun glistened through the windows onto the faces of the passengers with a pure and absolute white light.

But few people would look into the sea. It was full of unseen spirits and sharks.

In the morning newspaper was the funeral report of the death of Roberto Clemente, the baseball superstar of the Pittsburgh Pirates and the idol of the islands. His plane, laden with medical supplies for the earthquake victims of Nicaragua, had left the San Juan airport the day before, soared into the sun, and fallen into the sea. "All the good men die," said a young man, Marcos del Valle. "Roberto was a good man. I hope they find his body. His mother and father live near me, in Carolina. And I hope they find his body. The body of a man should not be lost in the sea." Clemente was "Mr. Puerto Rican Power" on the island and a national hero. But the sharks of the sea had devoured him and would not give him back. He was lost. The people on the plane knew Clemente was there in the sea beneath them.

Suddenly the plane was stilled. In seat after seat the people crossed themselves.

The sky darkened. In the gray clouds the gray towers of Nueva York pierced the air; the city appeared and disappeared. Everything became sunless and colorless. The sea looked like cement, sluggish and thick. And the jet either dipped or slipped into the grayness that was everywhere. The whole world vanished as a voice said, "Fasten your seat belts. We will land in Nueva York . . ."

And the people made the sign of the cross.

The Strangers in the City

"On the day I came to New York I decided to leave."

The day he had decided to leave, he had stayed. Where could he go? Like so many exiles he had spent his small savings on the ticket.

He had lived in El Barrio of East Harlem for twenty-five years. Still, he remembered: "I could not imagine living in those dirty buildings. So many families on each floor, who did not know one another, strangers, floor on top of floor of strangers in the city.

"It was so cold. Everywhere it was so cold. The faces of the people. The walls of the buildings. Where was the sun in New York?"

The tall man with the lean face of the mountains had become an urban *jíbaro*. He was a Nueva Yorker. He cursed in Yiddish. He was the janitor in a bank near Wall Street. Or was he the porter? He drank rye, not rum, ate pizzas, not *pasteles*. He had divorced his wife, instead of keeping a mistress. "Who can afford two women in New York?" The grayness of his face reflected the pall the city had cast over him. But in his bright eyes was the remembered sunlight of the island.

"On the island my family lived in a *bohío*. In the old thatched hut, with palm leaves on the roof. But it was more healthy than here. There was more room around the *bohío* to walk. There was more air around the *bohío* to breathe. There was more sun around the *bohío* than in a New York apartment. Even a nice one. And we did not live in a nice one.

"When I came to New York in 1947, the newspapers had just discovered the 'Puerto Rican Problem.' *I* was a 'Puerto Rican Problem,' they said. I wrote a letter to a newspaper that said I didn't think I was a 'Puerto Rican Problem.' We were not as they said we were, dirty, unhealthy, lazy, poor people. That was not the truth; the truth was that New York made us live that way. That was not the way it was at home.

"Everything is dirty here. On the island, the sun cleans everyone, everything. *Oh, why am I here?!*"

The rite of passage was a birth and a death. Being both, it was neither. It was remembered as a trauma that was too painful to remember. So it became nostalgia: that came later, when it had become a dream.

One man who had left the island forty years ago vividly remembered the pain of leaving: "I went on deck. There I saw the island lights, far, far away. I had a pain inside me. I couldn't imagine myself living away from the island. I imagined the island was leaving me. And I was nostalgic. I had hardly left the island and I was already feeling nostalgic." He knew it might be years before he could go home again. Still, the islander never really had left the island. "Wherever we go, there is the island," Governor Ferre had said. "I think we take it with us."

René Torres had left the island when he was three and returned when he was in his forties. "In his heart every Puerto Rican who goes to New York just wants to make enough money to go home," said Torres in his Cemi Folk Art Gallery in San Germán. "The European immigrants who came before us wanted to become Americans. We were born Americans.

"We are probably the only people in history who go to the United States in order that we can leave it!" Torres said.

In the nineteenth century the romantic poet José Gautier Benitez had written of the longing of the exiles of his day: "Borinquén! a name loving to the mind, as the memory of an intense love." It was with passion, not despair, that the poet wrote of the island, describing the land the way a man does a woman, "rising like Venus from the waves." Borinquén offered her lover, he said, more than any woman ever could:

> All is sensual and gentle in you,
> sweet, peaceful, flattering, tender. . . .

The exile remembered his island as his lost love, to whom he would someday return bearing gifts of his good fortune. Manny Diaz, a former city commissioner of New York, said wistfully: "We come to this country with the idea that if you work hard, you make a lot of money. Then you can go home and live happily ever after. Well, we work hard. But we never make enough money to go back home." Diaz had come to New York as a child forty-five years ago, and he remembered little of his birthplace. Might a man be nostalgic for what he had never known?

"This is not our house!" he said. "Even though we try, day by day, to get the American society to respond to us, to accept us, deep inside our feeling is that this is not our house, this is not our home. Our roots are elsewhere."

In their new homes there was nothing to make the islanders feel at home. The life style, the clothing, the language, the family life, the workday, the tempo, the streets, the emotional atmosphere, the psychology of the people, the crime, the fear, the streets, the tenements, the sounds of the city, the climate, the snow—all were foreign. Where was there any memory of the tropics, even the slightest, in the Nueva York?

El Barrio, as East Harlem or Spanish Harlem came to be called, was where the islander found an island of Puerto Ricans in the city. Here he learned that self-isolation was the first lesson of survival. Gerena Valintin, who was a "pioneer" and old-timer, having come to El Barrio in 1936, remembered the old neighborhood as a beleaguered island surrounded by Italians on one side and Jews on the other side. "El Barrio was self-contained. The Puerto Ricans lived from Fifth Avenue to Eighth Avenue, and from 110th Street to 116th Street. That was it! And you couldn't go beyond Fifth Avenue, where the *barrio* is now. They would attack you, brutally. They would write curses on the walls. Many Puerto Ricans were assaulted, maimed and killed by the brutalized gangs who didn't want a Puerto Rican to move into their neighborhood. Or even walk through it." Years later Valintin became the president of the Congreso de los Pueblos, the Congress of Puerto Rican Home Towns, and a respected community leader; he served on the city's Human Rights Commission and in numerous civic positions. But in his youth he had walked the streets with fear. "Anyone who walked east of Fifth Avenue took his life in his own hands," he said.

El Barrio was not a *barrio,* it was *the barrio.* In it the Puerto Rican was hidden, safe, invisible. "At the time we were unnoticed by New Yorkers," Gerena Valintin recalled. To be invisible was not to be free, or unaffected by prejudices, but within El Barrio, at least, one was not as vulnerable to the hostile city. A man might still find a sanctuary within the island of himself. "It was important to the *macho* of a man to know there was one place no one could touch him," Valintin said. "That was in El Barrio."

In the years after World War II, when the migration of exiles from the island became an exodus, it was no longer possible to be invisible. The change was dramatic and disastrous.

Manny Diaz, who lived through the history of the migration, talked of it with an ironic detachment, as if it were unreal:

"I came here in 1927. There were at that time maybe fifteen hundred Puerto Ricans in New York. We were nonexistent. We were nonpersons. Even in the 1930s we were no more than fifty thousand, probably less. And then, in the late 1930s and during World War II we were a 'manpower asset.' We were needed in the war factories. We were a 'positive asset to the city.' But after the war when we began to compete for jobs with older ethnic groups, and we began to ally ourselves with Blacks in attacking the closed doors of the establishment, and we were a million strong, we became a 'threat.' Suddenly, we were those 'lazy, dirty' Puerto Ricans.

"Evolution of the Puerto Ricans in New York from the nonperson, to the positive asset, to the negative threat was fascinating."

So many of the islanders came in the late 1940s and early 1950s that the older immigrants, from Europe, feared that they would be displaced. In his unabashed memoir of those years Richard Goldstein wrote in *New York* magazine: "These people were 'Spanish.' They came in swarms like ants turning the sidewalks brown, multiplied and settled in." The invasion of these people was so great "whole sections of the city had fallen" to them. And "the subway, the sky, Long Island Sound turned the color of dark rum by the sheer congestion of their bodies." His was a dark-skinned nightmare. "I did not hate them or fear them," Goldstein went on, "or even feel disgusted by them. I only knew . . . they were here irrevocably; the best you could do to avoid contamination was to keep them out of mind." The Latin was a stereotype, not a human being. If you sat beside "this greaser with hair like an oily palm tree," on the subway, "you just knew he had a razor up his sleeve.

"Spics. Specks. The name fit," he wrote. "They were barnacles."

The Puerto Ricans, beginning to overflow El Barrio into the older ghettos, soon learned not only how to do battle for their "turf," with "fighting gangs," something unknown on the island. They were expected to sing and dance at the same time, a cultural fete that was immortalized by *West Side Story*.

The flamboyant newspapers of the day began an unending chorus of stories of fear and despair about the "Puerto Rican problem." The New York *Mirror* of September 1, 1959, reassured the troubled city that the police "were on the prowl" in the "sidestreet jungle" of the *barrio* for teenagers:

1,400 COPS
TO WAR ON
TEEN GANGS

All the boys mentioned in this litany to "the murder of children" were Puerto Ricans. In the newspapers' journalese the *barrio* had become the "festering jungle" of the poor. The word "jungle" was the favorite of the time, used to describe any Puerto Rican neighborhood. And the culprits of the "wave of crime" that filled the newspapers were almost always an unnamed "group of Puerto Rican youth." The Mafia was not yet popular.

Some of the austere publications of academia agonized, in sympathetic tones, over the horrors of *barrio* life and the plight of the poor Puerto Ricans and created a stereotype of their own—that of the passive victims of the "culture of poverty." Either they were portrayed as knife-wielding, aggressive, murderous and raucous people who turned once-tranquil ghettos into high-crime areas, rampant with drugs and immorality; or they were lazy, unmotivated, passive, and humble peasants, happy as children, who came to the city "to get on welfare." "It seems whenever our people assert their rights we are classified as 'violence-prone temperaments.' Such comments do not jibe with our other stereotype as 'passive, humble people,' which used to be how 'expert liberals' referred to us," later commented the director of a South Bronx community center, Ramón Velez.

The institutions of the city were foreign to the islanders. And the

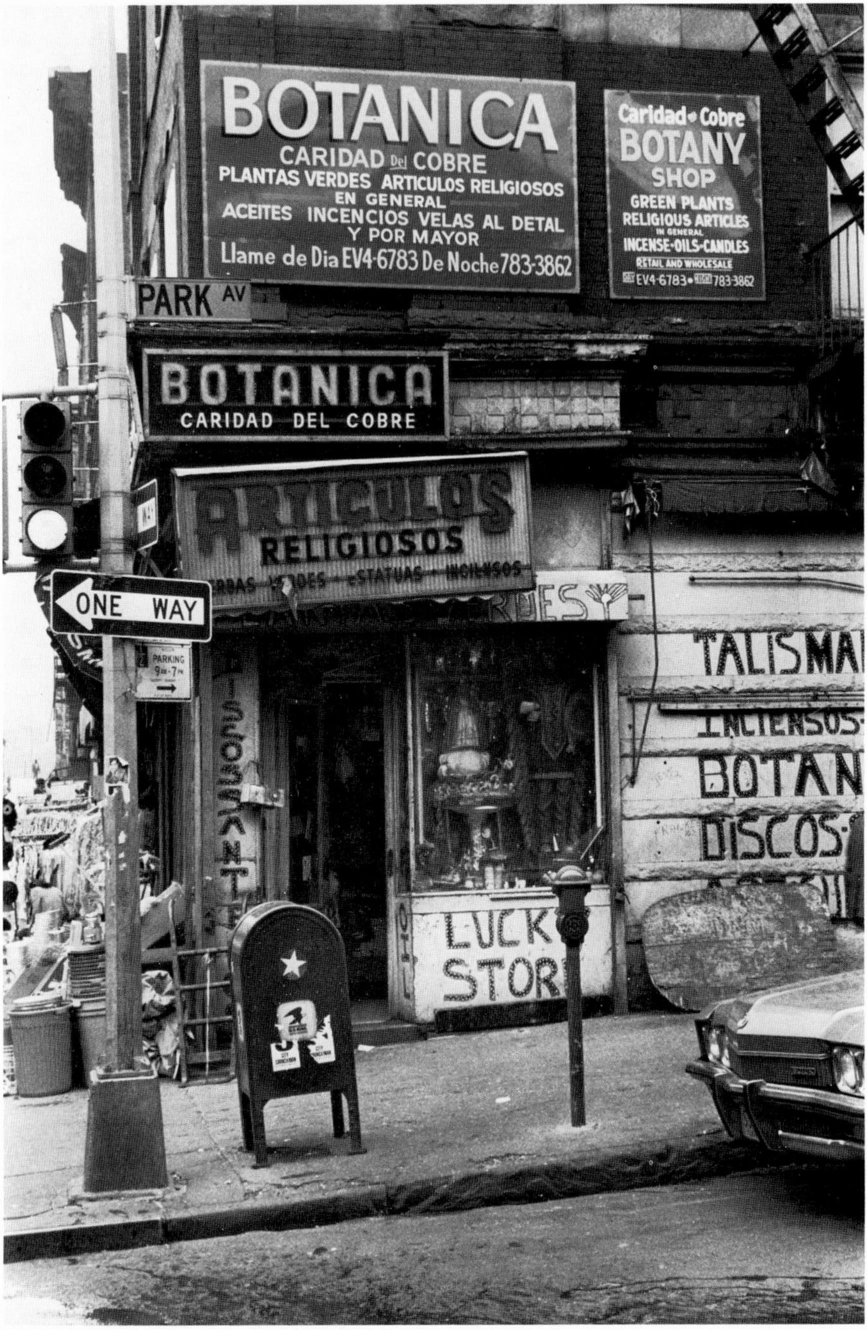

Botánica in El Barrio—"Living in New York you need the help of all the gods."

A cold family in a cold subway

Los projectos—a live canary in a plastic apartment

The tropical fountains of Manhattan

The domino players: *(above)* in a city park of San Juan; *(below)* beside an empty lot on East 103rd Street

A *bodega* on the island

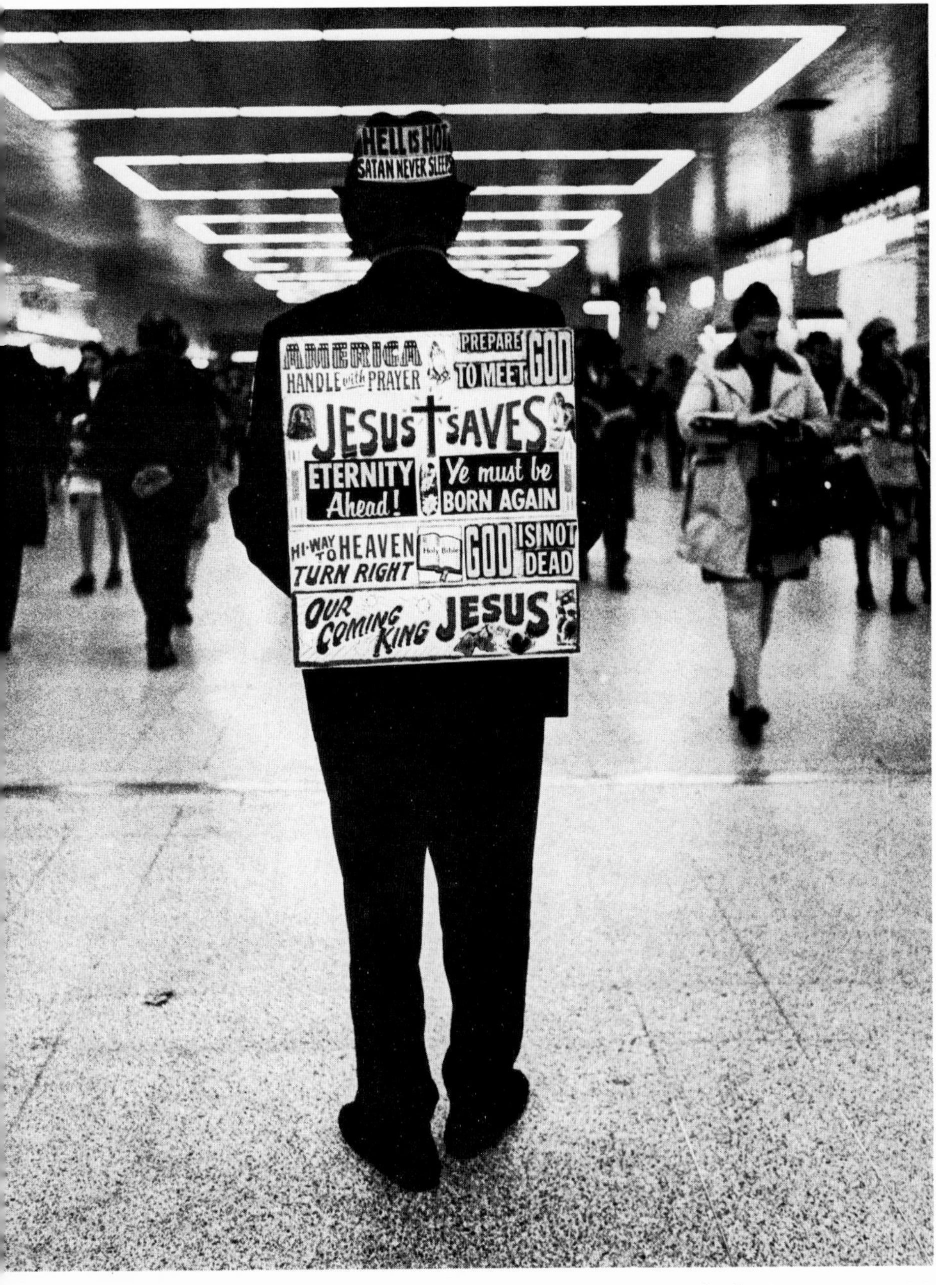

Puerto Rican evangelist in the Port Authority Bus Terminal

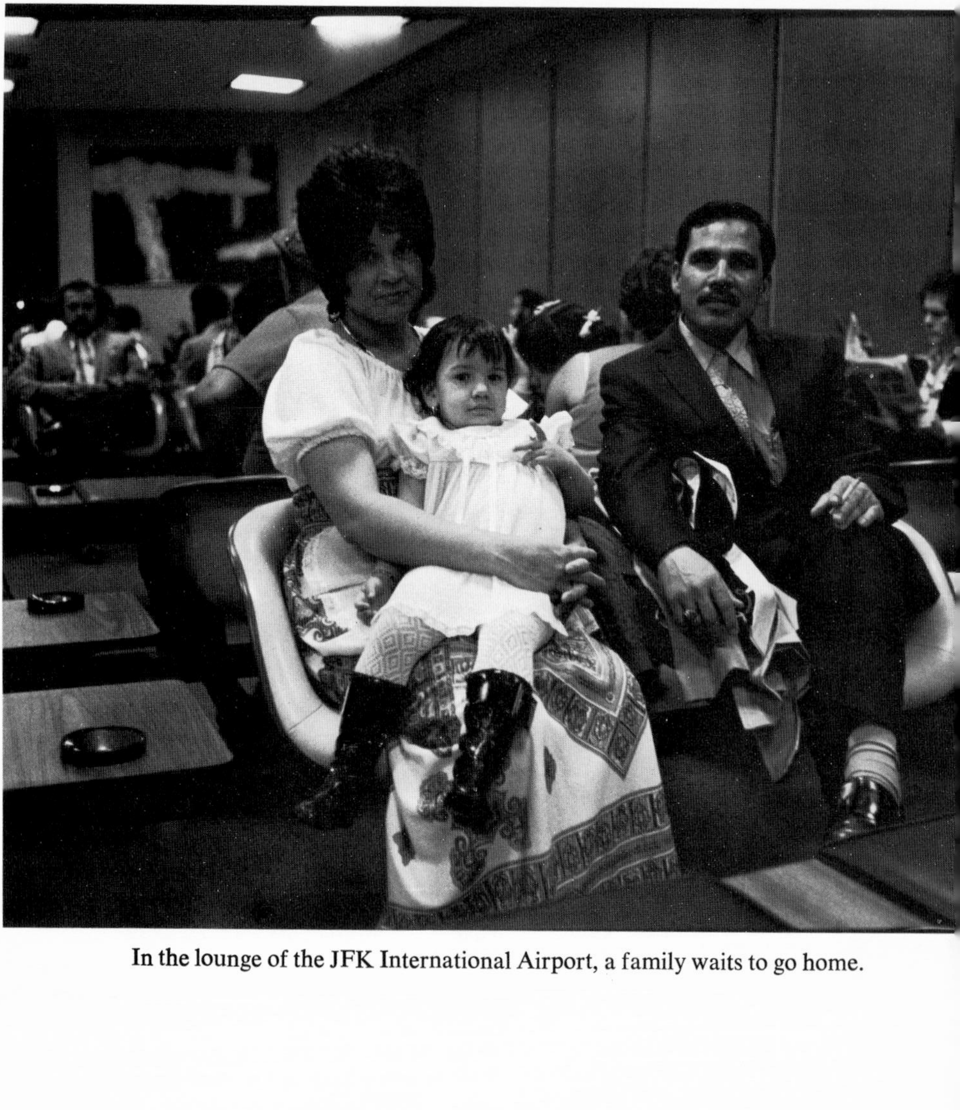

In the lounge of the JFK International Airport, a family waits to go home.

islanders were treated as foreigners by city officials. One young man, Herberto Sanchez Martinez, had brought suit against a former employer for back wages in the 1950s. The routine and humdrum case was heard before Magistrate Abner Surpless, in the Flatbush (Brooklyn) Municipal Court. Surpless, a former New York City Councilman, declared angrily in the midst of the trial: "It's too bad these people are citizens of the United States! Let's behave like Americans! Not like people over there [on the island] who are constantly jabbering and irritating!"

The young man told reporters that he had been cursed as a "bum" by the irate Magistrate, and berated in these words: "They [Puerto Ricans] cannot speak English, [but] they come over here! Where do they think they are!"

It was the temper of the times. The prominent Kings County Judge Samuel S. Leibowitz had proposed that all immigration from Puerto Rico be halted. He accused the islanders of responsibility for the increased criminal activity in the city, on the one hand, and the passive swelling of the welfare rolls, on the other hand. State Supreme Court Justice Emilio Nunez responded that it seemed "un-American" to bar American citizens from entering America. And the then director of the Commonwealth's Division of Migration, Joseph Monserrat, late member of the New York City Board of Education, politely suggested that Judge Leibowitz's approach to the *barrio*'s crime might be "pathological." Still, the proposal to prohibit, or limit, Puerto Ricans from the country they were supposedly citizens of received enthusiastic editorial support in several New York City newspapers.

Monserrat said: "The belief that our country has always stretched forth its arms to the 'poor and wretched' masses is simply not true! *No group has ever been welcomed with open arms by the nation as a whole.* . . . Remember when we whispered about the 'yellow threat'? Remember the history of the Know-Nothing party? Do you recall the reception given the Irish and German Catholics, or the Polish and the Russian Jews?" Monserrat, who was Commissioner of Migration at the time, had access to many official documents. He cited what was presumably one such report on newly arriving migrants to the city:

"They are satisfied with poor living conditions. . . . They don't want modern facilities. . . . They don't use bathtubs. . . . They're destructive and overspend money. . . . We've known about any number of illegitimate who have moved into an already overcrowded home with the mother. . . . I recall a family with thirteen of their own. Sister has four illegitimate children. . . .

"Is this New York City? Are these Puerto Ricans?" Monserrat asked: "No, the city is Cincinnati. The migrants are white Southern mountaineers."

Echoing through the years these stereotypes have been remarkably enduring. A front-page article in the *Wall Street Journal* in November, 1971, depicted the fear of residents in a remodeled brownstone and townhouse section of Brooklyn known as Park Slope, who dreaded the day Puerto Ricans might move into their neighborhood from an adjacent *barrio.* The intellectuals and professionals of Park Slope were threatened by an invasion of "raucous black and Puerto Rican children," wrote the reporter, Paul Goldberger. "On hot summer nights [the fear] creates the tableau of upper middle class white families tucked away in their elegant parlors listening to $1,200 stereos, while outside on the street the poor congregate to drink cheap wine, to listen to 'soul' or Spanish music, blaring from half a dozen transistor radios, and occasionally, to cut each other up with knives."

For two years I and my family lived on Seventh Avenue (as we had lived in the Lower East Side before that), the dividing line between Park Slope and the *barrio,* and never experienced the fear the *Wall Street Journal* reporter had seen. But that was no doubt due to our faulty perception of the ever-popular stereotypes.

Prejudice works best, however, when it is expressed with brotherly love. It is then universal and unconscious. Dr. Harold Wise, the founder of the Martin Luther King, Jr., Health Center in the South Bronx, believed the people of the *barrio* ought to be treated with love, like the whores of Saigon: "A nurturing has to occur. Like the prostitutes of Vietnam, who were given dolls and allowed to live a childhood they never had, the people of the South Bronx need to be nurtured," said the neighborhood doctor.

The language of social science was less sentimental. George Sternlieb, director of the Center for Urban Policy Research of Rutgers University, compared the fate of the *barrio* poor of the South Bronx to that of alcoholics; the poor were "drunk" on poverty. "You can pick a drunk up from the gutter. You clean him up. You put a new suit on him. But you don't change things from the inside. In ten days you got a drunk back in the gutter."

"Racism is usually very subtle, very creative, very real, in its ways of keeping Puerto Ricans down," said Manny Diaz. It need not be expressed vulgarly and brutally. "Not officially, because it doesn't have to be. It's built into the political and economic life of the city," Diaz said. "The role of Puerto Ricans in New York, for the last twenty-five years, has been to provide the manpower for the garment industry, the hotel industry, the custodian trades, and on the waterfront—all the menial, low-paying, sweatshop jobs that have been vacated by ethnic groups who have gone through the process—the Irish, the Italians, the Jews. . . .

"So we inherited the racism of everyone else, second and third hand, that was inhuman when it was new. And now it is hardened and institutionalized and invisible.

"We are not suffering our failures as Puerto Ricans, but are suffering the failures of the American system. It is just not built to absorb another ethnic group."

And yet they came to the city, by hundreds upon hundreds of thousands. There were 800,000 Puerto Ricans in New York, reported the 1970 census. When community leaders protested that the figures were "gross underestimates" Census Bureau officials admitted they had previously erred by as much as 30 percent in head counts in the New York ghettos. There were more than one million Puerto Ricans in the city, according to Diaz. Probably one million and a quarter, thought Hector Vazquez of the Puerto Rican Forum. Maybe as many as one million and a half, said Valintin.

No one knew. In the computers of the Tourist Development

Corporation of Puerto Rico, the data revealed that in the single year of 1968–69 an estimated 2,112,264 "arrivals" had visited the island, and 2,105,217 "departures" were tabulated. But looking behind the statistics revealed that of the 2,105,217 some 486,841 were American servicemen on shore leave; while 122,451 were tourists from cruise ships; and 361,741 were visitors from the Virgin Islands; and 237,584 were from "foreign countries." So about half of the computer's output—1,208,617—had left for New York. How many of these were vacationing tourists and how many were Puerto Rican exiles the computers did not know.

So many came. Why so many?

"The reconstruction of the island destroyed almost as many jobs—poor ones it is true, but jobs—as it made" was the explanation of sociologists Nathan Glazer and Daniel Moynihan, in *Beyond the Melting Pot.* It seemed an inevitable, and almost accidental, result of industrialization to them. But, to former Commissioner of Migration of the Government of Puerto Rico, Nick Lugo, Jr., it was neither inevitable nor accidental. Lugo thought the migration might have been planned by the government itself because agriculture couldn't cope with the population's growth.

"So, in order for them [the government] *to get started, or whatever, they saw a need to be able to get some people out of the island,"* the former Migration Commissioner bluntly declared; for it was by exporting the unemployed that *"those who remained on the island* [*were*] *employed."*

Was there a deliberate and predetermined policy by the governments of Puerto Rico and the United States "to get some people out of the island"? If such a policy was to work it would have to have been approved by both governments. Not so, retorted indignant officials on both sides of the sea, who vigorously denied the existence of any such agreements, written or verbal.

Many emigrants of the late forties, however, remembered being given leaflets by local municipal officials that encouraged them to leave the island, with promises of good jobs and wages in New York. Some said the speeches and songs from loudspeakers in the plazas of their small mountain towns, installed by the government, told of the wonders of life in New York.

One man, who worked in the late forties as a flight manager of a pioneer independent airline in San Juan, that carried thousands of jobless men to New York, remembered talking to *jíbaros* who boasted not only of promises of money they would receive on arriving, but of money they had been promised before leaving. He remembered labor contracts for migrant farm workers that were signed and ignored. He remembered that men were stranded in the city without money and without jobs.

The San Juan newspapers carried numerous exposés, in those years, of frauds and scandals that victimized the emigrants. Yet there were no Congressional investigations.

Rural poverty was not what had caused the islanders to come to New York. The exodus from the island was relatively small in the years before 1950, when the island economy was traditional and rural. It burgeoned after the industrialization began in 1950; in one decade, from 1950 to 1960, the exiles from the island increased from 226,110 to 615,384.* And these exiles were rural families, fleeing "progress," not jobless workers. Unlike the Jewish immigrants of the turn of the century, who were mostly skilled artisans in manufacturing or commerce, the Labor Department of the island reported that

* Every government figure of the numbers of Puerto Ricans in the United States has been a gross underestimate. Some believe these underestimates are as high as *one third* of the total. Why? The reason is partially that census takers can only count "visible" Puerto Ricans and is partially that families in the *barrios* move perhaps more often than any other group in the country. Nonetheless the figures do indicate certain trends, as do these population statistics for "Persons of Puerto Rican Origin in Coterminous United States":

Of Puerto Rican birth:			
1910	1,513	1950	226,110
1920	11,811	1960	615,384
1930	52,774	1970	581,376
1940	69,967		
Of United States birth:			
1950	75,265	1970	810,087
1960	272,278		

71 percent of those migrating had been employed in farming, or had "no work experience." Less than one in ten had ever worked in a factory.

After twenty years of migrations *from* industrialization, the island faced the same dilemma that it had a generation ago. Industrialist Amadeo I. D. Francis, director of the Puerto Rico Manufacturers Association, told a Congressional Subcommittee on Education and Labor in 1971 that the alternatives facing Puerto Rican industry "are an annual increase in unemployment of 20 percent, or a substantial increase in migration to the U.S. cities, which are already facing a staggering welfare burden." If the unemployed were not exported to the mainland, the unemployment rate might well soar to more than 50 percent.

So the poorest of the poor flew back and forth "like ping-pong balls" in the words of Commissioner of Migration Nick Lugo, Jr., who with his father owned forty-five travel agencies.

On a dirt road to Cataño, near the sea, a small dark man, with torn shoes and a jaunty black fedora, sat on a wooden crate and talked of his flight from New York on the "seven four and seven." The superjet "was a flying subway train." Borinquén to Manhattan, Manhattan to Borinquén, he had flown back and forth fourteen times. "I am in the jet set!" He liked the old days better; he liked to go by sea, because he liked to fish. That was one reason he came back to the island so often.

And how was the fishing?

"I yesterday catch not one fish, but three fish," he said. "They weigh five pounds. Each of them. More than I like anything I like to fish, if I catch the fish."

Where did he fish?

"On the island," he poked out to sea with his fishing pole. "I do not know the name in English. Maybe it is the Island of the Goat? Or something like that. My father has a place to fish. He knows the fish there. They wait for him to come.

"My father is the fisherman. I am not a fisherman, any more. I fish for quiet, a little quiet. In New York I work in a metal factory on

Ninth Avenue. So it is noisy as hell. Now I am on vacation. It is strange to come home on a vacation. On vacation a man should go away from home. But a Puerto Rican, where does he go on vacation? He comes home!"

Where was his home?

The little man looked incredulous. "My boss told me, 'Pancho, don't forget to come back.' He tells that to me every time I come home. He calls me 'Pancho.' That is not my name. But he calls me that every time. 'Pancho,' my boss told me, 'don't stay there and fish for the rest of your life. Don't forget, I need you on the job. And you need the job.' "

Would he prefer to stay on the island? And forget New York?

He laughed.

So why did he go back?

"The money," he sighed. "That is the reason everybody goes. The money."

And with that he walked down the dirt road to the sea. The lilt in his walk was that of a free man; it was a Puerto Rican way of walking. In New York he did not walk to work that way.

"I see you, maybe in New York?" he yelled over his shoulder. "Eh? We go fishing? For the money?"

The Odyssey of a *Jíbaro*

The son of a *jíbaro,* he had no money. He had landed in New York penniless in the depth of the Great Depression. He did not know there was a depression or what a depression was. He simply knew he was young and hungry. He came as a stowaway seeking adventure and a job. He remembered what he found:

I was illegal. . . .

When I came to America, I came in style. I traveled in a lifeboat on the deck of a United States Army transport, as a stowaway. That was in 1933.

Everyone on the ship was wearing khaki or white uniforms. But me. I was wearing a black suit. That was because it was the only suit I had.

My father died when I was a little boy. And my mother was so poor she had too many children to feed. She could not feed us. And she had to send us to different places. I was sent to a home for orphans. Even if I was not an orphan, I was an orphan. Later, when I was older, I joined the Army, maybe because it was like a home for orphans. That's how I knew about the Army transport.

In New York City I went up to Harlem, to 116th Street because I heard some Puerto Ricans were living there. But I didn't know any of them. So I used to sleep in Central Park. I had five cents in my pocket. The grass was nice in the park and I liked to sleep under the stars.

Every day I looked for a job. I didn't know there weren't any jobs in 1933.

One day I was sitting on a stoop on 116th Street. I still remember it. Some pieces of papers were lying in the street. I picked them up and smoothed them out with my hand and decided to write some letters. But I didn't have a pencil. So, I borrowed a pencil of someone. You will never guess who I wrote those letters to. I wrote to Mayor Fiorello La Guardia, who was Mayor of New York City, and to President Franklin Roosevelt, who was President of the United States, and to Santiago Iglesias, who was Resident Commissioner for Puerto Rico.

And I asked them to get me a job!

The stoop I was sitting on wasn't my address, because I didn't have one. But I wrote it on the letters anyway. And then I had to borrow some pennies for stamps, because I didn't want to spend the five cents I had in my pocket.

After that I waited every day on the stoop for an answer. On the second day I got an answer from Mayor Fiorello La Guardia. It wasn't a letter. It was a social worker.

She told me that I could get relief. That was what they called welfare in those days. It would give me money for a month's rent, so I could have a room full of cockaroaches to sleep in. I think that she thought it was unhealthy to sleep in the park, in the open air.

No! I told her. I didn't want relief and a room full of cockaroaches. What I wanted was a job. She shook her head and went away, saying, Another one of those crazy Puerto Ricans!

In a few days I got an answer from the President of the United States. He sent me one of his *social workers, who offered me the same things: relief and a room full of cockaroaches. But I just shrugged. No! I told her. What I wanted was a job.*

Of course, the Resident Commissioner for Puerto Rico, Santiago Iglesias, took a little longer to answer. It always takes a Puerto Rican a little longer. He has to think about it. That's something a Yanqui doesn't have to bother with. Anyway, the Commissioner sent me his *social worker, who suggested I walk across the street. On 116th Street, in those days, there was the Puerto Rican Government Office. It was right across the street from the stoop where I was sitting. So I walked it.*

They had no money to offer me because Puerto Rico was too poor itself. But they offered to get me some relief and that same room full of cockaroaches.

In America, I thought, there is no work. There is only money.

So I kept on walking. I walked so much looking for a job that my heel fell off my shoe. And, as I told you, I had only five cents in my pocket. But five cents won't pay a shoemaker. I went to a Puerto Rican shoemaker I knew, and I told him this:

Let me sew my heel on my shoe and I will sew some shoes for you. I know how because I learned how to sew shoes on the island. That way I will pay you by helping you in the store. That was how I got a job in New York.

A man who gets something for nothing loses something. His soul. His pride. His manhood.

They tried to buy my manhood from me with relief money. I learned that is what they try to do to Puerto Ricans. They are still doing that. They yell about welfare, but they like to give it. It is like the war. They yell about it, but they fight it. If they didn't like it, they would stop it. Welfare is like that. It is a cheap way to buy a Puerto Rican's manhood. It is a lie to say a man will come to New York to sell his manhood. He comes because he is dreaming of a break. And he gets broken.

22

In the Alien Fields

In the piny woods of New Jersey there were two palm trees. They were made of metal.

On the highway in the outskirts of Camden the palm trees grew in cement blocks beside a miniature golf course. The men from Aguadilla and Guayama, who worked on the farms, joked about the "palm trees of the *Yanquis,*" with riveted leaves.

The winter snow fell upon the metallic trees, and where it had melted in the spring sun, tiny icicles hung like a strange fruit.

It would soon be spring. The farms of southern New Jersey would once again become noisy with voices of Puerto Rican children, *arroz con pollo* would dominate the smells of pizzas, and in the evenings the songs of the islands would be heard in the lonely shacks of the migrants. In a few weeks the exiles would have returned to the alien fields.

The landless farmers who came to work in the fields of New Jersey were known on the island as the stubbornest, most independent and headstrong of men. *Jíbaros*—they were the equivalents of the old cowboys and ornery small ranchers of the West; they were artisans of the soil, knowledgeable in those archaic and ancient trades that had sustained mankind for centuries, before anyone had heard of farm machinery. The *jíbaros,* it was said, were illiterate, unschooled, simple-minded men who did not know anything except how to survive.

But these farmers-without-farms were contemptuously belittled. Even those who sympathized with their "plight" referred to them as "hopeless," "joyless," "uneducated," and "unemployable." They were none of these.

"Farmers have to have intelligent hands, quick minds, and strong backs and alert eyes, and a human heart. So do farm workers," said Moises Mendez, who had labored in the fields all his life. "The office and factory worker in the city, he would never 'make it' in the fields, on the farm. He wouldn't last a day. He would be *mierda* [shit]."

"The earth does not 'degrade' man," said another *jíbaro,* from Utuado. "It is man who degrades the earth. The farm work is not degrading to us. But those who hire us, and those who help us, it is they who degrade us."

In the early 1900s thousands of skilled Puerto Rican sugar-cane planters and cutters were sent halfway around the world, to Hawaii, not as cheap labor, but to teach the Hawaiians how to grow sugar. Skillful men, with a lifetime of experience in the sugar-cane fields, were sent to Louisiana and Texas in the pre–World War I years. The skills of the Puerto Rican sugar growers were to a large degree responsible for the cane fields that were, ironically, to undercut the island's sugar industry. As they were exported from the island, so the crops they harvested in the United States would be exported to the island. The migrants were treated as if they were farm produce.

And yet, these were men of inherited dignity. In the farm towns of south Jersey, as elsewhere, the *jíbaros* were insulted not so much by their work, or by their living conditions, as by the way they were treated by people. Living in a shack, with a torn mattress, or no mattress at all, was hardly new to them. It was the indignity of being thought of with contempt, or worse, with sympathy, that infuriated the *jíbaros,* whose name in the folklore of the island meant a "free man."

The small towns of south Jersey were clean and conservative. A farm town dies slowly and genteelly. Perhaps there was a new "bowling lane," where the old railroad depot had been. Perhaps there was a new "discount" junk store in an old cornfield. Not much more had changed. The main street was an old *Saturday Evening Post* cover. The people were decent and old-fashioned. And it was probably true that George Washington had once slept there on his way to or from Valley Forge, not too far away.

But they did not willingly, or pleasantly, serve Puerto Ricans in the local diner. The dark-skinned farmers, who had dirt under their fingernails, were not welcomed in the whitewashed and post-Revolutionary-period churches. On the streets they were arrested for the slightest violations of town ordinances they could not read.

"Migrant workers are suffering the consequences of the discriminatory structure of American society," a statement by the island's labor leaders said in the fall of 1970. "Our fellow Puerto Rican workers suffer four or five months of the year, every year. . . . Their civil rights are violated daily. They are jailed simply because they do not understand English. . . . They are not served in restaurants. They are mistreated and beaten by the police." Such indignities so troubled the signatories—Pedro Grant, leader of the United Labor Movement; Peter P. Huegel, of the AFL-CIO; Bishop Reus-Froylan, of the Episcopal Church; and Bishop Autulio Parrilla Bonilla of the Catholic Church—that they concluded with the *grito* "We must act!" But all they could propose was another investigation.

Once every year, at least, a television crew went into the fields in search of a "human interest" documentary. The newspapers regularly printed exposés. In between the visitations of the mass media there were investigations by Congressional and legislative committees, state and federal, who studied the misery of the exiled farmers, held hearings, issued detailed and impressive reports, and often offered bills that sometimes passed but were seldom enforced by the local officialdom.

Every once in a while a tragic newspaper story troubled the public. On a railroad crossing a farm truck, full of men, women and children, might be hit by a train, tossing the singing passengers to their death like squashed tomatoes. Or there might be a deadly fire, such as the one in Pilesgrove Township, New Jersey, in 1967, when five little children "died in a rundown four-room shack, while their mother was out picking leeks in a nearby field."* It was that terrible blaze that was partially responsible for Cornell University's closing of the migrant labor camp on its "research farm" that winter. The scholarly labor camp had been condemned by the State Health Department for several violations of the sanitary code, by a Senate committee, and by a report of the Migrant Legal Assistance Program, which stated: "Cornell's exploitation of the migrant laborers was a deplorable and unjustifiable act." The university's shacks were no better or worse than any others—holes in the walls, unlit toilets, few windows, and some so small that a family of eight was crowded into one and a half rooms. Like any farmer, a university department head complained, "It will cost the university more money" not to use migrants. The public disbelief and anger that a university would hire migrants in order to study them in its "research" projects forced the closing of the dismal camp.

These exposés of "bad conditions" in the migrant camps were "tremendously exaggerated," said Manuel Casiano, former Commissioner of Migration for the Commonwealth of Puerto Rico. He cited figures showing that one year 50,000 farm workers had earned $20 million. That came to $400 per migrant for four or more months in the fields. It came to about $25 a week. The government's "model" farm-labor contract did not require that employers guarantee the workers more than $25 a week "after all deductions."

So deep was the gulf of distrust that developed between the migrants and the officials of the Migration Office that the files on how and who was recruited to work in the fields were guarded as state secrets. "If it was known where [in what rural towns] we recruit, '*they*' would make trouble for us," said former Migration Commissioner Nick Lugo, Jr. " '*They*' would picket us!" he said. And why would migrants picket the Migration Office? He would not say. He merely muttered, frowning, "Politics."

"We try to make people feel a little comfortable here," said one of the officials in the Migrant Labor Office in downtown Camden, New

* *New York Times.* November 28, 1967.

Jersey, a white-haired, genial man, a Mr. Falcon. "But it is not easy.

"More and more, the farms will be mechanized. The machines are everywhere; even the tomatoes will soon be picked by machine," he said. In their belief that farm machinery will soon replace the farm workers some of "the big farmers, again, treat the workers badly." They believe they will "no longer need the Puerto Ricans," he said; so they treat them as if they were "expendable," not as "human beings."

"The big farmers do not understand the trouble they are making for themselves," Falcon said. "Soon our office will be replaced by a union. Cesar Chavez is coming to New Jersey, and Florida, and Wisconsin. And then they will see!"

Not only the white farmers but the Puerto Rican *barrios* were indebted to migrants, whom everyone insulted, Falcon said. "In every family, in every home, in every tenement apartment in the city, there is someone who originally came here as a migrant farm worker. Later on, when they earned a little money, they went to the cities. And so they brought their wives and children from the island. But in the beginning they worked in the fields."

It was the strength and courage of the *jíbaro* that made survival in the city possible, he said.

On the country roads the melting snows ran in rivulets along the fences. A man walked slowly along the country road, huddled in his jacket. He had come from the beaches of Aguadilla. He was one of the first of the work crews brought from the island to ready the migrants' camp, which had been boarded up and empty all winter. The nests of field mice and squirrels had to be cleaned out of the shacks and the old mattresses aired. In two weeks it would be seeding time.

23

The Birth of a *Barrio*: Division Street, Chicago

The man came out of a Polish bar on Division Street. He had "to check on my car." Some dark-skinned boys, Puerto Rican and black, who were leaning on his fenders did not move, but smiled. He smiled back at them. "I wanted to see if my car was still here." It was a joke.

In the eyes of one boy there was a flicker of anger.

"My God! this neighborhood has changed," the man muttered. He pointed to a high-rise apartment house. "All black in there," he said. "You know, I come here only twice in eight years. Once to a wedding. Once to a wake. I moved out eight years ago. Lived here all my life. And I don't ever want to come back. Ever!"

Why?

"It's a jungle," he said.

Had he been mugged?

"No."

Then what?

"Everything is changed," he said too loudly, looking at the boys. "For the worse!"

The boys leaned on his fenders looking blank. One of those *"¡No habla Ingles!"* looks. But the alerted eyes betrayed them.

In the auditorium of the Holy Trinity High School there was a concert of Polish song and dance. The posters, entirely in Polish, no English, promised a "gay memory" of the old country and the good old days on Division Street. The stolid men in black suits came with their careful-faced wives as if to church. The widowed grandmothers wore nylon *babushkas* bought at Sears. The girls were resplendent urban peasants, with embroidered blouses under the jackets of the pants suits. The little children were well behaved.

"Everyone is here," said a man. "The whole neighborhood. I mean, the *old* neighborhood."

The massive church, the school, the buildings of Holy Trinity were a sanctuary for the memories of the Polish families, who on Sunday afternoons had paraded up and down Division Street. It was their street. The sons and daughters of the Polish immigrants, unhappily affluent and in debt, came from the suburbs on such Sunday pilgrimages in search of a "gay memory" of their parents' past or their youth and did not wish to remember the harsher realities. All they knew was what they wished to remember. Across from Holy Trinity the Polish National Alliance Building still stood, sturdy as an empty bank. On Hadden Avenue nearby, Saint Stanislaus College was closed, its windows boarded up. The signs of the old neighborhood had faded on the abandoned taverns and the sausage shops, or they were repainted in Spanish.

Division Street had always been the battleground of immigrants. It was the street of strangers to one another, who never stayed there long enough to get to know one another. On such a street life was hard, and survival was harder.

In his hymn to Division Street of the old Polish ghetto, *Never Come Morning,* Nelson Algren had paid loving penance to its evil. The young hero, Bruno "Lefty" Bicek, in an often-quoted cry, uttered the pain of poverty that has echoed through ghetto literature ever since:

"I been hungry all my life, all the time," he told himself. "I never get my teeth into anything all my own." . . . Too hungry for the arid place he'd been born in. For lights, music, the women of the *gospodas,* all these awakened the hunger in a man. The same hunger that might, wolf-like, lie sleeping for an hour, or a day. Or else waken and keep a man in trouble the rest of his life. . . . These were things that made you a man if you possessed them, or a wolf—if you were born where such things were only to the hunter.

Later in the book, Bicek and his buddy Benkowski talked about what it was like to be "a Polack who ain't got much" on Division Street:

"All the hoods on Division got guts," Benkowski once told him, "but they got no brains. . . . How many guys, besides me, you think got brains . . . ?"

Bruno considered the answer now: the alderman had brains, the democratic committeeman had brains, One-Eye Tenczara at Potomac Street had brains. Even the precinct captain, Figura, had some brains. And the barber had brains or he wouldn't be getting twenty cents off every two dollars Mama Tomek's women earned. But that was all. That covered the ward. That's all the brains there were between Chicago Avenue and Division. That took care of all the penny matchers, all the jackpot sneaks, all the buck priests, the Gallaghers just off the boat, the bartenders and all the spooks [Blacks] on WPA.

"It's best for a Polack who ain't got much not to think too much about gettin' more," he philosophized easily.

Zgoda, the Polish ghetto's newspaper on Division Street, took offense at the book. It was an insult to Polish-Americans, the editors editorialized, and pro-Nazi propaganda; even though its writer was in the U.S. Army at the time, fighting Nazis. "No man is quicker to sense contempt than an outcast," Algren replied. "None is more swift to return contempt for contempt."

In those days one of the ghetto sayings was *"Grzmoty zabili diabla, a diabla zabili żydy"*—"When the thunder kills like a devil, then a devil kills like a Jew." There were no "Porto Ricos," no "spiks," on Division Street back in 1941.

The immigrant had to have a bad memory. If he remembered everything he did in order to live, life would be too terrible to endure. So his ethnic memories protected him for other immigrants. Since in the beginning the native inhabitants had been slaughtered, or driven away, almost all the settlers of Chicago were immigrants. In the early years it was the Irish who lived on the edges of the lake's swamps.

Their shanties of wood, where Mrs. O'Leary kept her mythical cow, to the north of the river, were like a peasant village, foul-smelling, with the "filthy, slushy miscalled water, a nauseous Chowder" of the Chicago River—the "Garlic Creek." Late in the nineteenth century the Polish immigrants came to build the largest Polish ghetto in the land.

By 1900 Chicago was the home not only of the largest Polish ghetto but of the largest Scandinavian, Greek, Lithuanian, Bohemian, Serbian, Croatian, and Dutch settlements of immigrants of any city in the country. One of every five Chicagoans of European descent was foreign born as late as 1960.

"Long before the white man set foot on this continent," declared a report of the Spanish Speaking Peoples Study Commission of the General Assembly of Illinois, "obsidian instruments manufactured by Mexican craftsmen in the vicinity of Tenochtitlán (the Aztec capital)" had reached Illinois. The expeditions of Conquistadors from Spain and Mexican Indians came to the area "before the Mayflower landed at Plymouth Rock." And a battalion of Mexican soldiers, under a Spanish commander, from St. Louis "fought in the American Revolution to help secure Illinois for the American."

As everywhere, the Puerto Ricans were "the last immigrants"; the Spanish-speaking had come to the prairies long before the English-speaking, but this prairie history was forgotten. Centuries later, in Chicago, Puerto Ricans inherited the ruins of the old Polish ghetto on Division Street, as they had inherited the ruins of the old Jewish ghetto on the Lower East Side, and the old Italian ghetto of East Harlem, in Nueva York. In the ghettos where no one else wished to live, or could survive, any more, the islanders were invited to rebuild their lives and raise their children.

"We get crumbs from the city," said Jesus de Torres, who worked for Mayor Daley's Human Resources Commission. "Because all that is left is crumbs. And because we got no political power."

Chicago's metropolitan area was as large as Puerto Rico; its population was twice as dense. The immigrants had come from the little rural villages and the *jíbaro* towns in the mountains and on the

Caribbean coast. "Most our people never had even seen a tenement," said Jesus de Torres.

In the beginning they came to work in the fields of Michigan and downstate Illinois. "Most of the food harvested for direct human consumption in Illinois is harvested by the hands of Spanish speaking persons," declared the report of the special commission on the "Spanish Speaking Peoples," set up by the state legislature. "Contractual labor from the sunny Caribbean lived through the winter in drafty box cars on Virginia Street, in Gary [Indiana]," the legislators reported. "Even the federal government" enticed Puerto Ricans to come "thousands of miles to work in the Savanna ordinance plant *after* congressional action had determined that plant was to be shut down in a matter of months." They were expendable workers in the labor market.

"Just people. Simple and poor people," said Monserrate Diaz, a former nun, a slight, intense "teaching sister," who left her religious order to help the poor of the *barrio*. She thought the people had been naïvely fooled by the government, or had "fooled themselves."

"Coming here means suffering. It means the cold. It means winters without a coat, without food in your house. It means losing your home to urban renewal. It means living like a gypsy, like a beggar," she said.

On Division Street a young and vivacious college girl, Beatrice Colon, one of the editors of a *barrio* journal, *The Rican,* talked of her own wandering: "I was born in Chicago. We used to live around LaSalle Street. That used to be the Puerto Rican community. Urban renewal came and destroyed our *barrio!* So people moved to Lincoln Park. Urban renewal came there, too. So people moved to Division Street. We keep moving west.

"No matter where we live, pretty soon there is urban renewal!"

In the offices of the Archdiocese Latin Center of the Catholic Church, Ben Rodriguez, a young and weary social worker, told a similar story: "We were pushed out of Old Town where the *barrio* was in 1950 by the city, by the real-estate developers. It happened once. It happened twice. It happened three times. We did not know what was happening to us. We thought this was how people lived in Chicago. We were strangers, so we accepted it. Later we became bitter."

The immigrants couldn't know, when they built their first *barrio* in Old Town in the 1950s, that the old, unwanted neighborhood was to become the new Greenwich Village of Chicago. But the urban renewers made the ghetto fashionable with boutiques and psychedelic shops for the tourists, after they evicted the *barrio* families. In a few years towering high-rent apartment houses, named ironically for Carl Sandburg, stood where the *barrio* had fallen.

"Urban renewal is not a housing deal, it's a business deal," said Jesus de Torres. "I have worked with these people. So I know how they operate. To make a buck. Housing is a money-making proposition. They do not want housing for the poor. They do not hate the Latins. They love the money.

"Where to go? Jump in the lake? They will urban renew the lake!" he said.

The rebuilding of the ghettos prophesied by the visionary planners of urban renewal had begun, modestly, as slum clearance. In the New Dealish National Housing Act of 1949, an unlikely trio of Senators, Robert Taft of Ohio, Robert Wagner, Sr., of New York, and Allen Ellender of Louisiana, instituted a federal program of slum clearance, to fulfill the postwar promises of a "better life for all." Long before urban renewal had become "Black removal," slum clearance had become "slum creation."

Segregation in housing was the earliest and most enduring result of the slum-clearance projects. In 1959, the New York State Committee on Discrimination in Housing reported "housing segregation" was sharply "on the increase." The "democracy of the slums" no longer existed, said Algernon Black, chairman of the committee. "The effect has been a disturbing increase in *racial tensions that can erupt into violence and physical strife* [my emphasis]," Black said. The pattern of polarization that was established in the guise of "slum clearance" was to haunt the cities for decades to come.

"We are spending millions to clear slums, and we are creating new slums all over the place," a former Congressman warned at the time. The urban-renewal projects, he said, were "making gypsies of the people of the city. I know of families that have been shuttled five or six times from one area that is to be demolished to another that is to be torn down six months or a year from now." Later, studies would be painstakingly made to discover what social phenomenon had caused the breakdown of family life among the ghetto poor.

The Puerto Ricans, newcomers to the city, were most easily victimized by the urban-renewal projects. A former congressmen said, "The Puerto Ricans can stay only for a time, until the developers are ready to tear the buildings down. Then they'll be dumped somewhere else." "Relocation" was the name given to this process of slum creation, and in New York the Commissioner of Relocation was a Puerto Rican, Herman Badillo.

The architect of urban renewal, née slum clearance, in the late 1950s was the irascible, resolute, and powerful Robert Moses, the chairman of the Committee on Slum Clearance, in New York, and the city's Construction Coordinator, the "Czar of Cement." Late in years, and long retired, but unsubdued, Moses was asked what he thought ought to be done about the *barrios*. "You must concede that this Bronx slum, and others in Brooklyn and Manhattan, are unreparable. They are beyond rebuilding, tinkering and restoring," he said. "They must be leveled to the ground!"

On Division Street the urban-renewal methods were more modest, on a smaller scale, but no less devastating.

In one shady, tree-lined, quiet side street there were several burned-out houses. The police suspected arson by the *barrio* youths. Beatrice Colon disagreed. She thought the landlords might be responsible "To get the insurance. To get rid of the Puerto Ricans. All I know is that, house by house, they are trying to destroy our *barrio*."

Families had just moved in, a few years ago. In their homes people did not feel at home yet. Everything was still too new, too uncertain, too strange. Perhaps in their minds they thought: When will we have to move again? How soon? Where will we have to go this time? "This community is very young," said Monserrate Diaz. "In years past

Puerto Ricans *worked* in the stores, but we didn't *own* a store. We have a few Puerto Rican storeowners now. We have a few professionals now. Not many. We even own a few of our homes now."

The signs of change, in Spanish, were everywhere. On Division Street there were the JOYERÍA CLOTHING FOR THE ENTIRE FAMILY . . . the LIBERIA GOMEZ, a bookstore . . . the BORINQUÉN BARBER SHOP . . . the SAN JUAN THEATRE, formerly the Biltmore Theatre . . . a dance hall, the CASTILLO CLUB, down the block from the ancient MEISTERBRAU tavern . . . and across the street from the LA PALMA CLEANERS was the old DIVISION STREET RUSSIAN TURKISH BATHS.

In the past, the old colors of Division Street had been gray and black and brick red. They had been replaced by tropical blue and green and yellow.

Some of the streets nearby were as polyglot. The Polish and Ukrainian and Jewish and Puerto Rican families lived door by door. It gave the neighborhood an atmosphere not so much of tension as of indecision, as if everyone were uncertain about what kind of neighborhood it really was.

A few blocks away, just off Division Street, there was an austere, carved Russian Orthodox Greek Catholic church, and on either side were prim little houses, with white picket fences. The faces of the residents were all white. Few, if any, Puerto Ricans walked these streets.

"There is hostility," Monserrate Diaz said. "If on this block a large group of Puerto Ricans were standing on the corner, singing or just talking, these people would call the police. Immediately!" Many of these houses look nice from the outside. But what is happening on the inside? Our people were inside the houses, not on the stoops or doorsteps as on the island. Most of the people on this block are not Puerto Rican. So our people hide inside of themselves. It is not because they are afraid of the neighbors. It is because they do not want to be insulted. Someday when this *barrio* belongs to us we will not have to hide who we are."

In Chicago, the infant *barrio* was helpless to protect the elementary rights of its residents. The Puerto Ricans "have not yet elected one of their number to public office above the most basic local level," reported the State of Illinois's legislative Spanish Speaking Peoples Study Commission. "Decent employment and a decent place to live [were] often denied to Spanish speaking residents . . . persons trained for employment are denied it . . . [in the schools there was] unfair and adverse discrimination to the children of such people. . . . Health care is a serious problem . . . they share in the chronically unmet health needs of the very poor. . . . Many brown skinned [Spanish-speaking] persons who are natural born citizens of the United States are subjected to a *life time* of harassment by police authorities."

Elsewhere, in the *barrios* of Hoboken, New Jersey, the police had installed a closed-circuit television camera on the main street, to spy on children at play, housewives doing their afternoon shopping, and the men who stopped for a beer at the local tavern on their way home from work in the evening. The public would not tolerate so Orwellian an invasion of their privacy or individualism for ordinary citizens. But the suspicion of Puerto Ricans was so deep that no public voice of protest was heard in New Jersey.

The birth of a *barrio* was as wondrous and frightening a thing to see as the birth of a child. In the urban ruin of the "death of the city" the Puerto Ricans had nonetheless created "an island" of life.

"Let's say some cultures have maintained their humanism," said Ben Rodriguez. "I feel the Latin people have that dignity about them. But it is being destroyed by the cities. We become lost in the jungle. We don't understand ourselves any more. We become confused, hating and destroying ourselves with alcohol, with dope. Our people, for the first time, are entering mental institutions. The insanity of the city is wounding our humanism.

"Our humanism is like an island in the city," he said.

"Everyone is an island," said Beatrice Colon. "In the *barrio* you have to be. Even the immigrants who came before us knew that. They settled in their own little communities for protection against the city."

In her dreams she recreated the *barrio* as she wished it to be: "I see trees. And I think how beautiful it is in Puerto Rico. In the city you hardly find any trees. I walk down streets where there are lots of trees. I collect the leaves. Whenever I write to someone I send them a leaf.

"A leaf to me is just like a human being. You have to be just as good to a tree as you are to a human being. The tree was made by God. You can't harm a tree and you can't harm a human being. You have to love everything. Lots of Puerto Ricans do feel that way. It's very natural to us to feel that way.

"Maybe our feeling comes from the island," she said. "I have been there, but I wasn't born there. So that's crazy. But that's how it is. In America you have to act a certain way, to act a role, to be aggressive. But that's not really you. That's not how we really are.

"I find beauty in Chicago. If you can't find beauty where you are, in what you are doing, you are going to die. Human beings need beauty to make them human. Like bread. At least, that's true for Puerto Ricans. If I couldn't find beauty in the *barrio,* in the city, I would die. But I can walk down a dirty alley and see the grass growing from the cracks in the cement, and that's beautiful to me. Because, you see, the grass is growing. Something living is growing in that concrete alley.

"Even in Chicago I see beauty," she said. "Maybe it is inside of us."

24

The People of the Sun

On the gray wall of the *bodega* in the *barrio* of Brooklyn four signs were painted in a row:

NO SITTING
NO PLAYING
NO LOITERING
NO DRINKING

The young mother sat on a dirty ashcan beneath the signs, wheeling a baby carriage back and forth on the garbage-strewn sidewalks. Where else could she sit?

In the city no one ever painted signs that said: YES! YES! ¡SÍ! ¡SÍ! That seemed to be a forbidden word. "Everybody says, 'No! No! Don't do this! Don't go there,' " said a man who pushed a clothing cart in the garment center. "Why can't they ever say Yes? It is more beautiful to say Yes!"

"A man who says No to living cannot live," a janitor on the Lower East Side said. "I tell you why all your laws are negative. Because you believe in nothing.

"You are afraid of living," he said, "so you are afraid of people."

Long ago the great statesman José de Diego had written: "We do not know how to say 'no,' and we are attracted, unconsciously, by the hypnotic suggestion of the predominant *'sí.'* Never does a Puerto Rican say, or know how to say, 'no.' 'We'll see,' 'I'll study the matter,' 'I'll decide later'—when a Puerto Rican uses these expressions, it must be understood, he does not want to. At most, he joins the *'sí'* with the 'no,' and he makes an ambiguous, nebulous, conditional conjunctive, in which the will flutters in the air, like a little bird, aimless and shelterless."

On the green hills of the island there had been no NO SITTING signs beneath the coffee trees. No one told children in the jungles to KEEP OFF THE GRASS. The sun and air were free and clear. "Even in the slums of San Juan we lived in the sun," said a young man. "The darkness of the city was strange to us." Stranger still were the laws of the city: NO SITTING ON THE STOOP, NO BALL PLAYING ON THE WALL, NO WALKING ON THE GRASS, NO LOITERING, NO DRINKING, NO SMOKING, NO DOGS ALLOWED, NO CHILDREN . . .

The islanders "were used to outdoor life, and freedom, access to fresh air, and sociability, and being with their neighbors, to communal living," said the commander of a *barrio* police precinct in New York. "So they were sort of stifled in their little tenement apartments and wanted to stay on their tenement stoops, either drinking beer or playing guitars. I could understand why they wanted that, but it was against the law. Puerto Ricans have to make *some* accommodation" to the city.

To worship a Sungod?

Aztecs loved a Sungod. So did I;
but the unchurched sky
was my rented ceiling.
Land Lords
evicted my Sungod.

No loitering, in the hall, sun!
No lovemaking, in the dark, sun!

The ballad of the *barrio* was a lament, but not a dirge.

Garden my slum
in human form?
adorn a Carib beauty
on nude tenements?

worship the sun?
Thats against
the Law Lords
in Nueva York.

"The people of the sun. That's what we are. Sun worshipers," said a Latin king in the *barrio* of Chicago. "But there is no sun here to worship." On the Lower East Side the wife of a prominent *barrio* leader said, "My husband, he goes crazy if he does not go to the island once a year. He has to 'see the sun to live.' "

A young office girl preferred Chicago to the Bronx. "In the Bronx the sun hardly ever shines. In Chicago it shines once in a while. Maybe twice a week."

In San Germán, on the island, a woman explained why she and her husband had left New York to come to the ancient, and proudly poor, town. "He liked New York. It was his home town. He had everything he wanted. But one day he said he couldn't stand living in the darkness any more. He had to be in the sun."

The far northern cold of the South Bronx was "Puerto Rico's Siberia," wrote island journalist Frank Ramos. "What happens to people when they move from an island with a tropical climate and experience a freezing winter?" He quoted the director of the *barrio* health clinic, Dr. Harold Wise, who, commenting on a *New York Times* report that half of the South Bronx *barrio* families had no heat "half of the time," said: "Something happens to the body when you spend the entire winter without heat." Ramos coolly responded, "One might add that under such conditions something also happens to the mind."

"Here I am dying of the cold," the poet Virgilio Davila once had written of an islander who went to New York to seek his fortune:

Borinquén calls me home,
this is not my country,
Borinquén is pure flame,
here, I am dying of the cold. . . .

In the cold each man was closed off from other men. Each man was encased in his own clothing. In the tenements it was the same.

The windows were shut tight. The doors were locked. A family lived as in a cave or a cell.

When it was said that someone was *frío,* it was meant that his being was cold, not just his body. He was lonely and alone.

"El invierno: Esta es la época mas peligrosa a la salúd"—"The Winter: This is a time that is very dangerous to the health." So said the brochure that the government Division of Migration gave to immigrants. The government brochure *Clima y ropa en los Estados Unidos—Climate and Clothing in the United States*—warned the islanders to prepare for the ordeal by wearing "a heavy coat of wool, or a jacket, *una chaqueta,* of wool, wool pants, strong shoes, a hat, wool gloves and a scarf to cover the head and neck."

In a handwritten and unsigned poem to a *tecato,* or junkie, an island writer said:

Cold as the river
    of thought
    that has slept through
time, Junkee—
    Caresses of cold hands
    Junkee—
dreams of devilish infants
    in search of
    a *solbeto.*
Junkee, Junkee, Junkee—
    in corridors of ice
    full of rabid words
    without end—
Junkee—
    No Exit—
    No Vacant Rooms—
Junkee—
    San Juan airport—
    New York—
The Bowery of the sweet child
    with the aroma of a man,
    Junkee—
    Junkee—

The injection of heroin was a small sun. It warmed the soul. "The pleasurable, whole-body, warm, orgasmic rush comes rapidly, and is more intense after a heroin injection," wrote Drs. George R. Gay and E. Leong Way, Ph.D., in "Pharmacology of the Opiate Narcotics." Heroin was like the French phrase for the act of love: it was orgastic as the "small death" of sex.

One *tecato* described it: *"Jesu,* man! This shit lights me up like I was the sun!"

In 1953 the Academy of Medicine in New York held two conferences on narcotic addiction of the city's youth. The scientists and doctors concluded then, as they might now, that addiction in the ghettos was due to "serious deprivations suffered by many children living in large and over-crowded cities." Children who were unwanted and rejected by the coldness of the cities, which gave them "no place in the sun," few playgrounds in the open air, fewer jobs, and the fewest "satisfactory living conditions," took dope "as a compensating factor," reported the experts twenty years ago. "NARCOTICS LINKED TO LIFE IN THE SLUMS" was the laconic headline of the *New York Times:* "REPORT OF EXPERTS HOLDS USE BY ADOLESCENTS REFLECTS DEPRIVATIONS IN CITIES."

In the ghettos the use of drugs had tragically increased in the post–World War II years. The Bureau of Narcotics in Washington had estimated that in less than a decade "addict-users" had doubled, to 600,000. But in New York alone the president of the City Council, Sanford Garelik, a former police inspector, said there were as many as 600,000 addicts.

"Dope is our worst enemy," said a member of the Young Lords. "It's worse than syphilis, worse than TB, worse than anything else."

On the island the use of drugs had never been part of the Borinquén, or Spanish, way of life. The sun had its own hallucinatory powers. If a man wished to see psychedelic visions he simply had to lie on his back in the grass and peer through his eyelids at the sun. If he needed a delirium the heat and rum were enough. And then there was sex. Sex, in a tropical atmosphere, had a languorous sweetness it had nowhere else.

"We have the 'soft' vices," a San Juan social worker said. "The hard drugs belong to hard climates. You have exported these tensions of your hard, cold ways of life to us. And you have now exported your hard drugs to soothe us, when we suffer from your cold heart."

It was a plague. Like the epidemic diseases that Europeans inflicted on the Indians, so the use of drugs spread throughout the *barrios* of the island. The young Puerto Ricans, like the Southern Blacks, seemed to have little immunity to the intoxication of heroin. And the children least of all. In little towns in the mountains where no one had ever heard of narcotics, suddenly it was discovered that heroin was being peddled to schoolchildren, in the school playgrounds.

"We have a couple of cases of heroin addiction in the seventh grade," said Mayor Jimmy Rosas of Guánica, the idyllic town on the farthest southern shore. "It is our biggest problem now with our young people."

The dream world of opium drugs was nothing new, however, to the people of the United States. In 1868 Horace Day, a former addict, estimated there were at least 80,000 to 100,000 "opium eaters" in the country—one addict for every 350 people. Oddly, the figure has been relatively constant through the years. In 1900 the AMA estimate was one addict for every 400 people, and in 1973 it was one addict for every 350 people. Day, in his book *The Opium Habit, with Suggestions as to the Remedy,* published by a reputable publisher of the time, Harper & Brothers, wrote that then, as now, the addicted included large groups of veterans of the recent war, the Civil War, as well as prostitutes and professional and literary men.

By the turn of the century the use of opium in "ladies' preparations" had become fashionable. Hundreds of thousands of Victorian ladies went to bed on "difficult days," slightly high and soothed by pharmacy panaceas. It was not then thought immoral to take opium, which was inexpensively available at the corner drugstore. Nor was addiction to opium, or to its derivative morphine, thought of as a criminal act.

After an "alarming increase in opium use by American troops" during and after the Spanish-American War, the strident moralist Theodore Roosevelt decided opium was not only immoral but un-American. By 1909 several states had banned opium smoking, and federal statutes followed.

Society, throughout history, had encouraged the use of the narcotics it later prohibited. In 1898, the year of the Spanish-American War, the Bayer Company of Germany developed a "wonder drug" they called heroin (from the German word *"heroisch,"* meaning "powerful" or "heroic") for medicinal use as a "cough medicine." Doctors were delighted when it was discovered that heroin helped "alleviate the symptoms of morphine withdrawal." So it was medically used to help morphine addicts, much as methadone was later used to help heroin addicts, in withdrawal. The drug has not yet been developed that will help the methadone addicts in their withdrawal. But it will be.*

The addiction of *barrio* youth to heroin had become as widespread as the addiction of the Civil War veterans and early pioneers and miners in the American West to "opium eating," or the addiction of the proper Victorian ladies to their "ladies' preparations" of opium and morphine "nocturnal powders." But there was one vital difference. The use of narcotics in the past was seldom associated with, or resulted in, crime. The addicts could obtain their euphoria without resorting to theft or death.

Some have thought the frustrating wars in Asia and the enterprising Mafia at home were mother and father to the growth of the narcotics problem. The childhood of an entire generation of *barrio* youth was marked by the Korean War and the war in Vietnam. Both of these "unpopular wars" brought home, as had the Spanish-American and Civil Wars, veterans who had become addicted to drugs and death.

In their despair over an unpopular and disastrous war, soldiers

* "We have created a lot of zombies," said the director of a *barrio* methadone program. "Half our clients have turned into alcoholics. They're off heroin. They're hung over, strung out, all the time. People can function on heroin. But they can't function on alcohol."

remembered "the ghetto in their existence," said Captain Brian Joseph, an Army psychiatrist who worked with heroin addicts in Vietnam. They believed that there is nothing wrong in taking an outside agent "to help you lift your problem." The Puerto Rican youths in the city, and the American soldiers in Vietnam, had a great deal in common, the psychiatrists thought.

"I just wanted to get out of the country and drugs took me out, for a while, at least."

"You're in a country where you don't know anybody, and it seems everyone's against you. It's hard to trust anyone, you know. All this works on you. The whole country is difficult to live with. Heroin? It kept me calm and able to keep a cool head."

"If I wanted to survive I had to take care of my pain, and make sure I got enough sleep and be able to forget days gone by."

"You see friends getting killed and you can't do nothing but take heroin to forget."

"Heroin makes you feel really happy, relaxed. Nothing bothers you. Anything anybody says, you can just take it, just shrug it off. If anyone hassles you, you just go for another hit."

These words might have been spoken by *barrio* youths on the city streets, but they were the words of soldiers in Vietnam. In the South Bronx, Hernan Flores, who had been a heroin addict, spoke as though *he* were in Saigon. "If a man falls into demoralization, he starts doing what I started doing. Shooting up drugs. I began to get very uptight about the way life was going. Shooting up drugs is a good escape, when you get very demoralized. So you just accept death, a slow death. It's very convenient. It's provided by the government anyway. So I decided I had to get it together. Or die. And I joined the Young Lords," Flores said. He became a leader of the *barrio* group.

The coldness of city life fed the dependence on heroin. Had not the philosopher Unamuno said, "We die not of the dark, but of the cold"?

"My father died inside," cried a social worker in the Catholic

Archdiocese Latin Center of Chicago, Ben Rodriguez. "Our family came from the hills near Lares. Just a little *barrio*. When we came to Chicago I watched my father die, day by day. That was a terrible thing to watch.

"His spirit died," the sorrowing son said. And when the spirit of the father died, so did the family's. "Who is a man from the mountains who loses his spirit?"

On the island the family was not only the center of life, it was a way of life. In a small town the local Mayor was asked to define what it meant to be Puerto Rican. He replied without any hesitation, "To be Puerto Rican is to love your family. My family is my life." The family not only comforted its members and protected them from society; it was a society unto itself.

"Living in a big city such as New York has broken this dependence of group living and the stress is on the individual," said a college student at a conference on "Neoricans," Lucy Ramos, from the *barrios* of New York, who had enrolled in an island university. In New York, she said, "what happens is a dependence on one's own self for existence." It was every man and woman for himself. "The family, once guardian of morals and cherished basis of social order, yields to the individualism of urban industry." Within "a generation" it was "broken to pieces," the girl said.

If the youth sought "compensation" in drugs, a family might seek it in welfare. A *barrio* leader said, "Welfare is like heroin."

What was "the welfare"? It was a family that "had no milk for the children sometimes in the past six months because of lack of money," as half the welfare families reported to the White House's study of *Poverty Amid Plenty*. Even when these welfare families had enough money for dinner, one of every three "had not enough furniture so that everyone could sit down while eating." One of every three welfare families "had not enough beds for all the family members." In the public bemoaning of the politicians (not shoeless, or without chairs to sit on or beds to lie upon) over the "waste" of welfare money, it was forgotten how little there was to waste. The "household budget" given by the City of New York to welfare families allowed for one bar of toilet soap a month for a woman, one can of dentifrice every six months, one comb every two years, one nail file every four years, one lipstick a year (if the woman worked she was allowed two), and one sanitary belt every two years.

One *barrio* leader thought the humiliations of "the welfare" could be correlated to the incidences of drug addiction. Welfare had institutionalized poverty, he said.

In 1970 the "subsistence level" for a ghetto family of four required an income of about $7,000, according to the government's Bureau of Labor Statistics. And the "poverty level" for an urban family of four, that year, was set at $3,968 by the Social Security Administration. It was just about what the average welfare family received. So, if welfare payments were set at the "poverty level," they were little more than half of the "subsistence level."

"Not enough to live on, and not enough to die on!" was the folklore of the barrio.

"The welfare" in the *barrios* was similar to the dole on the Indian reservations of the nineteenth century. The government's "handouts" of food and clothing to the Indians were consciously aimed at their "reduction to supplicants for charity," said Indian Commissioner Francis Walker in 1872, and so "break" their spirit. Whether or not this was the conscious aim of "the welfare" system of 1973, the effect was remarkably the same.

"In many ways being on welfare destroys a man," said Monserrate Diaz, who as a social worker had known hundreds of welfare families. "Welfare! If the social worker finds a man coming to the house because he loves a woman, and if the social worker reports the lovers, the woman loses her welfare money. The woman has no right to a private life, or a love life. Love is against the welfare regulations!

"So, in effect, the city says: If you are in love your children must go hungry."

The man suffered an even deeper humiliation because of his *macho,* Miss Diaz said. "A man says: I don't want to depend on anyone. I am proud of myself. Many conceal that they are on welfare. They are Latin. It is a humiliation to go to someone you don't know and ask: Give me money to live on. So it kills the man's pride": a lonely death. "Many people say Puerto Ricans come to New York, to Chicago, to go on welfare. I don't believe that. We are too proud. We come to find a job. And when we can't find one we have to depend on welfare.

"We don't want to die! But we die of humiliation."

In the *barrio* of the Lower East Side of New York a city government employee, who hid his name, cursed the indignity of the "welfare syndrome." He compared it to heroin addiction. But it was "even worse, because it was socially acceptable, you know, like oil depletion.

"Welfare does not help us," he said. "It feeds our children, yes. It maybe helps us to 'survive.' But to 'survive' as what? As the zombies of society. It does not help us to be men. To be independent, as a man ought to be.

"No! do not be fooled by this yelling about Puerto Ricans on welfare. Society wants it that way. You think the government would rather see a million Puerto Rican *independentistas,* with strong backbones and clenched fists? To me welfare is like heroin. It makes us addicted to poverty. It makes us beggars. It makes us liars. It destroys our pride. So it makes us dependent on society.

"If society, with its power, did not want us to have heroin it would stop it tomorrow. Like it would stop the welfare. It wants us to be addicted. So it feeds them both to us. And then it arrests us—for taking them."

On the yellow wall of a liquor store in the *barrio* of Brooklyn an addict had painted in bold, screaming letters:

FUCK THE PUSHER!

A few days later a civic-minded citizen had crossed out the word "FUCK." He was offended by the obscenity. The addicts waiting on the corner for their pusher thought the puritanical citizen was probably the owner of the liquor store.

25

The Unborn Addicts

The brown baby, small as a kitten and smaller than the rats in the basement, lay in an incubator in the old Lincoln Hospital.

In a hole in its stomach the doctors had inserted a plastic tube. The premature barely weighed three pounds and its twig of an arm was too thin for it to be fed intravenously, and it had to be fed. Being a five-month fetus, the baby was legally unborn (at the time, before the Supreme Court altered the legality of birth), and yet it was dying of a narcotic-withdrawal trauma. Its mother was a heroin addict who was addicted to methadone.

The incubator room was crowded with unborn addicts.

"Some of our babies have to die," said Dr. Cesar Costa, a young pediatrician who came from the medical school of the University of Puerto Rico "to help my people here." "They are born too small, too weak, to be able to survive the withdrawal symptoms and shock."

If the mothers were in the methadone program to keep them off heroin the babies were born addicted to methadone. They suffered the same withdrawal symptoms as from heroin. "If the New York City government gives methadone to the pregnant women, is it a pusher for unborn children?" Dr. Costa asked.

In the children's wards of Lincoln Hospital in the South Bronx, there were several healthy "methadone babies." "Most of them we save. So they can grow up to be addicts," an older doctor said.

"And when our babies die, is it the New York City government that is the murderer? Who is their murderer? Let the police go arrest the New York City government for every baby I have seen die here! Let there be a trial, with medical evidence, as to the cause of death. If the police or the government wanted to stop the heroin, they wouldn't need to use the methadone. But I know and you know and we all of us know that it wouldn't happen. They wouldn't do it. It's too profitable," said Dr. Costa.

In metallic cribs young addicts lay like abandoned and broken dolls, with big and empty eyes. Their addicted mothers had fled in fright. One mother had offered her baby "to the government."

"No one has even given them a name. We call them 'The Boarders,' " said Dr. Costa. "They have nothing wrong. Except for two things: they are poor—and they are Puerto Rican."

The children's wards were crowded with infants suffering from the "diseases" of poverty. "Sometimes we have to hospitalize babies just so they can be warm, because in the home there is no heat. We do not have one, or two. We have hundreds," said Dr. Costa.

"In the island our children do not die of the cold. Maybe they die of hunger. But here they die of hunger *and* cold," Dr. Costa said.

In the hospital corridor on a plastic chair a mother sat all day. On her lap was a languid little girl who was too ill to hold up her head. The mother cuddled and fondled and kissed her child all day long, without asking for anything or saying a word to anyone. All day she just sat there. She came every day.

None of the doctors or nurses told her to go. "There is no money for more nurses," a doctor said.

Among the *barrio* mothers the chance of giving birth to a premature baby is two to three times as great as it is among middle-class suburban mothers. Their chance of dying in childbirth is even greater. In 1930 about twice as many "nonwhite mothers" died in childbirth in the United States as did "white mothers"; but by 1960 for every woman with a white skin who died while giving birth there were *four* brown- or black-skinned women who died. In thirty years the advances in medicine had been reversed by the advances in ghetto poverty.

Even if their infants survived their birth the *bolita,* the numbers game, was against them. In the City of New York the official death rate for Puerto Rican children under the age of one year was thought to be about 30 in 1,000 live births. That was 150 percent higher than the infant mortality rate for white children. It was unofficially much higher.

"Poverty is the third leading cause of death" in the city ghettos, according to former Commissioner of Health of New York Dr. George James. Within the city 13,000 persons died of poverty in one year, he said, though their deaths were attributed to cancer, diabetes, pneumonia, influenza, cardiovascular disease, accidents, tuberculosis and VD. In these cases, said the Commissioner, the disease was the complication and poverty was the cause.

Was poverty then a "disease"?

Laboratory experiments had convinced medical men that malnutrition affected the brain cells and thought processes. And yet hunger was never listed as a disease, or a disease-causing agent, in health statistics. But then the doctors who diagnosed diseases were rarely poor, or Puerto Rican, or Black, and never hungry.

The "illnesses of hunger" were not wholly born of the city. One of the most insidious, infecting at least one of every ten Puerto Ricans, and possibly one of five, was a tropical malady known as schistosomiasis—the "disease of the snails." Schistosomiasis is caused by a parasitic worm that is excreted into the rivers and waters of the island by a tiny snail. It is the scourge of the tropics. From the waters of the Nile and the Congo to the islands of Japan and Indonesia, the disease has infected an estimated half-billion people. Some believed it was the most widespread disease in the world. And it thrived on hunger.

Dr. Chris Mengis, a former Army doctor, had found evidences of schistosomiasis in veterans of the "Bataan March" years after the American GIs had been imprisoned by the Japanese in World War II. Once the parasite entered the body it might live there for the victim's entire lifetime. It causes fevers, coughing spells, and dysentery. The visible sign of infection might be nothing more than the swollen belly of a child, often misdiagnosed by non-Puerto Rican *barrio* physicians unfamiliar with the disease. Inside the body the parasites damaged the liver, spleen, and lungs. Sometimes they entered the brain cells. And sometimes they caused death.

Schistosomiasis is not ordinarily fatal. "Those who are well nourished don't usually develop these complications," said Dr. Mengis. Once a patient recovered from even an acute infection, "if he has a good, well-balanced diet, he has a good chance of living amicably with his little inhabitants." The tropical disease thrived in the cold tenements, fed by the inadequate diets of welfare-budgeted and unbalanced surplus foods. Almost half (43 percent of its victims, according to the census of 1960) were unemployed or subemployed.

Poverty threatened to make the diseases like schistosomiasis epidemic in the city, said Dr. Costa. "In the hospital you cannot just take care of leukemia, broken bones, or parasites. You have to ask: Why does he have parasites?" the young doctor said. "Why do our children fall from three-story buildings? Because the windows are broken. Why are the windows broken? Because there is no money to fix them. Why is there no money? This, too, is a disease. Why is a baby intoxicated by lead? Lead poisoning is a disease of oppression." (In a health survey of the Lower East Side *barrio* 700 children, between ten months and seven years of age, were tested at random during the summer of 1970. Eighty-two had "suspiciously high levels of lead [from tenement paint] in their blood samples.") "The disease of oppression," Dr. Costa called it. "I am not talking of politics. I am talking from a medical point of view. Medicine cannot be separated from life. What is disease? The bacteria from the moon?

"From a medical point of view our people are sick not just because they are poor, but because they are not free," Dr. Costa said. "Our state of mind is not healthy because of that. And so the body is not healthy. The patient has good blood pressure, his pulse is good, but what about his mind? Why does he drink so much? Why does he take drugs? Why the aspirins? Because he does not feel free.

"Look at this hospital. Why do we have such trouble getting appropriations? They don't want to give money to a *barrio* hospital. They give it to the bigger hospitals, where they do research, where

Puerto Ricans are guinea pigs. Here is a poor hospital that is just treating sick people. They aren't interested in that."

In the children's wards were sixty beds. "Here we serve a community with four hundred thousand people. Mostly Puerto Ricans. Half of them kids," the young doctor said, his voice rising in anger. "In Pediatrics alone we have three hundred patients a day. Our emergency room is the second-busiest in the entire United States. Nowhere, except the Los Angeles County Hospital, do they have more emergencies."

He kicked at a large pile of refuse and garbage in the corridor. An orange peel rolled across the floor to the door of a laboratory. "Everywhere there is garbage," he muttered. "It is very depressing to work here. The conditions of the hospital are inadequate. The building is a disgrace. But who cares?"

A young nurse, walking past, smiled coldly. "We have lots of Band-Aids," she said.

Emergencies, the real ones, were put in Room 126. The "Dead on Arrival Room" a nurse called it. In the still room, on the examining table and covered with a sheet, was a "kid who fell into a bathtub and drowned." No one who knew him was at his deathbed.

"Many of the real emergencies we can't handle," Dr. Costa said. "If the skull is fractured we can do nothing here. We have to put the patient in an ambulance and transfer him to Jacobi Hospital. We don't have the equipment, the staff, the services that you need to handle things like that. We can do nothing."

The community leaders charged that victims of accidents had died while waiting for nonexistent medical services. One list of deaths, compiled by a community health group, had accused the hospital of responsibility for half a dozen.

Lincoln Hospital was one of the oldest and most dilapidated in the country. It had been originally built, in 1839, as a home for runaway slaves. Now it was run by one of the most modern and newest medical institutions in the country, the world-famed Albert Einstein College of Medicine of Yeshiva University, whose research facilities were staffed by a glittering array of illustrious names in medicine. The "elite" faculty at Einstein had little to do with the hospital. Few of them had ever visited it, or had reason to. In their well-endowed laboratories they were concerned with "pure research" and the hospital was "too political."

The Albert Einstein College of Medicine was the pride of the Jewish community. Its founding "was a little like the founding of Israel," wrote a reporter; for it "freed all Jews from the quota system" in the other medical schools. And yet many of the medical college's leading men, in coming to a school free of anti-Semitism, brought with them the psychological scars of anti-Semitism. Some of the researchers even requested the words "Yeshiva University" be removed from their letterheads because it was "too Jewish."

Up in the suburbs of the North Bronx the "elite" of Einstein were not about to be pulled back into the ghettos of the South Bronx by the sufferings of the Puerto Ricans. The paradox was one source of the conflict between the doctors and the *barrio*'s patients. A bitter moral and medical warfare developed, and the hospital was neglected.

On the corner of Cortlandt and 142nd Street bags and cans of bloody bandages, used syringes, and other medical refuse sometimes lay on the sidewalk for days. Rats were attracted to the feast. So were addicts, who came from all over the city to search for dirty needles in the rubble.

"We complained, we petitioned, we called the Mayor's office," said a *barrio* leader. "Nothing was done. One day we decided to act. We moved the garbage into the office of the hospital administrator; that same day the garbage got removed."

The battle of the garbage helped provoke the invasion of Lincoln Hospital. On the morning of a hot summer day, at 5:30 A.M., two hundred people of the *barrio* marched into the lobby and proclaimed the hospital "liberated." Led by the Young Lords, the Health Revolutionary Union Movement (HRUM), and the Think Lincoln Committee (made up of the hospital's own patients and personnel), they raised a Puerto Rican flag on the roof, and flung a banner across the front of the building, *"Bienvenido al hospital del pueblo"*—"Welcome to the Hospital of the People." In a volatile press conference full of laments and impassioned wrath—"My aunt died of a wrong blood transfusion"—the "liberators" issued a list of "revolutionary demands" for a children's day care and a senior citizens' service center, for door-to-door health teams to encourage preventive medicine, for more extensive drug-addiction care, and for a $140-a-week minimum wage for hospital workers.

In some of the city's newspapers the occupying of Lincoln Hospital was depicted as an "act of terror." The "liberators" included members of several street gangs whose names were emblazoned on their jackets—the Savage Seven, the Skulls, and the Bones.

When the New York police arrived in force that evening to reoccupy the beleaguered hospital, the "liberators" had gone and the only signs of the events of the day were the flag of Puerto Rico flying from the roof, which was removed, and the banner of welcome, which was torn down. The "liberators" had gone. In no time the hospital returned to its normal routine.

"Our brothers were dying there," a leader of the Young Lords explained two years later. "And they still are."

In a "confidential" staff memo released to the press by City Councilman Thomas J. Manton, the acting Chief of Surgery at the hospital, Dr. Everett Dargan, charged that the *barrio* residents had been terrorizing the doctors. The staff was forced to work "literally behind locked doors."

While surgeons were operating on a young boy who belonged to one "South Bronx Puerto Rican gang" the members of a rival gang tried, unsuccessfully, to invade the operating room to "finish him off," Dr. Dargan said. He cited incidents where doctors were "accosted," while in the nurses' home, a nearby residence for young women on the hospital staff, by addicts who demanded aid or money. Dr. Dargan's charges were dismissed by a spokesman for the city's Health and Hospitals Corporation. "What he omits to say," the municipal official noted, was that "no violence occurred" in any of the incidents. Neither man explained what doctors were doing in the nurses' home.

The hostility that erupted between the older medical staff and the community led a group of younger doctors, who called themselves "The Collective," to demand the removal of one of the older department heads, a doctor they respected as an "excellent clinician," but who was not willing to break "with traditional practices of medicine." The older Jewish doctors accused their younger colleagues and the *barrio* leaders of racism.

"The charge of racism clouds the real issue, is slanderous to us, and insulting," the younger doctors said: "We are working toward a future in which there will be one class of medical care for all people. The fact that day is remote is the shame of our society."

Racism was a medical problem to Dr. Costa. He felt it pervaded the hospital. "It is not efficient. You feel nobody trusts you as a doctor because of your color. Everyone is racist here in the United States. There is racism between white and Black, Black and Puerto Rican, white Puerto Rican and black Puerto Rican. It makes it difficult for a doctor to be a doctor. It is in the eyes. The way someone looks at you. Something you feel. I have felt it myself. Even I have become racist."

In a hospital where most of the staff, the doctors, and administration were white, the *barrio* patient felt like an intruder. He was suspicious and distrustful.

One woman in a Brooklyn *barrio* said: "Never go to a hospital unless you are dying. If you are not dying, they will kill you in there. The hospital is where our people go to die."

"If you are cured, it is a miracle," a patient said. "Every night when the light goes out I pray in the dark. If I go home from here, I will offer something to my saint for saving my life. The doctors have intelligence, I know. But that is all. What do they know about life? I am not afraid of cancer. I am afraid of them, the doctors. If I die, will they cry?" she said.

In the gloomy waiting room of the Lincoln Hospital a man and woman sat with a little girl on their lap. "I do not come here for myself," the woman said. "For my child." Her husband nodded. "If I can walk here, I do not go here. When they have to carry me, maybe then I go."

The fears and frights of the poor were not easily comprehensible to middle-class doctors. Was it possible to convey to them the nightmare of terrors that an old woman who believed in the spirits of the dead endured in the hospital bed where she knew so many had died before her?

A young boy might cry and curse that he was possessed by spirits beyond his control, that made him do things that he did not know or wish. His was a case of schizophrenia, might be the doctors' logical diagnosis. Psychiatric treatment was needed, or a juvenile home. (In Arizona, on the Navajo reservation, doctors now frequently called on medicine men to treat, and cure, their patients' psychic traumas. But any spiritualist woman who was found in a *barrio* hospital by the doctors was unceremoniously thrown out.) The medical studies had shown that Puerto Ricans suffered a higher incidence of psychiatric disturbances than any other group of people in New York. Sorrows of the souls seemed indigenous to the *barrios*.

"The doctors laugh at spiritualism," said Dr. Costa. "It is because they don't understand what it means to our people." The religious and cultural incomprehension between the doctors and the patients caused as many complications as the illnesses themselves.

On a winter day before Christmas in 1972, a young boy was admitted to the Adolescent Shelter on Rikers Island in New York harbor, a chintzy Devil's Island of a prison for youth. Michael Antonio Marerro was accused of threatening his mother with a knife. He was not accused of hurting her, merely of threatening to.

The boy was near hysteria. He was incoherent and feverish. In the juvenile shelter the youth, who was barely sixteen, watched how the young drug addicts, whose bodies shivered as his did and whose spirits pained as his did, were soothed by shots of methadone. So he told the doctors he too was a drug addict, in the hope of being given a shot of the comforting drug. He felt possessed by evil.

But the doctors who examined his urine and "inspected his arms" for needle marks "determined he was not an addict." He was set free.

On a bitter cold morning after Christmas, the boy came to

Bellevue Hospital begging to be admitted, it was said, for "he wanted psychiatric care."

Once he was in a hospital bed, he began to shiver convulsively. He trembled with fear. ("Evil spirits will make a man act crazy. He acts like he is dying," said an old spiritualist woman.) "The boy became difficult" was how the Chief Medical Examiner of New York, Dr. Milton Helpern said.

An "unidentified Bellevue physician" said the boy asked for a shot of methadone. The "unidentified" doctor telephoned Rikers Island to ask if there was a Michael Marerro in the methadone program. It happened that there was, but he was another Michael Marerro. Evidently the prison files could not tell one Puerto Rican youth from another.

"Let's say there was a Mike Marerro No. 1 and a Mike Marerro No. 2," said John Walsh, the public relations man for the Department of Corrections. "Mike No. 1 was admitted to Rikers on or about December 3 and was detoxified with methadone. Mike No. 2—the Bellevue youth—then told Rikers physicians that he was an addict and needed methadone."

So that evening the "unidentified" physician at the hospital injected the boy's unmarked arm with a forty-milligram dose of methadone. It was later charged by *barrio* leaders that the nameless doctor had inadvertently "killed the boy" merely to keep him quiet. The Department of Corrections publicist told reporters: "We never give a heroin addict more than a ten-milligram dose of methadone to start."

A senior physician at the eminent Rockefeller University laboratories, and a well-known authority on the use of methadone, Dr. Vincent P. Dole, said: "Although, normally, I would consider a forty-milligram dose small, and not enough to cause death, I would not categorically rule out the possibility."

On the morning of December 27, the boy was found dead in the hospital bed. Methadone was the official and "probable cause of death," Chief Medical Examiner of New York City Dr. Helpern said. He expressed his regrets.

A friend said, "He died of being a Puerto Rican."

26

Laws and Orders

Brother Against Brother

On the tenement stoop the two brothers leaned back on their elbows, enjoying the quiet of the twilight. At that hour of the day the block was most peaceful.

Suddenly one of the brothers jumped up, waving his fist and cursing his brother. In Spanish a curse was always more serious than it was in English. The brother who sat on the stoop now stood up. Leaping, with a sinuous twist of his body, he jumped his brother and they began to fight. A knife flickered in the lamplight. There was a scream.

The neighbors poured out of the tenements surrounding the wounded brother. He was bleeding and weeping. And so was his brother. Everyone knew they were close as twins. If one of them married, he would have to buy a bed big enough for three, they said on the block. So everyone offered words of comfort, advice, judgment, and love.

The policeman, who rarely patrolled the block, appeared at that moment. On his motorbike. He grabbed the wrong brother at first. The neighbors, to whom he was an intruder, said nothing. He realized his mistake and "apprehended" the other brother, announcing on his radio a possible "attempted murder."

A neighbor who was not Puerto Rican sought to calm the policeman. "I know these men. They are good men. They are brothers. They just had a family fight."

"Who are you?" said the officer.

"Just a neighbor. But I'd like to say something. It wouldn't do you any good to take him in. It will be a waste of everyone's time because no one will press charges. It was a family affair. It was between brothers. The family will take care of it. Why interfere?"

"You listen," said the officer, a bit sharply. "It's a criminal act to stab someone. He has to be booked. That's the law."

"Don't your brothers fight?"

"Not in the street!" said the officer. "Let them fight at home. In public, well, it's against the law, *our* law."

He booked one of the brothers that night. The neighbor wrote a report to the police of exactly what he had told the officer. In the morning, when no one pressed charges, the brother was released. His brother met him and they embraced and wept.

In the evening there was a celebration in the little social club in the basement of the tenement. The neighbor from across the street was offered four beers, which he drank to the toast *"¡Abajo la policía!"*

That was "Down with the Police!" By the fourth beer they were toasting *la policía.*

Later, years later, the fight of brother against brother was retold to Inspector Fink, who had been commander of the Ninth Precinct on the Lower East Side where the incident had happened, and now was retired from the force, teaching Criminal Justice at the John Jay "College of Cops." The Inspector recalled that he had been assigned to the precinct originally to calm the hostility that existed between the *barrio* residents and the police: he was "the cop with the master's degree," with a sociological understanding of the once Jewish ghetto where he had lived as a child.

In the streets the tense atmosphere had made police work difficult. There were accusations that policemen had beaten up two young Puerto Rican girls. On Avenue D, it was said that the hostility to the men in blue was so apparent that officers would not walk down that street. Not even in pairs. On the corners, the younger officers on foot patrol at night were often seen standing beneath the protective shield of lamplight, unwilling to venture into the dark side streets. Some were not afraid to admit that they were afraid. Those were the "long hot summers" of ghetto riots.

On Avenue C the "Thieves' Market" was held every Sunday morning in bold openness. "I found myself shocked," the Inspector recalled. "Someone would come to me: 'Hey, if you want to see where the swag is, where the burglars sell their merchandise, go to Seventh Street and Avenue C on Sunday morning. Every hallway is full of stuff.' And I used to rail about this to the detectives. I went there a couple of times and couldn't find the stuff. If they knew you were in the neighborhood the word would go out quickly.

"When I worked in East Harlem when you walked into a neighborhood—we used to go out at night to look for floating crap games—the mere fact that you weren't known (in the neighborhood) was enough to start a series of whistles, and signals, that shut down the whole neighborhood," he recalled.

Laws, said Inspector Fink, were "rules of conduct" that communities of men established to govern themselves. If the people of the *barrio* and the police lived by different "rules," they could not be enforced. The policeman was then like a soldier "in enemy territory."

The Inspector was an uncommonly thoughtful man, who was conscious of the inequities and paradoxes that beset law enforcement in a society of changing, and opposing, values. He was fond of rephrasing Plato's admonition that too much "individual freedom" in a democracy caused it to "break down," and created anarchy. But he was a social scientist as well as a policeman. He thought the dilemma was due to the "lack of communication" between different cultures. In an effort to create understanding he instituted lectures on Puerto Rican culture for his officers. He brought young Puerto Ricans and Blacks into the precinct as summer youth workers. And he urged that the police learn Spanish. In the window of the Ninth Precinct he placed a sign "¡AQUÍ SE HABLA ESPAÑOL!"—"SPANISH SPOKEN HERE!"

To the somewhat skeptical men on the force he explained in a leaflet:

> There's a new sign in our station house window. You might say it's a sign of our times. . . . Puerto Ricans are from a warm, friendly land. To them family and neighbors are important. . . . In this city they have sometimes found the people as cold and alien to them as the winter weather. They have been misunderstood because of their language and customs. Too often they have been discriminated against. . . . You might ask yourself, "Why don't they speak English?" "Why don't they learn our language?" They are trying, but it isn't easy. It wasn't easy for the other ethnic groups who settled here earlier. . . . Let's let them know that if they can't speak English, we'll speak Spanish. . . . And hopefully, in this way, the coming New Year will be happier for all of us.

The gap between the ghetto and the police was too deep and too old to be bridged by the Inspector's gestures of good will. When the Irish immigrants moved into the ghetto, known as Five Points before the Civil War, the Lower East Side was already considered dangerous and depraved. The hunger and poverty of the poor Irish was so severe that "policemen came into Five Points only in pairs and never unarmed," wrote Lloyd Morris in his history, *Incredible New York*. "It was the haunt of murderers, thieves, prostitutes and receivers of stolen goods." And the poor Irish women were "all of course prostitutes," warned a contemporary guidebook. That was in 1850!

The ghetto was run by a former New Orleans gambler and gang leader, Isaiah Rynders. He was "the law." He commanded a gang of hoodlums known as the Dead Rabbits and had won "control of the immigrant vote." Through his power in Tammany Hall he was appointed a United States marshal.

On the West Side there was as justly notorious an Irish gang, the Bowery Boys, led by the local Tammany Hall leader William ("Bill the Butcher") Poole, who challenged the power of Rynders. In the ensuing political battle Poole was assassinated. On the day of his funeral street fighting broke out. "Several thousand men and women armed with guns, paving blocks, iron bars and clubs milled through the streets from the Bowery to Broadway, fighting everywhere, looting houses, pillaging stores, and setting fire to buildings." The municipal police were helpless. So was Mayor Fernando Wood. In desperation the State Legislature in Albany "abolished the municipal police," and set up a new police force. And the second police force attacked the first police force. Not until the Seventh Regiment of the U.S. Army had surrounded City Hall and arrested the Mayor was peace restored to the city.

"Crime was endemic to the Lower East Side. The close collaboration between police officers, politicians and criminals was revealed in detail in the Lexow and Mazet investigations of the 1890s," commented Moses Rischin in his *The Promised City: New York's Jews.* The Slavic immigrants who came after the Irish, like the Polish and Russian Jews, were religious and law abiding; but the laws they abided by were their own. In one generation, by 1909, they had learned the laws of the ghetto so well that some three thousand Jewish youths appeared before the juvenile court. By the 1920s many of the Prohibition Era gang leaders, the forerunners of the Mafia, were former "good Jewish boys" of the Lower East Side.

So it was with the Puerto Rican youth. On the island, street gangs were unknown. The idea of "turf" was as unheard-of as switchblade knives, said the Police Superintendent Ramos Torres Braschi in the 1950s. Puerto Rico's juvenile delinquency rate was less than 25 percent that of the United States. But the young men returning from New York City had learned of gangs, drugs, and switchblades. "Some of the boys come back from the mainland with big ideas of becoming gang leaders," Governor Luis Muñoz Marín said in 1959. "We've got to watch them."

In each era "the major crimes and violence in the [Lower East Side] did not stem from the immigrants," wrote Moses Rischin. But the immigrants learned. The police, in any case, either could not enforce the established law or encouraged lawlessness.

On Seventh Street near Avenue D, a young woman described her frustration in seeking police protection for her tenement apartment that had been burglarized by drug addicts. Her story was typical of many:

"A man high on dope was out in the hall. I was here alone. My husband had gone to work. I put the chain on the lock and opened my door. There was this guy out there, about thirty years of age.

" 'What are you doing?' I said.

"He took an iron table leg that was lying there and said, 'I'm going to knock the shit out of you.'

"And I thought: He's going to break down the door. So I said, 'Put it down!'

"He said, 'Why should I?'

"And I said, ' 'Cause it's mine.'

"He was so high he put it down and left. Then I got frightened.

"I called the police. The Ninth Precinct. They told me they didn't have enough cops to send one. They said, 'Call the detectives.' So I called the detectives. They said, 'Why call us? Call the Ninth Precinct.' They didn't come either.

"The man came back twice. He made chip marks on the door. And we threw him out, personally. Then we had to go out. When we came home the whole door, even the police lock, had been bashed in. Our television, typewriter, camera, and binoculars were gone.

"So we had to stand guard at the door for two days while it was fixed. We took turns.

"About three days later I saw a man coming from our house. He looked suspicious. So I followed him. A police car came by, and I waved and jumped in. The man had gone into a restaurant. But the police won't go in and arrest him. I would go in myself, I said. So they went in. Around his neck was the binoculars and the camera that was stolen from us. It was ours. They had me identify it right on him. They found about twenty summons on him for drug arrests. He was real high. He babbled out the whole story to me.

"Why didn't they want to arrest him? I think they knew he was a pusher. And they wanted to protect him. This is my third robbery. And I can't be insured. It's like living in a state of siege."

On the same block, just across the street, the janitor of a tenement told her story:

"We have seventy-two tenants. Of the seventy-two one has been 'hit' every week. I'd say that twenty or thirty tenants have been broken into at various times. One tenant who had lived here for three days had his apartment broken into. He had freshly painted white floors. There were footprints all over the floor. He called the police. The officers walked right through the prints, scuffling their feet as they went, saying, 'Where's the footprints?' I was there. I saw it. Nothing is ever done. Nothing is ever returned. And most people do not call the police. Because they feel nothing will be done."

In the poorest *barrios* people accused the police not merely of not protecting them from criminals but of protecting the criminals. They were paid off by the narcotics pushers; they were pushers themselves, it was said.

The accusations were confirmed by Deputy Inspector Donald F. Cawley at the hearings on Police Corruption of the New York State Commission of Investigation. Police, said Cawley, "have accepted bribes. They have sold narcotics. . . . They have known of narcotics violations and failed to take proper enforcement action. They have entered into personal associations with narcotic criminals and, in some instances, they have used narcotics. They have given false testimony in court in order to obtain a dismissal of charges against a defendant. In one case, a police officer provided rental automobiles for the use of a known narcotics criminal [to transport narcotics]."

It was "a common practice," said Patrolman Robert Torres of the Narcotics Division, for officers to keep half of the narcotics they seized—to sell to addicts. Torres explained: if "an addict had fifty bags, you would turn in twenty-five and keep twenty-five." Was "this practice generally known not only to the patrolmen and detectives, but to your superiors?" Torres was asked by the investigator. It was, he said.

Chief Inspector Joseph McGovern, Commander of the New York City Police Department's Internal Affairs Division, at headquarters, testified that "gambling graft" was no longer the most lucrative form of police corruption. It was surpassed by narcotics.

One *barrio* leader said, "The dope is pushed on us because it turns our young men into zombies. It's the best way to kill their militancy." In its 1953 report on narcotics the New York Academy of Medicine had noted, as quoted in the *New York Times,* that "those youngsters who used narcotics no longer participated in gang behavior. It [narcotics] provided the nonconforming adolescent with an opportunity to express his aggression that is socially unacceptable, but did not, of itself, involve overt acts of aggression."

"The cops know they can't wipe us out with guns, or ideas. So they try to wipe us out with shit. I mean heroin," said a Young Lord.

"Drug abuse," as a term, is indicative of legal and law-enforcement ambivalence to *drug use.* Who defines the dividing line between use and abuse? Police have no alternative but to make their own definition. A bored suburban housewife may be popping tranquilizers but will never be judged guilty of "drug abuse," while a *barrio* youth, malnourished and depressed, caught with one cigarette of marijuana will be arrested and found guilty.

Nowhere was the distance between the police and the people of the *barrio* more evident than in the name given by the South Bronx community to the beleaguered and isolated Forty-first Precinct in its midst. They called it "Fort Apache." In a curious repetition of history the police often complained, as had the frontier soldiers, that the inhabitants were "hostile" to their efforts to bring the benefits of civic law and order. If the ordinary policemen imagined themselves to be the 10th Cavalry in "enemy territory," how many young Puerto Rican boys imagined themselves to be Geronimo? Was the reconquest of the West to be refought, day by day, in the streets of the South Bronx?

"LIFE IS CHEAP IN 41ST PRECINCT," a tale of the reported violence and homicides in the *barrio,* appeared in the New York *Daily News* in November, 1971. The reporter, Rudy Garcia, found no officer who was willing to be quoted; instead, he quoted an unnamed social worker, who voiced a prevalent opinion: "These are still fairly primitive people. . . ."

In the first nine months of that year, the office of the Chief Medical Examiner of New York had listed ninety-one "certified homicides" in the Forty-first Precinct. But in "Fort Apache" the local police in the same months had a record of only seventy-one. Apparently there were twenty murders in their own precinct that they had never heard of.

A *bodega* shopkeeper said, "So they don't know anything that's happening unless someone telephones to tell them the news."

The police in neighborhood precincts and the central headquarters spokesmen for the Police Department denied the implied accusation, pointing to their arrest records in the *barrio* as evidence of their diligence. And, besides, they said, these were "very tough neighborhoods" with a "high density of crime," where it was difficult for law enforcement "to successfully penetrate." "These people are suspicious of authority and often will not cooperate with law-enforcement officers," an Inspector said; why blame the policemen? "The men are frustrated by the hostility they face daily," he said. "If people would only cooperate with us."

But in the *barrio* it was often said that these high arrest records were evidence not of police protection but of police harassment. "The cops will have a different mental attitude when they investigate a robbery in East Harlem than they do when they investigate a robbery on Fifth Avenue," said Gerena Valintin. "In the *barrio* they treat the victim as if he was the criminal."

"Many brown-skinned [Spanish-speaking] persons who are natural born citizens of the United States are subjected to a lifetime of harassment by police authorities," the State of Illinois's legislative Spanish Speaking Peoples Study Commission reported in 1971. In the courts there was "undue harassment and a great deal of injustice to Spanish speaking residents," the legislators said.

In 1966, when the citizens of New York City voted down two to one the proposal for a Civilian Review Board, in the *barrio* precincts the vote for the Review Board was 71 percent *in favor*. "Undoubtedly crime in the streets is a concern in the Puerto Rican community, but so are the actions of the police," said one observer.

"Hostility, or even lack of confidence of a significant portion of the public [in a ghetto] has extremely serious implications for the police," commented the President's Commission on Law Enforcement study—*Task Force Report: The Police.* "Police-community relationships have a direct bearing on the character of life in our cities," the report said. ". . . the police department's capacity to deal with crime depends to a large extent upon its relationship with the citizenry."

On April Fool's Day in 1972 the student newspaper of the College of Criminal Justice at John Jay (part of the City University of New York) was a traditional lampoon of the ghetto. The edition was called *The Daily Dreck,* the Yiddish phrase for *The Daily Shit,* and in a column called "Afro-Latin Crap," a police officer mocked what he thought was the language of the ghetto:

> You dig, pig? Whitey owes me a lot. He owes me the will to help out in my community, he owes me a car to take me to register to vote. . . . He owes me a backbone. . . . While Whitey is paying his debts I'll keep playing my cards, taking my drugs, sipping my booze, messing over my women, and hoping by some benevolent gift from Whitey I can make it in the world.

In satirizing "Black–Puerto Rican Studies" the would-be police humorist wrote of ghetto youth: "I'm underprivileged, a member of a minority and a lonely dude whose father left the family afore I was born." Solace to the ghetto youth was offered by the mock advertisement of "Joe's Bait and Tackle Shop, Tijuana," Mexico, offering "Adolph's Abortions—No Fetus Can Beat Us."

Needless to say, the Community Relations Division of the Police Department did not distribute *The Daily Dreck* in the city's ghettos or *barrios.*

The *Putas* of Times Square

In their high black boots and miniskirts so tightly and briefly cut they barely covered the bottoms of their buttocks, the *putas*—whores—shivered on cold winter days. All but naked underneath their skimpy clothes as they waited for the fashionably overdressed men to come down from their uptown offices in search of the myth of passionate Latin women.

On the streets at the edge of the Lower East Side *barrio* there was a place where the *putas* gathered in the broad daylight and the *policías* of New York's finest were friendly, much of the time.

"The Latin woman," one police officer said, shrugging, "is a born whore."

But these *putas* were seldom Latin women. Few were Puerto Rican. Hardly a brown face was to be seen among the white and black faces. The men who came to buy a few moments of love were seldom Puerto Ricans.

Why then did they come to the *barrio?* So far from the uptown offices and hotels. It was safer to be a whore in the *barrio* than on Times Square. The suburban women, on their way to a matinee, would not be likely to see their men slinking in and out of the Bowery-like hotel along Third Avenue. Reporters came here only for a little local color now and then.

As it had for generations, poverty preserved the decorum of society. The ghetto had always been the whorehouse of the middle class. Once the Lower East Side had been the busiest red-light district of New York. It was so when the neighborhood was an Irish ghetto; it was so when it was a Jewish ghetto. In the 1890s a fatigued, but intrepid, researcher counted precisely 236 saloons, 118 "hotels" that catered to whores, and 18 "outright houses of prostitution" in the ghetto. The old slum became the new "Klondike, that replaced the uptown Tenderloin as a center of graft and illicit business." Its prime business was sex. Of women imprisoned in the New York State Reformatory for "soliciting," over the fifty-year period before World War II, one-fifth were Jewish and most of the rest were Irish and Italian.

"There were hundreds of prostitutes on my street," remembered the "Gorky of the Ghetto," Michael Gold, in his *Jews Without Money*.

> They occupied the vacant stores, they crowded into flats and apartments in all the tenements. The pious Jews hated the traffic. But they were pauper strangers here; they could do nothing. They shrugged their shoulders and murmured "This is America." They tried to live. . . . They tried to shut their eyes. We children did not shut our eyes. We saw and knew. . . . On sunshiny days the whores sat on chairs [in the daytime] along the sidewalks. They sprawled indolently, their legs taking up half the pavements. People stumbled over a gauntlet of whores' meaty legs. . . . They called their wares like pushcart peddlers. At five years I knew what they sold.
>
> Earth's trees, grass, flowers, could not grow on my street; but the rose of syphilis bloomed by night and by day.

Romanticism has since revisted the ghettos with nostalgic memories. The old "ethnic slum usually centered upon a stable family life," reminisced Michael Harrington in *The Other America*. But in the *barrios* Puerto Rican women were "the promiscuous, addicted, violent girls," Harrington wrote. He thought the *barrio* mothers "promiscuous." They "lived with one man for a considerable period of time, bear his [*sic*] children, and then move on to another man." Family life in the *barrios* was "female based"; a social phenomenon replacing the earlier "stable family life" dominated by the Irish and Jewish mother.

And yet most Puerto Rican girls were chastely and religiously brought up. In the home girls were taught that love and sex were intimate and almost unspeakable acts, governed by God and man. By the second generation, they had learned that in America "it was different." The public display of sex was encouraged and profitable. One by one the strict old codes of morality gave way to a "new freedom." This was, as Gerena Valintin said, a "buying and selling society. Everybody has a price. So they sold themselves."

Still, the family morality of the *barrio* was as religious as that of the Irish and Jewish families had been. The Puerto Rican *putas* had to go uptown to work. On the gaudy streets off Times Square they enticed out-of-town tourists like street beggars. The older professionals with established territories and a status officially recognized by the police haughtily and contemptuously referred to the newcomers to the trade as "amateurs," "spiks who have to work the kinky tricks." The girls of the *barrios,* who worked the streets uptown, were often too young and inexperienced to be protected by the strict rules that governed the business of sex. Some young girls no more than fourteen went into the streets alone to pick up men who had been rejected by the professionals as too sick or too cruel. These girls were easily abused not only by the men but by the police. In the business of prostitution a girl who had no protection, either from her pimp or the police, was every man's victim.

"A man respects a white woman or a black woman. He knows we won't let him shit on us. Let him get some little spik and he'll shit all over her," sneered one woman, defending her street corner with folded arms. "Even her own man treats her like shit. And a white guy or a black guy, he sees that. So he'll do things to her if he tried it with me I'd kick his balls up his ass for him. He knows it."

The male image of Latin women was simple-minded or mindless. In the guise of Carmen Miranda she had appeared in movies as a comic sexpot, an earthy and large-mouthed Mrs. Malaprop with a funny accent, vivacious but dumb. She was, as well, Dolores del Rio, forever *Flying Down to Rio,* svelte and mysterious, an unobtainable sex symbol whose dark eyes promised ecstasy and exotic tragedy.

Remembering his fantasy of *barrio* girls as a young man, Richard Goldstein wrote in *New York* magazine: ". . . the lower classes got nice asses. And Spanish girls had it even then. They were soft and tropical and made you think of words like papaya and Nicaragua." He was a bit embarrassed, but not much, by this "classic colonial situation" of imagined sexual conquest—". . . take the women and crush the men." In his youth, "Spanish men were no challenge. Dangerous (they had knives), but not threatening. They had no power."

The Borinquén women had rarely, nor willingly, been "taken" quite that easily by the Conquistadors of Spain, much less by the delivery boys of the Bronx. But, it was true that society did little to protect the young women of the *barrio* from the *machos,* whether Anglo or Latin.

Legally, prostitution was a "victimless crime," that is, its only real victims were women. So the lawmen, who protected the rights of prostitutes to be prostitutes, a right they paid for, were lenient in enforcing laws against the men involved. "Vice is usually considered to embrace prostitution" was the ribald comment of the staid President's Commission on Law Enforcement, *Task Force on the Police.* The locker-room double entendre was not thought improper, it seemed, because prostitution was loosely defined as a criminal act. Even the FBI reports on "rising crime rates," which included such offenses as "vagrancy" (sleeping in hallways) and the "disturbing of the peace" (singing at night while intoxicated), did "not include violation of vice laws" (such as selling a woman's body).

On the island, as on the mainland, widespread prostitution was a relatively recent phenomenon in the *barrios.* It was a "cultural adaptation" learned in New York, lately exported to the island; the idea of sex sold in the market plaza, opposite the church, was not native to the villages of Borinquén. Even in San Juan the prostitutes in the tourist hotels were mostly imported from the mainland of South and North America. Pimps went to New York and Miami "to bring girls to Puerto Rico," said Vice Squad Chief Angel David Gonzales. There were probably more Puerto Rican prostitutes in New York than on the entire island.

La Vida had told a very different tale. In his anthropological book of sex, Oscar Lewis reversed history by depicting a group of prostitutes who had come to New York from the San Juan *barrio* of La Perla, the ancient slum by the sea. He had based much of his theory of the "culture of poverty" on the life styles of these prostitutes. Many who read *La Vida* assumed the whores of La Perla were typical dwellers of the *barrios*. Lewis feared his book might be so "misinterpreted, or used to justify prejudices and negative stereotypes about Puerto Ricans," and cautioned, "This study deals with only one segment of the Puerto Rican population and the data should not be generalized to Puerto Rican society as a whole." But, Lewis went on to say, "It may also reflect something of the national character, although this would be difficult to prove. . . . However, I am suggesting the possibility that studies of the lower class [whores?] may also reveal something that is distinctive of a people as a whole."

"No, it is not a true picture of La Perla," said Clifford Depin, a San Juan leader of the Ladies' Garment Workers Union and a longtime resident. "The people there are poor, but there are many hardworking, stable families living there. And they have lived there for years. Besides," Depin said, "La Perla is not where the prostitutes of San Juan live. In fact, most of the prostitutes here, on the island, are not even Puerto Rican. To write that in a book is not true, at all."

The *barrio* of La Perla had been one of the oldest red-light districts in the Americas. Built in the sixteenth century, it was originally a village of Indian women kept by the Spanish soldiers who built the fortress of El Morro. Later it became a sexual barracks of the Spanish Army. Later still it was the whorehouse of the United States Army. The headquarters of the Commanding General was on the hill, overlooking the aging slum, within walking distance of the barracks of his soldiers.

"In my youth, when I was eight years old, I knew all about La Perla," said Jaime Benitez, then president of the University of Puerto Rico. Everyone knew about La Perla. That was where the whores were. So why did Oscar have to do those studies, and write that book to say what everyone knew? If a man wishes to write a book like that he does not need a typewriter. He can write it with his penis!

"And it was not even an honest book about our whores. If you go to Ashford Avenue, by the tourist hotels, you will see that most of the whores on the island come from the mainland, and so do their customers."

In his office, Clifford Depin agreed: "Whoring is not part of the Puerto Rican character," he said. "It is something we taught them."

27

The *Yagrumos*

When the wind blows, the leaves of the yagrumo *tree turn. The* yagrumo *is a softwood tree, with large leaves like fans. One side of the leaves is dark, and one side is light. So when the wind blows, the leaves turn from dark to light. And so when a politician is corrupt, it is said he is like a* yagrumo. *He changes with the wind.*

In the little café in Bayamón the sign over the bar read: "NO POLITICAL ARGUMENTS ALLOWED!"

On the island the politics of a man was not merely a matter of the political party he belonged to, or of whom he voted for. It was the way he articulated his dreams, his *corazón,* his *macho,* his philosophy of life. And a philosophy of life was not likely to be affected by the election of another man. Every man was unique. Then so was his politics. In the words "Do not give me your vote! Lend it to me!" Governor Luis Muñoz Marín had perfectly voiced the feeling of individualism of the *jíbaros* of the island. And, in politics, it was said, all Puertorriqueños were *jíbaros.*

The folk saying was: *If three Puertorriqueños get together to form a political party, they will form at least four political parties. . . .*

In a parable, the young lawyer Joaquin Marquez, in the Office of the Resident Commissioner in Washington, D.C., told about the political consequence of this "trait of the Puertorriqueño":

"Now, imagine if you put three Anglos in a deep pit. They would escape immediately. They would form a pyramid. One would climb out on the shoulders of the other two. He would then pull the others out.

"And, if you put three Puertorriqueños in the same deep pit, what would happen? They would immediately begin to argue about the best way to escape. Each would say he knows the best way to escape. Each would make a passionate speech about the way to do it—his way, of course.

"So none would escape from the pit."

The individualism of his countrymen was "noble in a philosophical sense," the lawyer said, but in "practical politics" it was "self-defeating." Every man talked, but no one acted.

On the island the Mayor of a small town said that the American politician "is not a man. He is a 'representative' of men. He has lost his *macho*. He does not honestly speak for himself. He says what he thinks others want him to say."

Wasn't that democracy?

"No!" the Mayor said. "That is cowardice!"

In a mountain town a lifelong political leader on the island shook an accusing finger. "You," he angrily said, "have made cowards of us.

"That is what your 'American democracy' has done to us," he said. "It has destroyed our manhood! How? *Secret ballots!* What is democratic about secret ballots? What is democratic about hiding your political belief in a voting booth? For a man to have to hide his belief in a voting booth, behind a curtain, inside the skirt of society, that is not democratic. That is cowardly."

He was a leader of his political party. Every election for the last thirty years had involved him; he regularly appeared on radio and television and at meetings, to urge people to vote. What was he talking about?

"A man who hides his belief shames himself," he said. "He will not vote for what he really thinks in secret. He will vote for his job. He will vote to feed the mouths of his children. Secret ballots cause men to be dishonest. Yes! Yes! It is true! That is because no one can see a man when he shames himself inside the voting booth by lying. Not even God.

"To be a man every man ought to stand up in the plaza and speak what he believes, for all to hear. He ought to defend his belief without fear. In the old days that was our way. That was democracy. That was the way of honor. Now you have taught us to hide in voting booths. A man learns to hide his belief even from himself. He learns how to lie. Even to God."

Nowhere in the Americas had a country been a political colony for as long as the island, he said. It may have become part of "our colonial way of thinking" to play political games. "Puertorriqueños have an independent heart and a colonial mind," he said. "The *jíbaro* knows, no matter how he votes, for four hundred and fifty years no *jíbaro* has ever been elected Governor in La Fortaleza.

"So we play your game," the old political *patrón* said.

In the *barrios* elections were an occasion for *fiestas,* for oratorical contests and debates in the bars and plazas that erupted into joyful fights. So often were there passionate fist fights and political shootings that when sociologists at the university asked islanders what they thought the most significant improvement on the island in thirty years, from 1930 to 1960, one-third replied, "No more fights at elections; before, people were killed."

The "colonial" mind had led to a "kind of duality" in politics, said Manny Diaz, a veteran of the New York *barrios'* political arena. On the one hand there was a "passive acquiescence" to the electoral process, and on the other hand there was a "personal resistance." In the Spanish era this was known as *"Se obedece, pero no se cumple"* —"Obedience [to the King], but not compliance."

In San Juan and in New York, it was not much different. The politician was the master of that "duality." He was the *yagrumo,* who like the leaf of the tropical tree turned whichever way the most powerful political winds blew. He was the man in between—half European, half native on the island, and half Puerto Rican, half American on the mainland. In the political tradition of Latin America it was the Creoles, *los criollos,* the half-castes, who were most often the government servants and political leaders. "What were the *criollos?"* asked Manuel Zeno Gandía, the Puerto Rican novelist of the nineteenth century. "A people of hostages," he wrote, "raving against the foreigners, but adoring them like idols."

The *yagrumos'* lack of political power was adorned by a refinement of style and a beautiful rhetoric. If the power of decision was not theirs, they concealed it. "Style is everything, when there is nothing else" was an old saying.

The elite of political *patrones* had governed the island for so long it seemed inconceivable that anyone else could, or would. Most of the legislators in San Juan had always come from the same families, and had gone to the same schools. Often they were related by blood or by love affairs, if not by commercial ties and country clubs. Whether they were believers in independence, statehood, or commonwealth in no way altered their social affinity.

In his paternalistic ways the conservative old Governor Luis Ferre may have differed from the paternalism of the liberal young Governor Rafael Hernández Colón. Yet, in the high society of Ponce, their families had intermarried. The problem of "democratic elitism," wrote the liberal political commentator and adviser to one Popular Democratic party Governor, Juan Manuel García Passalacqua, was "How can the people be made to understand what is best for them? . . .

"The attitudes developed toward the paternalistic government of Puerto Rico," wrote sociologist Nathan Glazer, "were easily transferred to the government of the City of New York." He believed these attitudes of compliance and apathy were so strong that "self-help [was] somewhat muted."

But there wasn't much evidence of paternalism toward Puerto Ricans by the political machines on the mainland. The gerrymandering of the *barrios,* to render the election of neighborhood politicians almost impossible, the long-standing literacy tests that disenfranchised *barrio* voters, and the undermining of political power bases in the *barrios* indicated a policy of deliberate exclusion of Puerto Ricans from the political process.

"No less than 200,000 Puerto Ricans were in effect disenfranchised" by the English literacy tests for voters, Nathan Glazer had once written. Since then, the courts ordered the tests be given in Spanish; then eliminated their use. Even so, voter registration has increased imperceptibly in only a few *barrios* and has perceptibly decreased in many *barrios* of the city.

Of all the people in the urban ghettos none have as small a percentage of registered voters as the Puerto Ricans. In the election of 1960 more than half (53.6 percent) of El Barrio residents of voting age did not vote. Although about 15 percent of the city's population, they were only 4 percent of the registered voters. In *Beyond the Melting Pot,* Glazer and Moynihan estimated that of 300,000 "potential" voters in the *barrios* of New York, no more than one in three had registered in 1960. City Hall in the days of Mayor Wagner's still powerful political machine had launched a "huge campaign" to register 100,000 Puerto Ricans, and so garner this presumably Democratic bloc vote. The politicians thought they had registered 130,000 new "Spanish-speaking voters." One year later Mayor Wagner's campaign manager complained that there were a mere 20,000 of these new voters on the rolls. "They [Puerto Ricans and Blacks] have abstained more in the 1960's than in the mid 1940's," Glazer wrote, "and the reasons are unclear."

Politics on the island was like the sun. Everyone basked in it. More than 82 percent of the eligible voters went to the polls in the election of 1972—considerably larger than the percentage of Americans voting in the presidential election in the United States. And yet the boycotting of elections was as popular a political act on the island as voting. For years the *independentistas* boycotted elections, keeping as many as one of every three voters away from the polls. In Latin America the "no vote" was an old tradition. So too in New York the largest *barrio* vote was the "no vote." It was too consistent and widespread to be dismissed. During the presidential election of 1968 fewer than one-third of the *barrio* voters registered and fewer than one-half as many voted that year as in the election of John Kennedy eight years before. The "no vote" case against both Nixon and Humphrey in 1968 equaled 85 percent of the eligible *barrio* voters.

In the tradition of the Populares, the Popular Democratic party of Governor Muñoz, the vote in the *barrio* had been overwhelmingly Democratic, even more so on the mainland than on the island. And yet, contrary to the popular myth of city politics, the Puerto Rican vote was not given equally and undiscriminatingly. John F. Kennedy won 75 percent of the vote in 1960, Lyndon Johnson won 86 percent against Barry Goldwater in 1964, Hubert Humphrey won 83 percent in 1968—but, as has been said, *fewer than half* as many *barrio* voters cast ballots for Humphrey as did for Kennedy. So the majority of Puerto Ricans had actually voted for no one that year. Two percent of the disenchanted *barrio* votes supported the independent party of George Wallace!

The thoughtful, often painful, choice of the *barrio* voters was seen in the vote of Congressman Herman Badillo, in the primary for Mayor in 1969. Badillo, who was touted as the "first Puerto Rican Mayor," was defeated by City Controller Mario Procaccino, when he received less of the *barrio* vote than any of the previous Democratic candidates for President, 71 percent. Since the vote was close, had he done better in the *barrio,* he might have won. The New York Puerto Ricans "were asleep at the switch," commented a political analyst; yet they had apparently *not* voted, quite deliberately, for a candidate, despite the fact that he was "one of their own" and a Democrat.

Badillo was not a traditional *barrio* politician. He was not a romantic poet or a street-corner prophet. In his speech he was soft-spoken, reticent, and cautious. Recognized in Congress, where he was the only Puerto Rican, as the representative of the *barrios,* his Congressional district nevertheless included the lower-middle-class suburbia of Queens. The image of his Puertorriqueñoism was purposely kept at a "low profile," one of his aides said. An old friend remembered an early campaign: "In his first political try for office Herman was asked by someone in the audience if he was Puerto Rican or Italian. He never really answered the question. He never has."

In his campaign for Mayor of New York City the hard-working Congressman built his candidacy upon the civic issues and programs he believed would benefit the "entire city," scrupulously avoiding appeals of ethnic rhetoric. A former Borough President of the Bronx, he had a practical, day-to-day familiarity with the workings of city government. But his political competence did not inspire political fervor in the *barrios*. His "cool style" was not in the island tradition. And his years as the city's Commissioner of Relocation had created a certain wariness among *barrio* residents whom his office had forced to move from tenements being torn down for urban-renewal projects.

"Herman is the most popular politician we have in the *barrio* because he is the only politician we have," one of Badillo's supporters said.

It was a black man who won the largest *barrio* vote ever cast for a Democrat. Basil A. Paterson, a Harlem State Senator who ran for Lieutenant Governor in the Democratic primary of 1970, was blatantly attacked on racial grounds. His color became "the chief issue" of the election. From the *barrio* he received what political commentators termed "an astounding" 91 percent majority. It was surpassed only by that of black voters in Harlem.

Still the people of the *barrio* had no elected officials of their own in any city administration, a Ford Foundation–funded group of professionals, the Puerto Rican Forum, complained in 1970. "Of 246 candidates for municipal offices in 1969, five were Puerto Ricans. None were elected. Of all the special-interest groups in the city, Puerto Ricans had "the lowest number of men in public position to bargain and broker the arrangements of the city," said Glazer and Moynihan.

"Powerlessness" was how long-time city official Manny Diaz described it. "The logos of power in a society such as New York has its genesis in the economic power of a group, and its expression in their political power," he said. "We are powerless in both economic and political terms. In the last five or ten years we have begun to develop a middle class. But the entrepreneur, the professional, the businessman in the Puerto Rican community is more concerned with 'making it' in his small storefront than with power. He does not own banks, buy and sell the corporate stock, deal in the real estate of whole neighborhoods, or control jobs the way an industrialist does." He thought the largest Puerto Rican employer in the city hired about two hundred people.

So small was the middle class, in a country that thought itself to be largely middle class, that Puerto Ricans, who were perhaps 15 percent of the population of New York, had fewer than one percent of the city's "two car" jobs. Of 9,000 municipal employees earning $12,000 a year or more, only 65 were Puerto Ricans, said Gerena Valintin.

In the days before the re-election of President Richard Nixon, fifty "Hispanic leaders" gathered in one of the small banquet halls of the Hilton Hotel in New York, at a $1,000-a-couple society dinner dance. "The black-tie, filet mignon affair," as the *New York Times* described it, brought together the wealthiest members of the Puerto Rican community: then Commissioner of Migration and travel-agency-chain-owner Nick Lugo, Jr.; the wholesale grocery supplier for hundreds of *bodegas,* John Torres; the president of the Puerto Rican Home Owners Association, José Colón; and the vice presidents of the Banco Popular and Banco Credito, Luis Abudo and Hugo Ruiz. The banquet itself was a cosmopolitan repast, with Alaskan king crab puffs, Singapore mushroom caps, Hawaiian basket pineapples, Russian piroshki, Parisian consommé jardinière, Swedish meat balls, Champs Elysées potatoes, Southern Cross salad, and baked soufflé Alaska. There were no Puerto Rican foods on the menu.

The President was delighted, and rewarded, by the $50,000 collected by the dinner guests for his re-election campaign fund. He sent a message that expressed his appreciation to the celebrants: ". . . in the big switch to the Republican party's way of life," said Maurice Stans, speaking for the President, the Spanish-speaking were "now participating." They too would "share with all other loyal Americans a mutual interest in the preservation of the great American way of life."

Just at that time the Committee to Re-elect the President in

Washington was being advised in a memo that the *barrio* voters were not to be trusted. They were "uneducated, apolitical," and "simple." It was recommended that the Republican party secretly begin a don't-get-out-the-vote campaign to keep the Spanish-speaking voters at home.

"A campaign that tries to sell the President would be hopeless," said the memo, dated June 19, 1972, and addressed by Alex Armendariz, director of the Spanish Speaking Voter Section of the Committee to Re-elect the President, to the deputy national director, Fred V. Malek. "The campaign must be conducted entirely as an effort to denigrate the opposition and keep the electorate home, leaving them with no candidate. . . . This should be fairly simple to organize. With one issue—attack—an uneducated, apolitical audience, addicted to media, could be drenched with simple slogans. . . . Far more important than organizing our support is disorganizing the opposition."

In the *barrios* of New York, the voters would be particularly simple to confuse. The Puerto Ricans "are undermotivated, easily self-divided and rely extraordinarily on luck for the betterment of their lives." They could be manipulated with ease.

On election day, needless to say, the Puerto Rican voters of New York's *barrios,* and elsewhere, voted overwhelmingly against the President. In few of the nation's ghettos did voters more unanimously support the Democratic candidate.

The stubborn and independent way of the urban *jíbaros* was captured long ago by the poet Luis Lloréns Torres:

A *jíbaro* came to San Juan
Where some Yankee lovers
Came upon him in a park
Hoping to win him over.
They told him of Uncle Sam,
Of liberty and voting,
Of dollars and habeas corpus,
And the *jíbaro* answered,
"Mmmmhmmmm."

Nevertheless the "poor have no power at all," said Manny Diaz. "The only power any of us have is rhetorical power. Like the power of a preacher who gets up and says moralistic and righteous things everybody hears but no one listens to. We make beautiful speeches."

If the Puerto Ricans did get together and elect a Mayor, "he would have no power," said *barrio* politician Gerena Valintin; admittedly Badillo could not change "the institutionalized political racism of this society. He has been overwhelmed and taken over by the political machine. He has to be if he wants to be elected Mayor. So the fact he is Puerto Rican will not help the *barrio,* which will be just as powerless as before."

Unlike the European immigrants, who in one generation had built recognized ethnic blocs of political power, the immigrants from Puerto Rico, after twenty-five years, had none. The exiled islanders were as large a voting bloc as the Irish, Polish, Jewish, and Italian immigrants who came before them, and often a much larger one. Legally they were American citizens before they arrived, and so were constitutionally entitled to vote. They were given less recognition, and fewer positions of power, by the established political machines than any previous group of immigrants.

The body of ethnic politics was divided into three parts—like Gaul. One part, the largest, belonged to the European immigrants. One part, smaller but growing, was claimed by the Blacks. One part, so small it was insignificant, was left for the natives of America—Indians, Chicanos, and Puerto Ricans.

Politics was the act of governing a nation. In ethnic politics the "ethnics" (from the Greek *ethnikos,* meaning heathens or pagans, literally "the clans outside the gates of the city") were offered participation in the governing process when they became part of the nation. The policy was sensible and practical. It had been enunciated at the turn of the century by Theodore Roosevelt, with his usual candor and honesty: "We have no room for any people who do not act and vote simply as Americans." European immigrants, in this sense, were classic ethnics. Once they were within the "gates of the city" they had to become part of the body politic. Still, the immigrants held on to their ethnic ties for generations. "The American hypothesis of the Melting Pot just ain't so" in politics, commented Mark Levy and Michael Kramer in their study *The Ethnic Factor: How America's Minorities Decide Elections:* "Ethnicity is becoming crucial in our political scheme."

But not for the Puerto Ricans, Chicanos, and Indians. They were not ethnic blocs, but were conquered nations. They had not come to this land seeking, and finding, freedom, but had fought against and had been defeated by this land. They had not come to the United States, but the United States had come to them. They were not white-skinned immigrants from Europe, but were rainbow-hued natives of America. They had not been outside "the gates of the city," but had been driven out by the ethnic invaders who had conquered and subjugated them.

The Puerto Ricans had little power, even when they were a majority. Like the Indians and the Chicanos they were politically suspect, and they looked with suspicion upon politics, for in the government structure of the United States there was no precedent, or constitutional provision, for nations or national minorities to exist within the government in peace and harmony.

A formidable man sat behind a formidable desk in a Midwestern office. He was the highest-placed "official Puerto Rican" in his state. "For five hundred miles in any direction," he said. As a city Commissioner, or "something like that," he worked for what he himself called "the racist bastards downtown." He was cynical about it. His jowled face, like a wary bulldog, was weary and defeated. But in the eyes of his admirers "he had it made"; he was a success who lectured on "the American Way" in school auditoriums and at civic conferences for "ethnics."

To his enemies he was a *vendito,* one who had sold out, a *puta* of the establishment. "He's got his," they said of him contemptuously.

"Since I work for the city I got many rewards," he said. "I tell you what I got. I got the ulcer. I got a bad liver. I got a bad heart. I got a heart attack. I got to be half an alcoholic." The Commissioner leaned across his desk and whispered, "And when I look in the mirror in the morning you know what I see? I see a lump of shit!"

"Maybe it should be printed," he said. "If you print it I will be fired. But why not? It will be good for my ulcer." He mused for a moment. "No! do not say my name. I have my family, and my ulcer, to feed."

28

Alien in Two Lands, Illiterate in Two Languages

De-education of a Child

The year Cristóbal Colón set sail for the Americas, the Spanish scholar Antonio de Nebrija completed work on his Grammática, *the first modern grammar of the Spanish language. He proudly presented his work to Queen Isabella.*

"What is it for?" the Queen asked.

"Your Majesty," replied the Bishop of Avila, who had accompanied the scholar, "language is the perfect instrument of empire."

The teacher picked up "The Primer" in English. He was saddened at the thought of "teaching English in English," but don Peyo was tired of fighting with his superviser. And so he said to his class, "Well, children, we are goin' to talk in Englis' today." He opened "The Primer" to a picture of a strutting cock. "Now, you know, *'gallo'* is 'cock' in English, in American," he began. "Read with me: 'The cock says *cockadoodle-doo.'* " The teacher called on Tellito: "How does the cock crow in English?"

"I don't know, don Peyo," the boy replied.

"But look, boy, you're just read it," snapped the teacher.

"No," the boy said.

"Look, dummy, the cock crows *cockadoodledoo,*" the teacher repeated.

"Don Peyo, that must be the song of the American rooster," the boy said apologetically. "The cock at home sings *'Cocoroco.'* "

In spite of himself the teacher laughed loudly. So did the class. The laughter frightened the *Camaquey* cock in the schoolyard, which strutted about flapping its luminous wings and crowing, *"Cocoroco"*!

The linguistic contest of the cocks was related by the Puerto Rican writer Abelardo Díaz Alfaro in his delightful tale "Peyo Merce Teaches English." After seventy-five years of the "Americanization" of the island, it seemed, the cocks still crowed in that uniquely melodious Puerto Rican "Spanish" of the *jíbaro*. For it took hundreds of years to unlearn a language, and to forget a culture. Even for a cock.

But the de-education of a child could be achieved in the lifetime of a child. Unlike a cock, a child could be taught to forget who he was as easily as he could be taught a different language.

On the island the de-education of the children began on a tropical winter day in February, 1901. It was the 169th birthday of *"Jorge Wasindon."* The schoolchildren of San Juan, more than twenty thousand of them, were dressed in red, white, and blue shirts, pants, and dresses, and, waving little American flags, were marched down the gracious old Avenida Ponce de León, then lined with leisurely Spanish colonial houses, beneath the royal palms by the sea, chanting a song they had been forced to memorize, in a language they did not understand, with words whose meanings they did not know:

America, America,
God shed His grace
On thee. . . .

In the plaza of every city on the island the schoolchildren were marched through the streets that day by their American teachers. Later that year, on June 14, the children were marched into the streets again, this time to celebrate Flag Day. Once again, "Each of thousands of pupils carried a flag, and many were costumed in the national colors [of America]," reported the Commissioner of Education Dr. G. G. Baumbaugh. "It was a field day of American patriotism," he said with pride.

All the schools began the day with the children saluting the American flag. They then sang uncomprehendingly, by rote and in

English, "America," "Hail, Columbia," "The Star-Spangled Banner" and other patriotic songs. By 1900 the schools had already been named in honor of Washington, Lafayette, Franklin, Jefferson, Jackson, Adams, Lincoln, Grant, McKinley, Longfellow, Prescott, Webster, Hamilton, Garfield, Horace Mann, and Peabody, the Commissioner reported. Everywhere the Spanish names were obliterated. The speaking of Spanish was forbidden in the classrooms. English was the new "instrument of empire."

In one teachers' manual on *The Teaching of English in the Primary Grades of Puerto Rico,* issued by the Department of Elementary Education of the University years ago, teachers were told: "Each morning the teacher should greet the children with, 'Good Morning.' She should not be disturbed if at first the children do nothing but look at her. She should *not* tell them in Spanish what *Good Morning* means. She simply repeats 'Good Morning' each morning until the children hear the expression so many times that they begin to respond more or less *unconsciously.*" But under no circumstances was the teacher to teach in Spanish, use a Spanish word or phrase, or permit the child to speak in Spanish.

Nursery rhymes were to be recited over and over, because the children who did not understand the English words would remember the rhythms. The picture books recommended for children in kindergarten and first grade were *Little Black Sambo, Mother Goose,* and *The Story of the Three Bears:*

> We played the Three Bears.
> Luis was the Father Bear.
> Blanca was the Mother Bear.
> Juanito was the Baby Bear.
> Maria was Goldilocks.

Of course, there were no bears in Puerto Rico. It was the English, not the story, that mattered, as "Here We Go Round the Mulberry Bush" became "Here We Go Round the Mango Tree." The educational aim was the de-education of the children, so that they would unlearn the nursery rhymes of the island, forget its folklore and culture, and become illiterate in the language of their fathers.

"The Spanish language is precious to these people. All their history, and their traditions, and their civilization are bound to it," Commissioner Baumbaugh had written. If the island was to be "Americanized," it was necessary for the Spanish language to be eliminated. "The logic of the situation is that the English language will become finally universal," he said.

One of the first commissioners of education, Dr. Victor S. Clark, in 1899, had stated bluntly that the "great mass" of "Puerto Ricans are as yet passive and plastic," and "their ideals are in our hands to create and mold." To do this would not be difficult, he thought, "if the schools were made American." Dr. Samuel McCune Lindsay of Columbia University, who became Commissioner of Education in 1902, was even more succinct: "Colonization carried forward by the armies of war is vastly more costly than that carried forward by the armies of peace, whose outposts and garrisons are the public schools of the advancing nation." The aim of the de-education was to "assimilate" the island, said Dr. Ricardo Alegría, the director of the Institute of Puerto Rican Culture, to prepare transforming "Puerto Rico [into] another New Mexico or Arizona. And the schools were the instrument of that cultural assimilation."

The new conquerors were merely echoing the words and deeds of the old conquerors. On their conquest of Borinquén the Conquistadors had used Spanish to subdue the native people, just as the Yankees used English. In the Congregation of Valladolid in 1519, the councilor of the King, Juan de Sepúlveda, had argued that "the rudeness of the minds of the people" made them "servile and barbarous by nature"; and, therefore, they were "bound to serve those of more elegant mind, such as the Spanish." Laws were enacted and schools established for the enlightenment of the Borinqueños, but *"being written in the Spanish language* [*the laws and the books*] *coerced the Indians into obedience, since they could not understand them,"* wrote Father de las Casas (emphasis added). "Saying that the Indians needed tutors, like children, because they could not govern themselves," the Conquistadors set about to teach them the Spanish language and Spanish culture, to make *españoles* of them.

"Always, language had been the companion of empire," de Nebrija had written in the introduction to his *Grammática,* to recommend it to his sovereigns. His concept of linguistic politics was to re-echo, word for word, in the educational policies of the Americans. When he became the island's governor, Colonel Theodore Roosevelt, Jr., elaborated on the age-old concept: "In brief, [our] policy was to Americanize Puerto Rico, and thereby confer on her the greatest blessing, in our opinion, within our gift. We felt we could do no higher, or nobler work than to model these other people on ourselves."

The policy was a failure. In 1920, when Harry Franck wrote *Roaming Through the West Indies,* he noted with dismay, "English is little spoken in Porto Rico." He was "surprised" because he was "old enough to remember what a splurge we made in swamping the island with American teachers soon after we took over." (At the time Commissioner Baumbaugh had sardonically said: "None of them [these teachers] knew Spanish, and some of them knew little English.") There had been "no progress made in teaching Porto Rico English in twenty years of American rule," Franck complained. If you stepped "out of one of the three principal hotels of the capital you are in a foreign country."

Governor Roosevelt voiced the same complaint in the 1930s. "When we arrived in Puerto Rico practically no one spoke English. Spanish was the language of the island." He "deliberately" set out "to change this and to make Puerto Rico English speaking." Some thought this policy was an "attempt to stamp out local customs and culture, and substitute English for Spanish," but that was "ridiculous," he said, for the United States, "at considerable sacrifice and expense," was seeking to reshape the island into "a real Pan-American center of culture, where Cervantes and Shakespeare, so to speak, sat side by side." If such was his policy, it too failed.

"In Puerto Rico the child comes to school with little or no knowledge of the English language," the teachers' manual of 1935 declared. That is still true of most of the children in 1973. Spanish is now, as it was then, the "language of the island." In the mid-1950s

Spanish was brought back into the schools, by the Puerto Rican government, as the language of instruction.

Paradoxically, as the schools on the island were abandoning the policy of enforced elimination of Spanish, and planned de-education, as an abysmal failure in education, the schools on the mainland were adopting the discredited and discarded policy for the hundreds of thousands of *barrio* children whose parents had been enticed to the United States in the 1950s. It was historically an old instance of a colonial policy, abandoned in the colonies, only to be embraced by the mother country. In school after school the old immigrant imperative was heard: "This is America! Speak English!"

Nowhere has this paradox been more poignantly written of than in the words of a Puerto Rican mother of four children in the Ocean Hill–Brownsville School District of Brooklyn, New York. In the *Forum* of the Center of Urban Education at New York University Mrs. Alma Bagu recalled her own years of de-education in the schools of the city, and those of her "Americanized" children:

> It was as if our teachers had taken upon themselves the task of straining every drop of Puerto Rican culture we possessed, to mold us into what they thought we should be. Some teachers would lecture us on how rude it was to speak a "strange" language in the presence of those who couldn't understand. Some teachers handed out punishment to those who spoke Spanish in school ("I must speak English in school," written five hundred times). Some Puerto Rican kids who found difficulty with English were considered retarded. . . .
>
> When I had my own children I wanted them to speak only English in order to avoid the same problems I had. For the sake of making things easier for my children when they went to school, I abandoned so many of the beautiful customs of my culture. I made little *Americanos* of them so they would not feel like aliens in the classroom. I finished the job on my children that my teachers started on me. I denied my offsprings some of my most beautiful memories. As a child I would ask for my mother's blessing as I left the house. *"Benedición,"* I would say. *"Dios te bendiga,"* she would always answer. God bless you. The candles of appeasement to the Saints and friendly spirits, which belong to the religion my mother brought with her from Puerto Rico, no longer burn. The rebelliousness and desire to be known as a Puerto Rican—whether out of pride, or a

feeling I couldn't make it in white American society—was gone. Because I wanted my children to be accepted by the *Americanos,* I closed the door on my own heritage.

The irony of the whole thing was that my children weren't accepted anyway.

In those years of de-education a social worker was said to have asked a little *barrio* child to describe how he felt in the schools of the city. The folklore of the *barrio* has often retold his sad reply. He was, said the little child: "Alien in two lands, and illiterate in two languages!"

In his "Broken English Dream" the young *barrio* poet Pedro Pietri had written:

> To the united states we came—
> to learn how to mispell our name . . .
> to fill out welfare applications—
> to graduate from school without an education. . . .

In a *Barrio* School

In Chicago a young mother hopefully brought her son to school to enter the first grade. He was a bright and alert child. José Gonzáles was tested in English. But he thought in Spanish. So he did poorly. It was decided he was mentally retarded. For nine years he was sent to a special school for brain-damaged and handicapped children. A school so neglected that the bathrooms had no toilet paper and the classrooms had few teaching materials. But then, the low-I.Q. children were thought of as little better than animals.

After nine years of his nightmare, the boy was retested. It was decided by the teachers that he was not mentally retarded after all.

"We made a mistake," the school social worker told the mother.

The boy, now fourteen, had been retarded by the school system. "Lives are being destroyed because of misplacement" of Spanish-speaking children "in mentally retarded schools," said the Superintendent of Public Instruction of the State of Illinois, Michael Bakalis. As José Gonzáles was trying to unlive his ordeal and return to normal boyhood, his youngest sister came of age to attend the first grade and to be tested, as he had been. His mother, Mrs. María Gonzáles, was frightened.

"I fear for her," said the mother quietly. "Someone [may] say she is retarded."

So widespread was the cruel disregard for the intelligence and gentleness of *barrio* children that in May, 1970, the Office of the Secretary of Health, Education, and Welfare, in Washington, D.C., had to issue a special directive to school principals and administrators ordering them to cease the "common practice" of sending normal children to schools for the mentally retarded, simply because they did not speak the same language as their teachers—English. "School districts must not assign national minority group students to classes for the mentally retarded on the basis of criteria which essentially measure or evaluate English language skills," ordered the government.

No sooner had Puerto Ricans begun to come to the cities in the 1950s than segregated "special" schools were set up for their children. These schools for "maladjusted" and "potentially" delinquent youth were often crowded with children whose failure was that they understood little or no English, and therefore "were not participating in classroom activities, were not learning, were quietly and unobtrusively 'sitting out' months and years of their school time." Once "silence was golden," but that was in a quieter era. Now, to be shy and silent in a classroom was a symptom of "mental retardation." So reported Dr. J. C. Morrison, former Assistant Commissioner of Education of the State of New York, in his survey of *barrio* schoolchildren in 1955, *The Puerto Rican Study*. In New York City these "special" schools were named the "600" schools, and by 1955 *barrio* children, who made up barely 12 percent of school enrollments, comprised 20 percent of the "600" schools' "backward" and "troubled" students.

In the generation since then the situation has not improved, but has gotten worse. Dr. Kenneth B. Clark prophetically said of ghetto children in 1955: ". . . their rate of learning declines the longer they stay" in school.

One hundred thousand children have been required to sit in classes for years, in the schools of New York City, hardly understanding a word the teachers said, the Board of Education reported, in 1971. In the city's schools there were at least "105,000 non-English speaking" children of "Spanish background" (*sic*), but only 4,418 of these children were given bilingual instruction—that is, were taught in a language they could understand—their own. These children were being "mentally retarded" by the schools. In reading levels (of English), general schooling and dropout rates they had the worst averages in the city. Of "about 250,000" *barrio* children in the schools, the Board of Education estimated, almost half, 42 percent, spoke little or no English, but fewer than 2 percent were taught in Spanish.

"Sometimes I wonder," a *barrio* teacher said, "what reading scores of Anglo, English-speaking children would be if we taught and we tested them in Spanish." Her eyes were perfectly innocent. "I think maybe we suddenly would have schools full of 'mentally retarded' English-speaking children, who would be judged to be 'slow learners,' and 'culturally deprived,' and 'backward in concept building,' and 'poor readers,' because they did not know the Spanish language and culture."

Why would anyone "teach" a child in a language the child did not understand? The children of the *barrio* were "expendable" in the educational system, thought Alfredo Lopez, a former student leader and editor of *Claridad*. "While the white child is taught to accept the system, the Puerto Rican child is taught to accept the fact that he or she is to stay out of it, never expecting more than being a cheap labor worker," he said bitterly. "The magic is worked . . . through the rigid refusal to teach the Puerto Rican his or her own history, language, or culture—robbing them of an identity, and of a sense of social essence."

"In a society that has institutionalized racism, the children that go to the schools are already tracked into low paying jobs even before they enter school" was the coldly laconic comment of a group of Puerto Rican educators, led by Jereno Hoyos, director of the National Puerto Rican Development and Training Institute. "Schools, while they may help individuals to climb, serve as a social agency for sorting and tracking children," declared the Puerto Rican educators in a research report prepared on a grant from the Office of Economic Opportunity in Washington, D.C. "In most cases the school is not the door to affluence," even though parents in the *barrios,* like most Americans, still "accept the myth of schools as avenues for self-improvement." For the children of the *barrio* "English-speaking chauvinism" ends that "American dream."

One "horrifying result" has been "the educational and emotional crippling of tens of thousands [of children] who have seen no choice but to drop out of school," commented Luis Nieves, director of Aspira, a Puerto Rican educational group devoted to better schooling for the *barrio* youth. Nieves thought that the Board of Education's study "documents years of planned neglect." After twenty years of conferences and studies that long ago had concluded that "the use of the native language as a medium of instruction, before English is acquired, will help prevent retardation in school," as the Board of Education once more reaffirmed, why had the school system chosen to ignore its own knowledge of what was educationally best for the little children it was dedicated to teaching? The failure of the schools was deliberate, and "planned," said Nieves.

Sitting in a classroom, mute and bored, day after day, was difficult. And yet, though one-fourth of the pupils in the public schools were Puerto Ricans, fewer than 1.5 percent of New York City teachers were bilingual—under 800 of 57,000 teachers. In simple language, most of these teachers were unable to teach the children of the *barrios*. They could not even speak to them. It was no wonder that of the quarter of a million boys and girls of the *barrios* some 86 percent were below the average reading levels (in English). Nor was it surprising that their rate of dropouts, some called it "pushouts," was 57 percent, compared to 46 percent for black children and 26 percent for those whom the Board of Education called the "others," *Los otros.*

The Losers was the title of education writer Richard Margolis's "Report on Puerto Ricans and the Public Schools," that chronicled his unsuccessful quest through seven states and sixteen schools for "decent" *barrio* education. His personal odyssey, undertaken for Aspira in 1967, began with the conclusion: "The public schools are like a giant sieve, sifting out all but the strongest, the smartest and the luckiest"; for "Puerto Rican children have nowhere to go but *out*—out of the schools, and into a world for which they are unprepared."

As for their parents in the *barrios* who believed the "American dream," Margolis observed, ". . . they often begin by thinking the schools can do no wrong, and end by suspecting the schools can do no right. Thus they proceed, over the disillusioning years, from a respectful reluctance to interfere to an angry readiness to protest. The path leads somewhat circuitously from authoritarianism to militant democracy, but the vital intervening stages—cooperation and participation—are usually missing."

"Our attempts at solutions," said Juan Cruz, a human relations specialist for the Chicago Board of Education, "are like trying to cover the sky with one hand."

The schools stood immobile and impervious through all this. Even in the *barrio,* where they were surrounded by the old tenements of the poor and the hungers of poverty, the school buildings were like fortresses of a resplendent civilization of foreigners. The government in an attempt to remedy the situation had built more and more modern school "plants." And yet the more modern the schools became, with their white plastic tiled walls, sterile, air-conditioned classrooms, and laboratories of computerized instruction, the more separate and isolated from the community of the poor they seemed to be.

Society had "created schools [that] are not very far from the common concept of a factory," wrote the Puerto Rican educators of the National Development and Training Institute. The schools were "plants" of "standardized, mass production" of the "consumer" society—efficient, well-planned factories of "educational products" and tested for "quality control." In the new schools "learners will be 'successful' to the extent that they conform as raw material," the disdainful educators said.

Being a *barrio* child in such a school, said Alfredo Lopez, "was like being a lobster in the Sahara desert."

If the schools were "outposts and garrisons" of the "colonizing" civilization, as the Commissioner of Education, Dr. Samuel McCune Lindsay, had said of the schools on the island in the early 1900s, what of the schools in the *barrios?* "Whites tend to dominate East Harlem schools," was the blunt statement of Patricia Cayo Sexton in her study *Spanish Harlem.* "All school principals are white and so are almost all administrators," she wrote in 1965. The citizens of the *barrio* "have little to say officially about what goes on" in their children's schools, except to protest from "the outside"; as school boycott leader Gerena Valintin had said, "You cannot 'liberate' a school."

The teachers in these "outposts and garrisons" often reacted as colonial soldiers might be expected to. Sexton interviewed one such teacher who said of the children of the *barrio* and their parents:

> They are animals. They don't care about their children. How can *we* be expected to do anything?

Another teacher told her:

> They are so poor and deprived and apathetic that they can't do anything. . . . What can the school do?

Another teacher told her:

> I won't try to teach them something like social studies. They don't have the basic concepts. This is even true in reading. You can't relate to them.

Another teacher told her:

> Puerto Ricans have incorrect perception. They probably see only vague outlines. This would explain why they do so poorly in reading [in English].

Another teacher told her:

> Things just don't make an impression on these children. We haven't found the way to reach them. For some reason they don't relate to school.

A teacher of docility, who had learned to live the ordered life of the suburbs, was emotionally uneducated and unprepared for the Puerto Rican child. She, the genteel teacher, had been taught from childhood to obey the inhibitions of urban society that made for survival amid the conflicts of city life, where to be too friendly and outgoing might be an invitation to "trouble."

But the boys and girls of the *barrio* had developed a *gusto* and verve not unlike their parents' *jíbaro* love of life. They were no longer subdued and intimidated by the city. They violated the inhibitions and restrictions of the educational system by their rebellious behavior, frightening the teacher "who leaves her middle class cocoon to venture out into a slum school," observed Sexton.

One *barrio* teacher told her: "They play too much. Discipline of themselves is a problem—perhaps it is the root!"

So the teacher became unnerved. Her response was often to hide her unease behind a mythology of "Latin" promiscuity. One teacher in talking of her students complained, "They love to dance and move their bodies. They can't sit still." At a party she gave for her *barrio* pupils she observed disapprovingly, "They all danced wildly," all, that is, "except one girl who was the best student in the school. She didn't dance at all." The teacher equated intelligence with inhibition, for to her it seemed as if the joy of dancing was sensual and "animal." "All the kids can think about is sex. No wonder they can't learn anything in school," explained an East Harlem social worker. "They have sex on their minds twenty-four hours a day."

In seeking to explain scientifically this mythology of "Latin" nonintellectual promiscuity as an intellectual obstacle that children of the *barrio* faced in becoming high achievers in English "intelligence tests," Sexton cited laboratory experiments with rats. Even "rats show abnormal sexual and social behavior" and "overactivity" when they are forced to live in overcrowded conditions, she wrote. "Slum dwellers [in the *barrios*] may be reacting in the same physiological way as the biologists' animals," she thought. Were then the Puerto Rican children to be studied and compared to rats?

The distance that separated the teachers and the students was not always expressed by such exotic racism. In the eyes of the *barrio* child his racist school experience was generally seen with much more realism and much less fantasy, observed Joseph Monserrat, the president of the Board of Education of New York: "The kid grows up in a Spanish-speaking house. He eats rice and beans, he has a language and a certain way of being. This kid walks into a classroom when he's six, and what the school proceeds to do then is knock his language out of him, in effect telling him that his whole world up to then is wrong. From an educational point of view, in terms of receptivity to learning and self-respect, the effect is negative to say the least."

In the school, as in the city, "the victim" was "usually seen as the cause of the problem," said the president of the Board of Education; "so we never solve the problem."

A child came to the school as to the house of a stranger. He was the stranger. The walls of the school were white as a hospital until he wrote on them. The rows of desks in his classroom were straight as in a welfare office waiting room until he moved them. The corridors were long and ominously still as a prison until he ran yelling through them. In the beginning he was timid, intimidated, shy. He was muted. He was tested, evaluated, and judged by his teacher, for his good behavior, or lack of it, before he knew why or how.

The child's "Puerto Rican" vocabulary was vibrant, expressive, beautifully nuanced, wide-ranging and grammatically incorrect. His verbal dexterity in "Puerto Rican" was therefore thought of as a weakness by his teachers, akin to illiteracy. Not English, nor Spanish, it was properly neither. It was nothing but the slang of the streets, vulgar and commonly obscene. If the child could not speak the pure Castilian Spanish, he could not speak Spanish at all. That no one spoke the pure Castilian Spanish, even in Castile, did not matter.

He fluently spoke "Puerto Rican." That was a demerit.

In the *barrio* "the emergence of this new language" had been hailed by Manny Diaz of the Urban Coalition as "a voice of clarity in the darkness." But it was not recognized in the schools. "If a people develop roots in a new place, as we have, they will develop a new language. And that language is legitimate," Diaz said. He argued for the "legitimizing" of this "new language" in the schools. *"Spanglish"* did not describe it, he said: "I hate that term." Then why not simply call it what it was—"Puerto Rican"? "Language, be it remember'd," Walt Whitman had written one hundred years ago, "is not an abstract construction of the learn'd, or of dictionary-makers, but is something arising out of the work, needs, ties, joys, affections, tastes, of long generations of humanity, and has its bases broad and low, close to the ground. Its final decisions are made by the masses, people nearest the concrete."

Not so in the schools. The teachers had just begun to recognize the importance of Spanish. And the vitality of "Puerto Rican" was still beyond the textbook conception of language as a static and grammatically measured inert body of words.

"Our Spanish is an emotional language," said Ema Ramos, a graduate student in psychology. "It is always changing. It is alive. Look at a word like *chico,* little boy, which we often say as *chicito,* little, little boy. If we feel that *chicito* is not expressive enough, we add a couple letters to it and make it 'Puerto Rican,' like *chicitito,* little, little, little boy. That is not 'correct' Castilian, but it is correct 'Puerto Rican.'

"And we do not express ourselves just with words," she said. "We speak with our bodies. The raising of an eyebrow. The movement of a finger. Body movements. Language ought to express what you are 'about,' what you feel. So you speak with your feeling. I mean, your feelings speak, if you are Puerto Rican."

If the child sat silent, simply "raising an eyebrow" at a teacher's question, he would be marked down as not answering. And yet the Puerto Rican child may learn a new language when he "begins to hear it kinesthetically. He begins feeling it in his mouth, on his tongue, in between his teeth, making new combinations" of sounds, said Dr. Vera John-Steiner, talking of the bilingual classroom.

"Rhythm is crucial," she said, in learning. "The development of language in the context of gestures, music, dance and movement is exceedingly important.*

"Space, for instance, could be a significant bicultural experience," she said. The child "who comes from a primarily outdoor way of life," as in Puerto Rico, or even the stoops of a city *barrio,* did not see the world the same way as a child who was used to "predominately indoor living." He created, if the teacher allowed him to, a "meaningful spatial environment" that was uniquely his own. In space, the child defined not only his world, but more than that, how he related "his own body to learning certain concepts of number, size and shape"; for space, too, was a form of speech. The *barrio* child had invented the "Open Classroom" long before it had become an educational institution, but no one listened to his spatial speech.

Learning was not always expressed, or limited, to words, said Dr. John-Steiner. What of a child who talked and thought in rhythm, to whom music was a form of intelligence that profoundly commented on the world, who knew the meanings of colors, and who defined life in visual and spatial forms more subtle than words? In English drills, in the classroom where reading and writing have so long been the main, if not sole, criteria for the testing of knowledge, the *barrio* child who could express himself brilliantly in a hundred subtle ways might as well be mute.

Was there a Puerto Rican way of learning and teaching? If so, how could it be fitted into and accepted by a school system that had been fashioned, for many generations, to comform to the ways of life and social aims of European immigrants. An Indio-Hispano people from a tropical isle had a different life style. The family life of the *barrios* was different from that of the suburban and the middle-class sections of the city. So were the religious beliefs. And to the communal way of thinking of so many Puerto Ricans, those of *jíbaro* heritage most of all, the aggressive individualism encouraged by the school system seemed uncultured and inhumane.

* Ralph Waldo Emerson had written: "He who has no hands, must use his tongue."

Schools existed in a "social and political context," the Puerto Rican educators had written. "Experience indicates the extreme difficulty of grafting on, or superimposing, a particular innovation and making it affect the general institutional status quo [of the schools]," they said. "It is impossible to see the bilingual school, as well as any school, outside of the culture and society in which it exists." Schools reflected society; they did not create the world.

The concept of community control and the decentralization of the schools originated as a plan to make schools more democratic and independent. But community control became a political as much as an educational battle. It too reflected society. The meetings of local school boards resembled political rallies, with organized cliques and claques, ethnic fighting for positions, backroom deals, ghetto "power of the powerless," and parents being urged to support one or another group in city politics.

"For ten years we have worked on the concept of community control of the schools," said Gerena Valintin, who organized several boycotts of the schools by tens of thousands of Puerto Rican parents. He now had doubts about the success of the concept of community control, much less its practice.

"We have no control," he said. "The school system is controlled by the white establishment. Since 1963, despite decentralization, the school system has not changed. At the time we said that community control for us in the *barrio* meant control, real control, of the purse strings, of the hiring of teachers, and of what our children were taught. That was real community control. It doesn't exist. It has never existed. It cannot be said to have failed because it has never been tried in any *barrio* anywhere in the United States. It is a charade. The establishment, in the schools and the unions and the government, beheaded that concept of democracy in its infancy. How? A few concessions were made to the demands of the *barrio*. But that was a political maneuver by politicians to divide the school pie, the educational budgets, a little differently.

"Nothing has changed. Really. Our children are still being educationally assassinated. They are mentally murdered by the schools," said Valintin.

On the Lower East Side, in the First School District and one of the oldest, the Puerto Rican parents, who were the overwhelming majority, tried for years to "take over" the neighborhood school board, which was controlled by the representatives of the older immigrants, Italian and Jewish. Most of these had long since left the ghetto, and were a minority among minorities. Finally, in the fall of 1972, the *barrio* parents and community groups succeeded and elected Luis Fuentes, the most controversial Puerto Rican educator in the city, as their community superintendent. Suddenly *they* were attacked as "racists." The "unrepresentative extremist groups" and "racial bigots" had captured community control, charged Albert Shanker, president of the United Federation of Teachers; "the outrageous had happened."

"I do not understand," a *barrio* leader said. "When we have no power we are nice, poor, humble Puerto Ricans. Everybody loves us! When we win power we become 'racial bigots.' Everybody hates us!"

Luis Fuentes was the quintessence of the neo-Rican—the Puertorriqueño New Yorker. He had been principal of Public School 155 in the embattled Ocean Hill–Brownsville district, a man famous for his headstrong, opinionated, tough, and independent policies. In the *barrios* he was admired by many for his aggressive, and biased, statements in defense of Puerto Rican children, as he was despised by many outside the *barrios* for the same reasons. Shanker, the union moyden, at once charged the Puerto Rican educator had been accused of "outright bigotry" against Jewish teachers, "anti-Semitic slurs," "ethnic slurs" against Italians and Blacks, and of instituting an "ethnic quota system" in hiring teachers—that is, of attempting to replace Jewish teachers with Puerto Rican teachers in proportion to the numbers of Puerto Rican students.

It was not "his fault," Fuentes said, that the establishment of the school system was largely Jewish. He believed that Puerto Ricans were where the Jewish immigrants had been a century ago, and his people were being held down by the establishment as the Jews had been. He believed this and he said it. Was this racism or anti-Semitism, he asked, or was it the truth?

As though in an offering of educational peace, Fuentes and the Puerto Rican–controlled local school board announced that District One was establishing a Jewish studies program and a curriculum on Jewish history and culture in their schools. They were among the first in the public schools. "Who will benefit from Jewish studies? Jews and all others," said Stanley Grossberg, special assistant to Superintendent Fuentes. "There is strength in diversity, unity in differences," Grossberg declared. "People of all ethnic and racial backgrounds [on the Lower East Side] work side by side."

In schools where Puerto Rican, Chinese, Italian, Jewish, Polish, Black, Ukrainian, Greek, Irish, and American Indian children sat side by side in the classrooms the slogan of the school board, *"En la Unión Esta la Fuerza*"—"In Union There Is Strength," was not political rhetoric, it was educational necessity. The school newspaper, *Numero Uno, Write On!,* was published in three languages, at least—English, Spanish, and Chinese. "Even our notices and memoranda are trilingual," declared Grossberg.

Bilingual education became trilingual, then multilingual. The school books, curriculum materials, and cultural programs in the classes began to resemble an international folk festival. In the school near Chinatown, P.S. 140, the new year, 4671, "The Year of the Ox," was celebrated by Chinese banquets, Chinese dances, and Chinese calligraphy done by the children under the banner "THE OX IS IN, THE RAT IS OUT."

The Community School Board was rechristened the Peoples' Board. In some schools Puerto Rican principals and administrators were appointed. "We are most happy because the Spanish parents, which are the majority, can go to the principal and speak to her without an interpreter. Our principal is Puerto Rican and we are proud of her. She treats everybody equally," said Lucy Martinez, a mother whose children attended P.S. 122, where the new principal was Carmen Enid Villafane Aponte. In the schools national pride became part of "an international spirit." The chairwoman of the school board, Georgina Hoggard, enunciated that policy: "Let us prove to this nation that there is a small place here where poor people can work together." And a high school student at the district's Central Commercial High, Michael Martinez, expressed it in his own way: "I really loved the way people were working as one, the Blacks, Whites, Puerto Ricans, and Chinese." They "forgot about prejudice," he exclaimed in amazement.

In a ghetto that had been torn by racial and national hatreds for one hundred years the "brotherhood of people" in the schools seemed unbelievable. For the first time in generations the "dream that was a nightmare," of the melting pot, was becoming a reality because the concept of the melting pot had been replaced by the concept of "strength in diversity, unity in differences."

Of all the innovations of the *barrio* teachers, parents, and students none intrigued and delighted the community more than the "decentralization of food" served in the schools, so that "real meals" of "ethnic specialties" could be cooked for their children. It required a long-fought court battle with the Board of Education. "The people were overwhelmingly in favor of hot meals rather than the frozen, TV-type dinners currently in favor with the central Board of Education," said Kathy Goldman, the food service coordinator. In the past, "Most of the food in the school lunchroom for many years went into the garbage. So we decided this is it! This is the only district that [has] the whole lunch program decentralized," local school board chairwoman, Georgina Hoggard, said, chortling.

"Such delicacies as fried chicken, *arroz con pollo* (rice and chicken), Puerto Rican rice and beans, chow mein, spaghetti and meat balls, corned beef and cabbage, fresh ham, chopped liver and Italian pizza" could now be served to the twelve thousand children who ate lunch in school. The tasteless and sterilized "frozen TV-type dinners" were gone. It was a "great victory for community control."

Not insensitive or unresponsive to the demands for multilingual education, the Board of Education announced that its central offices would henceforth publish its suspension notices to parents in English,

Chinese, Italian, French, and Spanish. The notices informed parents that their son or daughter had been suspended. Some 300,000 of these suspension notices were printed in Spanish, though there were at the time only 249,055 Puerto Rican students in the city schools.

It was not long thereafter that the Peoples' School Board of District One, and its superintendent, Luis Fuentes, were defeated by an old-line slate supported by the United Federation of Teachers of Albert Shanker.

29

Amerika! Amerika!

The Failure of the Elite: Manny Diaz

On Fifth Avenue, not far from the site of the townhouse where the "patroness of revolution," Mabel Dodge, introduced pre–World War I radicals of the IWW and the ghetto to the bohemians of Greenwich Village, at her famous "evenings," were the offices of the professionals of poverty—the Urban Coalition.

In an executive suite of the Urban Coalition was the office of a bronzed, distinguished-looking man of attainment and despair. He was one of the most highly placed, and paid, experts on Puerto Rican poverty in the city, if not in the country.

He had been "defeated" by that poverty, he said. And he might resign his position.

"I am whipped!" he said. "For twenty years I have headed these programs, and I no longer see any solution to poverty that gets me excited. I've heard no interesting new ideas or new concepts since the days of the OEO. For twenty years I have put so much time and energy into so many battles, and I have seen so few successes that I say to myself, we don't have any solutions. We don't know where the hell we are going. We don't see the realization of the American dream."

In East Harlem, Manny Diaz had begun as a street worker with youth gangs to become a leading member of the elite of the *barrio* community. In other offices, in other times, he had served on city commissions, the boards of foundations, the Mayor's stillborn Civilian Review Board for the New York police force, as a director of Mobilization for Youth, the Puerto Rican Development Project, and on an endless cycle of committees, task forces, and study groups. He had worked his way up into "high positions of powerlessness." Now, he said, "I have several secretaries to type my memos that no one will read."

His old friends said: "He has trapped himself in the Room at the Top. He is everyone's 'token' Puerto Rican. If the Mayor or the Governor needs a *barrio* face and a Spanish name on some committee, they call up Manny."

The government—city, state, and federal—even now offered to appoint him to a new "high position of powerlessness." He thought it would be wiser, and better for his health, if he got away to the island. "For a couple of years! Maybe I need to go back to my roots and live in Puerto Rico for a while. Maybe I should become a beachcomber or buy a sailboat and go around the world."

Not long after Manny Diaz made this statement, he did resign.

"So what have I learned? I have learned how to manipulate the system. But it hasn't provided any real solutions for my people.

"I could go into the federal government, or a university, and 'make it.' There have been offers. But I doubt my presence in the federal government will change that government, or that my presence in a university will change its ideology.

"Maybe I ought to write a book. It satisfies the soul. It is a monument to yourself, if you know who you are. It is a good question: Who am I?

"But I have just been whipped. Mentally and morally whipped. Not that I am going to perish as an individual; it is that the impact I wanted to have on society, and the things I wanted to do for my people, just haven't happened. And I feel very badly about it. Maybe there is no panacea. Maybe you nibble along the historical route and

Poet, psychologist, university teacher, and disc jockey, Felipe Luciano was founding chairman of the Young Lords.

Marchers of the Puerto Rican Socialist party parade through wealthy Upper East Side of Manhattan.

The Rican activist

Beer and patriotism in El Barrio

Herman Badillo, Congressman and leading Puerto Rican politician in Nueva York

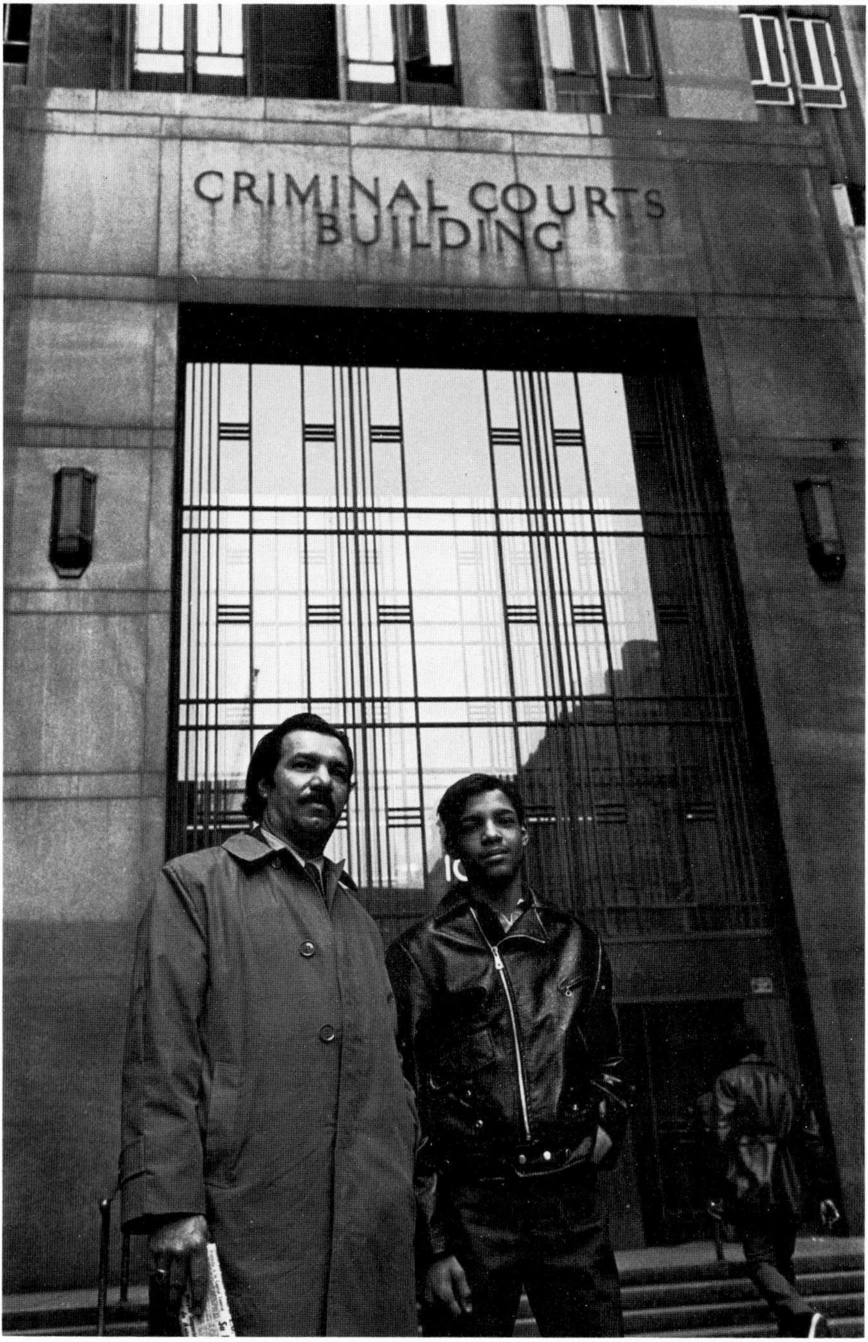

Carlos Feliciano, the nationalist hero, awaits his trial, with his oldest son.

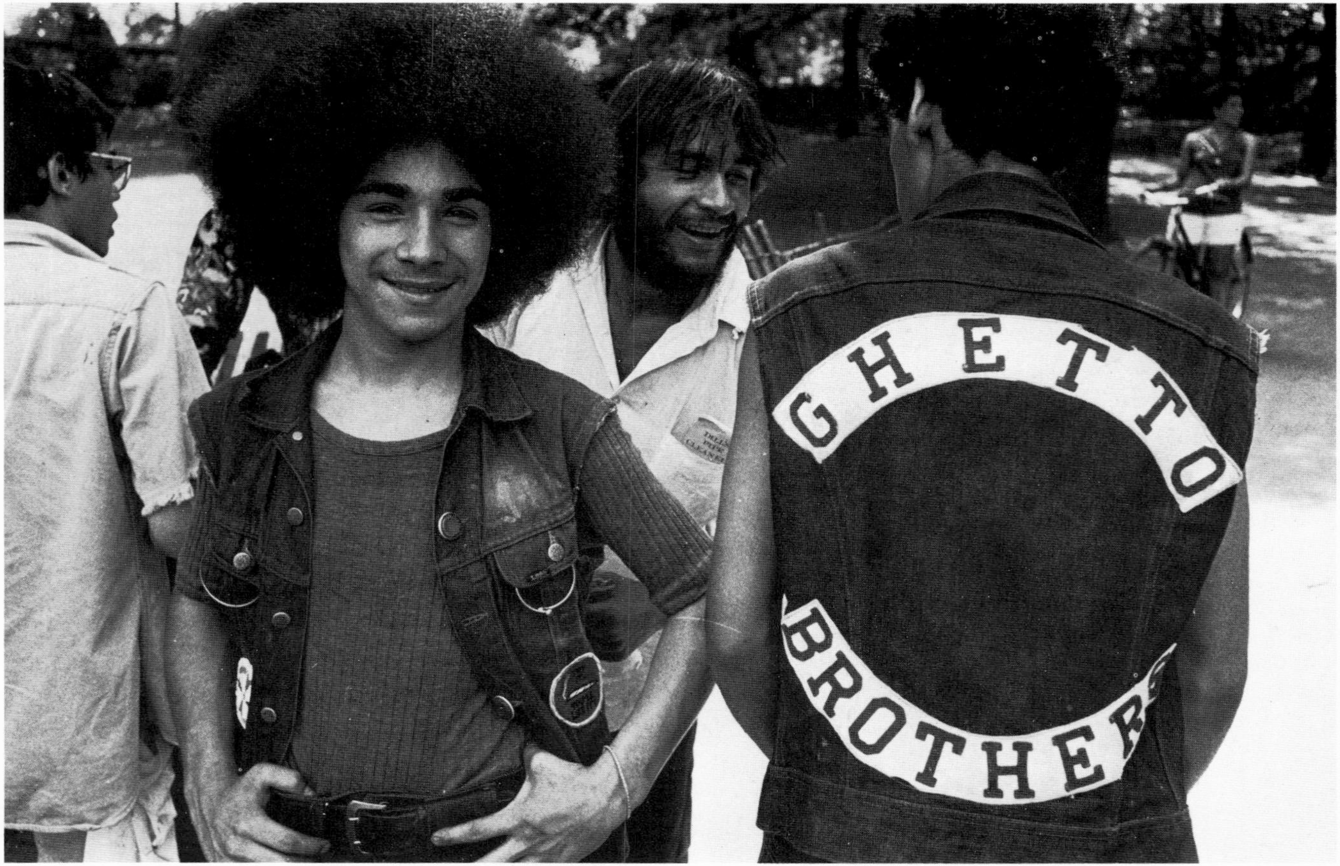

The Ghetto Brothers guard their *barrio* turf.

Don Pedro Albizu Campos *(Jose Garcia, Realidades Collection)*

Pedro Matos Matos

Manny Diaz

Gerena Valintin

The lovers

rip off what you can for your people. And you go somewheres else tomorrow morning, and rip off another bit of the establishment. I don't know.

"Has there ever been any group of newcomers in America who were accepted by the establishment? I know of none. The Catholics still see themselves as a minority. The Jews still see themselves as victims. After all these years, the Italians want civil rights!

"So, I ask myself, is there ever a time when America will ever fully accept anybody?

"I'm not even sure any more what it means to 'make it.' But I don't believe anybody ever fully 'makes it.' Now, don't get me wrong: I'm not ready to pack in my life, my career. There are many promises to keep. What bothers me is that I, as a leader, have to play roles that I am not convinced are going to provide any substantial solutions for my people.

"Of course I have knocked myself out getting bilingual education established, but I know that's not the solution. I have knocked myself out getting jobs for *barrio* people, but I know that's not the solution. I can knock myself out helping establish a Puerto Rican middle class, but I know that's not the solution.

"No! we are dealing with the amorphous mentality of racism. The Protestant ethic! The logos of Anglo-Saxon power! I don't know its genesis, but I know it is there. I can taste it. How can we change that? We need more than a revolution in social policy. We need a revolution in human values. People talk of socialism! The idea has influenced me, but I am not convinced that's the answer either.

"Where to turn? I am a man who is philosophically spent. A great many men in leading positions are spent. We have tried virtually every strategy. We have shot our bolt. So I have the hope that the young people who are coming in, who are fresher, more aggressive, more dreamy-eyed, less real, if you will, will be able to do better than we have done.

"Let me tell you a story:

"In the evening some time ago, I was down at the Municipal Building. It was summer, so it was still light, though it was maybe seven o'clock. Everything was closed down. There was no one about. And then I saw these two young Puerto Rican girls hovering around and looking lost. So I said to them, 'Can I help you?' 'Where is City Hall?' they asked. So I told them, 'It's right across the street. The building with the clock on it. Why do you want City Hall?'

" 'We are going to picket it,' they said.

" 'And what are you going to picket about?' I asked. The building was dark.

" 'We don't know!' they said. 'We haven't been told.'

"My first reaction was: that's horrible. I was bothered that our young people were more concerned with the process of the activity than the substance of what they were dealing with. But my second thought was, hell, that's beautiful! They don't give a shit what they are fighting for as long as they are there fighting.

"The young Puerto Ricans don't know where they're going. But neither do I. And yet they haven't quit fighting. The Puerto Rican intellectual has quit! And then I thought, Good grief! You know it's all bullshit! You know nothing is going to happen because they picket! Yet picket they must.

"If I look for hope in myself, I can't find it. Oh, I can come before an audience and offer them visions of paradise, and tell them how they will get there. But I am deeply in doubt. I am just not convinced that any of us is going to get to paradise in the United States.

"Perhaps this is what racism has done to people like me. The impact of racism on me is not that it has deprived me of a good job, a good place to live, and the so-called good life. It has deprived me of hope. It has deprived me of the ability to say to myself, Be happy you're alive!

"A portrait of Manny Diaz. Here is a man who has been effective, who has done everything, who has been a leader in a broad scope of engagements, not just in one field, who has had an impact, who has 'made it' again and again. So, you might say, here is a portrait of a successful citizen. But my soul tells me, Manny, you haven't done nothing!

"I started out as a romantic and a crusader. Then I became a pragmatist, dealing with monies and programs. Now what's the opposite of a romantic? A pessimist? No, I'm still a romantic. I'm still searching for something beautiful, that I know is never going to come about.

"Someone will say, Let's have a strike, a boycott, people marching up and down, picket lines. You can't argue with that. It's necessary. But that's an old play. Act one. Act two. Close the play. And I'm tired of going to these plays. It's as if I have given up hope in the American system.

"So there you are!

"What began as a commentary on the Puerto Rican elite ended up as a life history of Manny Diaz, the 'failure of the elite.' "

The Saga of a Dishwasher: Gerena Valintin

YANKEE, GO HOME!

The slogan was shouted in the halls of Freedom House, not far from Fifth Avenue and Forty-second Street, in New York City, half as a joke. But it was only half a joke.

None of the hearings ever were as full of *barrio* life as those hearings of the United States Commission on Civil Rights that were not held in the spring of 1972. In their brotherly wish to be elder brother to minorities the civil libertarians had been scheduled to hear the laments of the Puerto Ricans, but they had not expected to hear the cries of the street in Freedom House.

Spectators screamed, "We are not guinea pigs." In the streets hundreds of people marched beneath picket signs that read, "Investigate White Racists, Not Brown Victims," and "No More Hearings. No More Studies. We Want Jobs." The microphones in the hearing rooms were seized by young *barrio* activists who shouted insults and read statements and loudly reiterated the *grito* of the streets, incongruous as it sounded in the heart of New York City, "Yankee, Go Home!" In a few days, after his futile attempt to restore the decorum in which accusations of racism were officially heard had failed, Father Theodore Hesburgh, president of Notre Dame and chairman of the Civil Rights Commission, sadly canceled the hearings. He feared the "mood of anger."

The man who had organized the rout of the civil rights hearing was Gerena Valintin. Why had he done it?

"No one will speak for us. We will speak for ourselves," he told the press. "And we will hold our own hearings."

Gerena Valintin was a hard man to talk to. He burst forth with an unending flow of opinions and ideas on any subject. But he was difficult to talk to because he talked only when he wished, on his own terms. "I am too busy changing the world to waste words."

He was a legend in the *barrio*. A man of whom it was said, "Gerena is his own man; he is in debt to no one, and he fears no one." Even those who disagree with him, as did Candido de León, president of Hostos College, said, "Gerena is a necessity to the *barrio*. He has moral guts."

Of himself he said simply, "I am not a 'house Puerto Rican.' "

On his lean, drawn face, his gray bristle of a beard gave him the appearance of a sagacious Don Quixote who had fought many a windmill to a standstill. His eyes were deep-set and hardened, the eyes of an old organizer, rimmed with tiredness.

He had opinionated eyes. The beliefs of the man were clear in his look, firm and defiant.

To some Gerena Valintin was the "most successful" fighter for Puerto Rican rights in the city. He was merely the "most exhibitionist" to others. He was the "most individualistic." He was the "most old leftist." He was the "most mass media conscious." He was the "most oblivious to public opinion."

Some thought of him as a revolutionary. He had advocated "the overthrow of the capitalist system," hadn't he? And he was a vocal and open "believer in socialism." And yet in his advocacy he had helped organize the Puerto Rican parade, the Puerto Rican Folklore Fiesta in Central Park, the Puerto Rican Sports Council, working with, if not within, "the system." It was not enough to say, as the New Left youth did, that he was of the Old Left. No one ideology seemed to confine him, not even his own. In some ways his were the ways of the urban *jíbaro:* do not put your faith in words, but in deeds, do not expect anyone to do what you do not do yourself, and, above all, act! He was beholden to no one but himself.

Who, then, was he?

He was the creation of the life he had lived, he said.

"My family were farmers in Lares. Lares, you know, is where the revolution took place against the Spanish, and the Republic of Puerto Rico was proclaimed, for one day.

"When I had graduated from high school, in Lares, I decided to come here. Naturally, coming to New York was a big thing. When I came, I came by boat. It took five, six days. That was in 1936. My brother was here. He was a vulcanizer on tires, and he wanted me to work with him. But in Lares they told me to get a job in a restaurant. So I insisted in working in a restaurant though I hardly knew what a restaurant was.

"I had never seen the inside of a restaurant. Lares had no restaurant, at that time, or if there were, any families like ours were too poor to eat in them. There was no money. It was a depression. But Puerto Rico had been in a depression since the Americans came, in 1898.

"So, when I left the island, they told me to look for a job in a restaurant. That way I would be sure to eat—every day.

"Most of us got jobs as dishwashers. It was long hours and the pay was small, but at least you would eat. They paid me $7.50 a week. But they never paid me the $7.50. Maybe $3.50. They always kept the balance of my pay so I wouldn't quit. Once I got a job in a hotel, working all night, washing dishes. I remember it because I washed dishes for Jewish organizations that gave parties in the hotel. They were kosher. So the dishes had to be washed with special liquid, with special attention, in a special machine. The heat in the machine was about 110 degrees. And I had to wear special gloves to pick up the kosher dishes. For that they paid me 50 cents an hour. But I paid with my skin.

"On my job as a dishwasher sometimes I worked from six in the evening to six in the morning. I would rush home. And pick up my books. And go to City College.

"So I would be in college until maybe ten in the morning. Most of the time I would fall asleep in the class, because I was so tired. It is always strange to me when people say Puerto Ricans will not work hard. All my life I have worked hard. We all do. We have to. We get the hardest jobs.

"I was working in the Hotel New Yorker when the union began to organize. That was 1939. And I became active in the union. Since then I have been business agent and organizer for many unions, and I organized the workers in the Commodore Hotel, the Hotel Pennsylvania, the Waldorf-Astoria, and the New Yorker.

"Once the police beat me up on a picket line. I spent seven days in the hospital.

"The leadership of the Puerto Rican workers are not Puerto Rican. Most of us belong to unions that are led by racketeers, by labor bureaucrats, who do not represent us, but the system. We have not yet challenged the union structure. Eventually we will. Our organizers are going in now. We will pick some union that we will then hit. You will read about it.

"As a worker, before World War II, I joined the American Labor party. That's when Congressman Marcantonio represented El Barrio. That's where I learned to make speeches and I learned what parliamentary procedure was all about.

"Most of our people were farmers when they came here. They had never been to San Juan. They came from the small towns in the hills. They took a *público,* a small bus, from their town to the airport at Isle Verde, and came directly to New York. They had never been in a city. They had never seen a subway. They were never workers. They had never been in a factory. They had never seen a tenement.

"They were frightened. That was natural.

"The mentality of some of our people had been colonialized to the point where they were afraid to display their own flag. Or they coupled it with the American flag.

"Now our people, one million and three hundred thousand in New York, are mostly working class. The middle class is small. It will develop, we know, and become more affluent, and it will move away from the *barrios*. Let them go, if that's what they want.

"We no longer live in a little house with a *batey*. We live in a tenement or apartment house, full of rats and roaches. The landlord is a vicious man who makes profits on our misery. And when we become workers here, we work in sweatshops. So we recognize who our enemy is more clearly than on the island. Our movement is face to face with the enemy. It is stronger because of it.

"So we are being radicalized by life. We are taking the struggle into the streets. We are not afraid to confront the landlords. We are not afraid of the police, the jails, the schools. We are not afraid any more.

"I believe there is going to be a tremendous confrontation of Puerto Ricans and the white establishment in the cities. The Blacks will be aligned with us, not the Whites. In that struggle people will become aware of what democracy is all about.

"The Chicano, Indian, Black, and Puerto Rican movements will have to join forces, for their own interests. And the white workers will have to do the same. Even now the white working class is beginning to shape up. They see how their racism betrayed them into supporting Nixon's big businessmen. In the unions the struggle of the minorities will affect the thinking and the actions of the white workers. We have the same needs, the same enemies.

"Inevitably the capitalist system will collapse. I believe the capitalists are gearing for that confrontation.

"As a young man I knew there was something wrong in my having to leave beautiful Puerto Rico and come to this cold, strange land where I wasn't wanted. But I didn't know what, or why. We were apolitical. Now our community is learning what socialism is. Personally I believe in socialism. That's the only way we can change Puerto Rico, *and* the United States.

"Though I love Puerto Rico dearly, I was born there accidentally. I am an internationalist. I believe in the independence of all humanity.

"One time, you know, I worked for the City Commission on Human Rights. But I couldn't just sit there. Sit in meetings and say nothing and collect your money. So I told them I was not the 'house Puerto Rican.' So I was kicked out. They want Puerto Ricans who are not troublemakers. I am a troublemaker."

The Trials of a Revolutionary: Carlos Feliciano

On the old bureau in the bedroom in the box of mementos was the newspaper clipping. Lydia Feliciano brought it to her husband. He took it from her, holding it uncomfortably in his fingertips, and squinted at it—as though he still could not believe the words. The newspaper clipping was from the New York *Daily News,* dated May 19, 1970:

MORE ARRESTS EXPECTED
IN TERROR BOMBING PROBE

Spanish-speaking detectives have penetrated the revolutionary Puerto Rican group known as MIRA, and additional arrests are expected in the wave of terrorist bombings here, police revealed yesterday.

A major break in the international search for the bombers came over the weekend with the arrest of Carlos Feliciano, 41, asserted MIRA cell leader here on charges that he placed two bombs at a Bronx Army recruiting office. Cops got the bombs before they exploded.

The group, which seeks independence for Puerto Rico and is reportedly financed by Castro-ties with Communist money, has been accused of 41 pipe bombings in the city, including the highly destructive blast at the

Mobil building in mid-Manhattan, and General Electric Company facilities in Brooklyn and Long Island City, Queens.

Investigators also feel [MIRA] is responsible for the rash of fire bombings, 20 in recent months, at department stores here. Included are incendiary devices triggered at Alexander's and Hearns in the Bronx.

Hundreds of bombings in Puerto Rico, especially in San Juan hotels and American-owned stores, have been laid at the door of the militant group.

Feliciano of 313 E 118th St., a cabinet maker and building superintendent had in his apartment the components for bombs, including wiring, powder, pocket watches and transistors when police arrived Saturday with a search warrant, detectives said. . . .

In the modest apartment in the ghetto of Williamsburg, the rabbinical slum of Brooklyn's orthodox Jews and poorest Puerto Ricans, Carlos Feliciano, a quiet man and a good cabinetmaker, lived with his wife and six children. He read the newspaper's indictment of himself with a mock theatrical flourish, as an actor might read a bad review on the day he won an Academy Award. He laughed at himself. He was surrounded by family and friends and they laughed with him. There was an air of celebration.

Yesterday, in the court, he had almost become a free man. The District Attorney of the Bronx, Burton Roberts, now a judge, had offered to drop the charges, all twenty-two of them, if Carlos would plead guilty to "reckless endangerment," somewhat like reckless driving. Carlos had agreed. If they considered the time he had spent in prison, awaiting trial, he would face only a few years' probation, he thought.

The office of the New York District Attorney, where Frank Hogan reigned omnipotent, reneged on "the agreement," so Roberts openly put it in court. The Bronx D.A. told Presiding Judge Sidney Ash that Hogan's office had originally demanded a ten-year prison sentence. "After phone conversations with New York County it was agreed it would be six years. We went along."

Feliciano and his lawyers, Conrad Lynn and William Kunstler, objected that this was not "the agreement," as they had understood it. And they withdrew Carlos's guilty plea.

"This man is going to jail!" the enraged District Attorney shouted to the court. "I request your Honor sentence Carlos Feliciano! Sentence Carlos Feliciano today!" Since the jury had not yet been chosen, and the trial had not yet begun, Judge Ash smiled politely, and ignored the outburst. A few months later at the trial, the government case foundered when the arresting officer, Patrolman Philip Zimmerman, contradicted the prosecution's chief witness, Bomb Squad detective Andrew Gutierrez, and implied he had lied about the key evidence—a supposed bomb in a loaf of stale French bread. At a preliminary hearing, it was reported, Zimmerman had called Gutierrez a liar, and the two policemen had almost "come to blows."

So it was that after two years of preparation the jury took only a few hours to dismiss the government's charges and pronounce Carlos Feliciano innocent. He was promptly reindicted by Hogan's office in New York County, on almost the same charges.

In all of this the cabinetmaker sat calmly, as if it had nothing to do with him.

"Who is Carlos Feliciano?" said the signs in the *barrio*. Everyone knew. It was undoubtedly true that his name was as well known in the *barrio* as he was unknown outside the *barrio*. Unlike the Berrigan brothers, or Angela Davis, or Daniel Ellsberg, or Abbie Hoffman, few people knew of the political trials of the quiet cabinetmaker, who as a youth had fought in a revolution against the United States.

"The liberals and civil libertarians weren't interested in his case because he was Puerto Rican," said Father David Garcia bitterly. The Episcopal rector of St. Mark's in the Bowery was chairman of the Committee to Defend Carlos Feliciano. He had worked with the Black Panther bail fund, and he approached "the same people" to raise money "for Carlos' bail fund."

"As I telephoned these individuals I realized they weren't responding with the same enthusiasm or cash," Father Garcia said. "The Black Panthers were a glamorous thing, you see. But evidently a Puerto Rican political prisoner was not."

No prominent figures, in the beginning, spoke in Feliciano's defense. The news media were "totally uninterested." "I sensed a certain paternalism. There was a sense that all Latin Americans were crazy, or nuts anyway, or were incapable of developing a serious political movement," Father Garcia said. "So we collected the bail money in nickels and dimes. It came from welfare mothers. The old people on the *barrio* streets. And the poor, our poor, who gave to the poor."

To this Feliciano said, "But, of course, democracy comes from the poor."

He was an unassuming man. That meant, said a friend, "He does not assume his importance. He knows." Once he had told a group of students, "My case is not my case. It is the case of my country and my people."

In the Revolution of 1950 he had been one of the underground leaders, his associates said. "Other people were remembered—some dead, some in jail—but the name of this man, who was, in fact, a neighbor (a janitor), was not known," wrote his biographer, in a book issued by the Committee to Defend Carlos Feliciano. "Our collective ignorance, however, does not allay the fact: his part in the fifties was high level." Carlos, as a youth, had been a leader of the Cadets of the Republic, the uniformed corps that the Nationalists had established "to defend Puerto Rico." But there was no record of any public fame.

Once he was jailed in Arecibo for the killing of four policemen. He was sentenced to 465 years in prison. "They thought I was Methuselah," he said. When a government witness testified that he had seen Feliciano miles away, in the city of Mayagüez, at the time of the killings, the charges against him were dropped; but he was kept in prison anyway for five years. During his imprisonment he shared a cell with El Maestro, Don Pedro Albizu Campos. He recalled the years in prison as the "free-est" in his life.

"The most serene revolutionary I have ever met," said a man who met him for the first time. "If he is a revolutionary, then the word has a new meaning."

In a time when nationalism was so often prisoner of color and culture, Carlos Feliciano—the "symbol of Puerto Rican nationalism"—would go into a roomful of his *independentista* comrades, approach an American friend, and embrace him with a manly hug. "I will never forget the teaching of El Maestro, he would say. " 'The enemy of my enemy is my friend.' "

His humility had not diminished his beliefs. As a small boy, he remembered, "With stones, because I was small and had nothing else in my hands, I destroyed the signs on certain American properties [on the island], and all those that read 'No Trespassing.' " Even this was a typical act: a small boy throwing stones at the history of colonialism, a David?

This is his story of the trials of a revolutionary:

"My name is Carlos Feliciano, a Puerto Rican political prisoner, here in the United States. I am married, with six kids. At the time of my arrest I was working at two jobs to support my family. I worked for fourteen years with one company, in the Bronx, at my trade as a cabinetmaker. I worked for twelve years in the building where I lived as a superintendent, doing plastering jobs, plumbing, electric wiring. Sometimes I worked till midnight, and on Saturday, on Sunday. You know, I don't have the time to do other things than work.

"One night, in 1962, I remember it was about eleven o'clock when I went to bed with my wife. We were living then on 118 Street, between First and Second Avenue. On the first floor, in the back. That night some men shot through our window, eight times! at our bed.

"They wounded me in the arm. They almost killed me. I called the police. They said they would be there in five minutes. They didn't come. I waited forty-five minutes. I was bleeding. So I went in the street to look for a patrol car. I don't find one. When I went back to phone again, the phone, it doesn't work. Jesus! So a neighbor, she called the police. They sent eight patrol cars. They took me to Lincoln Hospital. It was already one o'clock at night. At six in the morning I was still sitting in the chair. No one pays attention to me. Finally, a doctor from India comes. He operates on me. They send me home. I walked. At home, the first thing I do is pick up the phone; it works. So I go to the backyard to check the telephone wire. It was the same old wire. Then I find eight

empty shells. So I took the shells to the police station. Never did they investigate this. Never.

"So I bought a rifle. I like to go hunting, and to protect myself I bought this 30–30 rifle.

"After the killing of President Kennedy there was the new Arms Control Law. So I had to fill out an application about the gun. So I went to a Notary Public and made an affidavit. If I am a revolutionary, and have the weapon for the revolution, I wouldn't tell the police that I have it. You know, that is the point. But because of my political cases in Puerto Rico, I was afraid if I say that they would take the gun away. So I said I was never in jail. I needed the gun to protect myself.

"On the day I was arrested, May 19, 1970, this is what happened. It is hard to believe. . . . The sun was shining. It was a beautiful day. It was Saturday. Not too hot. Not too cold. In the evening my brother was having a party. So I say to Lydia, my wife, go to the beauty parlor. I am going to the Bronx to fix the hunting scope on my rifle because the front glass was broken. When I come home we are going to the party.

"So I drove to Southern Boulevard in the Bronx, to Harry and Son, a sporting goods store. Harry knows me. Every year I used to go there for my gun license and supplies. But Southern Boulevard is a shopping street. It was very crowded. Especially on Saturday. There was nowhere to park. I drove around and around looking for a parking place. And then I said, I'm going home again.

"In the other block I saw a man leaving a parking place. So I change my mind again. I decide to park my car. When I park this patrol car came up behind me, and two policemen get out.

" 'What happen?' I say.

" 'Give me your paper,' one policeman say.

"The rifle scope was right there in the front seat. You know, open. You can kill no one with a rifle scope.

"So the other officer, he is so stupid, he saw the rifle scope and he said, 'Look what he have here!' Right there they handcuffed me. I said, 'Listen, man! I'm going to Harry and Son to get this fixed because it's broken. He knows me. Walk over there with me.' The policemen don't pay any attention to me.

"About a hundred people started to make a ring around us. From the crowd come two Spanish detectives. One is the Cuban Edward Rodriguez, and one is Andrew Gutierrez, from Spain [*detectives on the NYPD Bomb Squad*]*. Gutierrez took the ignition key and opened my trunk and began to search my car. Just like that. Without a warrant. Without nothing. In*

my trunk I have my tools, a spare tire, the beach chairs I use when my wife and kids go to the beach, and a loaf of old bread.

"The loaf of bread was hard and cold, old like a rock. For my dog.

"Gutierrez took the loaf of bread and began to hit the sidewalk with it, more than ten times. 'This is a bomb!' he yelled. 'This is a bomb!' If it was a bomb why did he hit the sidewalk so hard with it?

"They drive me to the Forty-first Precinct. They strip me. They search my hair, my body. You know, a skin search. After that, they dress me and handcuffed me to an old bench. So then they start to talk about politics—the Nationalist Party, the Young Lords. Now I know what is going on. I said, 'This is a frame-up!' So they start to beat me up. Rodriguez kicked me in the stomach. He talked very bad to me. For two hours they did this. This is illegal, too, because they are not the D.A.

"So after two hours they took my fingerprints and they drive me to Manhattan. This is in the Bronx, where they have courts and jails and a D.A. So why do they drive me to Manhattan?

"On the way they stop at an Irish bar. Some place near the East River. In the bar there were about thirty-five or forty white men, all drinking. They let me sit in a chair and they call the bartender. He's a big man, maybe seven feet. Looked like a policeman to me. I know he had a gun under his shirt. They talked to him and they start to drink Cuba Libre, you know, salt and lemon and whiskey and ice and things like that, in big glasses. They went to the back of the place, far from me. I was close to the door. Maybe they believed I was stupid enough to run and they would shoot me in the back. They did not handcuff me to the chair. But I know better than that.

"It was about six o'clock. That bar had a TV. And I remember there was what you call a hockey game on it. In the jail, in the D.A.'s office, you know, there is no TV. So you know I was there in that bar.

"So about seven o'clock they decided to take me to the D.A.'s office. They had been drinking very heavily. I thought, maybe they will drive me under a bridge and kill me, because they were already drunk.

"They brought me to the building where the D.A., John Fine, was. John Fine was at his desk. In a room they have a big table with about twelve or fourteen men, well-dressed men. I know the FBI by the way they dress. So John Fine, he already knew my name. He said, 'Feliciano, sit down at that table.' He didn't tell me, you have the right to have a lawyer. He didn't say, I'm going to tape your conversation, and use it against you in court. He said, 'Feliciano, what happen today? Why they arrest you?'

"At that time I still believed, a little, in North American justice. So I thought, if I tell him the truth, maybe he will call Harry and Son, and

look at my rifle scope, and see it is broken. And know that's why I was in this place. So he will release me. But, when I said what happened, he said, 'Okay, take him to the other room.'

"That night I had to sleep in a metal bin, in the Fifth Precinct on the Lower East Side. In the morning they took me to court. John Fine said, 'I want to indict this man for attempting, yesterday, to bomb an Army recruiting office in the Bronx.' That's what he said. So they send me out. In two hours they call me back to court. They claimed I had something to do with forty-one bombings in New York. They claimed I was a member of MIRA, the Puerto Rican underground movement. All these things, John Fine said.

"When they brought me back to court, one week later, John Fine didn't mention all of this. He said, 'I want to indict this man [*for*] *attempting to bomb the General Electric building somewhere.' I don't know where. Downtown, I think. So he changed it all again.*

"The judge said, 'Well, we can't let a man like that on the streets.' He put the bail at $150,000. After one month in the Tombs, they sent me back to the Bronx for more indictments. They put my bail at $125,000 more. [*In all Carlos Feliciano's bail eventually totaled $300,000.*]

"For twelve months I was locked in the Bronx jail. I went to the court forty-three times and brought twenty-two motions to drop the bail, based on my constitutional right. Well, they have a constitution, but it does not work for Puerto Ricans and Blacks. In court, the truth is, Puerto Ricans and the Blacks don't have constitutional rights. So I was locked in jail, even though I was not convicted of anything.

"In those twelve months, my lawyer, Robert Bloom, came to me and said, 'Carlos, the D.A. told me if you plead guilty, he will give you fifteen years.' Just like that! Fifteen years! So I said, forget it. One month later he came back and said, 'This time he offered you ten years.' I said, 'No!' Then he offered me seven years. Then he offered me five years. I said, 'No.' So I saw all these things as funny.

"One day I got a letter from the lawyer William Kunstler. He said, 'Carlos, I know what happened. Don't plead guilty. I'm going to defend you for nothing. Just send me a letter.' So I called him, and I called Conrad Lynn. Lynn is a black lawyer who knows more than I do about politics and Puerto Rican history, because in 1950 and 1954 he defended the Nationalists. No one wanted to defend them and he came and he said, 'I am here. I am going to defend you.' He made a good defense. He is a courageous man. William Kunstler, of course, is a very famous lawyer. So now I had three lawyers.

"So John Fine tried once more. One day Robert Bloom came to me

and he said, 'Carlos, the D.A. spoke to me this morning and he said if you plead guilty he will give you five years. But if you don't accept that, he is going to open a new case against you.'

" 'This is blackmail!' I said to him. 'Listen, tell Mr. Fine he can open twenty new cases. After sixteen months in jail it won't hurt me, it will hurt him. He can't hurt me any more.'

"Now the people, my people, began to come to court. Every day there were one hundred, two hundred, people there. In the courtroom they jumped up, brothers and sisters, and they shouted, 'Viva Puerto Rico Libre,' *and 'Free Carlos Feliciano.' Some days the judge said, 'Clear the room.' But one brother got up and said, 'Remember, Judge, we're going to be back here tomorrow.' The day after that they were all there. Lydia was in the front row, with all my kids. So the judge said 'O.K.! the bail is dropped to $25,000.'*

"So you see! How the real justice comes from the people! Not from their court! When they bring a man into court they say, 'The People against this Man.' When they convict a man, they say, In the Name of 'The People of the United States.' But they are not the people. Who are they? A young man, who is the D.A., and an old judge, maybe ninety years old. If he sees you in two hours, he won't remember who you are.

"There is no justice for people in a court. People are the only justice. It is the people who should judge the judge.

"Just before my trial was going to begin, William Kunstler came to see me and he said, 'Carlos, they have a new deal.'

"I said, 'What kind of deal?'

He said, 'They will dismiss all the charges in the Bronx, in Manhattan, even possible charges in Brooklyn, if you will plead guilty to something.'

"I said, 'Something? What do you mean, something?'

"He said, 'Reckless endangerment.'

"I said, 'Reckless endangerment?! What is that?'

"At the time all this happened I was driving my car. But I didn't hit anybody. Kunstler said, 'Carlos, it's just a small thing. They promise you probation. So you won't have a prison record. Think about it.'

"So I said, 'Okay. That doesn't sound too bad. I will speak to my people about it.' They said do it.

"But all those D.A.s couldn't make up their minds. So the trial was held. And the jury made up its mind. I was innocent, they said.

"I am innocent twice. First, because I am a Puerto Rican who is fighting for independence, for the freedom of his country. They are guilty because it is they who took our land, at gunpoint. We are innocent because we

are fighting for justice. Second, I am innocent because I didn't do the things they said I did.

"They can kill our body, but not our thinking, our beliefs. They have no beliefs, so they cannot understand that. We can't go back on our beliefs.

"In Puerto Rico, when I was jailed for five years, and when I was jailed here for seventeen months, I did not stop believing, I did not stop fighting. So they can put me in jail for twenty thousand years and it will mean nothing."

In the autumn of 1973 the cabinetmaker, Carlos Feliciano, was once again acquitted by a jury in the Supreme Court of New York, of placing a bomb and reckless endangerment. He was convicted by the same jury on four counts: of possession of a bomb, a blasting cap, explosive substances, and a pistol. On October 23, 1973, Carlos was sentenced to four years in prison. An appeal was submitted and granted the same week. Feliciano was free on $30,000 bail.

30

Revolución!

Go Left!
Pick Up the Gun!

GO LEFT . . .
RIGHT NOW . . .
PICK UP . . .
THE GUN!

Singing and shouting, the people filled the entire street from curb to curb—ten thousand Puerto Ricans arm in arm. Never in the history of the *barrio* had there been a march like this. In the forefront, waving the flags of Puerto Rico and the United States, came the Young Lords, boys and girls in army fatigues, chanting sharply as they came:

PICK UP . . .
THE GUN!

In the morning they had gathered on the corner of 124th Street and Lexington Avenue, where the pimps and pushers did business, but not that morning, for in the neighborhood of the *tecato* the Young Lords had the reputation of dealing swiftly with those who sold narcotics and women. Several pushers had disappeared. No one ever found them.

They were to march that day to the United Nations eighty blocks away, far downtown, through the old German and Irish neighborhoods and the wealthy Upper East Side, to demand that the international body "recognize the colonialization of Puerto Rico." To demand that in the *barrio* was one thing. To go into the hostile neighborhoods, where few Puerto Ricans lived, or even walked easily, was something else. Borinqueños didn't shout political slogans in the streets of Sutton Place. But these Young Lords were something else. Most of them seemed to be teenagers, jaunty in army fatigues and deep purple berets. Even a few green berets.

Singing as they marched with a dance step in a Latin-rock beat, they slapped their calves in tune with their chants. The rhythm of their feet kept the beat. It was a march without bands or floats.

An old man—one of the few—held a hand-painted sign in misspelled Spanish: DON PEDRO [Albizu Campos] IS NOT DEAD. HE LIVES [IN] THE HEARTS OF THE YOUTH. It was October 30, 1970, the twentieth anniversary of the Revolution of 1950, a "good day for a revolution," said one youth, whose sign said:

THE DUTY OF EVERY PUERTO RICAN
IS TO MAKE THE REVOLUTION.

Downtown in the streets, hundreds of police waited. It was said that as many as three thousand had been deployed on the line of march. The Young Lords were thought to be armed.

WE BELIEVE ARMED SELF-DEFENSE AND ARMED STRUGGLE ARE THE ONLY MEANS TO LIBERATION.

Point 12 of the Platform
of the Young Lords

The Minister of Education of the Young Lords, Juan Gonzales, later to become the Chairman, had issued a proclamation for the march:

"For years our people have been killed by the Yanqui. *We die of pneumonia in unheated apartments. We die from sterilization and unsafe abortions. We die from police bullets. We die from overdose. We die from garbage, anemia, hunger. We die because we are poor.*

"We fight, we protest, we demonstrate. Nothing changes.

"Our nation is a colony. Whether in Bridgeport, or Fajardo, we are controlled by the Yanqui. *We can't stand by anymore. This government,*

instead of protecting us, kills us. We have no choice, at this time, but to pick up those guns and say to our nation—ARM YOURSELVES TO DEFEND YOURSELVES.

"We were not born violent. We do not enjoy killing. But our daily lives are violent. This country is violent. Either we sit by, saying 'ay bendito,' *as our nation dies, or we stand up, organize and prepare for the revolution we know is coming."*

THE PARTY CONTROLS THE GUN!

GLORIA CRUZ

In the *barrio* everyone knew the march was coming, yet everyone was shocked by it. It was not right to go into the streets and shout. It was also dangerous. Still, it was a bold thing, real *macho.*

The old women in the tenement windows waved little Puertorriqueña flags in bony hands. On the crowded fire escapes whole families stood and cheered. The white-shirted and tired city employees in the storefront offices of the municipal rat-control agencies, the surplus food centers, the health clinics for addicts were uneasy and pretended not to see. In the schoolyards little children of ten or eleven waved clenched fists.

On 111th Street, they escaped from the yard, but their teachers chaperoned them back behind the steel-mesh fence. Three girls eluded them and joined the marchers.

On 106th Street a barber came out of his shop; he ran to his car and replaced the American flag on his radio antenna with a Puerto Rican flag.

From the hill, on 103rd Street, the march could be seen stretching for six blocks. The people of the *barrio* were not marching in neat lines. They filled the street, overflowing onto the sidewalks. In twenty blocks the few hundred had grown to thousands, who came out of the tenements, the stores, and parked cars. To their own surprise, they found themselves singing in the street.

On Ninety-sixth Street the marchers left the *barrio* and were joined by white university and youth groups, the American Servicemen's Union and Gay Liberation, who marched last.

In an old German frankfurter and würst stand on the corner of

Eighty-sixth Street several people watched the march. At the small bar two men from the neighborhood talked about the crowd.

"What is it?" one asked.

"I think it is a parade," his neighbor said.

"Who is parading?"

"Spics, I think."

"Spics?"

"Yes."

"Spics don't parade here."

"Maybe they're Irish."

"And what do they want?"

"Who knows?"

"I tell you what I think," said the first man. "They want to come in here and drink our beer."

In the unease that the neighborhood seemed to breed in them, the marchers began to chant loudly at the white faces that now lined the sidewalks. The chants became more vehement, and there was no more dancing.

SEIZE THE BUILDINGS!
SEIZE THE STREETS!
POWER TO THE PEOPLE!

SEIZE THE JAILS!
LET THE MADMEN AND MADWOMEN OUT!

GO LEFT . . .
RIGHT NOW . . .
PICK UP . . .
THE GUN!

On Fifty-seventh Street the students in the High School of Art and Design opened a window and were throwing confetti from their torn-up school notebooks. A group of black students joined the march. In a few moments they were joined by several dozen others—Chinese, Puerto Ricans, Whites, and Blacks. The marchers welcomed them with a chant:

ALL OUR BROTHERS
OUR BLACK BROTHERS
OUR WHITE BROTHERS
OUR YELLOW BROTHERS
OUR INDIAN BROTHERS
OUR CHICANO BROTHERS
OUR JEWISH BROTHERS
OUR AFRICAN BROTHERS
OUR CUBAN BROTHERS
OUR VIETNAMESE BROTHERS
OUR STUDENT BROTHERS
OUR ARTIST BROTHERS
ALL OUR BROTHERS
ALL OUR SISTERS

On Fifty-third Street a squad of mounted police was poised on a side street. They spurred their horses into the path of the marchers. They seemed to be attempting to separate the Young Lords from the rest. The mass moved quietly forward. The mounted police reined their steeds to one side, and the march passed them by.

A young girl screamed: "Death to the pigs!"

Palante, *the wrath-filled newspaper of the Young Lords, had printed a box with a black border of mourning that contained the words:* "THE ONLY GOOD PIG IS A DEAD PIG."

On the release of Huey Newton, the Black Panther leader, from prison, the Minister of Information of the Young Lords, Pablo "Yoruba" Guzman, had written an impassioned and rhetorical editorial of welcome:

"Say, 'Welcome Huey' to the strains of a twin explosion. Say, 'Hi, brother' to the music of pigs' bodies kissing the pavement as they drop dead from double-o buckshot in the back. Open your arms to embrace him as your mother mixes rat poison in Miss Ann's cake. Slap five with Huey while some official is whisked out of his car one night. That's how revolutionaries say hello."

"It may be rhetoric," said a police inspector. "But someone says, Kill the Pigs! Then someone reads it. And he goes out and does it."

On Forty-seventh Street at the Plaza of the United Nations, hundreds of policemen were waiting for the marchers. The barricades of the police had turned the broad plaza into a labyrinth. Several squads of uniformed officers and plainclothes detectives lined the sidewalks, or stood inside the lobby of the United Nations' Church Center; others waited around the corner in the Tactical Police Force buses. Another squad of the mounted police sat on their snorting, jumpy horses, ready.

As the youth marched down the street the helmeted police began to slap their clubs against their palms. Would there be a bloody confrontation?

The Lords halted the march. One of the leaders walked over to the police captain in charge, and he said, "We'd like to hold our rally. We have a permit for a rally."

"Yes," said the captain. "We are ready for you."

In the plaza a modest space was set aside for the marchers. Evidently the police had not expected so many thousands. No one had.

The Young Lord said, "If we lead them into there they would be so crowded there might be a riot."

A boy behind him whispered, "I think it's a trap."

"There's room," the police captain said.

"You will have to move the barricades," the Young Lord said.

"Our instructions are that you're to stay within the barricades. Let's get going."

"No," the Young Lord said.

The faces of the leaders and the police were adamant. In the lines of the policemen there was a noticeable stiffening. And the two sides glared at each other. No one moved.

In graceful and deft movements three young Puerto Rican girls knocked over the barricades with swings of their buttocks, and sweet smiles. The policemen rushed to stop them. But the three girls knocked over another barricade.

And so the marchers swarmed into the plaza past the leaders and the police.

Borinken on the Moon

The young man stood stiffly on the stage of Columbia University's venerable Ferris Booth Hall, his arms folded, holding a *machete.*

His *machete* was hidden within a black leather case that looked like a small attaché case. The young man was a "security" guard of the Young Lords, protecting the speakers at the student conference. All of the outsiders who entered the hall had been searched thoroughly and professionally in police fashion.

No reporters were admitted, few non-Puerto Ricans. As one of those who had been invited was frisked with extraordinary efficiency, the "Security" man, really a boy, who was searching his trouser legs and cuffs looked up with doleful and dark eyes. "I'm sorry, sir," the young boy said. "We got to watch out for pigs!" The quiet act of courtesy was the one indication that the student conference was being held by the daughters and sons of exiles from a gracious tropical island, not just the children of the ugly ghettos of Nueva York.

"Have you found any pigs?" the man said, putting down his hands. "Put your hands against the wall, palms out," he had been commanded.

"Man! I wish I did," the young boy said, smiling broadly.

Denise Oliver was talking. She was a beauteous and vibrant young black woman, with the profile of an Egyptian queen and the impassioned and deliberate rhetoric of a feminine Malcolm X. She had become the Young Lords' Minister of Finance. She could bring an audience to its feet in minutes by cursing the police, the pushers, the schools, the hippies, the world of the white man—the Man!

"High schools are prisons and high school students are prisoners," she chanted in a cool and clipped voice. "We got to go into the high schools, together, and push out the pushers. We don't need dope. We need liberation. We are not hippies. We don't have the option of dropping out of our middle-class families. We don't have middle-class families to drop out of. So we got no option to relate to. The dope is killing us! The dope is being fed to us by the Man! by the Mafia! by the pigs! by the government!

"Push out the pushers!" she said. Her voice was urgent. "If the police won't get rid of the pushers, we will!"

In the audience of more than a thousand young Puerto Ricans, half were high school students. Her words "Push out the pushers!" brought them to their feet, waving clenched fists and school books, and shouting their approval. Never had he seen anything like it, a veteran reporter said, but then he had "never heard anyone suggest that the youth should police themselves." Enforce their own laws? The *barrio* youth knew that the Young Lords did more than talk. If the *machetes* in the leather cases were merely dramatic symbols, the rifles they had publicly displayed in some of their street actions were not.

"Self-determination" gave the people "the right" to enforce their own laws, said a leader of the Young Lords. "If there is any power" in the *barrio,* "it is the righteous power of the Puerto Rican people."

Understandably, the police were disturbed by the rhetoric and the rifles.

"If they stab a pusher to death and throw his body in the river," said a retired, high-ranking New York City police inspector, "it is a great deal faster and serves to eliminate a condition. But . . ." He thought "vigilante groups operated at a very high cost" to constitutional liberties. "By force or fear or intimidation they say they are going to get rid of people who bring drugs into the neighborhood. In order to do that they 'oppress' a lot of good people."

The inspector had heard that *barrio* youth gangs had been "instrumental in ridding the neighborhood of criminals and drug pushers." As a police officer he could not condone their methods; there was "no hesitation on their part to use illegal means" in eliminating the pushers he said, for ghetto gangs executed their own "law enforcement" codes and practices; but he opposed the "law of the lawless."

A few years ago the Young Lords had been little more than a *barrio* gang. On the streets of Chicago, in the late 1960s, a group of boys had banded together to fight not for their "rights" but for their "turf." Like the Irish, Jewish, Polish, and Italian gangs before them on Division Street, they were neighborhood youth who sought protection in numbers. Their gang organizations were elaborate. They had a gang psychology. They believed in the gang mythology. A Chicago girl who knew the Young Lords then said: "A lot of the guys used to be on drugs. They used to gang-bang with the other gangs. But then they turned political."

A young man who had grown up in the gang recalled: "We had to get together to protect ourselves on the streets, not only from the existing gangs in Chicago—the Irish, the Polish, the Italians, the Blacks—but from the city.

"All our dreams had been shattered. This thing, this city, we had been thrown into treated us like nobody. It was a time of unrest. So we groped for something to hold on to. The way to get to feel like somebody was to belong to a gang. One of the main reasons gangs get together is to feel like you are somebody, to feel good inside. It is a positive thing. But it has lots of negative things too, like you develop the myth of the gang, the gang culture, like you are a world by yourself and if you stay together nothing can defeat you. That is really a myth."

Led by an elusive-faced boy by the name of Cha Cha Jiminez, the Young Lords gained the reputation of a cool and tough gang. Cha Cha became a legend on the street. He was a handsome and dynamic young man, with a face at times angelic, at times cruel. His gang was formed because "street brothers of high school age knew the pigs were killing spics and the situation had to be reversed," said Pablo "Yoruba" Guzman, who was to become one of the national leaders. At the time the gang had no program; its one political act had been to join the Young Patriots, a white street gang, and a new-founded ghetto group called the Black Panthers in the Rainbow Coalition.

In the summer of 1969, the Chicago street gang met with a group of young intellectuals and college students from New York in the Sociedad de Albizu Campos. Under the name of the Young Lords party the two groups merged. It was "a combination of the intellect and the gut, and theory with practice," Yoruba said. The leaders were of course the young intellectuals—Felipe Luciano, a poet and psychology student, who became the first chairman; Juan Gonzales, an SDSer from Columbia University, who was to replace him; José Martinez, an SDSer from Florida; Yoruba, a student at elitist Bronx High School of Science; and David Perez, born in Lares, who like Yoruba had become a student at the State University of New York at Old Westbury. It was not the coterie of a typical street gang, but then myths are not born of reality.

On entering their universities the young Borinqueños had left the *barrio* streets and the way back home seemed difficult. Felipe Luciano wrote of this conflict:

> The N.Y. Public Library raped me viciously
> Assaulted my nose with book smells
> Till I almost forgot
> Revolution was a thing of the streets.

"Seduced" by knowledge, he had forgotten what life was like. Luciano wrote to his books: "God, I wish I could fuck you."

> The library tempts me
> Sometimes worse than a woman
> With wide baby-holding hips
>   and thick calves
> Sometimes I wanna sleep on it,
>   in it, through it, and
> Wake up and say, "Good morning
>   books."

In the street philosophy of the street gang from Chicago the young intellectuals found their way back to the *barrio*.

One week after these groups had united in Chicago, the newly baptized Young Lords of New York had barricaded Third Avenue and 110th Street with garbage by tossing the uncollected refuse of El

Barrio into the streets in protest against the lack of garbage collection and the unsanitary conditions of the ghetto. "We decided that the first issue we could organize people around was the filth in the streets—since it was clearly visible," said Yoruba "By questioning this system's basic level of sanitation our people would begin to question drug traffic, urban renewal, sterilization [of our women], until the whole corrupt machine could be exposed." It was more than garbage that the young intellectuals were throwing into the streets.

The "garbage offensive" went on all summer. On block after block the people threw their garbage in protest into the streets. By the end of the summer, Yoruba remembered, "Our name and our image had become established. We set up headquarters."

In the fall they began door-to-door lead-poisoning tests for tenement infants. There was a free breakfast program for children. There was a free used-clothing give-away program, and the "liberation" of a Health Department chest X-ray truck to give free TB tests to hundreds of sufferers. There was their own Clean-Up-the-Barrio campaign, after the Sanitation Department had refused to lend them the city's brooms.

Reverend David Kirk was moved to say: "If Christ were alive today, he would be a Young Lord."

The youth "liberated" the Spanish First Methodist Church of El Barrio. Earlier they had begged that the church let them run their free community services from its usually empty building. They had been thrown out. Now, with a flourish of rifles, but with little or no ammunition, they occupied the church. Bishop Parrilla came from Puerto Rico to conduct an ecumenical service. The church was renamed Iglesia del Pueblo—the Church of the People.

All of these were simple acts. But to the young and idealistic intellectuals, these were signs of "The Revolution!" The dispensing of used clothing was nothing less than "Socialism in Action!" On the Lower East Side, when parents picketed for a traffic light on a corner where a child had been killed, it was "Rebellion on the Lower East Side." When homeless families "squatted" in an empty tenement it meant "The Land Is Ours! We Are Taking It Back!" The "garbage offensive" had become an act of "Insurrection!" And a minor riot in the *barrio* became "War in Newark!"

"Soon," wrote Juan Gonzales in the spring of 1970, "the revolutionary war will start and the oppressed people will slay Goliath, burn Babylon, throw the moneylenders out of the temple, and then we, the Last, shall be the First." Felipe Luciano wrote, "We must use urban guerrillas to fight this country on our own terms. Obviously, the underground must also provide this military training for the revolutionary brothers and sisters." All of the advice to the "secret" underground was publicly proclaimed in the pages of *Palante,* the Young Lords' paper.

"POWER TO GOOD SHOOTERS!" Richard Perez said. The slogan of the day was "The Party Guides the Gun!"

But the rules of discipline of the Young Lords were still those of a street gang, not a guerrilla army nor a political party. And their code of honor was written in the language of the street:

1. You are a YOUNG LORD 25 hours a day.
2. Any ORGANIZATION MEMBER busted on a jive tip which that member brought down on himself, or on others, can swim alone.
3. Any member found shooting drugs will be expelled.
4. No member may have any illegal drug in his or her possession or in their system while on duty. No one may get drunk on duty.

7. No one will point or fire a weapon of any kind unnecessarily, or accidentally, at anyone.

15. All contradictions between members must be resolved at once.

19. Each YOUNG LORD must learn to operate and service weapons correctly.

22. All members must read at least one political book a month, and at least two hours a day on contemporary matters.

28. All Traitors, Provocateurs, and Agents will be subject to Revolutionary Justice.

No ordinary student, clerk, or laborer needed, or would benefit from, these rules of discipline. He was not expected to. The "Organization" was aimed at the street people, the ex-addicts, the gang members, the school dropouts, the former inmates. Its élan, daring, and discipline were Brechtian—the democracy of the street—and not Jeffersonian—the democracy of the elected. "The street people" will be the "hard core" of the revolution, wrote Richard Perez.

Later the young intellectuals would expel some of the street youth, whose name they had used as a rallying cry, from the Young Lords. Cha Cha Jiminez had the "ideology of the lumpenproletariat," they said. The Young Lords of Chicago were not "politically responsible," they said; for they had no "political program," practiced no "revolutionary discipline," and above all, they did not follow "Marxism–Leninism–Mao Tse-tung thought."

Felipe Luciano, too, would be expelled as a "right opportunist." He dared to criticize the Black Panthers as "sectarian," for having "isolated themselves from the masses of the people." Luciano, who talked "like a poet or a defrocked priest," an elder *barrio* leader said, was accused of "extreme individualism" and of being "petty bourgeois." The leaders of the Young Lords would later admit they, too, were "petty bourgeois" in believing that the "lumpenproletariat [the street people] were the vanguard of the revolution," and they, too, as students, "came from the petty bourgeois, ideologically." But that was hindsight.

Their scene was the *barrio*. But their language was that of the Black Panthers. "We grew up through the reality of the Black Panther party," recalled Hernan Flores, a Young Lords leader. "Even culturally there is black culture in us. We didn't isolate ourselves from that. We looked at that and said: We have to form an organization similar to the Black Panther party." It took many years to differentiate between the culture of the ghetto and the culture of the *barrio*. "Many years of hardship. Many years of misery. Many years of history," said Flores. "Now, we identify with Blacks in some ways," he said, "but not in all ways."

And yet, for all their rhetoric of "pick up the gun," the Young Lords did not actually do so. There was no evidence they had ever attacked the police. But the authorities, who had listened to the rhetoric and to tales of police informers, began to arrest and jail the

Young Lords in New York as in Chicago. In Chicago the police arrested Cha Cha for the theft of $23 worth of lumber. He was sentenced to one year in prison, but disappeared before he could be jailed. One leader, in New York, Julio Roldan, was hanged in his cell in the Tombs prison in Manhattan. "Suicide," the police reported, but his friends charged that he was "murdered." Some fifteen FBI agents—or seventeen some said—were sent to arrest Juan Gonzales on the charge of draft evasion. Yoruba was indicted on several charges.

The defying of the law by the Young Lords had shocked and electrified the *barrios*. Puerto Ricans did not disobey the law. Exiles did not defy the government for the government was not theirs to defy. An old proverb said: *Never fight with anyone who is not a relative. He will show you no mercy.*

None of the old proverbs of the island or the new fears of the cities subdued the Young Lords. "DARE TO STRUGGLE! DARE TO WIN!" exhorted *Palante*. By defying the law the youth were proclaiming not only their lack of fear of the government, but that it was indeed their government to defy. The boys and girls of the Young Lords were the children of the city *barrios,* where most of them had been born. Unlike the parents, the youth were at home in the cities, the only homes they had known. In the schools they had been taught that the Constitution of the United States was theirs, too. And they refused to accept, as Juan Gonzales had said, that the government "instead of protecting us, kills us."

Self-confident, bold, aggressive and blasphemous, the *barrio* had never seen anything quite like these Young Lords. They defied not only the stereotypes of the "passive" and "humble" Puerto Ricans that non-Puerto Ricans cherished but those stereotypes of the easy-going, forever courteous and gracious people that the *barrio* believed about itself. The failure of their rhetoric of "revolution" to affect the government was less portentous than the effect it had on the psychology of the people.

The "nationalism of youth" was perhaps an even more significant and lasting phenomenon. In the past the exiled islanders had gotten together on a local and home-town basis. But the Young Lords, being of the second generation, born in the United States, were not confined by the nostalgia of their parents for home towns they had never known. One of the attractions of the Young Lords was that the people of the *barrios* were young. Sixty-five percent of those who had come from the island had been under thirty-five, and nearly half of the immigrants had been under twenty-five. In the *barrios* three of every four residents were under forty, and 40 percent were children not yet out of their teens, according to a 1964 New York Health Survey. And so the Young Lords, abetted by the youth of the exiles, quickly spread to several states, without the provincial pride and jealousy that traditionally limited organizations of Puerto Rican exiles.

"We come from home towns. So we formed our own home-town groups here. The Jewish people call them *Landsmannschaft,"* Gerena Valintin said of the older generation. The Congress of Home Towns, Congreso de los Pueblos, which he had founded and led was a federation of dozens of these social clubs where people met, not so much as Puerto Ricans as Aguadillaños, Utuadoaños, or San Juanites. On block by block, *barrio* by *barrio,* the older people had formed social clubs and cultural societies. Some of these became centers of local political power.

El Comité, a strong *independentista* club on the West Side of New York, was one of these. Its housing, welfare, and civil-rights campaigns had gained considerable support among the tenement families of the neighborhood. Its newspaper, *Unidad Latina,* voiced that combination of sorrow at the harshness of city life and the romanticized nostalgia for the island that the older generation so often echoed, poignantly and sadly. In the Christmas season of 1971 *Unidad* editorialized:

> Darkened skies, gray from the cold and rain; it is December. Now it is winter, but the cold of this country is felt all the time. In summer we can spend our time on the streets, or looking out of our windows—somehow the coldness isn't felt as much. But in the winter the cold creeps in our bones. We walk fast, all bundled up, with our hands in our pockets, as

if we were going somewhere. In the morning we go to work when it's cold and gray only to return home when it's late and dark and gray; we see the sunlight of the day through the grimy windows of the factories. . . . Winters are so hard.

"In Puerto Rico we had less but enjoyed more," El Comité said. The endless refrain of the exile. To the Young Lords such nostalgia was beautiful but somehow irrelevant. It was not that they did not feel the ambivalence of their parents, but their lives had begun at the opposite end of the flight from the island to the city, and so they saw the same thing from a different point of view. The Young Lords were simply PRs, Puerto Ricans, Ricans, or, as they defiantly sometimes called themselves, Spics. In the memories of the youth their "home towns" were the blocks of the city's *barrio* where they were born.

"Our mothers and fathers have a Puerto Rican identity," Hernan Flores said, but "after twenty years in the United States, they begin to consider themselves a part of this country." The older people had divided loyalties, because they had lived divided lives. But young people who had grown up in the city did not have the same conflict in the same way. "We helped make this country. We have to accept that. We are not going back. We intend to stay here. Our struggles are here."

In the city *barrio* the *jíbaro* from the hills was not the same man either, Flores said. He was no longer loyal wholly to *familia* and *pueblo*. The urban *jíbaro* had become a worker, and workers had to be loyal to each other. "That's what we are into now. Here the workers have to lead. So we say the workers have to have a heavy input. For a long time we'd thought the best way to work was to do everything ourselves. But in doing that we isolated a lot of people, especially the workers. They were very confused about our actions. Because we didn't involve them. We were sectarian. Now, we see that was incorrect. Like in Lincoln Hospital, where we decided to take over the hospital, to force them to treat our people right, medically. We isolated people.

"We used to say you had to be for 'The Revolution' twenty-four hours a day. You couldn't go to work. You couldn't go to school. All that did was to isolate us from the realities of the people," said Flores.

His own father was one of the people he had been isolated from. In the days when the Young Lords' *grito* was "Pick Up the Gun" he remembered that his father told him "he thought I was crazy!" The father and son were now closer politically.

"My parents had poor schools and not much opportunity of getting a job on the island. So they saw the best way of survival was to come to New York. To make some good bread," the youth said. "Like that was their American dream. It turned out to be a nightmare. We came here and they realized it was a lie. My mother had worked in a factory for twelve years, and she was laid off. My father worked in a factory, and after nineteen years he got laid off. He said, Wow! He began to understand things I was saying. He told everyone, Look what happened to me! Everyone knows he was a hard worker. He is a responsible person. He is forty years old! And now he comes to me and he says: I can see why you fight! He is reading all the papers now. . . .

"To say, I want to have freedom as a youth, the way we used to, that's bullshit! You got to have freedom as a human being, for every human being," the youth said. "For a while we were fooling ourselves."

In the summer of 1972 the now older Young Lords convened their "first and last Congress" to analyze their early acts of bravado and daring, which they now called "right and left opportunism." It was "extreme leftism," they said, to have youthfully thought they were the "party" of "The Revolution." Since they had "represented only themselves," a few students and a few street youth, they were not really a "party" at all, they decided. Where were the workers? And so they changed their name, hopefully and expectantly, to the Puerto Rican Revolutionary Workers Organization. From now on they would learn "Marxism–Leninism–Mao Tse-tung Thought," and they would become "communists," with a small "c."

The Puerto Rican movement was moving to the left. In the *barrios* poverty and economic depression were unabated and unrelieved. Civil rights were not granted. And the failure of the American society to satisfy the elemental needs of the poor had intensified the frustrations of the youth. They searched for new methods, new solutions, and new societies. Socialism was a tempting idea to the urban tribes of Borinquén with their traditions of communal living. Especially to these idealistic youths.

The Movimiento por Independencia had become the Puerto Rican Socialist party, the PSP, and its small New York chapter followed it to the left. It had begun quietly as a small group of exiled intellectuals, representing several viewpoints in the independence movement. On the streets of the *barrios* the "Vito Marcantonio Club" had few adherents among the poor. But as the "polarization of rich and poor" had grown intense on the island in the 1970s, said Juan Mari Bras, the Socialista leader, the *independentistas* turned their attention to "the problems of the workers," and began to advocate socialism. In Nueva York there was a similar leftward movement.

Socialistas had been prominent in the *barrios* before, from Don Luis Muñoz Marín to Gerena Valintin. In the past, however, they had been led by those outside the community, and the Puerto Rican Clubs were like auxiliaries to the national, non-Puerto Rican Socialist parties. As the Young Lords had been, these new Socialistas were born and bred in the *barrios,* and they were their own leaders.

The *barrio* Socialistas were remarkably like the ghetto Socialists of a century ago. Like the Jewish peasants of Eastern Europe who in becoming urban workers in the United States organized their first political power blocs in socialistic trade unions, so did the peasants from the hills of Puerto Rico. And, like the Jews and the Italians, too, the communal village life and family ties of the Puerto Ricans, with their humanistic and cooperative ways of thinking, were translated into a social ideology by manifestos and by conferences, instead of merely being a way of living as they had been in the "old country."

In a few years the Puerto Rican Socialist party, the "United States Zone," grew from a few dozen to "several" thousand. "Last year we tripled our organization bases," boasted Rafael Baerga, a national leader, in the winter of 1973. The "influence" of the Socialistas had begun to spread "over large sections of the Puerto Rican community," said José La Luz; for chapters had been established not merely in the *barrios* of New York, but in New England, in Boston, Springfield, and Hartford, south into New Jersey and Pennsylvania, and in the Midwestern *barrios,* as well. "We note the steady, consistent growth of the party," Andres Torres, a young New York official, said in self-congratulation.

The phenomenon went unnoticed in the press and on television. So did the worsening poverty and unemployment in the *barrios* that had caused it.

All of this activity "has not taken place in a vacuum," Torres said. "Conditions facing the Puerto Rican people here have continued to deteriorate," and the severe cuts in poverty programs and welfare funds were cutting deeply into the barest subsistence level upon which the poor lived. "These are programs which service and employ *hundreds of thousands* of Puerto Ricans," he said. Even more disastrous were the jobless rates. "Unemployment in the ghetto communities remains around 25 percent," Torres had estimated. Some thought it much higher.

It was among these—the poor and the jobless—that the prophecies of the Socialistas were the most enticing. Who else paid attention to them?

On the stoops of every *barrio* block the jobless men could be seen sitting, waiting for "something to happen." Some played dominoes. Some complained and drank beer. Some just sat and stared at the disappearance of the day. But some grew angry. The man who had gone from factory to factory and store to store, seeking a steady job, but who had been offered nothing but odd hours of janitorial work or a Sunday job as a part-time counterman, soon gave up hope of working. He gave up hope in "the system."

To the jobless man all the official words of economic prosperity were as meaningless as the official statistics of unemployment. He knew those "who make a living counting us who cannot make a living" have never sat on a stoop "for weeks, for months, forever," as one man said. They have never wondered, "Why was I born? Why am I alive? Why did I come here? How can I live?"

"Every morning I ask of myself, Was I born for nothing?" a young man said.

What did he answer?

"There is no answer. But I look for it."

One man in every two in El Barrio did not have a full-time job. Yet the government figures of unemployment in the *barrios* of New York were less than 10 percent. "The male 'undercount' is of very real concern in the ghetto areas," according to Herbert Bienstock, Regional Director of the Department of Labor's Bureau of Labor Statistics, for the figures did not include those youth who had never found a job, or the old who had given up looking. Nor did they count the "sub-employment rate for Puerto Ricans in slum areas" that stood at 33.1 percent in the *barrios* and 37 percent in El Barrio. If those who worked for less than the "poverty level" wage or who worked at part-time jobs were added to the government unemployment figures the *barrio* rates would approach 43.1 to 47 percent. And these figures, of course, did not include the women, whose lives were less easily reduced to statistics.

Congressman Augustus Hawkins of Los Angeles thought that the "uncounted unemployed" numbered 20 million. He accused the government of deliberately "underreporting" the jobless, and of ignoring the millions who "stop looking for jobs that don't exist." A man who had been cut out of the labor market was cut out of the unemployed statistics. Officially, he, too, did not exist.

The cold realities of life in the cities made the romantic ideas of revolution on the island seem to be a dream. "We have left behind all the simple notions concerning our role in the revolutionary struggle," Rafael Baerga said. "Now the study of Marxism-Leninism applied to our objective reality guides our practice." The new Socialistas of the *barrios,* like the former Young Lords, decided they too needed a "scientific analysis" to help them escape the poverty of their lives.

But the "scientific analysis" of their misery seemed to offer them more questions than answers. The cry of the jobless man on the stoop re-echoed in the words of Alfredo Lopez, an editor of *Claridad,* in his call to the Congress of the Puerto Rican Socialist party "in the Zone of the United States":

"What is the social character of Puerto Ricans in the United States? Are we a nation unto ourselves, or, as many *compañeros* believe, a national minority? Are we part of the Puerto Rican nation? . . . From that flows our conception of ourselves as organization. What do we propose as a party? Do we consider ourselves the vanguard of the American Revolution? If not, what historical role will we play?"

"They are questions which are plaguing our whole movement," Lopez said. If the Puerto Ricans lived in "the Belly of the Beast," as he believed, was there any escape?

In their Congress, convened at the church of St. Mark's, April 8, 1973, the Socialistas resolved these questions with a book-length resolution entitled *Desde Las Entrañas—From the Bowels of the City.* It evoked images of exodus and anguish—". . . Puerto Ricans living in the United States form an integral part of the Puerto Rican nation." Even unto the second generation. The former Young Lords criticized the Socialistas for romantic "petit-bourgeois nationalism" and "mystical" Puertorriqueñoismo. It was the old "divided-nation theory" the city-born youth said they had rejected when they felt the island had rejected them. But, the Socialistas replied, since 1968 when the MPI had demanded "double citizenship" for islanders on the mainland, they had believed that once a Puerto Rican, always a Puerto Rican: "As Puerto Ricans we function with a national perspective in mind," they said. The "generation born in the United States," they reassured the Nueva York youth, "would continue to be a part of the nation."

Puertorriqueños' "primary role in the United States is to unleash, in all its fury, the national liberation struggle in the very centers of the North American cities," the Socialistas concluded.

One thing alone remained constant. In all times and in all places a

Puerto Rican was a Puerto Rican. The *jíbaros,* the Young Lords, the workers, the Socialistas, and the newly proclaimed "Marxist-Leninists" of the city *barrios* remained faithful to their Puertorriqueñoismo, to their image of themselves, as Alfredo Lopez had said, and a people possessed by the "cry which was in the mass soul, the cry of Puerto Rico."

At the "student conference" of the Young Lords at Columbia University, years before, there had been a workshop held in Puerto Rican history. The teacher was a young woman, born in the *barrio* of New York. She spoke poor Spanish. Her workshop was crowded with young and old, teachers and students. At first she conducted the workshop in English, until someone chided her—"Talk Puerto Rican!" With a beaming smile she began again in faltering Spanish, halted in embarrassment, tried again, and faltered again.

"I am sorry," she apologized. "But it's too complicated and my Spanish is too simple. So I have to say it in English."

There was a quiet murmur of disapproval in the classroom. The displeasure of some of the older people—not with her Marxist-Leninist interpretation of Puerto Rican history, but with her English interpretation—was apparent on their frowning faces.

"Look! I am Puerto Rican!" the young woman almost cried. Her passion silenced the room. "I would be Puerto Rican if I were born on the moon."

31

The Ricans

The making of a Rican has been described by a young man:

"I remember stepping off that airplane in a light sweater, here in Chicago. And seeing the snow coming down, for the first time. That was the first snow I had ever seen. That was my first feeling about this country. That it was cold. It seemed to me to be a strange land.

"And it was a strange land to me. Where I had come from up in the hills of Lares it was the tropical jungle. I was fond of being a child of nature. I grew up with my friend who was a hunchback. He would teach me the secrets of the countryside. The birds. The trees. The fruits of the island. And we would go into the forest and hunt for birds. We would hunt for wild honey. As a boy I wanted to learn everything about nature.

"I was a child with the innocence of a child. Then, when I was thirteen, we came here [to Chicago].

"At thirteen I grew up. I had to. I grew up very angry at thirteen. I would come home from school, throw my books on the floor, bang things around. I didn't know where this bitterness came from. Except I knew that the streets, the concrete, the people around me, weren't part of me at all. My roots were not in this city, in these Yankee institutions that were destroying me.

"So I was angry. I was being torn up inside. On the outside I was an American, but on the inside I was still a Puerto Rican.

"At that time I was given two choices by society: I could go to school. But the teachers told me I was a Latin and was dumb and all the doors would be closed to me. So the teachers said there was nothing for me to do but to take workshop, and a general high school course. And then go to work in a factory and work as my father worked.

"I didn't want to go that way. For I could see the death inside my father. He was dying inside. Every day when he went to work I could see his spirit die.

"There was only the gang. In the gang you felt good, felt proud, felt you were somebody. So I thought I would go that way. All the dreams of the kids I grew up with in Chicago were to be hustlers on the streets. Either a pimp or somebody like that, who made it illegally. Because we could see no legal ways for us to make it on the streets. There were no other ways.

"But I could see the violence on the streets. And I didn't want to go that way.

"So I went to school. I learned to play the game. And I smiled. At thirteen I learned, kids all did, how 'they' could control us by telling us we were nothing. If a man was nothing, he had to be somebody else. Right? He had to be like 'them.' He had to become an Anglo. Or he would be nothing all his life. If the system can make you hate yourself for not being white, it has you!

"So I was an alien in the system. Being an alien I had no rights to live, to be.

"I was a Rican."

The Rican was many people. He, or she, was the *Neorican, Newyorican, Neorriqueño, Newyorikkan, Boricua, Borinken, Spic, Spik,* or simply the *Rican*—the Young Lord, the Latin King, the Ghetto Brother, the Latin Rock singer, the Marine in Vietnam, the scholarship student in the Harvard University Graduate School of Education. One thing he was not—he was not the hyphenated Puerto Rican–American.

On the island he was derided as the *Americuchi,* but the word conveyed a certain affection. The term Puerto Rican–American was too insulting even for an insult. It was rarely, if ever, heard.

Who then was he? The Rican was more easily described than

defined. It was simple to say the Rican was a second-generation son or daughter of a Puerto Rican family. But that too, was more a description than a definition. "He is neither black nor white. He is neither American nor Latin American. He comes from an island that is neither a state nor a nation," Samuel Betances wrote, in a youth journal cogently titled *The Rican*. That said what he was not. Betances, by way of explanation, quoted the parable told by Ramon Lopez Tames, who compared the Puerto Rican to "the plight of the bat who is rejected by birds and by rodents, belonging to neither family, [and] is condemned to live a solitary life between two worlds, misunderstood by both." That, of course, was an old *jíbaro* folktale and a portent of the future.

In one of his darker prophecies, the young Luis Muñoz Marín had written in the *American Mercury* of February, 1929: "Perhaps we are destined to be neither Puerto Ricans nor Americans, but merely puppets of a mongrel state of mind, susceptible to American thinking and proud of Latin thought, subservient to American living and worshipful of the ancestral way of life." But the Rican had a homeland. He had two. He was no longer an exile. He was not an alien in the usual sense, although he may have felt he was one. Most often he had been born in the United States, which had rejected him, as Puerto Rico had rejected his father. If he was an alien he was "an alien in two lands," as the *barrio* saying had it. And he suffered that double alienation that Louis Adamic had expressed in his description of earlier immigrants who, he said, even when they became citizens were still "ex-aliens."

A young college student, born in Chicago, who had tried to "go home again" to the island, where she never had been, voiced the pain of that experience:

"Where are we? In reality we are nowhere. When we go back to the island after living here, they say, 'You're not Puerto Rican! You're an American!' And when we come back to the United States, they say, 'Oh, you're nothing but a Puerto Rican!' So who are we? That just makes me wonder: Who am I? Why am I a Puerto Rican? What makes me a Puerto Rican? If I was born here, why doesn't that make me an American? If I am not, why am I not there, on the island?"

Beatrice Colon was not bitter, but her thoughts were painful. Her eyes were pensive, uncertain, doubting, as though close to tears. "Where is our place? In reality we have no place. Because we have no place to go back to. We have to learn to make it here. At first I couldn't accept that. I was saying to myself: You're not Puerto Rican! No! I am a Puerto Rican, I said! Then I started to think about it, and I said, Yes, it is true! I couldn't live on the island. I am preparing myself to live here. When my children are born they are going to be born here. There are a lot of people who don't want to accept that. But slowly it is being accepted. We are here! We are here to stay!

"I am a Rican," she said. "The Rican is someone who has Puerto Rican parents, who was born here and who has grown up here, and who has had all of their life experiences here. That's the new philosophy." She sighed with resignation and relief. It was as if she had cast off a burden.

"So I am a Rican." She nodded. "But *what* is *that?*"

No one was born a Rican. To be a Rican was not a state of being. It was an act of becoming, of birth itself. Everyone knew the trauma of his own labor pains, the blood and placenta, as the infant divided from the mother. Once it was born the infant began to have a life of its own, its own character and quality, as beautiful and creative as the moment of its creation. So it was to become a Rican.

"We must shape a culture," began the editorial dedication of the youth who founded *The Rican*. It was, in a sense, a declaration of independence of the youth. "We must develop a new vision, one which is not a carbon copy of the political and cultural system that now exists, or a total rejection of all its tools and instruments," *The Rican's* editors declared: "The time has come for us to identify ourselves according to our own standards and values."

The independence of the Ricans, in whatever way it was expressed, was seen as an affront by many of the older generation on the island. When the Young Lords sent organizers from the mainland to help "the struggle for independence" on the island they were met with curiosity and hostility that surprised them. It was more than a classic confrontation of parents and children, as poignantly described by Juan M. García Passalacqua in his column on the Young Lords, reprinted in *Notes of NeoRican:*

> Anyone who has observed the relationship between Neoricans and Puerto Ricans here has witnessed a strange phenomenon. On the surface a sort of camaraderie prevails. As the conversation progresses, however, the locals begin to fret. One can sense distinctions, rather than similarities, coming to the fore. The Neorican is harsh, cool, determined, high-powered. The Puerto Rican is suave, warm, hesitant, dubious. . . . They turn apologetic, edgy. One can sense a collective guilt feeling gaining strength. . . . At this point someone makes the inevitable remark: "But they are not really Puerto Ricans."

The industrialist and self-made millionaire Manuel Casiano expressed the same feeling of unease as had the Young Lords. He had come on the invitation of former Governor Ferre to be director of the government's industrial-development agency, Fomento. But he felt no more "at home" than did the rebellious youth. "Having been born in New York, I'm not regarded here as a 'true' Puerto Rican," Casiano said. "It's a ridiculous feeling, almost like being a man without a country."

Many of the older generation saw the Ricans' "new vision" of life as alien, insulting, and threatening to the traditional ways of life. Elena Padilla, in her pioneering work *Up from Puerto Rico,* written in earlier years of the migration, had said, "It is not possible to speak of a Puerto Rican culture in New York, nor even to pretend to understand the culture of Puerto Ricans in New York in light of the culture of Puerto Rico." But her depressing vision was bright if compared to the myopic insight of Nathan Glazer and Daniel Patrick Moynihan, who in *Beyond the Melting Pot* wrote that a "rich culture and strong family system" often gave "strength and grace and meaning to a life of hardship," but "In both these aspects Puerto Rico was sadly defective. It was weak in folk arts, unsure in its cultural traditions, without a powerful faith." Except for "love of dancing and singing," the Puertorriqueños had a "limited" culture. So the poor "culturally deprived" ones came to New York with no "network of culture" to sustain them. "One can hardly imagine what kind of human community will emerge from the process of adaptation," these sociologists wrote. They reflected the belief of Oscar Lewis, who in *La Vida* said, "The culture of poverty is a relatively thin culture." Lewis believed that on the island and on the mainland the Puerto Ricans' "native culture was relatively simple." Even their language was largely "inspired by bodily functions, primarily anal and genital," he said. As the Harvard sociologist Christopher Jencks was to comment later, "These observations rest on Lewis' studies of the ghettos of Mexico City and the Puerto Rican ghettos of San Juan and New York, where the breakdown of traditional peasant cultures has created a distinctive type of culture which comes close to being *no culture at all* [emphasis added]."

If these sociologists and anthropologists had studied the ethnic ghettos of the turn of the century they might have decided that "the breakdown of traditional peasant cultures" there too had resulted in the poor having "no culture at all." Fortunately for the Jewish, Irish, and Italian poor, they had escaped from their ghettos before the sociologists and anthropologists arrived to lock them into a "culture of poverty."

The culture of the Borinquén was buried by the decay of the city. But it was not destroyed. Nor was it assimilated or mercifully banished, but hidden beneath the debris, like seeds that could not yet be seen, the old "traditional peasant culture" of the *jíbaro* flowered in new forms. It was not recognizable to those who thought the new had to resemble the old. For the Ricans were born of Puerto Ricans, as sons and daughters were born of fathers and mothers, as flowers were born of seeds.

In the beginning the youth had "denied their fathers and mothers," Beatrice Colon said. All her friends wanted to "be accepted." She remembered: "Going to a white school, I wanted to be white. When you are not one thing, or another, you strive to become like whatever is closest to you. I had to hold on to some identity. Being white was all there was. Being Puerto Rican was denied to me by the schools, by the society."

Her white school friends didn't "really" accept her. They could not speak Spanish and made fun of her when she did. They insulted her "without even knowing it." Even going on a date was a cultural conflict. "I could date. But I couldn't stay out late. Boys had to come to the house. That meant they had to sit there with my parents. I couldn't be one of them.

"So I started to ask myself who I really was. I started to learn about myself."

In self-defense against the deprecations of her teachers, who treated her as if she were a victim of the "culture of poverty," she began to read about Puerto Rico. Her pride startled her. "I'm Puerto Rican," she told herself. "When you first become aware of who you are, it's really a big thing." The act of discovery was like birth. Once she had felt her parents had betrayed her. Now she felt she had betrayed herself. "I feel bad that I wanted to be white. And not who I am. Like denying my father for having his black blood, but praising my mother because she's white. But now I can love them both and not deny either one. And I can love myself."

The story was not her own, she thought. It was the story of her generation, for it was the making of the Rican. "You see, this way you are not part of the white world. You are not part of the old Puerto Rican world, either. You have found your own place in your own world—as a Rican. You are yourself.

"Now, most of the students see Puerto Rico as something to identify with. Why? They want the island to be independent because they want to be independent themselves. It gives them that one, little thing to cling to, to identify with, so they can find their own identity, and they feel they have some place, and they are someone." It was the Young Lords who in the beginning had exemplified this feeling, this sense of "being someone." That's why they had to be so angry, she said, in order "to break out of the nothingness we were all in."

"Ain't no piece of paper can make a *spic* a *yanqui,*" Pablo "Yoruba" Guzman, Minister of Information of the Young Lords, had said. "We are a people. We are a nation. We are not amerikkkans. We are Puerto Ricans. There is no such thing as a Puerto Rican-amerikkkan." He felt the pressure of colonialism wherever he was. "In the U.S. wherever a spic stands, sleeps, sits or shits, she or he is oppressed. Right on the spot, at that moment, we are being colonized. In the U.S., as on the island, we must struggle for liberation."

But, he too knew the Rican's ambivalence. "From Borinquén we moved to the U.S., where there is no defined land, except the ghettos we have been thrown in." Nations had to have land of their own. The Ricans owned no "defined" land.

In the Bronx High School of Science, where young Guzman had once been an honors student, he too had sought to "be accepted." He was a handsome, dark-skinned boy, too dark-skinned to "be accepted" by either the whites or the few middle-class Ricans in his class. The Blacks knew from his name and accent that he was not one of them. Those who knew him in those days said he pronounced his name "in a Jewish way." He was not then known as "Yoruba": that new identity came later.

These "spiritual problems of self-definition," of which Richard Pattee had written in the *Annals of the American Academy* as long ago as 1942, "strike at the very heart and reason for being of Puerto Rico," for it was "a fully developed and unified nationality." He believed the island was "ethnically unified," and foresaw nothing but "danger" in its relation to the United States.

Race, like nationality, was not acceptable as a mixture. It had to be one thing or another. The Ricans, if they could not be identified as either black or white, simply had no acceptable place within a racially exclusive society. Samuel Betances, the publisher of *The Rican,* commented sardonically: "In the racially polarized city they were not white, though they may be referred to as 'Puerto Rican white,' and they were not black, at least not black enough." He thought that the inability of the Ricans to fit into the stereotypes of a racial strait jacket caught them "in a maze of non-identities."

The young Luis Muñoz Marín, in his bohemian exile in Greenwich Village, had written in 1925: "Perhaps the island should be of interest to the American people chiefly as a laboratory experiment in racial ethics, as there you will find the nearest approach to social equality of this sort." At that time the Ku Klux Klan was riding high across the United States. The "race problem" was, as it is still, seen in whites and blacks. If the "wedding of races" on the island was then too far away culturally for the Norte Americanos to see, what of the children of Borinquén history in their midst? They were invisible.

"An Anglo sees his own skin as the only 'right' one. He is blinded by color. I don't know why," Beatrice Colon said. The shade of human skin did not matter to her. All that mattered was "the culture a person had." "Lots of Puerto Ricans are white, but their minds are not white." The "white world" wasn't defined by skin color: "It is the way people behave, whether they are kind or cold," that determined whether they were white or not. The whites were "cold," even when their skin was not.

In the "racially polarized city" the girl dreamt of a world where color would not matter. The whole world would be Puerto Rican or Rican. Everyone would be a beautiful mixture of colors and shades. And that meant, obviously, that if all the black and white skins were mixed together the dominant hue of the future would be brown.

"Everyone is going to become brown! In a few centuries everyone is going to be brown because that's *the color!*" cried Beatrice Colon. Her face was radiant at the thought. "If the Anglos were brown then they couldn't say *anything* about your color any more. They would still be Anglos, but *brown* Anglos! Then there wouldn't be any prejudices any more. That would be ideal! If everyone was *brown!*"

If she had a dream it was this: not that all people would be equal but that all people would be one. "I think it comes from our Indian, white, and black blood," she said. "The Rican, as I see myself, is all people in one. As much as I would love to hate other people, I can't really hate people. That's the way I am. That's the way we are." She laughed and laughed. "We are very strange that way."

Being many people in one was difficult. "It makes you more human, and that's hard. We have a split personality, split in three ways. We have three opinions about everything. We like to say, Yes and No and Maybe. Because that's the way life is. Because all three are right. We see life in three dimensions. We will get it together. Then we will become whole human beings."

The making of a Rican was not easy. It took a lifetime; even then it was not completed. By definition the Rican was incomplete—the human being who was in between, the odd man out, the Eve cast out to the east of Eden—all of these were Ricans, and they lived in every *barrio.*

> Lonely outcasts! In vain
> they lay songs aside
> as if the promised land
> lay within their souls.

So, long ago, Lola Rodriguez de Tio had lamented: ". . . why do we not have a homeland!" The fervent woman who wrote the national anthem of the island, *"La Borinqueña,"* lived as an exile in New York, and died as an exile in Cuba. As were the famous patriots, her friends Eugenio de Hostos and Dr. Betances, she too had been one of the first Ricans. And she sang of them, in her song of exile:

> Ay, sorrowed souls who dream
> when exile never ends. . . .

Once, in diaspora, the Jews had been the eternal exiles. After hundreds of years they had tired of wandering, and they had built a homeland. In diaspora the Ricans and Blacks now lived in the tenements where the Jews had lived, in Chicago, in Cleveland, in Philadelphia, in New York. The Ricans were now the eternal exiles.

A gentle scholar of the dying tradition of Jewish wisdom, Joshua Fishman of Yeshiva University, said of the Ricans: "They will not disappear into the American melting pot, as early immigrants did." He recognized the resemblances of history. In the Ricans, perhaps, he could see the strengths of diaspora that so many of his colleagues now deplored, but which he cherished. The exile of a human often made him not less human but more so; for the exile was stripped naked, he was shorn of the adornments of the society that cast him out. So he was no more, and he was no less, than he was. The old Jews knew that.

"I am me! I am not merely an American or a Puerto Rican," said a young woman who worked in the *barrio* health clinic on the Lower East Side. She was lovely. Her face was serene, and yet in her eyes there was a troubled look, more uncertain of herself than her smile dared acknowledge. At an early age she had married, had two children, and had left her husband. "That little boy," she called him. "He was my youngest child." Now she lived alone with her children and her work. Her life in the ghettos of New York was all she had ever known. Was there any other? Still, her mind wandered and she wondered about her life. Why was she alive? Who was she?

"My son asked me yesterday, 'Am I a Puerto Rican, Mommy?'

"I said, 'Yes.'

"He said, 'A kid at school told me I was a Puerto Rican.'

" 'What did you say?' I asked.

"I said, 'No! I am an American.'

"So I told my son, 'You are a human being.' "

Her eyes were dark. In her melancholy there was a defiant joyfulness. She seemed childlike and aged, at twenty-three. "And that's how I feel," she said. "I am a human being. Just a human being. I am me. I am not an American or a Puerto Rican. I don't feel patriotic about anything. I don't believe in anything. Just in being human."

32

The Women

On the ridge of the hill were two tire tracks barely wide enough for the wheels of the Jeep. The hill went up and down like a roller coaster that had gone berserk. In the deep valley on the steep slopes, the coffee trees grew precariously. The Jeep snorted up an incline. Its low gears growled as the wheels dug into the soft earth. A wrong turn would send the vehicle and its passengers tumbling hundreds of feet into the valley below.

"Here we go," the Jeep's driver murmured, her face beaming.

She held the steering wheel in both her hands, not because she was frightened but because her body was slight, weighing little more than ninety pounds. Her name was Dama María. Though she looked like a little girl, she was almost twenty.

The men in the back seat held tightly on to the sides of the Jeep. At each twist and turn of the narrow road they winced and tightened their lips. But they said nothing. They endured the ride in silence. Not one man offered to take the wheel nor did anyone joke about women drivers. The men knew there were few better mountain drivers than the girl at the wheel. Who wanted to risk his life just to be a *macho?*

"No girl, I bet, ever drove into these mountains in a Jeep before," an older *jíbaro* in the back seat said, chortling. He was delighted by the thought. "You can bet on that. She is dynamite, that little one!"

It did not describe her to say she was petite, for though her body looked fragile and feminine, the tautness of her muscles and the firmness of her hands revealed her enormous strength. Her eyes were dark and daring. In the university she had been a science major but she had gone to work in the mountains for the excitement, the challenge, and the danger. She wanted to "do something real for my people."

"In Nueva York you would be a hero of Women's Liberation," said one man in the back seat.

"A hero of what?" she asked.

"Of Women's Liberation."

"Ah," the girl cocked her head, as if someone had said something absurd but interesting. "Women's Liberation?" Her bemused eyes peered straight ahead, watching the narrow and winding road. Then she said, "Here we don't need that. Here in the mountains women have been 'liberated' for a long time. In Puerto Rico what we need is the 'liberation' for the men."

The mountain women had inherited many of the rural strengths and self-concepts of the Borinquén Indians, upon which village life was built. The family and *barrio* had been ruled by a matriarchy, and in some ways it was still. The *jíbaro* woman, no matter how traditional her day-to-day life, seemed to feel free to do "what was needed," when she so decided, or to tell her husband what was "for everyone's good," or to speak out and act herself in whatever personal or political uprising she thought necessary. Significantly, women were among the leaders of the revolution in Lares in 1868, and in Jayuya in 1950. As were the *jíbaro* men, so too the *jíbaro* women were willful and strong-minded.

The Spanish patriarchy and Borinquén matriarchy were wedded more unhappily in the urban and suburban cities, where colonialism had been more powerful. Even so, the tribal heritage of the women was not entirely suppressed.

In San Juan there was a young woman, a few years older, whom some of the *independentistas* had called "the Joan of Arc of Puerto Rico." She had been arrested on the island of Culebra, the target range for the U.S. Navy. And she proudly pointed to her penitentiary cell. There were few "pickets" she had missed. Boldly marching "in front of the noses" of the police, she delighted in crying *"¡Puerto Rico libre!"* "into their faces." And yet she modestly requested that her name not be used when she talked about the meaning of "Women's Liberation" to her.

"Men are not the enemy of women. That's foolish. Sometimes I think they hate men. No human is right when they hate another human just because of their sex," she said.

"Some of the things they say I do not understand. Like not wanting a man to help you, to hold a door for you. A man will hold a door for a man. Why not a woman? If a man will not help a woman, he will not help a man either.

"Of course, some things are true that they say. That men should look at women as human beings. In dignity. That is important in a Latin country where men sometimes believe in *macho*. That they are superior to women because of manhood, you know, *machismo*. Such men have contempt for women. But that does not mean it's right for women to have contempt for men."

There was a quiet decorum in her dress and manner. Even during a "picket" in front of the La Princesa prison she had dressed exquisitely to confront the police.

"Do you always dress so well to picket a prison?" she was asked.

She laughed. "Because a woman is political that doesn't mean she is not a woman. It doesn't mean that she has to act, and dress, like a man. She should respect herself. When you see a woman wearing man's clothes, to look like a man, that doesn't mean she is 'liberated' as some women say in the United States. All that means is that she has lost respect for herself as a woman."

She smiled. "A woman should be a woman, I think. Don't you?"

On Borinquén the women had the heritage of centuries-old traditions. So did the men. These island traditions gave both men and women a sense of serenity and of strength. Even when they rebelled against them. *Serenidad,* knowing who you were, where you lived in history, came from being surrounded by familial history. And that illusion of serenity still existed on the island in the behavior of women and men. In social life there were a graciousness and formality that were comforting, no matter how illusory. The vulgar society of booming industry and sprawling cities may have disrupted family life and brought emotional upheavals into the homes, but in the plazas there was a decorum and politeness of the older ways. The old Spanish saying was: *Behind the walls of your house you may do whatever you wish, but do not do it in the plaza.* Society was governed by polite illusions.

In Nueva York the illusions of the island could not last very long. The walls of the tenements in the *barrio* were too thin for dignity or *serenidad.* The gracious ways of the plaza could not survive the morning subway rush to work. And the Puertorriqueñas had no familial history to comfort and protect them from the city.

Until World War II, "housewifery was our sole profession," wrote the editors of a women's magazine in the *barrio* of Nueva York. "Our men being drafted, coupled with the great migration to the States, forced many of us to go to work for the first time." But, though everything had changed, nothing had changed. "Even though you worked in the factory all day," when the woman came home she was "expected to make up for a day's absence." These women had the worst of both worlds. "Our status as underpaid, live-in, full-time maids to our fathers, brothers and husbands [in that order] did not change," the editors of *La Mujer Puertorriqueña* had written.

Born in the urban *barrios* the young women often thought of themselves as "liberated" from the provincial morality of the island. They may have been. They were "liberated," as well, from the traditional ways of life that had given them self-confidence in being women.

Ema Ramos, a graduate student in clinical psychology, said sadly, "I see young girls saying how 'liberated' they are. And I feel very sad for them. They don't have any norms or patterns in the *barrios.* They have so many conflicts. They have nothing to relate to in the American tradition. They cannot say the feminist movement is something that they are going to join. They are not middle class. They are poor." In the city *barrios* the women had no "defined place," she said. The old morality and family life had "broken down," and nothing had replaced it. And so there was "no escape."

On the island the *serenidad* of the traditional family had flowed from the strength of the women. But in Nueva York the traditional family was weak and there was little *serenidad.*

The parochial and paternalistic beliefs of Spanish Catholicism, which had idealized and inhibited women, and the *jíbaros'* Indian idea of women as the soul and strength of the family and the village were fantasies in the land of *Playboy* bunnies and Marlboro *machos,* where reality for them was a garment sweatshop. Both of these island images of women were laughed at by the boyish bravado of so many Americano men, who were jovially and vulgarly sexual. In between the chaste and strict moral standards of the home and the loose and *laissez faire* lack of moral standards in the streets and schools the young Puerto Rican women were caught unprepared in a no-woman's land.

Gloria Steinem, an editor of *Ms.,* had gone to the island a few years ago, hopeful of "starting something like Women's Liberation," said a militant woman leader in San Juan. "But she started nothing. You know why? She had a press conference in one of the big tourist hotels on the Condado for the middle-class women. They came. They liked her. But our women in the *barrio* do not go to the big tourist hotels on the Condado. They are too poor."

On the island of Borinquén, and on the island of Manhattan, most of the women who worked worked at the poorest and worst jobs. In 1971, *La Mujer Puertorriqueña* wrote, "89 per cent of us still work in only low-income, factory type jobs" or as domestics. Less than 12 percent of these working women, and 4 percent of all women, had office or professional "middle-class" jobs. Such was *Nueva Vida,* the new life, in *"Amerika."*

In this new way of life, to be "liberated" was to be "alienated," Ema Ramos thought. The young Puertorriqueña was as much a victim as she was a revolutionary. She had to create a new way "of seeing herself." Her father thought "everything is falling apart" and did not know what to say. Her mother said, "What's this world coming to?" and did not know what to think. And her sisters, who were both angered and frightened by the failure of the moral authority of their mothers and fathers, were "liberated" by necessity as much as by desire. They began to develop "father hatred" and "mother hatred," Ramos said, forgetting that their parents were as lost as the younger generation, if not more so.

"So you could not talk to your mother [who did not know what was happening to her]," an embittered young woman said. "And so you could not talk to your father, who still demanded that you be a virgin [when you had not been a virgin for years], and that you don't get involved in 'intellectual things' [when you were in the graduate school at the university]."

If the old ways of their fathers did not help them, neither did the new ways of the young *machos* they married. *La Mujer Puertorriqueña* grew caustic. The voice of the young professional women in the *barrio* sought a new concept of womanhood, to "dispel the myth" that women were "nothing but a complement to a male." But in their professional lives the young women had not found it. "As we began to make it into high schools our aspiration grew," they hopefully wrote. "No more working in the factory for us. We would say—*I'm going to be a secretary.*" But the office was no utopia. "Even when we became a secretary, nurse or teacher" there was always "the mile long, solemn, decisive walk down the aisle" to become the *"mujer de la casa"*—the wife of the house, or the housewife, for their "little boy" *machos.*

The villain was not the man. He, too, was a victim of frustrations, said the young women. He needed his wife of the house to prove to himself that he was a man.

"Our men are 'de-balled,' " said Connie Morales, the Minister of Education of the Bronx Young Lords. "Since they can't prove their manhood economically, they try to do it sexually, at the expense of their women." In most of the *barrios* half of the young men were unemployed, without any trades or skills, school dropouts, who were angry and humiliated. Their *machismo* was the one pride of manhood that they still had. So, though the young women cursed the "ridiculous business" of *machismo,* as one college girl called it, they nonetheless sorrowed for their wounded men.

It was *machismo* that had created the worship of "the cult of virginity" in the *barrio,* said *La Mujer Puertorriqueña.* "We all know that men only marry good women, which is synonymous with being a virgin. They fool around with all those *mujeres malas* [bad women] but they will only marry the intact woman," the young women said. That means "you are judged not by your intelligence, by your awareness, or your uniqueness, but by your hymen."

Virginity in a woman, not a man, was important not for religious or sexual reasons, the young women wrote:

> Try to rationally figure out why a virgin is so necessary to a *macho.* To start with our men have been castrated by colonizers as far back as our history goes. They have been deprived of their freedom—economically, socially and politically. The result is a nation of very insecure men. Insecure in his masculinity and his right to be master of his nation. The only thing left to call his own becomes his woman. With her he can take out his frustrations. She becomes the only property left to him, so he holds on as tight as possible. He starts making demands on her he can't make on his oppressor. Since he is not allowed to release his normal aggressions in everyday life, he then throws it at us, the women.

The mirror image of "the cult of virginity" was the tradition of *la corteja.* "It is a well known fact that in our Puerto Rican culture married men are encouraged to have a woman on the side, or what we call *una corteja,*" said Connie Morales. "The wife is there to be the homemaker. She must be 'pure' to begin with—virgin—and remain 'pure' for the rest of her life, meaning no sexual pleasure. *La corteja* becomes [the man's] sexual instrument." One psychiatrist called this the "enforced desexualization of the mother."

La corteja was a woman of love. The word meant "lover," from *cortejar,* "to make love." The wife had children, said a young woman. "She was not expected to have orgasms"—that was the "mythology of *machismo.*" In the *barrio, machismo* was the worship of a "nonfunctional tissue, the hymen," said *La Mujer Puertorriqueña*. *"Machismo is fascism,"* said Connie Morales. *Machismo* was "the way our men will use physical force to show their manhood," said Ema Ramos. *"Machismo* is like idolizing a statue. Like Christ," said one teenage girl.

In a scientific attempt to discover the meaning of *machismo* a group of social scientists at the University of Puerto Rico interviewed 322 couples. Of these, 72 couples were given the "intensive" treatment. They were asked, "How does a man show his *machismo?"* To the surprise of the social scientists, who were Anglo, "an insignificant minority, about one-seventh, interpreted the term in an unfavorable light, as referring to a man who abuses women." One out of four couples thought of *machismo* as "sexual prowess," which they evidently didn't look upon unfavorably. The investigators decided they needed another investigation "to establish its [*machismo*'s] importance."

Since the success and fame of *La Vida,* by Oscar Lewis, the sex life of the *barrio* had become a fascination of social scientists. The New York Medical College established a Sex Therapy Center in El Barrio of East Harlem. In one year and a half, however, only fifty-two couples had come to the sex clinic, and "only two couples were Puerto Rican," complained the director, Dagmar Graham. These two couples needed only a week of treatment and they were "orgastic." Her colleague, John O'Connor of Columbia University's International Institute for the Study of Human Reproduction, remembered only one Puerto Rican couple who applied to them for treatment.

"Just when they were scheduled to begin treatment the woman flew to Puerto Rico to visit with her mother," O'Connor said. "I don't know what her mother said to her, but whatever it was it worked. When she came back to New York City the couple didn't need us any longer."

It was the fault of "the *macho* myth," grumbled the Sex Center director, Dagmar Graham. The *barrio* men were too *"macho"* and the women too "passive" to let themselves benefit from the scientific sexual techniques of the New York Medical College's experts on love.

One San Juan newspaper commented: "SEX THERAPISTS SEEK LATIN LOVERS." In the streets the clinic was the butt of laughter, mostly aimed at the naïveté of the Anglos when it came to lovemaking. The men and women of the *barrio* apparently had no need, or desire, to discuss their love life with the strangers, as the strangers did. Voyeurism was not in their tradition. Love was not thought to be a science.

Love in the urban *barrio,* or in the *campos* of the island, was not a technique to be learned in a clinic, or in a book. No man or woman bought love "on the installment plan as the Americans think," Ben Rodriguez said. In love every man was a Don Quixote, and every woman was a Dulcinea.

"For what did Don Quixote go to battle?" asked Miguel de Unamuno. "He fought for Dulcinea, for glory, for life, for survival. Not for Iseult, who is eternal flesh; not for Beatrice, who is theology; not for Margaret, who is the people; not for Helen, who is culture." He fought for Dulcinea, who is illusion.

"Love is the child of illusion and the parent of disillusion; love is consolation in desolation; love is the sole medication against death, for it is death's brother. . . . The delight of sexual love, the genetic spasm, is a sensation of resurrection, of renewing our life in another." And yet the act of resurrection was "a foretaste of death, the eradication of our vital essence." Unamuno wrote that a man and woman "unite so that they may divide."

That too was *machismo.* It was a duality, fragile and powerful, that only those who possessed, or who were possessed by, *machismo* knew.

"So, you see, we could never believe in the 'liberation' of women from men," said a woman leader of the *independentista* movement. "That is like the 'liberation' of the flesh from the bone. That is like the 'liberation' of birth from death.

"We are too romantic for that."

As with all immigrants, the first generation of women tended *"to stay close to home and marry our own."* The woman who moved away from the *barrio* was envied for her boldness and condemned for her betrayal. If there was an intermarriage it was an occasion for prayers, foreboding, gossip, and the lighting of candles. Fewer than 10 percent of older *barrio* women married outsiders. By the second generation one of every three young women married a man of another nationality, as had happened with the earlier pre–World War I immigrants. The second generation was "more American." It was not as bound to the *barrio* by what it thought to be the provincialism and *machismo* of its elders. Usually, among immigrants of the past, the men had led the way out of the ghettos.

Not so in the *barrios.* In matters of love the Borinquén women seemed to be bolder than the men. In the first generation of immigrants almost twice as many women as men married non-Puerto Ricans. In the second generation, too, more women fell in love with and married strangers (33 percent) than did the men (27 percent). The old traditions of *indio* and *jíbaro* women marrying foreigners, the Spaniards and Africans on the island, was continued in New York.

Were the women bolder? It was difficult to say. Romance, like sexual love, was as complex as it was perverse. It was enticed by social barriers and moral codes it rejoiced in defying. One thing was certain: the women seemed to feel freer in pursuing fantasies of their own creation, whatever the causes and consequences.

The men were more timid, more content to live with the *macho* of their inherited fantasies. It had been that way all through history.

One winter a young Puerto Rican girl came alone to the high snow of the mountains of New Mexico to teach in a rural village school. The school was in a beautiful and desolate valley between the Pueblos of the Rio Grande and the Navajo Nation. After some months the schoolteacher fell in love with and married a handsome young Indian. Her family came to the wedding from the *barrios* of New York. Like the bride, her parents had never been to the West, but were originally from a sugar-cane village on the island.

"Always I dreamed of coming to the West," said the father of the bride. "But my daughter comes. She comes and makes me come by getting married to an Indian." He shook his head. The *macho* had dreamt of the country of the cowboys, but it was his American-born daughter who fulfilled his dream. She was "a true Puerto Rican woman," he said, for she was "not afraid of anything."

Some of the older feminine traditions of the island had survived in the city. In time they emerged from the debris of the broken families. The strength of the women became visible again.

"The woman is more aware that fulfillment comes from closeness to other human beings," said Ema Ramos. "We grow up thinking it is fine, and necessary, to have feeling. And to love other people. It's conditioning. So you can't say it's a natural instinct. But women feel it more than men.

"Life is stronger in women, I think," she said.

In Chicago's *barrio* the young student Beatrice Colon said: "Women tend to be stronger than men. I can't explain why. Maybe it has something to do with the nature of *machismo*. A boy is more on his own. A boy always has to prove himself. Like when a boy throws his first rock and breaks some boy's head, he'll get spanked for it, but his father will say, 'Oh, did you see him break that boy's head.' So a boy has to do it again and again. He grows up to be a man, and he is still a boy, trying to prove himself, to show his *macho*. So he never grows up.

"Now a girl doesn't have to do that. The girl is educated more in the home. Everything in the home is directed toward her. My mother would always tell me, "You can't let anyone run you around. You have to be strong. You have to make your place!' So I'm pretty strong. I tend to dominate. That's how I was brought up. That's how a lot of Puerto Rican girls have been brought up.

"The women run the *barrio* organizations more than the men. The real fire is in the women. Yes, women are supposed to be weaker than men. From what I see men are weaker than women."

But that did not matter. "As I see it this is not a man's world. Or a woman's world. To me, a woman is a part of a man. And a man is a part of a woman. It's *our* world."

In the impolite pages of *La Mujer Puertorriqueña* the young women were troubled, and excited, by the same thoughts. "Already many are misunderstanding what we want. We are viewed as a strange tribe of lesbians seeking vengeance, because we hated our father. Let's get all this cleared up. We love and take pride in our men," the women wrote. "We do not want to take away their jobs. We, the women, want to join with our men to fight our common oppressor. . . . But we refuse to sit in the back seat, having our vision obscured by a male driver. We do not want to be treated either as *putas* [whores] or dolls." With a flourish of Biblical purgation they concluded, ". . . All together we will raise a new world on the ruins of Babylon."

In a poem by a "high school sister," Margarite Velez, the spirit and unique Puertorriqueña humanism of the *barrio* women's movement was strongly expressed. Her cry, and demand, was titled *"Yo, una Mujer Puertorriqueña*—I, the Puerto Rican Woman":

My past is a past of continual
    struggles,
I have been raped, beaten, used,
    by the invaders of my land.
But what is worse, when I look
    at my man,
I see him trying to prove he is
    a MACHO
by beating me, and leaving me at
    home, while he goes off
    and lays some "Joan."

I have been trained to accept
    this quietly,
(remembering my mother telling
    that this man can go out
    all night, but if the wife
    does that, the husband should

start worrying . . .
I remember asking why my brothers
are allowed to go out and
get high, while decent girls
stay home and cook and sew
and clean . . .)

Well, I have something to tell him
this time,
I WILL NO LONGER ACCEPT BEING USED,
'CAUSE THERE IS NO ROOM IN THE
STRUGGLE FOR WEAK WOMEN.

Don't think I want to be better
than you.
What I want is to join you.
This is a time for Brothers and
Sisters, to take the gun
in hand and fight together,
SIDE BY SIDE.

In words that were quieter and simpler, Ema Ramos said of the women: "Let's all become much more exciting people. It's like learning to stand up for yourself. I no longer feel I am alone. I am no longer alone, when I am alone. For years I have been fighting, I have been struggling, to find my strength. Now, I have found it."

The new strength of the young women came from deep within the island's history. Few would have recognized that they were heirs of the Indian matriarchs of Borinquén. Had she ever thought of female *machismo,* one young woman was asked. She laughed.

"*Machismo* is many things. In the struggle of humanity, of men and women, everywhere, for their independence, all human beings have to have *machismo.* That is a healthy *machismo,*" said the Nationalist hero, Carlos Feliciano. "But not in a bad way. Or in leadership. Or in the kitchen."

Carlos Feliciano was a young man, but an old revolutionary. He was a toughened veteran of a lifetime of jailings and shootings, exiles and revolutionary visions. It was not easy to imagine him in a kitchen apron; but he emphatically shrugged off any suggestion of irony at the thought.

"In the morning when I wake up my wife goes to the kitchen to make the breakfast. But I stay in the bedroom to make the bed. So, that way, we share that," he said. "When I go to the bathroom to shower, I take my towel and my soap with me. So I do not have to shout, 'Bring me the towel! Bring me the soap!' It is the same when I go sit down to have my breakfast. Always, I bring the glasses of water or the coffee to the table. So I do not shout to my wife, 'Bring me a glass of water! Bring me my coffee!' That is not *machismo!*

"And when we clean the house she takes the broom, and I take the mop or she takes the mop and I take the broom.

"In the past too many men put everything on their wife. That was not right. Every woman has the same right as a man. The man is not the master and the woman the slave. That was fake *machismo.*

"Some of the greatest heroes of Puerto Rican independence have been women. Some of the women have been greater heroes than the men. And I will tell you something else: the women, our sisters, have never sat in the chair in court to testify against their brothers. Men have done that! Men have been cowards! Men have lost their *machismo!* But never a woman. Not one woman has ever done that. In the struggle for independence there have been hundreds of our sisters who have been heroes. Like Blanca Canales and Lolita Lebrón and Carmen Pérez. Have you read the letter that Lolita wrote from prison a year ago? After twenty years in the prison her belief is stronger than ever, her thinking is more beautiful than ever."*

In the neat and modest apartment of the Feliciano family in Brooklyn, a young man who had listened intently to the talk of *machismo* leaned forward. The button of a rifle on a map of the island was pinned on his purple beret. "If she was released from prison tomor-

* Lolita Lebrón had been arrested in 1954 after the armed attack on the House of Representatives in Washington, D.C., when five Congressmen were wounded; Blanca Canales had been arrested during the Revolution of 1950, when she led the attack on and capture of the city hall of Jayuya; and Carmen Pérez had been arrested that same year, as a "Nationalist woman leader."

row, she said, she would pick up her gun again and do the same thing!"

"No, she did not say exactly that," replied the quiet voice of the former leader of the Cadet Corps of the Nationalist party: "Lolita said that if they offered to free her from the prison because she was a woman, she would not go. She would not go out until all of her brothers were freed too.

"That was real *machismo!*" Carlos Feliciano said.

33

The Gods of the Ghetto

The Church

On the evening of a summer day, the pimp leaned low on his right elbow as he cruised onto Wabash Avenue near the shore of Lake Michigan in his old, stylish black Cadillac. It was his signal to the smiling policemen on the corners and the expectant businessmen on their way to the lakeshore hotels that he was in business. His "girls" were ready to go to work.

Elegant and tall young women, his "girls" were specially selected for the high-priced trade. In fashionable couturier clothes they sat in the shadowy back seat of the Cadillac, inhaling one last leisurely cigarette before their long journey into night began again.

One was black. One was brown. Their clientele were those lonely executives who couldn't fall asleep alone in their hotel rooms and the academicians from professional conventions and the delegates from men's clubs conventions, who were not as racially exclusive in the dark as they were in the daylight.

"Black is beautiful!" a pimp said, laughing harshly in a nearby bar.

"And, baby," purred his brown "girl," a Puerto Rican woman, "brown skin is *in!*"

South Wabash Avenue was the urinal of Chicago's Loop. The official tourist guides did not list its attractions, but they hardly had to. Nor was the pimp's signal noted in the police manuals, for everyone knew it. The modern and massive building, equipped with the latest computers and sophisticated crime-detection devices, in the midst of the desolate streets of winos and whores, was the impressive headquarters of the Chicago Police Department; but if the nightly route of the pimps was marked on their data-retrieval cards, there was no evidence of it in the streets.

"In the Syndicate-run [Mafioso] strip joints about three blocks from police headquarters, the dancers busied themselves between numbers, performing fellatio in the booths for ten dollars a spasm," wrote Chicago journalist Mike Royko, in *Boss,* his would-be political eulogy to Mayor Daley.

Just a few streets from there was the Archdiocese Latin Center of the Catholic Church. A neighborhood social worker for the church waved to a pimp on the corner when he left work that evening. The pimp came by every evening; that was "his" corner.

"Christ would have known His way around here. He knew this sort of scene," said the church worker. "Our priests are uncomfortable here. They don't know how to talk to pimps. A whore embarrasses them. If they met Mary Magdalene they would react with self-righteousness. It's not a ministry they are taught in the seminary. Hell, no.

"Our priests feel more at ease in the lakeshore hotels. That's where their relatives are, waiting to go to bed with the Latin 'girls.'

"In the *barrios* the chasm between the Church and the people has grown. Now our people need spiritual help more than ever in history. But the Church doesn't give people that spiritual help. How can I tell a man who has no more hope that he should go to church and pray for a 'better life' in the hereafter? He sees his daughter becoming a whore. He sees his son becoming a pimp. He sees his children sticking their arms into a needle. What can a priest who's never suffered any of these things say to help him?

"When he does go to church he sees the priest, in his rectory, eating his steak, while the poor man at home feeds his family rice and beans. He is not going to believe anything that priest says."

The Church is "the worst obstacle to religion our people face," he said.

From the year of its coming to the Indies the Church was a "Church of the Conquerors." It was "imposed" on Borinquén by the Europeans, as Bishop Autulio Parrilla Bonilla had said, as "an instrument of the Conquest"; the cross had not followed the sword, but the sword had followed the cross. Every *entrada* of the Conquistadors was accompanied, and often was led, by the priests, from the voyages of Columbus onward.

One of the first of the clergy to come to the Indies was the monk Fray Ramón Pane, who sailed with Columbus on the second voyage. On the island of Española (Santo Domingo) he settled to convert the "pagan," but admittedly intensely religious, Indians. In doing so, "the poor anchorite," as the monk called himself, opened a wound in the bond between the Church and the people which has never wholly been healed.

The monk built a chapel in the village of Guarionex, the chieftain who later went to Borinquén to become a leader of the natives in their war against the Spaniards. One day, when the chapel was unguarded, Guarionex sent six tribesmen to steal the "sacred images," the crucifixes of Christ and the statues of the saints. Ramón himself described what happened in this earliest of religious conflicts between the European and American religions:

"After leaving the chapel the men threw the images on the ground, heaping earth on them, and pissed on top, saying, 'Now will you yield good and abundant fruit'; they offered this insult because they had buried the images in a tilled field . . . of yams. . . . Several days later the owner of the field went to dig up some yams, and in the place where the images had been buried two or three yams had grown together in the shape of a cross."

Guarionex's mother thought it to be a sign. Her son led the people in revolt against the Church.

Not all of the Indians were as rebellious as Guarionex. Some "became Christians merely by being taught that there was a God," the monk wrote. But some "afterward mock what was taught them:

such require the use of force and punishment," Fray Ramón Pane said in 1496.

The Church had enormous secular power, not only over the Spanish government but over the lives of the Indians. In the Indies that power was visible in the personal possessions of the Spanish priests—gold, slaves, and women. Father de las Casas, the "protector of the Indians," himself had been the owner of slaves. And the brilliant Father Bernal Díaz, the chronicler of Cortéz's conquests, was the "Keeper of the Branding Iron" that was sanctified and kept to burn the initials and coats of arms of the Conquistadors into the flesh of their slaves.

Lesser priests than these were even more lustful for conquests. In Peru "the monasteries are transformed into public brothels," wrote Ulloa and Jorge Juan in their journals of life after the Conquest. Priests who were "living in constant concubinage [with Indian girls] is so common," they noted, that it was "a point of honor." The Bishop of Cuba proudly brought his Indian mistress with him during the Conquest of Mexico. Even the Mass of the Ordaining of the Priests became an orgy; there was "no abominable act left uncommitted, no indecency not indulged in" by the novitiates. The reputation of the Spanish priests was to be a curse upon the Church for hundreds of years. On the island, at the turn of the century, a Church layman said of the Spanish clergy: "We dare not send our daughters to confession."

"Devotion was lined with lechery," wrote historian Salvador de Madariaga. "For Spain had grown in hypocrisy and was rotting with it." As the Bishop of Puerto Rico, the scholarly Bernardo de Balbuena, had written of the Spaniards' greed on the island during the seventeenth century:

> Wrench from this giant, Greed, his sway over men,
> And you will turn to chaos and distraction
> The order that frames his law. . . .

"Theology was abandoned," said de Madariaga, "in favor of economics. The feeling of fraternity in Christ yielded to an idea of order and sense in society." And that meant the preservation of the colonial wealth of the Spanish Empire became the mission of the clergy.

Spain's reign over the clergy tightened as its empire crumbled. In the nineteenth century on the island, "the proportion of native-born clergy with respect to the total population decreased," said the Jesuit Father Fernándo Picó, and the Church underwent an "intensive process of hispanization." The chasm between the Church and the people widened; for more than ever it was the "House of the Foreigners."

One hundred years later, after the Spanish had gone, the foreign-born clergy remained. "We have over seven hundred priests here, but I don't believe there are more than fifty Puerto Rican priests," said Bishop Parrilla in 1972. "We have Dutch. We have Americans. We have Cubans. We have Spaniards. Historically, we have not had the freedom for the free development of a Puerto Rican Catholicism. In the past we, the Church, had tried to impose a religious colonialism, to impose European ways of being a Catholic." By this, the Church had "alienated itself from the realities of people's religion."

"The Bishops of Puerto Rico are alienated from the people," the Bishop said. He thought this might be due to the type of seminary training for the priesthood. "Our formation [of priests] is in abstractions in a very alienated way, to such an extent that we are unable to make a judgment of reality," he said. But in the Church the main fault lies not in the teaching methods of the Seminary, but in "the mentality of the colonized." The island had been a colony for so long it was "a victim country." So was the Church. His friends the bishops did not wish to see the colonial state of their religion because they were frightened. "They are frightened because for centuries we have been taught to be frightened. What is wrong with the bishops is wrong with the priests, and is wrong with the people—the colonial mentality. See, they are afraid!"

Parrilla leaned forward. "Have you read Fanon?" he asked.

Autulio Parrilla Bonilla was a new sort of priest. He was "so Puerto Rican that he made a *jíbaro* look like a foreigner," said a fellow priest. He was born in a poor rural village, the son of spiritualists. He had become a Catholic late in life, while serving in the U.S. Army, and later still had become a Jesuit. "I was a Socialist before I became a Jesuit. So now I'm both," he said casually. A rugged man, his brusque manner hid a pained compassion. Of commanding intelligence, he had been a bishop for relatively few years, but had already been Chaplain of the National Guard, director of Social Action and of the island's major seminary for priests. His fellow bishops refused to assign him a diocese, for he advocated that the Church give its properties to the people, to be run as a cooperative "in the name of Christ."

Lately he had been accused of having "radical" ideas. "Christianity is more radical than all ideologies," the Bishop replied, "because it is grounded in love."

The *jíbaro*'s individualism was in him. He had taken "many controversial positions," commented the *National Catholic Reporter:* he was a "pacifist," he "supported the movement [for] Puerto Rico's independence," he denounced the "colonial and capitalist system" of the United States, "and he marches for peace." The Papal Nuncio, Archbishop Antonio del Guicide, visited him to suggest he retire to the Society of Jesus and refrain from voicing his political opinions. He said no. In a few months he was visited by the Vatican's Father Ricardo Lombardi, founder of the Better World Retreat movement, who suggested that the Bishop go into voluntary exile. Curiously, Father Lombardi had himself been exiled from Rome by Pope Pius XII, and was not reinstated until Pope John XXIII had ascended the Papal throne. If the Bishop smiled is not known, but he said no. "I'm an equal to the Pope in the sense that we both are bishops," he said. "And they can't push a bishop around like that."

In his spirited words he spoke for "a new generation of Catholics." Most of all he wished for the independence of his country and his Church from the history of colonialism. He wished to see Puerto Rican Catholicism become as respected and distinctive as "Italian, German, Spanish, or French ways of being Catholic. There are many ways of being a Catholic. You can be an Indian Catholic. You can be a Puerto Rican Catholic."

And he wished to see the people bring their religiosity out of their homes, their *fiestas* in the streets, and their *jíbaro* rituals, into the Church. "In the cathedral in Mexico I have seen the Indians dancing before the Blessed Sacrament. That was an act of worship, very authentic and very cultured. There are many good things in the pagan religions that we *have* to adapt to really bring the message of Christ," he said. For if the Church did that, "with love, not manipulation," it might bridge the chasm that had separated it from the people of Borinquén for more than four hundred years.

"So let the people breathe and act and demonstrate the way they love God the way they want," said the Bishop Autulio Parrilla Bonilla.

"Religiosity is more common outside the church," wrote Kal Wagenheim. He spoke of an old ritual known as a *rogativa.* The *rogativa* was a ceremony held in an open field, or on a road, in which a whole village gathered to sing and dance and pray. It was a combination of a Catholic processional and an ancient Indian ceremonial. During one dry spell in 1928, the people of a rural *barrio* held a *rogativa* for the rain. Not two weeks later the hurricane San Felipe struck the village. An old man told Wagenheim: "They haven't celebrated a *rogativa* there since."

The most popular Church services were still the more ceremonial ones. People flocked to a pageant or a parade for their patron saint; it was the occasion for a *fiesta* that might last for several days. But few attended an ordinary morning mass. Fewer still would go to communion or confession.

In Borinquén of old the gods of the Indians had been worshiped in the open and in communal ceremonies. Where else would one pray to the gods of the wind, the sun, the fire, and the water? So today the people gathered by the thousands to pray on the beach where the airplane of the baseball hero Roberto Clemente had crashed into the sea, that "the water give back his body," as one man said.

Life and death were not lived in a church. So why celebrate them there? The people were too religious to be Sunday worshipers.

The homes of the religious in many countries had shrines. But in

Borinquén almost everyone's home *was* a shrine. The crucifixes, statues of the Virgin, figurines of the saints in plaster or candle wax, and images of Christ adorned the walls of living rooms and bedrooms in village *bohíos,* or suburban condominiums, or tenement apartments. That was the way it had always been. In the old days the *cemis,* or saintlike idols of the Indians, had been kept in the *bohíos.* Now the *cemis* were saints. But the traditions of very personal prayer between the worshiper and his God protector still continued. The people did not have to go to church to worship their Gods when they brought the Gods home with them.

In Utuado, Father Dimas Young complained: "Let me give an example. We have one class in our church elementary school with thirty-nine children. But only three go to mass. Their parents hardly come at all. When they do come they pray to the statues.

"Our church had five statues of the Virgin! Five!" the priest exclaimed. "I told the people there was one Mother of God. Not five! When we remodeled the church I had the statues moved to the rear of the church. And I told the people that the mass came first. Not the statues. But they do still come to church and pray to the statues and they do not stay for the mass!"

Father Young thought the adoration of the statues was uncomfortably similar to the "pagan customs" of the Indians. And that disturbed him. His parishioners "say they all are Catholics," but he wondered what kind of Catholics they were. "They may be Catholics by culture," the priest said. But they were not "Catholics by religion" as he knew it.

"I don't think they know what Catholicism is, or what Christianity is," he said. "They love God. But not the Church."

In the village of Loíza Aldea the priest had angrily cursed the people as "Pagan!" The Fiesta de Santiago, renowned throughout the island for its profound and frightening religious symbolism, was just "an excuse to drink and dance and have a good time," said the priest. "To be a real Catholic one must attend the mass. But most of them don't, and even fewer go to confession," he said. His was the eternal lament of missionaries since the Conquest began.

"Loízans are half-Christian, half-pagan," he said in disgust.

Agreeing that the Indian religion had been disguised as Catholic ritual, Father David Garcia, pastor of St. Mark's in New York, believed it was a sign of strength, not of weakness. "In Puerto Rico there is a very pronounced influence of the Borinqueño Indians in religion. The gods of the Indians have been maintained in Catholic disguises. And the saints in the churches do not represent the saints in the European tradition, but as the Indian gods. That is why people pray to the statues of the saints the way they do. And that has continued unto the present day."

Some dubbed this the "Creole Catholicism" of the Puerto Ricans. In reshaping the rituals of European Catholicism to fit their Indian and *jíbaro* beliefs and ceremonies, the islanders had literally taken religion out of the Church, as had the Pueblo Indians of the Southwest; they had brought it home to be used to satisfy their spiritual and practical needs and desires.

The church on the plaza might dominate the town. But in the religious life of the people its influence was less imposing. In politics after nearly five centuries the power of the church was embarrassingly slight. Led by Bishop Davis, a Norte Americano, in 1960, the Bishops of Puerto Rico had sought to defeat the government of Muñoz Marín by circulating a pastoral letter that threatened to excommunicate any Catholic who voted for the Populares Governor, a nonchurchgoer. Said the Bishops: "The philosophy of the Popular party is anti-Church and anti-Catholic, and is based on heresy." Muñoz Marín, in the elections, nonetheless won overwhelmingly with the vote of 68 percent of his "heretical" Catholic countrymen. Evidently the threat of excommunication was not too threatening to Catholics who rarely attended church anyway to worship God, supplicate to Christ, or adore the Virgin, when they could be just as religious at home.

The decline of the church, in the European and American sense, as a center of religion, caused an Army chaplain who visited the island after its invasion by the United States in 1898 to quip: "Puerto Rico is a Catholic country without a religion." His idea of religion, defined by churchgoing, was of little help in judging the "unchurched" gods of the island. In any event, his words of contempt were to be repeated often by priests when the Puerto Rican immigrants began to bring their "Creole Catholicism" of the island to the mainland.

Catholics in the United States looked upon their co-religionists from the island as "superstitious" and "not really Catholic." The Irish and German priests were particularly "scandalized," a Catholic writer said, by the Puerto Ricans' "consensual marriages." Curiously, when the Puerto Ricans arrived on the mainland, the American Church decided to end the practice of establishing "national parishes," as had been done for immigrant groups of Catholics who had arrived before them. In the "Catholic establishment" the islanders had no power, no churches of their own, no "national parishes," few, if any, priests, and not one bishop. On the island there had been one priest for every 7,000 Catholics, compared to one priest for every 750 Catholics in the New York Archdiocese. Even if only Puerto Rican priests were considered there was one for every 56,000 islanders. But, in New York City in 1960, there was one lonely Puerto Rican priest for the entire population of nearly 750,000.

Once again the Church was "the Church of the Conquerors," and the new priests were "foreigners." If there was only one Puerto Rican priest in the forty-two Spanish-speaking Catholic parishes in New York, in Chicago there was none at all.

Nonetheless, there were priests who earned the love of the *barrios* by their devotions. There was Monsignor Fox in El Barrio of New York, and there was Father John Ring in the *barrio* of Chicago.

In that conservative Archdiocese John Ring was thought of as one of the "heretic" priests. He had been parish priest to a street gang that called themselves the Young Lords long before they were known anywhere but on the streets of Chicago. And he had translated the works of Father Camillo Torres, the martyred Jesuit, who had died in the jungles of Colombia in a guerrilla army of peasants. "If he were not a priest I would say he was a Communist," said a fellow priest of Father Ring, "but since he is a priest I can only say that the Church is catholic indeed in who it ordains into the priesthood in these strange times."

Someone said he looked like an All-American boy. He smiled. "If you really mean All-American then you have to include the Latin Americans, the Central Americans, the Caribbeans, and, of course, the Puerto Ricans. They are all," he said, "Americans."

The handsome, tall, athletic young priest wore no collar. He had the look of a man who did not like to be fettered by stereotypes. In a crowd of Puerto Ricans his slouch, like an off-duty baseball player's, seemed more pronounced, as though he was unconsciously uncomfortable being the tallest one in the room. One young girl who knew him in the *barrio* said, "I think Father Ring is confused enough about his identity to be one of us."

As an inexperienced priest, he recalled, he had been assigned to a suburban parish church. Religion in the suburbs had not been "too demanding," he said, but it was not what he thought of as his "pastoral mission." He was reassigned to a parish in the inner city, the sociological pseudonym for the slums. Some of the original Young Lords were in the parish youth group. "I didn't know who they were. I didn't even know they were Puerto Ricans until I met them," he said. "When I discovered that my parishioners were speaking Spanish I decided to learn Spanish. So I could talk to them. When I could understand them I discovered they were wonderful people.

"If the Church and the people could talk the same language," Father Ring said, laughing, "it might help."

He became so elated by their "joyful religion" that he went to live on the island for a year, to discover the source of their "humanistic faith." He lived with Bishop Parrilla, who became his teacher and his "brother" and his friend.

And the Bishop taught him the meaning of Puerto Rican Catholicism as he knew it. "I have great faith in the Church," the Bishop would say. "By the Church I mean not the Church in the sense of a sect, but in the sense of love. My idea of the Church is that of love between brothers. By loving man you necessarily love God. And I believe that because I believe in the body of Christ and in the people of God."

Father Ring did not have the faith of the Bishop. He was younger and more cynical. On returning to Chicago he became "director of sorrows" at the Archdiocese's Latin Center, on South Wabash Avenue, "a test of anyone's faith." But he was resigning, he said, so that a Chicano or a Puerto Rican could become director. "Isn't it time," he said, "that the people of the *barrios* run their own Church agencies and their own Church?"

"Would a Puerto Rican priest be replacing you?" he was asked.

"No," he said.

"But why not?"

"There aren't any Puerto Rican priests in Chicago."

"None at all?"

"There was one. He left."

"Left Chicago?"

"No, he left the cloth."

"Isn't there a single Puerto Rican priest in the entire city?"

"No."

Suddenly he looked older. He frowned and his young face became lined.

"Let me put it this way," the young priest said. "The problem is: can a priest stay in the Church and still remain a Catholic? Or, to put it another way: can a Catholic stay in the Church, and still remain . . . a priest?"

The Spirits

In the old tenement on Third Street there lived a witch who dyed her hair orange.

She was not old, nor young, not beautiful, nor ugly. She looked like an ordinary warm and buxom housewife in her middle forties. But her neighbors knew of her witchcraft and respected her. On the streets when people met her they would not talk to her, and when she talked to them they would lower their eyes before replying. She was known to possess *el mal del ojo,* the evil eye.

One day a trembling young woman who lived in the tenement of the witch went to a neighborhood center on Fourth Street and whispered this story: *La bruja,* the witch, had cast a spell on the tenement and all those in it. Every week mysterious fires burned in the hallways. Every week the fire engines came to put out the fires. But one day the fires would burn up the building. And the young woman was frightened for the life of her children.

Couldn't someone help us! the young woman pleaded. By evicting the witch and her evil spirits!

The social workers were amused but dared not smile. So they promised to phone the proper municipal agency that handles these matters. If there was a Department of Evil Spirits in City Hall, they said, laughing, afterward.

An investigator from the proper municipal agency did come to inspect the tenement, in due time. The tenement ought to be condemned, he reported. The fire escapes were unsafe. The hallways were deathtraps. Someone *had* been setting fires in the building. If he encountered any evil spirits he did not report them; that was not his job. He recommended that all of the families be moved to one of those once-palatial hotels which had degenerated into havens for whores and addicts, where the city fathers liked to house mothers on welfare and their children. In spite of the fears and protests of the tenants, all the families were ordered to move to such a hotel. Even the witch was told she had to move, for she too was on welfare.

Not long after the families and the witch were moved into the hotel it caught fire. Some tenants were badly burned. It was said that *la bruja* was angered when the city officials ordered her to move from her home. Her evil spirits had probably set the fire. The social workers no longer laughed.

"A spirit woman has power," one said, "if it is only power over the minds of the people."

The *espiritista,* or spirit woman, knew the good as well as evil spirits. She could call on them to cure as well as punish. On the island the *curioso,* sometimes called a *santero* in the city *barrios,* would be consulted for remedies for the ills of the heart and mind, as well as the body. *Espiritismo* was especially potent in curing the maladies of love. And this alone made a spirit woman a respected, and feared, member of the *barrio*. She was treated with the ambivalence that people sometimes treated a psychiatrist.

Spirit worship was not simply a matter of belief. The medicinal herbs and oils the believers bought had been used for thousands of years. In the prayers, signs, and aromas that were used to influence the spirits the history of humanity could be retold, from Biblical days and before. After consulting a spirit woman the sufferer went to a *botánica*—a botanical pharmacy, though that did not describe it at all—to buy a magical potion, a medicinal herb, an incantation, a holy candle, or a mystic oil or amulet, whose origin may have predated Moses.

The "medicines" of spiritism were practical and purposeful. If the rituals of mysticism did not overwhelm the doubts of the nonbeliever, the names of the potions promised tempting and practical cures: *Vente Comingo* (Come with Me), *Yo Puedo, Tu No* (I Can, You Can't) *Abre Paso* (Make Way), *Estate Quieto* (Keep Quiet). And the spiritual sprays with English names and aims, the Blessed Spray, the Double Fast Luck Spray, the Gamblers Spray, and the Love Spray, created an aromatic mist at the push of a button and simulated the spirits with a scientific speed.

In the ghettos, where poverty was a way of life, the physical world necessitated spirits who alone could lift its burdens. Who else could? The spirits, and spirit women, had been the healers and lawyers of the ghettos for generations, dispensing good fortune and punishment. The doctors prescribed pills and the social workers offered charity, but neither knew how to cure the psyche or soothe a poor man's soul; for these were matters of *espíritu,* the spirit.

The old Jews of the ghetto had their own spirits and curers. In his boyhood, not far from Third Street, one Yiddish writer remembered when his mother had called a "speaker woman" or "witch doctor" to cure him of the trauma and blood poisoning caused by a Fourth of

July firecracker that had torn a hole in his shoulder. The family doctor had failed to cure him of his nightmares. So a "speaker woman" was summoned. His mother assured him: "She knows more than many doctors." But, as an "American boy," he was ashamed, he said. "This foreign hocus-pocus did not appeal to me."

Tanti beovati!
Tanti sabatanu!
Tanti Keeliati!
Tanti lamachtanu!

An old woman dressed in rags—"poorly as any synagogue beggar"—the "speaker woman" spoke in tongues. That is, she spoke in the voices of the spirits. Her way of curing would today be called Yiddish voodoo. Her religion would be dismissed as that of "semi-illiterate peasants." But in the ghetto she was the "magic maker," "Baba Sima, the witch doctor."

Praying for the boy's spirit, she evoked the ancient spirits that were remarkably like those a spirit woman of the *barrio* might have called upon, almost a century later, with prayer: "To him, and to her, and to us, and to it! The serpent, and the fire, and the ocean, and the sun! God is Jehovah, and Jehovah is God! *Rushyat! Cum! Tum! Sum!"*

The sick boy was then given a potion made of "horse droppings gathered in the street, mixed with a spider's web, honey, grits, thyme, my own urine and pepper." Every day the potion was smeared on his forehead. He was told to go to the East River. If there was a moon, he was to drink a glass of river water. And then he was to throw the glass into the river, saying, "Cum! Tum! Sum!"

So "I was cured," he said. His nightmares ended. His wounds healed. His spirit was at peace. "Baba Sima, the witch doctor! It was she who cured me."

On the Lower East Side, "there were many such old women," the Jewish writer recalled. "They were held in great respect. The East Side worshiped doctors, but in nervous cases, or in mishaps of personal life," the "speaker woman" was often called. In the mysteries of love, and of sex, the superhuman force of the spirit was all that might help. "Lovers sought philters of the old Babas to win a victory over a rival in love. Deserted wives paid these women money to model little wax figures of their wandering husbands, and tortured them until the false one returned." In the *botánicas* in the *barrio* similar little wax figures still could be bought, though they had Spanish, not Yiddish, names.

The old *babas* of those Jewish ghettos and the spirit women of the Puerto Rican *barrios* were spiritual sisters. And yet they came from different worlds, and they spoke in different tongues.

Where then did the spirits of the *barrio* come from? The fecundity of the island bore them.

In the early 1600s the genius of Shakespeare had perceived the tropic abundance of the spirits who inhabited the islands of the Caribbean. Caliban, his imaginary native in *The Tempest,* thought these spirits were everywhere on the island. He thought the Europeans were spirits, too, at first. In seeking to explain his spiritual world to the rational men of the Renaissance, Caliban told them:

> Be not afeared. The isle is full of noises,
> Sounds and sweet airs that give delight and hurt not.
> Sometimes a thousand twangling instruments
> Will hum about mine ears; and sometimes voices. . . .

The sweet sounds were "dreams," Caliban said. But to the Europeans they were nothing but music, or "music for nothing."

On Borinquén the spirits were everywhere. They rose from the mist of the rivers, blew in from the sea on the *juracán* winds. They sang in the voices of the *coquís,* the tiny tropical frogs in the hills. They hid in the dreams that haunted suburbanites in the cities. And in the evenings they walked the ancient streets of Old San Juan so visibly that one could almost see the spirits in the moody air where El Morro brooded by the harbor. All of these beliefs were so ancient that people who believed them did not know where they had come from or when they had begun. It was merely known that it was so.

In the night these spirits of the island came to life. So the Indians of Borinquén had believed. They believed it still.

In death, the dead did not die. The spirit became a *jipia.* It went to live in a secluded region of the island known as *coaibay,* a lovely and green valley. The *jipia* lived there sensually; for the Indians believed the body and soul were one, so the *jipia* was both spiritual and sensual. By day the spirits of the dead slept. At night they awoke. They roamed the island "eating wild fruit and visiting living relatives." When the *jipia* came to visit it was considered friendly to leave fruit on the table for it to eat. In the suburbs of San Juan and in the *barrios* of New York there were people who still did this, though the offering of fruit was often plastic. Still, it was good to be friendly to a *jipia,* for if insulted it might haunt the dreams of the living.

The Indian belief had survived in strange ways. People who believed in these spirits most often did not know why they did, or where their belief had come from.

Spirits had "existed long ago, but not nowadays," said some believers. In saying this they were remembering religions they had forgotten or never known. The reincarnation of tribal memories of the Borinquén Indians and African slaves was visible on the candles and amulets sold in the *botánicas,* where the face or name of an Indian or African was an indication of healing power. Few who believed this knew why it was so.

"In ancient days, Indians used herbs in Spiritual ceremonies," read the label on an "Indian Spirit" spray can—for quick action—of the "Jinx Removing Incense." The sweet spray of "nine Indian Herb Oils" was selected for "mystic importance" in the bathing of "People [who] believe they are Jinx, or Evil Eye. Use Spray with Conviction." The prayer candles offered to the "Indian Spirit" were no less potent, with the promise of strength, symbolized by a tomahawk representing a "medicine man," by "good fortune" represented by an Indian arrow, and by "success" represented by a bag of money. Under these signs were the words "Concentrate on the Indian," and "Let Us Pray." The Indian symbols had been combined with the rituals of Catholicism to bring the believer the rewards of American materialism.

One of the most popular—and powerful—of the *botánicas'*

prayers were the beads for "The Prayer of the Seven African Powers." It was recited to the glass beads of a rosary, with a prayer that began, "In the Name of the Almighty Jesus Christ," and "In the Name of the Father, Son and Holy Ghost," but that ended in the name of the "African Saints":

> Listen, Chango!
> I Call You, Ochun!
> Help Me, Yemala!
> Look Upon Me With Grateful Eyes, Obatala!
> Come To Me, Ogun!
> Be Good To Me, Orula!
> Intercede For Me, Elequa!
> All Seven African Powers!
> Amen!

The supplicant was then told to "Make the Sign of the Cross." In the heart of each glass bead of the "Seven African Powers" was a depiction of Christ's crucifixion.

Spiritism was ecumenical. In the Indians' belief that all living things had spirits, in the sea, the sky, and the earth, and that all things were living, spiritism by its nature had to be ecumenical. There was an amulet of "The Egyptian Scarab" that evoked "the creative force of the Sun, the Sun God or Sun Power." There was the "Goddess of Love and Beauty" in the "Seal of Venus." There was the talisman of "The Prayer to the Star of David, with Mazzuzah," for a "Happy Home." There was the "Star of David" in the center of which was the "Eye of the Lord." There was the "Four Leaf Clover" in the center of which was an "Egyptian Scarab." And there were amulets and prayers to all the Christian saints, including Joan of Arc: "I Call on Thee to do Justice for Me."

Of all the sacred amulets of spiritism one of the strangest was the "MahaRajah's Mascot." It had the face of a Borinquén Indian god, encircled by two snakes, from which three naked legs emerged in the shape of a three-legged swastika. The crux of the design was the face set in the groin of the legs. One of the feet pointed to "Protection," one to a "New Home," and one to a "Cadillac"; while the face was the symbol of "Romance." In buying the amulet the wearer was told, "Carry this 'MASCOT' with you at all times, even in the tub. Then put it under your pillow at night. Keep it for nine days, then throw it into the River water, and make a wish." Curiously, the Borinquén Indians had worshiped the god of the rivers as a god of fertility and abundance.

Some of these mystical charms were refreshingly practical and prosaic. The "Love Soap" came with the advice that the user was to wash her, or his, lover with it. Once bathed, the lover ought to respond more lovingly to loving. "Try your lover with it," said the instructions, and "true happiness could be yours."

Botánicas offered to believers a wide variety of useful prayers, as well, for a penny or two. One was the "Prayer to the Worker" that beseeched "Joseph, working man, come with me when I obtain my bread with the sweat of my brow," and asked the Three Angels of Jesus to "talk for me when I go to solicit"—the salesperson's dream. The "Prayer for Peace in the Home" was as commonplace, imploring, "Lord, I want peace as much as bread in my home"; while the "Prayer to the Intranquil Spirit" cursed the unfaithful lover, or wayward husband: "Let him not rest in peace, either seated, standing or sleeping," and "Neither a divorcee or a married woman or a widow will love him." The rejected lover cried, "Nobody calls you. I call you. Nobody wants you. I want you. Nobody needs you. I need you," conjuring the lover with prayer and magic, "You are to run after me, as the living run after the cross."

In the arts of conjuring and sorcery and witchcraft there were hundreds of prayers, chants, candles, amulets, and secret powders. "We sell everything that's related to witchcraft," said Miguel Rivera, the owner of a prominent island *botánica.* His boast of commercial witchery was as true of every *botánica.* Of the prayers to the "Cabalistic Circle" the "Revocation to Saint Michael Archangel" was typical, with its curse, "Come sorcery and corruption and revoke yourself in my body. Let my enemies suffer as Jesus suffered upon the Cross."

So the devil was summoned to invoke the sacrifices of Christ upon one's enemies. These spirits of evil, like the spirits of love, seemed to be all too human.

All of this, at times, was too spiritual and exotic to be a "real" religion, to the churchmen and scientists (social) from the north. " 'Spiritualism' is a religion which is more akin to an occult science like astrology," wrote Glazer and Moynihan, in *Beyond the Melting Pot;* "to a few Puerto Ricans [it was] a religion," they reluctantly admitted. Even so loving an *aficionado* of the Puerto Rican scene as Kal Wagenheim, in his *Puerto Rico: A Profile,* voiced the commonly held belief of outsiders that it was merely "in some remote villages [that] semi-illiterate peasants harbor beliefs in witches and spirits," and only "among the uneducated" was there fear of *el mal del ojo,* the evil eye. Curiously, in the same book, he approvingly quoted Nathan Leopold's work that had concluded that though spiritism had its roots in the beliefs of the *jíbaros* it had "spread to the learned professions [where] many doctors, lawyers and professors are firm believers" in the spirits.

The belief in Indian "spirits" and African "saints" was a modern corruption of the Borinquén religion, some thought. Ricardo Alegría, director of the Institute of Puerto Rican Culture, believed that many of the rituals of Haitian voodoo had been adapted by the *"botánica* culture," especially in the *barrios* of New York. On the Lower East Side, the pastor of St. Mark's in the Bowery, Father David Garcia, disagreed: "In the *barrio* we do not have a mixture of Haitian and Dominican voodoo. We have a contemporary and urban Indian religion.

"Our people have taken the religion of the island, the Indians' gods and ceremonies, and have brought them into the *botánicas* and store-front churches," the Episcopal priest said. "If you look behind the Catholic rituals and Pentecostal phenomenon and magic of spiritism and compare these things to some of the Borinquén Indians' beliefs and ceremonies that existed on the island it all seems very Indian. That is what it is. It is not voodoo. It is not Christianity. It is not European. It is Indian."

Up in the hills of the island, in Utuado, the local Catholic priest

Father Dimas Young talked of spiritism as he had experienced it in his church. "Spiritism thrives," he said, "in the hills. But it thrives in the Church, too. It is closely related to Catholicism." In his Catholic church the belief had turned the Holy Water into an Indian "medicine." "At first, I was surprised to see people drink the Holy Water in church. They would drink it from the font. They washed the afflicted parts of their bodies with it, as though it was a medicine. Some women, I was told, bathed their private parts with Holy Water before making love, to bless the conception. But I did not believe that! I thought, how primitive. And then I remembered that my mother, who was German-Irish in ancestry, would sprinkle Holy Water around our house. So I thought, maybe they know more about Holy Water than I do."

Religion was "very humanistic" to the people, the priest thought. It was as real to them as "the spirits they talked to." These spirits were the embodiment of life, so that every human body possessed, and was possessed by, "a spiritual reality."

When he came to the island he had been assigned to a parish church in Río Piedras, the home of the University of Puerto Rico. He had a "real shock" there, he recalled:

"One day a young girl came to me in the church. She had her beautiful long hair in her hand. Her mother had cut it all off, so that the girl was bald. It was her sacrifice for some evil she felt she had done. She begged me to place her hair on the altar. I didn't know what to do. I had been in Puerto Rico for only a few months and had never seen anything like that before in a Catholic church. My housekeeper in the rectory told me to take the hair. Puerto Rican women often promised to God to cut off their hair in penance, she said. But at the time I thought: My God, the Indians used to do that! At the time I was shocked, but I know now that the young girl's devotion to spiritism was very religious. She was truly penitent. She had offered a part of herself to God.

"If that was not a religious act, deeply religious, what is?" the priest asked.

In La Casa de las Almas, the House of the Soul, on Antonsanti

Street in Santurce, San Juan, the islanders' intimate way of appealing to the spirits had been institutionalized as an intellectual philosophy and religious ideology. The bodily reincarnation of the soul within a spiritual reality beyond the known reality of science was the quest of the spiritualists of La Casa. It was supported by wealthy benefactors and businessmen, such as Luis Rodríguez, the builder of the first condominium in San Juan.

One group of spiritualists in La Casa was led by Vincenti Geigel Polanco, a lawyer in his sixties. A man of eminence, he had been a founder of the Popular Democratic party, Governor Muñoz Marín's floor leader in the Senate, a former university teacher, and Attorney General of the Commonwealth. He had been a believer in spiritism for a quarter of a century. In his legalistic mind he defined "the philosophy of spiritism" in four parts, the most important being the belief that "man is basically a spirit with eternal life"; his spirit never died, as the Borinquén Indians had taught. The human being, for all its self-conceit, was merely one part of the earth and the universe. If man could lay aside his petty self-conceit, and live in peace with life, he might achieve *serenidad,* the serenity that every Puerto Rican believed was "the good life."

Geigel had conducted séances where mediums talked to the spirits. The urban spiritualist preferred the word "medium" to "spirit woman," which was too identified with the *jíbaros* of the hills. Séances were to him after all merely experiments in extrasensory perception, that was now being "recognized scientifically." There were many levels of reality, and man knew only a few.

"We are, above all, spirit." So "we must not be possessed by 'things' since our reason for being is in the process of perfection, our goal being eternity," said the former Attorney General of the Commonwealth.

Ramón Fernández Marina looked upon spiritism from a quite different perspective. He was not a believer but he believed in its value. As the clinical director of the Puerto Rican Institute of Psychiatry, Dr. Fernández observed: "Man's nervous system is constantly evolving to find ways to relate to the changes of his environment, which is also termed 'progress.' Spiritualism for some people is an explanatory release. That is, while some may blame their ills and despairs on another person, in spiritualism it is projected to invisible spirits . . . to the supernatural. In this way, spiritualism serves a distinct emotional purpose. Religion has a definite function in our society. It offers a deep-rooted psychological security which man needs. Spiritualism adds to religion a pseudo-scientific explanation of miraculous occurrences which religion cannot explain." Unlike "churched religions" he thought spiritism was more democratic, in that "it gives its adherents a sense of direct participation." He did not say "more Indian."

"Spiritualism serves the population, the upper middle class as well as the poor, as a common defense against anxiety and guilt" when life is beyond their control, Dr. Fernández said.

But the force and strength of spiritism paled with intellectual explanation. It was an earthy religion, paradoxical as that may have seemed. The spirit became part of the body of the believer. There was nothing of the flesh that was not of the spirit as well.

Lovers whose passion had been sterile could buy fertility candles. The candles, in the shape of naked lovers, were often lit by the bedside during lovemaking. By lighting these candles the lovers evoked the spirits, and gods, of fertility. Though they may not have chemically affected the ovum or sperm, when the candles in the shape of a comely black woman and a handsome black man burned by the bed of the lovers their effect was surely to heighten the romantic reality of their passion. The vision of a flame igniting the wax breast of the woman, or the fire burning in the wax groin of the man, was an intensely spiritual and sensual experience.

In the *botánicas* every desire and need of the body could be met. The spirits were human.

The Masses of St. Mark's

In this Vault lies buried
PETRUS STUYVESANT
late Captain General and Governor
in Chief of Amsterdam
in New Netherland now called
New York
and the Dutch West India
Islands, died Feb AD 1672
aged 80 years

The historic tomb of the city's first immigrant governor was dug into the old stone wall of the church. On the vestry door nearby was a newer inscription:

VIVA PUERTO RICO LIBRE

In the courtyard of the church of St. Mark's in the Bowery, on Second Avenue, lay the large flat stones that covered the burial vaults of some of the city's most aristocratic families. On the gravestones were carved the names of the Beekmans, Livingstons, Ingersolls, Vandenheuvels, Goelets, Winthrops, Grahams, Fishes, Barclays, Babcocks, Bibbys, and Bells. Then there was the grandiloquent slab "Erected by the Veterans of the War of 1812" to the memory of Daniel D. Tompkins, who died in 1825—the former Governor of New York and Vice President of the United States, for whom the battleground of the Lower East Side *barrio,* Tompkins Square, was named.

On a funerary statue a ghetto youth had drawn a hammer and sickle, in Magic Marker red ink, beneath a motto not unknown to the dead of the American Revolution:

POWER TO THE PEOPLE!

It was an old gray church. One of the oldest houses of worship in the city, St. Mark's had been built by the first American revolutionaries. The cornerstone was laid on the 25th of April, 1725, when the ghetto of the Lower East Side was the upper northern suburb of New York, where English gentlemen built their country estates and stately manor houses. Seven years before the birth of George Washington the building had been begun, but the church was not consecrated until May 9, 1779, when the American Revolution had been won. The Tories had by then fled the city. So its first parishioners were the triumphant revolutionaries.

And now the descendants of the revolutionaries had become Tories. On Tenth Street a few of the old aristocratic townhouses remained. But they were the haunts of the sons and daughters of immigrants who had lost their own revolutions. The hallowed church and the graves of its builders, some of them the founding families of the country, were surrounded by the tenements of the *barrio*. At night the winos and drug addicts were seen in the shadowy graveyard, pissing on the tombstones.

St. Mark's was the sanctuary of a new revolution. The church was the meeting place for the Puerto Rican Revolutionary Workers, the Committee to Defend Carlos Feliciano, the street gang known as the Ghetto Brothers, and the first Congress of the Puerto Rican Socialist party. Once, the Black Panthers had gathered in the vestry. And once a week the poetic remnants of the long-haired street people, the Yippies, Hippies, and Motherfuckers, gathered where the altar had been, to read poetry to one another.

"Our parish reaps the rejects of society," said the parish priest, Father David Garcia. "Here we are the church of the derelicts of the street, the winos of the alleyways, the young drug addicts, the abandoned welfare mothers, the street gangs, the *barrio* militants, the angry university students, the political prisoners. In doing this our theology had led us into prison revolts, to peace demonstrations, to establish free clinics for the hippies and the homeless, to work with the poorest and the angriest of the *barrio*.

"In doing this," Father Garcia said, "we have learned how demonic, inhumanly demonic, life in New York is for people. Love is difficult in the streets. Not in the pulpit, but in the gutter. In the *barrio* streets love is revolutionary."

A young man who had come into the city from the *barrios* of Texas, David Garcia was seeking "the power of love." He had become an Episcopal priest to learn that power. "For us Jesus responded to the power of love and He sacrificed everything He had." Could he, David Garcia, do less? "The power of love calls men to the higher forms of Truth, Justice, Community, and Love," he said. The young priest spoke in capital letters. In his voice there was a subdued fervor that was perhaps subdued so that it would not explode. Episcopal priests, even revolutionary ones in the *barrios,* do not forget their dignity.

He believed in righteousness. A man did what he honestly believed; his father had been a dedicated career officer in the Air Force and the son was apostately devoted to his "way of love."

In the old church there were two parishes in one. When he came to St. Mark's, said Father Garcia, the old families of the descendants of the American Revolution and the poor of the *barrio* worshiped together, but they hardly spoke to one another. The church was very formal, musty and rigid with the revered traditions and familiar refrains of the Common Prayer Book. It was comforting to some to know that nothing had changed since 1779. And the vestrymen, who were all white, wished to keep it that way. Some of the Puerto Ricans and Blacks came to the young priest and said they "were not satisfied with the services on Sunday and the soft pews."

The poor parishioners demanded four of the vestry seats, a gift of $30,000 from the church fund for *barrio* work, and that the Sunday service be changed to include the words: "We are here in the name of peace and justice, and in the name of all those who have died in that quest—Malcolm X, Martin Luther King, Che, and Albizu Campos. . . ." And they demanded that the American flag be removed from inside the church. On either side of the altar they requested there be two banners, one with a black fist on a green background, and the words "FREEDOM NOW!" in Swahili, and the other, representing the liberation movements of Latin America, bearing a *machete.*

"Our congregation responded in shock and amazement," recalled Father Garcia, with a slight smile. But they met and voted that four new vestrymen and women be named and they gave a gift of $30,000 for the work of the poor Puerto Ricans and Blacks in the parish. "Some people said it would go for guns! A lot of white people left the church. They have not come back. Of course, they took their money with them." Father Garcia sighed: "But the people who stayed began to initiate a process of healing."

And then the poor parishioners began to change the church. The altar was moved into the center of the hall. The pews were removed. Instead of the pews there were rows of aluminum folding chairs, placed in a circle around the altar. On Sundays the worshipers sat in a circle and passed bread and wine from hand unto hand. Sometimes they would stand, holding hands, as they sang the new psalms they had written themselves.

There was a "Psalm of Protest," a "Psalm of the Abandoned," a "Psalm of the Liberated," a "Psalm of the Ghetto," a "Psalm of the People," and a "Psalm of Deliverance":

Christ, deliver me
from the S.S.
from the N.K.V.D.
from the F.B.I.

Christ, deliver me
from the Councils of War.

"In the name of Jesus Christ and all of us who have suffered and fought for justice. In the name of Betances, Campos, Torres, Zapata, Bolívar, Che, Martínez, and all our brothers and sisters," the mass was rewritten to praise and exalt "PEACE!" and "POWER!" and "LOVE!"

"We do not have sermons any more. We sit about the altar and we talk about the problems of our lives," said Father Garcia.

"To quote the old platitudes, to quote the old prayer book, would not lead us anywhere. So our service was written by the people of the congregation about their real lives and their need for real salvation.

"The service says: Jesus did not come and leave. He began a battle and He lost the battle. But He established some principles we live with—to seek the Truth. And we feel the Truth is that God is not God in an abstract sense, but that He is the sense of power that is lived out in the lives of every human being, the power for Truth, Justice, Community, and Love."

Even the Order of Holy Matrimony was rewritten to offer the lovers "power" over their love. It began with the words:

"Brothers and Sisters, and all those who fight for the People: We are gathered here . . . in the midst of oppression, with the purpose of uniting in Holy Matrimony this man and this woman, so that they may become one body in the struggle for liberation. . . . Before declaring this couple man and wife, let us think about the Revolution."

In the betrothal itself the priest said to the man, "Do you take this sister as your wife, and promise to live together according to the wishes of God, that men and women shall be free? Will you remain with her until one of you dies?" The same was asked of the woman. Then the rings were given and the man and the woman said together:

> With this ring I marry you.
> With my body I will worship you.
> Everything I am and possess
> I give to you.

And then, when the Communion was given, to conclude the wedding, the entire congregation said, "Long live Free Puerto Rico!" The marriage ceremony was a requiem for more than *machismo.* It offered to the lovers "an offering of love" in "communion with the people."

"In St. Mark's we are seeking a new humanity," Father Garcia said. "We are seeking to create a society of truly human beings, that may not be possible in the present structure of society. So we have restructured our church service. We, in St. Mark's, realize that human liberation takes many forms. The mandate of the Church, for those who dare to believe, is guided by the idea that the Church has come of age. For a man to come of age is for him to realize all of his potential. So, too, the Church.

"Ours is a 'theology of the people.' When one speaks of Christianity one cannot abstract it from life, or universalize it. You have to speak of very specific human beings. So our theology is not defined by the Church's formulas for salvation, but by the human conditions in the *barrios* of the city.

"To me, the Church and organized religion have had their day. I am unsettled by the Church. As many of us in the Church are. But I believe that the Church can bring something unique to Marxism and modern materialism. Of course, that goes counter to the Marxist understanding of history based of materialism. Social science is against eternal truths. But I believe we have an absolute spirit that is both dialectical and is never ending. And that is the basic tension between the Christian position and the Marxist position. I live within that ambivalence daily. I am very much aware of that contradiction in my personal life. Every man is. All of us give it different names. But that's the spiritual crisis of our time.

"I consider myself a utopian," he said. "Some would say I am a utopian Christian. Some would say I am a utopian Marxist." He spoke the words with an equal diffidence. "Maybe they are both right."

Father Garcia thought of himself as a disciple of Jesus, of Don Pedro Albizu Campos, of the young Marx ("Not vulgar Marxism"), and of Camillo Torres, the Jesuit martyr, of whom he admiringly said: "He joined the guerrillas, not waiting for them to join him. And he offered his body for his beliefs." In the church built by the American revolutionaries of two hundred years ago, the young priest quoted the American revolutionary who died so recently, Father Camillo Torres:

"The Christian imperative now is Revolution!"

Epilogue: Father and Son

The father sat like a king in the modest living room that was the dining room and kitchen as well as a spare bedroom. He leaned back on the shabby sofa with comfort and pride. He was a thoughtful man, with a gray, wistful mustache and worldly manner. Living "for half of my life" in the United States, he had come home to the mountains of Puerto Rico, to his hometown of Utuado, to his little apartment in the beautiful tropical valley. He had "come home again."

"Life in the United States is not living," he said.

In the beginning he had worked in the fields. As a migrant laborer he had traveled the same road as many who came from the island to the farms of southern New Jersey to harvest the crops. It was all he knew how to do. Then he had worked in a factory for fifteen years. Then he had worked as a salesman. In time he had "made it." That is, he had made enough money to go home.

"When I was a boy I walked to school barefoot. Seven miles!" he remembered. "My father had a farm here in Utuado. We were poor. We were very poor. That was when I thought I had problems. But it wasn't. When I went to the United States, that was when I had problems. There is something worse for a man than being poor. This is not being respected as a man."

Felipe Rivera had come home with his family. The father looked at his son, as if to say, Have I done the right thing? And the son, who had listened quietly, nodded his head.

Danny was sixteen. He was tall for his age, a likable boy with a shy, gracious smile. He had been born on the mainland and had spent his boyhood in Trenton, New Jersey. Until he was fourteen, when his father brought him to this mountain town, the boy had never been on the island.

"Oh, at first I thought it's all right for old people. Like my father. He wants it quiet. It was too quiet," the son said, "for me."

He was worldly at fourteen, the world traveler. After all, he had come from the big city; he knew everything. But then "a strange thing happened," he said. "I learned how dumb I was.

"In this little town the kids really know their 'thing.' They know their town like it's theirs. They know what they're talking about. You know, they don't talk big, full of hot air, like we do in the States, but they know what they think. Sometimes a Puerto Rican comes here from the States and he says, 'Man! this town is dead!' And then the kids tell him what's what. Like, what is life? It's not dead just because it's not a madhouse. There's not much doing. There's enough. There's a good movie for only thirty cents. [Antonioni's *Zabriskie Point* was playing.] There's a lot of games and dances and all that. But mostly it's a good place to *live*. To be *alive*."

The son said: "Yes, I like it here. Sure, I might want to go back to the States to see my friends. But I don't want to live there any more."

A motherly woman, her hair in a gray knot, with a sweet smile but a hard mouth, said: "I thought I was a Puerto Rican, living in New York. But when I came home I was an outsider. Puerto Ricans on the island are friendly, kind, and generous. Puerto Ricans in New York steal the smile off each other's faces."

She owned a gift shop in Old San Juan for the tourists. It had been eight years since she had "come home," and she "would never go back."

"Was it the city that changed Puerto Ricans in New York?" a tourist asked her.

"No, it wasn't the city," she said. "San Juan is a city, too."

"Then what?"

She smiled and said: "It's you."

The children of Felipe Rivera had not suffered as others had. None had fallen victim to the diseases of the ghettos. His son had not become addicted to despair or narcotics. His daughter had not been seduced by the cosmetic five-and-dime culture. And he and his wife had somehow survived with their love of life and each other. Still, he had been worried.

In the United States he had been many men. But he felt none of them were himself. Now, for the first time in years, he felt that he could be himself.

"Life is more real here," the father said. "In the United States everything is not real. People are not real. You are not real. Sometimes I think that the only thing that is holding the United States together is money. Without money everything there would fall apart."

Pascual Martinez had worked at jobs no one else would do. He worked "like a horse," for four years. He became ill. Lung disease, the doctor said. When he won $100,000 in the New York State lottery he was on welfare. The State of Connecticut impounded $25,000 of his prize, in payment for the welfare money he had been given: it was only a "loan," said the state. And then the federal government demanded $41,000 for taxes. "Since they are a great government and I am a poor soul they wanted to take advantage of me," said the poor rich man. "I'd rather give all the money to the government of Puerto Rico than let it stay with the government of the United States." He suffered an attack of ulcers.

And so Pascual Martinez decided to go home to Puerto Rico. If you have to be poor, isn't it better to be poor where it is beautiful?

The mountain river behind the Riveras' house was swift and silvery, for the current was fast as fishes. It was a few steps to the small bridge which crossed the river on the way to the plaza. Up the hills, on the sides of the valley, were groves of coffee and banana trees. In the back yard of the house were *flamboyan* and breadfruit trees, blooming in a tropical rainbow of colors.

In the evening air there was a sweet smell. "That's the smell of the earth," the son said. "It took me a while to get used to it.

"Every weekend I go to visit my grandmother and my uncle on their farm. I want to get a farm like that. And then I want to marry a Puerto Rican girl from here. A girl who knows how to live. A girl who knows what life is all about.

"When I grow up I want to be the Mayor of Utuado," the son said.

"I want to be the first Puerto Rican born in the United States who came home to be the Mayor of his father's home town.

"And when I die I want to be able to have something real to leave to my kids. I want to leave them something alive."

In a way that was unique and unexplained by father and son the generation gap seemed to have been narrowed by them. Among the families of immigrants that was unusual. The family of Felipe Rivera had been immigrants twice over, going from the island to the mainland and back again; so the closeness of father and son was all the more unusual. What was it that did it?

"Puerto Rico!" the son said.

In autumnal Washington, D.C., as the leaves fell on the football fans going home to their Ivy League televised games—he was a "Cornell man" himself—a young Puerto Rican lawyer in the Office of the Commissioner disdainfully spoke of those who do not "make it" and "go home again": "If a man loses his job, he goes home. If a woman has marriage problems, she goes home. If there is family trouble, the family goes home. More than anything else, what keeps Puerto Ricans from being assimilated into the mainstream is the $50 air fare.

"Everyone would go home again," he said, "if it cost only $50."

In the house of Felipe Rivera there was silence. There was an anger in the face of the father. He spoke slowly now.

"I think in the United States people become ignorant. The way they talk about the island, what is that but ignorance? The way they treated me was out of ignorance. What else is it? If you say it is racism, what is racism but ignorance? Our own people become ignorant about themselves. Why are Americans, who are intelligent, so ignorant? And when they come to Puerto Rico to write books and studies all they express is their ignorance. They might as well not come.

"A man," the father said, "must know where his heart is."

The father and the son looked at each other, and nothing more was said. It was a look such as brothers give one another.

Sources: An Intimate Assay

To write a book about people it is helpful to go to the people one is writing about. It is not a law, but it ought to be.

For a book that begins by "researching," that is by "searching again" in other books, ought to be suspect. Is that not like attempting to look at life through a series of mirrors? No matter how precise and clear these mirrors may be they are merely reflections of one another. They are not human. So it is that these books become reflections of reflections. And it is difficult enough for us to see beneath the surfaces of our own lives with our own eyes, without diffusing what we see of life around us through the eyes of others, who often have eyes like mirrors of their minds.

So, then, the source of this book is the people. In their eyes, my eyes have sought to see. In their touch, my feelings have sought for feelings. In their words, my ears have sought to hear their hearts. To do that one cannot be an outsider.

Long ago, in the year after World War II, when I came to the island of Manhattan, to a neighborhood known as Yorkville, the people of the island of Borinquén were coming to a neighborhood to the north, known as El Barrio. For fifteen years I lived there. When the islanders in their exile began to move to new islands in the city of their creation, I too moved, for reasons of my own. After a few years on the edge of the *barrio* of the Upper West Side, my family lived for four years in the heart of the *barrio* of the Lower East Side, near Avenue D and the river. Then, for two years, as this book was being written, we lived on the anguished and dulled edges of the *barrios* of Brooklyn, exiled from my home as were my neighbors, journeying with them on their pilgrimages to the "Blessed Isle" of Puerto Rico, seeking that nostalgia that refused to become a memory.

The sorrow I knew, in being an exile, was theirs as well. For it is not enough for the writer to be a neighbor; he must become his own neighbor, if he can. He must not be an observer. He must see with the eyes of another. He must become his brother and his sister.

Not that I have not been taught by books, by and about Puerto Ricans. As the long list of books that will follow testifies, many books have been my teachers. It is necessary to read when one wishes to learn of history. Or about things that it would take a lifetime of living to learn. Even then I have preferred to listen to the voices of people who lived, or relived, that history—the unwritten, unrecorded memories that demeaningly have been misnamed "oral history." And why these? Because in the myth and memory, legend and reality, of the history that is imbedded in the bone and blood of people the very contradictions express the complexity of life more fully than any logical study.

My writing of the tribal past and present of Borinquén was guided in this way by the tribal memory of the *jíbaros* of the hills. The books of scholars merely provided the scenery, the background, the stage setting of artifacts and ideas, for the real drama of life. A book, any book, this book, can do no more.

So it is with statistics. In my past books I have argued that the more governmental, meticulously official, precisely tabulated, and accurately computerized statistics are, the less meaning and truth they reflect about human beings. And many scholars have been angered by my statements. One sociologist had her revenge by referring to my last book, in a learned journal, as "raw data." But the Census Bureau of the United States, upon whose statistics so much of our knowledge of ourselves is based, has conjectured that as high as 33 percent of figures concerning the poor may be subject to "miscalculations." The Acting Director of the Census Bureau, Robert Hagan, has admitted that the statisticians had "missed counting" some 5.3 million people in the 1970 census, most of them the poor of the inner cities. And the 1970 census was the "best ever taken." "Like its predecessors [the census] was imperfect," he matter-of-factly said.

If the Census Bureau's statistics are "imperfect," so is every analysis and conclusion that is based upon them. As it is with statistics, so it is with books. They, too, should be read with a wary eye, with a doubting mind, with forgiving love.

Where then to go for the truth? I have gone to the people.

These are some of the books I took with me. For, knowing that there are as many truths as there are people, and that each of us possesses a truth of own own, I have taken on the journey the books that I will list as a balance, a ballast.

Be it remembered that this is not a bibliography, nor is it my wish to list all of the hundreds, perhaps thousands, of books and papers that I have read in writing this book, as is so often done to testify to the writer's scholarship and impress the readers. This is an intimate assay of the books that I have found useful. Sometimes for the right reasons. Sometimes for the wrong reasons.

And for every book there were hundreds of people who guided me. . . .

Los Indios

Since the people of Borinquén were declared to be officially "nonexistent" by their conquerors nearly five hundred years ago, it was not thought necessary to write much about them.

The natives of the island, the so-called "Taino"* Indians—who never called themselves that since it was not their name—hidden in their mountain villages, beneath whatever cultural guises most effectively disguised them, were not about to reveal themselves in writing. Like so many conquered tribal people they decided it was safer to be "nonexistent."

Not until the rise of the independence movement and search for national roots, in the late nineteenth century, was the native history and culture rediscovered. One of the rediscoverers was the historian Cayetano Coll y Toste, whose works, *Prehistoria de Puerto Rico* (San Juan, 1907) and *Leyendas Puertorriqueñas* (reprinted by Orion, Mexico City, 1959), are classics. Unfortunately, few if any of his works have been translated into English. His work has been carried on by Ricardo Alegría, director of the Institute of Puerto Rican Culture, and his ethnological colleagues. Alegría has been more successful, though not necessarily more fortunate, in having his work translated; for most have been published as children's books: *History of the Indians of Puerto Rico* (Colección de Estudios Puertorriqueños, San Juan, 1970); *Discovery, Conquest, and Colonization of Puerto Rico, 1493–1599* (Colección, San Juan, 1971); and *The Three Wishes* (Harcourt, Brace & World, 1969), a book of island folktales.

Of older books and papers that are difficult to find, but well worth the attempt, homage must be paid to Agustin Sthal's *Los Indios Borinqueños* (Puerto Rico, 1889), Pablo Morales Cabrera's *Puerto Rico Indígena* (Puerto Rico, 1932), J. A. Mason's "Puerto Rican Folklore" in *Riddle's*

* In the language of the original people of the islands *taino* simply meant "good." The chronicles report that when the ships of Columbus first lay anchor the natives greeted them by shouting, *"Taino! Taino!"*—that is, "Good! Good!" Whereupon the Conquistadors, who were illiterate in the islanders' language, named the people the *Tainos*.

Journal of American Folklore (New York, 1918), and the intriguing *Porto Rico Collars and Elbowstones* by R. W. and S. K. Lathrop (London, 1927). And most of all the detailed jottings of the anthropologist Walter J. Fewkes, whose *The Aborigines of Puerto Rico* (Bureau of American Ethnology, Washington, D.C., 1907) offers the sum of his dozen-odd scientific papers reporting the work of cultural exploration he did on the island, soon after he was asked to leave the Hopi villages by that tribe.

And then there is Fray Bartolomé de las Casas's sixteenth-century defense of *los Indios*, his *History of the Indies* (Harper & Row Torchbooks, 1971), which, if read within the context of the religious and political polemic it was written as, offers the reader an insight into the origins of the "noble savage," and "savage savage," beliefs of the Conquistadors. The little-known notes of the monk Fray Ramón Pane, who sailed with Columbus to the Indies, undoubtedly are a more realistic portrayal of native life (*The Life of Admiral Cristóbal Colón by His Son Ferdinand,* Rutgers University Press, 1959). Pane described the people of Santo Domingo, who were related to the Borinqueños, and whose chief, Guarionex, went to Borinquén to lead the revolt against the Spaniards. In his notes, hailed as "the first anthropological study by a European of the Americans," the monk wrote of beliefs still common among the *jíbaros* in the mountain villages of modern Puerto Rico.

Some of the more contemporary enquiries into the past include Adolfo de Hostos's "Ethnology of Puerto Rico," in his *Anthropological Papers* (1941), and that fascinating dictionary of the native language of the island, with its lasting influence, *Diccionario de Voces Indígenas de Puerto Rico,* by Luis Hernández Aquino (Editorial Vasco Americana, Spain, 1969). The most comprehensive work in English, full of useful information, some more so than others, is still the *People of Puerto Rico: A Study in Social Anthropology* by Julian Steward (University of Illinois Press, 1957); though, in my opinion, it is weakest on the strongest influences of the Indians.

Then, too, there are a few background studies of interest—at least they interested me: *The Indian Background of Latin American History,* edited by Robert Wauchope (Knopf, 1970), and *Race Mixture in the History of Latin America* by Magnus Morner, the Dutch ethnologist (Little, Brown, 1967). Of necessity these are based on Spanish, not Indian, versions of history.

Lastly, there is the newest book, and to my mind the finest: the brilliant, provocative, humanly rich, theory-smashing, and beautifully printed *Art and Mythology of the Taino Indians of the Greater West Indies* by Eugenio Fernández Mendez (Ediciones El Cemi, San Juan, 1972), which seeks to recreate the scope and grandeur of the history of the Borinquén natives by conjecturing about the place of their seagoing island culture within the universe of the Mayan empire and religion.

The Coming of the Conquistadors

To understand those most misunderstood of men, the Conquistadors, it might be best to begin with the many cultures of Spain, from which they came. For Spain was then not quite Spain.

In seeking to comprehend the influence of the Islamic minds and mores of "the Moors," who had ruled Spain for seven hundred years, upon the Conquistadors, *A History of Islamic Spain* by W. Montgomery Watt and P. Cachia was a revelation of my own ignorance. So were its companion books, *Islamic Political Thought* by W. Montgomery Watt and *Classical Islam: 600–1258* by G. E. von Grunebaum. These books are part of the comprehensive Islamic Studies Series of the Aldine Publishing Company of Chicago.

Some of the romantic fervor, religious faith, and mathematical skills of the Conquistadors, as mariners and explorers, had their origins in the cultures of their enemies. As the historian Salvador de Madariaga relates in his works, the Conquistadors were driven by the historic duality of these ironies. His *The Rise of the Spanish American Empire* (Free Press, 1965) is a treatise on this theme of Don Quixotism, upon which Miguel de Unamuno based his passionate philosophy, *The Tragic Sense of Life* (Dover, 1954).

Was Don Quixote a Conquistador? In the letters, diaries, and chronicles of the Spanish explorers that quest for the reality of illusion suggests itself. The dreams of Columbus, voiced in *Christopher Columbus: Four Voyages to the New World: Letters and Selected Documents* (Corinth Books, 1961), might easily be mistaken for those of the Man of La Mancha; an illusion not dispelled by his son's biography, *The Life of Admiral Cristóbal Colón by His Son Ferdinand* (*op. cit.*), or by Jacob Wassermann's retelling of his quest for the "Earthly Paradise," in *Columbus* (Martin Secker, London, 1950). The chronicles of Governor de Oviedo of the Indies, and his contemporaries, de Peralta, de León, López de Gómara, and others, which are not generally available in English, reiterate the Quixotic beliefs that guided their conquests, and still influence the life of their progeny on the islands. And whose echoes I listened to among their descendants in the plaza of San Germán.

Of the too many books that seek to rationally relate that era of irrationality I thought *The Conquistadors* by Jean Descola (Allen & Unwin,

London, 1957) useful. It seemed to have the veracity of those times, not ours, to be found also in *Daily Life in Spain in the Golden Age* by Marcelin Defourneaux (Praeger, 1971). The beautifully researched works of Carl O. Sauer, an exemplary scholar of original documents, were equally helpful; to wit: *The Early Spanish Main* (University of California Press, 1969) and *Sixteenth Century North America* (University of California Press, 1971).

Most of the English versions of the history of the Conquest seem simplistic by comparison. *The History of Spain* by Sir Charles Petrie and Louis Bertrand (Collier, 1945) and *A History of Spain* by Charles Chapman (Free Press, 1965) like most such books seemed to me to contain much useful information and useless prejudices. An antidote to their historical biases is to be found in *Tree of Hate: Propaganda and Prejudices Affecting United States Relations with the Hispanic World* by Philip Powell (Basic Books, 1971). Exceptional in their insights, as well, are the thin, seemingly slight volumes by J. H. Elliot, *The Old World and the New World: 1492–1650* (Cambridge University Press, 1970), and Ronald Syme's *Colonial Elites: Rome, Spain and the Americas* (Oxford University Press, 1958).

And yet, when all these books, and so many more, have been read, it is perhaps best to return to that most illuminating of all books, *Don Quixote* by Miguel de Cervantes, and to forget the rest.

The Unique Island

On the island there was a marriage of the diverse cultures of Borinquén, Spain, and Africa, by rapine at worst, and by seduction at best.

Borinquén was never truly Spanish. Its unique character was recognized from the beginning of the conquest by the sixteenth-century poet Juan de Castellanos in his *Elegies of Illustrious Men of the Indies* (*Elegy, La Gesta de Puerto Rico,* edited by María Teresa Babin, San Juan, 1967), and by the seventeenth-century Bishop of Puerto Rico, Fray Damian López de Haro in his famous "Sonnet" (*Borinquén: An Anthology of Puerto Rican Literature,* edited by Dr. Babin and myself. Knopf, 1974).

Of the many historians of the island none, it seems to me, have interwoven its many-faceted cultures as sonorously and skillfully as Salvador Brau, in his *Historia de Puerto Rico* (Editorial Coquí, San Juan, 1966). His work, like that of Lord Macaulay and Charles Beard, has become a national classic. It is worth learning Spanish "just to read Brau," says a Puertorriqueño friend, "even though his best work ends with the end of the Spanish Empire."

The colonization of the island during four centuries of Spanish rule was as quixotic as was its conquest. It was gentle and brutal by turn. On the one hand, the island was a mercantile fiefdom of the Spanish Empire, writes Arturo Morales Carrión, a former foreign-policy adviser to Governor Muñoz, in his objective study *Puerto Rico and the Non-Hispanic Caribbean* (University of Puerto Rico Press, 1971), and as is disdainfully detailed by Gordon Lewis in the first part of his *Puerto Rico: Freedom and Power in the Caribbean* (Harper & Row, 1963) and by Eric Williams, former Prime Minister of Trinidad, in his angrily Marxist history, *From Columbus to Castro: The History of the Caribbean, 1492–1969* (Harper & Row, 1970). And, on the other hand, the mythology of the "Grandeur That Was Spain" was, and still is, idealized on the island by those known as "The Sixteenth Centuryers."

Still, the island's culture was not quite so decisively divided. It integrated the mores of its conquerors into its own, as in a romance, says María Teresa Babín, in *The Puerto Rican Spirit* (Collier, 1972).

The "soft nature" of the island was romantically celebrated, as well, in the early 1800s by Juan Rodríguez Calderón, in "To the Beautiful and Felicitous Island of San Juan de Puerto Rico" (*Borinquén Anthology, op. cit.*), by the poet Santiago Vidarte's *The Puerto Rican Album* and *The Song Book of Borinquén,* by Alejandro Tapia y Rivera in his numerous dramas and essays, by the Balzacian stories of that master of the "social novel" of the nineteenth century, Manuel Zeno Gandía.

Little known beyond the island, there exists a vast and varied literature. It is unique in its abundance for so small a country. There are excellent collections: *Antologia de la Poesía Puertorriqueña,* edited by Cesareo Rosa Nieves (Las Américas, New York, 2 vols.); *Poesía Puertorriqueña,* edited by Carmen Gómez Tejera (Orion, Mexico City, 1957); *Lecturas Puertorriqueñas: Prosa,* edited by Margot Arce de Vázquez and Robles de Cardona (Troutman Press, 1966); *Historia de la Literatura Puertorriqueña* by Francisco Manrique Cabrera (Las Américas, 1956); the works of Tapia y Rivera, especially his *Biblioteca Historica de Puerto-Rico* (San Juan, 1854, reprinted, 1954); *El Cuento,* edited by Concha Meléndez, a collection of essays and folktales (San Juan, 1957); and hundreds of obscure, intriguing works, such as the *Early Ecclesiastical History of Puerto Rico* by Salvador Perea and Juan Agusto Perea (Venezuela, 1929), that are difficult to obtain.

The philosophical and political writing of Eugenio María de Hostos, Dr. Ramón Emerterio Betances, José de Diego, Luis Muñoz Rivera, Luis Muñoz Marín, Antonio Pedreira, and Pedro Albizu Campos, that have so profoundly influenced the thought and history of the Caribbean and the Americas, are hardly known at all in the United States. For they do not exist in English.

Books that depict the lives of some of these men have been written, mostly for children. *Heroes of Puerto Rico* by Jay Nelson Tuck and Norma Vergara (Fleet, 1969) and Marianna Norris's *Father and Son for Freedom* (Dodd, Mead, 1968) are typical of this childish genre. Thomas Aitken's biography of Governor Luis Muñoz Marín, which reads somewhat like an uncritical campaign biography, *Poet in the Fortress* (American Library, 1964), is the sort of book that the president of the University of Puerto Rico, Jaime Benitez, referred to as a "Walt Disney–Horatio Alger story." The drama of the humanitarian dreams that became political tragedies in the lives of these men has yet to be translated, or published, beyond the island.

So few of their works have been translated into English one wonders why. One reason may be that Borinquén, lying between South and North America, and being a blend of Indian, Spanish, and African cultures, is unique. The unique is always suspect.

The *jíbaros,* or country folk, are the source of this cultural uniqueness. Nowhere else in the Caribbean or the Americas have the cultures of the three continents—America, Africa, and Europe—combined, and survived in so deeply integrated and singular a manner. It is symbolic of the importance of the *jíbaros* that the book that signaled the emergence of modern, national Puerto Rican culture was *El Gíbaro, The Jíbaro,* written by Dr. Manuel Alonso in 1849. His romantic vision of country life paled in the glare of the twentieth century. One hundred years later, or nearly so, Dr. José C. Rosario, in his landmark study *The Development of the Puerto Rican Jíbaro and His Present Attitude Toward Society* (University of Puerto Rico, *Monograph Series C, No. 1,* 1935), expressed the opposing, then contemporary view, of the *jíbaro* as "barefoot, ignorant and sickly, superstitious and dreadfully inefficient"; he was the island's "greatest problem."

Whether the island's greatest strength or its greatest "problem," the reaction to the *jíbaro* determined the intellectuals' viewpoint. He was the pivot of Puertorriqueñoismo.

In the mountain villages and rural *campos* the unlettered *jíbaros* have given their culture to the world of letters. Enrique Laguerre, one of the distinguished novelists on the island, has recognized the influence of the *jíbaros* in his anthology *El Jíbaro de Puerto Rico* (Troutman, 1968), which strangely has not been translated into English, though Laguerre's novel, *The Labyrinth* (Las Américas, 1960), has been. Similarly, the works of Manuel Zeno Gandía, most especially his nineteenth-century novel of the life of the *jíbaros* in the countryside, *La Charca* (San Juan, 1966), which influenced the development of modern Borinquén literature much as the works of Émile Zola did France, or Theodore Dreiser did the United States, have never been translated or published in Norte America.

The uniqueness of the island's literature has remained uniquely its own. Few beyond its shores know of it, even today.

Americanization: Conquest and Resistance

On the twenty-sixth of June, 1903, the President of the United States issued the *Proclamation: Porto Rico Lands for Naval Purposes* (Government Printing Offices, Washington, D.C., 1903).

Seemingly, in the beginning, the invasion and occupation of the island were a small part of Colonel Theodore Roosevelt's "Splendid Little War." In *The War with Spain* by Henry Cabot Lodge (Harper & Brothers, 1899) the conquest of Borinquén is an insignificant chapter of his dream of empire. And William Jennings Bryan hardly mentions the island in his collected papers of 1900 (*Bryan on Imperialism,* Arno Press, New York Times Books, 1970). The tropical riches of the island and the sugar interests soon changed this oversight. *Puerto Rico and Its Resources* by Frederick Ober (Appleton & Co., 1899) was followed by a flood of books that explored the financial opportunities the island offered investors: *Opportunities in Puerto Rico* by C. H. Allen (1902); the *United States and Porto Rico* by L. S. Rowe (1904); *The Porto Rico of Today* by A. G. Robinson (1899); and, finally, *Selling in Puerto Rico* by William Aughinbaugh (1915).

The journalistic books and political papers were encouraged by a host of government surveys, documents, and reports, many of which are mentioned in the text. One of the most influential was the *Report on the Island of Porto Rico* by Henry K. Carroll (GPO, Washington, D.C., 1900), which guided the policy of the United States on the island for years to come.

In perspective the emerging colonial power of the United States can be seen in the historical musings of the statesmen of the mid- and late-nineteenth century: such as the papers and autobiography of Ulysses S. Grant and Carl Schurz's biography of Henry Clay, with its blunt depiction of strong-armed foreign policy in Latin America and the Caribbean. The stark portrayal of *The Racial Attitudes of American Presidents* by George Sinkler (Doubleday, 1971) illuminates one side of the picture; much as *Anti-Imperialism in the United States* by E. Berkeley Tompkins (University of Pennsylvania Press, 1970) does the other side. Further background studies that I found of interest were: *Pan Americanism: A View from the Other Side* by Alonso Aquilar (Modern Reader, 1968); *The United States and the Caribbean,* edited by Tad Szulc (Prentice Hall, 1971); *The United States and Disruption of the Spanish Empire: 1810–1822,* an early delineation of the Pan-American geopolitik, by Charles Griffin (New York, 1937); and *The Death of the Imperial Dream* by Edward Grierson (Doubleday, 1971), written in acerbic wit, to describe the rise of the idea of the "imperial commonwealth" as a political device to preserve the British Empire.

Some interesting insights into the emergence of colonial policy, as an extension of Indian policy, may be seen in *Roosevelt's Rough Riders* by Virgil Carrington (Doubleday, 1971) and in Roosevelt's own *Rough Riders and Men of Action,* appearing in Volume XI of the *Works of Theodore Roosevelt* (Scribner, 1926). But the continuation of the Wars against the Indians, as foreign policy, has not been deeply studied, or understood, by historians.

The Americanization of Borinquén that colonization sought to achieve is hailed, and lamented, in many books. Legally the process is described in the invaluable *Documents on the Constitutional History of Puerto Rico* (Commissioner of Puerto Rico, Washington, D.C., 1964). In the schools, where the earliest and the most intensive campaigns for Americanization were undertaken, the calmest history of this controversial subject is offered in *A History of Education in Puerto Rico* by Dr. Osuna (University of Puerto Rico, 1923); while *Americanization in Puerto Rico and the Public School System: 1900–1930* by Aida Negrón de Montilla (Editorial Edil, San Juan, 1970) presents a polemic condemnation of the educational attempt "to destroy Puerto Rican culture." The methodology of Americanization used in the schools is described in *The Teaching of English to Primary Grades in Puerto Rico* by Maude Owens Walters (University of Puerto Rico, 1938), a governmental "teachers' manual."

In English, there have understandably been few books that depict the resistance to the policy of Americanization. As far as I know there is no book that tells of the guerrilla bands that fought the American Army during the War of 1898. Nor is there a historical account, in English, of the rise of the independence movement or the Nationalist party, except for journalist pamphlets such as *Albizu Campos* by Federico Ribes Tovar (Plus Ultra, 1971) and political broadsides such as Juan Antonio Corretjer's poetic and impressionistic *Albizu Campos and the Ponce Massacre* (World Wide, New York, 1970). The wide opposition to the Jones Act of 1917, by which Puerto Rican citizenship was abolished and American citizenship was imposed on the island, exemplified by Commissioner Luis Muñoz Rivera's speech to the United States Congress, has been largely ignored. Muñoz's plea has been rarely reprinted until recently (*Borinquén Anthology, op. cit.*).

The conflicts created by the policy of Americanization have, however, produced a shelf of books by its proponents. Former Governor Colonel Theodore Roosevelt, Jr.'s *Colonial Policies of the United States* (Doubleday, 1937) has recently been reprinted by Arno; as has *Changing Colonial Climate* by the last American Governor, Rexford Guy Tugwell. Some of these books are valuable as historical landmarks in the development of colonial policy, as seen by the colonizers; Victor Clark's study for the Brookings Institution, *Puerto Rico and Its Problems* (Washington, D.C., 1930), is one such. Many are, however, more valuable as historic curiosities, in which visiting experts seek to impose their ideas upon island life, than as studies of realities of Borinquén culture.

For myself, I feel an unassuming and personal journalistic account, as contained in the chapters of Puerto Rico in *Roaming Through the West Indies* by Harry Franck (Blue Ribbon Books, 1920), its eyewitness stories of the successes and failures of Americanization as it affected the daily lives of ordinary people, often has more veracity, and almost always has more humanity. Here *is* history.

The Modern Times

In the computerizing and industrializing of a rural tropical island that was once an "Earthly Paradise" is written the major story of the twentieth century.

The story begins with statistics. Soon after the end of World War II the University of Puerto Rico published a series of books that analyzed the floral, agricultural, industrial, and human problems of the island in precise figures. Eminent among these books were Planning Board director Rafael Picó's study of economic geography, *Geographic Regions of Puerto Rico* (1950); *Money and Banking in Puerto Rico* by Biagio Di Venuti (1950); and *Ships and Sugar* by S. E. Eastman and Daniel Marx, Jr. (1953).

As the scholarly heralds of the economic upheavals that were to change life on the island forever, these books were in turn elaborated by a series of directive and critical studies that plotted the future of the islanders: *Puerto Rico's Economic Future* by Harvey Perloff (University of Chicago Press, 1950); *A Comprehensive Agricultural Plan for Puerto Rico* by Nathan Koenig (U.S. Department of Agriculture, Washington, D.C., 1953); *Puerto Rico, Middle Road to Freedom* by Carl Friedrich (Rinehart,

1959); *Puerto Rico: A Study of Democratic Development* (*The Annals*, American Academy of Political and Social Science, Philadelphia, 1954); *People, Jobs, and Economic Development: A Case History of Puerto Rico* by A. J. Jaffe (Free Press, 1959); *Fomento—The Economic Development of Puerto Rico* by William Stead (National Planning Association, Staff Report, 1958); and so on. . . .

Curiously, none of these programmatic books were written by Puertorriqueños. They should be read with that in mind.

Not long after these studies appeared, the policies projected by their writers were proclaimed a success by another series of studies, written by non-Puertorriqueños, as in *Puerto Rico Success Story* by Ralph Hancock (Nostrand, 1960), and in David Ross's *The Long Uphill Path: A Historical Study of Puerto Rico's Program of Economic Development* (Editorial Edil, San Juan, 1969), an unemotional study noteworthy for its balance and understatement.

So surprising and swift was the change on the island from a rural to an urban way of life that it was declared "the Puerto Rican miracle." The planners and corporate leaders were hailed as tropical Horatio Algers. "Forceful Ferre Family" in *Fortune* magazine (October, 1959), which huzzahed millionaire Luis Ferre, soon-to-be "Governor from M.I.T.," is rather typical. *Puerto Rican Businessmen, a Study in Cultural Change* by T. C. Cochran (University of Pennsylvania Press, 1959) is more restrained, but no less celebrant, as is *Transformation, The Story of Modern Puerto Rico* by Earl Parker Hanson (Simon and Schuster, 1955) —a story Hanson helped to write as a member of the island's Planning Board in the New Deal years. None of these books, oddly enough, deals extensively with the effect of the industrial "cultural change" on the newly created factory workers and their unions, but there is a forceful book on the subject in Spanish: *Lucha Obrera en Puerto Rico* by Quintero Rivera (CEREP, San Juan, 1971), which surveys the early years of labor-union activity and change.

The social conflicts created by the "transformation" inspired still another series of books. Economists were replaced by sociologists, psychologists, and anthropologists. Few of these questioned the inevitability, or social value, of industrial "progress," but sought to report objectively the problems it had caused. *La Vida* by Oscar Lewis (Random House, 1965) is such a study. Its lurid and ugly story of a few families of prostitutes is no more typical of the island than *Tobacco Road* is of the mainland, but it has been ignorantly used as a textbook of Borinquén life. More thoughtful and more complex, and therefore less popular, is *The Modernization of Puerto Rico* by Henry Wells (Harvard University Press, 1969), which suffers from the conceits and misconceptions of an outsider, but which deals with the changes that affected the majority of the populace. In politics, too, methods and goals had to be re-evaluated, as chronicled in three books from three points of view: *Puerto Rican Politics and the New Deal* by Thomas Matthews (University of Florida Press, 1960); *La Crisis Política en Puerto Rico: 1962–1966* by Juan Manuel García Passalacqua (Editorial Edil, 1970); and Manuel Maldonado-Denis, *Puerto Rico: Una Interpretation Historico-Social* (Siglo XXI, Mexico City, 1969).

In a gentle and humane mosaic of interviews mostly with *jíbaros* and country people, Henrietta Yurchenco has evoked the hopes, confusions, and sadness that these changes have brought in her little book *¡Hablamos!* (Praeger, 1971). The mirror image of this subdued picture is sharply outlined in Juan Angel Silen's condemnation of the industrial "colonization" of the island in *We, the Puerto Rican People: A Story of Oppression and Resistance* (Monthly Review Press, 1971). Silen seeks out the historical basis of the growing independence movement, which he presents with impressionistic style and sweep.

A kaleidoscopic view of the acquiescence and resistance to the industrialization of the island, and the traumatic effect it had on the people, is presented in *Problems of Social Inequality in Puerto Rico,* edited by Ortiz, Rameriz, and Levine (Ediciones Libería Internacional, Río Piedras, 1972).

The former *New York Times* Man-in-San-Juan, Kal Wagenheim, has attempted with *Times*esque clarity and cohesion to combine in a single book the historical, economic, political, social, and cultural changes on the island, from the time of the Borinqueño Indians till the present. It is an impossible task, but Wagenheim is remarkably successful in his *Puerto Rico: A Profile* (Praeger, 1970) in offering an encyclopedic, instant history. Naturally, in writing of so much, he can dwell on so little.

Rural life on the island is all but forgotten by most of these writers. The travail of the agricultural villagers has been painfully described by many old books, such as *The Stricken Land* by Rexford Guy Tugwell (New York, 1947) and Sidney Mintz's singular study, *Worker in the Cane* (Yale University Press, 1960). But the decline of farming and the destruction of the rural economy have been largely ignored by the scholars. One compassionate and impassioned economy study, if one can imagine such a work, exists. It is a thin, incisive pamphlet, *Sugar Cane and Coffee in Puerto Rico* by Raymond E. Crist (University of Puerto Rico, no date), which is reprinted from the *American Journal of Economics and Sociology,* April and June, 1948, and which depicts "the bitter fruit of industrialization."

Since the exodus from the island has come from the dying rural towns it is strange that so little has been written about them.

Exodus

The islander is born in exile. Wherever he goes he is in exile.

In the old days the ancient mariners of the island journeyed to the shores of the continents to the north and south. Eugenio Fernández Mendez has written of their extensive trade in cultures and goods with the Mayan kingdoms to the west, in *Art and Mythology of the Taino Indians* (*op. cit.*). There is no known evidence that they sailed east, to Africa. But they may have. English and German archaeologists of the nineteenth century have suggested this.

And, of course, Ponce de León, the first Governor of Puerto Rico, was one of the earliest explorers to set foot on North America. Unhappily, no definitive book of his life and journeys has been written that recommends itself.

So the modern exodus from the island has an ancient history. The political exiles of the nineteenth century and the economic exiles of the twentieth century are chronicled in *El Libro Puertorriqueño de Nueva York* (in Spanish and English) by Frederico Ribes Tovar (Spain, 1968). Although Tovar's work has been criticized for its flamboyant style and textual errors, his book is the most comprehensive compendium on the exodus. It is well researched and full of pathos, accented by personal statements and documents that are rarely available elsewhere.

The early migrations are briefly discussed in *The Puerto Rican Migrant in the United States* by L. R. Chenault (Columbia University Press, 1937). But a more human and poetic account is found in Jesus Colon's reminiscence, *A Puerto Rican in New York* (Mainstream, 1961). Colon, who came to the city around World War I, tells his story in an anecdotal style and offers an excellent companion volume to Elena Padilla's more formal and analytical *Up from Puerto Rico* (Columbia University Press, 1958). Her title reveals her attitude.

It may be that exile is too painful for a personal narrative. The Kafkaesque state has been depicted most forcefully in the *cuentos* of Victor Hernández Cruz (*19 Necromancers from Now,* edited by Ishmael Reed; *Rhythm Section, Part One* by Cruz, Doubleday, 1970); in the short stories of José Luis González (*Borinquén Anthology, op. cit.*), and the novel of exile by Pedro Juan Soto (*Ardiente Suelo, Frío Estación,* published in English as *Hot Land, Cold Season,* Dell, 1973). And the masterpiece of the exodus remains the play by René Marquez, *La Carreta,* which had a long run off-Broadway in New York City, in its English version *The Ox Cart.* One critic referred to *La Carreta* as the *"Grapes of Wrath* of Puerto Rico," which in its own way it may be.

As the exile returns, a new literature has arisen, of which Soto's *Hot Land, Cold Season* is a forerunner. The *Return Migration to Puerto Rico* by José Hernandez Alvarez (University of California, Population Monograph Series, 1967) foretells this growing trend.

In El Barrio *and Other Mysteries*

It is a mystery that a generous and gentle, easygoing and outgoing people from an exquisitely beautiful and bright tropical island have survived in an ugly, gray, cold city like New York.

El Barrio may be the quixotic reason. It is not merely a slum. It is an island of warmth amid the cold. Piri Thomas in his unforgiving books of *barrio* life, *Down These Mean Streets* (Knopf, 1967) and *Savior! Savior!* (Doubleday, 1972), depicts the emotionally rich life of the economically poor with a harshness and cruelty that are humanized by the Puertorriqueñoismo of the people. The survival of the exiles is due to their inner strengths. In his evocation of the *corazón y alma,* heart and soul, of *barrio* misery the novelist has captured more mysterious strengths and truths that men and women live by than most sociologists, and other ologists, dare to grasp in the cold hands of analysis.

The fervor of life in the *barrio* has been illuminated, as well, in the work of young writers such as Felipe Luciano; in *The Puerto Rican Poets,* edited by Alfredo Matilla and Ivan Silen (Bantam, 1972); by Victor Hernandez Cruz, in his *Snaps* (Random House, 1969); and by Pedro Pietri, in the threnody of his requiem "The Puerto Rican Obituary" (*Palante: Young Lords Party,* edited by Michael Abramson, McGraw-Hill, 1971).

In seeking books of *barrio* life by *barrio* writers, one is dismayed by how few there are. One writer said to me, "We're not a fad yet, you know. Like the Indians!" Very, very few of the Puerto Rican writers, poets, photographers, or playwrights are known, or published, outside the *barrio.* So one turns with hard eyes to the books of the outsiders.

Much of the literature of the *barrios* has been written by those outside the *barrios.* It need not be faulted for that alone. Rather it is that these writers most often write as outsiders because they are outsiders. They rarely come into the hearts and homes of those they are writing about. They rarely feel their pains. And so they misinterpret what they are told. They do not see with the eyes of others.

The Island in the Sun by Dan Wakefield, a book of earlier *barrio* life (Corinth, 1960), is exceptional. Wakefield wrote of El Barrio as if he lived there. He gleaned the buoyant and fervent élan of the Puertorriqueños and Neo-Ricans with warmth and enthusiasm, though he did not shy away from the brutalities the people suffered. Nor did he blame them for their suffering. In writing the book he talked to hundreds of people, and he listened. Patricia Sexton, a sympathetic writer, on the other hand was so horrified by the miseries of *barrio* life that she compared El Barrio to Maxim Gorky's *Lower Depths,* and the life of the poor to the life of rats. Her *Spanish Harlem* (Harper & Row, 1965) has been criticized as a well-intentioned but superficial outsider's view that in the end is one-sided and insulting. In writing the book she seems to have interviewed mainly *barrio* "leaders." And then there is *Beyond the Melting Pot* by Nathan Glazer and Daniel Moynihan (MIT Press, 1963), which reflected the tenacity of Puerto Rican culture. But their opinions are more ideological and abstract. In my opinion, their conclusions are arbitrary and inaccurate. In writing their book they seem to have relied largely on the studies and statistics of others, not on day-to-day *barrio* life.

Of the three ways of entering *barrio* life from the outside, that of Dan Wakefield seems to be the least popular among writers. Unhappily so. For it is one of the most rewarding.

The surveys, studies, statistics, and reports proliferate, however. Some of those prepared by the Division of Migration of the Commonwealth of Puerto Rico are exceedingly helpful, though they are occasionally contradictory, depending on their political source and purpose; and some, compiled from the United States Census Bureau statistics, are admittedly partial and incomplete.

No Congressional or federal-agency survey of *barrio* life has yet been issued that is comparable to those of other ethnic or nationality groups; for, unbelievably, no comprehensive government hearings have ever been held on the needs of the Puertorriqueños in the United States. The documents of the Status Hearings (*Hearings Before the United States–Puerto Rico Commission on Status,* 89th Congress, Government Printing Office, 1966) are vast and thorough, but these volumes (*I. Legal; II. Constitutional; III. Social-Cultural*) are devoted almost exclusively to the island, not the *barrios.*

In his books Federico Ribes Tovar has undertaken, almost single-handedly, to fill this void; a Herculean task for one man. His compilations, *Handbook of the Puerto Rican Community* (El Libro Puertorriqueño, 1968), the *Enciclopedia Puertorriqueño,* in Spanish and English (Plus Ultra Educational, San Juan, 1970), together with his previously noted

El Libro Puertorriqueño de Nueva York (Spain, 1968) give some idea of the panoramic endeavor he has attempted. Symptomatic of the lack of interest and neglect of *barrio* life is the fact that Tovar has had to publish his books on his own.

One of the more reliable, although limited, surveys of individual *barrios* is *A Study of Poverty Conditions in the New York Puerto Rican Community* (Puerto Rican Forum), which is outdated and somewhat selective. There are theses and studies of the *barrios* of Philadelphia, Boston, Chicago, and Honolulu, but these, to my knowledge, are thus far unpublished and unavailable to the public. In Chicago, studies by *barrio* writers have begun to appear in *The Rican, a Journal* (Chicago, 1972–74). And the local and *barrio* newspapers are a source of journalistic and polemical articles—as in other *barrios*. There is as well a sporadic scattering of city and state surveys, either civic or academic, such as *The Spanish Speaking People of Greater Bridgeport, Connecticut* (University of Bridgeport, Sociology Department, 1962), and the *Reports of the Legislative Committee of the Spanish Speaking* (Legislature of Illinois, 1972). But there are fewer of these than one might wish for. These most often consist of mimeographed sheets filed away in the recesses of specific governmental or university departments.

A mosaic of *barrio* life is more vivaciously portrayed within pages of *barrio* and Puertorriqueño movement newspapers. *Claridad,* the Puerto Rican Socialist party weekly, and *Palante,* formerly the Young Lords' paper, are especially interesting; though, of course, they represent the opinions of their parent organizations.

Life is seemingly easier to study when it is dissected and isolated. In the narrower aspects of *barrio* life there is therefore a much wider range of studies.

Schools are analyzed by a group of Puertorriqueño educators in a perceptive and probing study of bicultural and bilingual education, and its hopes and realities, *A Proposed Approach to Implement Bilingual Education Programs* (National Puerto Rican Training and Development Institute, New York, 1972). In the well-known *Early Childhood Bilingual Education* by Vera John and Vivian Horner (Modern Language Association, 1971), many of the pioneer programs were critically discussed. *Schools Against Children,* edited by Annette Rubinstein (Monthly Review Press, 1970), adds its harsh evaluation of the ghetto schools to those of books by Kozol and Holt. It is noteworthy for the studies by David Rogers and Eleanor Leacock, as well as Doxey Wilkerson's "The Failure of Schools Serving the Black and Puerto Rican Poor." Still other studies with national implications are *Bilingualism in the Barrio* by Joshua

Fishman (Office of Education, Bureau of Research, HEW, Washington, D.C., 1960) and James Conant's acerbic *Slums and Schools* (McGraw-Hill, 1961), which is fortunately not yet out of date.

On the streets, the effect of police work in the *barrios* and ghettos has been the subject of a great number of books: *The Enemy in the Streets: Police Malpractice in America* by Edward Gray (Doubleday, 1972), *Police Power* by Paul Chevigny (Random House, 1969), as well as the standard texts on criminology by Sutherland and others. To my mind, however, the most judicious, and therefore damning, of all studies of the inadequacies of law enforcement among the poor is the report prepared by the nation's leading police and legal officials, the *Task Force Report: The Police* (President's Commission on Law Enforcement and the Administration of Justice, Government Printing Office, 1967).

Unlike crime, which inspires flamboyant and insistent headlines, the health problems of the *barrios,* which kill and injure many more innocents, have suffered from a lack of public airing. I can think of no books and few reports that are worth mentioning.

Similarly, the unemployment and employment problems of the *barrio* workers seem to create no sensational headlines. And few books. The unbelievably cruel nature of the problem is touched upon by Herbert Bienstock in his *Report to the Workshop on Employment Problems of Puerto Ricans* (Center for the Study of the Unemployed, New York University, 1968). Of value, too, is the *Summary of Proceedings of the Workshop* (New York University, *ibid.*). A handful of specialized reports on specific trades exists, to wit: *Bias in the Building Industry* (City of New York, Commission of Human Rights, 1963–1967) and James Haughton's "The Role of the Board of Education in Perpetuating Racism in the Building Trades, and Vice Versa" (*Schools Against Children, op. cit.*). But I know of no similar report on the garment or hotel trades, which have been a traditionally large employer of Puertorriqueño men and women. One is needed.

A sad footnote to the above: Though many, if not most, of the earlier exiles from the island came to the United States after World War II to work as migrant laborers in the fields, there is no study to compare to the compassionate books written about the toilers of *La Causa* in California. *Migrants: Agricultural Workers in America's Northeast* by William Friedland and Dorothy Nelkin (Holt, 1971), a powerful and moving book, somehow manages to all but ignore the tens of thousands of *jíbaros* in the fields of the United States. It is devoted almost exclusively to the experiences of Blacks. Why?

Family life and religious faith seem to be more interesting subjects to researching students and church missionaries. The studies of sects and sex abound, especially in the scholarly journals. Still, I cannot banish the feeling so often expressed in the *barrios* that these studies too often use Puertorriqueños as guinea pigs. And so treat them. It seems especially true of their familial and spiritual lives, which are viewed as exotic curiosities.

If I feel this way, it is not difficult to imagine how those who have been studied feel. Or why they are angered.

The tenements are less subjective. On the *barrio* streets the houses were visibly and easily defined as abused long before the Puertorriqueños moved in. Since then there have been endless books describing the obvious. One of these, in the early years, was *Forbidden Neighbors: A Study of Prejudice in Housing* by Charles Abrams (Harper & Brothers, 1955), with its chapter on the dilapidated housing awaiting the newly arrived exiles—the "Puerto Rican Airlift." Fred Cook, in his in-depth probe into the urban-renewal, slum-clearance, and relocation programs, *The Shame of New York,* that filled an entire issue of *The Nation* (October 31, 1959), described the civic reasons for the further decline of the *barrios.* Living conditions of those conditioned to the unlivable are chronicled in the books of Federico Ribes Tovar, Dan Wakefield, Patricia Sexton, and Piri Thomas.

Of generalized books that do not specifically deal with *barrio* life, but which I found useful, I might mention *The Poorhouse State* by Richard Melman (Dell, 1966), on welfare systems; *The Other America* by Michael Harrington (Macmillan, 1963); and *The Poor Pay More* by David Caplovitz (Macmillan, 1963).

And then there are the sensitive writings of Joseph Fitzpatrick of Fordham University, whose work has appeared in many journals, on many subjects. His *Puerto Rican Culture* (Puerto Rican Family Institute, no date), *Delinquency and Puerto Ricans* (Puerto Rican Family Institute, 1959), "The Integration of Puerto Ricans" (*Thought,* Autumn, 1955), and "The Adjustment of Puerto Ricans to New York City" (in *Minorities in a Changing World,* edited by Milton Barron, Knopf, 1967) are of enduring interest, although some of his perceptions are historically outdated.

It may be that those in the *barrios* affected most cruelly by *diaspora* are the youth. *The Shook Up Generation* by Harrison Salisbury (Harper & Row, 1958) is a realistic description of youth and youth gangs in the *barrio,* which were romantically depicted in the musical tragedy, *West Side Story*. Salisbury's harsh book has its novelistic counterparts in Warren Miller's *The Cool World* (Little, Brown, 1967) and Sol Hurok's *The Warriors.*

Conditions such as these have inevitably created a changing political climate in the *barrios*. It has just begun to burst forth from the *barrios* into the larger cities and into the national consciousness.

Unlike the Black, Chicano, and Indian movements, this aspect of Puertorriqueño life has as yet been little reflected in popular literature. *Awakening Minorities,* edited by John Howard (Trans-action Books, 1970), offers a few essays on the *barrio* upheaval, most of them by outside observers, such as "The Puerto Rican Independence Movement" by Arthur Liebman. In the past, when the *barrio* was represented by Congressman Vito Marcantonio (see *Vito Marcantonio* by Salvatore John La Gumina, Kendall-Hunt, Iowa, 1969, and *Vito Marcantonio* by Alan Schaffer, Syracuse University Press, 1966), studies of *barrio* politics in terms of Anglo politics had more validity. Now a book on Congressman Herman Badillo, yet to be written, would seem to be in order. *The Ethnic Factor: How America's Minorities Decide Elections* by Mark Levy and Michael Kramer (Simon and Schuster, 1972) not only discusses the continuing influence of nationality groups in the political picture, but points to the need for a detailed analysis of *barrio* politics.

The phenomenon of the Young Lords that electrified the *barrios* in the late 1960s is recorded in *Palante: Young Lords Party,* edited by Michael Abramson (McGraw-Hill, 1971). It presents personal testimony and striking photographs that chronicle the rise of this street gang which became a political force and catalyst for change. *Carlos Feliciano,* edited by Ruth Reynolds (Carlos Feliciano Defense Committee, 1972), describes some of the political repression that greeted the movement as it affected the older nationalist and independence groups and leaders.

A new book has come to my desk, as I write this. It is *The Puerto Rican Papers: Notes on the Re-Emergence of a Nation* by Alfredo Lopez (Bobbs-Merrill, 1973). Though I have not read it closely, it seems to me it may well be "the path-breaking" work that Manuel Maldonado Denis says it is. Lopez is a young journalist and editor of *Claridad,* whose writing on the Puertorriqueño experience is both intensely personal and political. His book ranges widely, from the culture and history of the island to the nature of nationalism on the mainland, and the cultural confrontations that arise from its tenacity. Even my unhappily hasty reading, as this book goes to press, recommends his chapters on "Strategy of Miseducation," "The Political Economy of Bodegas," "Culture: Roots, Development and Genocide," and the until now unwritten "The Movement: A History."

One awaits, with excitement, books like this. Hopefully, it is the first of many. . . .

Still, as I said in the beginning, the books that I have listed are offered as scenery, a background to the lives of the people. The thoughts of their writers, as in all secondary sources, are seen through the prisms of their opinions. Wherever the books have been contradicted by the voices of the people, I have not hesitated to listen to the voices of the people.

Of the hundreds, the thousands, of Puertorriqueños who have talked, taught, argued, guided, and misguided me through these pages, let me mention a few to whom I must pay homage. Some of them are very old friends, like Manny Diaz, whose experience and generosity offered me a brotherly helping hand. Some are new, young friends, like Magali Soto, whose spirit and enthusiasms offered me sisterly love. And there were many more: Don Pedro Matos Matos; the *independista* leaders Juan Mari Bras and Ruben Berrios; Governor Rafael Hernández Colón and former Governor Luis Ferre; Jaime Benitez, now Resident Commissioner in Washington; the indefatigable Gerena Valintin; Hernan Flores of the Young Lords, and Denise Oliver; Commissioner of Migration Nick Lugo, Jr., and his effervescent father, Nick Lugo, Sr.; Ema Ramos; the novelist, Cesar Andreu Iglesias; the artist, José Olivo; Piri Thomas by his books, and Miriam Colon and Rita Moreno by their illuminating genius; my literary *compañero,* María Teresa Babin; and my boyhood *compañero,* René Torres; Carlos Feliciano, Jesus Colón, Reverend Richard Gillett, my dear friends; the Bishop Autulio Parrilla Bonilla and Father David Garcia; Beatrice Colon, Monserrate Diaz, and the staff of *The Rican;* Geno Rodriguez, whose photographs in the book spoke their own language to me; the old Spanish woman who mothered me on my stays in San Juan, and the courageous woman, who in modesty asked me not to mention her by her family name, but who cannot object to my gratitude, in my thanking her by her given name, Violetta.

For this is the book of all the people of Borinquén whom I have known. . . .

Index

About the Author

The research for *The Islands* began on the day in 1946 Stan Steiner moved to Manhattan into a neighborhood of European immigrants known as Yorkville. It was then "that the immigrants from Puerto Rico began to move into El Barrio, just to the north." Steiner says, "For fifteen years, I lived there and watched the exiles come from the islands. For four years, I lived in the barrio of the Lower East Side. For two years, I lived in the barrio of Brooklyn."

Born in Brooklyn, in 1925, "when there were still farms in our neighborhood," he knew the anguish of a rural way of life turning to urban decay. Steiner now lives on a mountain in Santa Fe, New Mexico, and does "not wish to come down. Ever." He was an overseas correspondent, magazine and sports writer and anthologized poet. Author of *The New Indians* and *La Raza: The Mexican Americans* and co-editor of *The Way: An Anthology of American Indian Literature* and *Axtlan: An Anthology of Mexican American Literature,* he is now writing a sequel to *The New Indians.*

74 75 76 77 10 9 8 7 6 5 4 3 2 1